ADOBE® PHOTOSHOP® CS3 EXTENDED:
RETOUCHING MOTION PICTURES

Gary David Bouton

Course Technology PTR
A part of Cengage Learning

Australia, Brazil, Japan, Korea, Mexico, Singapore, Spain, United Kingdom, United States

Adobe® Photoshop® CS3 Extended:
Retouching Motion Pictures
Gary David Bouton

Publisher and General Manager, Course Technology PTR: Stacy L. Hiquet

Associate Director of Marketing: Sarah Panella

Manager of Editorial Services: Heather Talbot

Marketing Manager: Jordan Casey

Executive Editor: Kevin Harreld

Project Editor: Dan Foster, Scribe Tribe

Technical Reviewer: Mara Zebest

PTR Editorial Services Coordinator: Erin Johnson

Interior Layout Tech: Bill Hartman

Cover Designer: Mike Tanamachi

Indexer: Katherine Stimson

Proofreader: Gene Redding

© 2008 Gary David Bouton

ALL RIGHTS RESERVED. No part of this work covered by the copyright herein may be reproduced, transmitted, stored, or used in any form or by any means graphic, electronic, or mechanical, including but not limited to photocopying, recording, scanning, digitizing, taping, Web distribution, information networks, or information storage and retrieval systems, except as permitted under Section 107 or 108 of the 1976 United States Copyright Act, without the prior written permission of the publisher.

> For product information and technology assistance, contact us at
> **Cengage Learning Customer & Sales Support Center, 1-800-354-9706**
>
> For permission to use material from this text or product, submit all requests online at **cengage.com/permissions**
> Further permissions questions can be emailed to
> **permissionrequest@cengage.com**

Adobe and Photoshop are registered trademarks of Adobe Systems Incorporated.

Library of Congress Control Number: 2007931841

ISBN-13: 978-1-59863-461-7

ISBN-10: 1-59863-461-5

Course Technology
25 Thomson Place
Boston, MA 02210
USA

Cengage Learning is a leading provider of customized learning solutions with office locations around the globe, including Singapore, the United Kingdom, Australia, Mexico, Brazil, and Japan. Locate your local office at: **international.cengage.com/region**

Cengage Learning products are represented in Canada by Nelson Education, Ltd.

For your lifelong learning solutions, visit **courseptr.com**

Visit our corporate website at **cengage.com**

Printed in the United States of America
1 2 3 4 5 6 7 11 10 09 08

There have been four people during my school years that had a passion for art equal to, or surpassing, my own. They taught me how to think, and they taught me that art without a concept displays skill, but it's art without heart.

I dedicate this book to the late John Sellers, Dean of the School of Visual Communications at Syracuse University, a true mentor and a friend. I thank him for his unflagging belief in my gifts even when I demonstrated none.

To Bob Kaplan, for his guide to living a creative life and reconciling fine art with commercial art. It's all just art, right, Bob?

To Curtis Crystal for helping me build a system, then the tools, and finally the design. It's the only recipe that leads to true original work.

And to my art history professor, Ludwig Stein, who showed me the convergence of art through the ages and brought it all home with a style of presentation that was an art form itself.

It's all to the grace of visual communications that you don't feel all that small standing next to real giants such as these.

Acknowledgments

Without the help from some of the kind and generous individuals I thank here, there either wouldn't have been this book, or this book would have been greatly diminished in content and there would be one more strange person roaming the streets wearing an aluminum foil hat, muttering something about a Lasso tool.

- Product Manager John Nack at Adobe Systems: I want to thank John for his patience and time helping me and other pre-release testers understand what Photoshop Extended was developing into at the time this book was written. John has an unusually deep interest in his product; his participation in the online discussions were eventful and educational, and John helped tease apart some of the finer points of this version.

- Chris Cox at Adobe Systems: As a principal architect of Photoshop, you'll see Chris's name all too briefly on the splash screen to Photoshop. I'd like to give the reader a longer chance to read it. Thanks, Chris, for your detailed explanations of Photoshop Extended as it evolved.

- Silas Lepcha and Vishal Khandpur at Adobe Systems: You people were instrumental in getting pre-releases out on a regular schedule, and I want to thank you as much as any of the members on the Adobe staff. Thank you, gracious and patient souls!

- My agent Matt Wagner: Thank you for believing in this book and the unflagging dedication you demonstrated to find the right place for it.

- Kevin Harreld at Course Technology for his patience through the months getting the manuscript into a human-digestible format, and for allowing me to tell the story the way I see it.

- Editor Dan J. Foster: Thanks from the heart for the work you did polishing the manuscript and getting it into production with speed and grace even at times when my screen figures were as clear as football play directions.

- Technical Editor Mara Zebest: Thanks to my friend and colleague for more than 14 years, working on yet another Photoshop book with pinpoint accuracy and the attention to details I occasionally smudged, all for the benefit of our readers.

- Layout technician Bill Hartman for the speed, the beautiful layout, and the reproduction of the color work.

- Ross Hignett at White Oaks for Grass Valley: Without your time and generosity we would have been hard pressed to show how the Canopus unit can help in the pipeline between archived Super 8 movies from 50 years ago to a beautifully restored digital state.

- Diana Lee at Maxon: Thank you Diana, and the other folks at Maxon for the pre-release of Cinema 4D version 10, used in this book to show animation, compositing techniques, and some truly awesome modules for generating particles, grass, and sundry other items much needed for our home movies.

- Bob Bennett and Brad Peebler at Luxology: A larger-than-life thanks for the use of modo 301, featured in this book to demonstrate the use of synthetic scenes happily coexisting with actual video footage.

- Thanks to Charles and Kate Moir, Bhavesh Bhavan, and the other gifted programmers at Xara, Ltd. for the advance copy of Xara Xtreme Pro, which I used for original artwork and to edit and annotate the screen figures in this book.

- Debbie Rich and all the support folks at Digital Anarchy: for the use of Knoll Light Factory and Primatte, shown in this book.

- Lisa Deutch and Amedeo Rosa at Alien Skin Software: for the use of Alien Skin Exposure, featured in a tutorial in the book.

- Eric Wingaard at Shinycore: for the use of Path Styler Pro, used in several examples in the tutorials.

- The Wegman family: for permission to do a location shoot in one of their fine supermarket locations.

- Peter Muserlian of Pemco Group: for granting us location shoot permission at the mall.

- Christine Wilhelmy at Apple, Inc: for the use of publicity photos of Apple Final Cut in this book.

- Robert Stanley: for actually giving this book its title, and as an invaluable resource for some of the finer points on Hollywood productions.

- Our actors and actresses! Special thanks to Melissa Feidt, her children Hayley and Nolan, and cooperation with LaValle's for the karate green-screen example shown in this book. Thanks also must go to David Bouton, Barbara Bouton, Jackie Schneider-Revette, Karl and Elkie Puettner, Dr. Michael Couch, Hector Couch, and Maddie and Drew Shuff for letting us stick a camera in their faces, usually on their only day off, for their patience and willingness to do embarrassing things, to sign a release cast in negative 2-point text, for making all of this possible, and for being friends, neighbors, and family.

- My wife Barbara: for her encouragement and countless hours spent as DP, gaffer, foley, prop manager, and for building the pirate costume.

About the Author

Gary David Bouton is the author of more than 20 computer graphics books, including the *Inside Adobe Photoshop* series and other titles ranging from vector drawing to modeling and Internet media. The author is also a trained illustrator and has been awarded four international awards for design and desktop publishing. A former advertising agency art director, Gary has worked on numerous television commercials for 7-Up and has designed print ads for various name-brand products. In the spare time he doesn't have, Gary composes original music and is currently working with film editors to provide special effects for music videos.

With his wife and frequent co-author Barbara, the couple host TheBoutons.com, which offers a forum for discussions on Photoshop, video, graphics and audio software, as well as tutorials and free content for anyone who has a passion for self-expression.

Contents

Introduction .... *xi*
How to Download the Example Files .... *xiv*

PART I: ENTERING THE WORLD OF VIDEO

Chapter 1: The Timeline and Importing Video   3

Preparing for Video Import. *3*
Importing Videos to Hard Disk *6*
A First Look at Importing Video. *11*
A Tutorial on Trimming Video Footage *19*
Working with Audio in Photoshop *23*
An Experiment with Losing Placed Files. *26*

Chapter 2: Working the Timeline Palette: Creating Videos from Still Images   29

Adobe Bridge and Color-Synching Animations. *42*
Timelapse Animations. *52*
Creating the Ken Burns Effect. *53*
Filtering a Video, Post-Production *60*

Chapter 3: Reconciling Different Media in a Composition   65

An Outline for the Composition. *66*
Broadcast Standards and Photoshop Compositions *67*

PART II: VIDEO SWEETENING

Chapter 4: Cuts, Wipes, and Fades — 93
Hands-On with the Animation Palette's Menu 93
Scripting 103
Building Transitions 105
Editing Transitions into a Composition 115
Two More Transitions to Complete Your Collection 123

Chapter 5: Video Color and Tone Adjustments — 131
Correcting Color Within a Composite Video 131
Colorizing a Moving Video Area 143
Keeping Your Color Adjustments Broadcast Legal 152
A Special Effect Using Color Correction 153

Chapter 6: Video Restoration — 161
Video Transfer Hardware and Software 162
Firing Up A-D Convertor Filtering 167
Retouching Motion Pictures 169
Enhancing Focus 181
Polishing the Presentation and Exporting 181

Chapter 7: Titling and Animating Text — 185
Measuring Screen Safety 185
Creating Subtitles 190
Creating a Crawl 195
Text Warp and Animated Text 205
Animating Text Manually 213
Creating Typewriter Text 220
3D Animated Text (with a Helper Application) 223

PART III: ANIMATION AND ROTOSCOPING

Chapter 8: Basic Animation and Rotoscoping — 231
Rotoscoping a Walk Cycle 232
Fleshing Out Your Animation 239
Cartoon Physics 249
Creating Cycles from Non-Cycling Videos 259
Mixing Animation with Photography 264

Chapter 9: Advanced Rotoscoping and Wire Removal — 275

Rotoscoping Away Unwanted Scene Areas *276*
Using Live Action as a Rotoscope *286*
An Exercise in Fantasy Composition *297*
Saving Time by Retouching Rendered Videos *303*
Wire Removal *306*

PART IV: 3D AND 3D ANIMATION

Chapter 10: 3D and CS3: An Introduction — 313

Understanding the 3D Tools *314*
Hands-On 3D: Experiment 1 . . . . *319*
Retexturing a 3D Model *324*
Google Earth and 3D Architecture *327*
Texture Replacements and Basic 3D Animation *342*

Chapter 11: Basic CGI Compositing into Video — 357

Everything's Coming Up Lilies *358*
An Example of Simple 3D Character Animation *372*

Chapter 12: Creating 3D Scene Props — 383

Working with Vanishing Point *383*
Putting a Neon Sign in a Video *388*
Putting a 3D Prop Into a Scene *397*
Combining Animation with Models and Videos *416*

PART V: SFX AND COMPOSITING TECHNIQUES

Chapter 13: Creating Fun, Simple, Effective fx — 427

Adding a Cross-Star Sparkle to a Clip *427*
Simulating an Earthquake *450*
Adventures in Split-Screen *455*
Warping Time *461*
Reversing Time *472*

Chapter 14: Advanced Compositing: Green Screening — 475

Lighting and Why We Use Green for Screening 475
Cutting Your First Key 478
Adding Polish to a Production 492
Green Suiting on the Cheap 496

Chapter 15: Compositing and Motion Matching — 511

Adding Elements to a Camera Pan 511
Complex Motion Matching 520
Creating a 38-Second Situation Comedy 534

PART VI: OUTPUT

Chapter 16: Codecs, DVD Authoring, and Saving for the Web — 551

Different Recipients Require Different File Formats 551
Examining the Structure of Digital Video 552
Publishing for the Web: QuickTime Codecs 557
Après-Codec: Setting Other Parameters for Publishing 561
E-Mail Attachments and Cross-Platform Issues 566
Publishing for the Web 567
Exporting for Collaboration 571
Codecs for Authoring 571
Archiving Your Video Work 575
Fade to Black; Roll Credits 577

Index — 579

Introduction

Moving pictures, from their very beginnings, have used the property of motion to do a single thing: tell a story. The story begins in the artist's mind as a concept and, to make a long story short, the artist films the idea.

So what separates the movie maker from the Photoshop artist? We all begin with a concept; we open Photoshop, bring in images, drawings, painting, or scans; we compose a scene and add lighting and color to direct the audience's eye. What we've been lacking is the element of *time*: how to express ourselves in pixel width and height with the additional dimension of changing these pixels across a duration of time—and time is exactly what Adobe Systems has provided as the big new feature in Photoshop Extended.

I wrote this book because I wanted to tell a story to two converging audiences: the Photoshop professional and the After Effects user. I wrote this book for the Photoshop professional who wants to add an element to a composition but was previously limited to a little GIF file whose star was confined to flashing text or a bouncing ball. With Photoshop Extended, depending on your ambition and your system resources, you can now import video clips with audio, create video segments from scratch to layer on top of the video, apply your existing retouching skills to an idea you have in mind, and export a polished, professional video that is as visually sumptuous as your still-image retouching work. As a perk, once you've worked completely through this book you'll be better prepared to tackle Adobe After Effects, if this is one of your goals, because many of the conventions for video editing in Photoshop Extended and After Effects are quite similar. I also wrote this book with the After Effects user in mind. For years, After Effects users have sought out Photoshop's rich set of pixel editing tools as a finishing touch for video compositions; After Effects professionals will be pleased to find a lot of documentation in this book on Photoshop "how to's." Pore through this book and you might just discover an easier way to achieve an effect using Photoshop Extended; its memory handling is superb, you can work with a fairly large number of layers with speed, you have over 50 filters you can apply to videos (plus there's a way to apply third-party filters), and the Animation palette in Photoshop will make you feel right at home.

Adobe Photoshop CS3 Extended: Retouching Motion Pictures is organized much like, well, a *story*: the first few chapters and parts are an orientation, and exposition of sorts, covering how to get existing videos and audio clips into a document, and a detailed explanation of both operating modes for the Animation palette. Along the way, I show you new features such as the Clone Source palette, how to work with some of the new UI elements such as the docker strip, how video durations are measured, and how to work with *pixel aspect ratio*, a pixel attribute many Photoshop users have not had to understand until now.

You'll find the meat in the middle of this book. Beginning in Part II, I demonstrate how to not only cut video clips together, but also how to build transition effects such as clock wipes and dissolves that are the staples of After Effects users. I move on to working in Frames mode with the Animation palette in Part III to show how to create animations from the ground up, and also how to perform retouching work such as wire removal and a little rotoscoping. Then there's the special effects: Photoshop Extended can also import 3D objects from modeling applications such as 3D Studio and Maya, and, as always, Photoshop is a superb integrator of different types of media created in different applications. I show you the ins and outs of working with video that has alpha transparency, green screen techniques for putting an exotic locale behind your actor or actress, and how to achieve stunning simulations such as slow motion, split-screen compositing, and motion matching a CGI element into an actor's hands…standard Hollywood stuff, except you're the one doing it on your desktop.

The finale is how to get your work *out of* Photoshop, out of your machine, and on to your home TV set, your friends' TV sets, and YouTube and the other video salons. I also touch on archiving and transporting your original work. You might have worked with large files in previous years in Photoshop, but we're talking a magnitude larger need for storage when dealing with several high-quality video clips.

I've provided content for working through the many tutorials in this book, so be sure to check out the section "How to Download the Example Files" immediately following this Introduction to see how to download the media before you begin. The files are not hard-drive busters in size; I tried very hard to keep the video file sizes as small as possible for folks with dial-up connections, but at the same time provide good quality so the examples serve as good ones when you get to your own personal and professional work. As far as the *content* of the content goes, it's light, a little on the surreal side at times, and as polished as an author could get without scheduling three years' worth of cinematography! The reasons I went for the broad strokes in content are twofold: I enjoy a good laugh, but more importantly, this book is about storytelling. The examples in this book necessarily need to be concise and brief; humor and the extraordinary by their nature can be quite succinct—the audience gets the point right away, and therefore this small story can be told in its entirety in a short span of time. I wanted closure in the tutorials: You'll learn how to begin, tell, and conclude a tale through retouching and editing.

I hope you enjoy this book as much as I did writing it, and learn as much as I did while writing it. Let's cut to the chase now!

Bonus Content and a Third-Party Guide

In addition to the downloadable videos and audio tracks to use with this book's tutorials (see the following section), there is a special gift to our readers on the download area; the folder is called "Bonus Chapter." Within that folder you'll find 11 animation sequences that you can use as composite footage in your own work. There are some effects and very nice simulated aerial photography that are terrific for green-screen work. There's also a chapter on applications that play nice with Photoshop, in PDF file format. Because Photoshop is the *el primo* professional integrator of media created in different applications, we thought it would be helpful to list what the author used to prepare this book and demonstrate their value in mini-tutorials. The links to third-party software listed in this chapter are live links; with an active Internet connection, you just click the link to check out the specs and demo versions of some spectacular complements to Photoshop CS3 Extended.

How to Download the Example Files

We'd like you to get started right away with the techniques in this book. All the example files for the chapters can be downloaded from http://www.courseptr.com/ptr_downloads.cfm. Type **Bouton** in the Search Downloads field and you'll arrive at the book's examples main folder pronto.

Because we want to provide access to readers who have a dial-up connection in addition to broadband folks, the book's example files are broken down into chapters. Before you begin a chapter, download the files in the example_files folder, and if you'd like to see what a completed project looks like, download the files in the gallery folder. If a particular example file proves too large to download in its original state, the files are compressed using the ubiquitous ZIP file format—easy to extract in Windows or Mac OS X.

You'll also occasionally find bonus files in a chapter folder. These are free for you to experiment with, and the only stipulation is that you don't post or sell the files as your own. But do feel free to use them in your personal and professional work; there are animated backgrounds of nature and high-tech scenes that'll perk up a home movie or just about any board room presentation.

Get ready to roll 'em; video editing in Photoshop is one of life's few experiences where work is fun!

Part I
Entering the World of Video

The Timeline and Importing Video

1

The (Animation) Timeline palette might feel familiar to you if you've used ImageReady in previous versions of Photoshop. And if you own Premiere, After Effects, or similar video editors, you'll feel right at home in CS3 Extended. However, I won't *assume* familiarity—my high school gym teacher had a saying about assuming things!

This chapter gets you up and running with the timeline with a specific focus on trimming a video clip. Additionally, I show you how to add audio to the footage, play back the video and audio mix, and export the trimmed video to a high-quality file format that retains all aspects of the composition. Let's begin with getting your footage off of your camera and onto a hard disk. Depending on a camera's saved file format, this process runs from difficult to impossible to work directly from your camera's media in Photoshop.

Preparing for Video Import

Remember when you made the big leap from editing 1MB images in the early 1990s to editing press-ready, 300 ppi full-page compositions? Probably the first thing you did was get a better computer, and the second thing was to add a hard drive. I heartily recommend that you buy a new 500GB hard drive and dedicate it to your video work; I've seen this size (and larger) for as little as $125 online. You'll also want to buy a spool or two of DVDs and regularly back up your original footage and edited videos. Write them as data and not movie files because

Camcorder Shopping Tips

If you haven't taken the plunge and bought your camcorder yet, there are an unprecedented variety of cameras at more price points than ever before. Fortunately, you will need to narrow your criteria to a list of precisely two things before you plunk down your plastic: the quality of the video recorded (audio is a secondary consideration) and the ease of loading your video in Photoshop or another video editing suite you might spring for after recharging your plastic.

Here is the skinny on what is available, what I chose for a camera, and things you want to steer clear of:

The Standard Definition (SD) Digital Video (DV) format was introduced in 1994. DV is the most widely used industry format; everyone from professionals to consumers use one variation of it or another. The cameras that use SD usually take MiniDV tapes as media. MiniDV tape is written to DV-AVI format (Audio-Video Interleave), which can be compared to the properties of a TIFF file—everyone can read, write, and edit SD video coming in DV-AVI format taken from a MiniDV tape. DV-AVI fits into today's standard workflow, but the sun is setting on this level of technology because the age of High Definition (HD) video is dawning.

You can buy a great SD MiniDV camcorder at very attractive prices. For example, Panasonic's top-of-the-line prosumer MiniDV camera sells for under $500, which is less than a high-end iPod. The new High Definition prosumer camcorders cost twice this much in 2007, and not many HD models are available yet. But it is not just about the cost of the camera.

As expected when governments, technical bodies, businesses, content providers, and even Wal-Mart get involved in the evolution of a technology, not one but several standards currently exist for HD. Therefore it is premature to predict the clear winner(s). Predictably, without a sole standard for HD, hardware such as DVD burners and players for HD has been announced by Sony and other manufacturers but is not yet shipping.

As far as this book and Photoshop Extended are concerned, you need a camera that can produce a file in one of the following formats:

- MPEG1
- MPEG4
- MOV
- AVI
- MPEG2 (MPEG-2 is supported if an MPEG2 encoder is installed on your computer. Apple charges for this encoder.)

SD cameras that write to MiniDV tape produce AVI natively, so these kinds of cameras are probably your best choice for PS CS3 Extended work. Also, the DV-AVI format is not as compressed as other video formats. You'll get good video luminance and chroma with SD camcorders.

SD camcorders that write to MiniDVD discs or to in-camera hard disks write data in MPEG-2 format. Flash media-based camcorders write to the MPEG-4 format. SD video saved in either of the MPEG formats is of lower quality than SD video written to tape. The MPEG footage is more highly compressed and as a consequence contains more artifacting (noise). Most editing software must *transcode* (reformat) MPEG footage to an intermediate format (usually DV-AVI for editing) and then transcode it back to MPEG. With MPEG footage it is easy to get into a situation similar to editing the same JPEG images three or four times; you lose quality each time you resave the files. It is my recommendation, therefore, that you avoid all SD camcorders that write to anything other than tape.

All professional, prosumer, and consumer HD camcorders write data in some variation of MPEG-2 or MPEG-4. The recently released AVCHD (Advanced Video Codec High Definition) cameras by Sony and Panasonic aren't an exception. AVCHD is really MPEG-4 AVC (H.264).

As when MPEG compression is used with SD, HD video is compressed and can display artifacting, but because so much more information is gathered compared to SD, the resulting images do look better than SD that was not MPEG compressed. You start out with more pixels captured of higher color quality, so you end up with more.

HiDef original data is a compressed file and can't be edited directly by most software, including Photoshop Extended. There are a number of variations of MPEG-2 and MPEG-4 used on HiDef. Even though Adobe Systems tells consumers that Extended will open compressed HD footage, Photoshop might not be able to *parse* (understand, interpret) the specific type of MPEG compression produced by the camera. If this is the case, you'll have to use your camera's software utilities or a third-party program to convert the MPEG footage into DV-AVI or MOV, as these are the most compatible and capable formats that Photoshop Expended can work with.

High Definition video is very exciting, and it is the way of the future. And in 2007 it is a headache, it is expensive, difficult to get, and difficult and time consuming to work with. You've faced this problem before and surely will again: the transition from film photography to digital, from 2-megapixel to 10-megapixel file sizes, from JPEG to RAW. However, it is clear that if you lay out the cash for emerging technology today, your media will remain fresh and up to date longer, but you invite workflow miseries in the here and now.

I therefore recommend that your initial video investment be a high-quality, cheap SD camera for now. You're assured that everything will work well because you are working with the current mainstream technology and not "bleeding-edge" technology.

The media clips that accompany this book were produced using a $400 Panasonic SD camcorder, and I couldn't be happier for the while. But I'll probably be buying a HD camcorder—in a few years.

movie files use lossy compression (standard video titles are written using MPEG compression).

Also, you'll want to set up a directory structure on your new hard drive; you'll want to arrange your source files and edited work by project—for example, P:\Video\Sunday on the Beach, P:\Video\Carousel Ride, and so on. I suggest that you create folders for your projects before launching a Photoshop session because when you export finished footage, Photoshop doesn't provide you with a New Folder option in the Export dialog box. Put all project-related media in the proper folder—video, audio clips, still images, and Photoshop PSD animation work. (I explain shortly why organizing files by file type instead of in project folders will get you into PhotoTrouble.)

Importing Videos to Hard Disk

The first video I took with my new camera was hardly as simple as downloading RAW images from my digital still camera, and if you're a first-time-outer, I have some suggestions to reduce the inevitable stress. First, chances are your camera came with a CD or DVD that contains a rudimentary video editor but also a program for downloading your footage to hard drive. Install this program! If by chance you misplaced the disc, I show you later in this section how to use your operating system's utility for bringing in the footage.

> **Note**
>
> Different manufacturers have different terms for the act of copying data off a video camera and onto your hard drive in a file format readily accessible by your system tools, video viewers, and Photoshop. *Import, capture, transfer,* and *download* are the most common terms for the same thing. None of these terms includes erasing your data from the camera's media, so you've got your footage safe until you remove it manually.

Using Your Camera's Download Program

Let's say you had your camera's software CD on hand and you've installed it. Following are the steps that apply to today's MiniDV tapes. If your camera stores video on Mini-DVDs, memory sticks, or a mini hard drive, the footage has already been written to a specific file format:

1. Make sure the camera is powered on and in Playback mode.

2. Hook the camera up to a USB (or FireWire) port. Your OS should signal you when it has found the device.

3. Go to the download program. (I'm using Panasonic's DV Studio Light). Choose your input device from the program's menu (or icon).

4. Use the on screen controls to rewind the media to the beginning of the take you want to download.

5. Mark your In point using the program's controls. (In Figure 1.1, you will see that DV Studio has a Mark In button.)

6. Play or fast-forward your video to the end of the clip and mark the Out point.

7. Save the clip to hard drive; this will take a few minutes. (In DV Studio, I double-click the timeline where the highlighted clip is to save to disk.)

In Figure 1.1, you can see the UI of the DV Studio program that came with my camera. This figure captures a download in process from my camera to the AVI file format on my dedicated hard drive.

Figure 1.1
The editing programs that come with your video camera usually include a downloading capability.

Downloading Video Using Windows Movie Maker

The steps to downloading video data using Windows Movie Maker are very similar to the steps used with most cameras' OEM download software. Vista and XP have slightly different menus and tool buttons in their respective versions of Movie Maker, but the procedure is essentially identical. Get your camera plugged into a

USB port, wait for the system audio signal that tells you Windows has found the new device, and then follow these steps.

1. Make sure the camera's powered on in Playback mode, the media is in the camera, and you've got it connected to your PC via USB or FireWire, whichever standard the camera manufacturer adopted.
2. Launch Movie Maker from the Programs group on the Start menu.
3. In Movie Maker, choose Import from Digital Movie Camera. You'll see a Video Wizard dialog box.
4. Click the Create Clips when Wizard Finishes checkbox, and then click Start Capture. In general, it's good to save scenes as individual clips instead of downloading one (several gigabyte) video, so click Stop Capture after a Scene Is Concluded. If you took your scenes in a tight sequence with very little blank space between takes, let the first video run a second or two into the following video, capture it, and then use the onscreen VCR controls to back up your camera's media a little and capture (download) the next scene. Later in this chapter I show you how to trim saved videos. In Figure 1.2 you can see I'm in the process of saving my third clip.

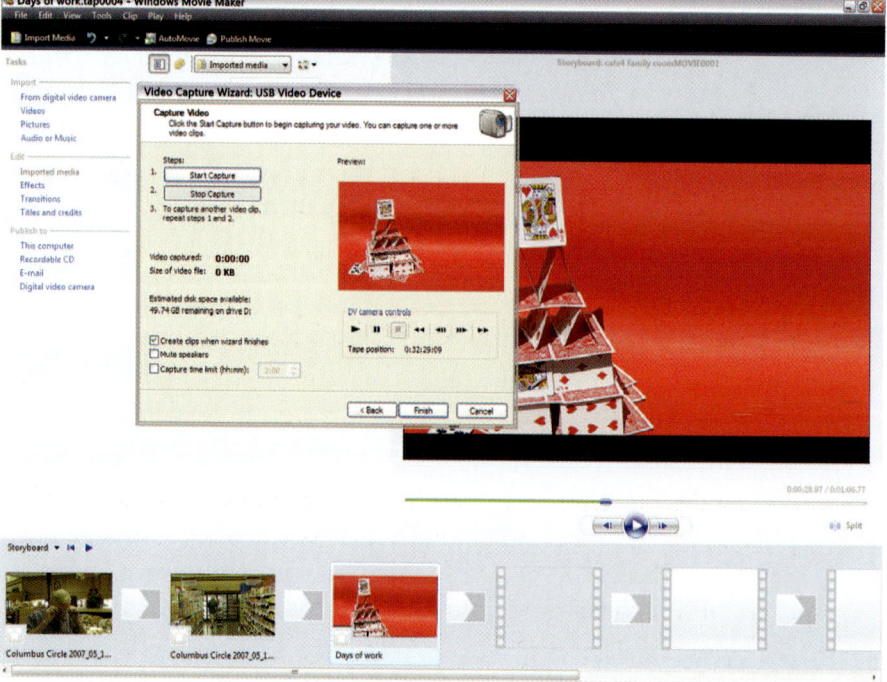

Figure 1.2
Downloading your videos using Windows Movie Maker is as simple as using your camera manufacturer's download application. The file format will be the same.

5. After you've captured the videos, click Finish. It's time to save them to hard disk. Movie Maker displays a dialog with three options. Although the first one, Best Quality for Playback on My Computer, sounds good, it's not. Choose the *second* option, Digital Device Format (DV-AVI). The first option saves small, very compressed, and artifacty WMV files that Photoshop will not import, and that's not how you want your original videos transferred! See Figure 1.3 for the correct option to choose before clicking Next.

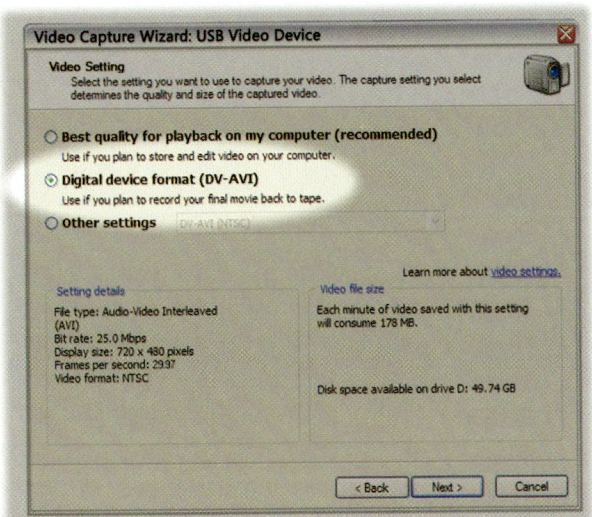

Figure 1.3
Save your video captures to DV-AVI file format.

6. The next dialog box asks you where you want your AVI files saved. Choose the folder you created on that new huge hard drive, in a subfolder designated for a specific project, such as footage of your spouse, vacation, and so on.

Downloading Your Videos in the Mac OS

iMovie comes with Mac OS X, and this is the place to begin downloading your camera footage if you don't have the camera's software utility. Here's how to get your video copied over to hard disk:

1. Make sure that you have your media in your camera, the camera's hooked up to your Mac, and your camera is in VTR (playback) mode. Alternatively, if you have a card reader, you can plop the appropriate media into a USB 2, FireWire, or Flash card reader.

2. In iMovie, you might want to set your preferences to the auto-length to which iMovie trims the footage as it imports it. Choose Preferences.

3. Click Create a New iMovie Project in the dialog that automatically appears, give it a name, and click Create.

4. Basically the download is automated and is a very simple process. You click the Import button in the preview window, and iMovie brings all of your video in and divides it into scenes. You also have the VCR controls for forwarding and rewinding the footage on your camera to import only the scenes you want to copy over.

5. When you're finished, you can arrange clips into a single export or (more prudently) export individual clips by selecting them. Then choose Share > QuickTime. Choose a movie format from the pop-up menu. I heartily recommend choosing None in the compression area.

6. Click the Share Selected Clips Only checkbox. Then click Share.

7. Name the movie and then click Save.

In Figure 1.4 you can see iMovie HD in action (you don't have to load high definition media to use iMovie). Photoshop can import MOV, AVI, MPEG-4, and various other file formats; I recommend you stick with non-lossy compression such as MOV, and if you need to share your file with a Windows co-worker, the AVI export from iMovie works fine.

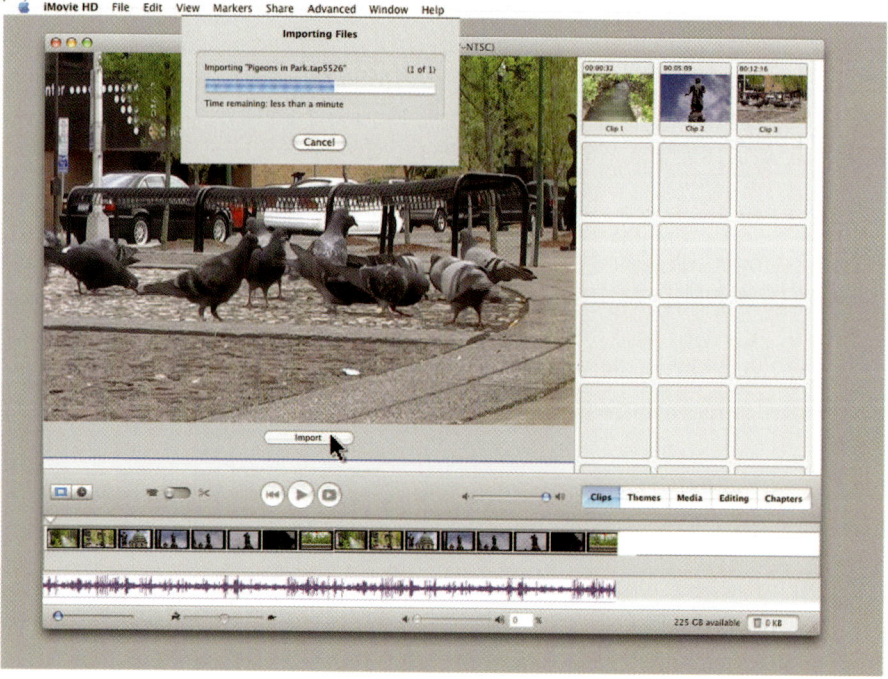

Figure 1.4
Whether it's your camera's utility, Movie Maker, or iMovie, you should download your videos and save them in uncompressed file format.

> **Note**
>
> Photoshop's video engine is based on QuickTime, although it can import and export to many different video file formats (QuickTime is a technology; the MOV file format is only one implementation of QuickTime). Windows users must have QuickTime installed on their system to use Photoshop Extended's video features. If you inadvertently deleted this utility or need an upgrade, visit apple.com/quicktime/download/.

A First Look at Importing Video

If you don't have a video camera, the following sections describe how to perform a simple footage trim using the Animation palette. The following sections take you through the how-to's of correcting pixel aspect ratio, an explanation of what some of the timeline controls do, and some hands-on steps for polishing a video to export from Photoshop.

Correcting Aspect Ratio

Unlike 99% of the image files you import from cameras and graphics created in other applications, video footage can have a non-square pixel attribute because, for reasons explained in later chapters, NTSC standards define a video pixel aspect of 0.9 (1.0 would define square pixels). Therefore, your typical standard definition DV footage will come into Photoshop a little narrower than looks right. Although the footage will play correctly in the Windows and Mac OS media players, this distorted (called *scaled* in Photoshop) appearance will most assuredly interfere with accurate editing work. The way to change your view of the .9 (expressed as .9/1 as a fraction) aspect for the pixels video *without changing the data* is to choose View > Pixel Aspect Ratio Correction. When data looks wrong, first change your view, and only as a last recourse do you change the visual data itself. As you can see in Figure 1.5, at top left (before correction), the title bar of the document says (scaled) after the file name, but your own eyes will inform you of the .9 pixel aspect.

Exploring the Timeline Editor

The Timeline Editor is where half of the video editing action takes place in CS3 Extended; the other half is on the Layers palette. Peek ahead to Figure 1.6 to see what the icon for the Animation (Timeline) palette looks like on the docking strip. If it's not there, you can either choose Window > Workspace > Video and Film (which rearranges your workspace and puts all the palettes you'll need in the workspace, overwriting your current workspace) or just choose Window > Animation to display the Animation (Timeline) palette.

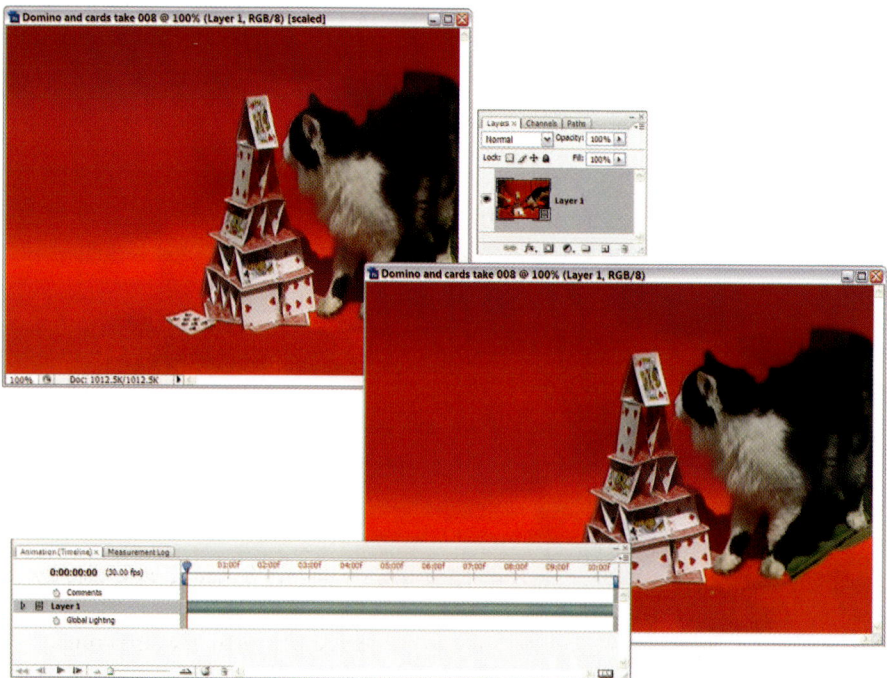

Figure 1.5
Change your view of the non-square video pixels so you can edit videos accurately.

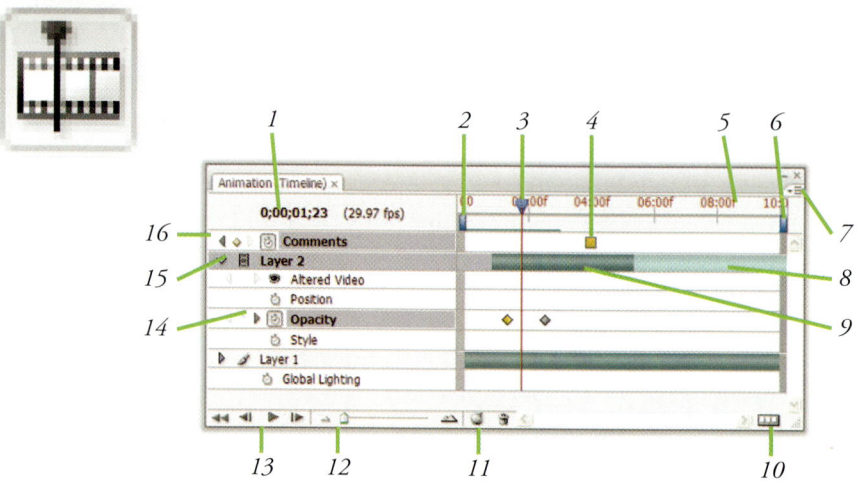

Figure 1.6
The Animation (Timeline) palette.

> **Note**
>
> Because both CS3 and CS3 Extended have UIs that are slightly different than previous versions, let me digress for a minute and walk you through the docking strip.
>
> The arrows to the top right above the palette title minimize and maximize palettes to icons with text titles. To further minimize docking strip items to just the icons, you drag the left edge of the strip to the right; your cursor turns to a double-headed arrow when it's in the right position for dragging. You can have several docking strips. If you'd like to build one next to the default strip, you group undocked palettes (they stick to the bottom edges of one another) and then drag the gang to the left of the default strip.
>
> Unless you use two monitors, you can get cramped for workspace real estate very easily with all of Photoshop's palettes out. I prefer to display the palettes I use most frequently reduced to icon buttons, with the Layers/Channels/Paths grouped palette floating in the workspace. To convert a docked group to floating in the workspace, you drag the top tab of a docked palette (or group) into the workspace. If you feel you're not going to use a grouped palette for a while, you can return it to the docking strip by dragging its title bar to the bottom of the strip. You get a visual signal—a blue bar beneath the strip—when your cursor is in docking position.
>
> Finally, the Tools palette (it's not officially a toolbox anymore) can be undocked by dragging its top tab—the screen element just above the PS Web button and just below the dark gray dock element—into the workspace. You also have the option to display the Tools palette in two rows or in one row by clicking the arrow icon on the top tab of the palette.
>
> Closing palettes, grouping individual palettes, and accessing the options for palettes on their flyout menus are accomplished exactly the same way as in previous versions. Minimizing and maximizing a palette is done by single-clicking the tab area above the palette titles.

With my video loaded in the workspace (File > Open) and the Animation (Timeline) palette at the ready, here's a walkthrough of the features and functions on the palette (refer to Figure 1.6):

1. The Timeline Current Time counter. This area displays the current time in the displayed video as defined by the timeline marker (3). This is an active area; you can drag the numbers left and right to advance the frame displayed in the document window and move the timeline marker. (I explain the meaning of the numbers shortly in this section.) You can also double-click the timeline counter to display the Set Current Time dialog box where you type in a precise value to then move to that time in the video.

2. The Start of the Work Area marker. This blue element marks the beginning of the video workspace, not to be confused with Photoshop's graphics workspace. By default, when you open a video file, the beginning marker is flush to the left of the timeline, but you can change this, as I'll demonstrate in this chapter. The End of the Work Area marker (6) is the end of an imported video, by default.

3. The timeline marker. This indicates the current time as displayed in the document window, and it can be dragged to fast-forward or rewind to any point in the Work Area. This UI element is commonly called the "thumb"; I call it the thumb often in other chapters, and it's called the thumb in professional nonlinear video editos such as Apple Final Cut Pro, Avid Studio, and Adobe After Effects.

4. A comment. Comments are sticky notes unique to the Animation (Timeline) palette. You can create a comment to remind yourself that there's an action or cut at a specific point in the timeline, and this is a more convenient method for making notes than using the Tools palette's Notes tool. In (16) in Figure 1.6, you see the controls for toggling between notes in the timeline. The stopwatch icon is for arming video, Styles, and comments for key (frame) changes; you click it to its active position to auto-create key changes, and a second click deactivates auto-keying and also deletes all keys, including comments. You can see a comment by double-clicking a gold comment icon, or if you hover over it, you'll see the message in a tool tips-style message box.

5. The timeline. This displays the increments of the animation, and the timeline marker points to it to tell you the current time in the video displayed in the document window. Time is measured in two different ways in traditional video and in CS3 Extended: in chronology (hours, minutes, seconds) and in frames—each unit of measurement serving a valuable purpose in video retouching and editing.

6. The End of the Work Area marker. See (2).

7. The flyout menu button. This UI element is common to all palettes in Photoshop. I cover some of the basic options you access off this menu in this chapter and get into others as you proceed through this book to advanced techniques.

8. Hidden area of placed video. When you bring in a video, the Animation (Timeline) palette displays it as a video layer, a green shaded bar, and it takes up the width of the Work Area. However, one way to trim a video is to shorten the play length of a video layer. You do this by dragging on the end of the video layer green shaded bar toward the center of the Work Area; the lighter green area is the hidden video.

> **Note**
>
> As you get into the tutorials in this chapter, you'll notice that the document window has no file extension; the document, even when saved to Photoshop's PSD file format, is merely a vessel for applying edits to a video that remains untouched on hard disk. It's similar to placing an image in Quark or InDesign; a video file is linked to its saved Photoshop document. All of this has its advantages and disadvantages, which I'll cover shortly.

9. The visible video in the Work Area. This green shaded bar indicates video that is visible in the Work Area—your composition. See (8).

10. The Frames/Animation toggle. Video you place in a document can be manipulated in the Animation mode of the Animation (Timeline) palette, but clicking this icon takes you to the Frames view of your composition. You will severely mess up your video if you click to toggle to Frames mode and then perform any editing; Animation edits are performed by keyframing, while Frame animation is accomplished with a frame-by-frame method. I'll walk you through all of this, starting with Chapter 2. For now, don't click the Frames toggle when you're just beginning to work with placed video footage.

11. Onion Skin. This is a feature used by traditional animators to see previous frames and future frames to better tween an effect into the composition. I show working with Onion Skin in Chapter 8.

12. Timeline zoom. Especially when working with long footage, it's hard to see a specific point on the timeline where you want a mark in or mark out point. You drag to the little hills icon at left to shrink your view of the timeline and drag right to the mountains icon to zoom into the timeline. It works exactly like the slider on the Navigator palette, except it zooms time instead of image view.

13. The VCR controls. These are used to stop, play, rewind, fast forward, and move your document view by single video frames—very useful in rotoscoping and retouching. Alternatively, you can press Enter to start and stop a video.

14. The stopwatch icons and layer properties. Part of the power of PS CS3 Extended as an animation tool is the capability to change certain attributes of the video layer over time. For example (and as shown in Figure 1.6), suppose you want to fade a layer to complete transparency, displaying underlying layers over time. First, you pick a time point using the timeline marker and click the stopwatch icon, then on the Layers palette, you decrease the opacity of the target layer. A diamond appears on the timeline on the Opacity track, and the stopwatch icon changes color—a visual indicator that you have

one or more keyframes defined. If you click the stopwatch icon again, it deletes all keys, saving the state of the video layer to the current opacity, position, and/or Style (so don't do this). Use the forward and backward arrows bracketing the stopwatch icon to preview the keyframes.

Keyframing is a method for building sophisticated video edits and animations; Photoshop handles smooth or sharp time transitions between keyframes, removing the mental calculation traditional animators have had to perform for almost a century.

15. The video layer icon. This is the default icon that reminds you that the layer is a placed video and not a standard pixel layer; it also appears on the Layers palette. You can display a thumbnail instead of the icon via the palette options you access on the palette's flyout menu. You can see the tracks for standard video layer properties in Figure 1.6; don't get confused over Adobe's name for filters you can change over time on the timeline (in combination with using the Layers palette). It's called Styles on the Animation (Timeline) palette, but in addition to the Styles on the Styles palette, you can also animate *filters* you apply to a Smart Object video layer. You can only animate filters that you can apply on the Filter menu; some, but not all filters are available for video layers.

> **Note**
>
> A video layer can also exist on a layer as a *Smart Object*. See Figure 1.6 inset for the icon that is tagged to the video layer image thumbnail as it appears on the Layers palette. A Smart Object, as it applies to a placed video, is a sort of "wrapper" for the video that enables you to apply various filters in a nondestructive way to the video layer. I get into working with Smart Object-placed video footage in Chapter 3.

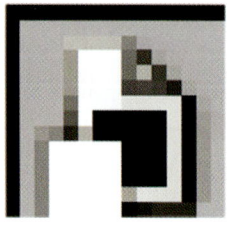

Figure 1.6 Inset
A Smart Object will accept additional editing properties as you work with the video.

16. The comments stopwatch and controls. As shown in (4), a comment is a handy placeholder for text to remind you of an event at a specific time. To make an initial comment, you click the stopwatch icon and then enter your text message. To create your second and all other future comments, you put the timeline marker at a point in time and then choose Edit Timeline Comment from the palette's flyout menu. When the current time is over a comment marker, the diamond between the forward/back icons to the left of the comments stopwatch lights up; you delete that comment by clicking the diamond icon. You progress through comments on a layer by clicking the forward/back arrows. Or simply hover over a comment mark on the timeline, and a message box displays your comment text.

There are two more things about the Animation (Timeline) palette I need to show you to complete the basic tour. First, tiny green marks that look like screen artifacting might appear on the Work Area track (the area directly below the timeline) as shown in Figure 1.7. This is a visual indicator that Photoshop is busy buffering its read of a placed video, and playback of your composition will be slower than real time until Photoshop has stored the area of time you're playing in buffer memory. The green will turn solid when the time has been completely cached. One way to partially prevent Photoshop from taking time off to buffer is to increase scratch disk allotment in Preferences (Ctrl+K) > Performance. Another way to preview a slightly jerky video in real time is to choose Allow Frame Skipping from the Animation (Timeline) palette's flyout menu.

Figure 1.7
RAM frame buffering is performed on-the-fly when necessary in Photoshop to play back a video sequence.

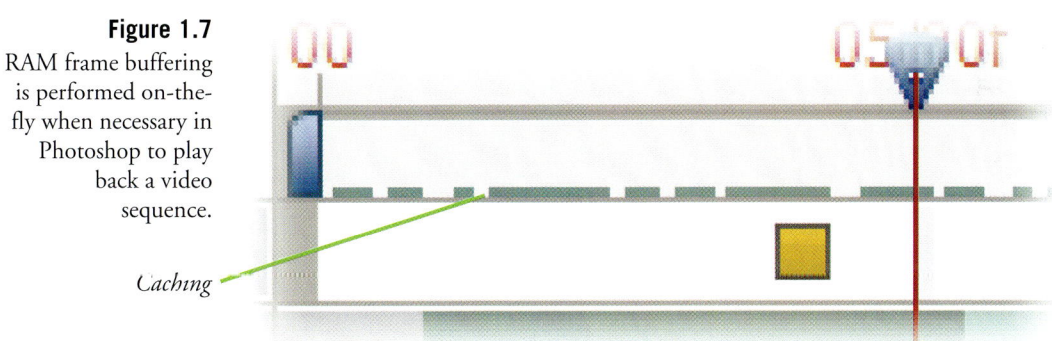

Related to frame buffering is the fps (frames per second) field in parentheses to the right of the current time field (callout 1 in Figure 1.6). When the fps is displayed in black, you're working in real time, and frame buffering is not necessary (this is typical with small video clips). The value, as I mentioned earlier, should be 29.97 fps for most video imported from digital camcorders. When the field appears in red, you'll also notice that the fps value is less than real time. This means

Photoshop is attempting to buffer the playback, and motion will appear to stutter in the document window. When the field is green, this means that buffering is done, and you should be playing back sequences in real time. See Figure 1.8 for the three states of the fps field.

0;00;01;23 (29.97 fps)

0;00;01;23 (7.09 fps)

0;00;01;23 (29.97 fps)

Dropframe timecode — 0;00;01;23

Standard timecode — 0:00:01:23

Figure 1.8
The fps field in buffering state, buffering finished, and real time state.

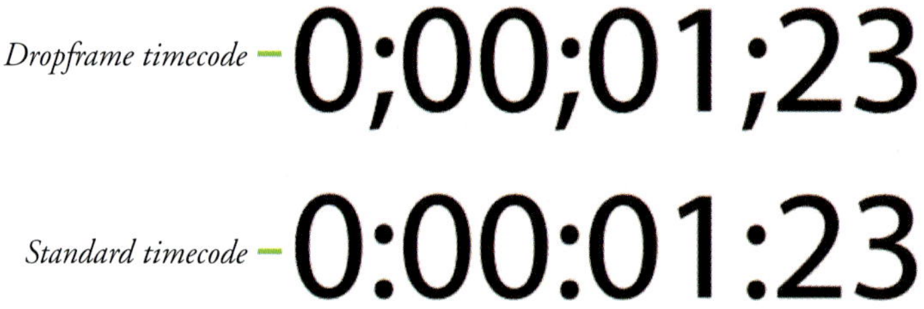

When playback on the timeline is in time (as opposed to frame) display, the delimiters between hours, minutes, seconds, and frames are displayed in one of two ways, depending on the media you have placed. When digital camera or other broadcast media is loaded, 29.97 frames per second is the National Television Standards Committee's (NTSC) standard for broadcast frame rates in North America, Japan, and several other countries. The delimiters appear as semicolons, as shown at the top in Figure 1.8. Also called *dropframe* timecode, 29.97 fps was devised to reconcile the differences between black-and-white and color TV broadcasts. The term *dropframe* does *not* mean your computer will drop frames (skip frames) if the processor can't handle the data stream; the term is used to describe the way broadcast TV transmits the frames as video—the effect of dropframe timecode is invisible to the audience. In other words, the dropframe timecode skips (or drops) *timecode values* at a predetermined rate in order to keep the standard timecode rate synchronized with the video data.

When you use media created on the computer, such as an animation created in Poser, Cinema 4D, or another animation package, you typically save to 30 fps, and the video in Photoshop reads with colons, not semicolons, as shown at the bottom in Figure 1.8. Here's the skinny on proceeding with this disparity in frame rates: If your finished video is never going to air on broadcast TV, you can safely output your work to 30 fps. If you intend to publish your composition and have it aired, choose 29.97 fps when you write the finished footage; doing this ensures that black-and-white and color footage is timed with the fudge-factor reconciliation we presently live with. You also have the option to write your video animations to 29.97 fps to perfectly synch with camera footage—most professional animation packages offer this frame rate. The only time you'd want to stray from the NTSC convention is if you're airing a video in Europe, which uses the PAL standard rather than NTSC and has adopted 25 fps for standard broadcasts.

A Tutorial on Trimming Video Footage

When you create a terrific Photoshop image, you begin in the shooting phase. A lot of times you pad the still frame when you take a picture, standing farther away than necessary from the desired subject, and then crop it later. This action has an analogy when shooting video footage—to capture an exact moment, you begin the camera prior to the anticipated action and then press the Pause button only after you're certain nothing interesting will happen afterward. Therefore, if you adopt this strategy, you need to trim the excess head and tail from the video to use the clip as a finished, polished cut in a larger composition.

In the following steps I take you through placing the video footage you downloaded early, trimming it, and then making a copy of your trimmed composition. The concept behind the footage was to tell a very simple visual story: Someone put some exquisite labor into building a house of cards (try it sometime—it's harder than it looks, and we wound up using a glue gun to hold the house together), and then a housecat saunters in and threatens to wreck it. Cats by their nature are uncooperative, and therefore I ran into the problem of getting Domino into and out of the scene; you can see my wife's hands putting Domino on the seamless at the head of the video (and it needs to be trimmed out). Additionally, we ran out of red seamless, and this video is a work in progress you'll complete in a later chapter that covers rotoscoping away unwanted visual elements, the part of the picnic table that shows beyond the extent of the seamless.

Here's how to work with the Animation (Timeline) palette; the steps are based on your new knowledge of the features on the palette:

1. Double-click an empty area of Photoshop's workspace (the gray background) to display the Open dialog box and then open Domino and cards take 008.avi from hard disk. You might get a Missing Profile dialog box, depending on how you have Preferences > File Handling and Edit > Color Settings defined. I make it a practice to work in Adobe RGB color space because it's very wide

and tends not to clip colors I need preserved in my original media. I recommend choosing Assign Working RGB: Adobe RGB (1998) at this point if you get this dialog box. Then click OK.

2. The following dialog box informs you that Pixel Aspect Ratio Correction Is for Preview Purposes Only. As I explain in other sections of this book, video that is meant for television broadcast is formatted with pixels that are non-square, specifically 1 unit tall, but .9 units wide. So the video of Domino is going to look weird, but it would not look weird when broadcast on television because TV sets compensate for the non-square pixel aspect ratio. For now, I'd recommend that you check the Don't Show Again checkbox and then click OK. Just remember the View command described in Step 4 whenever you work with video that will be played on a TV set, either from the airwaves or from a playback device such as DVD.

3. Save the file as Domino and cards take 008.psd now.

4. Go to View and uncheck Pixel Aspect Ratio Correction. This changes your view of the video so it's no longer smooshed in appearance, and you can edit with accuracy. However, the video is still formatted with a .9 pixel aspect ratio; if you check out Image > Pixel Aspect Ratio you'll see that the video does not use square pixels. All is well, though; you change your *view* of data and not the data itself as a rule, because changing data usually creates a permanent and often unwanted change.

5. Because I need you to trim to specific start and end points in this document, click the flyout menu on the Animation (Timeline) palette, choose Palette Options, and then click the Frame Number button. Click OK to apply the change. Now on the Animation (Timeline) palette, the timeline is displayed in the frame number increment; see Figure 1.9.

Figure 1.9
Choose to display the timeline increments in frames to better locate a specific point in the footage.

6. With your cursor, scrub the timeline by dragging right from the beginning of the clip to where you can see Domino clearly entering the scene. *Scrubbing* is simply an industry term for moving the timeline marker back and forth to locate a specific point in time. To my eye, my wife's hand appears to be in the clear by frame 43.

> **Quick Timeline Browsing Techniques**
>
> As you get into more complex composition with more video layers (and more altered video layers), you'll find that simply dragging the thumb offers resistance because Photoshop is sort of going through a reading-ahead process; the more data, the more the thumb will fight you when you want to scroll through the timeline.
>
> One way to avoid delays is to pinpoint a time on the timeline and then make a decisive click on that point. Doing this prevents Photoshop from browsing all the frames between the current time and your desired time. Another method for going to a specific point is by double-clicking the Current Time indicator, the bold text at upper left above the comments stopwatch. Doing this displays a dialog box where you type the time in when you want the thumb located; click OK and you're there. Additionally, if you hover your cursor over the Current Time indicator, you'll see it turns into a double-headed arrow. You can scroll the current time exactly like you do using the thumb by dragging left or right on the current time.

7. Click the comments stopwatch with the timeline marker at frame 43. This is just to give you some experience with comments; type **Mark in at Frame 43** in the Edit Timeline Comment dialog box and then click OK (pressing Enter doesn't close the box but instead starts you on a new comment line of text), as shown in Figure 1.10.

8. Scrub the timeline toward the end until you find the place just after Domino has leaped off the seamless; I put this event at about frame 164.

9. You now have your start and end marks decided upon. Drag the Work Area start and end markers to 43 and 164, as shown in Figure 1.11. Alternatively, you could drag the video layer's beginning and end points in to match 9 and 264 on the timeline; doing this eliminates the out-of-range footage from playback, and for export purposes for a single-layer composition, it's the same deal as redefining the Work Area.

I have a little surprise in the section to follow. Writing the trimmed video will come a little later in the chapter. Now's a good time to update your edits by pressing Ctrl/Cmd+S.

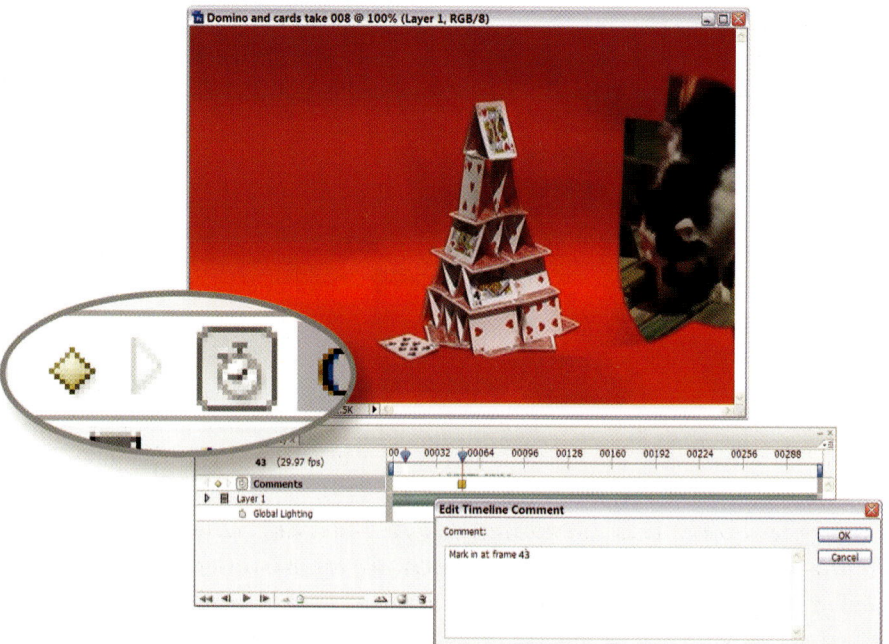

Figure 1.10
A comment will be saved to the PSD document, easy to recall in future editing sessions.

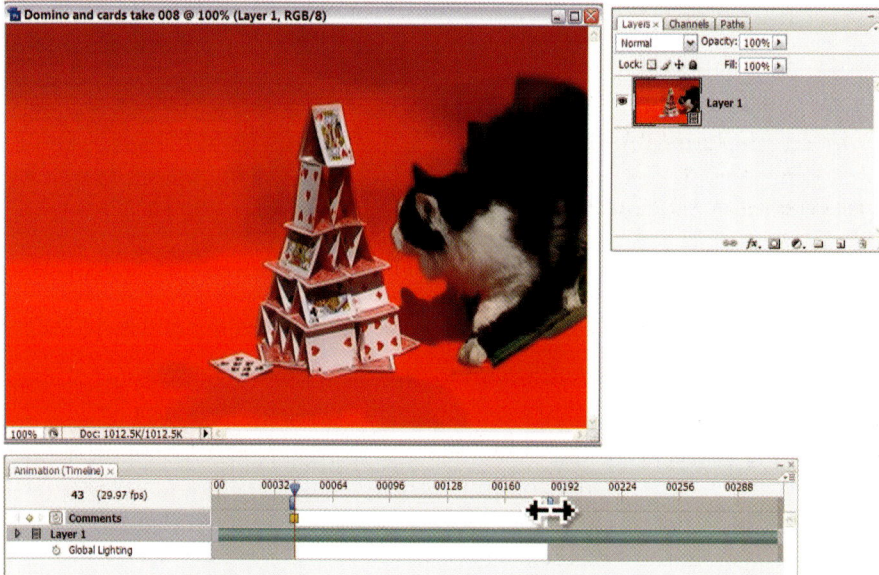

Figure 1.11
It's easiest to define a precise start and end to a video clip in Frames Timeline display.

Working with Audio in Photoshop

Although Adobe Systems did not name the program PhonoShop, *Photo*shop CS3 Extended handles audio at a rudimentary level in video editing work. Here's the deal:

If you import a video that has sound (the Domino and cards take 008 video has no sound), you can play back the audio along with the video by pressing the Play button in the VCR area of the Animation (Timeline) palette while holding Alt/Opt. I believe Adobe "hid" this capability to alleviate the annoyance of auto-playing audio while a user is busy editing video. Audio can be added to a video composition by copying a file into the composition as a layer. Here's where it gets less than straightforward: Adobe Systems licensed QuickTime video technology from Apple to build the video rendering engine in Photoshop. Audio files such as AIFF, WAV, MP3, and Ogg-Vorbis and audio embedded in QuickTime (MOV) file format can be placed in a Photoshop Extended video composition, but only via (in Windows) the File > Open As > QuickTime movie file type, and on the Mac the Open dialog box has to show that the file is a QuickTime movie. It helps to think of the phrase, "A rose by any other name would smell as sweet." In other words, Photoshop doesn't care whether you bring in an MP3 file or a QuickTime audio file; it just has to be brought in as a QuickTime.

For example, you find a royalty-free song that suits your video, read the royalty agreement carefully so as not to violate public exhibition criteria *before* you post your work to YouTube, then open your audio (File > Open As, and then choose QuickTime movie (*.MOV, *.AVI, and so on) in the Open As drop-down box. Ignore the color mismatch attention box (audio rarely has color, except for Blues), and life is good.

Download Scary music.mp3 from www.courseptr.com, and put the file in the same folder where Domino and cards take 008.psd and the placed AVI file are saved, for the sake of organization.

> **Note**
>
> If you fancy yourself a Jack or Jacqueline of all trades and want to create your own incidental music for videos, check out Chapter 16 where I cover digital audio workspaces (DAWs). You can also import MIDI tracks to a DAW in case you're not a Broadway composer; there are scores of free MIDI download sites on the Web, such as http://www.freemidi.org/. You import these files to a DAW, assign what are essentially music notation data some synthesized instrument sounds, render the file to audio, and off you go to Photoshop to enhance your video.

Follow these steps to add some very threatening music (in the spirit of John Williams' "Jaws" score) to the trimmed video:

1. Open the Scary music.mp3 file in Photoshop. Photoshop might alert you that the file has the wrong color profile; dismiss the attention box—there is no video or even pixels in the file, only five seconds of high-fidelity music.

2. On the Layers palette, drag the layer title for the Scary music document into the Domino and cards take 008.psd document window. Your composition now has a soundtrack. Although it's far from polished, audio in a video enhances its entertainment value almost as much as fancy special effects or even terrific original cinematography.

3. This is just a tutorial example, so timing is not of paramount concern. The audio file is a tad short of the Work Area video: The audio is 3.8 seconds. If you followed the steps you'll see that the video marks in and out for a total video duration of about 4 seconds (164 – 43=121; 121/29.97=4.04 seconds playlength). If this was a paying gig, you'd scout down exactly 4 seconds worth of audio, but it's not; I created the audio track to mismatch the video deliberately to show you a technique. By default, all video, audio, and still image layers you duplicate to a video composition are placed at the head of the Work Area. With your cursor, drag the green (the live) audio track on the Animation (Timeline) palette to the middle of the Work Area, leaving a brief silence at the head and the tail of the composition, as shown in Figure 1.12, and then hold Alt/Opt and click the Play button. "Just when you thought it was safe to build card houses"!

Now you know how to move the in point of a layer in your composition to the beginning of the composition's Work Area. There are a lot more sophisticated video edits you can perform using layer properties, which I cover in future chapters.

Let's pretend that the half-finished mask I've painted around Domino is finished and you want to save the file as a movie clip to show around. Here are the steps to export the video in a format that retains the audio and can be used as part of a different composition:

1. Choose File > Export > Render Video.

2. In the Location field, specify a hard disk location. I recommend saving the video to the same folder as the scary music and the PSD file in the workspace; again, good housekeeping prevents you from practicing new curse words down the road.

Figure 1.12
Audio layers behave identically to normal pixel and video layers when you manipulate them on the Animation (Timeline) palette.

3. In File Options, you really have only one choice for a video with sound: QuickTime. Click the Settings button and then click Settings in the Video area.

4. Compression Type: Choose None from the drop-down list. Frame Rate: 29.97, the same as the original MOV file. Compression: Millions of Colors; and Quality: Best on the slider. Millions of Colors means 24-bit, RGB, 16.7 million possible colors. Click OK, then click OK in the Options box to back out to the Render Video box.

5. You don't have to fuss with the other File Options in this example; you set the Size to Document Size, and Photoshop then writes the file to the dimensions of my original AVI footage, 720 by 480 pixels. Also, you're in fine shape with the Pixel Aspect Ratio settings because you did not change the document pixel aspect ratio but only your onscreen view earlier in this chapter.

6. In the Range field, click the Currently Selected Frames button; the fields at the right show you the in and out points you defined by clipping the Work Area earlier. The Render Video box should look like the one in Figure 1.13 now.

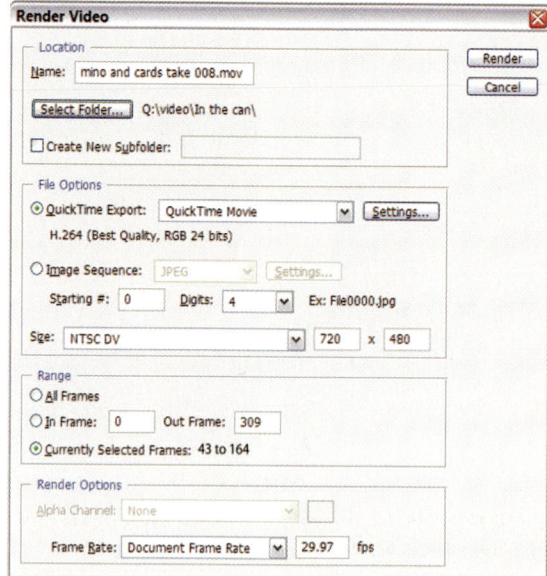

Figure 1.13
Set up the format specifications for the rendered video.

7. Click Render; there's no alpha channel information in this movie, so you can safely ignore the Render Options field. I show you some alpha channel tricks in future chapters.

8. Press Ctrl/Cmd+S again. You can never save too often, and one of the quirky and remarkable things about many software programs is that you can perform several Undos to the file as long as it's loaded in the workspace. If you want to back up to a historical point before you added the scary music, choose the History palette from the Window menu or the docking strip and then click the saved state prior to copying the QuickTime layer to the video. If you do this, save again.

It's showtime. Open QuickTime Movie Player, load your video, and play it. The file should be about 150MB, and if this is too costly for your current hard drive's free space, you can delete it after the amusement has worn off; you can always write another video now that the PSD file is saved to hard disk.

An Experiment with Losing Placed Files

As mentioned earlier, the saved PSD file contains references to the original video but doesn't contain the original content. The good news is that you haven't altered my video in any way, and as a "pointer" file, the PSD document is quite small and contains barely more than editing information: in and out point markers, keyframe markers, and a low-res still image of the time in a video when you last saved the PSD file. The bad news is that if you move or delete the resource files, the PSD file verges on useless for generating new edited footage.

Humor me and try this very unwise thing; I'm getting paid to show you examples, but also how to avoid pitfalls. Follow these steps to ruin and then restore the PSD file:

1. Close Photoshop.
2. Move the original Domino MOV file to a different location on hard disk, somewhere where you can find it easily, like the Desktop.
3. Launch Photoshop and then load the PSD file from File > Open Recent.

As you can see in Figure 1.14, your Open session begins with an attention box. Photoshop is yelling at you that it can't locate missing footage referenced in the PSD file. And the attention box tells you the remedy: You click OK and then go directly to Layer > Video Layers > Replace Footage. Then you locate the AVI file you moved to your Desktop. Better still, minimize Photoshop and move the QuickTime file back to your project folder and then use the Replace Footage command.

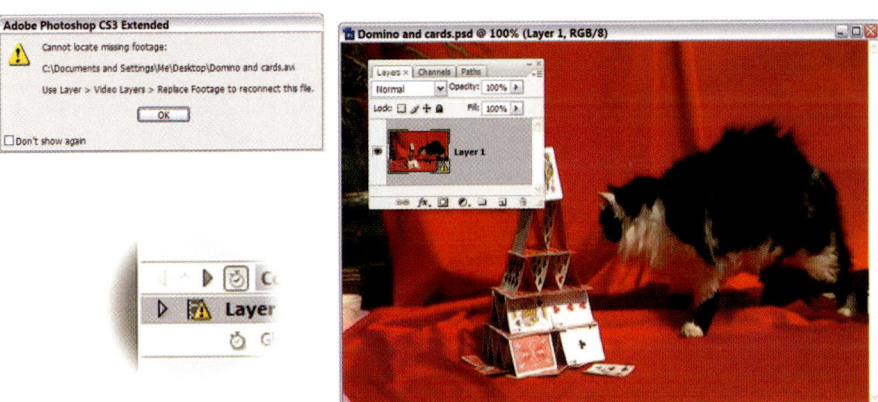

Figure 1.14

If you misplace a resource file, Photoshop alerts you, and you can easily relink to the misplaced resource file.

At this point, there are a lot more pages under your right thumb as you're reading this book than there are under your left thumb—there is a lot to explore in Extended with video editing. For starters, did you notice that the command to relink the footage is called Replace Footage? Consider this: You've edited away for hours, specifying different filters, adjustment layers, and keyframes for opacity on a piece of placed footage. Then the boss hands you *today's* footage and asks you in a nice way to apply your day's work of edits to the new footage and forget about yesterday's video you were using. This is a real simple one: You delete or move yesterday's video, open yesterday's PSD file, suffer the attention box, and then replace yesterday's footage with today's! All the edits are local to the PSD file, and the new placed footage will display with all of your cuts and dissolves and other fancy edits. This is called *slipping video* in professional circles.

It seems like we're moving beyond the Lasso tool and Gaussian Blur in Photoshop CS3 Extended, eh? Bring your already learned skills from previous versions and take a stroll with me into the following chapters to apply all your image editing talents to motion pictures.

2

Working the Timeline Palette: Creating Videos from Still Images

As a Photoshop user, you probably have a healthy archive of beautifully retouched still images, and the good news is that you can animate a lot of them as I describe in this chapter. I'm not a firm believer in learning to walk before running; however, still image animation is a very good way to become proficient with the Animation palette. Consider this: Ken Burns is best-known for the *Ken Burns Effect*, a technique of creating animation from still photos by panning and zooming, best displayed in the 1990 documentary *The Civil War*. So well-received is this effect that it's included in Photoshop Elements and Apple's iMovie—and you can manually achieve this effect in Photoshop.

This is going to be great: You'll learn how to make movies without the need for a movie camera!

GIF Animations

ImageReady is gone as of Photoshop CS3; however, the Animation palette provides all the functionality for GIF animation creation that ImageReady did, and creating GIF animations is a worthwhile topic to cover before proceeding to more complex animated photography.

In Figure 2.1 you can see a close-up of the toggle button on the Animation palette. At left is its appearance by default when you first open it, and it has the parenthetical Timeline appended to its title. In this mode, you're editing video by creating events called keyframes, but this is not the mode for building animated GIFs. At right is the Animation palette in Frames mode; you get to this mode by clicking the toggle button at the lower right. It changes its appearance from a filmstrip to something suggesting transition sliders.

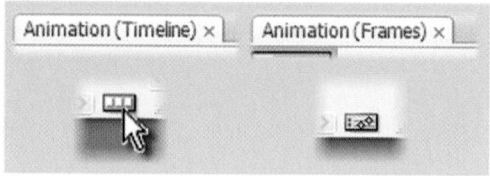

Figure 2.1
The Animation palette has modes for video editing (Timeline) and for creating traditional cell and GIF animations (Frames).

In the following steps, I take you through the process of creating a simple three-step animation using the Frames mode of the Animation palette. You begin with a *concept*, as always: The "story" you can build from Ped Xing.psd can be used on the Web to tell people to stop or go to an URL, which is easy to understand because practically everyone is familiar with a pedestrian crossing light. The PSD file contains three layers: a blank sign, a layer with the stop symbol illuminated, and a layer with the go symbol illuminated. Creating the file from photographs was fairly easy—I stood around an intersection for a few minutes, camera mounted on a tripod, and then shot three photos. The reason I masked off the go and stop symbols on layers was not only to conserve file size but most importantly *to preserve animation continuity*. It was a windy day when I took the photos, and the clouds in the scene during the go and stop crossing light cycle moved. The result would be a jarring, distracting, and disorienting animation were you to animate between the full frames I took. I also enhanced the stop and go symbols by increasing the saturation and brightness to make the animation read quickly.

Here's how to create the pedestrian crossing animation:

1. Open the Ped Xing.psd file and then open the Animation palette. This file is larger than desired for a Web page, but I found the dimensions provided good detail for editing work. You'll work with the file at its original dimensions, but you do not have to scale down a graphic when making a GIF animation; Photoshop's export filter can scale original photos to the size you need.

2. Click the toggle button if necessary to move the palette's controls to Frames mode.

3. The little triangle to the right of the Duration display is a drop-down where you set the time that a frame plays. Choose 1.0 from the list to make the first frame play for one second.

4. Click the triangle on the field below the Duration drop-down and set the number of times the GIF animation will play to Forever. This action does not increase the saved file size, and I've found that only rarely do you want an animated GIF to stop playing on a page on the Web.

5. On the Layers palette, hide the Stop and Go layers so that the animation begins with a blank crossing sign. Your workspace should now look like Figure 2.2.

Figure 2.2
Set the visibility of a layer, the duration, and the number of plays for your GIF animation.

Warning

Before proceeding, click the flyout menu on the Animation palette and be sure that Create New Layer for Each New Frame is not checked. You'd enable this feature if you were painting an animation, but this feature only creates unnecessary new frames in a PSD file that already contains all the elements you want to animate.

6. Click the Duplicates Selected Frames icon on the Animation palette, the dog-eared page icon, to create the next frame. By default, the same duration as the preceding frame is applied to Frame 2 (which is okay for this example, and you know how to change duration now), and the contents of the second frame are identical to the first.

7. Click the visibility icon for the Stop layer on the Layers palette. Now Frame 1, which plays for one second, is blank, and after one second the stop symbol appears.

8. Click the Duplicates Selected Frames icon on the Animation palette and then hide the Stop layer on the Layers palette.

9. Click the Duplicates Selected Frames icon and then unhide the Go layer on the Layers palette.

10. In Figure 2.3, the animation is complete; because the animation loops forever, it returns from Frame 4 to Frame 1. You're done, and it's time to export to GIF file format.

Figure 2.3

A four-frame animation that loops forever is an economical method for providing a movie for a Web audience.

11. Choose File > Save for Web and Devices. This is a new command in Photoshop; the device the command refers to is usually a cell phone—if you have one hooked up, you can save an image as your cell phone wallpaper.

12. Choose GIF from the Preset drop-down list; the Save for Web command is very similar to the feature in CS2. The name of the game in this command is how small you can make your animation with the highest quality. Although Adobe still offers you a "How long will this file take to open in a browser" area on the status bar for 56.6kbps (dial-up) connections, it's a good practice

nevertheless to be considerate of the ever-shrinking dial-up audience and keep your GIFs under 60K or so.

13. Choose the Image Size tab and then scale the image to "play to the cheap seats," the audience who still runs 800 × 600 screen resolution. For this example, type **400** in the Width field, check Constrain Proportions, use Bicubic Sharper as the Quality option, and then click Apply (which affects your export, but not the document in Photoshop's workspace). Check the status line to see the proposed Save GIF file size.

14. If necessary, lessen the number of unique colors saved to GIF (GIF can store a maximum of 256 unique values) by experimenting with the Quality slider in the Preset area. Click the arrow to reveal the slider. In Figure 2.4, I've first opened a 2-Up view from the top right tab area to compare my original to what I'm going to export. I've also zoomed in by choosing a zoom from the lower-left drop-down box, but only so you can see the amount of dithering clearly in this book. In the Preset area, I've chosen 64 unique colors, Selective dithering type (usually provides good quality with the best compression), and some lossy compression that degrades the image somewhat but offers a noticeably smaller file size. At 100% viewing resolution, the audience will not see such massive loss of image detail, because the Web audience usually doesn't or cannot zoom into Web graphics.

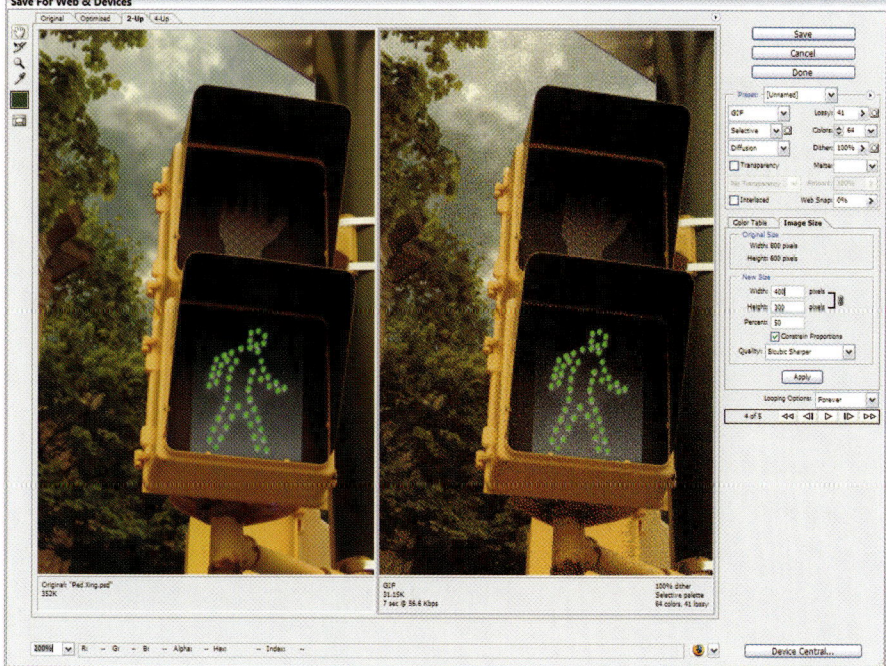

Figure 2.4
Save for Web & Devices will write a GIF animation to disk, as well as other static Web graphics file formats.

You can play the animation by operating the VCR-like controls, and at the bottom of the command's UI, you can choose to preview the animation in an installed browser. You can see the tiny Firefox icon in Figure 2.4.

15. Click Save, choose a hard drive location for the GIF file and you're done and returned to Photoshop's workspace.

16. Press F12. Why? Because technically Save for Web & Devices is a different module than Photoshop proper, and with file types such as JPEG, Save for Web & Devices changes the metadata tag information in the file. Photoshop recognizes the change and will flag you when you go to close the file. "Do you want to save changes?" when ostensibly you've made no changes can be confusing and introduce errors in your workflow, so it's just a good practice that whenever you Save for Web & Devices, you press F12 (File > Revert) directly afterward.

You're almost finished. Any GIF animation that features a blinking effect can cause viewing problems for audience members who suffer a disability such as epilepsy. Part of being a good online performer is to practice social responsibility, so go to http://www.webaccessibile.org/test/check.aspx and upload your finished GIF animation. In Figure 2.5 I've done this and captured the test results, and as you can see, the flashing animation is slow enough to be considered responsible entertainment.

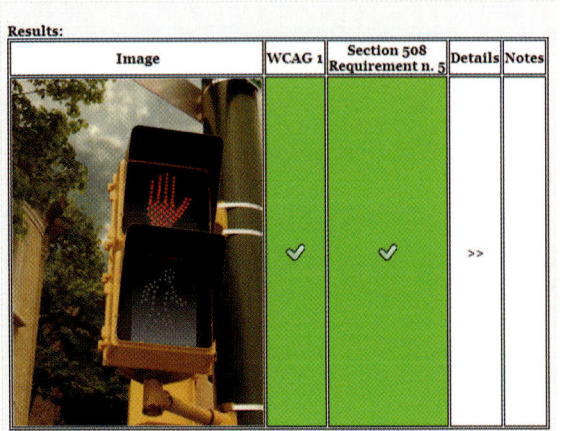
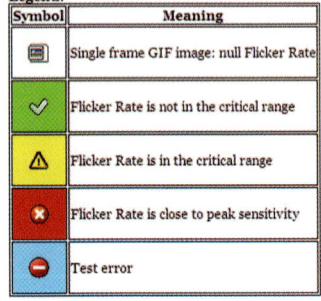

Figure 2.5
Any content you create for the Web should be tested for accessibility and conformity; most of these online tests are free of charge.

Creating a Potter's Wheel Animation

In the world of 3D modeling and rendering, one of the first types of animation is called the *potter's wheel*; it's still a visually exciting way to show off all sides of a 3D object on a 2D surface such as your monitor. The term is derived from folks who work in clay, who lathe a pot, vase, or other laterally symmetrical piece by turning the clay on a wheel.

All you really need to create a potter's wheel animation is a visually interesting object and some sort of turntable. In Figure 2.6 you can see what I did to set up the scene. The ceramic sculpture rests on a wooden kitchen turntable I marked with a grease pencil in ticks corresponding to a clock face. Then I put a plant stake next to the turntable for reference as my wife rotated the frog. A tripod is necessary, and choosing an outdoor location for the pottery wheel dictates no winds and keeps moving clouds out of the shot.

Figure 2.6
A potter's wheel animation is easy to set up.

Tip

The Salvation Army is an excellent resource for props; it's where I bought the Frog Prince in this tutorial for $3. The Salvation Army is a worthwhile charity; you can turn around and redonate a prop when you're done, and it's a tax deduction.

Let's talk about frame rate for a moment. Some experts in cinematography and animation will tell you that about 15 fps is the least you can get away with before the viewer detects choppiness in the animation, thus dampening the illusion. For GIF animations, you are somewhat reliant on your audience's computer speed and Internet connection, and through experience I've concluded that 10 fps produces acceptable motion for short animated sequences. This equates to the 0.1 seconds choice on the Duration drop-down menu. Therefore, you want the frog to spin in a cycle that loops back from the last frame to the first. There are 11 unique rotation points on a clock as it travels from 1 to 12, so a single potter's wheel cycle will be a little over a second, a comfortable speed for the audience without boring them.

New to CS3 is the File > Scripts > Load Files into Stack command. This is your automation shortcut to copying still frames into layers in a single PSD document you can then animate. "Stack" is a misnomer here; you're loading copies of individual files onto their own layers in a PSD file, and Adobe Bridge image *stacks* are unrelated to this Photoshop command. When using this command, files must be named in a numeric sequence—image001.tif, image002.tif, and so on—or Photoshop's script will fail. I recommend that you get a batch file renaming utility off the Web if you're going to use Load Files into Stack a lot; alternatively, you can manually rename your target images or use Bridge to make the task marginally easier.

Unpack the Frog Prince folder you downloaded earlier and then follow along to create an animation from the still images:

1. In Photoshop, choose File > Scripts > Load Files into Stack. You'll then see a Load Layers dialog box. For this example, *don't* check the checkboxes that refer to Smart Objects and Aligning Source Images. The Use drop-down context menu enables you to you to load an entire folder of images that meet the sequential numbering criterion (the Folder option) or to load individual files with the Files option. If you choose Files in your own work, you can Ctrl/Cmd+click only the files you need, sidestepping sorting and renaming files when necessary. In this example, click the Browse button and navigate to the files in the Frog Prince folder. You want all 11 files as shown in Figure 2.7; select them all and then click OK.

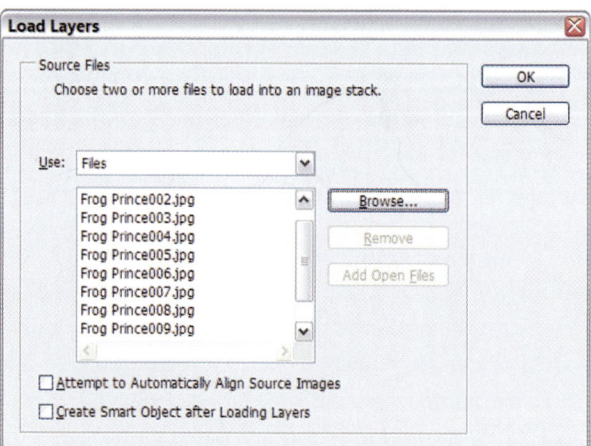

Figure 2.7

The Load Files into Stack script takes the manual labor out of copying and aligning source images for animations.

2. Wait a moment while the script runs, and then you should have a new unnamed document in the workspace. Save the file to PSD file format.

3. On the Layers palette, you'll see that all the layers from the source files are arranged in order and are all visible. You want to begin the animation on the Animation palette's Frames mode first frame with the top layer, unless you want the frog to spin counterclockwise. To do a counterclockwise animation or reverse the appearance of any imported frame sequence, you first make the bottommost layer visible. So expand the Layers palette and then click+hold and drag down the Visibility column on the palette to batch-hide all the layers except the bottom one. Then build your animation by unhiding layers on the Layers palette from bottom to top. Now, ignore this trick and proceed with Step 2 to make a *clockwise* frog potter's wheel animation.

4. On the Animation palette, set the first frame to 0.1 seconds and the play time to Forever, and then click the Duplicates Selected Frames icon.

5. Hide the top layer, exposing the following one below on the Layers palette. Because there are no transparent regions on any of the layers, it's okay to leave the underlying layers visible as you create the animation.

6. Keep moving downward on the Layers palette, hiding layers and creating duplicate frames on the Animation palette until you have 11 frames. As you can see in Figure 2.8, the work goes fairly quickly because Photoshop sorted the frames for you.

Figure 2.8
Create the animation by progressively hiding the document's layers.

7. You're done and can now export the animation to GIF by using the File > Save for Web & Devices command described earlier. Keep this file open, though; I show you a trick next that demonstrates a relationship between Frames and Timeline modes on the Animation palette. You can repurpose this GIF animation into a full-blown (4-second) QuickTime movie with very little effort.

> **Creating Persistent Layer Properties**
>
> At the top of the Layers palette are several controls that can get you out of a jam when you've made a mistake creating a frame-based animation. The Propagate Frame 1 checkbox can be used to create a cascading change to all attributes to a layer as it appears in your animation. For example, you have a drawing of a tree on Layer 9, and it's hidden in Frame 1 of your animation. You want it to be visible throughout the animation, so you make it visible by clicking the layer's Visibility icon (the eye), then click the Propagate checkbox with this layer selected (highlighted on the Layers palette), and every new frame will have the Tree layer visible.
>
> The Unify icons to the left of the Propagate checkbox are used to create persistent properties for layers at any time in the animation creation process. It's very easy to have a frame in your animation jump around because you moved the contents of a layer at a point in the Animation palette's Frame mode event line. To correct such a headache, you go to the frame on the Animation palette that has the layer's contents properly positioned (you click the frame on the palette, highlight the layer in question by clicking on it on the Layers palette, and then click the Unify Layer Position icon. Similarly, you can not only hide or unhide layers in your animation's event schedule by clicking the Unify Layer Visibility icon, but also adjust the amount of opacity—for example, if you want a layer to be 50% opaque throughout all frames, you set 50% on the Layers palette and then click the Unify Visibility icon. Finally, you can animate an effect and style in an animation, and to unify a styled layer across time, you use the far right icon on the Layers palette.

Moving from GIFs to Video

The relationship between the Timeline and Frames modes of the Animation palette is a simple if not straightforward one. The Timeline is used to edit video layers footage of digital film because an understanding is presumed that the duration of a video clip is calculated by a fractional value: fps (frames per second), also expressed as frames/second. This is the playlength resolution, and it is immutable: You do not speed up a video by exporting it to greater than 30 fps. Doing this only increases the smoothness of playback, but a 4-second clip will still play back at 4 seconds in length. It helps to think of a 300 ppi image. You can change this image to 72 ppi without resampling the image by using the Image Size command. Right-click over the document title bar to access it quickly and be sure the

Resample Image option is unchecked. The image doesn't change because ppi is a fractional relationship between the image pixels and how many are measured within an inch—pixels/inch.

On the other hand, in Frames mode, a single frame can be onscreen for a tenth of a second, a second, you name it. On the Animation palette in Frames mode, a frame is a frame, and you can change the temporal resolution—the play length—to anything you choose by working with the Duration drop-down list. This is why it's important not to edit in Frames mode and then switch to Timeline mode and perform other edits. Photoshop will warn you if and when you do this; Photoshop does not reconcile the different measurements of playlength between fps and the Frame mode's "this is a frame. How long do you want it onscreen?"

Your own personal reconciliation is to use this technique: If you need to add a hand-crafted frame-based animation to video footage, you write the hand-crafted animation out to a QuickTime full-blown fps-timecoded movie and then import the result to a video layer in a new composition. I show you how to accomplish amazing things in future chapters using this technique. In a nutshell, when you want to edit video, you use the Animation palette in Timeline mode, and when you want to make cartoons, you use the Frames mode.

All of this should *not* lead you to conclude that you cannot export a frame-based animation to a timecode-based video. Let's say you want to use the Frog Prince animation as a piece of video instead of a relatively low-quality GIF. I deliberately composed the still images to allow for some text at 9 o'clock in the composition and will show you how to animate text in the video in Chapter 7. Follow these steps to making a video from this simple potter's wheel cycle:

1. A 1-second GIF animation doesn't play for 1 second because you can loop it 5, 10 times, or forever, but it's a nuisance for an audience using QuickTime Player to have to set manual looping or to ask your audience to replay the segment on a DVD player. Therefore, you'll play this animation out to 4 seconds (brief, but not tedious) of video now. Shift+click Frames 1 and 11 on the Animation palette to select them all.

2. Click the Duplicates Selected Frames icon, and Photoshop creates 11 duplicate frames and puts them at the end of the existing frame animation. In Figure 2.9 you can see that I have 22 frames now. Repeat this step until you have 44 frames.

3. Just to review the preceding explanation of timeline and frames, do a quick mental calculation of how long 44 frames, each with a duration of a tenth of a second, are going to play at 30 fps video. It's a trick question: The fps rate is precalculated in the Frames mode of the Animation palette. It's all relative; click the toggle to switch to Timeline mode on the Animation palette and you'll clearly see at upper left that the duration is 4 seconds, 11 frames (4:11).

Figure 2.9
In GIF animations, looping to create a cycle is automatic. In video, you must be explicit and render all the frames you need for cycles.

4. Let's spice up the video with some audio I created that happens to be 4:00 in length. In general with short clips, if the audio is shorter than the playtime of the video, you have more ease working the clip in and out of a large composition. Mac users should choose File > Open and then choose Calliope.mp3 as a QuickTime movie, and Windows users, choose File > Open As, choose Calliope.mp3, and choose QuickTime Movie from the Open As drop-down field. Photoshop might tell you the colorspace isn't correct for your color profile preferences, but you can safely ignore this box by clicking OK because the file has no color, only an audio track.

5. Click the toggle on the Animation palette to switch to Timeline mode and then drag the layer title of the calliope document on the Layers palette into the Frog Prince document window. You can close the MP3 file without saving now.

6. Notice that every layer in the animation has its own track in the timeline view. Don't experiment with moving the tracks; this would change the animation. Just open a track layer by clicking the triangle icon to the left of a title on the Animation palette. As you can see, the animation as a timecode changes the opacity of layers across time; it's indicated by a keyframe marker for the track. To slide the audio track so it begins and ends toward the middle (leaving silence at the head and tail of the animation), drag the track in the composition space to the middle. The green bar indicates the track should look like the one in Figure 2.10.

Figure 2.10
A track on the Animation timeline shows where a track begins and ends in a video composition, and you can set the entrance and exit points.

7. You're finished editing. Don't switch back to Frame mode because this will slide the audio track to the head of the video; you'll get a warning box from Photoshop, and all you will discover is that a new frame has been added to the animation in Frame mode. Choose File > Export > Render Video.

8. QuickTime is the only file format that Photoshop can write with audio, so choose it in the File Options field, then click Settings, and then click Settings in the Video field.

9. I cover compression types in future chapters. Video compression uses a codec—a compressor/decompressor—and there are several choices for the QuickTime format, but the one that appears to be of the best rendering quality but with fairly high compression is H.264. Choose it, allow two-pass encoding by clicking the Best quality (Multi-pass) radio button, and set the compression quality to about 38 (a numeric value will pop up as you drag the slider left or right). This will create a file that's about 500K, which is pretty good for 4 seconds of 24-bit color with no noticeable artifacting and high-fidelity audio. H.264 is also known as MPEG-4 and AVC encoding. Unlike earlier versions of the H.2XX codec, 264 does not restrict file dimensions. H.261, for example, restricts dimensions to 252 × 288 pixels, and saved file sizes will be larger. This choice could get you into trouble later on because even though you'd choose Original Size in the main Render to Video dialog box, your file would be 252 × 288 pixels.

10. Click OK twice, and then in the main Render Video dialog box, in the File Options field, choose Document Size from the Size drop-down list, in the Range field click All Frames, and then in the Render Options field make sure the fps is 30. At the top, name your movie, choose a hard disk location, and then click Render.

11. Get some popcorn and sit back. Save and then close the Frog Prince document.

Adobe Bridge and Color-Synching Animations

Another type of animation you can create using still images is called *a build*; you make a transition between the changes made in the scene from photo to photo. In the example in this section, I photographed an apple, starting from a whole one, to bites taken out of it, and finishing with an apple core in the last frame. So this example is sort of a reverse "build." If you want to try something like this, I recommend that you drive a stake through the apple or other edible object, through a disposable seamless, and into something stable such as flower arrangement Styrofoam as I did. This makes the positioning of the object more or less consistent between frames as you create changes such as eating the object.

Working Between Bridge and Camera RAW Editor

I explain the first part of this example because I photographed the frames using camera RAW, and there's little sense in asking you to download scores of megabytes of RAW files when I'm demonstrating a technique and not patience. Inevitably, there will be color balance and possibly levels variations when shooting a sequence such as this over a period of 10 minutes. This is why RAW is such a blessing; you can synchronize exposure settings for a group of images because RAW is essentially undeveloped film. Adobe Bridge came with CS3, and it's more than a bridge between Photoshop and other Adobe programs you might have—it can create groups of images for RAW processing (called *stacks*) and call the RAW Editor outside of Photoshop to perform color corrections. In the steps to follow, I show you how to get your series of camera RAW images in and out of Bridge, in and out of the RAW Editor, and into a new folder that you can load as a Photoshop stack (each image is on its own layer in a single document) to then animate.

Here's how to prepare your camera RAW files for Photoshop animation:

1. Launch Bridge by clicking its icon on the Options bar in Photoshop or, if you're not in Photoshop, by double-clicking its icon in the folder in which you installed Photoshop.

2. In Bridge, point it to the folder where you saved an image sequence. This is done by treeing down the hard drive folders on the Folders tab at the top left of the screen.

3. Pick the images you want in the animation by Shift+clicking them. The collection you are making appears in the Preview pane.

4. Right-click over any of the images in the Content window and then choose Stack > Group as Stack from the contextual menu, as shown in Figure 2.11. A stack is represented as a thumbnail of the top image with the frames of the other images peeking below it, like a badly shuffled deck of cards, with a number icon at the top left corner telling you how many images are in the stack.

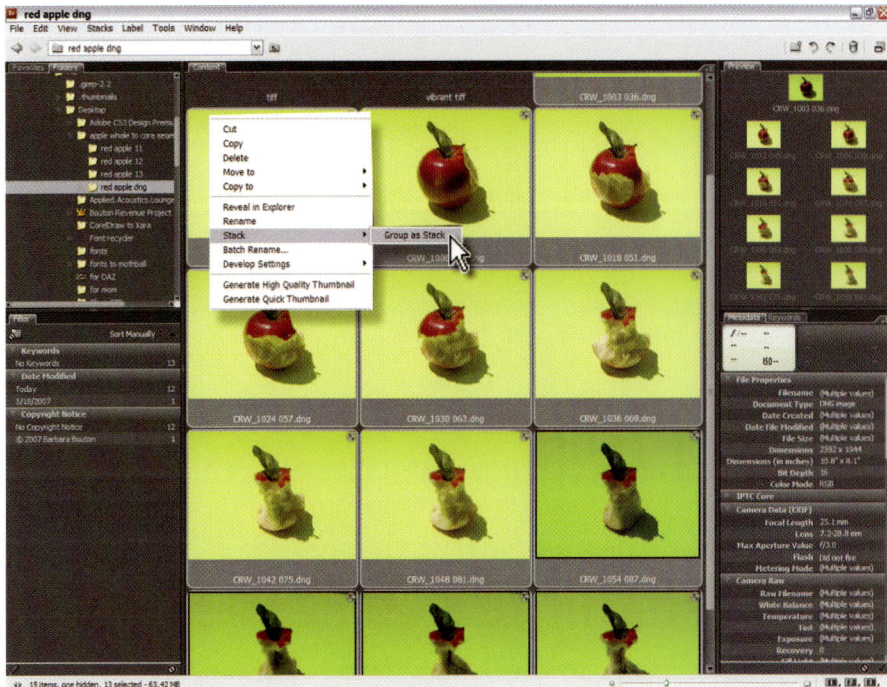

Figure 2.11
A Bridge image stack is a collection of photos you choose. Stacking photos does not affect any of the visual file data.

5. Right-click again on the stack and then choose Open in Camera RAW from the contextual menu.

6. On the left side of the screen you'll see your stack as individual images. Pick the one that has the best target exposure by clicking each one and examining it in the main window. Once you have the best of the lot, perform any additional enhancements you feel necessary from the tabs at the right of the screen. By default, you have Basic tone and color corrections, and hopefully you don't have to perform a lot of adjustments. Click through the other icons—Tone Curve, Detail, and so on—to find any adjustment features your image might require and then tune the image to perfection.

7. Click the Select All button at top left and then click Synchronize. A dialog box appears, asking you what features of the current image in the main window you want corrected in all the other images. I choose the defaults by simply clicking OK in this box; if you want to apply only specific changes, check or uncheck the boxes—you can also narrow down the list by accessing the choices from the Synchronize drop-down list at the top. See Figure 2.12.

Figure 2.12
Perform adjustments to an image and then apply the same corrections to all images in a stack.

8. Click Save Images. Name the file to name the whole sequence, choose a folder, and then choose a file type for the saved copies. I recommend TIF or PSD because JPEG uses lossy compression and you're probably going to compress the finished video; you lose a lot of detail when you compress more than once.
9. Close the Editor, close Bridge, and launch Photoshop.

Importing and Aligning a Photoshop Layer Stack

In this section you'll get hands-on experience with a "hands off" automation that Photoshop performs: auto-aligning layers. As hard as I tried, the apple sequence didn't line up perfectly, and this would create a jarring, unsuccessful animation build. In the following steps, you'll work with the JPEG files in the Zip file you downloaded. Notice that the files are numbered but are nonsequential—there are gaps in the numbers because not every photo I took was ideal. This is okay in your work; you can have a numbered sequence of files that is missing numbers in the sequence as long as Photoshop can load an ascending order of numbered files. If your own photographic sequence and the number sequence of files you want to animate are out of order, Photoshop will load the files, but they will be on the wrong layers. This is a simple problem to fix, however: You just rearrange the layers by dragging their titles on the Layers palette list.

Follow these steps to dig deeper into Photoshop's animation capabilities:

1. Choose File > Scripts > Load Files into Stack.

2. In the Load Layers dialog box (yes, Adobe's dialog box name doesn't match the command), choose the JPEG images you downloaded in the Red Apple archive and then click the Attempt to Automatically Align Source Images checkbox (see Figure 2.13) and then click OK. It will take a moment or two to run the script, and you may see empty document windows popping up as Photoshop executes the script.

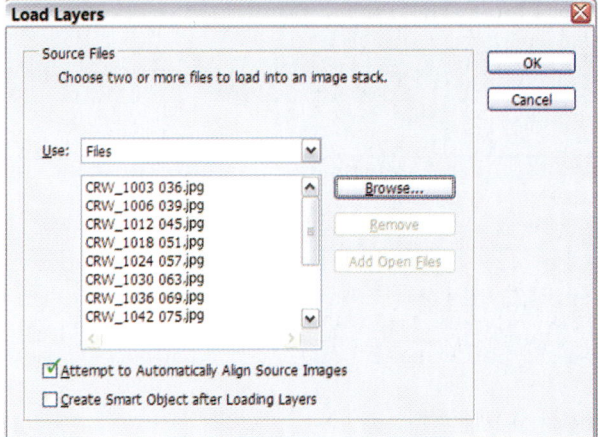

Figure 2.13
Photoshop usually does a good job of aligning image content in a collection of photos with similar visual content.

3. Once the document has been compiled, you'll see that Photoshop needed to expand the extent of the document window beyond some of the photos to align the visual content. This causes no problem in this example; to clean up the composition, choose the Rectangular Marquee tool and then on the Options bar, choose Fixed Ratio from the Style list. Type **4** in the Width field and type **3** in the Height field. The 4:3 aspect ratio is perfect for onscreen display of the animation and for playback on a television from DVD.

4. Drag a marquee around the inside edge of the apple photo on any visible layer in the document window, as shown in Figure 2.14. You can leave a little transparent area if you like; later in this example I show you how to create a persistent outside frame around the animation to give the apple a more polished presentation.

Figure 2.14
Crop the image to create more of a close-up on the apple in the finished animation and to remove superfluous transparent areas.

5. Choose Image > Crop. Save the file as Red Apple.psd. Now press Ctrl/Cmd+D to deselect.

6. If the completely eaten apple appears at the top of the Layers palette stack, you can fix this by clicking on the top (eaten apple) layer and repeatedly press Ctrl/Cmd+[(left bracket key) until this layer has been moved to the bottom of the Layers palette stack. Choose the Frames mode on the Animation palette. Set the duration of the first frame to .5 seconds. The layer of the apple completely uneaten should be visible on the Layers palette.

7. Click the Duplicates Selected Frames icon and then, on the Layers palette, hide the pristine apple and reveal the frame with one bite taken out (of the apple).

8. This animation would look jarring and quite ineffective as a build sequence if we went from half a second of apple to half a second of apple with a bite missing. Instead, you'll now gradually dissolve from one image to the other via the Tweening function. Shift+click both frame thumbnails on the Animation palette to select them and then click the Tweens Animation Frames icon, directly to the left of the Duplicates Selected Frames icon. The Tween dialog box appears.

9. Through experience you'll learn more about timing, but for this example using 4 frames works in between the first and second frame, so type **4** in the Frames to Add field, and you can leave the other fields at their defaults. See Figure 2.15; click OK to add the frames.

Figure 2.15
Tweening creates a gradual transition between the opacity and other attributes of the frames you choose.

10. Tweening presumes you want all the in-between frames to be the same time duration, but in this example you don't—it would make a stultifying animation! Shift+click Frames 2–5 to select them and then set any of the frames' duration to .1 seconds to adjust all the selected frames, as shown in Figure 2.16.

11. Repeat the technique you just used in Steps 7–10; make sure each new frame you add is .5 seconds in duration and that the tweened frames are .1 second. You should have 61 frames after defining each of the 13 layers and then tweening them.

12. One of the advantages Photoshop has over a movie editor is its robust set of tools. You'll see in the last few frames that I goofed and took a little too big a bite out of the apple, and the stake we used to anchor the apple is visible. No big deal. Make the layer visible on the Layers palette; it has the most stake visible.

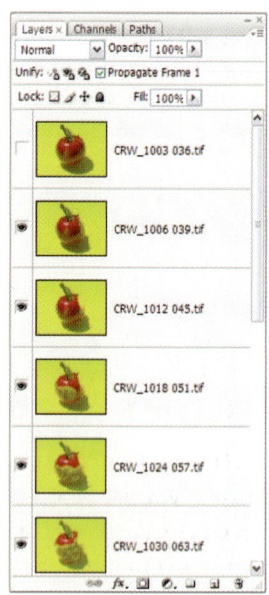

Figure 2.16
When you change a duration, it applies to all highlighted (selected) frames.

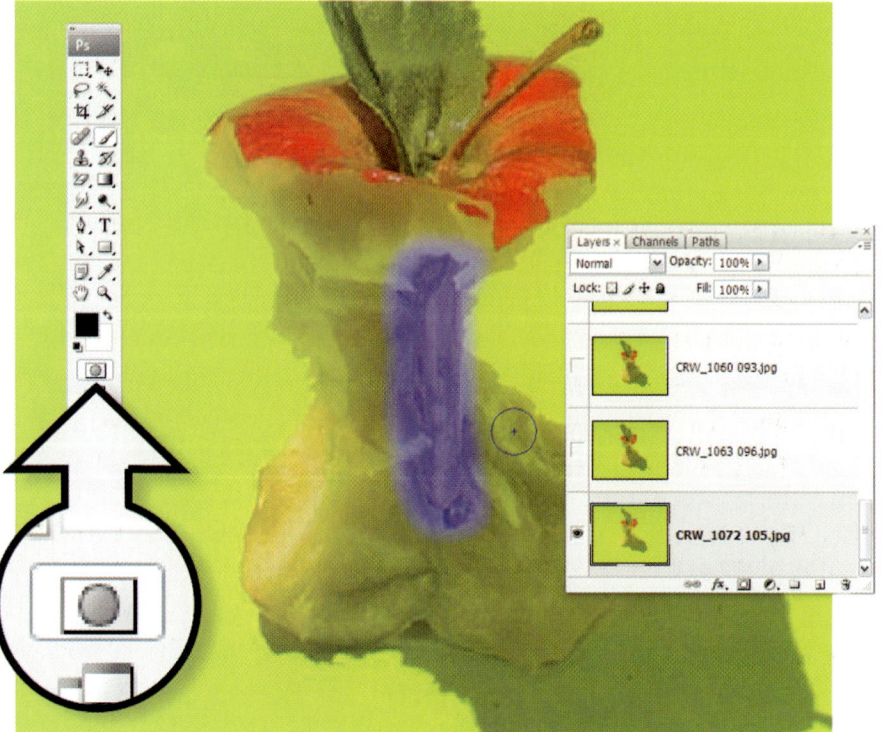

Figure 2.17
A bum frame is easy to fix when a "build" sequence usually contains an image area that can be used for repairs.

13. Click the Quick Mask Mode button on the Tools palette, and then with about a 30-pixel diameter brush at 100% opacity and foreground black, stroke over this stake area to define it. See Figure 2.17; I have Quick Mask defined as blue in this figure so you can see it (default red doesn't cut it when painting a selection over a red apple).

14. Click the Quick Mask Mode button to toggle back to Standard Editing mode, and then scroll up to the layer containing the 87 photo, the last in the sequence without the stake visible. Make this layer visible and highlight it to make it the current editing layer. Press Ctrl/Cmd+J to make a copy of the selection onto a new layer (alternatively, click the Layer menu and choose New > Layer via Copy). Be sure to turn off layer 87 when you're finished to avoid messing up the animation frames.

15. Move the new layer containing the copied image area down in the layer stack on the Layers palette (by dragging it down) to the first bum frame (93), duplicate the copied image area's layer by dragging the layer title into the Creates New Layer icon on the bottom of the palette, and then hide the duplicate.

16. Right-click over the original new layer's title and then choose Merge Down from the context menu. Repeat this and Step 15 for layers 96 and 105. Turn off visibility for all but the bottom layer; you can click+drag down on the eye icons on the Layers palette to do this most quickly. Press Ctrl/Cmd+S to save at this point.

Finessing the Animation

Before creating the animation, I'd like to demonstrate how a persistent area in an animation can be added after you're finished animating the main character. Also, it would be nice to create a simple opening and closing to the animation through a fade up and fade out. To continue:

1. Click the top layer title on the Layers palette to highlight it and then click the Create New Layer icon on the palette. A new empty layer is created on top of what was the current editing layer (saving time dragging new layers around to reorder them on the palette). Make sure the Propagate Frame 1 box is checked on the Layers palette to ensure the new frame doesn't go disappearing during the duration of the video.

2. Let's create a spotlight effect around the apple, thus hiding any edge areas we might not have cropped away earlier. With the Elliptical Marquee tool, drag an oval selection around the apple and then right-click and choose Feather. Specify about 25 pixels for the Feather amount; click OK.

3. Press Shift+F7 (or Ctrl+Shift+I, which is the same command for Select > Inverse).

4. With the Eyedropper tool, sample a medium-olive shade on the leaf of the apple. Usually, when you're framing a scene, it's best to choose a color from the scene to make the frame harmonious with the contents.

5. Press Alt/Opt+Backspace, then Ctrl/Cmd+D to deselect. Your document should look like Figure 2.18 now.

Figure 2.18
Create a green mortise to highlight the star of the scene.

6. Click on the Creates New Layer icon and then click the foreground color swatch on the Tools palette.

7. In the Color Picker, make the olive color you chose last a deep olive: R: 37, G: 55, and B: 0 is good.

8. Press Ctrl/Cmd+A, Alt/Opt+Backspace, then Ctrl/Cmd+D. This layer is the beginning and end of the fade for the animation.

9. On the Animation palette, click the toggle to Timeline mode.

10. Click the triangle next to the top layer title on the Animation palette's tracks area to expand it and then click the stopwatch icon for Opacity.

11. Move the timeline marker to about 1/4 of a second (about seven frames as measured in timeline units) into the sequence. On the Layers palette, drag the Opacity slider for the top layer to 0. Now you have the fade in, and it's time to do the fade out.

12. With the timeline marker positioned at the fade in keyframe (at about seven frames into the animation), click the flyout menu on the palette and choose Copy Keyframe(s). Put the timeline marker at about 9 seconds and then on the flyout menu choose Paste Keyframe(s).

13. Copy and paste the first keyframe at time 0 and to the very end of the animation timeline and adjust the opacity on the Layers palette to 100% for the very beginning and end keyframe opacity positions. Your screen should look similar to Figure 2.12, where I'm scrubbing the timeline to preview the fade out. The reason I give the fade out a longer duration than the fade in is for storytelling reasons—the audience will probably anticipate the end (but not the opening), and so we can let the fade out linger just a little longer than the fade in. Asymmetry is more visually interesting than symmetry in all types of entertainment in the arts.

Figure 2.19
Create a fade in and fade out by adjusting the opacity of the top layer over time.

The rest is academic; if you like, use the eating an apple.mp3 file to add sound to your animation, and then export the animation as you did in the Frog Prince example to a QuickTime movie. When exporting, be sure to specify 640 × 480 pixels for the document size in your own work. The original RAW files I used in this section were on the large side for animations, and yours would be, too.

Timelapse Animations

Like build animations, timelapse animation can be effectively created using still photography, and the additional perk is that by using still images, you'll most certainly achieve more detail and better color than is possible using today's affordable digital camcorder (DCC). I am not going to show a tutorial on creating timelapse sequences in this section; you shoot your stills and then bring them into Photoshop using the Scripts > Load Files into Stack command with the Attempt to Automatically Align checkbox highlighted, exactly as you did with the apple sequence. Take a look at cocktails timelapse.mov in the Gallery you downloaded. I set up a scene that I knew would change dramatically from sunrise to sunset. The glasses are filled with food coloring, and the interaction between each other and the sunlight provides an interesting animation you could use for a number of advertising purposes. I pulled four stills from the animation you can see in Figure 2.20. The biggest trick was to make a good judgment call—although I took over 150 photos, almost one every half hour, the scene is not the type of timelapse such as a flower opening or clouds racing across the sky. Upon playing back all the frames in a single sequence, it looked boring; there was not enough visual contrast in the timelapse. So I wound up using only six key frames and then tweening them.

Figure 2.20

Timelapse animation can be easily created from a sequence of perfectly aligned still images.

Creating the Ken Burns Effect

One of the new features in PS CS3 is Photomerge, an elegant script that auto-aligns a sequence of images you take from left to right, up to down, or any other way you choose to pan a still camera. Setting up a sequence for Photomerge requires a little pre-planning. A tripod is a must; it really helps to keep your exposures the same (Bridge and RAW Editor can assist you), and your photos should overlap by at least 15% so Photoshop has common reference points in its calculations.

Performing a Panoramic Photomerge

I thought it would be interesting to pan across a row of beautiful houses, so I photographed a sequence for you to use in the Howard Street archive you downloaded. In the sections to follow, you'll create an animation in the style of Ken Burns, and I also show you how to stylize the animation to visually heighten the charm of the row houses. The first step if you're doing this with your own photography is to create an image stack in Bridge as shown in Figure 2.21 and then edit the exposure in RAW Editor as I showed in the apple sequence earlier.

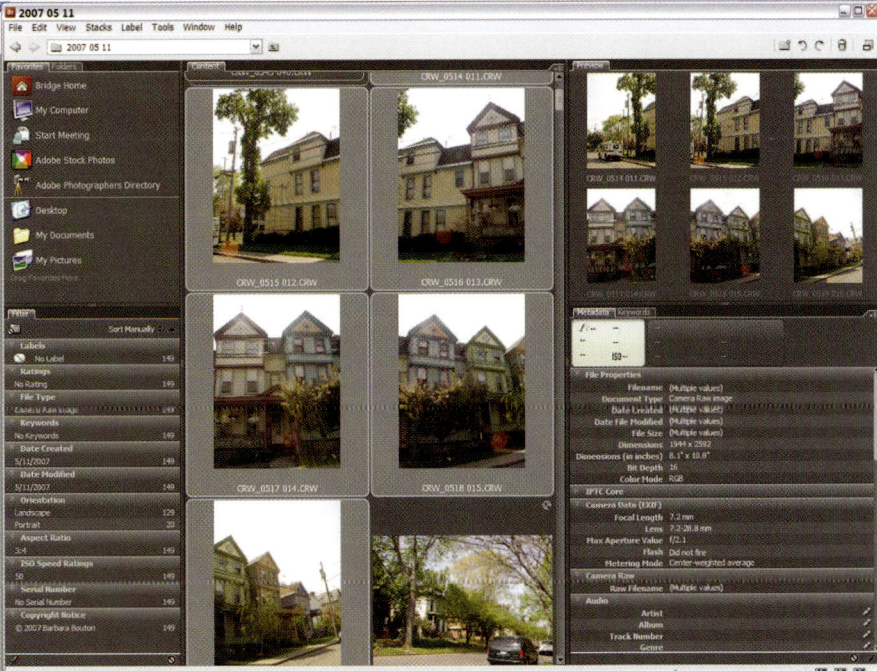

Figure 2.21
Stack the images you want to use to create a panorama and then edit them for color matching in the RAW Editor.

Here's how to take the JPEG files after editing them in the RAW Editor and create a panorama using the Photomerge feature:

1. Choose File > Automate > Photomerge.

2. Click Browse and browse for the files.

3. At left, you can see different types of merging called Layouts. For this example, leave the setting at Auto and click OK.

4. Wait for the script to run, and in a moment or two you'll get a document that's quite wide, with all of Howard Street pretty neatly aligned, as shown in Figure 2.22. The center of the image bows outward, and that's because my camera was closest to the center of the street as I yawed the camera for panning instead of performing what's called a tracking shot (where you move the camera parallel to the focal plane). I sort of like the bulge, and it will play well in the panning animation. However, if you want a more linear scene and shot your sequence the way I did (by rotating a tripod from one point of view), you can choose Perspective instead of Auto in the Photomerge folder box (Step 3). Notice that the layers are masked, and they are all selected. Don't deselect them for the moment.

Figure 2.22
The Photomerge automation shaves hours off creating a perfectly stitched panorama from a series of still photos.

5. In this example, the photos merged pretty well—certainly well enough to continue building the animation. However, if your images have different color casts, the panorama will not work visually. If this is the case, you now choose Edit > Auto-Blend Layers. Photoshop then attempts to color match the images across layers.

6. The Howard Street panorama features pretty scenery, but the houses are backlit, and the sky was hazy when I shot the sequence. If this happens to you, don't fret. First, right-click over any layer's title (not the image thumbnail) on the Layers palette and then choose Merge Visible. Save the file to PSD file format.

7. Because the sky is a fairly uniform shade of blah, you choose the Magic Eraser tool, set it to about 24–32 Tolerance on the Options bar, and then click over the sky area(s) to remove them to transparency.

8. Find a good (wide) stock photo of a better sky, put it on a new layer beneath the scene, and then choose Merge Visible. In Figure 2.23, I used a synthetic, rendered sky. Aurora, by Digital Elements, is a plug-in for Mac and Windows that operates off the Filter menu in Photoshop. In about 30 seconds I have a sky that is visually compatible with the Howard Street scene.

Figure 2.23
Synthetic or photographic, your panorama should look picture-perfect before you create a panning animation.

The Secret to Creating an Animated Pan

Because Photoshop can retain image areas that lie outside of a document window (this is called *Big Data* by Adobe engineers), you need a smaller document window to pan the image over time. You cannot adjust the canvas size because this will clip areas outside the document window. Therefore, you need to copy this layer to a new, small document window and then animate the pan.

In the following steps I walk you through the procedure for setting up a document to hold the panorama image for animating:

1. Create a duplicate of your work. Right-click the title bar, choose Image Size, and then scale the duplicate down to about 1984 pixels in width, which should yield about 716 pixels in height. Save the file to PSD format; don't close it, but you can close the larger original now; you no longer need it for this example.

2. Create a new document; Ctrl/Cmd+double-click the workspace to call the New dialog box.

3. Make the Height 480 pixels and the Width 853, Background: White, 72 ppi, and then click OK. To be cool here, you've created a widescreen HDTV-proportioned document window, one that will play letterbox style on an SD television. It will enhance the drama of an otherwise static piece of video.

4. Drag the layer title from the Howard Street document into the new document window, as shown in Figure 2.24, and then with the Move tool, drag the image so its left side is the focus of the document window, the beginning of the pan. This document size also helps cover a "sin"; I didn't stand far enough away from the street, and as a result, the Photomerge command created a somewhat uneven, visually awkward bottom to my document. Therefore, this example will feature a pan that is tight and hides the unsightly edge of the panoramic photo outside the document frame. The lesson is to stand farther away from your scene that you are imaging when planning to do a panoramic pan.

5. If you like, you can apply a filter to the copied panorama. I used a Colored Pencil filter in the finished Gallery movie to stylize and enhance the appearance of houses that beg a little additional romancing. If you apply a filter to a Big Data layer, even the areas outside the document window are filtered.

6. You'll want to fade in and fade out of this animation because there is no visual opportunity to loop the animation, as with the apple video. Create a new layer beneath the panorama, and then fill it with a color that's harmonious with the panorama. I used warm brown and then applied Filter > Render > Difference Clouds about six times to get an organic, almost marble texture when the pan fades in and out.

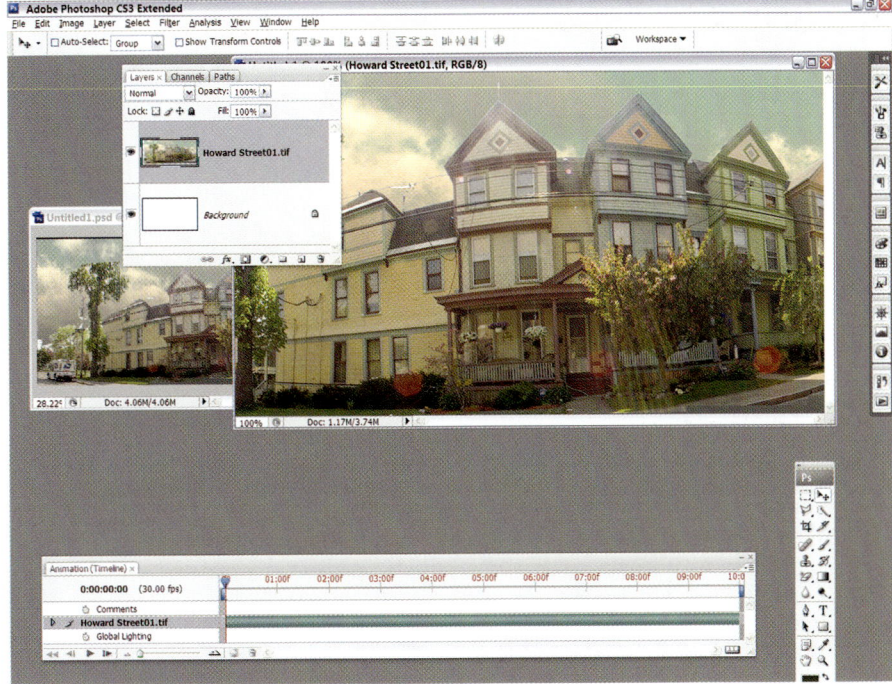

Figure 2.24
Put a copy of your panorama in a document whose size is scaled to the size of your finished video.

7. Hide the top layer and click on the Panorama layer on the Layers palette. On the Animation palette in Timeline mode, click the flyout menu icon and choose Document Settings.

8. Make the Duration 20 seconds long, and because this video is destined for playback on TV, change the fps to 29.97 (see Chapter 3 for details on broadcast standards). Click OK to apply the setting. Twenty-five seconds isn't really a long time and will give the pan a leisurely pace. The best way to calculate this duration is through experimenting. If your initial duration plays back too fast or slow when previewing it, add or remove five seconds.

9. Click the Position stopwatch icon for the Panorama layer and then move the timeline marker to about 10 seconds.

10. Here's a real trick for creating smooth pans: Don't move the layer but instead use the keyboard arrow keys. With the Move tool chosen, hold Shift to "power nudge" the layer's contents by 10 pixels per keystroke until the center of the document features the right side of the ochre house, as shown in Figure 2.25.

11. Move the timeline marker to the end of the animation workspace on the Animation palette, and then with the Move tool chosen, power nudge the layer's contents to the left (left keyboard arrow key) side of the panorama.

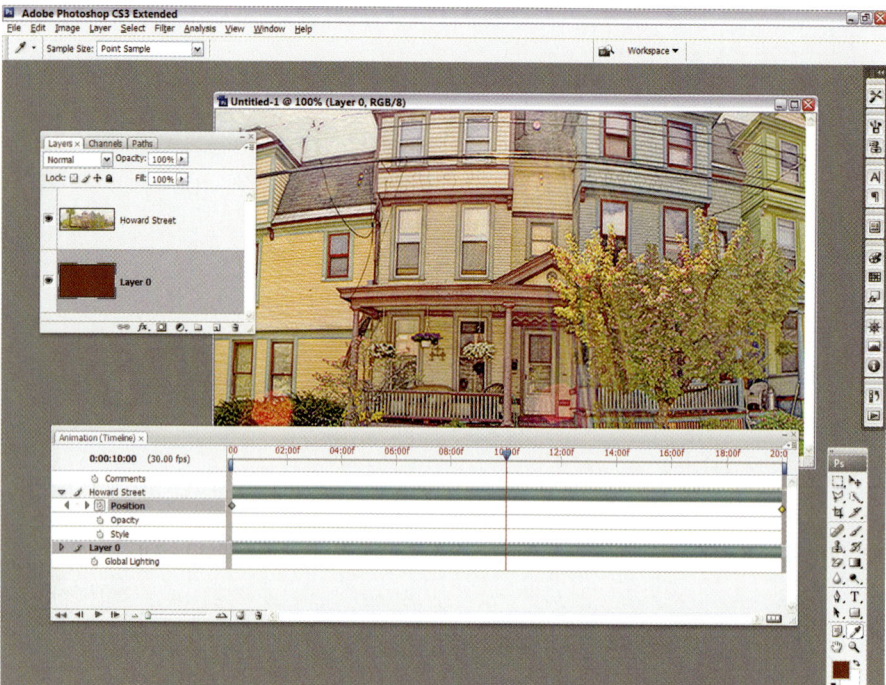

Figure 2.25
Achieve a steady pan effect by arrow keyboarding the layer with the Move tool chosen.

12. Let's get more ambitious than a "straight pan" from left to right. As long as additional scenery is hidden outside the document window, drag the timeline marker back to 10 seconds and then down arrow key nudge the scene down by about 20 pixels so the crest of the houses is the focal point.

13. You'd imagine that you now have an interesting pan, but you don't. If you press Enter and preview the pan, it glides upward and then makes a sharp descent at 10 seconds. It would look more professional to gently glide up to the house roofs and then down again. To do this, set the timeline marker at about 9;29 and then use the down arrow keyboard key to nudge the layer down by about 10 pixels, moving the view up a little. Then do the same thing at 10;29. What you've done is create an arc across time; it's not obvious or intuitive, but you've "eased" the animation so the midpoint doesn't have a sharp directional change. See Figure 2.26.

14. You're almost ready to write the video. To make the pan fade in, click the stopwatch icon for Opacity for the Howard Street layer, but first go to the head of the video on the Animation palette. Click the Opacity stopwatch and then change the opacity to 0% on the Layers palette. Then move the timeline indicator (the thumb) to 1 second, set the Opacity to 100%, and then copy and paste the keyframe at 19 seconds. Then go to 19;29 on the timeline and decrease the Opacity to 0%. Try this to humor me: right-click a keyframe marker, as seen in Figure 2.27. You have Hold and Linear Interpolation; leave

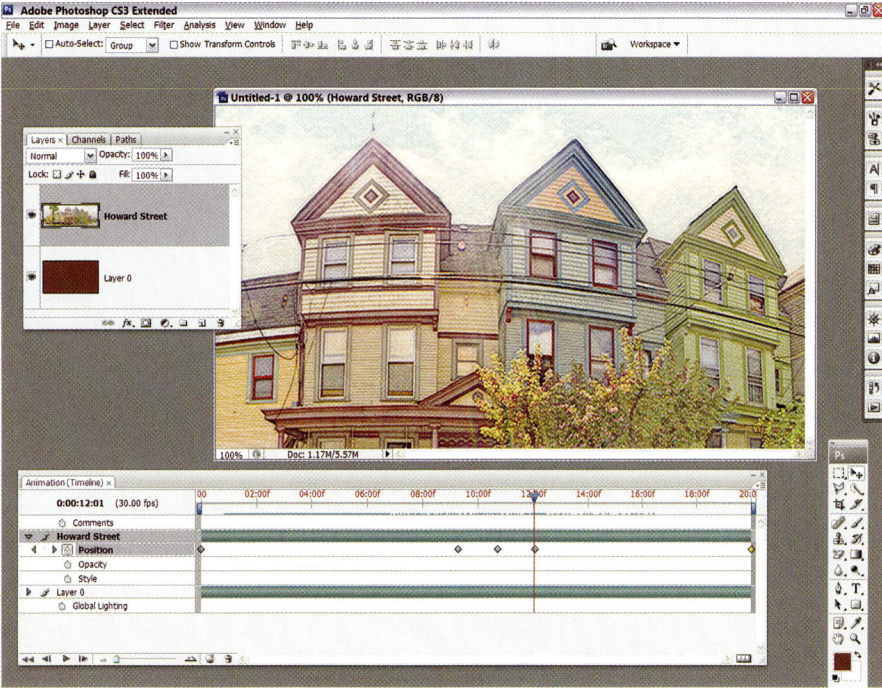

Figure 2.26
Create a gentle pan across the timeline by creating intermediate position changes to a layer.

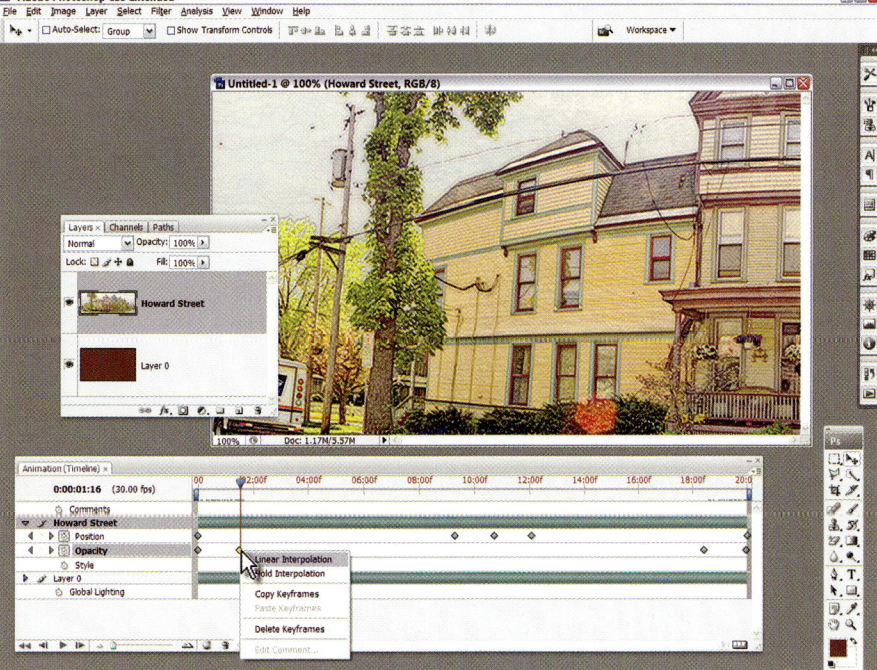

Figure 2.27
Create a fade in and fade out for the panning animation.

the key at Linear. Linear Interpolation has an equivalent on the Frames mode of the Animation palette—it's called tweening; the frames make a slow, smooth progression from one keyframe to the next. Hold Interpolation is equivalent to a cinematic cut—there is no gradual transition between one keyframe and the next. I show you some creative uses for Hold Interpolation in Timeline mode in future chapters.

15. Add the piece of music in the Howard Street folder to the document and then write it out to QuickTime from File > Export as you've done earlier in this chapter.

Filtering a Video, Post-Production

There are some effects you can add to an animation only after the animation has been written. Photoshop can treat a placed QuickTime or other valid movie file format as a Smart Object—a Smart Object can be filtered, and the filter can apply to only a part of the onscreen movie by using the Smart Object's masking feature.

Here's the challenge—I photographed a sequence of a beautiful Art Deco building, panning from top to bottom. It's simple enough to animate the pan using the steps in the Howard Street section. But I'd like some barrel distortion to add visual interest and bloat the building a little to make it look more impressive. And I didn't shoot the building with a wide-angle lens. This is a task for post-production editing work, and in the steps to follow you'll learn how to make a visually stunning piece of video from a nice but otherwise pretty ordinary skyscraper. First, I made an image stack in Bridge and then color-matched in RAW Editor to create the Niagara Mohawk JPEG images you'll use to build the animation.

1. Choose File > Automate > Photomerge.

2. Choose the Niagara Mohawk JPEG files, click the Blend Images Together checkbox, and this time, click the Interactive Layout button—I'm going to show you how to pre-build some drama to the composition. Click OK.

3. You now have a new UI—the Photomerge area of CS3 Extended. Zoom out of the composite scene by Alt/Opt+clicking with the Zoom tool (the same zoom and navigation shortcuts work in all Photoshop UI dialog boxes) and then click the Perspective option.

4. Choose the Vanishing Point tool, the middle one at left of the UI. What you'll do is make this building look tiny at top and huge at the bottom. With the tool, click (don't drag) at the base of the flagpole. Your panorama should look like Figure 2.28; click OK to apply the changes and run the script to create the panorama.

Figure 2.28
The Interactive Layout feature enables you to create very dynamic panoramas using Photomerge.

> **Tip**
>
> If you have a document composed of image sequences on layers, you can Photomerge them *in situ* without calling File > Automate. Use Edit > Auto-Align Layers after selecting all the layers on the Layers palette (Shift or Ctrl/Cmd+click to additively select).

5. Choose to Merge Visible as you did with the Howard Street tutorial. Okay, the panorama doesn't fill the document window due to the distortion you added in Step 4. The solution is to carefully clone in missing areas with the Stamp tool. Fortunately, architecture usually features repeat areas that are easy to clone from, as I'm doing in Figure 2.29. You might want to press Ctrl/Cmd+K to scoot to Preferences > Transparency & Gamut and set some different colors than the default gray for transparency, seeing as the building and sky have gray. I set up bright blue and red for the checkers that indicate transparency on layers.

6. Create a new 640 × 480 pixel document to hold the panorama and then copy the panorama to the new document.

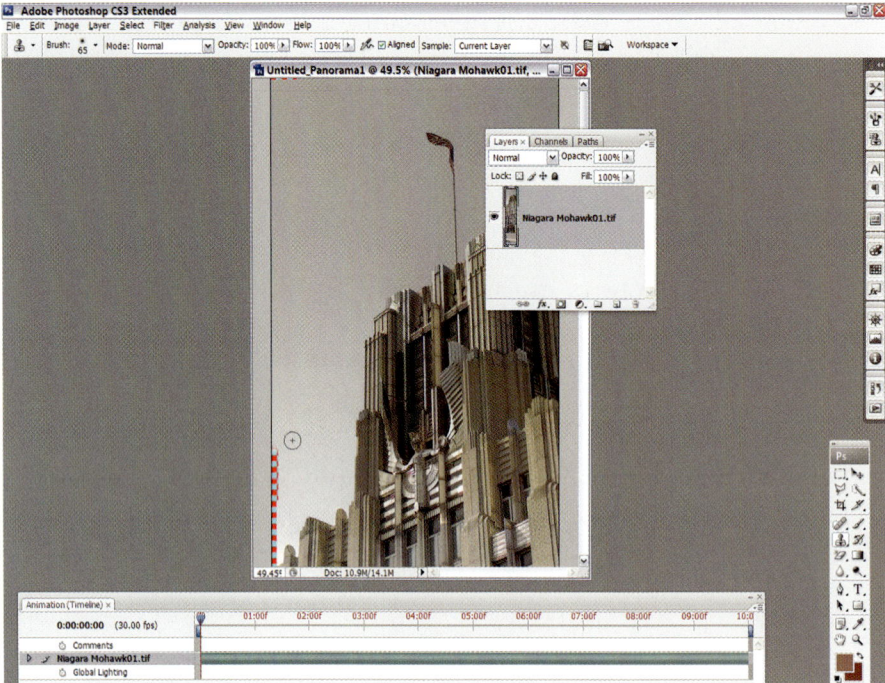

Figure 2.29
Correct the panorama before you animate a pan.

7. Make the animation about 25 seconds in duration. As with the Howard Street pan, you created a fade and fade out to the pan. For this example, do the same thing; this animation doesn't need to weave from side to side as you pan.

8. Export the file to QuickTime video. If you have the spare hard disk space, don't compress the file when writing it to video, thus retaining some quality. You're going to bring the QuickTime movie in as a Smart Object, and the second time you write the animation, you can use H:264 compression.

9. Close the files in the workspace after saving, choose File > Open as Smart Object, and then choose the QuickTime movie you exported in Step 8.

10. Choose Filter > Distort > Lens Correction. Notice that some but not all filters are available for Smart Objects. I show you in future chapters how to skirt this limitation for various useful filters.

11. Drag the Remove Distortion slider to about −31. Yep, you're distorting, not correcting the footage. The reason you couldn't do this to the panorama you wrote as a QuickTime is because the Lens Correction would look at the whole image, even the areas outside of the document window, and the flick would be a dud. As a Smart Object measuring 640 × 480, the Lens Correction

applies to the whole document's dimensions over time. Now vignette the piece a little to add emphasis. Drag the Vignette Amount to about –57 (darker); the midpoint is fine in the center of the window. See Figure 2.30—there are some creative advantages to abusing the intended use of a filter!

12. I worked very hard to compose and record some appropriate music for this dynamic, breathtaking pan, so add the MP3 file in the Niagara Mohawk volume you downloaded to the composition and then write the file to QuickTime with compression to your hard disk. Save, exit, and get a front-row seat for the debut!

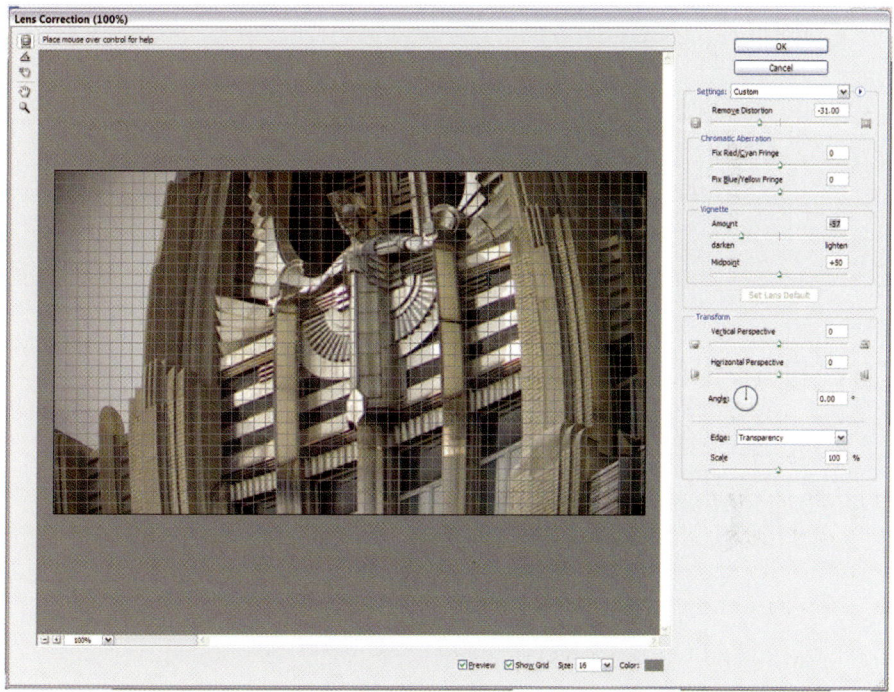

Figure 2.30
Make a fisheye pan of the building using Lens Correction.

Figure 2.31 shows four stills from the finished video. Please check out NiMo.mov in the Gallery folder. You'll notice one or two touches I didn't cover in this chapter, but I will in future chapters. The lens flare at the beginning of my movie was accomplished through an ActionScript I'll teach you how to write in Chapter 9, and the neon sign flashing on and off was accomplished by turning layers on and off using a painting of a neon glow. I moved the neon's position to match the movement of the pan. I explain how to do this, too, right around the corner, so don't touch that dial.

Figure 2.31 Four stills from the finished video.

Clearly, Photoshop Extended is well versed in video, but as you've experienced in this chapter, the core tools that have been in Photoshop since version 5 play a determining role in not only polishing your presentation but also achieving stuff that would be time consuming or impossible any other way.

3

Reconciling Different Media in a Composition

Photoshop Extended invites you to don several different creative hats: those of a cinematographer and/or animator, director, producer, and editor. However, rooting your core competence in one role—that of video editor—is a very good place to start before you run out of heads for all your hats. And realistically, you'll probably get more paying gigs sooner if you hang your shingle out as digital video editor.

In this chapter I teach you how to play the role of editor, and I'm going to play the largely unloved role of The Client. Like most clients I'm going to hand you media that is of different dimensions, different video durations, a few files that aren't video at all, and then pose the perennial question, "Can you make something out of this?"

Yes, you can, and you will. I show you how to assemble a visually exciting, fast-paced video composite that makes up a short fictitious TV commercial out of media that, as individual pieces, aren't stimulating or interesting in the least. In the process, you'll gain experience resizing, timing, and creating a composite (a comp) video that looks as good if not more polished as anything that's aired on prime time.

An Outline for the Composition

Imitation is a sincere form of flattery, and it's also a good springboard for education. Therefore, this mock TV commercial uses a visual device you've seen before: the checkerboard—an array of small videos appearing as a progressive build onscreen. This treatment is quite effective when you're trying to coax a story out of actions that are not very dramatic: The treatment *is* the story, and this hook doesn't exactly fit the old advertising jibe, "when you've got nothing to say, you *sing* it." The commercial is for ShadeTree Home Centers and is made up of two parts: the checkerboard build, composed of nine video clips of beauty shots of a hammer, a saw, a drill, and so on. Close-ups were a must because at one-third their original size (three across and three down in the composite), the audience needs to see more than fly specks. The second part of the commercial is a signature shot for the fictitious store; it's an imitation camera snorkel past all the home goods, arriving at a paint can with the store logo. I used a computer animation application to create the clip; it looks somewhat less than real, but the animation is visually exciting, and I don't own a rig for snorkeling a camera three inches above a surface at 35 miles per hour.

This sounds like a very ambitious project, but don't feel that it's daunting: It's all about editing; Photoshop has the tools, and I've created all the media for you. Concern yourself with procedure and logistics in this chapter. Figure 3.1 shows the finished checkerboard.

Figure 3.1

A checkerboard treatment of nine videos composited using Photoshop.

Broadcast Standards and Photoshop Compositions

By the National Television Standards Committee (NTSC) regulations, video broadcast in North American and other countries (Europe uses PAL standards, see following Note) is done at a frame rate of 29.97 fps, and standard TV resolution is 720 pixels in width by 480 pixels in height, with a pixels aspect ratio of .9. You need not concern yourself 99% of the time with the 29.97 frames per second frame rate; in fact, if you're posting a video to an online site such as YouTube, you can think, and use, 30 fps. This fractional value is an NTSC kludge that came into being when color broadcasting entered our living rooms; it's also known as drop-frame rate, but it *should* be called "averaging the technical disparity between color and black-and-white broadcast signals." Simply put, it's black box stuff for creative individuals; you don't need to know why 29.97 evens out two different broadcasting formats as they're simultaneously transmitted, and frames are *not* skipped (there is no stuttering with 29.97 fps).

The .9, less-than-square-pixel convention is also a byzantine NTSC convention; an engineer discovered that to speed up transmission, you could take video, smoosh it, and then have the audience's TV set electronics unsmoosh it. 720 by 480 by .9 pixel aspect ratio works out to a 4:3 image once you let Photoshop do the math. In the examples to follow I show you how to change your view of a .9 video without resizing or resampling it, so after you've created a composite you can write the piece to video that conforms in all ways to NTSC standards.

> **Note**
>
> The most significant difference between NTSC and PAL standards for readers who want to broadcast in most South American countries, Poland, the Nordic countries, the Middle East, and a few other regions is frame rate. PAL standards are 25 fps versus NTSC's 29.97 fps, and many engineers will tell you that 25 fps provides better video fidelity than NTSC. The inside joke, in fact, among broadcast engineers is that "NTSC" stands for "Never Twice Same Colors." In this chapter, if you want to create a PAL-compliant video, substitute 25 for 29.97. The aspect ratio for PAL DV is slightly different than NTSC; it's 720 by 576 at 1.07 pixel aspect ratio, but overall conforms roughly to 4:3, the dimensions of most monitors and essentially NTSC aspect ratio.
>
> There are other attributes to the PAL standard such as luminosity, audio quality, and so on that do not impact on your Photoshop composition at all. Broadcasting is the responsibility of broadcasters; like printing, you ensure that your Photoshop files are CMYK-legal and of sufficient resolution, and then the printer handles the hardware-specific details to "broadcast" your piece.
>
> I just *love* "standards"; there are so *many* of them!

Creating an NTSC Base Layer

A composition has to begin somewhere; when compositing two or more videos it's usually a good idea to start a new Photoshop document. Fortunately, with video, Photoshop has a preset designed especially to conform to video standards. Follow these steps to define the attributes for a working background layer, and then we'll move on to placing the first piece of video content:

1. Ctrl/Cmd+double-click Photoshop's workspace to display the New dialog box.

2. From the Preset drop-down list, choose Film & Video; by default NTSC DV will appear as a Size option. I recommend that you leave this option as is for this tutorial; my DV camera shot a lot of the clips you'll use at NTSC dimensions and fps. See Figure 3.2. Click OK, and click OK again when the attention box appears regarding Pixel Aspect Ration Correction. You'll notice that the new document has two sets of guides; you'll use them later—the outer guides are for action safety, and the inner guides are for titling safety. Standard definition televisions tend to overscan a broadcast signal, and these safety zones assure you that important action and titles you add to video are not cropped out when played.

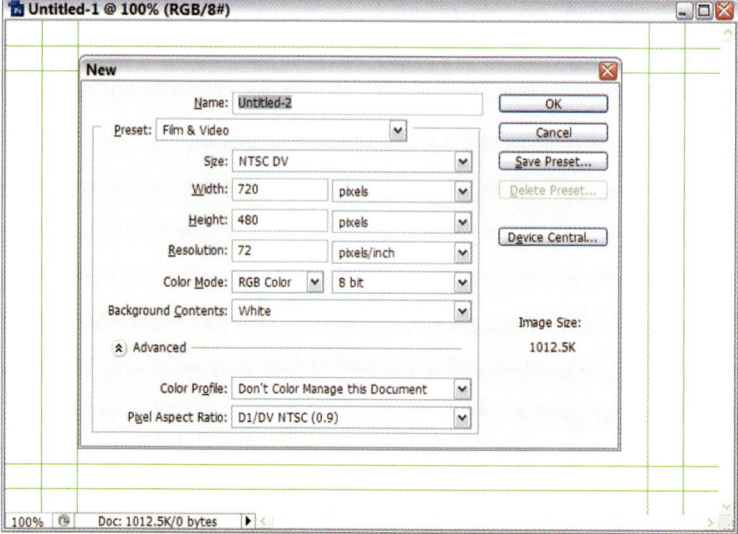

Figure 3.2
Create a new document of correct dimensions, aspect ratio, and action and title safeties to boot.

3. To ensure that you're editing in future steps with an accurate view of the document, choose View and then uncheck Pixel Aspect Ratio Correction. Most of the clips you'll be placing have the same .9 pixel aspect ratio, and what you've done is correct your view of the document window *without changing any data*. In general, in computer graphics, if something looks wrong, you change your view first, and only as a last resort do you alter the visual data, which is usually a permanent, irrevocable change.

4. Open the Animation palette to Timeline mode. Notice it's blank; you have no action in the document, so you have no timeline.

5. I usually like to first place a video as part of a composition routine, which then triggers the Animation palette to display the timeline; you accomplish two things in one edit. Choose Layer > Video Layers > New Video Layer from File. Choose Saw.mov from the folder you unpacked at the beginning of this chapter and click Open.

6. Because the movie is smaller than the dimension of the document, it's not centered, but this is okay for this example. Additionally, notice that the timeline's Work Area extends to 10 seconds, a default for new movie documents. The fictitious TV commercial will run about 18 seconds, however, and it's a good idea to extend the duration of the Work Area right now to avoid clipping durations from future placed videos. Choose Document Settings from the flyout menu on the Animation palette. Type **29;29** in the Duration field, to give you extra room for positioning clips in the Animation palette's Work Area. Be sure to use a semicolon and not a colon as the delimiter: Drop-frame fps values are delimited with semicolons; other film rates such as computer animations can take a colon because most applications used to build CGI (computer graphic images) were engineered with the presumption that your final output would be film or medium other than broadcast television.

7. Choose 29.97 as the Film Rate and then click OK. See Figure 3.3.

Figure 3.3
Choose a duration and film rate compatible with your intended playlength for the composition and your intended output (broadcast TV in this example).

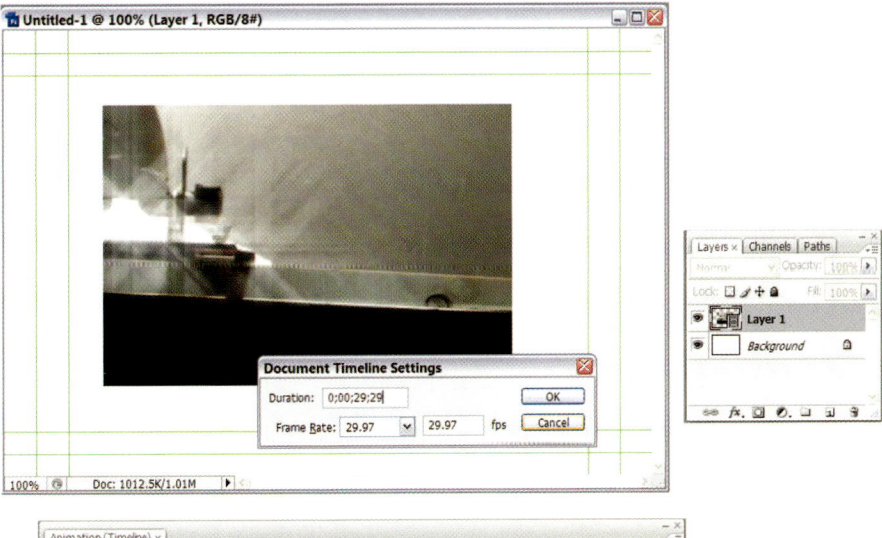

8. Save the composition (but don't close it) in the native PSD file format to the same folder on your hard drive where the media is located for this chapter. Doing this helps keep your project intact; if you move a clip used in a PSD composition and then open the file later, you'll have the hassle of relinking the clip.

Letting the Concept Drive Your Editing

Take a deep breath and help me think here about how to stage the nine videos filling the screen, checkerboard style.

1. I'll tell you in advance (as The Client) that the videos are of different durations, different dimensions, and in different file formats. I guide you through all these reconciliations.

2. I want the checkerboard to complete the build in 8 seconds. Therefore, let's think "good cinematography" here. The opening of the commercial should be a black screen; it would look awkward to begin the commercial with one checkerboard already in place. So there are actually 10 screen changes and not nine. The nine videos should ideally pop onscreen at regular intervals (trust me on this one; it looks unprofessional and irritates audiences to have differing duration times). Therefore, each "slot," including the blank opening, will enjoy a .8 second lag behind its neighbor. In this example, I'll round 29.97 fps to 30; 30 × .8 equals 24 frames. This is your magic number when staging the entrance of the checkerboard videos.

3. I, The Client, have a strong preference for which frames go where in the checkerboard, so I've removed some guesswork from this assignment. However, consider this if you ever get an assignment like this: The component videos of the checkerboard necessarily will have different durations. I, The Client, have not been very tidy with the vids I've handed to you. Some clips will support the whole 8 seconds onscreen, while others will not. A good solution, given the checkerboard treatment of this commercial, is to hold the last frame of a clip that needs to be onscreen longer than its duration; I show you how to do this later in this chapter.

Editing Clip Dimensions and Entrance

The clip of the saw needs to occupy 1/9th of the total dimensions of the composition; additionally, it needs to enter the scene (the Work Area on the Animation palette) at Frame 24 and hold until the 8-second point (frame 240) in the composition. Guides are of great assistance in precisely scaling the saw clip and can then serve for aligning the clips as you add them. You'll add guides to the composition in the following steps and also a comment, an Animation palette feature that visually indicates an editing point—in this instance, where all the videos need to conclude.

1. Press Ctrl/Cmd+R to display the rulers around the document window. You can't add or delete guides without their "source," the rulers.

2. Right-click over either ruler and then choose Percent as the value.

3. Drag vertical guides to 33 and 66 percent. Then drag horizontal guides to 33 and 66 percent.

4. Choose View > Snap > To > Guides.

5. Press Ctrl/Cmd+T to put the current layer, the video of the saw, into Free Transform mode. Click Convert to convert the video layer to a Smart Object.

6. With the Move tool, move the video so it meets the top left of the document window. Smart Guides are enabled by default (you can activate them at any time if they're not on through View > Show), and they're of invaluable assistance in this example. When the video is perfectly aligned to the top left, you'll see magenta lines at top left.

7. Hold Shift to constrain scaling to proportional, and then drag the bottom right bounding box handle up and to the left until the video snaps to your guides, as shown in Figure 3.4. Then press Enter or click the check icon on the Options bar to apply the scaling. Notice that the video layer now sports a different tag; instead of a little movie, it now has a Smart Object tag. It's not, strictly speaking, a placed video anymore but belongs to the PSD file as an *altered video*.

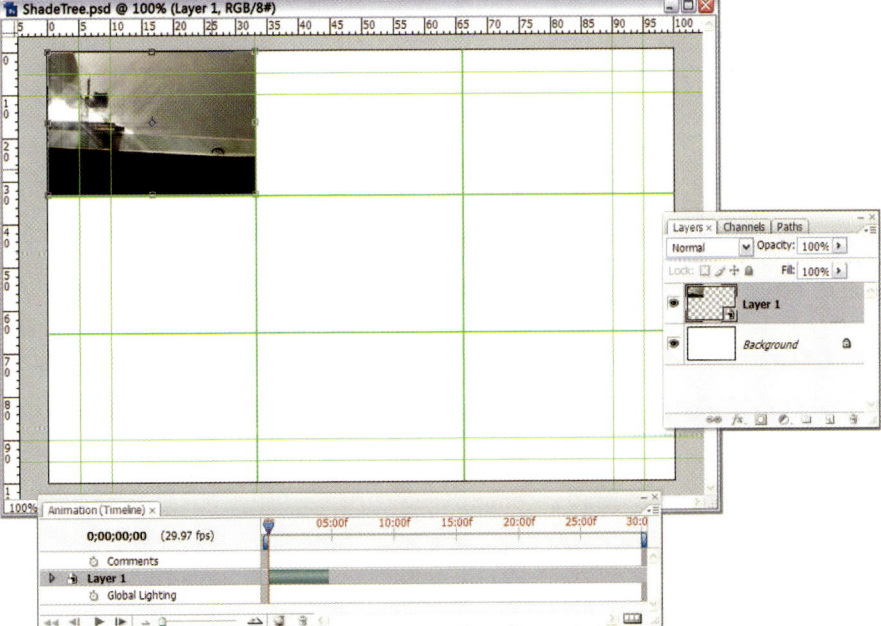

Figure 3.4
Scale a video via the Free Transform feature.

> **Tip**
>
> You can't adjust several video attributes directly when a video exists on a layer as a Smart Object; however, indirect editing can be done by temporarily extracting the video from its Smart Object "shell." You can do this by right-clicking a Smart Object layer on the Layers palette and then choosing Edit Contents.

8. Double-click the current time indicator on the Animation palette and then type **8;00** (seconds) in the Set Time field to immediately scoot to the 8-second mark in the Work Area on the Animation palette. Click the Comment stopwatch on the Animation palette and then in the Edit Timeline Comment box type **Dissolve** or something equally evocative to remind you that this is the end point for all the checkerboard videos. See Figure 3.5.

> **Caution**
>
> In Step 8 I asked you to scoot ahead to 8 seconds on the composition's timeline. This area doesn't feature the saw movie because by default all videos added to a composition go to the beginning of the Work Area, and the clip doesn't play for 8 seconds. Don't use Free Transform on video layers that show no content at a specific point on the timeline; you'll get erroneous behavior and inaccurate editing. Instead, always make sure you have a thumbnail on the Layers palette before calling Free Transform and/or make sure the current time indicator (the thumb, the element with which you scrub the timeline) is set within a video layer's bounds before trying to scale, rotate, or perform other transformations.

9. Click the menu icon on the Animation palette and then choose Palette Options. Click the Frame Number option and click OK. The timeline indicator on the Animation palette now shows frame numbers, and timing all the clips for their entrances will be a lot easier.

10. You might need to zoom the Animation palette's timeline using the slider at bottom left to see the 24 frame mark. With your cursor (there is no special cursor when you're in the Animation palette's timeline and tracks), drag the head of the saw video to 24 frames, as shown in Figure 3.6. Clearly, the clip doesn't play until my specified end point at Frame 240, but you'll fix this in the following section.

Figure 3.5
Define a comment on the timeline you can refer to later.

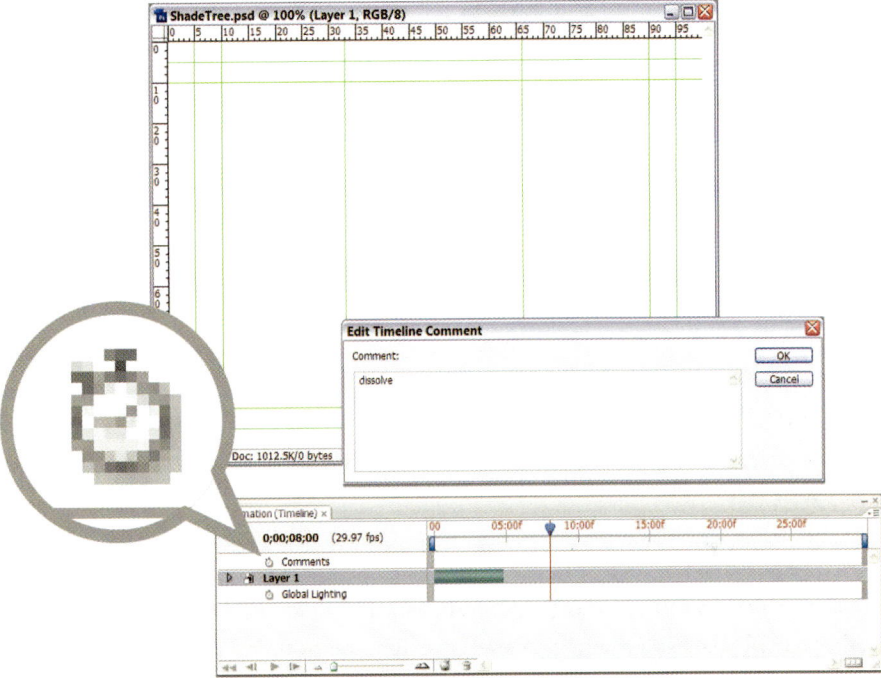

Figure 3.6
Start a video at any given frame by dragging the head of the layer's track to a point on the timeline.

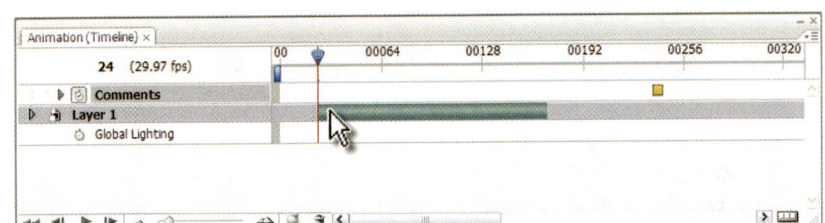

Freeze-Framing

A hold, also known as freeze-framing, is accomplished in Photoshop by duplicating and then rastering a video layer, be it a regular video or a Smart Object. Follow these steps to freeze the saw until the 8 second mark.

1. Move the current time on the Animation palette to the very last frame of the saw video. What I do usually is drag the thumb close to the end and then click the Selects Next Frame/Selects Previous Frame VCR buttons on the palette to target the frame. If the document window goes blank, I've gone one frame too far and need to back up by one frame.

2. On the Layers palette, drag the video Smart Object layer into the Create a New Layer icon to duplicate it.

3. The duplicate layer will default to the head of the timeline, so drag its track to match the positioning of the original. Choose the bottom of the two layers and then right-click over it. Choose Rasterize Layer from the context menu as shown in Figure 3.7. When freeze-framing, it's critical to have the current time at the last frame. For example, if you rasterized a duplicate layer at its midpoint, your "frozen" frame would not be the last frame.

4. Because several of the videos you'll place don't run for 8 seconds, they too will need a hold at the end. Therefore, it's a good idea to get highly organized with this composition, starting at this step. First, by default, all rasterized videos run the length of the Work Area on the Animation palette. This is unwanted, and you need to hide the unwanted areas by dragging the track—the green bar—that represents the playlength of the rasterized layer, at its ends toward its center. You know you have hidden play areas when you see a pale green bar to the left or the right of a track. Drag the ends of the duplicate layer on the Animation palette so it starts at Frame 24 or later but ends at Frame 240.

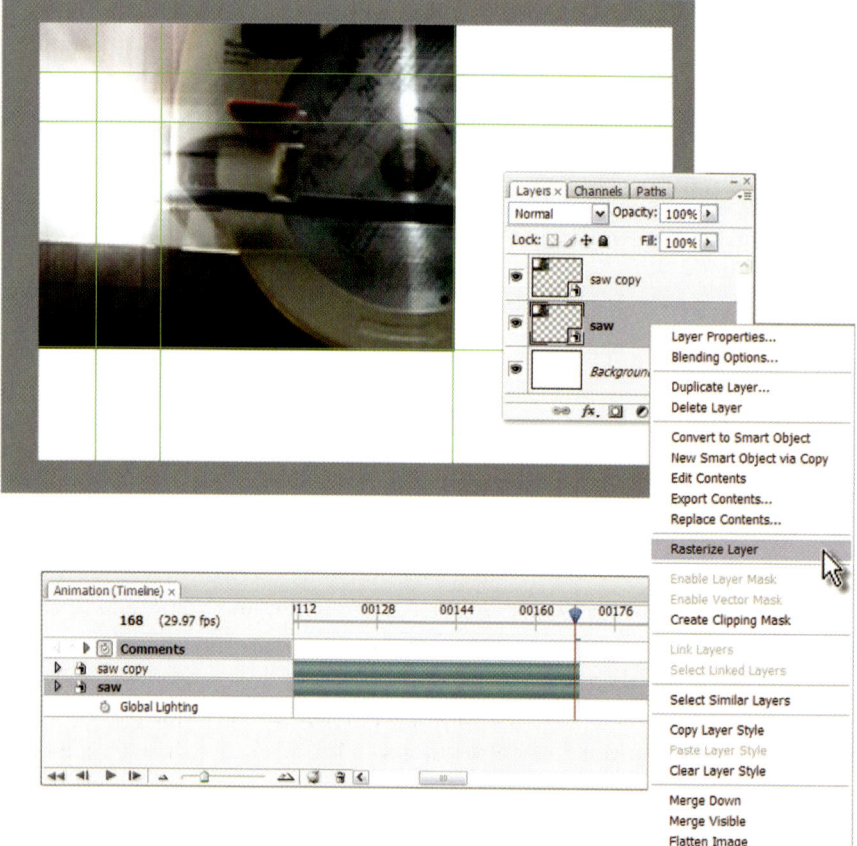

Figure 3.7

Rasterize a duplicate of the video to create a still, non-video image of the final frame of the original.

5. Click on the folder icon at the bottom of the Layers palette to create a new group. Name the group saw; double-click the default name and then type away.

6. Drag the saw and then the rasterized duplicate layer into the Group folder. Make certain the video is above the still image on the list; if you don't you'll be showing almost 8 seconds of still image in the finished video composition. In Figure 3.8, I've opened the Group folder so you can see what the arrangement and timing should look like.

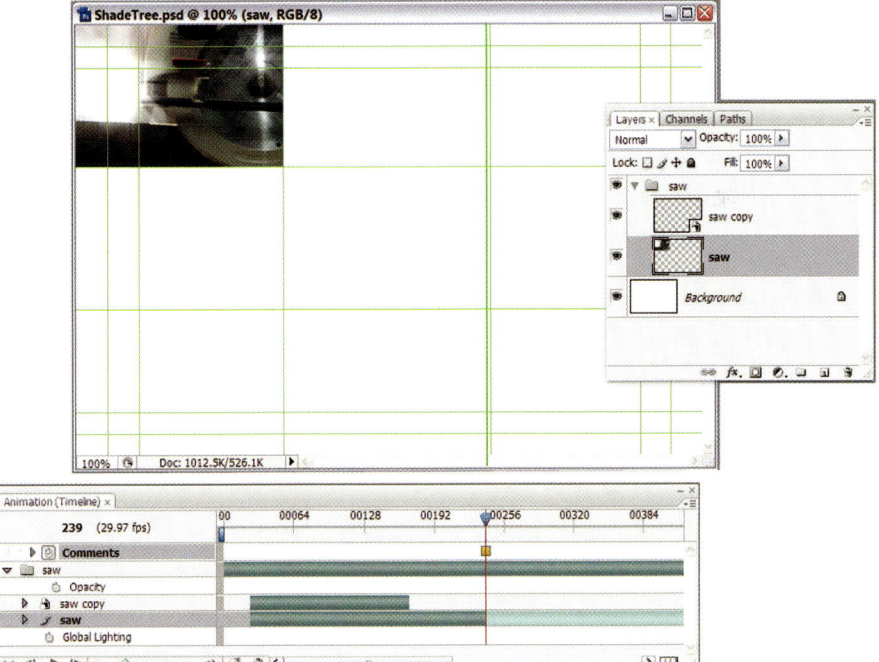

Figure 3.8
Label and group layers for easier scrolling and reference later.

Adding the Second Checkerboard Element

There are one or two novelties to adding the second video to the checkerboard composition, but you've already set up the composition for order and precise placement, and you know how to scale a video. The next steps show how to introduce the next video, which will occupy the 12 o'clock position in the nine-slot grid. Oops: I, The Client, called you five minutes ago and told you I want the build effect to happen clockwise, with the ninth, center square filled last ("Sorry, you don't mind, do you? It's easy for you to do, right?"). There's a hitch: This clip of a drill doing its thing on a piece of wood runs longer than the 8-second cut-off for the sequence.

But you know how to hide a portion of a video track, and I'll point out where in the following:

1. Click on the saw folder so the top item in the Layers palette is active. Choose Layer > Video Layers > New Video Layer from File, and then choose Drill.mov and click Open. Alternatively, you can use File > Open and then drag the movie's layer title into the composition window. My "approved" technique, though, spares you opening and then closing and answering an attention box about saving the file.

2. Scale the video layer down and position it to the direct right of the saw movie in the document window.

3. Twenty-four and 24 is 48; move the track's beginning on the Animation palette to the Frame 48 mark on the timeline.

4. Drag the right end of the layer track so it meets your Comment mark on the timeline, as shown in Figure 3.9. Now the excess is trimmed from the Work Area, and the clip ends synchronously with the saw movie clip.

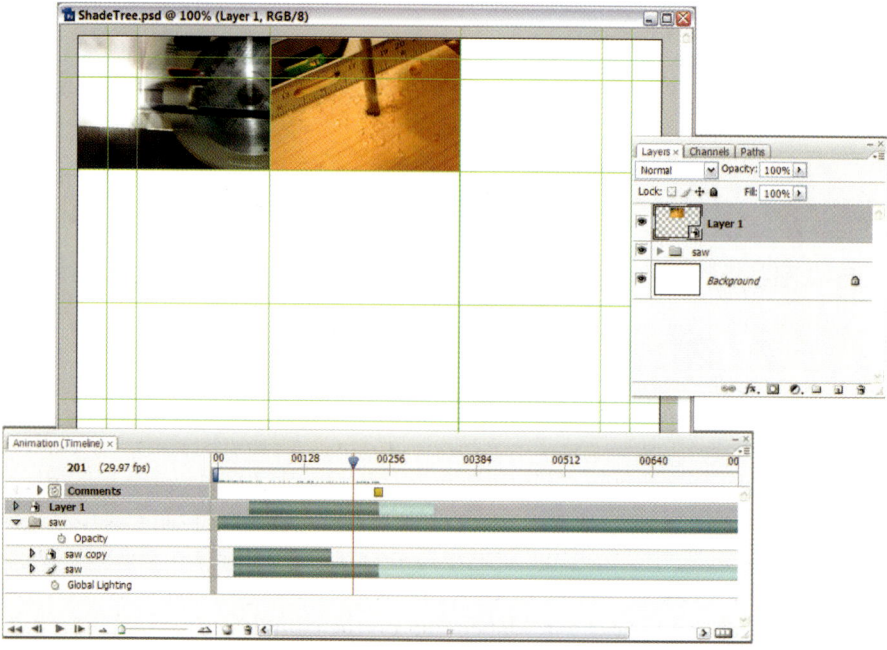

Figure 3.9
Trim a video's play length by hiding the head or tail on the Animation palette.

Compiling a Video from Frames

Procedurally, make sure the current time indicator is at the beginning of the video for when you transform the additional videos. You now add the Cascading screws.mov at top right, beginning play at Frame 72. It needs a hold, and you do this exactly as you did with the saw video. Then it's on to Triangle.avi at center right, a short video that also needs a freeze-frame; it begins play at Frame 96. I'm tossing in an AVI file just to give readers using both Windows and the Mac OS some experience with "the other side"; Photoshop treats AVIs exactly the same as MOV files, but you cannot *export* an AVI with audio due to the rendering engine Photoshop uses (QuickTime).

The Caulking.mov file (goes at bottom right) runs in excess of the 8-second mark; begin its play at Frame 120, and drag its tail to the left on the Animation palette to end it at 8 seconds (Frame 240). Put Painting.mov at the beginning mark of 144 at bottom center; this clip needs a freeze-frame. level.mov goes at bottom left beginning at Frame 168; it needs a freeze-frame. The audience is probably not going to notice all the freeze-frames per se; it's the overall *composition* that is the "star"—the clever way all the little videos appear—and not really the motion content of the individual videos.

Now here's the head scratcher: A hammer needs to go at left, above the level video, but it's not a movie—it's a sequentially numbered series of still frames. Follow these steps to learn how in a few clicks you can create a video from files—as long as they are consecutively numbered—and thus add to your repertoire as a DV editor who can handle most any type of media:

1. Double-click Photoshop's workspace to display the Open dialog box.
2. Go to the Hammer folder you unpacked for this chapter's files and open it in the dialog box.
3. Click on any of the filenames and then check the Image Sequence box before clicking Open, as shown in Figure 3.10. I created this sequence by loading the video, then I chose File > Export > Render Video. In the File Options drop-down list you have the Image Sequence choice. Although I did this to present you with a challenge in this chapter, you might consider doing this in your own work, particularly when you need to send videos across the Internet to a collaborator or client. Depending on the complexity of the image content in each frame and the file format to which you export (JPEG high quality works well), you can use Zip or StuffIt to compress the still images to achieve a file size smaller than the native video clip. Click Open.

Figure 3.10
Open all the files in a folder as an image sequence.

4. The next box wants to know the frame rate of the image sequence you're opening. Choose 29.97 and click OK. Click OK to the next warning for Pixel Aspect Ration Correction and toggle the Pixel Aspect Ratio Correction off from the View menu. Your composition has a frame rate of 29.97, and you gain nothing by specifying a higher frame rate. On the other hand, were you to specify a lower frame rate than that of the composition, the hammer video might suffer from stuttering. See Chapter 17 for thorough documentation of frame rate and other considerations when you render a composition to video.

5. Drag the thumbnail of the hammer video from the Layers palette into the composition document window. Notice that the layer is tagged with a little filmstrip. It's inside Photoshop, so it's not a true video file one could distribute to others, but it has all the attributes of a motion picture. You can now close the hammer document window without saving it.

6. Position and then scale the dimensions of the hammer video using Free Transform so it's at nine o'clock in the composition, just as you did with the other videos.

7. Notice that the duration of the hammer video exceeds the comment mark on the Animation palette. The head of the video starts at Frame 192; drag the tail of the track to meet the comment point. The composition should look like Figure 3.11 now, and only Mr. Fixit is left to add. Notice how the Animation palette video layer tracks are arranged and notice that I bothered to label all the video layers on the Layers palette; it's a very good practice, especially when you have so many layers in a single video comp.

Figure 3.11
Arrange the Animation palette and the Layers palette so the components of your work are well organized and easy to locate.

Shifting the Time with a Clip

It's a good time now to play the composition. First, drag the Work Area's end to meet the Comment mark; Figure 3.12 shows a close-up of the beginning and ending Work Area markers—think of them as the beginning and ending of the finished video you'll render. In addition to marking the duration of a composition, limiting the Work Area to the area you want to play back (to preview) allows Photoshop to buffer the video into system memory more quickly. Play the defined Work Area for the comp a few times. The first time you play a composition, Photoshop needs to buffer into memory, and the video does not play back in real time.

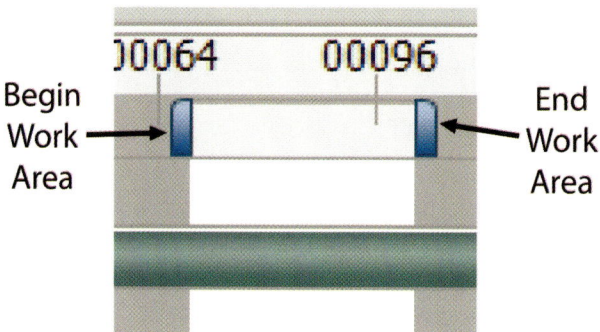

Figure 3.12
The Work Area markers define the beginning and end of a composition.

I noticed something when I played back the comp: The hammer video, as it appears in the comp, is *boring*! It doesn't begin with any action. Fortunately, I've provided several seconds of the hammer doing its thing, and what you'll learn in the following steps is how to shift a clip on the Animation palette so the duration is the same, but the video features different (in this case, better) visual content:

1. You might experience some "drag" if you try to scrub the timeline indicator (the thumb) to an exact point in the composition, mostly because you have eight clips and they're all altered video, and this makes Photoshop write temp files to disk, access system RAM, and all that good, processor-intensive stuff. Instead, double-click the current time indicator and then type **192**, the point of the hammer clip's entrance. The thumb immediately scoots to this time without scrolling through other frames.

2. Extend the tail of the track by dragging the end of the green bar to the right.

3. Drag the hammer track back and forth until you find a point where the hammer animates instead of resting poised. See Figure 3.13.

4. Drag the head of the track to Frame 192, hiding the frames that precede this point, and then drag the tail of the track to the left to hide everything after the comment mark at 8 seconds.

5. Save.

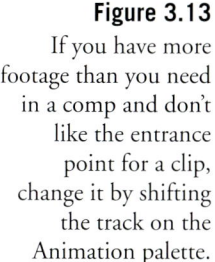

Figure 3.13
If you have more footage than you need in a comp and don't like the entrance point for a clip, change it by shifting the track on the Animation palette.

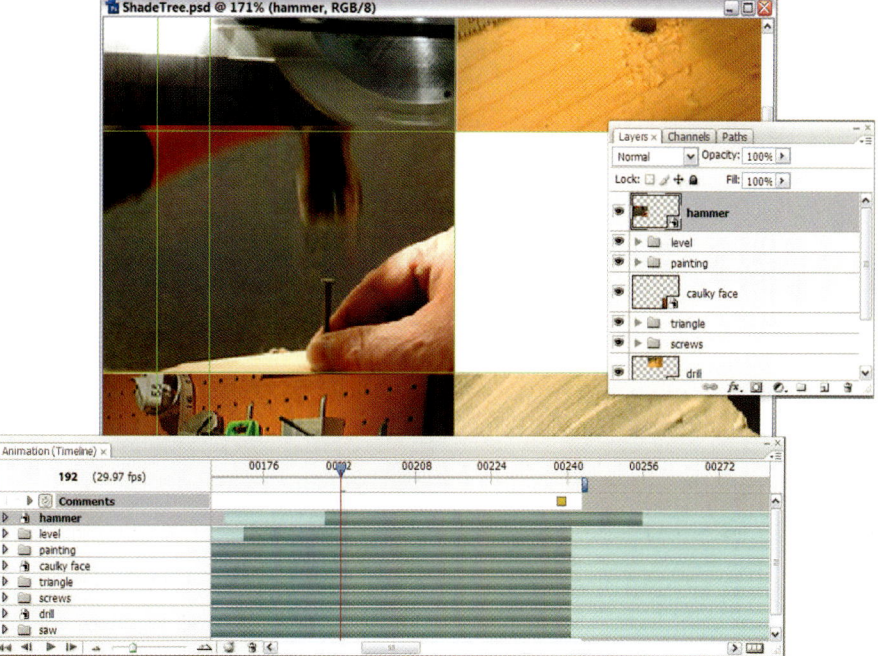

Finishing the Checkerboard

Mr Fixit.mov completes the checkerboard in the center square; place the clip now via Layer > Video Layers > New Video Layer from File. Scale and position the clip and notice that the clip runs long for the comp, so, as with the hammer, find a good place in the clip to begin it—start it at Frame 216—and then hide the head and tail by dragging on the ends of the track on the Animation palette.

I, The Client, feel that the presentation would look cleaner if the checkerboard were framed with one of the corporate colors, orange. Follow these steps to accommodate The Client:

1. The Background layer has been white up 'til now because placing the videos is easier working against white. However, the commercial should start with a black screen; click the Background layer on the Layers palette to make this the active layer.

2. Choose black as the current foreground color on the Tools palette and then press Alt/Opt+Backspace to fill the layer with black.

3. Click the Mr. Fixit video layer on the Layers palette, and then click the Create a new layer icon on the Layers palette. Doing this puts the new layer on the top of the stack.

4. Use the Eyedropper tool to select an orange foreground color from the checkerboard of video clips; sampling a color from the triangle worked for me.

5. Choose the Line tool from the Shapes group on the Tools palette.

6. On the Options bar, set the type of shape to Fill Pixels (I've highlighted the button in blue in the following figure). Also set the Weight to 5 pixels, which will be noticeable, but not a "hit you over the head" effect in the finished video. It's important to work at 100% viewing resolution with documents in which there's text or other elements such as the border you'll add. It's also important to make drawn elements thicker than 2 pixels for broadcast because very slender text and other elements tend to twitter onscreen.

7. Hold Shift to constrain the angle of your drag. Drag lines where you have guides in the document so they frame the video checkerboard, as shown in Figure 3.14. Then, because this new layer plays the duration of the Work Area, drag the tail of its track on the Animation palette to the comment mark, aligning its exit with all the other videos.

Figure 3.14

Adding a grid adds polish to the comp and also reinforces the corporate color of the fictitious company.

Adding and Fading Up the Signature

In later chapters I cover all sorts of fancy transitions, but for now all we need is a cross-dissolve from the checkerboard to element #2 in the commercial, the snorkel animation, which is called a *signature shot* in advertising.

Cross-dissolves require only one element to fade up, as long as the underlying video remains. In the steps to follow, you'll change the opacity of the signature clip over 15 frames (half a second) to make what is also called a soft cut from the completed checkerboard to the snorkel animation. As you might imagine, you'll lose 15 frames of the checkerboard comp as a clear video graphic. This is okay in this example because I budgeted this in when I timed the composition, and in your own work, plan some wiggle room for clips to accommodate transitions.

1. Choose Layer > Video Layers > New Video Layer from File. Choose the Signature.mov file and click Open.

2. Choose Timecode from the Animation palette's Palette Options on the flyout menu. There's no sense in viewing frames on the timeline from this point on; the hard work of timing the entrance of the checkerboard elements is completed.

3. Extend the end Work Area marker to 18 seconds, the finished duration of the mock commercial.

4. By default, placed videos are put at the head of the Work Area, and the signature animation needs to go later. Drag the track on the Animation palette to about 7 seconds, 15 frames (7.5 seconds).

5. Put the thumb on the Animation palette at 7 seconds, 15 frames—the head of the animation video.

6. Open the track on the Animation palette by clicking the little triangle. Click the Opacity stopwatch.

7. On the Layers palette, set the Opacity for the animation video to 0%.

8. Go to the comment mark on the Animation palette with the thumb and then set the Opacity for the animation video to 100%. Notice in Figure 3.15 that keyframe markers are automatically added to the track on the timeline—this happens whenever a stopwatch is active and you make a change to a layer attribute along time.

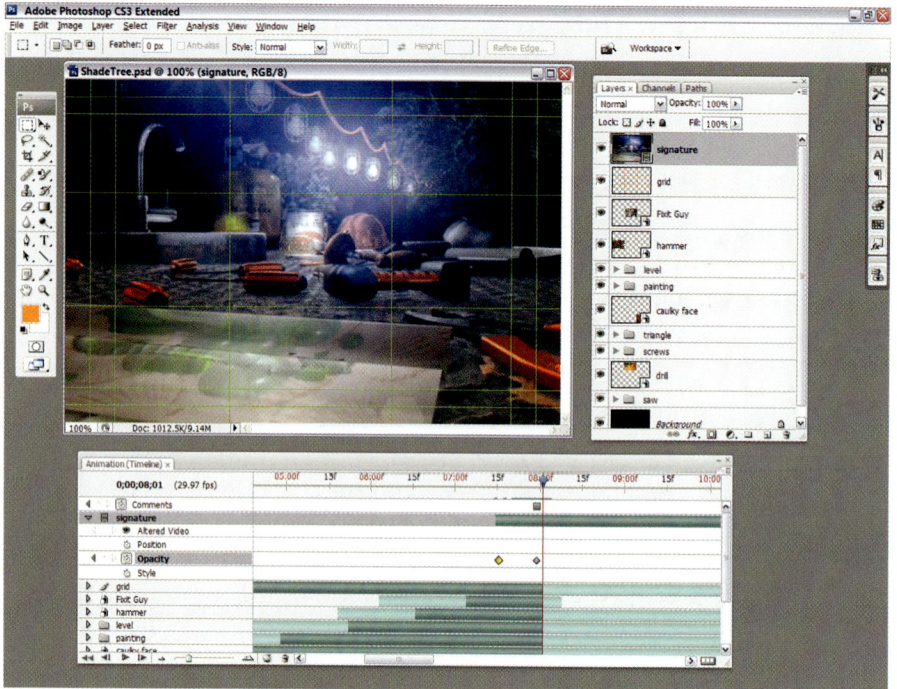

Figure 3.15
Change opacity for a layer at points along the timeline and you can create a dissolve.

Adding Titles

The end of the animation fades to black, but before it does, it would be right and proper to close the commercial with a logo and a selling slogan. In keeping with the frantic pace of the commercial, I created two short text and graphics animations—they perform a zoomy blur into frame from the left and right. I created the animated text and logo in SwishMAX, an inexpensive Flash-compatible Web content creation package, but the unfortunate thing is that SwishMAX doesn't export AVI files (or any other true video format) with transparency. Therefore, it would seem that superimposing the titles over the product shot at the end of the animation is problematic.

Not so, as you conclude editing the video in the following steps. If you are faced with an animation package that doesn't support transparency, you can choose black as the background color and then use a blending mode in Photoshop to hide the black.

1. Click the top layer to make this active so the logo will come in at the top of the stack. Choose Layer > Video Layers > New Video Layer from File. Choose logo.mov.

2. On the Animation palette, drag the track so it begins at about 14 seconds. Note that the animation has a very short duration and does not extend to the end of the commercial at 18 seconds.

3. On the Layers palette, choose Screen as the blending mode for the layer, and instantly you have white text against a clear background so the underlying animation can be seen.

4. With the Move tool, move the logo to center it onscreen, but use those titling safety guides. Make sure the logo is in the clear.

5. Duplicate the video layer and, since it will default to the beginning of the timeline, drag the duplicate to the same location on the timeline, go to the last frame, and then rasterize the bottom duplicate's last frame, exactly as you did to freeze-frame the checkerboard videos earlier.

6. You need to butt the static duplicate layer so it doesn't appear until the last or next-to-last frame of the animated logo on top. Because you're dealing with a background on the top video layer in Screen mode, the static layer will show through, spoiling the animation, unless it appears only after the animated logo has "landed." Drag the head of the static layer track so it looks like that in Figure 3.16. It's okay to hold the title through the 18 seconds of the commercial and even extend beyond the end of the Work Area. Nothing outside the Work Area on the Animation palette is ever rendered to video.

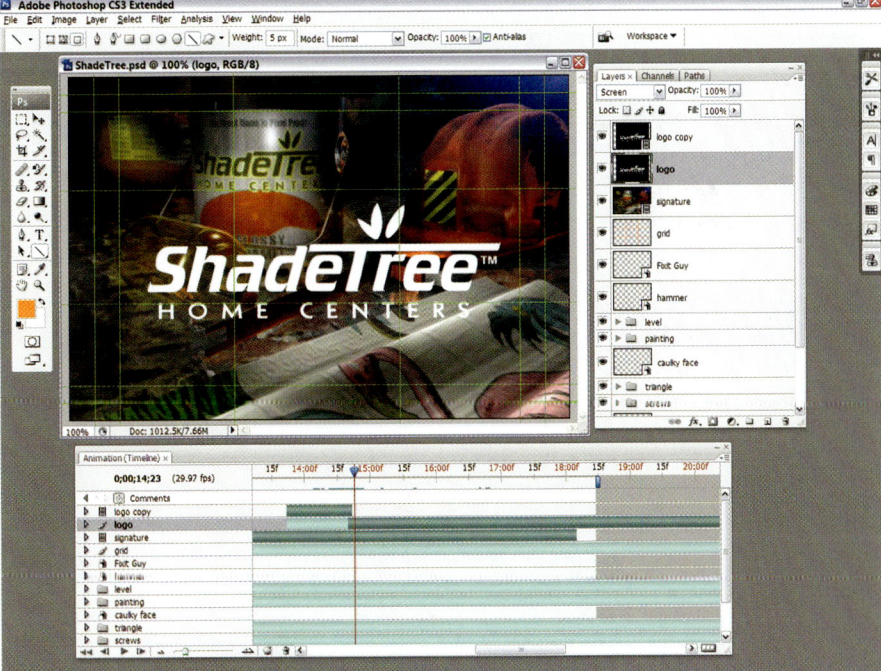

Figure 3.16
Add a logo by using Screen blending mode to hide the black background in the logo.

7. You're almost home free. Add the snappy slogan at the top of the layer stack via Layer > Video Layers > New Video Layer from File. It's the slogan.mov file; it needs to be in Screen blending mode and centered in the video window as you did with the logo file. You'll need to duplicate the video and then rasterize the bottom copy at the end frame, like you did with the logo animation. Let it enter the composition just after the logo appears at about 14;15 to keep the audience breathless. Remember to keep this slogan within title safety, as shown in Figure 3.17. Save at this point but don't close the file.

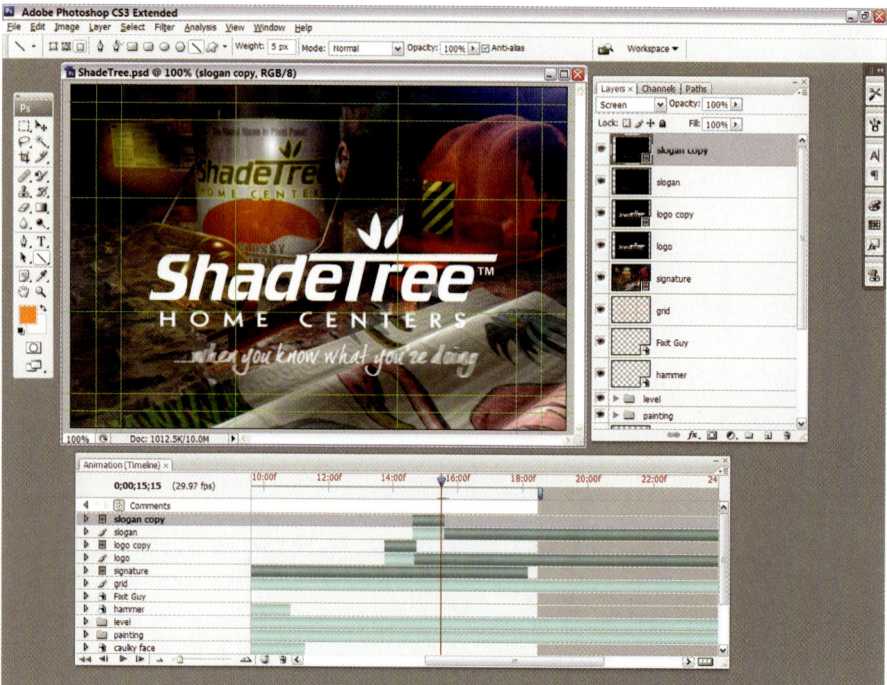

Figure 3.17
Add the slogan right after the logo begins to settle.

Adding Audio and Rendering Your Work

Any video that has an audio track can be played back with sound by holding Alt/Opt before you click the Play button on the Animation palette. None of the videos in this composition have audio (it would be a confusing mish-mash cacophony because there are no audio tools in Photoshop, so I scrubbed the videos of sound), but the piece really should have some driving music with a hint of domestic fix-em-up machismo.

Photoshop can place an audio file in a composition, but it's done in a less-than-straightforward way because audio support, like video rendering, is QuickTime technology Adobe licensed for this build. You can import audio in QuickTime file format with audio only and no video as long as the file has been written this way, and you can bring in Windows WAV files, MP3 files, and even Ogg-Vorbis (*.ogg) audios, which audiophiles boast has higher quality than MP3 at similar compression rates.

The trick for Windows users is that you have to choose File > Open As and then choose QuickTime movie as the file type, even though the file might be a WAV or MP3. The Mac OS doesn't concern itself with file types *vis a vis* Photoshop and can open an audio file simply by making sure the audio is defined as a QuickTime in the Open box.

I wrote a little jingle that's a fraction over 18 seconds expressly for this assignment, using a digital audio workspace application. Follow these steps to place the audio track in the composition, and then I'll show you how to export the composition to a file format others can appreciate:

1. Choose File > Open As, and then choose ShadeTree Theme Song 18.mp3 from the archive folder you unpacked at the beginning of the chapter. For Windows users, choose QuickTime Movie from the Open As drop-down menu at the bottom of the dialog box. Ignore any colorspace attention boxes and don't freak that the music file appears as a document window whose contents are totally transparent. All is well.

2. On the Layers palette, drag the layer title into the composition window. You can close the original file without saving changes.

3. By default, the track's beginning starts at the beginning of the Work Area, so you really don't have to do any adjusting now because I timed the song to match the duration of the composition. Make sure the end of the Work Area meets the end of the audio track, as you can see in Figure 3.18. The layer order of audio doesn't matter; when rendered to video, any composition with one or more audio tracks will play back, even if an audio "layer" is on the bottom of a layer stack.

> **Note**
>
> You can perform minor audio editing in Photoshop. You cannot adjust volume, but you can mute audio at any point by hiding its track on the Animation palette, exactly like you hide video content you don't want to show. You hide part of the track by dragging the ends of the green bar that represents the layer so that the light green areas represent hidden data (muted audio).

Figure 3.18
Add audio to your composition by placing an audio file as a layer element.

4. Play back the composition to check for any errors in timing and visibility while holding Alt/Opt before you click the Play button on the Animation palette.

5. Choose File > Export > Render Video.

6. The Currently Selected Frames button should have been selected for you, but click it if it isn't.

7. Choose QuickTime Movie from the File Options drop-down list. Again, QuickTime is the rendering engine for video that Adobe has licensed, and only this file format will export with audio. Windows users shouldn't be concerned; QuickTime Movie Player should have been installed when you installed Photoshop Extended. It's hard to buy an application today for Windows that doesn't auto-install the Movie Player. If you're positive you don't have it on your system, go to Apple.com and download a free copy. Alternatively, if you absolutely must have a Windows-native video with audio, there are several inexpensive, occasionally free MOV to WMV convertors. Do a keyword search on the Web for one; you'll find dozens.

8. Click the Settings button to the right of the drop-down list. In the Movie Settings box, click Settings.

9. Choose either Sorenson 3 or H.264 as your codec (compressor/decompressor). Sorenson offers very good color, while H.264 (a variation on the MPEG-4 codec) excels at compression. It's always a choice between quality and file size when compressing videos. And you do want to compress your composition, at least for passing around to your friends. Uncompressed, this composition would take up hundreds of MB on your hard drive, QuickTime Movie Player would not play the video without halting several times as it caches to memory, and qualitatively, the difference between uncompressed and compressed movies using either of these codecs is nominal. The only times you'd want to specify None as a compressor is when collaborating or writing files you need to edit later or for rendering to physical film for motion pictures. Motion pictures need each frame to be at least 2K (2,000 by 2,000 pixels), so let's forget about this consideration with this example. Set the Frame Rate to 29.97, set the compressor to High (best quality/large file size), and then click OK.

10. Click OK in the Movie Settings box to return to the Render Video dialog box.

11. Choose a location on hard disk for the rendered movie, then click Render.

12. Wait a while. I recommend that you make some popcorn.

13. Save and then close Photoshop. Open your MOV file in QuickTime or a QuickTime-compatible player. Decide you're very happy with your first composition, send it to The Client, collect wheelbarrows of non-sequentially numbered, large denomination bills.

For a chapter that's as early as this one in this book, I realize I might have tossed a lot at you. But ask yourself what you really had to learn compared to what you already knew and applied from your existing skills with previous versions of Photoshop. Free Transforming a video layer is almost exactly like scaling a still photograph, video layers are listed the same way as composite layers for still imaging on the Layers palette, and transparency in videos is the same as transparency in still image composition.

What I hoped to take you through in this chapter is working with the aspect of *time* in a Photoshop composition. The Animation palette is well laid-out and fairly intuitive to work with; between the Layers palette and the Animation palette you can create just about anything you can envision, except the pictures are *moving* pictures. Use the Photoshop tools with which you have experience the same way as you have for years with still images, use the new features with the aspect of time as a consideration, and hopefully you've seen that Photoshop doesn't care whether you edit a still image or video layer.

Your document merely contains pixels that change color from time to time!

Part II
Video Sweetening

4

Cuts, Wipes, and Fades

With the exception of Alfred Hitchcock's *Rope*, the timeline of a video story is usually segmented. Cuts and fades just make sense. After all, what audience would want to watch the cops drive all the way to the airport to catch the bad guys? When you make a video transition, you're performing the equivalent of a comic book caption that says "Meanwhile..." or "Later in the day...." However, unlike static comic book panels, transitions have become as elegant as the video content itself—they become an integral part of the visual story, and the best transition effects play a subordinate role to the main characters, the video clips.

Photoshop Extended has a number of features on the Animation palette for making cuts, but that's only part of this chapter's story. I show you not only how to best cut some raw footage into a well-paced, visually interesting video short, but also how to build transitions—specifically wipes and fades. You'll use Actions and Adobe Bridge to make reusable transition effects, so now it's time to cut to the chase!

Hands-On with the Animation Palette's Menu

Cuts and dissolves are covered in this section: They're the workaday connective tissue for videos of just about any content. The example video in this section, Bubble kids.mp4, derives most of its entertainment value from the very simple interaction of two children chasing soap bubbles around the yard on a sunny summer day. If you've ever photographed kids under seven at an event, you'll immediately sympathize with the plight I had—you can chase them around with a hand-held DV unit (producing nauseatingly unstable framing, more or less like camera phone coverage of a disaster), or you let the camera roll for several minutes and spend your time more wisely coaxing the kids into frame. Doing this leaves a lot of boring, static "in-between the moments" footage, and instead of imprecisely chopping footage into chapters using the system's DV download utility, this is a great opportunity to really time and massage the footage into segments that make chronological sense. In a very real way, video editing helps tell the story, just as cropping a photograph in Photoshop helps emphasize the important compositional elements.

Splitting, Extracting, and Lifting Video Layers

You have three basic commands available on the Animation palette's flyout menu for making cuts:

- **Split Layer.** Splitting a layer in two occurs at the timeline point where the thumb is located when you click this menu command. For all intents and purposes, you have the beginning on one layer and the end on the layer directly above it.

- **Extract Work Area.** This operation, technically, is a multiple cut; it puts the layer segment that is bounded by the Work Area markers on a new layer and creates a gap in the remaining video. This is a great command for clearing static, unwanted segments from a video, and it performs the operation on all video layers (tracks) in the composition.

- **Lift Work Area.** If you want to delete a segment from a video but not from *all* the clips on the timeline, you use Lift Work Area; you can lock or hide video layers you don't want edited.

Unlike traditional film editing, your cuts are not permanent, for two reasons:

1. Photoshop is working with a *placed* video file; the original is only *referenced* in the Photoshop document window.

2. The footage that you command to be cut is actually hidden: The dark green tracks on the Animation palette are visible video, and the light green bracketing the dark green represents hidden footage. You can unhide the hidden cuts at any time by dragging the light green track ends to the left or right of the timeline. Therefore, you can't mess up original footage, and you can't even mess up your composition. Even if you use the Trim Document Duration to Work Area command, at any future point you can use the Document Settings command to lengthen the composition, and yep, the light green hidden tracks are revealed in the timeline.

Therefore, the following steps are completely nondestructive. Using Bubble kids.mp4, here's how to make your cuts:

1. So I can provide you with specific timeline points, choose Palette Options from the Animation palette menu. Then click Frame Number instead of Timecode, and click OK.

2. If you scrub the timeline from the beginning, you'll see that the little girl doesn't enter until Frame 98. However, it would be an artistic mistake to cut at Frame 98 because that leaves no "easing" into the scene. Instead, leave a little less than a second for an intro to the clip by moving the timeline thumb to 76, and then drag the left edge of the green track to this point. Doing this turns Frames 0–75 to the light green color, indicating hidden frames.

3. Move ahead to Frame 427. We have a long static period with no children until the little boy re-enters at Frame 620. Give a lead-in of about one second by moving the Work Area beginning point to Frame 450 and then move the Work Area end marker to Frame 600, providing almost a second's worth of ease room to the static segment's surrounding video.

4. Choose Lift Work Area from the Animation palette menu, as shown in Figure 4.1. A gap is created in the video, and the footage after Frame 600 is copied to a new layer.

Figure 4.1
Photoshop automatically copies footage to a new video layer when you lift out a segment.

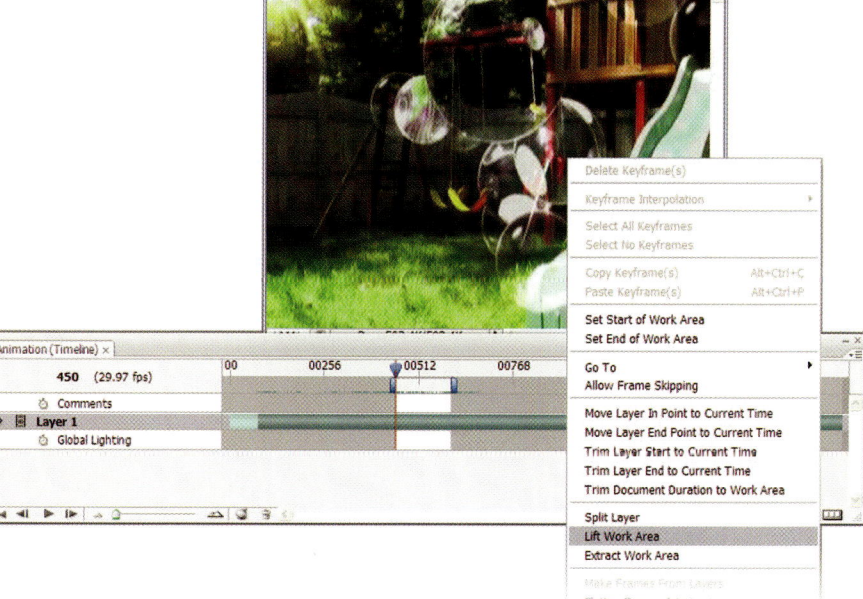

5. It's important that a layer is selected to perform splitting, and Photoshop's method of splitting video requires it to leave both the original and the copy selected; you therefore need to click the top layer (thus deselecting the lower selected original) before making other splits and lifts. You can highlight a layer for editing by clicking on either the Animation palette track or the title on the Layers palette list. Rename the bottom layer "sunshine, both kids" for easy future reference.

6. Return the Work Area beginning and end points to the original perimeters on the timeline. Click the top layer to make it the active layer. At Frame 710 I unwisely paused the camera, and although everything from Frames 600 to 710 is fine and packed with action, there is a lighting change at 710. Move the thumb to 710 (the easiest way is to click the Time Ruler; performing scrubbing on large videos exhibits dragging performance even with muscle machines) and then choose Split Layer from the menu (see Figure 4.2). Now rename the middle layer on the Layers palette "short clip of Drew." Save the comp as Bubble kids.psd; keep the file open.

7. Frame 1074 begins a new scene, as does Frame 1231. We managed to get a really nice portrait sequence with the little girl, Maddie. Click the top layer to make it active. Move the timeline indicator (the thumb) to 1074, split the layer, and then click the top layer again and move to 1231 and choose Split Layer. Name the 710–1073 layer "less light, both kids" and the 1074–1230 layer "Maddie."

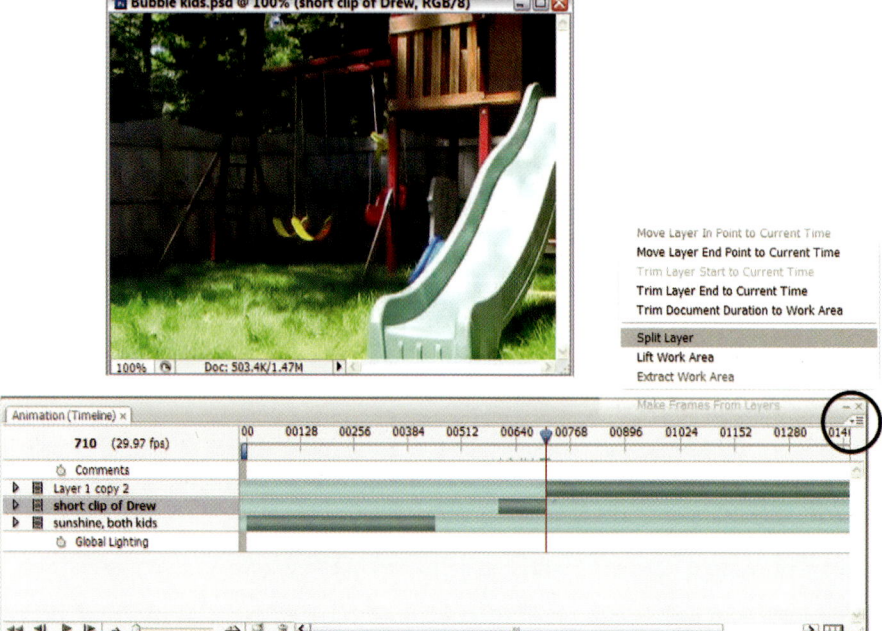

Figure 4.2

Split the video at frame 710 so the preceding Frames can be isolated and manipulated as an individual clip.

8. You have five segments now. Although the content of the video is homogenous, look at Figure 4.3; I've labeled the appropriate clips with Drew's name, Maddie's name, and then the twosome in segments where the sun produced a little lens flare, and the slightly dimmer scenes. Labeling the layers makes it easier to create a mental storyboard for the whole video.

You've performed some good cuts, but they're not yet arranged in a logical or artistically pleasing sequence of events. It's time to move to the editing chair.

Figure 4.3
Creating cuts is the first stage of video editing.

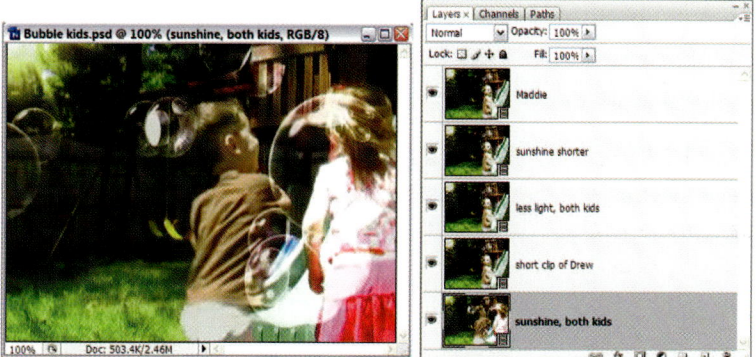

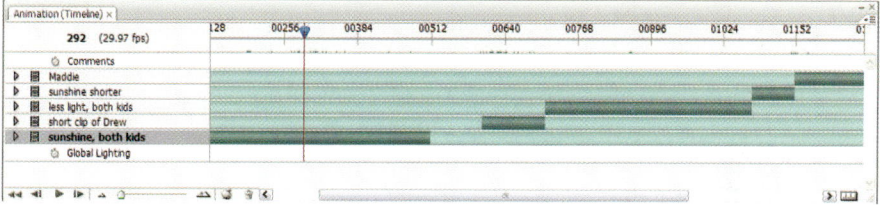

Ordering and Blending Video Layers

Feel free to experiment with your own creative sequence of events at this point. My sequence is to begin with the original beginning, then cut to the short clip of the boy (Drew), to the close-up of Maddie, onto the scene with less sunlight, and finally to the segment with more sun. There's a finite number of arrangements with five clips; I thought a good flow was an establishing shot, move to Drew, who isn't in much of the footage, change scenes to a close-up on Maddie, and a temporal zoom out to the two shots for the remainder of the produced video.

Humor me and accept my "Director's cut" for the following tutorial. You arrange the video layers by dragging them up or down on the Layers palette list.

Here's how to time and then add some cross-fades to keep the video interesting and smooth:

1. On the Layers palette, move the "sunshine, both kids" layer to the top of the stack to use as the introductory segment.

2. On the Animation palette, slide this layer track to the beginning of the Work Area by dragging it with the cursor. Now the hidden area from Frame 0 to 78 is completely gone from the Work Area, and the film begins at (the original) Frame 78.

3. Choose Palette Options from the Animation palette menu and then choose Timecode. When editing clips together, you need a sense of time and not empirical frame numbers.

4. Move the "short clip of Drew" to beneath the "sunshine, both kids" layer on the Layers palette; it'll be the second sequence. Then arrange the remaining layers so "Maddie" is third from the top layer, "less light, both kids" is fourth from the top, and "sunshine, shorter" is the bottom layer.

5. One track at a time, move them so they overlap each other on the timeline. In Figure 4.4 you can see I've allowed about one second to ease in and out of a segment, which you'll do shortly. You don't want them to butt segments against one another in this example. Why?

    - The segments are relatively short, so straight cuts would be visually interruptive.
    - A cut in film is used to redirect the audience to the character that's speaking or active, not because you ran out of footage.
    - You can then fade segments in and out.
    - In the previous section on making cuts I asked you to give some legroom to the in and out points. This is "fade time," and if you made cuts in the produced video, your timing would have nasty lags of static footage.

6. Because your first segment is on top of the layer stack, to cross-fade to the second segment requires that you fade out the top layer, and the second segment does not need to be faded in. Go to about 11;25 on the time ruler with the thumb, click the first layer, open the track to get to the properties on the Animation palette, and click the stopwatch for Opacity (a keyframe is created on the track at the present opacity, 100%).

Figure 4.4
Overlap the segments in the timeline.

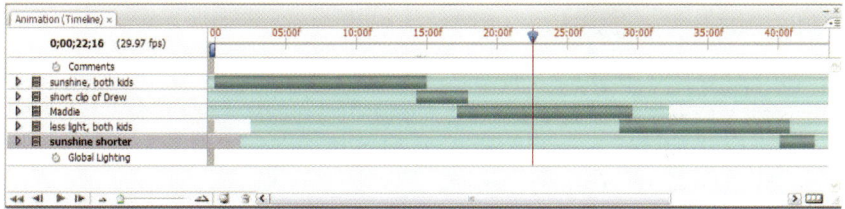

7. Move to 12;21. On the Layers palette, set the opacity for this layer to 0%. You've not only maximized the time for the cross-fade by going to the last frame (fades under a second are usually visually jarring), but you've also squeezed every available frame out of the composition. This will be important to the client; I wouldn't want to tell Drew and Maddie's parents that I left a lot of footage on the cutting room floor just because I'm a novice video editor!

8. You have the option to simply fade out scenes to reveal the following segment or fade a segment up and then down; visually, it makes no difference. So proceed with the fades. In Figure 4.5 you can see I've chosen to fade the clip of Maddie up and then down, making a fade up on the following segment unnecessary. I found that a good shortcut to creating a key that has the same opacity as the one directly before it is to drag the Opacity slider to a little under 100% and then back to 100%. This forces the auto-creation of a key at the opacity you need without the need to copy and paste a key. Additionally, use the Go To Previous/Go To Next stopwatch icons on the Animation palette for keyframes (the arrows bracketing the keyframe icon to the left of the stopwatch. They'll toggle you between successive keys a lot faster than scrubbing the timeline.

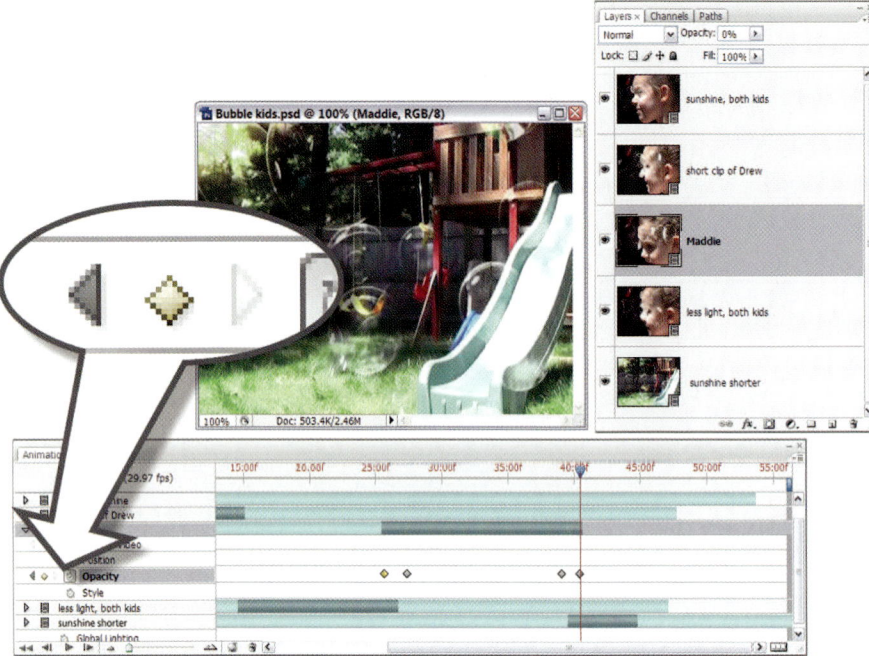

Figure 4.5
Fade between segments on the timeline.

9. Don't hesitate to zoom in and out of the timeline to set precise keys. When you're done, drag the Work Area marker at right to the end of the last segment (see Figure 4.6). You could trim the Work Area now by choosing Trim Document Duration to Work Area, but I see this as an overly fastidious gesture. As long as the Work Area brackets the footage you want in the finished video, File > Export > Render Video has the option to clip the rendered video to the currently defined workspace.

10. I dumped the sound to this clip because there was no fun in it but rather a lot of us shouting directions to one another. So I created JSBach-Sheep May Safely Graze.mp3. It's in the Zip archive you downloaded and is an arrangement of a classic, almost meditative piece by Bach. Not only is the MP3 file thematically appropriate for the video, but without it, it's a return to silent 8mm home movies. Audiences are conditioned to expect audio, and I also added some ambient outdoor sounds to the song so the composition can feel like the ice cream man is playing his tunes down the street instead of a sterile, overproduced (and creatively dissonant) home video. Windows users should choose File > Open As, pick QuickTime as the file type, and then drag the open file's Layers palette title into the kids video document window. Mac users can simply open the file as a QuickTime file because Photoshop for the Mac doesn't use the file type convention Windows does.

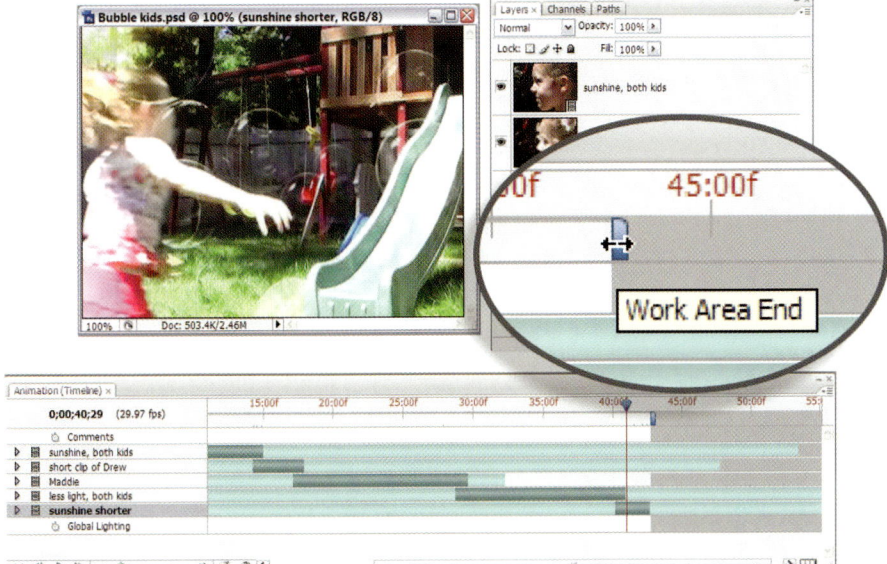

Figure 4.6
Bracket your production using the Work Area markers.

11. The audio track is perhaps 10 seconds longer than your production. I recommend sliding the audio track to the head of the composition in the Animation palette, and the audience will get 10 seconds of audio with no video. You really need something such as Premiere to fade audio to synch with video; sadly, you cannot adjust volume for audio in Photoshop.

12. Choose File > Export > Render Video. In the main Export box, click the Currently Selected Frames button in the Range field.

13. Choose QuickTime in the File Options area and then click the Settings button and choose Sorenson (for better color) or H.264 (less saturation but smaller files).

14. Choose a location on hard disk for your production and then click Render. Save the file again after the render completes. Keep the document open for the tutorial in the following section.

Fades: Up and Out

To conclude a production, it's a good idea to have the video transit to a color. This is the simplest of video transitions and is easy to accomplish in Photoshop. The classic fade to black feels a little ominous and depressing for the kids chasing bubbles, so let's instead create a fade to white at the end of this composition (it's currently quite in fashion on TV commercials).

Follow these steps to copy a single segment from the composition so it can stand on its own, and then make a fade up and out.

1. Move the timeline thumb to the point where you have the clip of Maddie in close-up.

2. Right-click the layer on the Layers palette you marked with the close-up of Maddie, and then choose Duplicate Layer. In the Duplicate Layer dialog box, choose New as the Document Destination, and then call it Fade Experiment.psd or some other similarly evocative name. After the new document appears in the workspace, you can close the larger composition.

3. Notice on the Animation palette that there's a lot of hidden video at the head of the track, because Photoshop did not destroy the footage when you made the Split Layer command. For editing comfort, move the visible track to the center of the Work Area on the Animation palette (drag the track with the cursor), and then move the beginning and end markers for the Work Area to bracket the "live" area (the dark green) of the footage. On the Animation palette menu, choose Trim Document Duration to Work Area.

4. Create a new layer on the Layers palette, drag it beneath the video layer, and then fill it with white.

5. Open the video track's Opacity properties and click the Selects the First Frame button (the far left one on the VCR controls).

6. On the Layers palette, drag the opacity for the (top) video layer down to 0 and then click the Opacity stopwatch.

7. Move the timeline to about two seconds in from the head and then drag the Opacity slider to 100%.

8. Move the timeline thumb to about 12 seconds and then drag the Opacity slider on the Layers palette back and forth to force the Animation palette to create a key at this point, making sure the opacity is at 100% before continuing.

9. At the tail (which should be about 15 seconds), drag the Opacity slider to 0. As you can see in Figure 4.7, the progression is appropriate for the content of the video. Check out Bubble kids.mov in the Gallery folder to see how the cross-fades look and how the fade to white serves as a subtle signal to the audience that the movie is over. In general, you should reserve a particular transition for only the beginning and end of a video to avoid sending false prompts to your audience that the film has concluded.

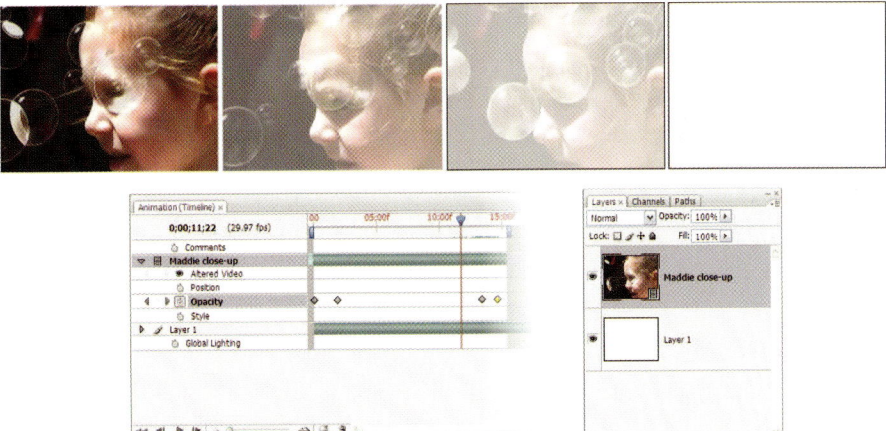

Figure 4.7
Fades up and out serve as a "frame" for your moving picture. They make it a tidy, polished package.

Scripting

In the sections to follow I show you how to build an animated transition effect. It doesn't merely move onscreen, but its *shape* changes. To make iris wipes, Venetian blind wipes, and other professional transitions, you need to build the animation yourself, with some help from the Actions palette and a little scripting knowledge. Photoshop Scripts help you to avoid tedium and potential carpal tunnel syndrome, and they enable useful functions. The samples provided with Photoshop Extended come in three formats, but all essentially perform the same operations. AppleScripts and Windows Visual Basic Scripts are platform specific; therefore, I discuss JavaScripts here, which are platform independent. I've found that JavaScripts run almost exactly as fast as platform-specific scripts within Photoshop.

In the next section I show you how to cobble appropriate transitions for a specific set of video clips. The transitions need to be of certain lengths, none of which is under 45 frames (1.5 seconds at approximately 30 fps). So you see that because Photoshop has no feature to repeat an Action, you'd have to click the Play button on the Actions palette at least 45 times, and that sort of defeats the point of using a calculating machine to make movies!

Enter Photoshop's sample scripts. Go to Adobe Photoshop CS3\Scripting Guide\Sample Scripts\JavaScript now and load ExecuteMoltenLead.jsx in a plain text editor (do *not* use Word or a DTP program that formats text). Okay, unless you have programming or scripting experience, this is a mish-mash of instructions. However, all you need to do is add a line or two of instructions and change two other lines, and the result is a script that will repeat an Action you've created 10 times or a thousand times. I'm sorry I can't provide you with the finished script, but you'll note at the top of the file that it's Adobe's property. No big deal—just follow along and you'll learn a trick or two about hacking a copy of a file to repurpose it for your work:

1. Go to the line:

   `"$$$/Presets/Actions/SampleActions/MoltenLead=Molten Lead" );.`

   Change the `MoltenLead=MoltenLead` to x=x. You've now genericized the Action the JavaScript points to, and to run this script all you have to have is an Action on the Actions palette located in the Default Actions folder and that the Action is named x (it was easy for me to type).

2. Right after the x=x you have a close quote, then a close parenthesis, and finally a semicolon. Insert your cursor at the end of the line and then press Enter to carriage return and create a new line. It should be line 21 if your text editor counts lines. Type **var i=0**. It's a command that sets iterations, the number of times a routine is run, and now half of the job is done.

3. On the line after `( File(fileName) );` is a close curly bracket, signifying the close of a section in the script. Press Enter to force a new line below the close curly bracket.

4. Type **for (i=0;i<=63;i++)**. You're done! 63 represents the number of Action times you'll create and x will run. I can see you're guessing ahead, and yep, you can put any integer you like after the = symbol; however, the next tutorial needs a transition built that runs for two seconds (about 60 frames). Save the file as Execute x 63 times.jsx. JavaScript filenames such as this one are not dependent on spaces between words or characters; you'll see plenty of spaces in the filenames in the Presets\Scripts folder. However, the text in the files is indeed sensitive to capital letters, punctuation, and spaces; make sure *everything* is typed exactly the way it's shown here.

5. To better prepare for all the tutorials in this chapter, also write out a repeat for 45 frames, for 90 frames, and for yourself, create a 100x and 300x for editing long segments of video. This will take a good 30 seconds and less than a dozen keystrokes.

6. Copy the files to Adobe Photoshop CS3\Adobe Photoshop CS3\Presets\Scripts. Your script can now be accessed though the File > Scripts menu in Photoshop after restarting Photoshop.

Figure 4.8 shows at left the original JavaScript (dimmed) and at right the new script with the edits you made highlighted in color.

Figure 4.8
You only have to work through five steps to create an invaluable utility for Photoshop.

```
var strPresetActionDefaultActions = localize(
"$$$/Actions/DefaultActionsName=Default Actions.atn" );
var strPresetActionSampleActionsMoltenLead = localize(
"$$$/Presets/Actions/SampleActions/MoltenLead=Molten Lead" );

if (!app.documents.length > 0) {   // open sample file if no
document is opened.
   var fileName = app.path + "/" + strSamplesFolderDirectory + "/"
+ strSamplesFilenameDune;
   var docRef = open( File(fileName) );
}
try {
```

```
var strPresetActionDefaultActions = localize(
"$$$/Actions/DefaultActionsName=Default Actions.atn" );
var strPresetActionSampleActionsx = localize(
"$$$/Presets/Actions/SampleActions/x=x" );
var i=0

if (!app.documents.length > 0) {   // open sample file if no
document is opened.
   var fileName = app.path + "/" + strSamplesFolderDirectory + "/"
+ strSamplesFilenameDune;
   var docRef = open( File(fileName) );
}
for (i=0;i<=any number you like, such as 300;i++)
try {
```

Building Transitions

I'd like to bundle the film effect called *wipe* with the one called *fade* into merely *transitions*, because after you've built the transition, you can use it to transit to a color (which makes it a fade) or as a mask to gradually reveal a different video layer in a composition (often called a wipe). The effects I show you in the sections to follow, when used with some artistic sensibility, rival the canned transitions found in editing suites such as Avid Studio and Premiere. So think of the following sections as practicing ingenuity and economy (if you don't already own a video editor) and really working out your Photoshop chops with past and present features.

The project is called "Role Call" and consists of three segments: an alarm clock going off, a dad and his son traipsing through the woods to get to a fishing stream, and finally mom, who is charged with the distasteful task of cleaning and cooking the tasty fish. You'll shortly see how to build transitions between these scenes that enhance the storytelling in a compatible and highly inventive fashion.

Creating a Venetian Blinds Transition

The Venetian blinds effect is typically used as a black-out to close a scene, but in this project you'll use it as a transition, mostly because the opening scene has Venetian blinds shadows casting on the alarm clock. To begin, you'll need to create a document with transparency at 2048 pixels wide by 1064 pixels high. This is much larger than a standard video frame size, but you need to create this size for two reasons:

1. A large animation can later be angled (rotated to a degree of your choosing) and still cover the frame of a typical 720×480 video, providing you with multiple returns on a single investment.

2. This particular effect cannot be created at a comfortable duration, such as two seconds, due to some hard geometric realities. You simply cannot open or close the blinds in two seconds using a 740 by 480 image file because of the limited number of pixels; if you have a 1-pixel wide slot on the blinds times five or six slots and increase the width of the slots by one pixel per frame, mathematically, the blinds would draw closed in less than 40 frames, providing a Venetian blinds effect of about one second, as though someone *slammed* the blinds. The solution is to work big to create a longer duration and then resize the compiled file.

Here are the steps for building the Venetian blinds transition you'll later animate:

1. In the document, choose the Single Row Marquee tool and then click anywhere in the document.

2. With black as your foreground color, press Alt/Opt+Backspace to fill the selection, switch to the Rectangular Marquee tool to prevent future selection mishaps, and then deselect.

3. Create five duplicate layers and then arrange them so they're equally spaced. A quick way to do this is to use the Move tool to move one layer's line to about 100 pixels from the top (use the rulers as guides for this), put another one of the lines at 100 pixels from the document's bottom, Shift+click all the layers on the Layers palette, and then with the Move tool selected, click the Distribute Vertical Centers button on the Options bar. You need a line (a Venetian blinds slat) toward the top and bottom but not touching the document's edges because the blind would not close completely when you try to animate them. Now right-click over any layer title (not the thumbnails) and choose Merge Visible.

4. Open the Actions palette, choose the Default Actions folder, and then on the flyout menu, choose New Action and name it x.

5. Ctrl/Cmd+click the layer thumbnail to load its nontransparent contents as a selection.

6. Click the Creates New Layer icon.

7. Choose Select > Modify > Expand, and then expand the selection by three pixels.

8. Press Alt/Opt+Backspace to fill the selection, and then Ctrl/Cmd+D to deselect.

9. Click the Stop button on the Actions palette, and you're done.

10. Choose File > Scripts and then choose Execute x 63 times. If for some reason the script is not showing on the menu, choose File > Scripts > Browse and then navigate to the JavaScript folder and choose Execute x 63 times from the menu and sit back for a moment while all the frames are created. See Figure 4.9.

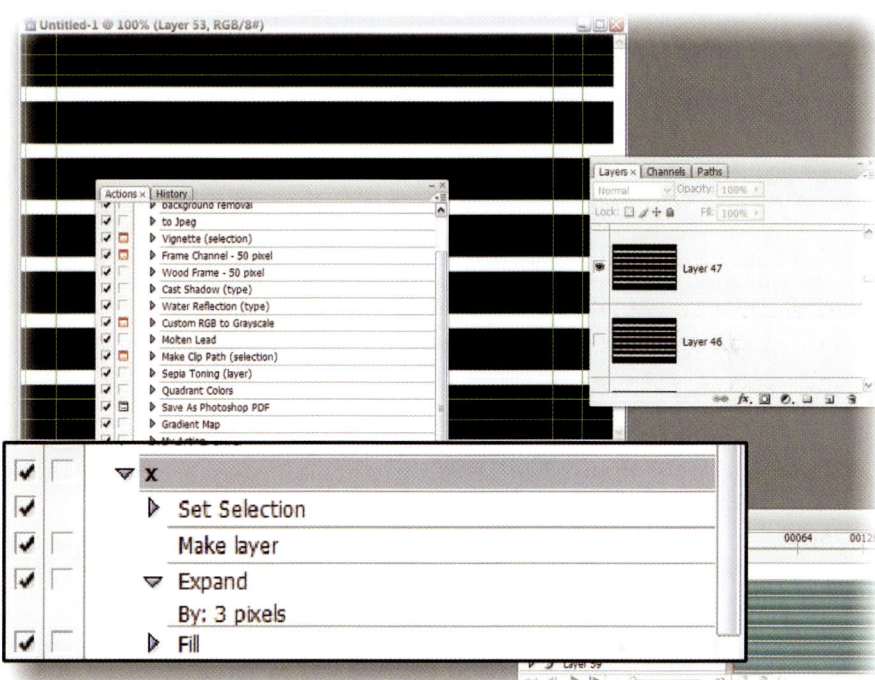

Figure 4.9
Between Actions and a custom script, building a Venetian blinds animated transition is easy.

11. Click the Animation palette menu and then choose Make Frames from Layers.

12. Drag the end Work Area marker on the Animation palette to the end of the top frame. Then choose Trim Document Duration to Work Area from the Animation palette menu (see Figure 4.10). What you have now is a 66-frame animated transition where the blinds close—it would have required more steps to animate it opening using Actions. But this is okay; you won't use this transition in the upcoming tutorial, but you now have it for your own use and will find it handy to put a fancy ending on a movie of your own.

You have all the frames you need, so choose File > Export > Render Video. Choose QuickTime and click Settings. For your compression, choose Animation. Animation not only compresses losslessly but also retains alpha transparency. Choose Straight-Unmatted in the Alpha Channel drop-down menu in the main Render dialog box after setting the codec, and then Render.

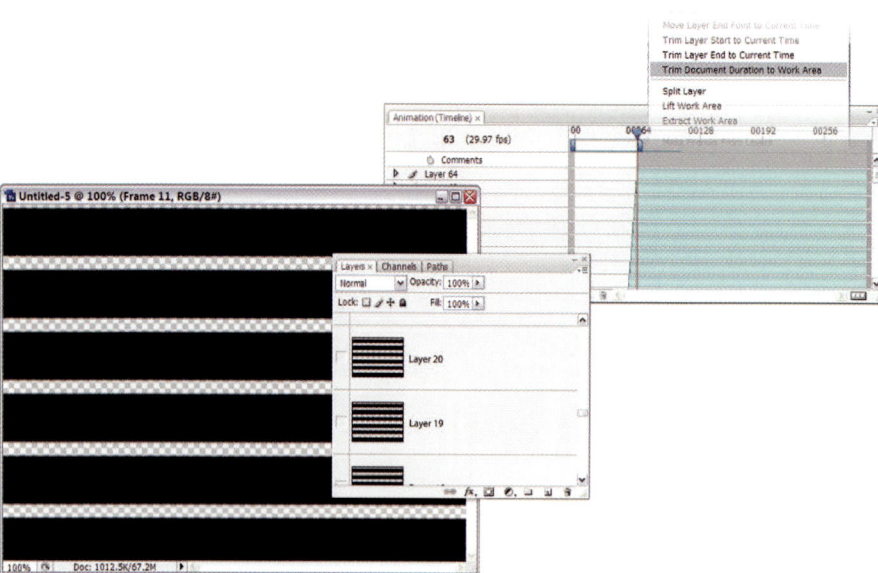

Figure 4.10
Trim the composition's duration.

Reversing Footage

This trick involves using Bridge as a (free) batch renaming utility and can be used to reverse any type of footage rendered out as frames. (I cover "warping time" later in this book.) Follow these steps:

1. The layers you have now in the document have been cast in time and as a consequence will not export and then import properly as still images; opacity on the single layer files turns on and off as part of the Animation palette's video process. Create a duplicate of the document (right-click on its title bar for the command), and then with the duplicate in the foreground in the workspace, click the menu on the Animation palette and choose Flatten Frames into Layers. Delete all the layers named Layers now.

2. Choose File > Scripts > Export Layers to Files. Choose a directory you can easily locate later and then save to PSD file format. This process will take a few minutes even on a fast machine, and you'll soon see that the filenames are a mess, and Photoshop will not import them as a video without some name massaging in Bridge.

3. Open Bridge and navigate to the folder to which the frames were written.

4. In Bridge, click the arrow I've encircled in Figure 4.11 and then choose Ascending order, which you'll see reverses the order of the Venetian blinds progression, making them open as file numbers increase.

Figure 4.11
Bridge comes as a free utility with Photoshop. Batch renaming is only a small feature in this powerful program.

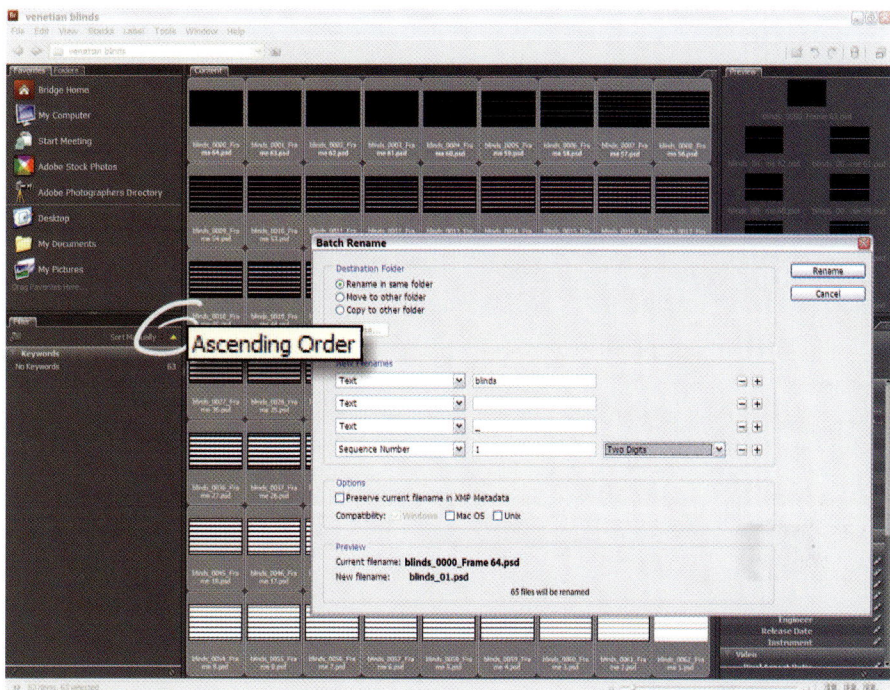

5. Shift+click the first and last frames files to select them all, and then choose Tools > Batch Rename.

6. In the top Text field, type **blinds** in the right entry field.

7. In the Sequence Number field, type **1** in the entry box to begin renumbering with 1 and then choose Two Digits from the drop-down menu to the right of the number entry field.

8. Click the Rename in Same Folder button in the Destination Folder field, and then click Rename, as shown in Figure 4.11. You're done. Close Bridge and return to Photoshop.

9. Double-click the workspace to display the File > Open box, click any of the Venetian blinds files in the folder, and then click the Image Sequence checkbox. Choose 30 fps as the frame rate in the next Frame Rate dialog box.

10. Choose File > Export > Render Video, choose QuickTime, click the Settings button, choose Animation as the codec (the compression type), click OK to return to the main Render dialog box, choose a convenient location for the video, and then click Render. Close the document without saving; you'll bring in the Venetian transition a little later, after you've designed the other transitions for the project.

Creating a Clock Sweep

I have a personal fondness for the clock sweep transition because it telegraphs the passage of time while actually being a subtle effect that doesn't club the audience over the head with gee-whiz pyrotechnics.

You need a clock sweep to make the transition between the clock (appropriately enough!) and the dad and kid tromping off to fish. To build it, you need a wedge, and in the following steps you need to use the Frames mode of the Animation palette to make a progressive build. I suggest you use pie slice.png in the Zip archive; you can always build your own design after you understand why I designed it with little red markers at the edges and other things. Notice that it's slightly larger than a standard video frame size; this is for coverage when the animated transition wipes the underlying video layer.

The Action you'll create requires that the wedge shape rotate around a point in the center of the document window. This is very hard to accomplish as an Action or command with an off-center wedge shape, so the two almost invisible dots in the layer mark the edges of a hypothetical circle and *force* the Free Transform command to rotate the wedge piece around a point in the center of the document.

1. Click the toggle on the Animation palette to go to Frames mode, and then set the first frame to 0 seconds. Actually, you want 0.03 as the duration, but the Frames mode will round off the value to 0, and it really doesn't make any difference to accomplishing the animation—it's just a queer rounding-off thing that Photoshop and other applications do, and your FPU on your chip is not to blame.

2. On the Actions palette, rename your Venetian blinds Action from x to something else. Then click the menu and choose New Action and call it x.

3. Duplicate the current layer by dragging it into the Creates New Layer icon on the Layers palette.

4. Click the Duplicates Selected Frames icon on the Animation palette.

5. Click animation frame 1's thumbnail on the Animation palette.

6. On the Layers palette, hide the current layer.

7. Click the second frame thumbnail on the Animation palette to select it and turn the visibility for the current layer back on.

8. Press Ctrl/Cmd+T to put the current layer's contents into Free Transform mode.

9. On the Options bar, specify a 4-degree positive (clockwise) rotation. Press Enter to apply the transformation.

10. Click the Stop button on the Actions palette.

11. Run the Execute x 90 times JavaScript. In Figure 4.12 I've called out the original wedge shape with a dotted red highlight so you can better see the start point and then how the shape fans out to complete a circle shape.

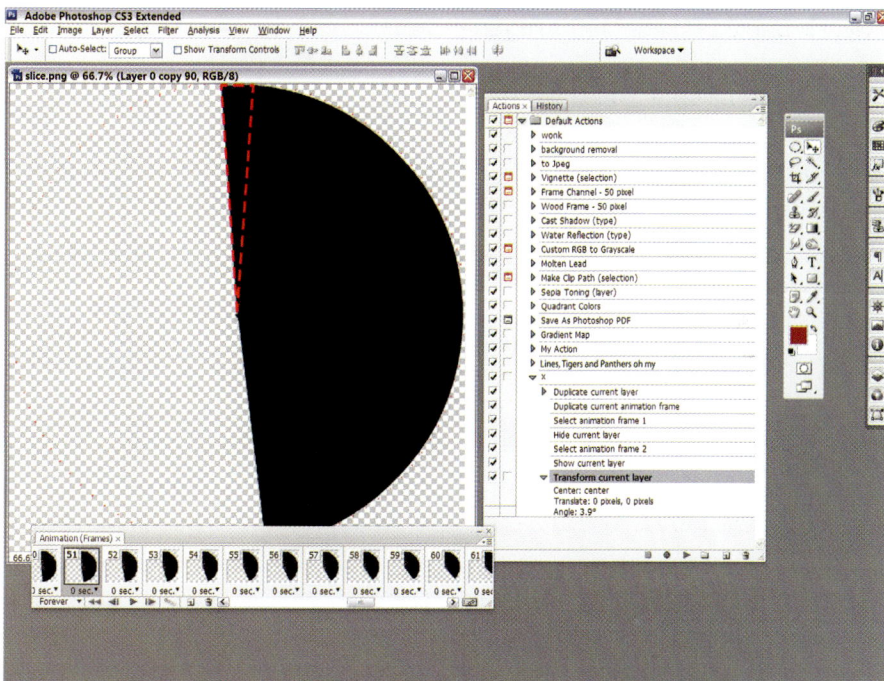

Figure 4.12
Animate a clock wipe with a hand-built Action and a JavaScript to drive the automation.

12. Switch back to Timeline mode on the Animation palette, just to see what it's doing. Note that unlike the Venetian blinds transition, all the tracks are totally occupied with keying; there's no entrance or exit or pale green hidden areas. This is because in order for this build to work, frames are turned on at certain points and remain on. Click the Play button to watch your work and then save it as a video via File > Export > Render Video. Use the QuickTime Animation codec to preserve transparency. Done! See Figure 4.13 and note that appearances are deceiving for the Layers palette, which shows a layer at any given frame in time but not the animation build you clearly see in the document window.

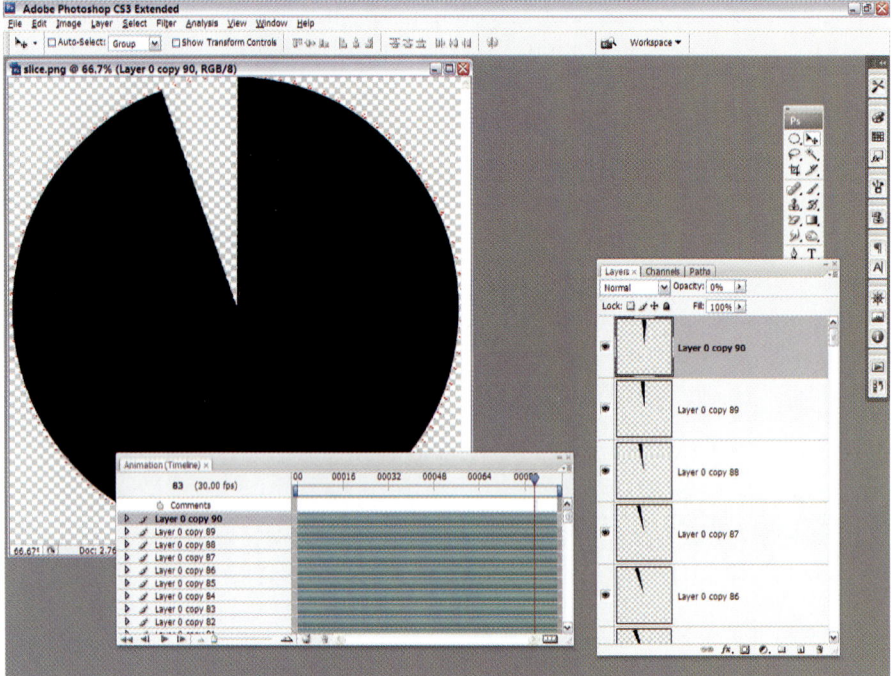

Figure 4.13
A build animation should show layer visibility, progressing from layer to layer, throughout the play time.

Creating an Iris Wipe

Iris wipes will serve you in a number of editing situations, and they're easy to build and animate. For the conclusion of the composition, my little Poser animation pulls out from mom's face to an establishing scene, sort of a reveal from her expression of revulsion to *why* she's revolted. From a cinematic point of view, an iris-out wipe accomplishes two things: First, it centers attention on her entrance and bursts the cheery scene of dad and junior in a way that's marginally more subtle than a clown bursting through a paper hoop. Also, it distorts depth; mom is zooming out, the iris is zooming out, so you achieve double the perceived depth effect over time. It visually broadens the scene, which needs it because it's a computer graphic (CG) and not real footage.

Follow these steps for creating a closing iris wipe; you can then use the previously described steps with Bridge to reverse time and get the iris *opening* transition needed for the scene (it's just easier to build the iris closing):

1. Ctrl/Cmd+double-click Photoshop's workspace to display the New dialog box.

2. Choose the Film & Video preset, choose Transparent as Background Contents, click OK, and turn off the Pixel Aspect Ratio Correction from the View menu.

3. Right-click the title bar of the untitled document, choose Canvas Size, choose Percent from the Height and Width fields, and then type **200** in both the Height and Width fields. You do this because to create an iris wipe that extends beyond the video layer dimensions, the wipe has to be larger.

4. Press Ctrl/Cmd+R to put rulers around the window and then drag a vertical and then a horizontal guide out of the rulers, placing them at the center to cross-hair the document.

5. Choose the Elliptical Marquee tool, hold Alt/Opt+Shift, and then start your drag away from the center, at the cross-hair point until the circle marquee is a little shy of touching the edges of the document window.

6. Press Ctrl/Cmd+Shift+I to invert the selection, fill it with black, and then deselect. Your document should look like Figure 4.14.

7. On the Actions palette, create a new Action and call it x. You can have duplicate names, but they'll confuse the JavaScript, so you'll rename the x Action you created in the previous section later. You're recording now.

8. Duplicate the layer.

Figure 4.14 Holding Shift+Alt/Opt constrains the selection to 1:1 and draws from the inside out instead of marquee-style.

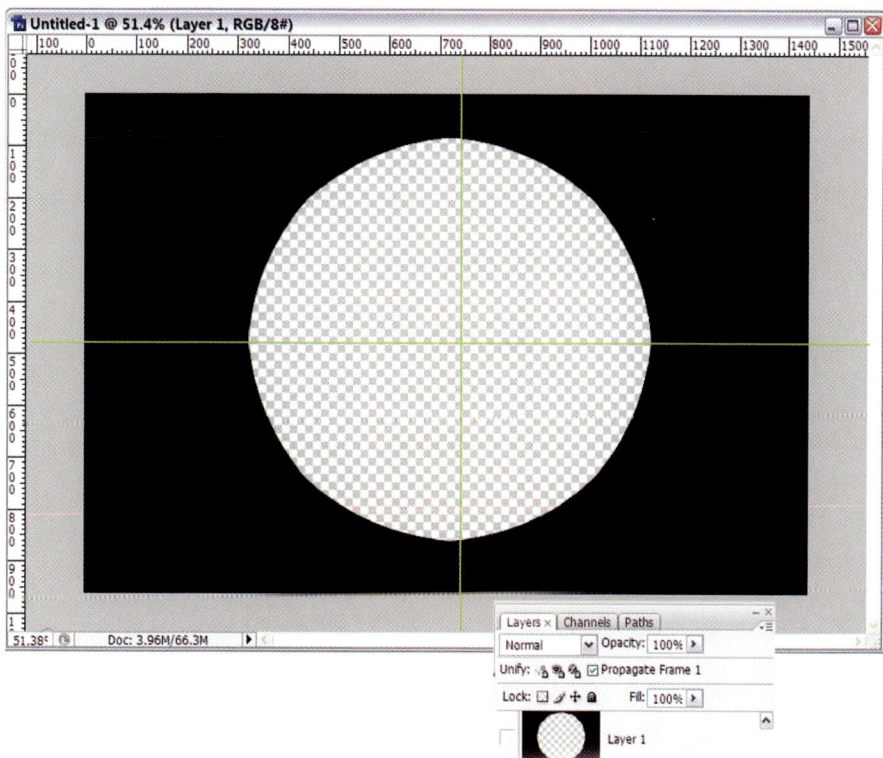

9. Ctrl/Cmd+click the layer thumbnail of the duplicate and then choose Select > Modify > Expand.

10. Expand the selection by 7 pixels. Click OK.

11. Fill the selection with black; then deselect, stop the Actions recording, and rename the first x Action on the list to something you'll remember such as Clock Wipe.

12. Run a JavaScript you create to generate enough frames to close the iris; it'll be about 60 frames (two seconds of animation). By the way, if you want a longer iris opening or closing, you modify the Action to make the Expand command fewer pixels in diameter. Four pixels, for example, will create an iris effect of nearly four seconds. In general, an animating transition of less than a second is unacceptably abrupt, and anything longer than eight seconds becomes a movie in and of itself—a boring movie.

13. Choose Make Frames from Layers on the Animation palette menu. Now move the Work Area end marker to the last frame in the animation. Notice in Figure 4.15 that the iris is not circular but instead has visible polygonal sides. This is an unfortunate function of the Expand command on smooth shapes, but all is well. Later in this chapter you'll feather the edges by blurring them, and the audience will not notice anything because there will be video content emerging from the iris.

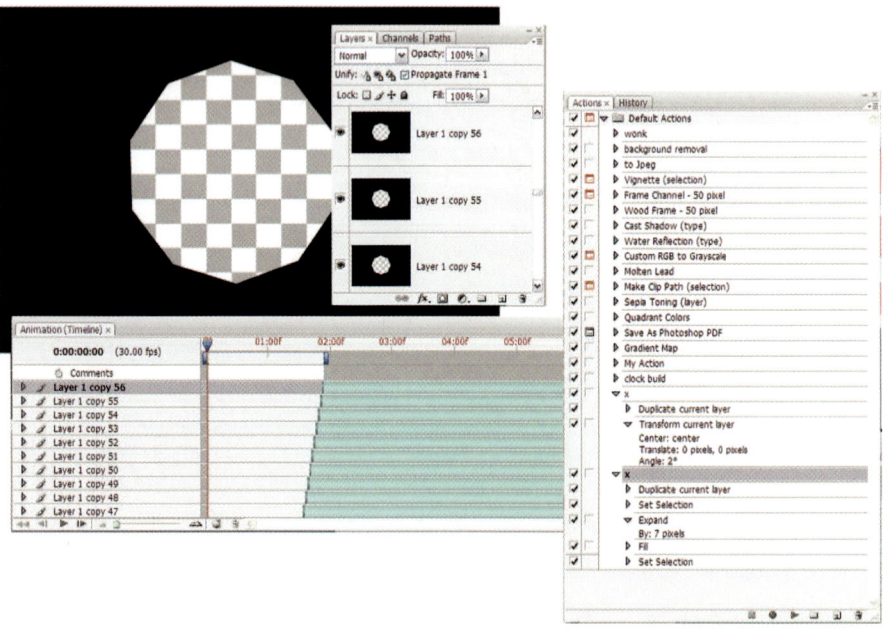

Figure 4.15
Create an iris effect by progressively expanding the selection and filling new duplicates of the layer.

Exactly as you did with the Venetian blinds effect earlier, choose File > Scripts and then Export Layers to Files. In Bridge, rename and reorder the files to make an opening iris. Then open the files in Photoshop with Image Sequence checked. Render Video from File > Export with alpha support enabled (use QuickTime's Animation codec), and you have the needed iris effect for the video compilation.

Editing Transitions into a Composition

This section is the fun part; you have your transitions done, you have my clips, and now it's time for some tricky staging, timing transitions, and generally fussing with layers to get them to appear in the right chronology.

Setting Up the Composition for Transitions

You need to integrate the videos I've provided into a single document and then adjust the entrance and exits for the clips. Follow these steps to massage the clips into working order for the wipes you built earlier:

1. Open Fishing at Sunrise.mov, alarm clock.mov, and Mom 'n' fish.mov.

2. Duplicate two of the movies to the third's document window. If you hold Shift, you can drag the thumbnails into other document windows so the content is centered. The movies are all the same dimensions, so this is a quick way to duplicate and align the content.

3. Order the layers so that the alarm clock is on top, followed by the kid and dad, with mom and her fish on the bottom layer. After you've completed duplicating videos to the composition, you can close the originals without saving.

4. Click the Animation palette's menu, choose Document Settings, and increase the Duration to 30 seconds.

5. Slide the tracks to positions as shown in Figure 4.16 so each segment overlaps the next one. This is just like editing the clips of Maddie and Drew and the bubbles, except instead of cross-dissolves you'll be adding transitional wipes as connective tissue.

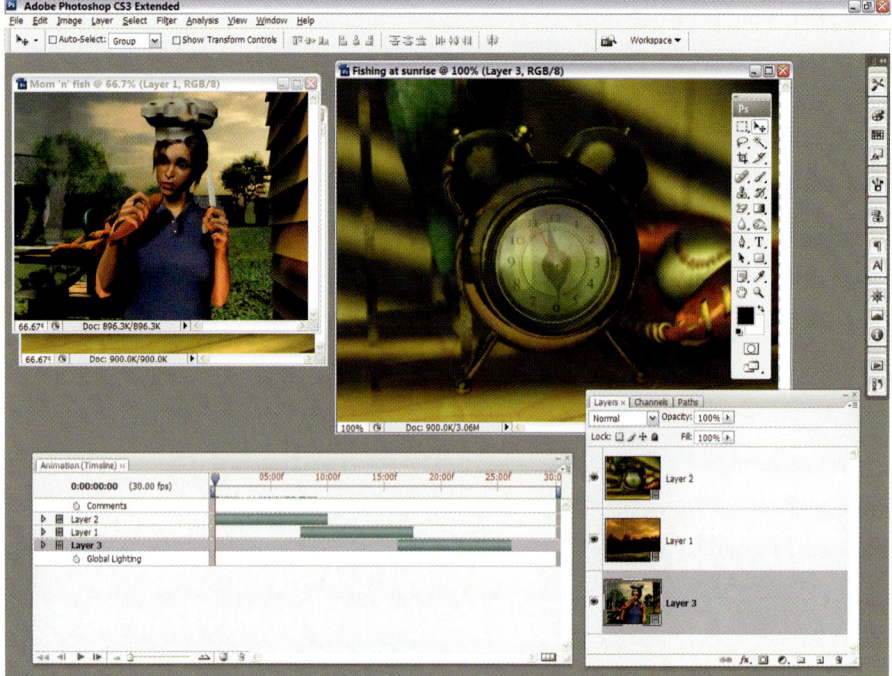

Figure 4.16
Overlapping the heads and tails of video segments provides stretch room in the composition for transitions.

Bring in the fx!

Let's open the Venetian blinds animation you rendered earlier to use as an opening for the composition. Follow these steps to create the beginning two seconds of the polished movie:

1. Choose File > Open as Smart Object, and then choose your Venetian blinds movie. Doing this saves a step later; you can't rotate a video clip as a movie but only as a Smart Object (which doesn't affect the video quality in the least).

2. Drag the layer thumbnail into the composition document window. Move its track on the Animation palette to the head of the composition. Close the Venetian blinds movie without saving changes.

3. On the Animation palette, set the current time to when you can see the Venetian blinds partially open. Then press Ctrl/Cmd+T (Free Transform).

4. Using either the Move tool cursor or the Options bar's Rotate field, rotate the Venetian blinds object about 25 to 35 degrees positive so that it aligns with the Venetian blinds shadows in the underlying alarm clock scene, as shown in Figure 4.17. If your Venetion blinds transition doesn't seem large enough for the composition, you can scale it up; you're eventually going to blur it, so the scaling transformation will not introduce harsh edges. Finally, click the check icon on the Options bar to apply or press Enter (keyboarding is faster, I feel).

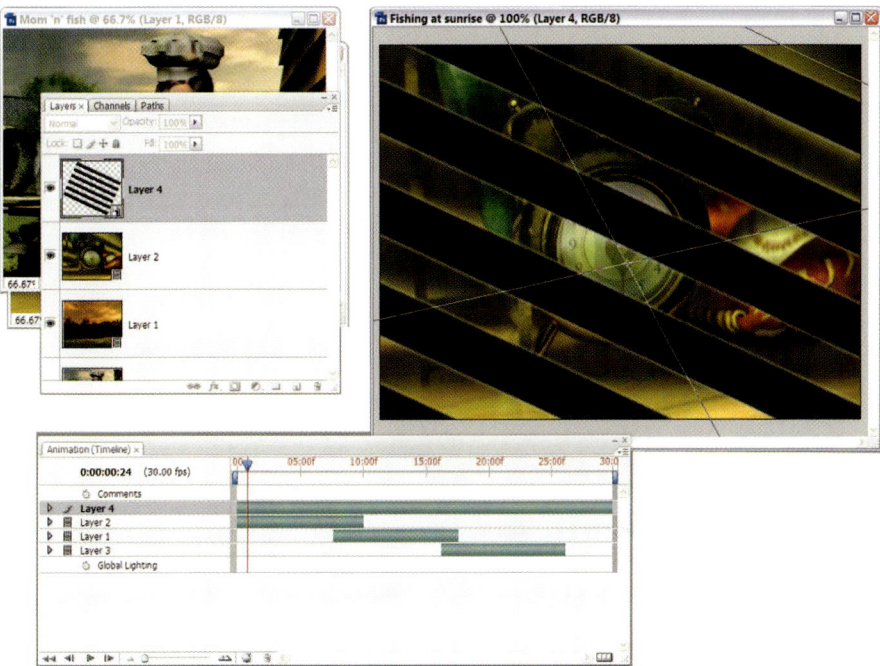

Figure 4.17 Rotate the blinds so they are compositionally agreeable with the underlying video content.

5. Choose Filter > Blur > Gaussian Blur. Use your artistic eye to tell in the document window when the Venetian blinds wipe looks very close to the shadows in the video. Your screen should look like Figure 4.18 now. Press Ctrl/Cmd+S at this point.

6. Label the layers by double-clicking their titles on the Layers palette and then type in an easy-to-remember name. Thumbnails really don't help you locate a clip on the Layers palette because they update from the current time displayed on the Animation palette, and frequently the thumbnails will go blank. The composition should be saved now in PSD file format as Role Call.psd.

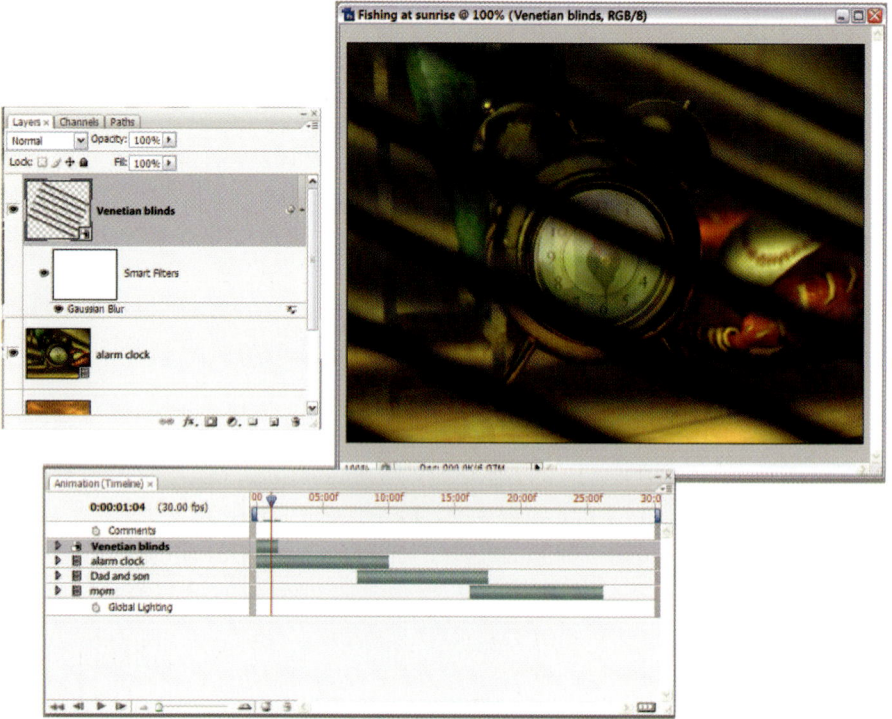

Figure 4.18
Blurring the Venetian blinds transition helps integrate it into the underlying video.

Transitions and Clipping Masks

Somewhat trickier is establishing the transition between the alarm clock and the dad and son walking across screen because unlike the blinds, the transition segues between two clips and not a fade out from the beginning of the composition. Additionally, the clock wipe is intended as an effect and shouldn't be seen per se, but rather used as a mask to reveal the dad and son clip.

You might be familiar with layer clipping masks used in still compositions; I walk you through the steps regardless—the big perk in Extended is that you can use a video layer as a clipping mask for a different video layer. Here are the steps for making dad and his son appear through a clipping mask whose parent object is the clock wipe transition:

1. Open the clock wipe.mov file you created earlier as a Smart Object and then Shift+drag its thumbnail on the Layers palette into the composition. You can close the clock wipe file without saving now.

2. Center the clock wipe in frame using the Move tool in the document window and then use Free Transform to scale it up to about 140%. To do this, you have to go to a time when the clock is only partially wiping so you can see the

edges. Hide the dad and kid clip on the Layers palette so you can see what you're doing.

3. Drag the clock wipe to below the dad and kid layer (the top layer) on the Layers palette; it will be the clipping mask for the layer directly above it. Drag its green strip on the Animation palette so that it completes before dad and kid enter the composition. If needed, shift the alarm clock and the dad and kid's timelines, too. The trick here is to make certain that the tail of the clock wipe matches the tail of the alarm clock clip and the head of the clock wipe matches the head of the dad and kid clip. In other words, the transition has to cover the entrance and exit points of the clips it connects. See Figure 4.19.

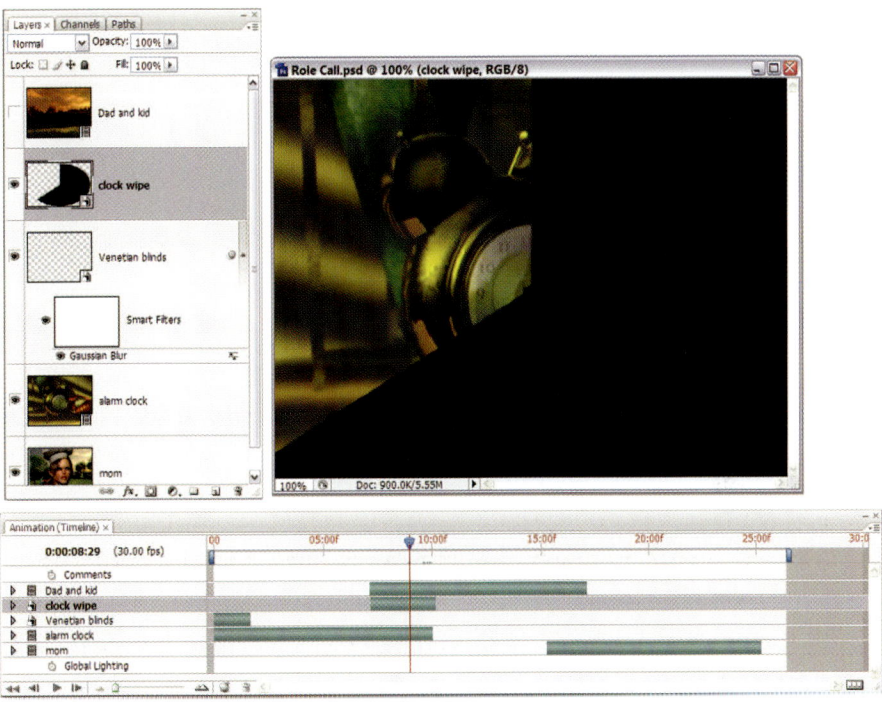

Figure 4.19
The transition video has to match the entrance and exit points of the clips it is supposed to artistically bind together.

4. Unhide dad and his son. Hold Alt/Opt and click between the dad and kid and the clock wipe layers on the Layers palette, as shown in Figure 4.20 (where the cursor is enlarged for better reference). This *is* magic! Play this segment of the clip to see what you've created. To help Photoshop with video playback buffering, drag the beginning and end Work Area markers to surround the transition on the Animation palette; playback will happen much more quickly when Photoshop doesn't have to buffer all 30 seconds of the composition.

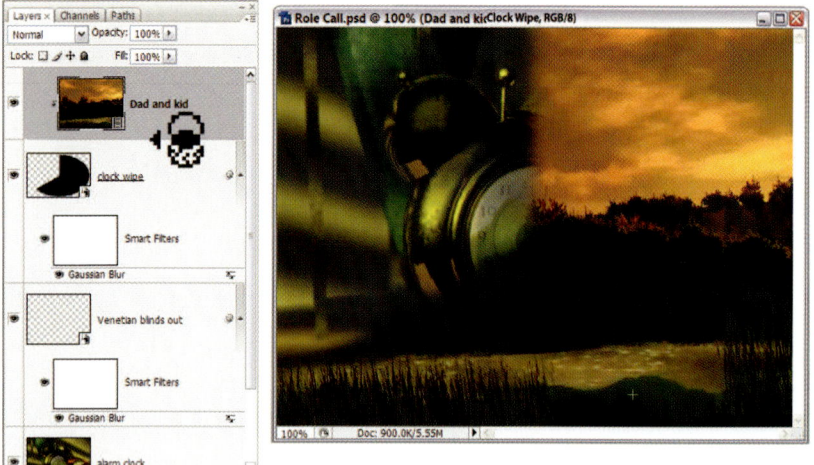

Figure 4.20
The clipping mask creates the effect of the dad and kid scene wiping over the alarm clock.

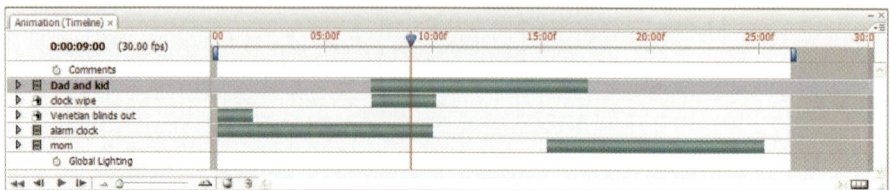

Exits and Entrances Through Layer Duplicates

The opening Venetian blinds "reveal" works great, as does the transition between the clock and dad and his kid. However, on the timeline directly after the clock wipe is completed, the mask is complete, the layer is 100% transparent, and dad and kid are completely masked for the rest of the segment. This is because clipping layers show areas above when there's corresponding non-transparent areas on the clipping layer and hide areas where the clipping layer is transparent.

Not to fret; the simple solution is to duplicate the dad and kid layer as a non-clipped layer that plays synchronously with the clipped original, and by putting it beneath the original clipped layer, it magically fills in at the point where the clipped layer drops out.

Follow these steps:

1. Drag the dad and kid layer thumbnail into the Creates New Layer icon on the bottom of the Layers palette.

2. Drag its position on the Layers palette list to above the mom clip.

3. A duplicate clipped layer retains its clipping attribute when duplicated, so position your cursor between the duplicate and the mom layers on the Layers palette list and then Alt/Opt+click to remove the clipping attribute. In Figure 4.21 you can see that the duplicate has the same entry and exit points on the timeline, and the thumb is clearly in the play area (after the clock wipe transition), and dad and his kid are proceeding as usual.

Figure 4.21
A non-clipped duplicate of video helps continue the composition after a transition effect.

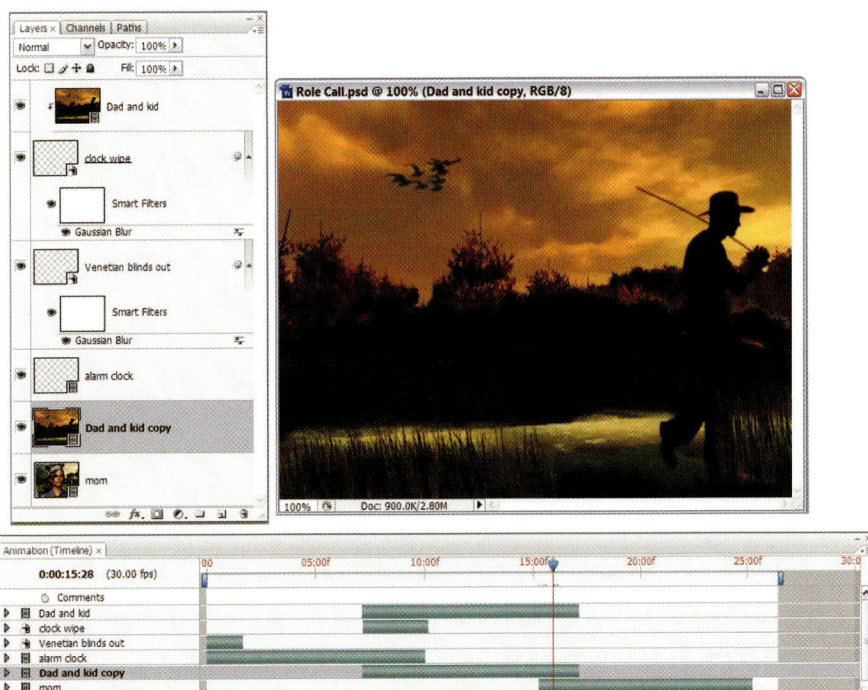

Now it's time to add the iris transition. Just like the clipping mask hid dad and his kid after the clock sweep completed, dad and son are going to vanish from their play time after you clip the duplicate to reveal mom and her fish at the ending. So follow along and you'll create a second duplicate of dad and junior to make both the transition and the play time work.

1. Load the iris movie you created earlier as a Smart Object and then duplicate it to the composition by Shift+dragging its Layers palette thumbnail (thus centering it). You can now close it without saving.

2. Drag the iris video layer to below the dad and kid duplicate, above the mom layer.

3. Play with the track positions on the Animation palette so that the iris transition matches dad and kid's exit and mom's entrance. This is why I asked you earlier to make the composition 30 seconds long even though the finished play length will be shorter. You can always crop the duration using the Work Area markers, but to make a short film longer, you have to go to the menu and respecify the document settings. I'm not big on any application process that takes your cursor away from your work.

4. Duplicate the dad and kid duplicate and then remove its clipping mask attribute. You have two duplicates in a row on the Layers palette above the mom video layer.

5. Click the bottom duplicate, hold Alt/Opt, and click between the duplicate and the iris video layer to clip the dad and kid copy to the transition.

6. The layer above dad and kid is going to play over the iris transition, so you need to hide the tail up to the point of the iris transition, as shown in Figure 4.22. Drag the tail with your cursor.

7. Create a new layer on the bottom of the Layers palette stack and fill it with black.

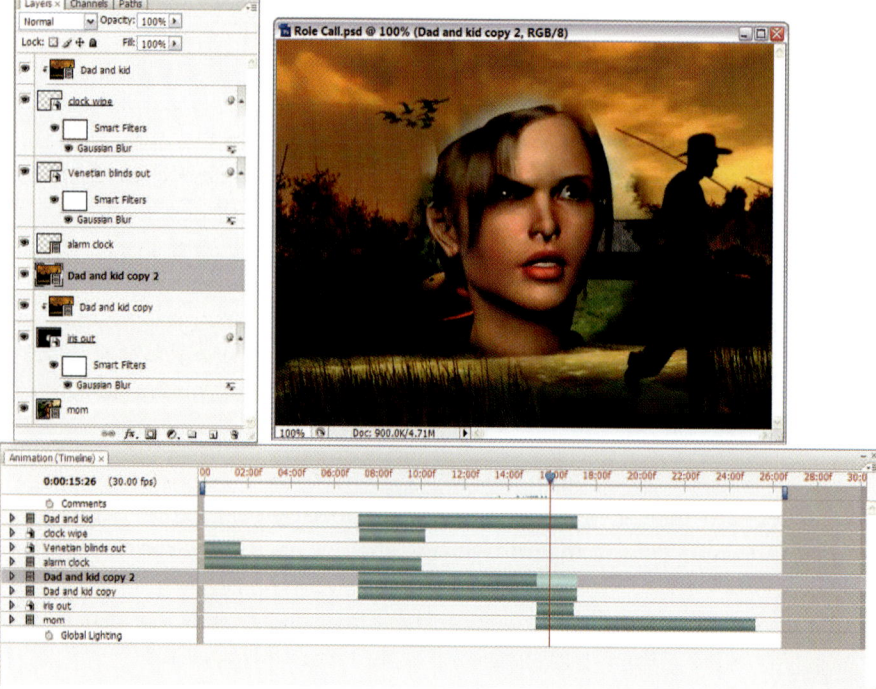

Figure 4.22

Three transitions for three clips creates a highly polished video composition.

8. Just as you did with the close-up clip of Maddie earlier, fade mom to black at the end of the composition by first establishing a key of 100% opacity for the mom layer approximately 1.5 seconds in from the tail, and then key the clip to 0% Opacity at the end of the mom clip. For a little poignancy, you can hold the black at the end of the composition for an additional second. To do this, just drag the end Work Area marker out for an additional second.

9. Add some music. I've timed Joplin-Weeping Willow Rag.mp3 to match the action and transitions; you do this sort of thing in a sound editor such as Adobe Audition or Sony SoundForge. Windows users, choose File > Open As and then open the file as a QuickTime movie, and Mac users just use the open box with QuickTime specified. Drag the thumbnail of the audio layer into the composition and then on the Animation palette drag the audio track so it butts with the beginning of the composition.

10. Choose File > Export > Render Video. Select QuickTime (because Photoshop can only export videos with audio tracks to QuickTime), don't specify an alpha channel, in the Compression Settings choose H.264 or Sorenson 3, and then render the movie. Trust me: It's a lot of fun watching your editing work come to life.

Two More Transitions to Complete Your Collection

Finally, I have three more clips I want you to assemble to demonstrate two more types of transition animations: the clapboard wipe and the push-in. Interestingly, as motion pictures and broadcast television matured during the mid-1950s, there was some cross-pollination with respect to transitions. TV copied what motion pictures were doing, and then motion picture directors asked film editors to copy some of the neat stuff TV editors were using. It's a little unsettling to see small TV transitions on the big screen, but perhaps George Lucas used the effects most successfully in his *Star Wars* sagas—big sound effects, sweeping landscapes, and larger-than-life transitions.

Therefore, in the best spirit of a tribute film, my clips emulate three of the most memorable clips in *Star Wars*: First, we have the setup with the bad guy commanding his lackey to go fetch some robots from a planet where they're wandering aimlessly and probably will welcome the company. Then we have an establishing shot of the robots wading through the sand on a desert planet, and finally a space shot of the lackey cruising down to the planet. In a ship.

Yes, it's a fun assignment, but also a productive one. You'll see how to build a wipe that is similar but distinctly different from the clock wipe, and you can repurpose the effect to flip the angle from which the transition happens. Push-wipes are extremely easy to create and add excitement to your action videos.

Building a Clapboard Wipe

The clips I've provided in the Zip archive are unusually proportioned; they're 720 pixels wide by 327 pixels high. I did this to simulate the big screen, double-wide 70mm framing used in *Star Wars* and many other classics. Photoshop has a setting called Anamorphic as a choice when you pick the Film & Video preset, and it's roughly the same aspect ratio as 70mm, 2:1. Naturally, I didn't use Photoshop to cobble the 3D animation clips, but if you'd like to wow your friends with rotoscope animation (see Chapter 8) in "wide screen," Anamorphic aspect ratio would be a good choice.

So here's the setup: You need to create the clapboard wipe (also called a Radial Wipe in After Effects; the pin for the rotation distinguishes it from a clock wipe—a clapboard wipes from a corner of the frame). You need to create a new file that's twice as wide as the final frame in which it appears, so we're talking 1440 by 1440 pixels because the clapboard needs to animate from a center point even though it will eventually wipe from the corner of the frame. Create the 1440 × 1440 document (File > New > Width: 1440 pixels, Height: 1440 pixels, Background Contents: Transparent, Resolution makes little difference but you can use 72) with a transparent layer and then follow these steps:

1. Display the rulers (Ctrl/Cmd+R) and then drag guides to the center, 720 and 720 as measured in pixels. If for some reason your rulers do not display pixels as the increment, right-click either ruler and choose Pixels from the pop-up menu.

2. Choose the Elliptical Marquee tool, and then place your cursor at the crosshair of the guides. Hold Alt/Opt+Shift to constrain the ellipse to a circle and to draw from the center and then drag away from your starting point, releasing the cursor when the marquee just touches the edge of the document. You might want to zoom the window out to see the document edge. If you have a wheel mouse and have zoom defined for the wheel in General Preferences (Ctrl/Cmd+K), drag the wheel toward you to zoom out.

3. With black as your foreground color, press Alt/Opt+Backspace and then deselect. You have a black circle now.

4. With the Rectangular Marquee tool chosen, go to View > Snap To > Guides. Remember to turn the Snap To off after this example or all your paying assignments will feel sticky to work in.

5. Select the bottom of the circle and then delete it. Then select the right side of what's left and delete this. The result should be a 90 degree pie wedge facing right and down. This wedge will not rotate properly frame after frame using Free Transform, hence the following step.

6. Pick an easy to locate color such as red from the Color Picker, and then choose the Pencil tool (it's in the Brush tool's group on the Tools palette). Set the size to one pixel from the Options bar. Yes, the stroke will be hard to see in such a large document, but it's not really for you to see so much as it is for the Free Transform feature to see, just like the pie wedge clock wipe example earlier.

7. Zoom in and then click a 1-pixel dot at the bottom edge of the guide and then a dot at the right side of the horizontal guide, as shown in Figure 4.23. Close the rulers; you don't need to be tidy and get rid of the non-printing, video-invisible guides.

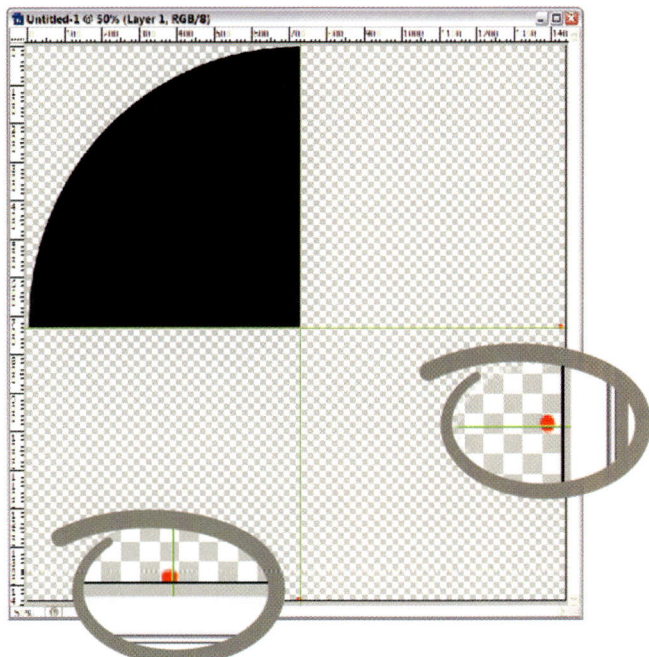

Figure 4.23
The dots you create will not show in the video, but they force Free Transform to put the rotation point for the layer at the center of the document window.

8. The neat thing about this transition is that you have total flexibility over the duration; if you want a short duration, you increase the degree of Free Transform rotation in the Action you'll now write.

9. On the Actions palette in the Default Actions list, rename your x Action to Iris Wipe, and then click the menu and choose New Action. Name it x.

10. Duplicate the layer.

11. Press Ctrl/Cmd+T and then type **2** in the Degrees of Rotation field on the Options bar. Press Enter to apply the transformation.

12. Stop recording. You're done. From the File menu, choose Scripts > Execute x 45 times (or whatever you name the file you saved earlier in this chapter).

13. Delete the two unnecessary top layers; because of the way the script executes, it overshot our target to make a total of 27 and not 45 layers. On the Animation palette, choose Make Frames from Layers and then drag the end Work Area marker to 1;30 seconds (45 frames). See Figure 4.24.

14. Render the animation out to QuickTime, Animation codec in Settings to preserve the alpha channel. Save and close the file.

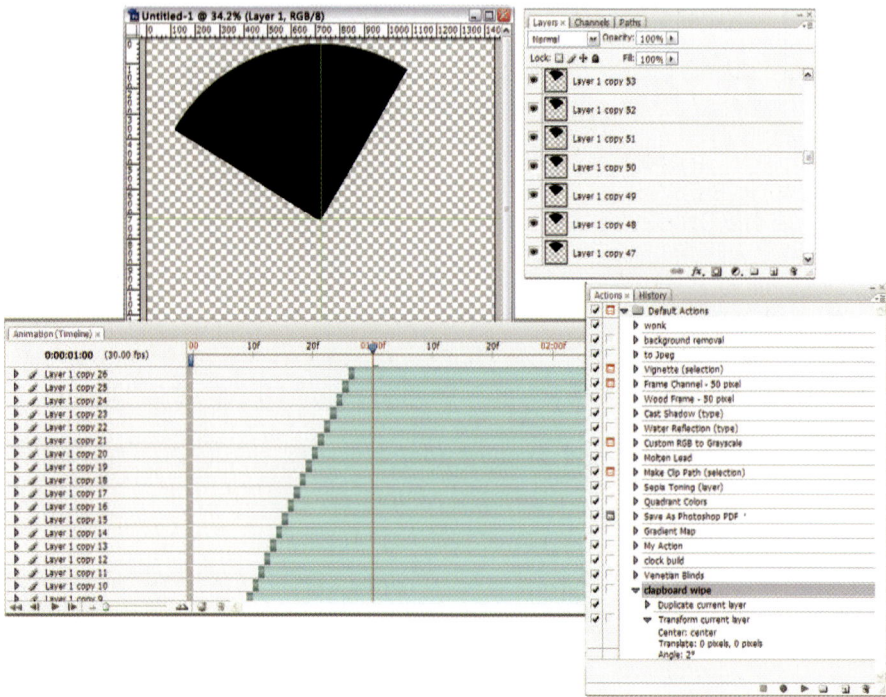

Figure 4.24
Create your video in a single click from the layers that your Action and script produced.

Adding the First Transition

The following steps will feel familiar to you if you worked through the fishing trip example earlier in this chapter. Open Lord Carburetor & Lackey Boy.mov and Bots.mov and then follow these steps:

1. Shift+click and drag the bots thumbnail from the Layers palette into the Lord Carburetor document window to duplicate and center it. Close the Bots.mov file without saving changes.

2. On the Animation palette, click the menu, choose Document Settings, and increase the duration to about 30 seconds. Don't forget to enter a Frames value after the seconds (0:00:30:00); if you don't, the Animation palette won't give you 30 seconds of time, but instead only a few frames.

3. Put the bots sequence on top on the Layers palette and then duplicate it and hide the duplicate layer (for the same reason you needed several dad and kid layers in an earlier example).

4. Shift+click the bots and the bots duplicate layer on the Layers palette to select them both. Overlap the head of the bots sequence with the Evil Guy clip by 45 frames (a second and a half) by dragging either track on the Animation palette. Because they are both selected on the Layers palette, when you slide one track, the other moves in perfect sync along with it.

5. Open the clapboard wipe movie and drag it into the composition, then close it without saving.

6. With the Move tool, first find a frame in the duration that clearly shows the point of the pie shape and then drag it so the point meets the lower left corner of the document window.

7. Order the layers as shown in Figure 4.25 so that the clapboard wipe is below the original bots video layer and turn the visibility back on for the copy layer.

8. Hold Alt/Opt and then click between the bots original top video layer and the clapboard layer to create the clipping mask, as shown in Figure 4.25.

Figure 4.25
Clip the layer so it intrudes upon the first scene. The duplicate sustains the second clip after the clipping mask video has run its duration.

9. Convert the wipe layer to a Smart Object by right-clicking over its title on the Layers palette and making this choice.

10. Choose Filter > Blur > Gaussian Blur and then use your eye to evaluate when the edge of the clapboard wipe is soft and aesthetic looking.

11. Save your document to PSD file format; don't close it.

Creating a Push-In Transition

To conclude the 25-second long sci-fi epic, you need to add the space scene. The video itself is the wipe in a push-in style transition. This is a very simple but exceptionally exciting and effective way to introduce a new segment.

1. Open the Lackey in really cool spaceship.mov file. You might see here that this scene and the scene of the bots will not cut well. It would be better if the spacecraft enters from the left, sort of chasing the pesky bots. No big deal; choose Image > Rotate Canvas > Flip Canvas Horizontal. Photoshop pops you a prompt that the video must become a Smart Object first and then offers to do this for you. Click OK and then flip the spacecraft.

2. Shift+drag the layer thumbnail of the spacecraft into the composition and then put it at the end of the Work Area on the Animation palette, overlapping the out point for the bots by about 90 frames. The spacecraft layer should be on top. Close the original spaceship file without saving changes.

3. Create a new document and make it 900 pixels in width by 500 pixels in height, Content: Transparent.

4. With the Rectangular Marquee tool, drag around the left side of the document, leaving about 25% of the right side in the clear.

5. Fill the selection with black and then deselect.

6. Choose Filter > Blur > Gaussian Blur and then blur the black rectangle by about 7 pixels in radius.

7. Drag the black layer into the composition, beneath the spacecraft.

8. Click the stopwatch for the position of the spacecraft video layer.

9. Choose the Move tool. Use the keyboard arrow keys to nudge the spacecraft video offscreen to the left at its entrance point at the beginning of the bots playtime.

10. Go on the timeline to the end of the spacecraft clip and then nudge the clip so it's centered fully in frame. Holding Shift "power nudges" non-transparent objects on layers by 10 pixels per stroke.

11. Repeat Steps 8–10 with the black layer that has the fuzzy right edge. The layer was built outside of the composition because there's no way to show only one blurry side without blurring the three others (spoiling the effect) unless the clipping object is larger than the finished video. Adobe calls this "Big Data"; an object can be larger than the document window. As you can see, this is a handy feature.

12. Clip the spaceship video layer to the black layer. See Figure 4.26.

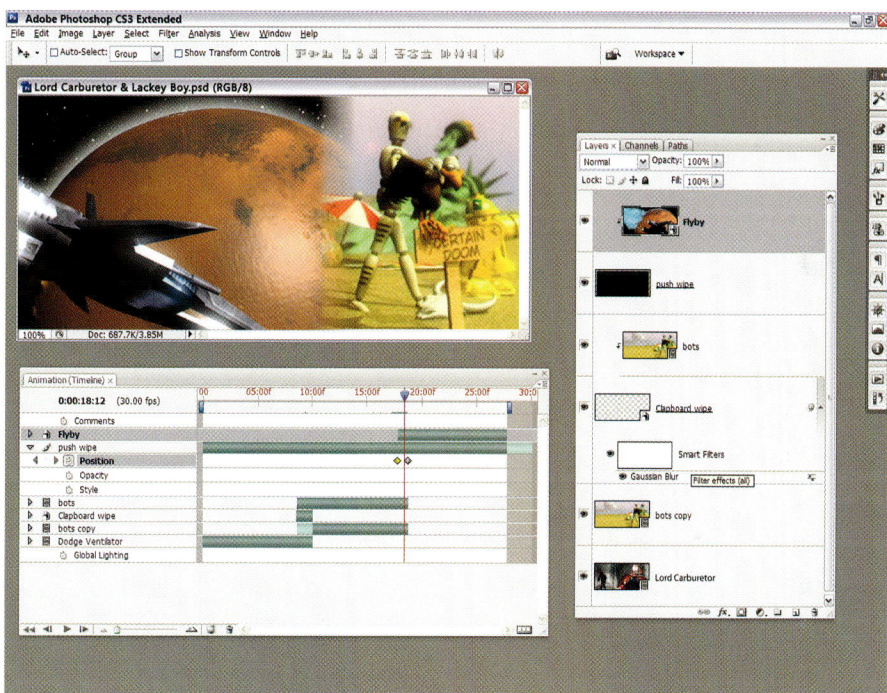

Figure 4.26
The clipping mask moves in tandem with the video layer to always present a blurry right edge, softening the push-in effect.

13. Add my epic score to the composition, Sci-fi short.mp3. It contains mildly amusing dialog over the music, and you can get away with approximate synching of dialog to a video when your characters have no mouths or they're not facing camera. The music is public domain: Henry Purcell's "Funeral March for Queen Mary" and Dukas' "Sorcerer's Apprentice." I think the pieces sound quite in the spirit of John Williams' brilliant scores for Mr. Lucas. I just couldn't afford John's services, so I settled for a MIDI score I arranged in a digital audio workspace (DAW).

14. Drag the end marker on the Animation palette to 2 seconds after the spacecraft clip ends, put a black layer under the composition, and create a fade to black.

15. Render the file out to QuickTime (Sorenson works better in this example than H.264 for the saturated colors), and you have exactly enough time to eat one malted milk ball at the film's opening.

Digital video is pumping a lot of new life and creativity into the traditional art form of the motion picture. And one of the nicest things is the quality of edited video. When I worked in advertising over 20 years ago, a lot of times you'd see a color or tone shift when a transition came in because the editor was literally working with a sandwich of film. The film not only visibly dimmed the layers it was on top of, but you also were at least one generation removed from the original footage, and this, too, led to degradation of the finished movie or commercial.

You now have the skills to produce just about any type of transition. Play with variations on what you've learned in this chapter, and soon you'll have a stock library of effects you can truly call your own.

5

Video Color and Tone Adjustments

Occasionally, the color casting—blue from the sky or colors from nature, buildings, or other objects—spoils an otherwise beautiful piece of footage you've taken. You might be able to perform a little compensation when you dump the DV data to hard disk, but perhaps not to your satisfaction, and naturally you can't do any pre-filtering if a client hands you the clips.

This chapter is all about playing with color and exposure of your digital media in Photoshop. I show you how to balance color so a composite piece shows a color balance you want, how to perform steps that range from the subtle to dramatic alterations, and even how to degrade color and film quality to imitate the look of an old television broadcast. Much of what you learn in this chapter features Adjustment layers, which dynamically adjust *all* frames in a video clip. You can use almost every command on the Image > Adjustments menu. I also show you how to shift hue over time using styles to create quite a visually arresting blend of video and a little animation.

Correcting Color Within a Composite Video

The technique I show in this section can be used for video composite work or simply with a single video layer. I chose to show a composite technique for the challenge and also for the real need to get video elements looking compatible in a video presentation. For single layer, non-compositing assignments, if you learn my technique here your assignment will be a piece of cake.

Here's the story with the example files: I thought it would make an interesting piece of very human composite work to show the classic, "I can't get in touch with my spouse because she is yacking on the telephone again!" I filmed my friend Michael over the course of several minutes dialing and redialing on his cell phone, growing frustration evident in his body posture. I compressed minutes into seconds by cutting and creating overlapping dissolves (covered in Chapter 4), and then it was on to shooting the object of the fellow's frustration. I didn't shoot the two clips the same day or in the same location. In fact, the artificial couple I created never met each other; I just directed them, and they did their respective shtick.

The heart of the example to follow is to get the clip of Jackie a little color corrected—the exposure is fine, but she's casting into magentas and greens compared to Michael. You might initially wonder what's wrong with that; Michael is clearly not in proximity to Jackie, and their respective complexions would not be expected to be identical. However, it's the composition, the composite, you need to consider. You compose for geometry and also for overall color in a scene, and I don't think the clips in their original state present a cohesive story because of the color casting. By lessening the color differences in the two clips presented onscreen simultaneously, you focus the audience on what's happening without the distraction of colors failing to reconcile. Figure 5.1 shows the two videos you'll put together in the sections to follow.

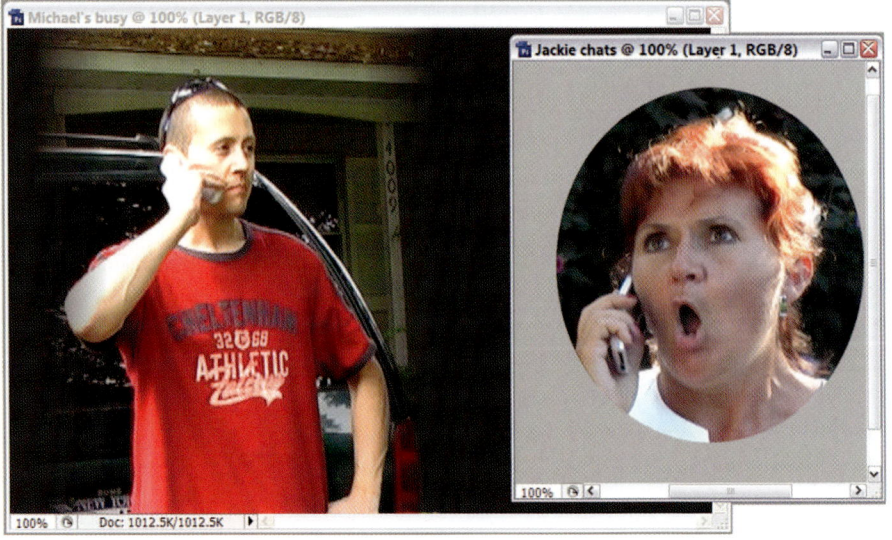

Figure 5.1

The acting and overall composition will work fine, but the clip of Jackie introduces color casting that will spoil the composite video.

Clipping the Video Layer for Composite Work

The first thing to do is to get the clip of Jackie (as the top layer) into the video with Michael. Then I show you how to create an oval mortise for the Jackie layer that can be freely animated into the composition at the appropriate entry point. Yes, we could do a split-screen in this example and avoid some steps, but using a clipping mask layer is simple and provides a certain elegance to a Production akin to putting an important photograph in a handsome frame.

1. Open Michael's busy.mov in the workspace and turn off Pixel Aspect Ratio Correction.
2. Open Jackie chats.mov and turn off Pixel Aspect Ratio Correction.
3. Press Ctrl/Cmd+R to display rulers in the Jackie document.
4. With the Move tool, drag guides out of the rulers and position a left and a top guide to meet the top and left extent of the oval that Jackie's within.
5. Create a new layer in the document and put it below the video layer.
6. With the Elliptical Marquee tool, drag a selection to match the shape of the ellipse in which Jackie is framed.
7. With the bottom layer chosen on the Layers palette, press Alt/Opt+Backspace to fill the interior of the selection, then press Ctrl/Cmd+D to deselect. The current foreground color doesn't matter. You're going to create a clipping mask, and Photoshop evaluates the mask based on layer content opacity and not color.
8. Hold Alt/Opt and then click on the edge of the layer titles on the Layers palette. As you can see in Figure 5.2, you now have a mask that clips the Jackie video to the selection you filled in Step 7. If it's not a flawless mask, if a pixel or two shows behind Jackie's oval, this is okay; I have a frame that you will apply shortly that will disguise any imprecision.

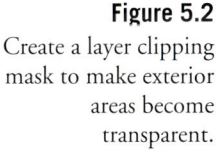

Figure 5.2
Create a layer clipping mask to make exterior areas become transparent.

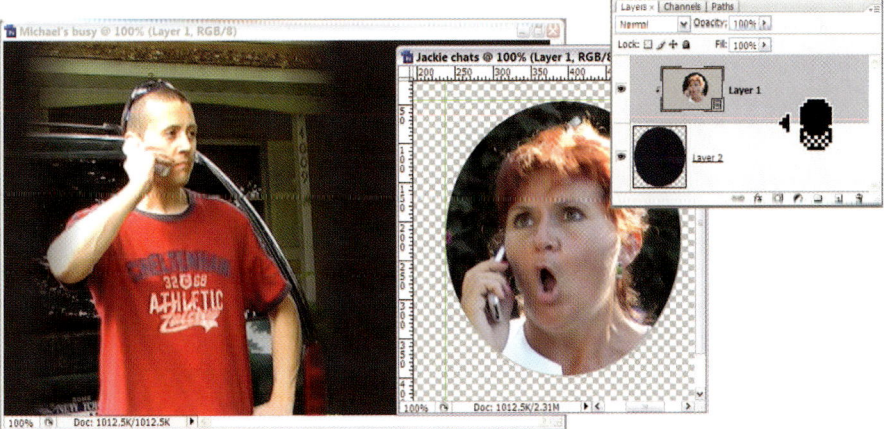

Color Correcting Through Adjustment Layers

It's a simple duplication move to get Jackie and her clipping mask into the video document of Michael. From there you'll add an Adjustment layer, specifically Color Balance, to bring Jackie's complexion more in line with that of Michael and the overall composite. Adjustment layers initially cover the entire layer and all layers below, so a problem arises that can be fixed in one or two steps. Here's the deal: An Adjustment layer is a mask, in much the same way the clipping mask now hides the exterior of Jackie's oval. By applying black to the Adjustment layer in all areas where Michael is featured, you tell Photoshop not to adjust anything.

Here's how to make the composite and color balance the Jackie video:

1. Hold Shift. Click both the Jackie video and the clipping mask layers on the Layers palette to select them.

2. Drag and drop the layer title into the Michael video document to duplicate them. You can close the Jackie document without saving now.

3. While the duplicates are both selected in the Michael document, with the Move tool, drag them to the right of Michael, so Jackie clears Michael. This is a coarse composition you'll refine shortly.

4. On the Animation palette, with both layers still selected, slide the Jackie and the clipping mask tracks (the green bars) so their tails are at the end of the Work Area. My concept is that we introduce Michael first and then Jackie a few seconds later. Notice that the Jackie clip is shorter in duration than the Michael video.

5. Click the Create New Fill or Adjustment Layer icon (it looks like a Moonpie) on the bottom of the Layers palette to expose the menu. Choose Color Balance from the menu.

6. Just click OK at this step to create the Adjustment layer but not make any changes using it.

7. Choose the Rectangular Marquee tool and then create a selection over Michael extending to the right but not including the mortise of Jackie. Peek ahead to Figure 5.3. Then fill the selection with foreground black (set the foreground to black and then press Alt/Opt+Backspace). Then deselect.

8. On the Adjustment layer entry on the Layers palette list, double-click the Adjustment icon (not the layer mask thumbnail), and the Color Balance dialog box appears.

Figure 5.3
Black on an Adjustment layer hides underlying layers from the effect of the layer.

> **Tip**
>
> Layer masks can be inverted, in case you want protected areas to be exposed to Adjustments and vice-versa. You click the mask thumbnail on the Layers palette and then press Ctrl/Cmd+I to invert the tones on the mask. You can also paint using shades of black to create partial Adjustment layer effects; using gray colors or a black color with the Brush tool at partial opacity accomplishes similar results. To globally reduce the effect of an Adjustment layer, you choose it on the Layers palette and then decrease the opacity.
>
> If you've toiled on a mask that you might want to use as a selection in future steps on the same video, you go to the Channels palette—the Adjustment layer mask is right there (but it's a temporary entry)—and then drag the title into the Create New Channel icon on the bottom of the palette to make the mask selection a regular, permanent alpha channel.

9. Tune the colors for Jackie now, but not for Michael because the mask for the Adjustment layer is white (exposed) for Jackie but black (protected) over Michael. I recommend that you begin with the midtones (click the radio button on the bottom) with Preserve Luminosity enabled; Jackie's color cast is not quite magenta, but skews toward blue, so drag the Yellow/Blue slider toward yellow, drag the Magenta/Green slider just a little toward green, and then drag the Cyan/Red slider to about +5 toward red. Luminosity should be preserved in color correction because color influences brightness; Photoshop internally uses a color model that mimics real-life color response—in short, Jackie's exposure is fine, and you don't want to change it. My recommendations for Color Balance are derived through trial and error. There is no formula for color correction; you use your artist's eye.

10. Click the Shadows button and then play with the Color Balance. This will affect more of Jackie's foliage background than the actress herself because she's well lit and tonally balanced, while the background falls into shadows. I recommend that you skew the shadows regions into green and away from cyans and magentas to warm up the green and make the overall video layer more color-harmonious with the Michael video layer, which is quite warm and casts toward yellows. In Figure 5.4 you can see the adjustments I've made in Steps 8 and 9. Click OK to apply the settings when you're happy with the composition, and remember that Adjustment layers are dynamic, and you can revisit the dialog box at any time in the future by double-clicking the icon for the Adjustment layer on the Layers palette list.

> **Note**
>
> You'll notice that the entry for the Adjustment layer on the Layers palette list is auto-named Color Balance 1. You can rename the layer by double-clicking the title and then typing in anything you like. More importantly, this Color Balance 1 suggests that you can add more than one Adjustment layer to the stack of layers in a composition. If you need to, you can add a Levels Adjustment layer and others—the theoretical limit being your system resources. You just need to remember that an Adjustment layer affects *all* layers below it. Therefore, you can use the mask by painting black on the Adjustment layer to confine adjustments, and you can also put video layers on top of Adjustments layers—to keep the video from being affected by the Adjustment layer.

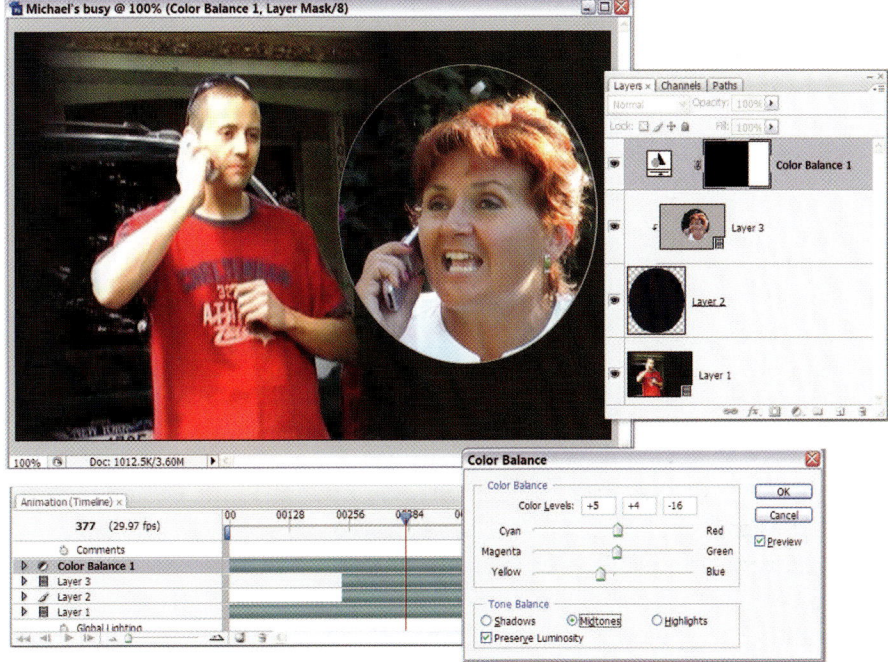

Figure 5.4
Use Color Balance to bring Jackie's colors in line with the overall composition.

Tidying Up the Mask and the Composition

The mask you created earlier for the Adjustment layer has a hard right edge, and the effect of the Color Balance is seeping into the Michael layer noticeably because Michael is matted against a color that's not quite black in the video. So you'll correct this in the following steps. Additionally, Adjustment layers and clipping masks are by default created to play the duration of the Work Area on the Animation palette. For the Adjustment layer, playing it throughout the 25-second composition doesn't visibly harm anything, but the clipping layer needs to be trimmed. When a clipping layer plays for a duration longer than the video layer it's clipping, you (and your audience) will see the clipping mask pop into the video—it has nothing to mask.

Let's address these issues in the following steps:

1. On the Animation palette, drag the head of the track marked Color Balance to match the head of the Jackie layer.

2. With the Brush tool, choose the 200 soft pixel brush and about 75% Opacity on the Options bar.

3. Choose White as your current foreground color and then click on the mask thumbnail for Color Balance on the Layers palette. Painting with white exposes adjusted areas, while painting with black hides the Color Balance adjustment in this example. And painting with partially opaque white partially exposes the adjustment effect.

4. Scroll the timeline indicator on the Animation palette to a point in time where Jackie is present in the video composition.

5. Stroke once along the edge of the layer mask. Stroke again and then perhaps a third time until the edge of the layer mask is not visible in the document window. At any time if you've overdone the editing and the mortise of Jackie looks wrong, press X to swap foreground/background colors and then stroke using foreground black to hide your previous editing strokes. See Figure 5.5.

Figure 5.5
Soften the edge on the layer mask to prevent a hard edge from showing in the darker areas of the Michael layer while Jackie is in the composition.

Adding a Frame, Moving the Mortise

I mentioned earlier that the oval edge masking Jackie doesn't have to be a perfect match because you can put a fancy frame above the video layer to hide imperfections. I created coily cord frame.png using Xara Xtreme; you could use Photoshop or Illustrator. I was able to export a PNG file from Xara with transparency; shortly, you'll place the PNG file at the top of the composition layer stack, and Jackie will show through.

Additionally, I didn't think it's good video to simply pop Jackie into the composition, but rather to travel her video into the composition from frame right at an appropriate time. The appropriate time is 1 or 2 seconds after the squeak toy chattering begins on the audio track that's embedded in the Michael video. Although the humorous sound effect (and I already apologized to our actress) is audio, by moving Jackie into frame slightly after the sound begins, you're essentially "cutting on action," an editor's trick to keep action from looking too paced and staged. It's very stiff to cut to an actor at the beginning of his line and then cut to the other actor when he has a line.

Here's how to add the coily cord frame element and then define a position change for multiple elements all in one go:

1. Move the timeline indicator (the thumb) on the Animation palette to a point in the composition where Jackie is in frame.

2. Open coily cord frame.png and then duplicate the layer to the composition and close the original PNG file without saving changes. Put the frame layer on the top of the layers stack on the Layers palette and then with the Move tool position it so it fits over the oval of Jackie. If it helps, rename the layers for easy identification purposes.

3. On the Animation palette, trim the duration of the frame by dragging the head of its track to match the other tracks associated with Jackie as you edited in the previous section. It might be a good idea to save your work to hard drive in the native PSD format at this point.

4. You can hear the audio by holding Alt/Opt and then clicking the Play icon on the Animation palette to see where Jackie should enter, but I'll make it easy here: The squeak toy sound begins at about Frame 267. Move the timeline indicator to Frame 320, and then on the Animation palette, click the Position stopwatch for the Jackie layer, the coily cord layer, and then click the stopwatch for the clipping mask layer. Doing this sets a key for all these layers' positions at the current time.

5. On the Layers palette, Ctrl/Cmd+click the coily cord, the Jackie layer, and the clipping mask layer to select them. *Don't* select the Adjustment layer, and be careful to click the layer title area. Ctrl+clicking a thumbnail will load the nontransparent layer areas as a selection (this is not the intention here). You're all set now to move all the selected layers into frame in perfect synch.

6. Move the timeline indicator to Frame 256. With the Move tool, hold Shift (for power nudging, nudging by 10 instead of 1 pixel) and then use the right arrow keyboard key to move Jackie so her left edge is just out of frame. Although you've got the beginning position in advance of when the squeak toy noise begins, remember that the Jackie layer is in motion and doesn't really become the co-star of the video composition until about one second after the sound effect begins playing. In Figure 5.6 you can see my setup.

Figure 5.6

Moving a little after a sound event is similar to cutting on action.

7. Proof your work. Hold Alt/Opt and then click the Play icon. Let Photoshop buffer the composition into memory for its first play, and then let it repeat with audio enabled a few times. I show you the steps, but it's you who's doing the editing. If you think Jackie moves into scene too fast, Ctrl/Cmd+click on the three Jackie component layer titles on the Layers palette, move the timeline indicator to first position point, and then with the Move tool chosen, nudge the layers farther to the right. This will slow the entrance, but it's only one of several different editing moves you can quickly make when multiple layers are selected and have at least one key frame defined. In Figure 5.7 you can see the composition about halfway through the duration, with Jackie established in the scene.

Figure 5.7
Time and retime the move in, if necessary.

Creating a Fade to Black

Play the composition to its end and you'll notice that Michael does a freeze-frame and then his video fades to black. Hmmm…Jackie should match the fade, right? Like the Michael video, Jackie also does a freeze at the end. I did this by duplicating the video of the Layers palette and then choosing Rasterize Layer to create a still frame at the end of the video. Then I wrote the composition out to a new video.

To make Jackie fade to black along with Michael is not difficult. In the following steps you'll create a new layer in the composition, fill it with black, and then alter the layer's opacity over time, from zero to 100%.

1. On the Layers palette, click the top layer to make it the active layer. Click the Create a New Layer icon, press D (default colors, black is now the foreground color on the Tools palette), and then press Alt/Opt+Backspace. Make sure this is the top layer in the stack.

2. Hide the black layer on the Layers palette so you can see what you're editing.

3. Move the timeline indicator to about Frame 724; this is where Michael has already frozen and the fade begins. See Figure 5.8.

4. Unhide the black layer. Click its Opacity stopwatch on the Animation palette and then set the opacity for this layer on the Layers palette to 0%.

5. Move to the end of the Work Area on the Animation palette. On the Layers palette, set the Opacity for the black layer to 100%. Then play the video. The Michael fade should happen fairly synchronously with the overall fade. See Figure 5.9.

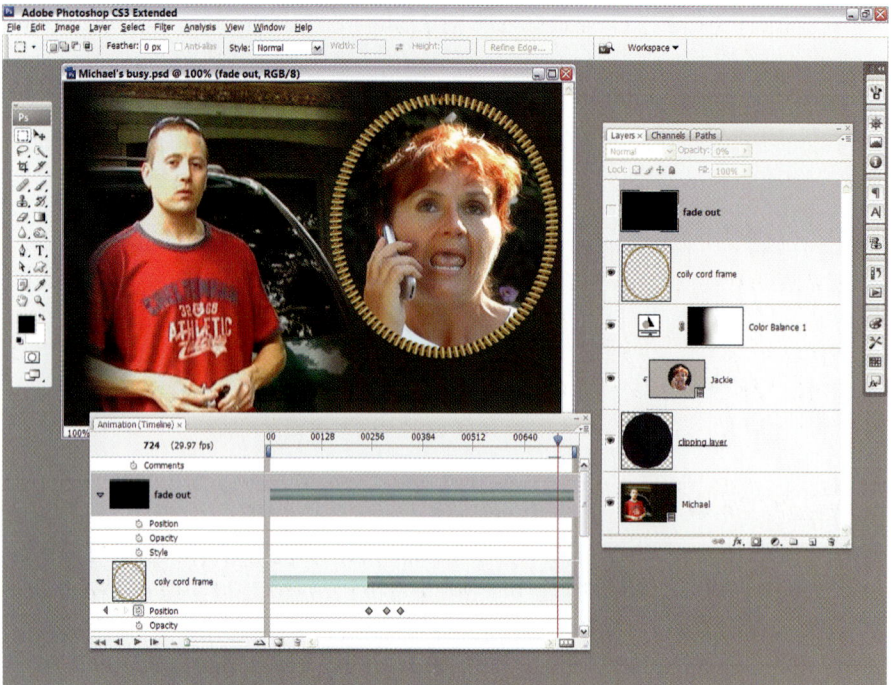

Figure 5.8
Move the timeline to the point where you need to match the fade to black.

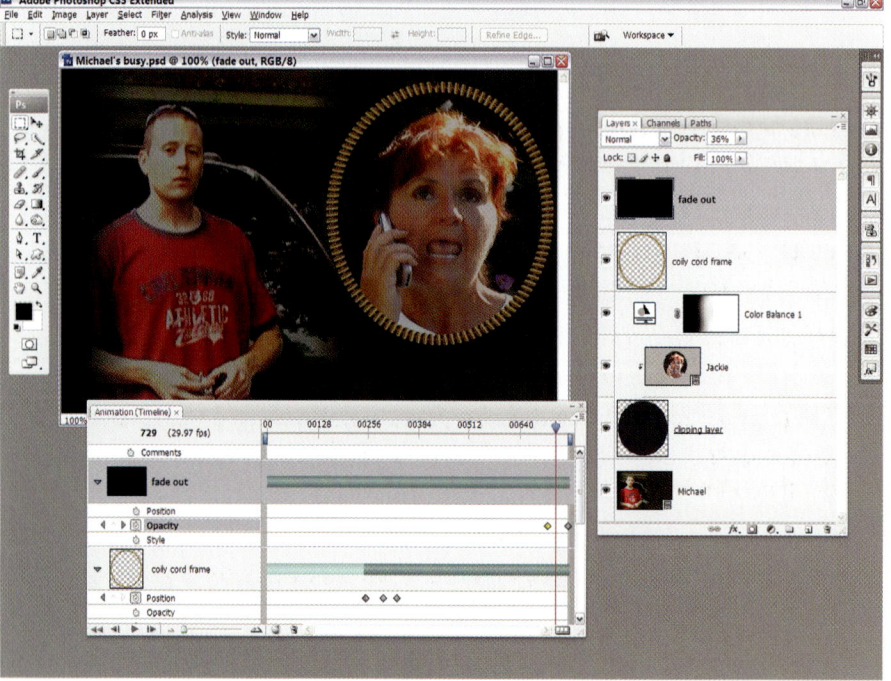

Figure 5.9
The freeze, then fade to black, is a classic and sophisticated end to a clip.

6. Choose File > Export > Render Video. Render the video to QuickTime file format using the Sorenson Video 3 codec (for better color than most other codecs). With most codecs the option to export with alpha masking is automatically dimmed, so click Render and you're done.

Colorizing a Moving Video Area

Suppose you have a client who, after the video has been shot, wants to change the color of an item in the movie. And the object is moving. This is not a big deal after you learn the steps in Photoshop; like the moving Jackie mortise, you can move an Adjustment layer over time. The following sections bridge reality and fantasy as you see how to make a dart hitting a dartboard change color over time.

Setting Up a Comp for Traveling Masks

The professional challenge in this example creates a dramatic change in the video's visual content: The fictitious client wants the third dart to hit the dartboard in SloMo dart.mov to have a red shaft and feathers, to better even out the scene. Ordinarily, you can move an Adjustment layer's mask around a composition, but you can't move it in and out of the document window's extent because it's not Big Data. *Big Data* is Adobe's term for image content on a layer that exceeds the extent of the document window.

The trick to overcoming this apparent limitation, because the dart in the video enters the scene, is to extend the canvas of the composition, thus allowing the Adjustment mask to extend out of the scene. To finally get the video for rendering back to video proportions, you duplicate everything to a new, properly sized video document. The excess becomes Big Data, and life is fine.

Follow these steps to set up the composition, mask an area to use for adjustment, and then apply a Hue/Saturation Adjustment layer.

1. Open SloMo darts.mov and then go to View and turn off Pixel Aspect Ratio Correction.

2. The canvas needs to be extended to frame right by the length of a dart. Click and hold the Eyedropper tool to choose the Ruler tool (which is grouped with the Eyedropper tools).

3. Scrub the timeline until the fourth dart has hit the board. With the Ruler tool active, click+drag the length of the third dart. If the Info palette is not currently displayed, press F8 to display it.

4. The width the Info palette reports should be about 465 or so pixels. Right-click over the document title bar and choose Canvas Size from the pop-up menu.

> **Tip**
>
> The Info palette is useful for measuring areas using American and European increments, as well as percentages and pixels. If the Info palette is not set up to measure using pixels as the increment, you click the tiny crosshairs icon in the lower left field (the X,Y coordinates) and then choose Pixels from the list. Doing this affects not only the readout from the Ruler tool but also the rulers in a document window when you have them displayed. In general, we measure video in pixels, so this is a good Info palette setting for the examples in this book.

5. Click the anchor chicklet at the 9 o'clock position to anchor left so you can expand to the right.

6. To be on the safe size, type **1200** in the New Size > Width field and then click OK.

7. Add a new layer, put it on the bottom of the stack, and then fill it with gray so you can see what you're doing in future steps. Save your work by saving the file as a PSD file. Your document should look like that in Figure 5.10.

Figure 5.10

Extend the canvas size and add a background layer.

To change the shaft and feathers of the dart, you need to build a mask that's shaped like this silhouette:

1. Double-click the Quick Mask Mode button on the Tools palette. By default, your Quick Mask overlay color is probably red, which will be useless seeing a mask around a dart that will eventually become red. Choose white or slightly off-white. Also, make sure Color Indicates: Selected Areas is the active option and then click OK in the Quick Mask Options box. You're editing in Quick Mask mode now.

2. Use what you're familiar and comfortable with to select the shaft and feather area. In Figure 5.11 you can see I'm just using the Brush tool; you could use the Magnetic Lasso tool or other selection tools as well. The previous exercise changed the Opacity setting for the Brush tool, so be sure to adjust the Opacity setting back to 100% on the Options bar.

3. Press Q to return to Standard Editing mode so you can see the marquee. By default, Photoshop defines masks created in Quick Mask mode as Masked Areas, which would be the inverse of what you seek, selected areas, in this example. This is why I had you change this preference in Step 1 to Selected Areas. If a mask is inverted in your own work, press Shift+F7 (you can tell if the selection is inverted if you see the marching ant selection appear around the border of the document window).

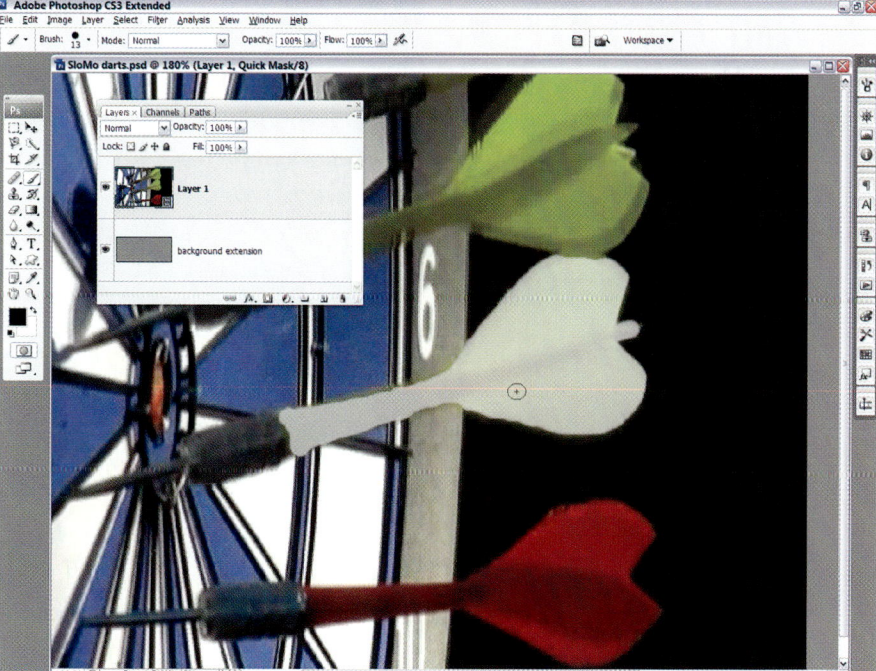

Figure 5.11
Select the shaft and body of the dart in Quick Mask mode.

4. Click the top layer on the Layers palette to make sure this is the active layer and then click the Create New Fill or Adjustment Layer icon on the Layers palette. Then choose Hue/Saturation from the menu.

5. Here's where your artistic eye is needed. When the Hue/Saturation dialog box comes up, click the Colorize box, and then strive for a good color match for the colorization, so this dart's body looks like the one at bottom right in the frame. In Figure 5.12, I believe I created a good match by specifying pure red Hue (0 degrees on a color wheel), 55 Saturation, and −10 Lightness to give the red color some heft. Click OK when you're happy with the new color; you can respecify the color at any time in the future by double-clicking the Adjustment Layer icon on the Layers palette list of layers (*not* the thumbnail image for the Adjustment layer mask).

Figure 5.12
Change the color of the dart's shaft and feathers using a Hue/Saturation Colorize Adjustment.

Moving and Putting the Mask in Motion

Here's the fun part: In the following steps you'll animate the Adjustment layer mask, moving its Position in time to match the motion of the underlying dart. Additionally, you'll notice that the dart is blurry until it hits the board due to the speed of the dart.

To make the Adjustment layer blurry is not difficult: You blur the mask.

1. On the Animation palette, click the Position stopwatch for the Adjustment layer's Layer Mask Position; a keyframe is created.

2. Set the current time to about Frame 90, just before the dart moves into frame.

3. With the Move tool, move the Adjustment layer mask out of frame in the document window. You can use the keyboard arrow keys in combination with the Move tool to nudge it, but the dart moves both horizontally and vertically from out of frame at 90 to resting in the dartboard at Frame 120 (30 frames total), and I found while running this example that inadvertent lateral moves over time didn't show up in the video.

4. Scrub the timeline between 90 and 120. At any point where the mask comes detached from the underlying dart, use the Move tool to correct its relative position. The whole sequence will take perhaps four position keys, as you can see in Figure 5.13.

5. Even with proper position, the blurring of the dart in the video makes the mask look awkward. With the layer mask selected on the Layers palette, choose Filter > Blur > Motion Blur.

Figure 5.13
Photoshop automatically sets new keys it will then animate when you change the position of the Adjustment layer mask.

6. Drag the Motion Blur filter box to a position in the workspace where you can compare the angle of the blur you need to the dart. I think 25 degrees works well here, and that dart is very blurry in the video, so set the Distance to about 80 pixels. See Figure 5.14; this is a *permanent* edit, so make sure the interactive preview in the document window looks right before clicking OK.

Figure 5.14
Blur the layer mask so it appears to move in frame like the dart does.

Impressing Your Client with a Variation

I love to get a difficult assignment and not only complete it but also add an element of the *impossible* to the difficult. What do you say we change the color of the dart over time? You can't change an Adjustment layer's parameters over time, but you can indeed change a style applied to an Adjustment layer (not the video itself). The bonus here is that you're not altering the video and can save the composition to a relatively small PSD file size as a consequence.

Here's how to change the color of the dart over time:

1. Double-click the Adjustment Layer icon on the Layers palette list to display the Hue/Saturation box.

2. Uncheck the Colorize box and then click OK. The Adjustment layer now has no effect beyond holding a blurred, traveling mask around the dart. As such, it's a lot easier to predict the result of an Overlay Style's color.

3. With the mask selected on the Layers palette, click the Add a Layer Style icon (the "fx" on the bottom of the palette). Choose Color Overlay from the list.

4. In the Layer Style box, choose Color from the Blend Mode drop-down list and then for this example choose an orange (H: 45, S: 100%, B: 56%) by clicking the swatch to display the Color Picker. Click OK after adjusting the HSB color values. Lower Opacity to 80%. Color blending mode occasionally produces unexpected results—overly saturated color, for example. In this step, however, bright orange contrasts well against the red and yellow darts, and my suggested color values appear to play okay. See Figure 5.15.

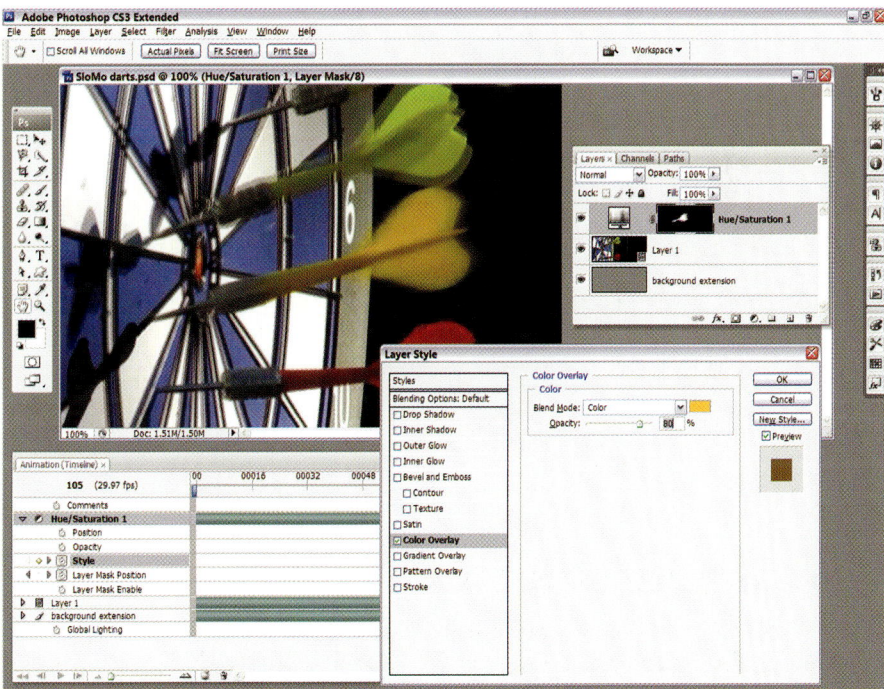

Figure 5.15
Use a Color Overlay on the Adjustment layer mask to recolor the dart's body.

5. To now cycle the color of the dart over time, first set the current time to about Frame 106, just after the hit.

6. On the Animation palette, click the stopwatch for Style for the Hue/Saturation layer. This sets a key.

7. Advance the current time to about Frame 125.

8. Double-click the Color Overlay entry on the Layers palette to display the setting box. Here I suggest that you choose a color with not a lot of brightness or saturation. Color mode can influence brightness and saturation already existing in the underlying video—the dart in this example. You have some creative latitude if you go with green because there is no deep, saturated green dart in the video for comparison (although the yellow darts are leaning toward green, picking up the blue on the dartboard). If you choose Hue: 109, Saturation: 71%, and Brightness: 55%, the green will look fairly natural for the dart color compared to the red and yellow ones already in the board. I also adjusted Opacity to 95%. What you've accomplished is to create a style change that occurs from Frame 106 to Frame 125, a little less than a second's worth of transition time. See Figure 5.16.

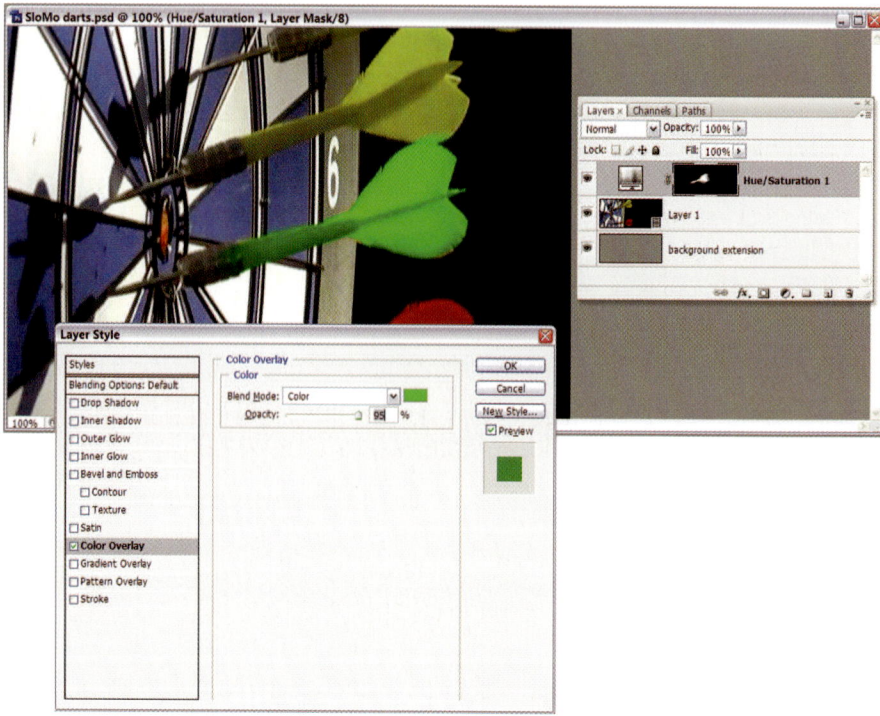

Figure 5.16
Change styles over time to animate colors.

I'd like to stress the quality of timing when what you're doing here in reality is adding animation to a video. The frames I chose for you work well in this example: A 25-frame transition from orange to green is noticeable and comfortable—also because the laws of physics when applied to digital media state that you have to cycle through hues without skipping any. For example, if you wanted a transition between orange and purple, Photoshop would have to include intermediate hues of green and blue, creating too many color changes in this span of time.

Resizing the Canvas of the Composition

As I mentioned earlier, a canvas extension was needed to hold the layer mask in all positions over time. To get the video back to "normal" now, follow these steps:

1. Ctrl/Cmd+double-click the workspace to display the New dialog box.
2. Choose Film & Video from the Presets drop-down list and then click OK. Turn off Pixel Aspect Ratio Correction.
3. Hold Shift and click all the layers except the gray background in the darts composition to select them.
4. Drag the layer titles from the Layers palette into the new film and video document window.
5. Make sure View > Show > Smart Guides is checked.
6. With the Move tool and all the duplicate layers still selected, drag using the Move tool in the document window until you see magenta highlights on the top and left of the document window, the indication that the duplicate layers are aligned to the document, as shown in Figure 5.17.

Figure 5.17
Duplicate your video work to a document window that's correctly sized for rendering.

7. You don't need the blank video layer on the bottom of the document; delete it by dragging it into the trash icon on the Layers palette. Also, preset Film & Video documents play for 300 frames (10 seconds), but the video only plays for 147 frames. Before you render the video, drag the end of the Work Area to meet the end of the playlength for the layers you duplicated.

8. Choose File > Export > Render Video. Choose any codec you like but use QuickTime as the file format because there's an audio track in the darts video layer. Done; collect huge amounts of money from the fictitious client, and then relax with a game of billiards.

Keeping Your Color Adjustments Broadcast Legal

On the topic of color and color correction it's important to discuss what NTSC colors are. Broadcast-legal colors don't pertain only to a TV broadcast, but to any signal sent through a TV set—the most common in households today being standard definition.

The average computer monitor and video subsystem (your video card and so on) have a broader color capability than a television set. One of the more obvious unwanted side effects of trying to play a DVD that was mastered from film or DV is called *blossoming*. Particularly evident are colors that go beyond the saturation point of the television's colorspace; you'll see a bright red jacket on a person "blossom," growing beyond the silhouette of the jacket and looking like a flat, evenly lit blob onscreen.

To prevent or reduce broadcast-illegal colors, here are three strategies:

1. Bring your finished video into Photoshop. By finished, I mean a video that's already been rendered via File > Export, not a file with multiple video layers or with retouching, static layers in it. Choose Filter > Video > NTSC Colors. This is a "one pop" filter; there is no dialog or preview box or any options. You might not see any change in your video, but chances are good that any colors that might have been out of range (gamut) for TV playback have now been brought into range. Render the file to a document with a different name via File > Export and then write it to DVD.

   Mind you, the NTSC Colors filter will bring your video (all of it) into broadcast-legal colors, but it does not ensure the *best-looking* broadcast-legal video. What this filter does is move out-of-range colors to the nearest (arbitrarily assigned) legal color, and any discrepancies are handled by diffusion dithering. As an example (so you don't need to try this), I created a three-frame video of pure red I applied using a soft brush tip. I applied the NTSC Colors filter, and Figure 5.18, the foreground document window, shows the result. This is a "worst-case scenario," but it's a good piece of information to tuck away.

Figure 5.18
The result of applying NTSC Color filter to a video that is way out of broadcast range.

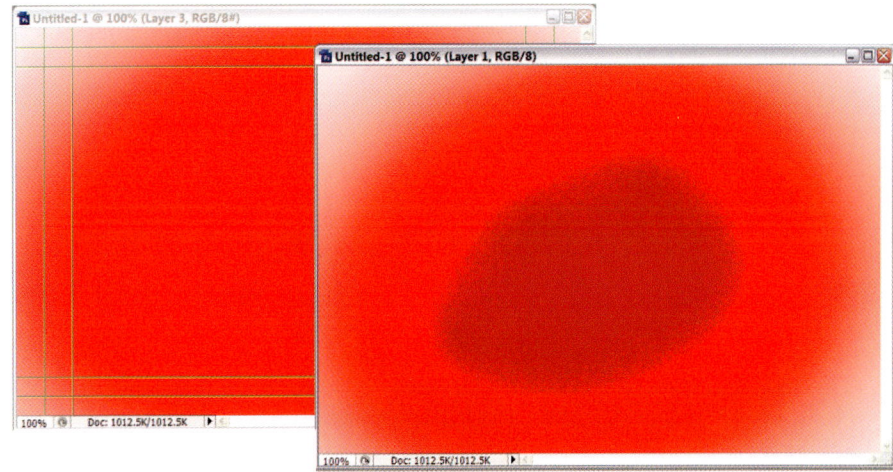

2. Invest in an inexpensive color TV; The Salvation Army usually has color TVs in stock, and you'd be turning a good deed, to boot. Remember you're always playing to the "cheap seats" when you author a video, so a cheap TV ensures that if your playback looks okay, it'll only look better on the majority of TV sets. Then you find the four-pin S-Video or RCA connector on your computer video card's out port, hook up the TV, and play your video.

3. Burn a DVD with your video, go into the family room, and play the video on your home entertainment center. This is not as good a method for ensuring broadcast-legal colors as hooking a cheap TV set to your computer; additionally, if you see video blossoming, you've wasted a 50¢ DVD.

Check out Chapter 17 for the details on getting your video work out of your computer and onto a professionally authored DVD.

A Special Effect Using Color Correction

People in the cinema trade just *love* to pay homage to earlier broadcast years. We see little snippets of television shows in motion pictures all the time, and they've usually been degraded intentionally using one technical method or another to make the image look more authentic, like someone filmed a TV set, and the raster bars are visible because TV fps timing is different than motion picture fps rate.

Using several different Photoshop features, the next example shows a good way to "crummify" a DV clip to make it look as though someone filmed a 1950s TV broadcast using a Super 8 camera. I chose to emulate the Saturday morning science programs with Professor Wizard in color.mov, with a comedic twist at the end (yes, this shtick has been done with scores of variations over the decades).

As you can see in Figure 5.19, the original DV footage doesn't work because although the costume, the shoe polish hairdo, and the beakers look "period," the color presentation spoils the clip. But you'll fix this shortly.

Figure 5.19
This "science show" DV clip doesn't work because it's in color.

Getting the TV Blue Look

Black and white television sets had a bluish cast that you'll add through a Hue/Saturation Colorize Adjustment layer in the next steps. You want to be careful not to overdo the bluish cast; I've seen some extremely blue, extremely tricked-up faux footage in movies, and it spoils what was supposed to be an unnoticed special effect. Don't mind the fact that the Adjustment layer will degrade the brightness and contrast of the underlying video; you'll correct this with an additional layer later. The important point is to degrade without totally ruining the clip you want to make look old-fashioned.

1. Open Professor Wizard in Color.mov and turn off Pixel Aspect Ratio Correction.

2. Click the Create New Fill or Adjustment Layer icon on the Layers palette and then choose Hue/Saturation from the menu.

3. Click the Colorize box and then choose H: 207, S: 8, and leave the Lightness alone, as shown in Figure 5.20. Click OK.

4. Save the document to PSD file format. You can keep it open in the workspace. You need to cobble a special file next.

Figure 5.20
Black and white television sets had a bluish cast in real life and especially when portrayed in mock "period" films.

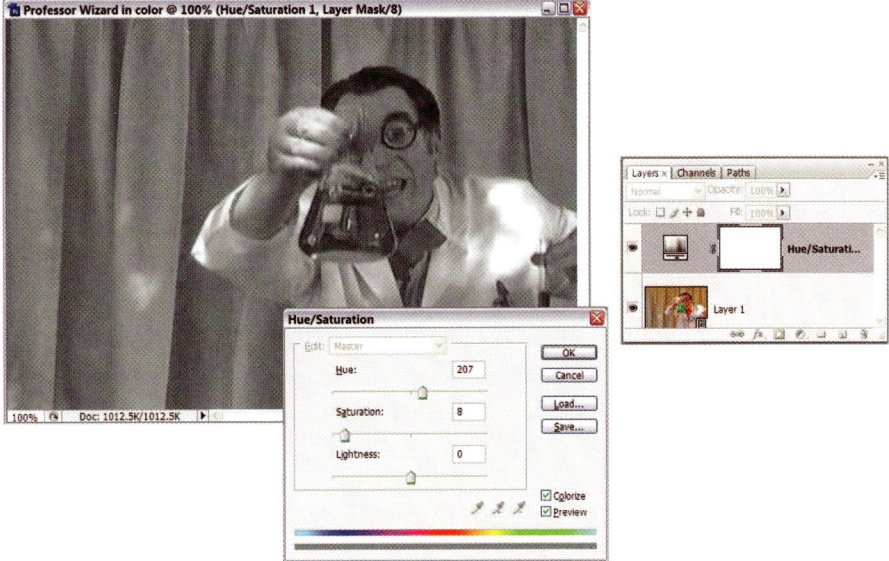

Creating and Applying a Raster Pattern

The stripes you'll occasionally see in old black and white television broadcasts are due to two things: the relatively low resolution onscreen—scanned at 525 lines per inch (lpi) as of 1953—and interlacing 60 fields per second, at a ratio of 2:1. Today, affordable DV cameras need to interlace to handle the massive amount of visual data acquisition, but at a 1:1 ratio, which is far less noticeable.

Let's coarsen the lpi value in the next set of steps; television is a medium of close-ups, and short of obliterating the details in the Professor Wizard video, I believe we can telegraph the idea that this is a capture off a black and white TV set from the 1950s.

1. Ctrl+double-click the workspace area to display the New dialog box. Choose the Film & Video preset and turn off Pixel Aspect Ratio Correction.

2. Create a new blank layer on top of the current Background layer and then delete the Background layer.

3. With the Rectangular Marquee tool, create a selection that spans the document horizontally but is only 5 pixels or so in height. Use the Info palette if necessary to guide you to achieve this shallow vertical dimension.

4. Fill the selection with black and then deselect.

5. Choose Filter > Blur > Gaussian Blur. Blur the document by about 1.8 pixels.

6. Ctrl/Cmd+click the layer thumbnail on the Layers palette to load the non-transparent pixels as a selection. The marquee will be slightly taller than this raster due to some partially opaque pixels included in the selection; this is perfect because you've achieved a good spacing for the raster as a pattern with zero effort.

7. Choose Image > Crop. Then choose Edit > Define Pattern. Save the pattern by naming it rasters as shown in Figure 5.21. Now that the image has been saved as a pattern, you can close the document without saving it.

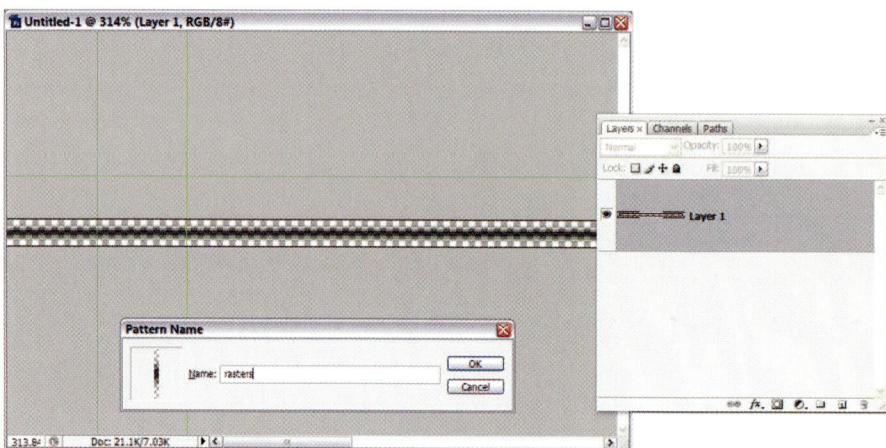

Figure 5.21

Save the document as a pattern to use as a fill later.

8. With the Professor Wizard document, choose Layer > New Fill Layer > Pattern.

9. Click OK in the New Layer box (there are no options you need for this example) and then in the following box, Pattern Fill, choose the raster pattern if it's not currently displayed at the left and then scale the pattern to 50 or 60% of the original. Click OK.

10. Now's your big opportunity to adjust the TV's reception. On the Layers palette, for the Pattern Fill layer, choose Overlay blending mode. Doing this darkens dark areas in the underlying video and bleaches out highlights somewhat.

11. Fiddle with the horizontal controls and the antenna. I'm kidding! Reduce the opacity of the layer to about 63% or to whatever you feel looks good to your artistic eye. Then play the video using the Animation palette. As you can see in Figure 5.22, the video looks fairly good and awful now. If the Hue/Saturation or the settings for the pattern fill don't display the video to your satisfaction, you double-click the layer icon on the Layers palette (not the mask thumbnail), and the dialog box for that attribute pops up, and you can adjust the settings.

Figure 5.22
Don't touch that dial. Professor Wizard will be right back.

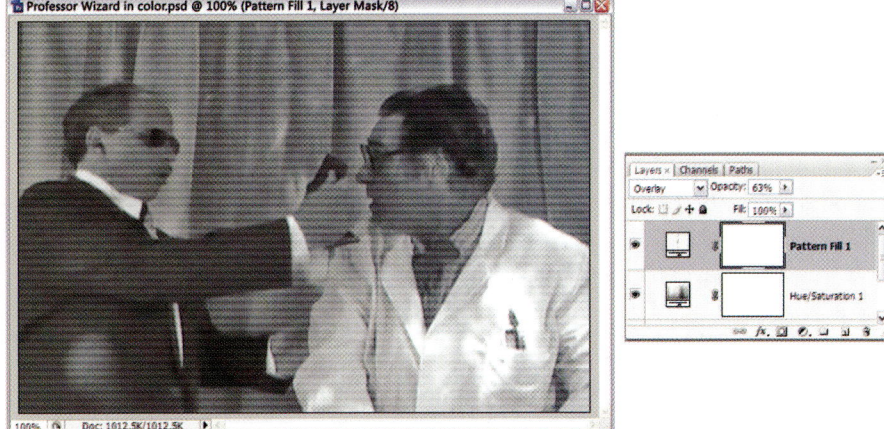

Adding Ghosting

Another wonderful byproduct of 1950s technology was poor broadcast reception, specifically in the form of ghosted signals. To create a little video ghosting:

1. Drag the video layer into the Create a New Layer icon at the bottom of the Layers palette.
2. Choose the Move tool.
3. Use the keyboard arrow keys to nudge the duplicate layer to the right by about 6 pixels and down 2 or 3. Ghosting traditionally occurred to the right of the original signal.
4. Decrease the opacity of the duplicate layer to about 59% and change the blending mode for this layer to Lighten, as shown in Figure 5.23. Because the duplicate is below the Pattern and Adjustment layers, it is affected exactly as the original is. If the fuzziness bothers you, do what they did in the 1950s and bang the side of your monitor once or twice. Cursing helps, too.

Figure 5.23
Even though the picture is degraded, your special effect will get a terrific reception.

Using a Plug-In to Degrade Video

Although the most straightforward way to change color, levels, and occasionally video content is done through Adjustment layers, you can use any plug-in (Photoshop native or third party) to change video. You need to bear in mind that a filter applied to a video only does so for the current frame. Therefore, if you check out Chapter 4, there's a hack to a JavaScript that ships with Photoshop that will run any Action any number of times you like. The Professor Wizard video is 433 frames; I suggest that you cobble a script to run an Action called X 433 times right now.

Here's the deal: Alien Skin Exposure 2 provides Photoshoppists with film simulations that are extremely authentic. You can download a 30-day fully functional trial at http://www.alienskin.com/downloads/getmail1.asp. I think after running the trial version you might decide to pop for it because it's also a great little plug-in for editing and enhancing *still* images. I used it as a video pass in my finished video in the Galley folder.

Exposure 2 provides many different film types; to create a different type of vintage video, you use the TRI-X 400 pushed two stop setting. This delivers a graininess reminiscent not of TV, but of the educational films the gym coach might have shown you (on hygiene or similar social concern) if you were around in the 1950s and 60s.

You can also choose to run Filter > Noise > Add Noise 433 Times and then stack up Black and White and Exposure Adjustment layers to achieve an interesting but not as authentic effect as Alien Skin Exposure does in one step. Here's how to create the look of a black and white film that's been scuffed around the floor a few times:

1. The video layer should be the current editing layer. Make sure the current time indicator is at the beginning of the video file. On the Actions palette, if necessary, delete or rename any action already named x from previous chapter exercises. Click on the Default Actions folder to make it active and choose New Action on the Actions palette's menu, and then name the Action x.

2. Choose Filter > Alien Skin Exposure 2 > Black and White Film.

3. Choose B&W Films > Kodak TRI-X 400 - Pushed 2 Stops from the Settings list and then click OK. In Figure 5.24 you can see the result. Click the Selects Next Frame icon at the bottom of the Animation palette.

Figure 5.24
Exposure 2 provides a film response whose haloing and grain can't easily be achieved with native filters.

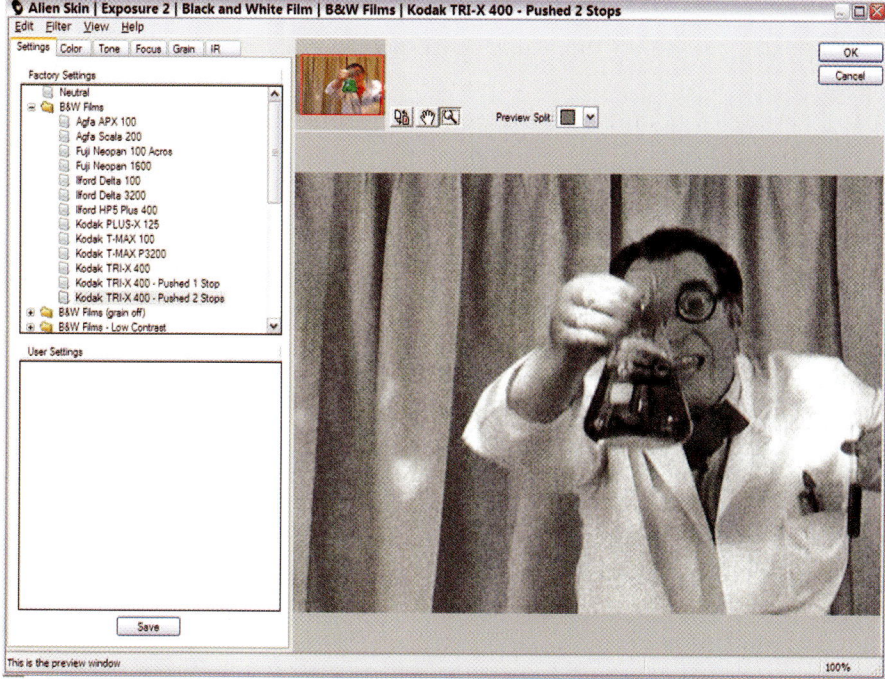

4. Stop recording the Action. Again, click on the Default Actions folder to make it the active folder if it's not still selected.

5. Choose File > Scripts > Execute X 433 Times—the script you adjusted at the beginning of this section (based on Chapter 4 instructions).

6. Wait a while for the script to run, and then choose File > Export > Render Video. Use codec settings you feel comfortable with and choose QuickTime as the export file format because the clip has audio. You can now close the document without saving. Every frame has been altered, and even with Photoshop's good compression, the document saved to PSD would be upwards of 300MB.

I've covered color correction and overall color degrading, plus a little fanciful color animation in this chapter, but I'd like to point out that anything you find on the Adjustment Layer drop-down list on the Layers palette can be used to alter the appearance of a video without altering the video itself and incurring a huge saved PSD file. Color Overlay, also, is but one of several layer styles you can add to a video. By the careful editing of the mask associated with a layer style, you can do creative and wondrous things with Pattern Overlay and Gradient Overlay, used at partial opacity in Overlay, Color and other blending modes.

Remember that your net goal is to change the meaning of the video through the use of color and other adjustments, either to correct or to enhance. To fancy up, to disguise rather than to reveal and illuminate a video that's not a good one to begin with isn't worth your time or effort as a Photoshop professional.

6

Video Restoration

I can't think of anyone who uses current video technology who doesn't have a sizable stash of video that was recorded using *legacy* technology. Whether it's for the family or for serious archiving purposes, videos recorded on videotape and film might not be in mint condition. It's the purpose of this chapter to walk you through a pipeline from translating physical and electric media to digital, and then see what you can do to restore or retouch the content.

First, I'll guide you through some recommendations for the hardware and software you'll need to render your old media to new media. The hardware is a significant but not wallet-breaking investment, and alternatively you might find a rental place or borrow a friend's setup for an afternoon. I don't recommend letting a service digitize your heirloom footage. Services vary in quality, and you could be the lucky customer who enjoys a service mishap with your one-and-only media. Also, retail stores such as pharmacies don't do the digitizing in-house; if you were dead-set on outsourcing video transfers, you'd be best off finding the name of the actual service to which the drug store mails their work.

Then in this chapter I show you a number of different approaches to restoring color, correcting color balance and exposure, and a few last-ditch efforts to retouch heirloom videos; generally, it's better to try to restore than to retouch—if you remember the early "colorized" videos of Laurel and Hardy shorts and *It's A Wonderful Life*, you realize that the bonus of adding color is stolen by the *distraction* of adding color.

Video Transfer Hardware and Software

It all begins with procuring the hardware you need to dub analog media to digital, by outright purchase, loans, or a rental or two. There's a very old computer phrase, "GIGO: Garbage In, Garbage Out." If you shave a few dollars in the required hardware for the transfer process, it will show, and you'll spend more time than necessary coping with a punk transfer in Photoshop. It's sort of like retouching a severely compressed JPEG image when you could be working with a high-resolution PSD file.

Video Transfer Hardware

Let's assume the bulk of the video you want to archive is on VHS videotape format; I'll get to other video media types later in this chapter. What you need to copy the data to digital format on your hard disc are the following items:

- A VHS playback device—a tape deck in good working condition. Today, this might be a hard item to come by if you've retired your own unit. I recommend searching eBay or finding folks whose hobby is restoring and reconditioning VHS tape decks. Perform a search on Google using "VHS tape deck" as a key phrase. Alternatively, you might take an older VHS unit you already own and have a local electronics shop do some repair work on it. Of paramount importance is the quality of both the transport mechanism (the drives that pass the tape across the heads) and the condition of the playback head(s). You want them demagnetized and checked for any scratches that might cause a physical drop-out of video data when playing cassettes.

- An analog to digital (A-D) convertor. I was fortunate enough to work with a Canopus loaner unit while writing this book, and having grown familiar with its features, I cannot recommend anything else if you're serious about high-quality dubs. Some video cards come with video capture circuitry (some are good, while others are as sophisticated as an SD television tuner) and you can find "kits"—hardware and software that claim to make video transfers a fun and automated task—for as little as $89. (My response as a professional is a polite, "No, I don't think so.") You can expect to pay about $500 for a purchase of an A-D box that runs in the same league as Photoshop.

- A FireWire connection on your computer. Today, 99% of new Windows machines come with at least one FireWire port; all Macs come with one. If your PC doesn't have a FireWire port, you'll need a card and an empty slot on your motherboard. The good news is that cards can be had for around $30 from reputable manufacturers.

> **Note**
>
> *FireWire* is actually Apple Inc.'s brand name for this serial bus technology. When shopping, you might encounter the phrase "DV cable"—it's a FireWire connector. Similarly, the IEEE 1394 interface is a generic term for FireWire, and Sony likes to call it i.LINK in literature on their video products.

- Connector cables. You'll want to add to your shoebox collection an S-Video cable, a FireWire cable, and three RCA phono connectors, also called CINCH/AV connectors. RCA phono connectors are easy to come by at electronics stores, and although some might be labeled "best for digital video," what you're looking for is solid connectivity and throughput. The gold-tipped connectors are the darlings of audiophiles, and there is empirical evidence that these cables provide good throughput because gold doesn't oxidize. And gold connectors cost up to 10 times what you can get off the shelf at a department store. There's also a slim chance that you'd know the impedance of the A-D box; if you do, try to find cables that match the impedance for a clearer signal.

Video Transfer Software

To work backwards here, you want a digital copy of your analog movies in a file format that has lost the least amount of data during the process, and ideally it should be in a file format that you can work with in Photoshop. It is the job of the A-D convertor to encode the stream to a format that then goes to a host program for saving to disc in a specific file format.

There are some convertors, particularly the inexpensive ones, that offer a host application and will write to several different file formats. I caution you *never* to choose MPEG-2; although this is the standard for DVD encoding, it isn't the type of encoding you want for archiving. Within a few years, MPEG-2 will become a legacy file format, giving way to MPEG 4 or similar higher quality file encoding for commercial movie titles. MPEG-2 not only delivers quality that's inferior to other file compression/decompression (codec) schemes, but Photoshop cannot read an MPEG-2 formatted video.

Nearly ubiquitous is the DV-AVI digital video stream; most DV cameras use this as an encoding scheme, and it offers good compression and very good video quality. Photoshop, Adobe Premiere, and other products can read a DV-AVI encoded video. Usually, an A-D convertor comes with a host application, but you can indeed use Premiere, iMovie on the Mac, and Windows Movie Maker as host for getting the data stream from the tape deck, digitized through the A-D box, and then onto your hard disk.

Output Connects from the Source Media Player

Getting the connections set up correctly is the next step. Although I use a VHS cassette deck in this example, actually I can think of three electronic legacy media you might want to digitize, and the connections differ. For video tape decks, get your color-coded RCA cables, hook a white one to the left audio out and a red one to right audio out. The audio signal captured by the video camcorder was in all likelihood mono, but your video tape deck doesn't know that: It's probable that only the left channel originally had data, but the tape deck is splitting the mono signal so your home entertainment center has audio coming out of both (or more) speakers. Then hook a yellow RCA cable to the video out.

With most affordable video tape decks, the video out sends *composite* video data: it's a somewhat arbitrary blend of all the video information, and chances are good that the A-D box you bought or rented has a single composite video in jack.

> **Tip**
>
> Don't mistake *composite* video for *component* video. Composite video signals are "pre-mixed"; there is no way for a user to separate color or brightness attributes of the video. Component video comes in several standards, but the most common splits the RGB data into separate outputs, yielding a better signal. Component video outputs on a video deck are a high-end feature most consumers aren't likely to see, and as you might expect, you'd need a compatible A-D convertor to accept multiple channels of data.

However, it's possible that you have home movies recorded using a compact Video 8 camcorder, which takes those little cassettes that look quite like an audio cassette. Whether it's Video 8 or you still own a working VHS camcorder, check to see whether it has an S-Video out jack. Sometimes called "Super-Video," the "S" technically stands for "split video," also known as Y/C video. This is called *component* video splitting, and although it's a relatively low-end implementation of component video, it's better than a video composite stream. The signal is split into a luminosity channel (Y) and a chroma channel (C). In Figure 6.1, you can see an illustration of the back of a generic videotape deck and what should go where. If your tape deck has a coaxial connector, don't use it—it delivers a lousy signal and is intended to hook a deck up to the antenna in on an SD television.

For 15 minutes in history, read/write LaserDiscs were available; the ultimate demise of the storage system was due to the Helium-Neon laser tubes' expense and short life. The playback units have an S-Video output jack as well as RGB component jacks out. Unless your A-D box has separate R, G, and B leads, you'd use the S-Video out to the A-D box.

Figure 6.1
Use RCA cables to connect the videotape deck to the A-D convertor box.

From the Source to the A-D Unit

The reason I mentioned buying and using color-coded cables is because it's just easier to mate the signal outs with the corresponding signal ins on the analog to digital convertor box. Standard color-coding definitions are white = audio left, red = audio right, yellow = video, and S-Video cables are usually black. The Canopus ADVC 300 unit I used to digitize the media used later in this chapter as an example looks like the illustration in Figure 6.2. For videotape deck transfers I used all the RCA connections, and I also had some Video 8s, which took only the RCA left audio channel and the S-Video connector.

My Video 8 camcorder went belly up over 20 years ago, but fortunately I was able to buy one in mint condition on eBay for $100. The camera can play back as a standalone; a playback unit for these tiny videocassettes was manufactured, but today such a unit is more expensive than buying the camera.

> **Tip**
>
> The playback heads on Super 8 camcorders varied from manufacturer to manufacturer. If you don't have the camera used to record the Super 8 cassettes, and quality is of ultimate importance, take the camera you intend to play back the cassettes on to an expert at an electronics store and ask him to check the alignment of the playback heads to the media path—the little gate through which the tapes spools through the cassette. Realignment, and usually *un*alignment, can make the cassette play back with greater fidelity, and your digitizing process will yield better quality.

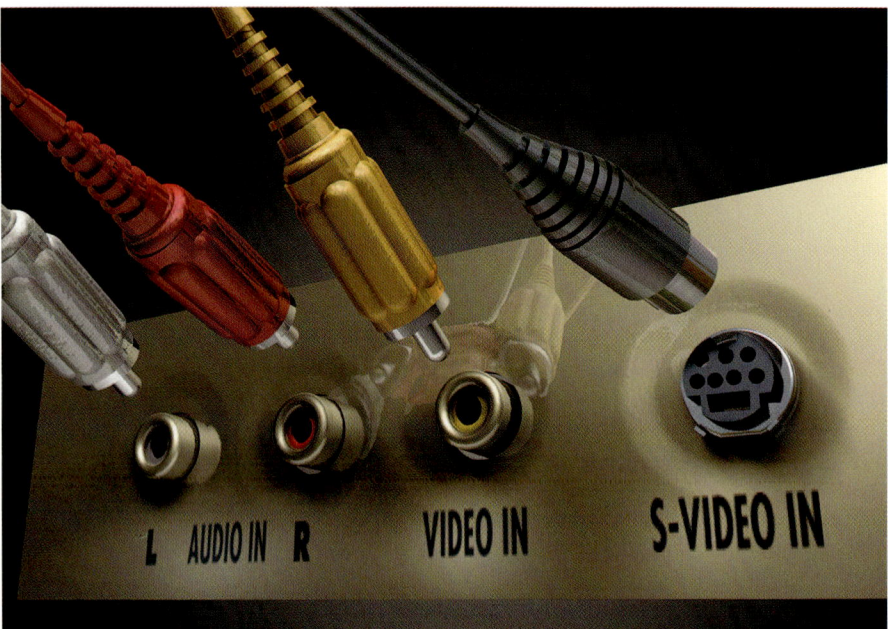

Figure 6.2
Use the corresponding inputs on the A-D unit for the videotape transfers.

> **Caution**
>
> Generally, it's a bad idea to try to jam a connector into an unyielding jack, along the lines of "don't run with the scissors." S-Video cables and jacks come in two different configurations: The four-pin (two grounds, a Y and a C pin) and the seven-pin. Today, almost all jacks are configured for seven pins, and a four-pin connector off a cable fits fine (the extra receptacles are not used). However, in rare instances you might have a seven-pin *connector* and a four-pin *receptacle*. Seven doesn't go into four evenly, not in math and not with electronics hardware, so don't even consider the brute force school of technology! Pay a visit instead to "the Shack," and the solution will cost you under $5.

FireWire Connection from A-D to Your Computer

As I mentioned previously, you need a FireWire cable to send the signal the A-D unit creates to your computer and ultimately to the application that hosts the transfer. In Figure 6.3 you can see my illustration of the back of the Canopus unit and what is called the DV/in-out port. Again, FireWire has many different names, and DV, contextually, is the same difference as FireWire. Don't worry; due to the "clipped rectangle" physical layout of the FireWire connector, you can't connect the cable to the wrong receptacle, and you can't put it in the wrong way except by using a hammer, which is not on my previous hardware list!

Figure 6.3
FireWire goes to FireWire. It's that simple.

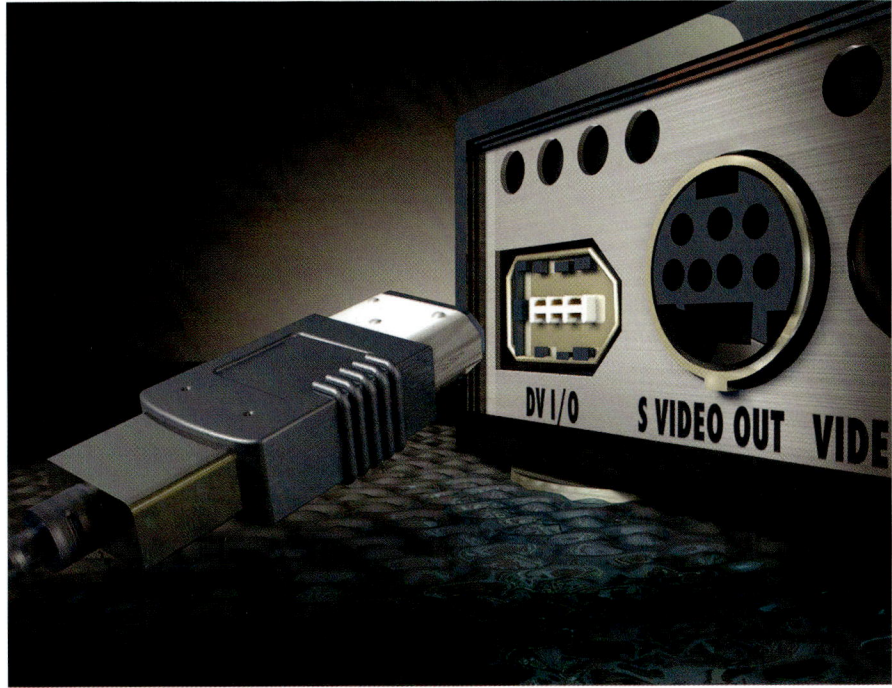

Firing Up A-D Convertor Filtering

The Canopus ADVC 300 comes with software; it's filtering software and not a host for raster image processing (ripping) the analog movies to digital format. This is where I found a clear difference between typical A-D boxes and the Canopus.

Here's the deal: First, the Canopus unit is "intelligent" in that it examines the data stream and offers corrections and enhancements as "pre" stage to the host application. It analyzes signal strength, improves it where necessary, and evens it out to prevent (or reduce) flickering. Additionally, it performs an audio lock to video, which many A-D boxes do not perform. Audio signals read from analog media are usually clocked by your computer operating system, and the bad news is that they can drift in time away from the analog video signal to the tune of one second per two minutes. After a few minutes, your heirloom movies (those that had audio) can sound like a foreign film dub. However, the Canopus unit has a dedicated chip inside to correct and lock original audio to video. Figure 6.4 shows two tabs of the Image Controller Panel, a utility you install, run, and then keep running while you rip your videos using your host application. The Canopus box directs the host application to correct for color, exposure, and other parameters and locks the audio to the video.

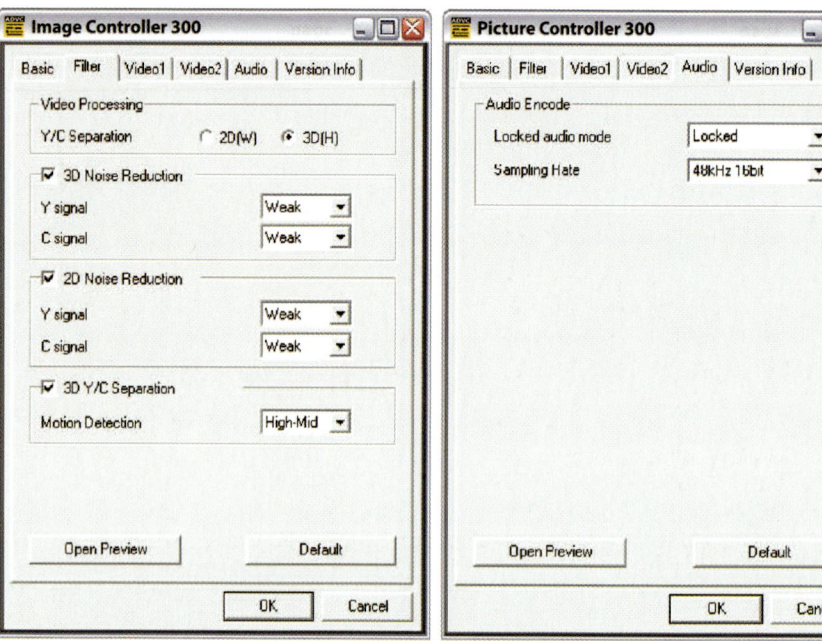

Figure 6.4
The Canopus and few other units can synch analog sound to its video source.

Using a Host Application for Transfers

With an A-D box, basically your rip from a videotape deck follows the same pipeline as a DV cam into the same host you use for downloading media from your camera. The connections are different, but essentially you're translating signals from a proprietary format to a format Photoshop and other applications can read and you can work with.

A lot of people on forums and several professionals I've spoken with prefer Adobe Premiere as a host; however, iMovie and Windows Movie Maker can be used successfully for ripping the videos. In Figure 6.5, I've launched Movie Maker; this simple host application enables me to split the original content into appropriate clips, for organization's sake and also to keep the saved files manageable in file size.

The monologue between the A-D unit and the host application for capturing the data stream is an important element, worth discussing for a moment here. The Canopus box with my transfer is interpreting analog data and passing it along in a language it speaks. With the Canopus, the data stream is DV-AVI, although other brands of A-D convertors speak anything from AVI to MPEG-2 and MPEG-4. Actually, the makers of the unit, Grass Valley, call this "Canopus AVI"; the term "AVI" isn't a Windows-ism in this sense, but merely means "the audio and video are being interlaced so they don't drift later on." This is also called *quantizing* (changing floating values to whole number, fixed values) a stream of information. The host application must understand the language; in my situation,

Figure 6.5
The A-D convertor "talks" to the host application.

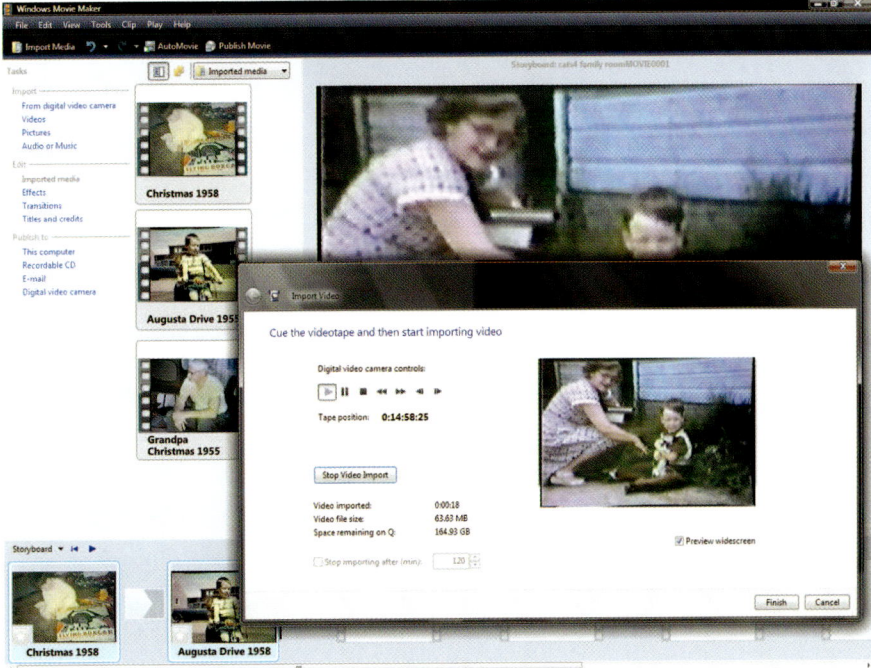

Movie Maker is being told there's a device sending data, it doesn't care whether it's a DV cam or a videotape deck, and it recognizes the stream as AVI. Therefore, I save from Movie Maker to Windows AVI file format, and life is good; Photoshop can indeed open the video with audio intact. End of hardware story.

Retouching Motion Pictures

For all the Canopus ADVC 300 unit was able to do to comb the data stream and improve color wherever needed, Christmas gift.mov, the example file with which you'll work in the following sections, is not a flawless memory. There are a number of color and exposure corrections I show you how to perform, and it's both a creative and emotional kick to work with videos of yourself as a child!

Super 8 to Digital File Format

Physical film transfer to digital format cannot be done at home. However, there are services who can write a DVD from your Super 8s, avoiding the cost of an A-D unit.

As with shopping for anything, services vary in quality; you have video service bureaus and then there's the corner drug store (which sends the work to a video service bureau, charging you less, taking less of the bureau's time to deliver lower quality). On the high end of quality and expense, every frame can be scanned. More affordable and of less finished quality, most transfer places use a projection rig that transmits light through the film as it passes through a gate, onto a micro-polished mirror, and then into a lens system that records onto digital media.

I should warn you that if you do opt for the cheap route, the sacrifice is always quality. With the Christmas gift.mov clip, I had no choice; the film was transferred to videotape 30 years ago, and I can't locate the film. As a partial consolation, you might notice that quality often takes a back seat to the emotional impact of just seeing one's family in motion decades ago, albeit through sepia-tinted glasses.

Specifically request a service to clean the film for you, and if you clean it yourself, I don't recommend making physical contact. Instead, use a can of air. If possible, if the service is in town, ask if you can watch. Not only can you learn, but you might also kibbutz. For example, the folks who did my transfers didn't close the gate on the transfer machine quite tightly enough; I pointed this out along the way, but many rips show inward-bowed frame edges. As far as delivering the digitized movies to you, do not request an authored DVD, which uses MPEG-2 compression, subpar quality as a consequence, and Photoshop cannot read MPEG-2s. Ask for the original digital file (no lossy compression) on one or more DVDs.

Many commercial services also offer at a premium to put a stock soundtrack to your silent home movies. Nahhhhh; I show you in this book how to add your own audio and how to time it.

Smart Objects and Adjustments

Figure 6.6 shows a frame from Christmas gift.mov. Here's the scoop on correcting color and exposure with placed video files (Chapter 5 has more complete documentation): Movies are made up of frames. You have every menu item and every tool available to you when you edit a movie in Photoshop, but only frame by frame. This means you'd need a script to apply, for example, the Watercolor Artistic Filter to 30 seconds of footage (see Chapter 4 for a useful script). However, if you put the placed video in a Smart Object "wrapper," you have fewer menu options from which you apply an adjustment (and virtually no Tools palette tools), but this Smart Object enables you to apply, for example, the same Filter > Artistic Filters > Watercolor to the entire video clip.

If you need to directly edit one frame—perhaps there's a hair in one frame that was trapped in the projection gate—you choose Edit Contents from the context menu by right-clicking over the Smart Object layer. Doing this extracts the unretouched video from the Smart Object container "wrapper," and you do your single or multiple frame retouching.

The good news about Smart Objects is that they, and most media on layers, accept an Adjustment layer placed above them in the layer stack. As a bonus, all filters and Adjustment layers come with a layer mask; you paint over the mask using shades of black to hide or expose the effect of the filter and/or adjustment.

"Smart" Restoring the Video Clip

Analysis is the first step before changing Pixel One in digital videos. Open Christmas gift.mov now; then choose View and uncheck Pixel Aspect Ratio Correction. Doing this doesn't change the video, but rather it changes your view of it. This video was intended for burning to DVD and, as such, required a .9 pixel aspect ratio for playback on a standard definition (SD) TV set.

The list of defects is as follows:

1. The color is casting warm due to age. If you're experienced in Photoshop still-image restoration, you know that color and brightness are interrelated; you change one, and the other takes on a different quality. So one of the first things you'll do is experiment with levels first, see if this doesn't take some mud out of the video, and then proceed to a little selective color balancing.

2. The overall focus is poor. I show you later some methods for enhancing focus. A blurry image is never going to become sharp, but you can improve edges in the picture's visual content.

3. There is some vignetting. Notice how there's light falloff at the edges of the frame. This is partially due to a very directional floodlight when the movie was taken and also because the video transfer uses a single-source, somewhat directional light to project the image onto a receiver for scanning. This can be corrected, too.

4. The gate wasn't tight when the film was digitized, so the edges of the frame are bowed. Actually, you probably don't want to ask an operator to "keep the gate closed tight, please" because scratching the original film might occur.

Figure 6.6 is a frame from the movie. You'll address color and exposure in the following set of steps.

1. Right-click over the video layer on the Layers palette and then choose Convert to Smart Object from the context menu. Notice that the tag on the lower right of the layer thumbnail changes from a tiny filmstrip to an icon that indicates something is contained in a document.

2. Click the Create New Fill or Adjustment Layer icon on the Layers palette and then choose Levels from the list.

172 Adobe Photoshop CS3 Extended: Retouching Motion Pictures

Figure 6.6
This digitized Super 8 movie suffers from both physical aging and a less than professional capture.

3. I tried experimenting with the Eyedropper tools to sample the white point (the white of the toy box, apparent 3.5 seconds into the clip) and set a black point. Actually, in this example, clicking the Auto button can work. As you can see in Figure 6.7, not only does detail come out of the murk, but colors have been greatly improved.

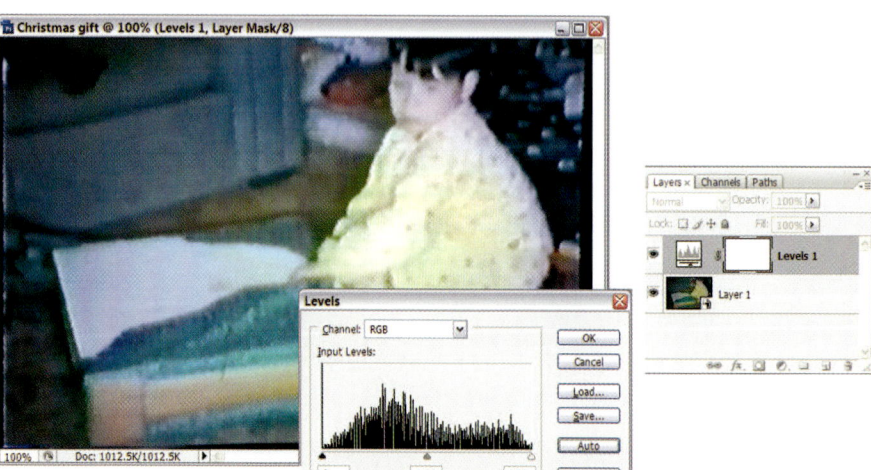

Figure 6.7
Correct levels first and see if this doesn't solve a lot of color problems.

Traveling Masks and Local Adjustments

If your vintage video is really important to you, and you're unhappy with an area of an Adjustment layer, you have two Photoshop features at your disposal to create local corrections: the layer mask that accompanies an Adjustment layer and the position change on the Animation palette's video tracks. In this example I'm content with the overall levels correction but not with the pajamas—the chest area is too hot and lacks the detail of the pattern. This can be corrected by first isolating an area of the footage where the kid remains fairly static (Frames 72 through 190 in Figure 6.8). Then you paint using black to hide the Levels Adjustment layer areas using partial opacity (about 45% in this case) and the Brush tool over the areas that are too bright. You then click the Layer Mask Position stopwatch on the Animation palette to set a key. Scrub the timeline to arrive at a point where the kid has moved significantly and then move the layer mask with the Move tool, automatically setting another key on the timeline. Additionally, in Figure 6.8, I needed to locally adjust the color casting of the pajama top because when I hid some of the Levels the brightness adjustment to the pajama top took on a yellowish cast. This can be done by copying the Levels mask as I show later in this chapter.

It's important to use partial opacity and a soft brush tip when editing the Adjustment layer mask; from this point, you isolate and then refine the other video segments until you have a completely restored video clip.

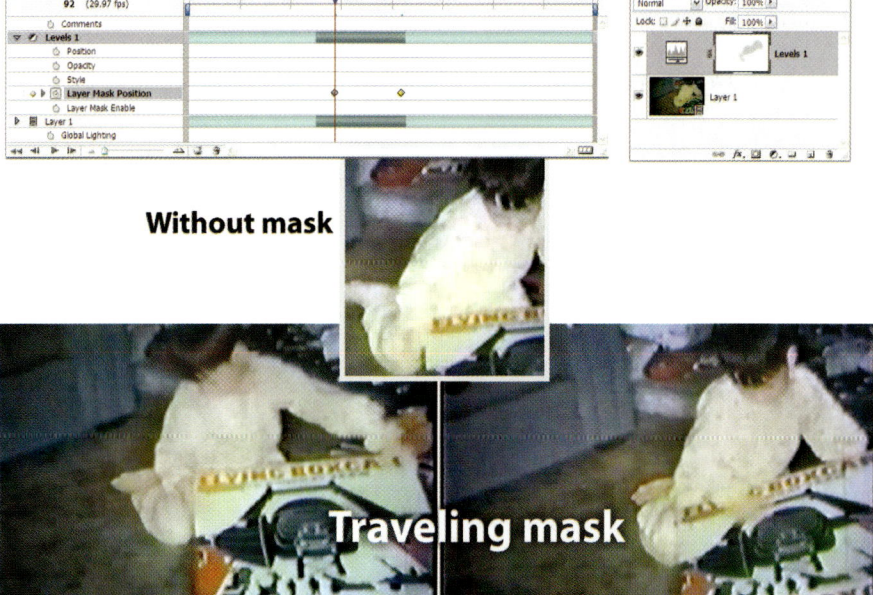

Figure 6.8
Hide Adjustment layer mask areas and then move the mask over time to create local corrections.

> **Tip**
>
> If you need to readjust the settings for an Adjustment layer, double-click the Adjustment icon on the Layers palette list—the icon to the left of the thumbnail of the mask.

Adjustment Mask Editing and Duplicating

The preceding sidebar, "Traveling Masks and Local Adjustments," is a taxi driver's tour of a technique for applying local correction to a short video sequence and, where necessary, moving the local adjustment over time. Due to the use of floodlights with mid-twentieth century home movies and the uneven aging of the original film, you'll probably find yourself in a situation where areas, but not all of a scene, needs fine-tuning. Christmas gift.mov provides a good test-bed to selectively correct the levels of the scene; from Frame 24 through 74 the boy and the camera are pretty static. Notice, however, that the uniform Levels Adjustment layer results in the kid running exceptionally bright, and details are lost in certain areas. Without animating the Adjustment layer, you'll simply retouch the mask in the following steps to tone down the areas in frame that show over compensation for lighting as a "nearly the best method, I can accomplish this within a lifetime" sort of edit. The result will be a much better overall exposure for this segment, but it will also introduce some unappealing yellow color casting. You correct levels locally and then move on to correcting the color balance; it's the smartest SOP for this video restoration.

1. On the Animation palette, drag the start and ends of the tracks for both the video and the Levels layer to begin at about 24 and end at 74. Doing this will result in only editing Frames 24 through 74; to retouch the entire 8s15f clip you have to work in segments, write the segments out as rendered video, and then do a final compile using all the rendered video.

2. Click the mask thumbnail for Levels 1 on the Layers palette to edit it. Choose the Gradient tool, set the current foreground color to black and background to white (pressing D does this), and choose the Radial gradient style at about 45% opacity on the Options bar.

3. Drag in the document window starting where the pajamas meet the box and then release the mouse button when you reach the red toy doctor's kit. As you can see in Figure 6.9, some detail has returned to the pajamas, and because the Radial gradient makes a smooth, progressive transition to white, there are no hard edges between the hidden mask areas (black) and active mask areas (white).

Figure 6.9
Use a Radial gradient on the Levels Adjustment layer mask to tone down a central area, fading the mask outward in the video frame(s).

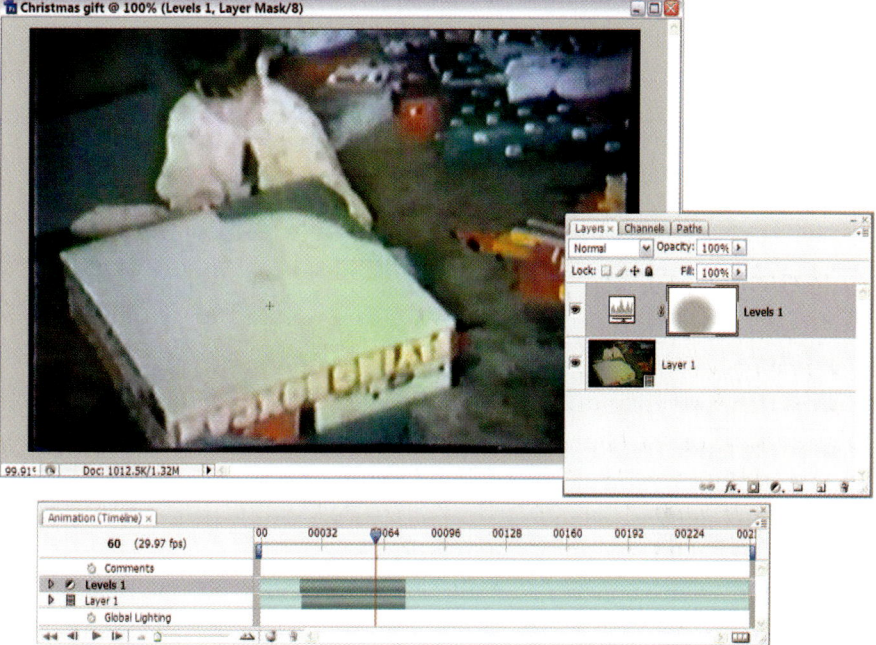

4. Because there are more brightness levels in the pajama area, there's more space to display color casting; the kid's pajamas were originally off-white, not pale yellow, and surrounding facial areas that are yellowish is the clue here. Click the Create a New Fill or Adjustment Layer icon on the bottom of the Layers palette: choose Color Balance.

5. With Midtones selected in the color Balance box, try +25 Red, −14 toward Magenta, and −8 toward Yellow. Doing this helps correct the kid's skin tones—skin tones with Caucasians display the most color in the midrange of brightness scales. Doing this also creates very little color correction on the pajamas because their tone lies in the highlight region.

6. Click the Highlights radio button and then try moving the Yellow/Blue slider about +30 toward blue. Click OK to apply.

7. You only want to color balance the same areas that are adjusted for levels; hold Alt/Opt and then drag the Levels mask (thumbnail) up to the Color Balance mask. Reply Yes in the following box, which asks if you want to replace the Layer mask. You've duplicated the masked area from your levels work, and the video should look a lot better, as shown in Figure 6.10.

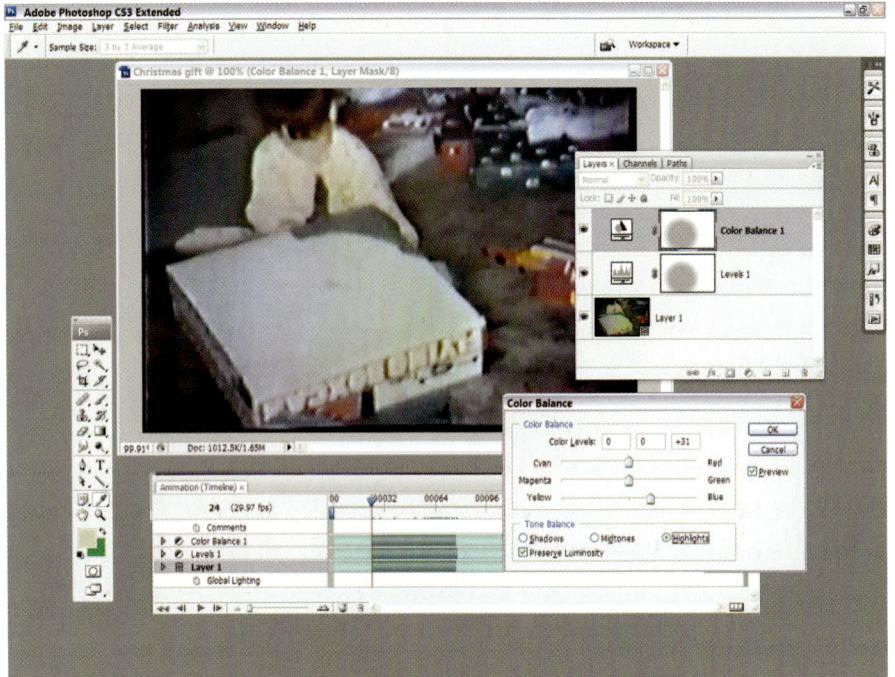

Figure 6.10
Color correct the same areas that you corrected for brightness values.

Working with the Photo Filter

Whether it's a still image or video footage, occasionally you need to work backwards before moving forward. Although the sequence between Frames 24 and 74 is much improved, I believe that using a Photo Filter Adjustment layer now will help separate the star of the clip (the kid) from a background with respect to color temperature. The kid's face is now running a little too warm, the pajamas are close to but not exactly neutral, and the box he's unwrapping should be showing bright primary colors, but they too are casting warm.

Between 24 and 74, the box is almost completely static in the scene and the areas I've mentioned move, but they don't move a lot. Therefore, in the following steps you'll apply a cooling photo filter as an Adjustment layer and then edit the mask to affect the pajamas at partial opacity, the kid's face at less opacity, and the front of the box at full opacity:

1. Peek ahead to Figure 6.11; I've altered this screen capture to show frame areas where you need to select, partially and fully. Go to Quick Mask mode and then use the Polygonal Lasso tool to select the front of the toy box and then fill the selection. Deselect and then with the Brush tool set to about 65 pixels in diameter at about 50% opacity, stroke over the pajamas and the kid's

face. Then set the Brush tool to Clear Painting mode, about 50% opacity on the Options bar. Stroke over the kid's face in one pass to make the mask less opaque (less selected when you apply the Adjustment layer mask).

2. Go back to Standard Editing mode. You want the areas you filled with Quick Mask to be selected and not masked; if your Quick Mask options are set up as Color Indicates Masked areas, your marquee is inverted right now, and you'll see a marquee around the border of the document window. If this is the case, press Shift+F7 and you're good to go.

3. Click the Create a New Fill or Adjustment Layer icon on the bottom of the Layers palette, and then choose Photo Filter from the context menu. Notice that your selected areas are immediately understood by the Adjustment layer, the selected areas are written into the Adjustment layer mask, and your on-screen preview is accurate and as intended. Choose Cooling Filter 80, click OK, and your document should look like that in Figure 6.11. Understand that my color corrections in this and the previous section are based on my own artistic sensibilities, which you might not share. Therefore, as long as you get the principles I describe here, you can riff on them with this video and, more importantly, your own. So if in Color Balance you feel the highlights should go more toward blue and yellow than values I've suggested, trust your own eye on this call.

Figure 6.11
Use the Photo Filter adjustment to reduce warm casts in selected areas.

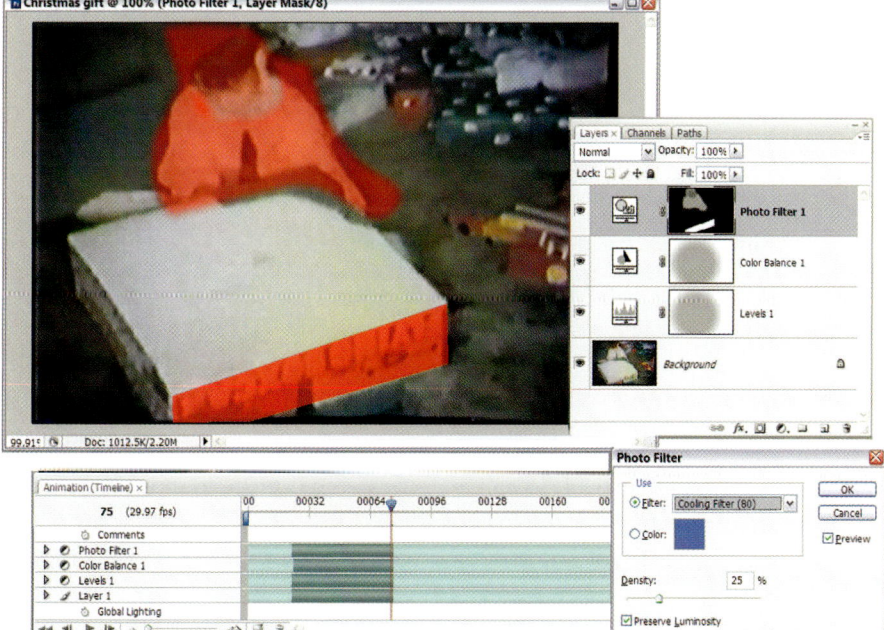

4. Remember that you've only enhanced Frames 24 through 74; if you specify this range in the Render Video box, there is no need to adjust the Work Area start and end markers on the Animation palette to bracket the frames to write to video. Choose File > Export > Render Video, choose QuickTime as the file format, use None in Compression Settings, return to the main Render Video box, click the In Frame radio button, type **24** in the first field, type **74** in the Out Frame field, choose a convenient location on your hard drive to render the video, and then click Render. Keep the file open for the following section.

All the corrections I've described in previous sections are local to a specific time range, such as Frames 24 to 74. When a cut or a change in lighting (or scene content) occurs, it is at that point you want to isolate the segment using the techniques described earlier, and then most likely work with new Adjustment layers, different masks, and different settings. However, this is as tedious as it gets, remembering the value of the completed, restored video.

Now that you have the steps tucked away for local changes, the next section moves to creating global changes, changes that affect the entire video clip. To create global changes, you need to first bring all the retouched segments into one document and then arrange the segments into a continuous clip; see Chapter 4 on creating cuts and arranging segments into a video composition.

Using Lens Correction

As you can see in Figure 6.12, brightness falloff (vignetting) is a problem throughout the video; it becomes particularly evident after adjusting the levels of any of the segments.

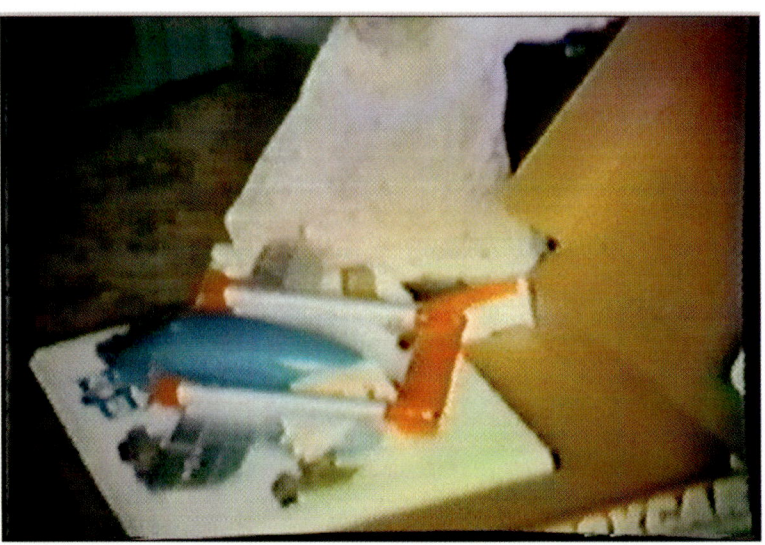

Figure 6.12
Lighting falloff can occur for several reasons; fortunately, Photoshop has a cure.

Lens Correction is in the Distort group of filters, I imagine because it actually *does* distort images—back to their intended state. Because a filter applied to a Smart Object video is a global change, it plays throughout the duration of a video unless you hide part of the track as you did with levels.

1. If you edited all the segments, stitched them together, and rendered a video, bring the video into Photoshop. If you didn't, use the current video at a time on the timeline where you have active Adjustment layers in place. Click the Smart Object video layer on the Layers palette to select it.

2. Choose Filter > Distort > Lens Correction.

3. Turn off the grid (the checkbox is at the bottom). Make sure Preview is enabled so you can see the cumulative effect of your editing work if you're using the original clip with Adjustment layers. Set Vignette Amount to +45 (lighten) and then set Midpoint (the falloff of the vignette; lower values make the "gradient" that corrects the vignette less contrasty) to about +45, as shown in Figure 6.13. Click OK to apply the filter. You'll see that a lot of the background toward the frame edges is now visible, but unfortunately, there's an upper limit to the restoration, so in this example file, you can't restore areas where lighting has fallen off to 100% visibility. There's no real way to cull visual information from pixels that are R:0, B: 0, G: 0. The good news is that via Adjustment layers, a lot of compensation performed earlier helps support this anti-vignetting step.

Figure 6.13
Lighten the edges of the video by using Lens Correction.

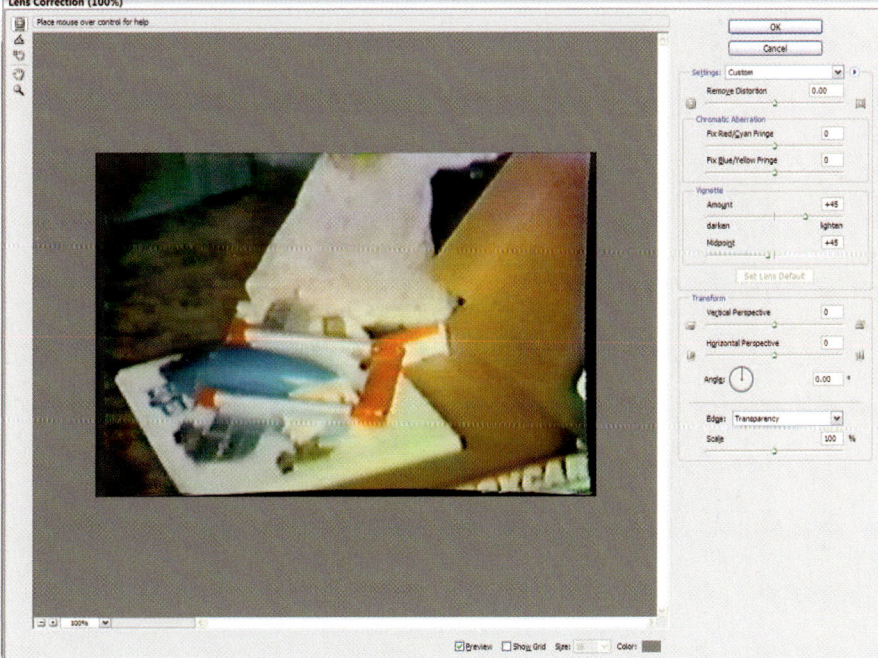

Manually Correcting the Film Warp

As I mentioned earlier, and as you can see quite well, the right side of the frame bows inward due to the film not passing accurately through the device that transferred the film to digital file format. You could use Lens Correction to remove bowing on all sides of a video (called *pincushioning* and also *barrel distortion*), but only one side of the film looks wrong. To fix this, you Free Transform the video, which means temporarily taking it out of its Smart Object shell, as follows:

1. With the video layer selected on the Layers palette, press Ctrl/Cmd+T.

2. Click OK in the attention box. It tells you that smart filters need to be disabled while you edit the video.

3. Right-click in the document window and then choose Warp from the context menu.

4. You can use the bounding box handles to warp a video, but in this example, it's easier and more accurate to put your cursor at about 3 o'clock and then click+drag (push) to the right until the warped edge looks unwarped, as shown in Figure 6.14. Actually, the overall look of the video will improve noticeably now that the edge is straightened, pushing the video out and to the right a little (undistorting it). If necessary, fix the bottom edge slightly, too. Click the check icon on the Options bar to apply the Warp Free Transform.

Figure 6.14
Use the Warp Free Transform to selectively restore an edge of a video clip.

Enhancing Focus

The example movie, as I mentioned earlier, is a rip from original Super 8mm film. Super 8s were actually of decent resolution: A frame size of 5.6mm (0.22 in) by 4.14mm (0.163 inches) actually yields a frame of 756 by 553 pixels, greater than SD broadcast TV. However, most of the problem with restoring Super 8 footage is due to the Silver Halide clusters—the grain—which varies in size, depending on how the film was pushed during processing.

Sharpening videos that have noticeable grain is usually problematic; most Photoshop filters will heighten the grain while sharpening the video content because the filters see the grain as an object. However, if you follow these steps with less-than-razor-sharp videos such as Christmas gift.mov, you stand a much better chance of crisping up edges without emphasizing the film grain:

1. On the Layers palette, click on the video layer and press Ctrl/Cmd+J to duplicate the video layer.

2. Click the top duplicate video layer title on the Layers palette and then choose Filter > Other > High Pass. The image will look all gray; the goal here is to find a setting through which edges of the objects in the video preview window are visible and well defined. A Radius setting of 3.9 pixels works well for this video example. Click OK.

3. On the Layers palette, change blending mode for this layer to Overlay. If you turn the visibility of this layer on and off, you can clearly see the difference in this layer's contribution to sharpening the video image.

The advantage to this method is that the sharpening effect is completely isolated to a separate layer, and the pixels on the original layer are not changed in any way. Additionally, because the sharpening effect is on a separate layer, you also have the option to lower the opacity for the layer if you feel the overall effect is too strong.

Polishing the Presentation and Exporting

Because this eight-second clip is hardly worthy of the silver screen, and because my relatives who don't all own computers want to see the clip, writing the composition out to DV is the logical next step. However, playback on a television set, particularly a standard definition TV, is going to crop out some precious border pixels in the composition. TV sets don't play back videos edge-to-edge as computer monitors do. Largely analog devices, TV sets overscan the media (more expensive TV sets allow adjustment of scanning, but don't count on it); approximately 10% of the outside of video is clipped through overscanning, and therefore a really good idea is to pad your video by at least 10% as a measure of overscanning compensation. The following steps take you through this simple trick; then I show you how to render the composition to video.

1. Right-click the document's title bar and then choose Canvas Size.

2. In the Canvas Size box, set the units to Percent, and then type **110** in both the Width and Height fields, as shown in Figure 6.15. Click OK.

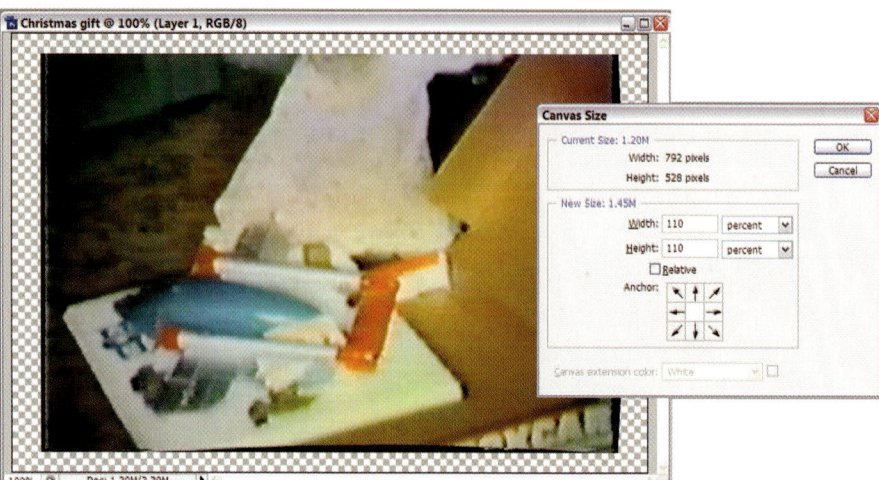

Figure 6.15
Increase the size of the canvas without enlarging the video itself.

3. Create a new layer on the Layers palette, drag it to the bottom of the layers stack, and then fill it with black.

4. Choose File > Export > Render Video.

5. In the File Options field, choose QuickTime and then for the Size drop-down list choose NTSC DV (or PAL if your audience is South American, Nordic, or another nationality whose standards are PAL; most of the world uses NTSC). What you're doing is rendering to a document size that is the same aspect ratio as TV even though the document in Photoshop is 10% larger. This means you have not messed up your composition and can re-render it in the future for different output needs.

6. Click the Settings button and then click Settings to display the Compression Settings box. Choose None from the drop-down list, choose 29.97 fps as the Frame Rate (see Chapter 17 for details on compression schemes), Best Quality, Millions of Colors, and then click OK to apply the settings. Click OK again to return to Render Video.

7. Choose a location on hard disk that has at least 200MB of free space and then click Render. See Figure 6.16.

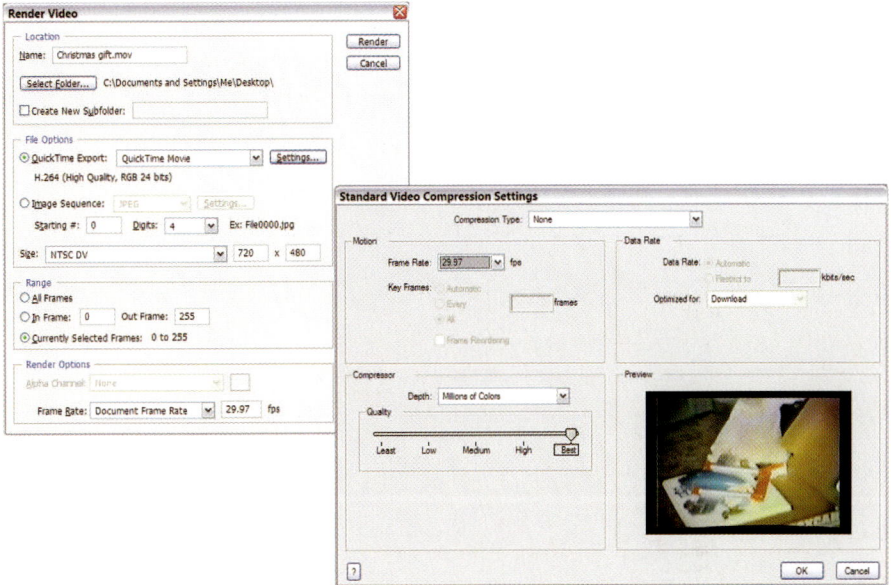

Figure 6.16
Use these settings to write a high-fidelity video from your edited and enhanced vintage video.

You'll need DVD authoring software to get the resulting rendered video on to a DVD. I recommended QuickTime as the file format in the previous tutorial because Photoshop only supports audio in rendered video using QuickTime file as the export. Photoshop's rendering engine is licensed from Apple, Inc., and other file exports will not render with audio. This then becomes problematic with Windows users looking for an authoring program because even though you specified None as the compressor, there's a kernel of MPEG-4 in QuickTime technology, and some authoring programs such as Nero can't transcode MPEG-4 to the necessary MPEG-2 to write to a DVD that'll play in a TV set's DVD player. Here's the deal: MPEG-4 at Highest Quality setting doesn't lose original video information, but it does remove redundant pixels in neighboring frames to gain a little lossless compression. Windows users can buy Adobe Premiere Elements for less than $100, and it reads all QuickTime codecs fine, and it will write to DVD standards fine. Alternatively, you can write a rendered video to AVI file format with no audio and then add a soundtrack to silent original videos using most DVD authoring apps; even Microsoft's Movie Maker, the free utility that ships with XP and Vista, enables you to add audio.

All in all, you now have the steps and techniques for preserving analog video. It helps to think of video restoration using Photoshop as a very similar process to restoring still images. Between Smart Objects and Adjustment layers, it's a slightly longer route to restoring a video, but the process is quite similar to scanning an heirloom family photograph and then bringing out the details hidden by aging.

7

Titling and Animating Text

Although video has been accompanied with audio since 1923, text continues to appear on screens everywhere for several important reasons. Professionals who contribute their expertise to a motion pictures sort of appreciate seeing their name during the credits. Ad agencies optimize a selling message in 30 seconds by repeating what the announcer is saying in 3" tall block lettering. And let's not forget accommodations for the hearing impaired and audiences who don't speak a certain language—subtitles call for a handy-dandy Type tool!

This chapter takes you through the use of Photoshop's Type tool and various techniques for animating text: fades in and out, scrolls (crawls), special effects treatment of text, and the gamut of creative things you can do with the printed word on film.

Measuring Screen Safety

With standard definition (SD) televisions, which still occupy the family rooms of 90% of today's homes, you are completely at the mercy of a broadcaster and the television owner for the accuracy and fidelity of the work you've published. TV sets are notorious for overscanning, and the consequence is that most of the time at least 10% of your video area is clipped outside of the screen. NTSC standards were developed a long time ago to compensate for inaccurate display by publishing screen safety standards that happily Adobe has adopted and implemented in CS3 Extended. The first thing you want to do when creating a title for a video is to measure the video aspect ratio; for the following example let's assume you want to put a title on a video that came off a prosumer camera—720 × 480 pixels with a .9 pixel aspect ratio. Ctrl/Cmd+double-click the workspace to open a new document and then choose Film & Video from the Presets drop-down list as shown in Figure 7.1. If your target video is nonstandard in aspect ratio, you can choose from the Pixel Aspect Ratio drop-down list. Do not choose to manage the color profile. Video does not use the same color space as your past still-image Photoshop work for screen or print; your exported work will look lousy if you've color profiled your work and chosen a video codec such as MPEG-4.

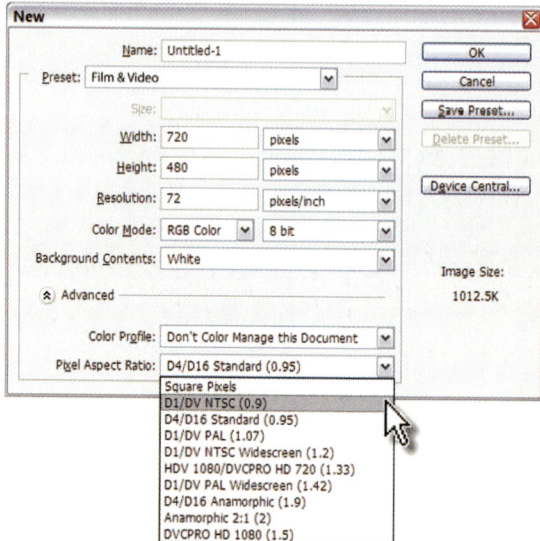

Figure 7.1
Choose a standard size and aspect ratio for your video titling work from Presets in the New dialog box.

> **Tip**
>
> Similar to TV display, theaters also don't usually project films accurately on the screen. If you sit in the front row sometime, you'll notice a light-absorbing material bordering the screen to hide projection spill and present the audience with a clean, rectangular image.

Notice that the new document by default has guides already positioned for you. The outside guides define the "best case" scenario—10% clipped from the video by television overscanning (and most likely an area clipped by poor projectionist aligning work in movie theaters). The worst-case is defined by the inside guides, at 25%. I suggest that you play to the "cheap seats" as a regular practice and keep your titles inside the 25% guides. In addition to the newly created document, load any video clip you like for the following tutorial.

In the steps to follow I show you how to get a title onto a video clip and then make the title legible to the audience.

1. With your clip in the foreground in the workspace, choose View and then uncheck Pixel Aspect Ratio Correction so you're working with an undistorted view of the video composition. On the Layers palette, click+drag the Video layer into the new document while holding Shift, which forces Photoshop to center the duplicated layer. You can close the original video clip without saving at any time.

2. Choose the Type tool (give it a second or two to parse your list of installed system fonts) and then choose a font, a font size, and a font color (I recommend white or black, whichever contrasts with the overall underlying video) from the Options bar. I recommend center alignment, available on the Options bar—you can then click in the center of the document window and type away and the text is basically centered onscreen. Now type some text that is appropriate for your chosen video.

Fonts for Video

There are a number of do's and don'ts for type specification for video titling that depend on the media on which your video is played. As far as size of text is concerned, video podcasts are usually played on a very small screen, and therefore your video should be designed within medium of close-ups, including your text. For example, a 320 by 240 phone screen demands a titling point size of no less than 30 points for "subtle" text. For playback on a monitor that is at least 19", full screen, although your video dimensions are 720 by 480, the playback onscreen will be larger, and 48 point text will be legible, particularly if you use a bold typeface. Also, you probably want to render the text using the Sharp anti-aliasing setting on the Options bar for small videos (YouTube, phones with screens, or video tutorials you might author for online access), and you can ease off to Strong or Crisp for presentation on TV sets. For motion pictures, video files are usually written to 2 to 4K (2,000 pixels on a side to 4,000 pixels on a side), so if you're lucky enough to get a gig doing motion picture titles, you'd set your title document size to match the dimensions of the film you are titling. A clear, legible subtitle for widescreen films is about 225 points.

Your choice of typefaces must be subordinate to the film and legible. For years I didn't understand why character generators for videotape had such uninspired font selections, but a font face such as Helvetica Condensed bold is used over and over again in film and video for a number of good reasons, beginning with perfect legibility. Serif typefaces are not as legible; although serif fonts (Times, Garamond,

> Palatino) are a "quick read" for the printed message in physical books, researchers discovered years ago that sans serif typefaces (Helvetica, Optima, Futura) are read more quickly on the Web and in video than the same message cast in a serif font. Similarly, consistent stroke within a font's characters allows the audience to read the message more quickly than Roman fonts that have thick and thin strokes in their glyphs.
>
> Especially on broadcast TV, the weight of a font must be more than 2 pixels; if you use a Roman typeface whose characters have strokes less than 2 pixels in breadth, the audience will see *twittering* in your text message. Strive for a font weight and height where all strokes are at least 2 pixels; 5 is better.

3. After you've typed your text, it might be time to fine-tune the size and perhaps the proportions. Because text is vector in nature in Photoshop until you do something to rasterize it, it can be scaled and distorted while remaining crisp and legible. Try this: Press Ctrl/Cmd+T to put the text into Free Transform mode and then with the Move tool, drag a corner handle to scale the text (or hold Shift to constrain the proportions, to not distort the text). When the text looks more to your liking, press Enter to apply the transformation (or double-click inside the Free Transform bounding box…or click the check icon on the Options bar; there are several ways to do most things in Photoshop). In Figure 7.2 you can see that I wanted a slightly taller look from my font than was originally cast. In general, experts advise that condensed typefaces do not slow down a reader significantly, and the benefit to a designer is that you can get more words to the line.

4. Unlike page layout, it's difficult to choose a solid text color that separates from the underlying video because color areas move while a text message appears onscreen! A traditional solution has been to use a contrasting drop-shadow, but you can do better using Photoshop. On the Layers palette, click the fx icon and then choose Outer Glow from the drop-down menu.

5. In the Layer Style dialog box, set the Blending Mode choice to Multiply, not Screen. Then click the color swatch and pick black from the Color Picker. Because you're previewing live (see Figure 7.3), you can fine-tune the opacity and the Spread and Size until the text reads well, but the effect doesn't steal from the text or the content of the video. Unfortunately, you can't advance the video to see how the text reads across the duration of the video. Therefore, you apply the Layer style, press Enter to play the video, and if or when the text fails to read, press Enter to stop the video and then double-click the Outer Glow entry on the Layers palette, and then adjust the effect.

Chapter 7 ■ Titling and Animating Text 189

6. Export your video with the tiling. See Chapters 1 and 2 for the rough details on using File > Export > Render Video, and see Chapter 17 for file format options.

Figure 7.2
Text can be tweaked using the Move tool in combination with Free Transform.

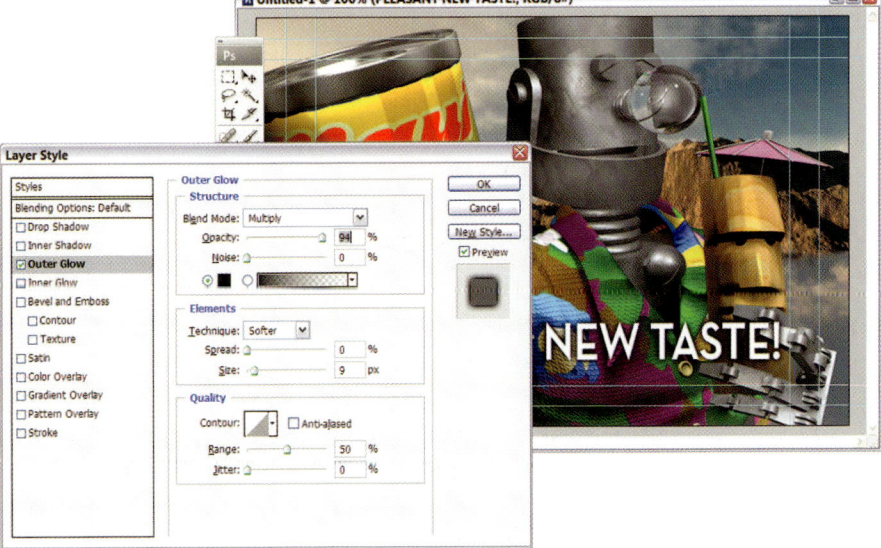

Figure 7.3
Apply a Layer style to enable the text message to be read.

Creating Subtitles

My family has grown up in the United States for over a century, but I still have relatives in France, and yep, they speak French—and I thought I'd send them some videos of my late grandmother, whom they've only heard about. I thought it would be a friendly and familial gesture to subtitle the videos, and Photoshop makes this an easy process. First, when you need to create subtitles, you use the rules I mentioned in the previous section concerning font size and other attributes. The next step, for the sake of convenience and accuracy, is to have a text editor or word processor open in the background while you work, loaded with the translations you need to cast. I use Microsoft Word because Photoshop recognizes extended type characters copied from the clipboard: all the acute accents, grave accents, and cedillas that are part of the French language, and even proper quote marks (curly quotes), whereas a plain text editor usually doesn't know about proper quote glyphs.

Open GrandmaBouton.mov and French.pdf in Acrobat Reader, a document with the text for the following tutorial. Fortunately, you don't need to own a word processor to copy text containing extended characters when someone has written the text to PDF. There are two sentences in the video clip and two phrases I translated to French in the PDF file. What you'll learn is how to time a subtitle, how to make it appear and disappear in rough synch with the audio dialog in the video.

1. In Acrobat Reader, load French.pdf and then with the text and image Select tool, highlight "Oh, qui est cela?" and copy it to the clipboard. Keep Acrobat Reader open and switch to Photoshop.

2. In Photoshop, create a new document based on the Film & Video preset.

3. Shift+drag the loaded GrandmaBouton.mov layer on the Layers palette into the new document window. You can delete the Background layer and close the original Grandma clip without saving. Because new Film & Video documents have a default duration of 10 seconds, the document is shorter than its contents (GrandmaBouton.move plays for 13;19). Click the Animation Palette menu, choose Document Settings, and then adjust the duration to 13;19 so my grandmother isn't clipped. Save the new document as GrandmaBouton.psd.

4. In Photoshop, with GrandmaBouton.mov loaded in a document window, choose the Type tool and on the Options bar set the typeface to a sans serif font (I'm using Helvetica Condensed bold in these figures), white, and about 42–48 points in size, center justification.

5. Click an insertion point in the vertical center of the window, right over my hands in the document, where one would expect a subtitle, above the 25% safety guide. Then press Ctrl/Cmd+V to paste the clipboard text into the document window. With the Move tool, reposition the text if necessary.

6. Add a Drop Shadow style to the text to allow it to be read more clearly, just like you did in the first tutorial. In Figure 7.4, I've clicked the fx icon on the Layers palette and chosen Drop Shadow, and I'm playing with the Spread, Size, and Opacity. Alternatively, you could use the Outer Glow style and modify it exactly as you did in the first tutorial—it's really just a question of aesthetics.

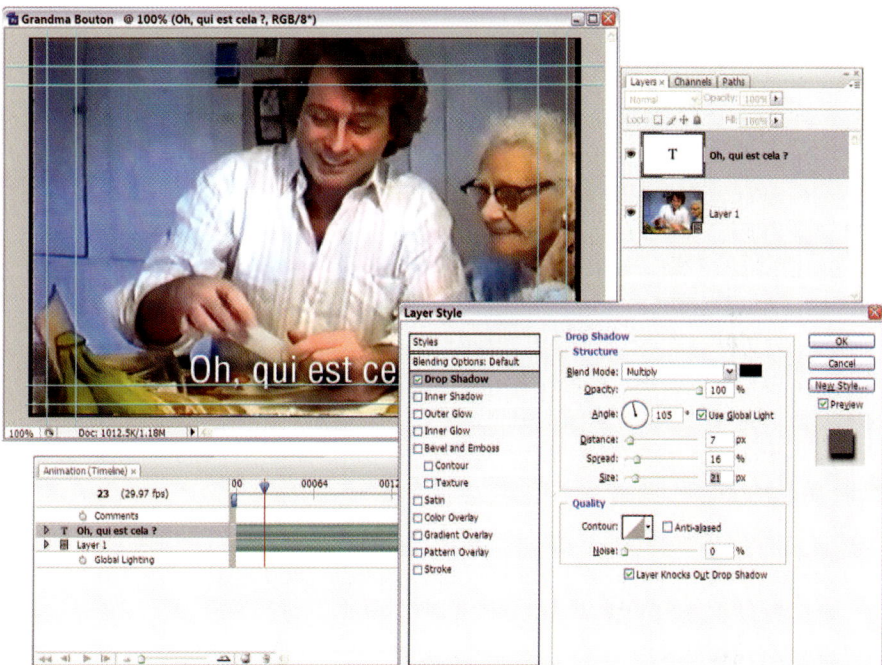

Figure 7.4
Add an effect (a style) to text to make it more legible above your video.

7. Find the point in time in the video where I say, "Oh, who's that?" I put the time at about 4 seconds, 14 frames in from the head of the clip. Drag the timeline marker to this point so you can add a comment for easy visual reference, and then from the Animation palette's flyout menu, choose Edit Timeline Comment.

8. In the Edit Timeline Comment dialog box, type "Oh, who is that?" and then click OK. As you can see in Figure 7.5, there is a marker on the Comments track now. Now you can define in and out points for the subtitle. Ignore the Adjustment layer in Figure 7.5 on the Layers palette. I used it while cobbling this tutorial to perform a little color correction on a copy of the video clip, and you can learn about color correction in Chapter 6 on video restoration.

9. A good question to ask right now is how long to keep a subtitle onscreen. The average person can read for comprehension at the rate of 200–400 words per minute in his native language. Reading for memorization and learning is much less, but the audience won't be quizzed on your subtitles in the future,

Figure 7.5

Add a comment to mark a point in the video where a subtitle should appear.

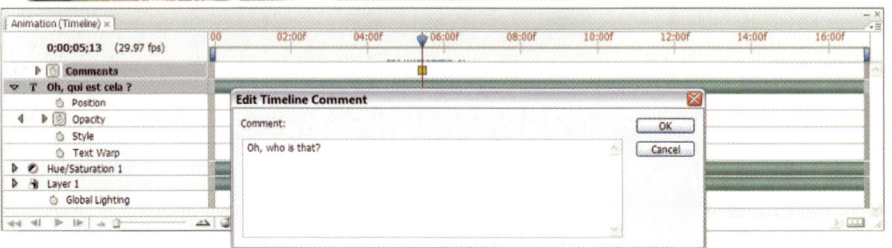

so this subtitle can last for approximately one second onscreen. With the timeline marker at 4;14, click the Opacity stopwatch icon for the text track on the Animation palette.

10. Right-click over the 4;14 Opacity change marker on the text track and choose Copy Keyframes.

11. Move the timeline marker to 5;14 and then from the Animation palette's flyout menu choose Paste Keyframe(s).

> **Tip**
>
> You might want to set up keyboard shortcuts for copying and pasting keyframes to speed up your work. Go to Edit > Keyboard Shortcuts and then choose Palette Menus from the Shortcuts For drop-down list. You can safely overwrite the Canvas Size command, which is available whenever you right-click over a document title bar, and use Ctrl/Cmd+Alt/Opt+C to copy a keyframe and Ctrl/Cmd+Alt/Opt+P to paste a copied keyframe (this key combo is not reserved at all). If you have an existing keyframe marker, you can copy, paste, and delete at this point in a video by right-clicking over it to access the command from the context menu, but you cannot paste new keyframes on a track at a point where there is no existing keyframe. That's why I recommend setting up keyboard shortcuts.

12. Here's an artistic call to make. I don't like subtitles that pop in and out, but instead I prefer a fast fade in and out. To quickly fade up the subtitle, paste a keyframe half a second before the 4;14 initial time and paste another at half a second after 5;14. Now, set the timeline marker to the first icon on the Opacity track and then, on the Layers palette, set the Opacity for the Text layer to 0%. Drag the timeline marker to the 4;14 marker and then right-click over it and choose Hold Interpolation. A hold interpolation creates a sudden change in a track's attributes; the default is linear interpolation, which eases a transition between one marker and the next that signifies a change in a layer's attributes, such as Opacity. In Figure 7.6 I've drawn a sort of legend for these timeline keyframe markers. At left is the diamond-shaped linear interpolation marker. Next to it is a hold marker, and it has a hybrid shape between a diamond and a rectangle to signify that a linear interpolation keyframe precedes it. Moving to the right, there is a hold keyframe that's rectangular because another hold marker precedes it on the timeline and then finally a linear marker that is selected (so it's gold).

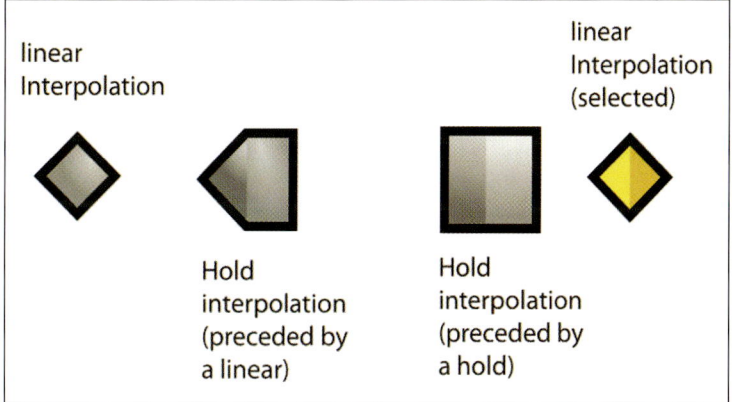

Figure 7.6 Keyframe markers on the Animation palette.

13. The subtitle should fade up at the first linear interpolation keyframe (marker). On the Layers palette, set its opacity to 0% when you've moved the timeline marker over this point in the video. The second marker (at 04;14) should be a hold interpolation at 100% opacity, as should the third marker. The fourth marker should be linear and 0% opacity. If you'd prefer to have your subtitles pop instead of using quick fades, you set up your keyframes, three of them, as all hold interpolation: the first at 0% opacity, the second right on the pop-in point at 100% opacity, and the third at the pop-out point at 0% opacity. See Figure 7.7 for my quick-fade setup.

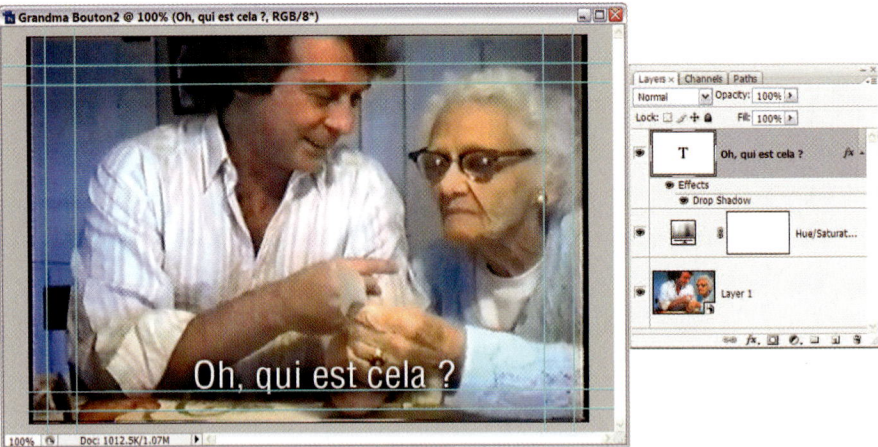

Figure 7.7
You have the option of holding from one keyframe to the next or gradually transiting from a track's key attribute to the following one.

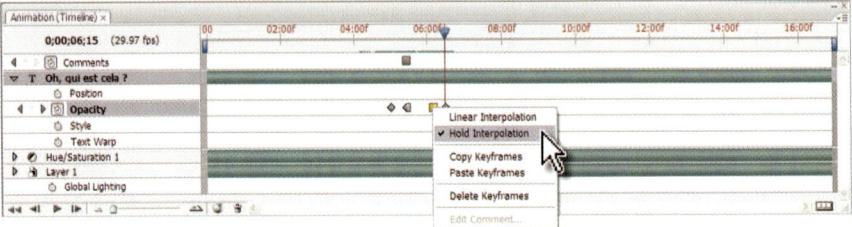

14. To finish subtitling this clip, you first want to put a guide through the vertical center of the first subtitle. You want to align the second subtitle relative to the first subtitle (and all the subtitles you might create in a clip) vertically. You do this so the audience has a consistent focal point, and their eyes don't have to jump all over the place! Press Ctrl/Cmd+R to display document rulers and then drag a horizontal guide from the ruler at the top.

15. Copy the second phrase from the Acrobat document and repeat the preceding steps. You mark the phrase in at the audio "Notice there's no writing…" and give the subtitle about a 3-4 second duration. Here's an artistic call to make: The second subtitle is quite long—you can break it up and display single lines of text for short durations or do what I recommend here and display the subtitle in whole on three lines. It is less interruptive for the viewer because the "actor" speaks the phrase as a continuous line without pauses. It also helps if you understand the subtitle so you can manually break lines (Shift+Enter/Return creates a forced, soft break), because it's poor form to create an awkward text line break in any language. For film, which is traditionally displayed in wide format, you can usually get away with a single line of text at a large point size for lone phrases.

In Figure 7.8, I'm finishing adding the second subtitle and am using a guide to center the second subtitle relative to the first (by scrubbing the timeline back to the first subtitle to align the guide).

Figure 7.8
Use the same technique to add subtitles. Consistency is important for font size and type, as well as location onscreen.

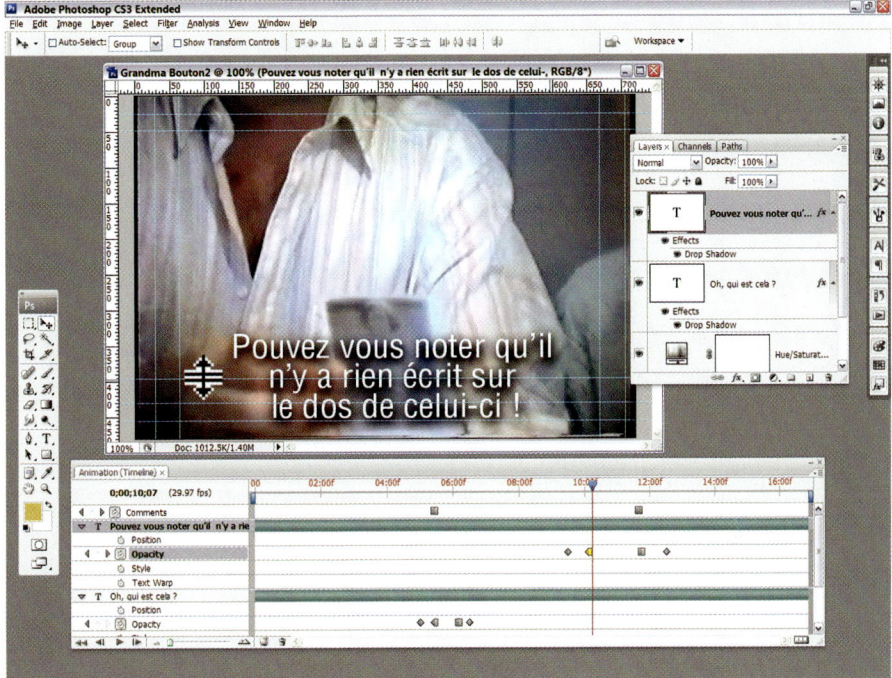

Creating a Crawl

George Lucas is credited with inventing the cinematic perspective crawl for the prologues to his *Star Wars* epics. I teach you how to create this effect in this section, but note that a simple, non-3D crawl is the staple of Hollywood. Film credits tend to appear in one of two presentations: fade ins and outs or crawls. I professionally prefer the crawl treatment for motion picture credits because the audience has a lot more time to read them; although single credit fades can present a credit at a much larger point size.

In the following sections, you'll gain experience copying and pasting text as paragraph text into Photoshop, which has supported long blocks of text since version 6. Then I show you how to create a crawl. And finally, I show you how to apply perspective to the crawl. Note that some effects you'll want to achieve cannot be accomplished in a single pass in Photoshop—you need to create an animation, export it and then bring it in as a video layer to accomplish a certain effect. Fortunately, digital media can be lossless, so you could in practice create astounding effects by doing five or six passes of exported video.

Importing and Animating Paragraph Text

Paragraph text in Photoshop has almost as many options as a genuine desktop publishing app such as Quark and InDesign—90% of the trick of creating flawlessly kerned and justified blocks of text lies in knowing where to find the features. I will help you out on this one in the section to follow; you'll need typesetting expertise if you're ever going to design the credits to a motion picture. Although Photoshop has a spell checker, it's probably best to create long blocks of text in a word processor and proof your copy for both spelling *and* grammar. Microsoft Word dominates the world of word processors, and Photoshop can read clipboard data copied from Word with proper punctuation, curly quotes, and extended characters.

The following tutorial walks you through importing some text I've written and saved to plain text format, Chapter 7.txt. Follow these steps to get a handle on working with paragraph text that you'll later animate along the audience's screen:

1. Launch a plain text editor such as Windows Notepad or OS X TextEdit. Load the text file Chapter 7.txt and then select all the text. Copy it to the clipboard and then exit and switch to Photoshop.

2. In Photoshop, create a new document that's about 720 pixels wide by 800 pixels high. Although you'll be creating a crawl animation that appears to go on for several yards, it's the animation that creates this effect and not the document height. Additionally, the final background for the crawl is Starfield.mov, and it measures 853W by 480H (DV widescreen), clearly wider than the new document here. However, because the text will appear to stretch to infinity, the width of the text is relative, and at its horizontal center the paragraph text will sit comfortably on the 853 pixel wide background. Fill the Background layer with solid black.

3. Choose the Type tool and then open the Paragraph Text palette, quickly accessed via the icon directly to the right of the Type Warp icon on the Options bar. Drag the palette free of the docking strip by dragging on its top tab; separate the Character palette from the Paragraph palette by dragging the Character palette's title off the grouped palette and then dock the Character palette beneath the Paragraph palette; it snaps to the palette when it's in range. You need to work with both palettes to finesse the block of text, and as individual palettes your work will go quicker than toggling between groups.

4. On the Character palette, choose Helvetica Condensed bold (or a similar sans serif condensed face) and pick bright yellow as the text color and about 34 points in font size with 48 point leading (so the lines are clearly separated for easy reading as they crawl). On the Paragraph palette, click the Justify All icon

at top at far right and uncheck Hyphenate (hyphenation is for books and magazines and not for headlines). This setting is equivalent to forced justification in desktop publishing; it forces lines of text to fall flush left and right within a column and usually prevents rivers (unsightly gaps between words from line to line of text) from occurring.

5. Marquee-drag in the document window to create a target shape for the text you'll "pour" into a new layer. Make the shape nearly fill the window from top to bottom and leave about 90 pixels of margin on either side. You can scale the container for the text at any time after pasting into it by manipulating the container corners with the Type tool.

6. Press Ctrl/Cmd+V to paste the clipboard text into the marquee container. As you can see in Figure 7.9, the text is neat and clean and justified, but the headline looks wrong, as does the last line of paragraph text. No problem, only solutions: I show you how to perform some typesetting next.

7. Take a look at the word count for each line in the paragraph. In Western literature—for headlines—seven words per line is the maximum; readers lose their place with more than seven, and you cause readers to snap their heads excessively using fewer than five or so words per line. If any line has more than seven words, put your cursor before the word you want to kick down and then press Enter. However, don't create "bad" line breaks; keep words that belong

Figure 7.9
The Justify All option on the Paragraph palette is a good choice for setting even columns of paragraph text.

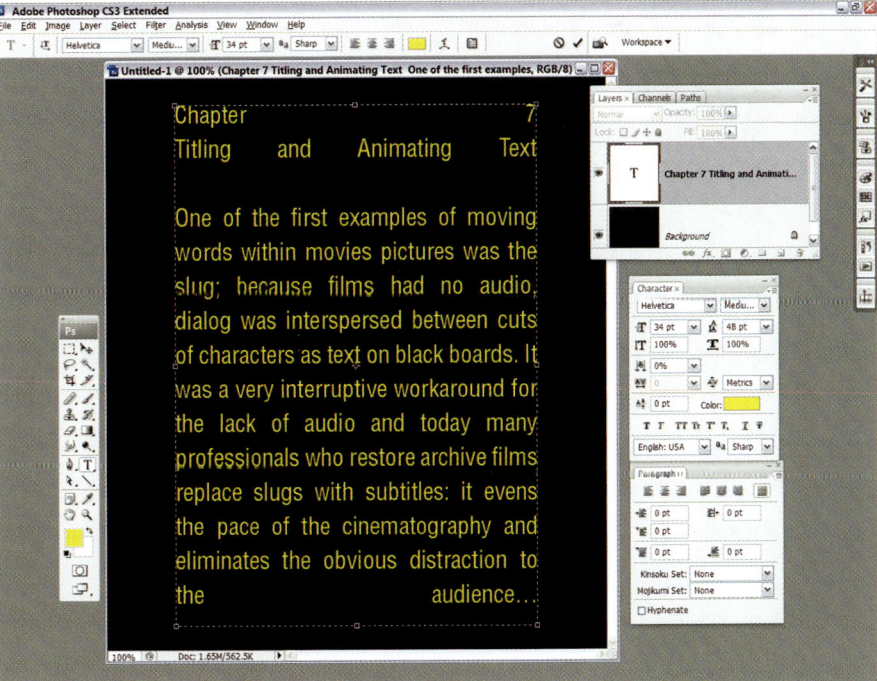

together, such as "first examples" and "the pace of the cinematography" as unified phrases on one line. The last line shouldn't have a single word at the end; words that are "stranded" from the rest of a paragraph are called widows, and they just plain look awkward. Put your cursor before the word "to" on the second-to-last line and then press Enter to bump it down to complete the last line, for spacing and as a standalone phrase. Then insert your cursor in the last line, triple-click to select the whole line, and then click the Justify Last Left button on the Paragraph palette.

8. On the Character palette, the Tracking control can be used effectively to remove rivers and excess space between words; it's almost synonymous with the typesetter's term *kerning* and controls character spacing. Pick a line of text that has too much space between words (I'm using "the lack of audio and today many"), insert your cursor, and then triple click to select the whole line. Photoshop's typesetting features include successive clicking to select additional text: A double-click selects a word, triple-clicking selects a line, and four or more successive clicks selects multiple lines, depending on line breaks. Now drag the face of the little "AV" icon as shown in Figure 7.10 to the right until the line of text looks easier on the eyes and more professional. If you overdo the positive tracking and kick a word to the following line, type a slightly smaller value in the field at right. It's trial and error, but fortunately the errors pass quickly.

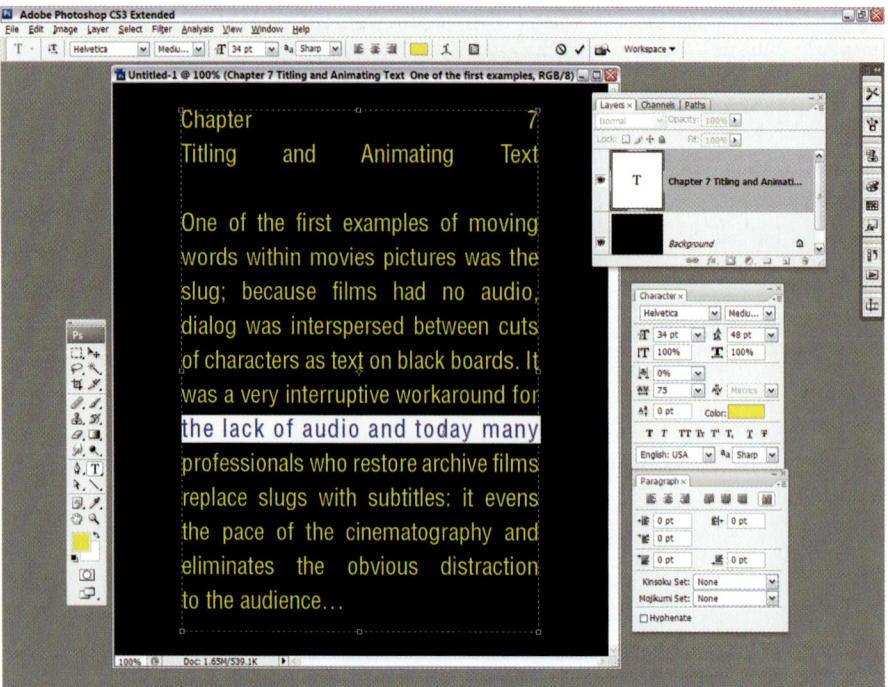

Figure 7.10

Use the Tracking feature to expand the space between characters in selected text.

9. Now here's an inspired idea: Notice I describe the terms "slug" and "subtitles" in the paragraph text. Why not emphasize these words to set them off from the body text? With the Type tool, highlight one of the words, and then on the Character palette, italicize the word (or bold it) and then choose white for the text color. Do this to both terms.

10. The headline and subhead need some work. Highlight *Titling and Animating Text* and then choose 45 points on the Character palette. Then click the Center text icon on the Paragraph palette.

11. Highlight the *Chapter 7* line and give it about 72 points height. Then highlight the title and the subtitle and specify about 23 points for Add Space after Paragraph on the Paragraph palette. Doing this helps line spacing between the title, the subtitle, and the body of the paragraph. These values are arbitrary; I arrived at them by evaluating, adjusting, and perhaps doing a little more evaluating. The quick way to "spec" paragraph text is by highlighting and then dragging on the faces of the icons on both Type Tool palettes; most of these icons are "live" and act like sliders. See Figure 7.11.

Figure 7.12 shows how the text should look before you save to disk. You're going to commence animation in the following section.

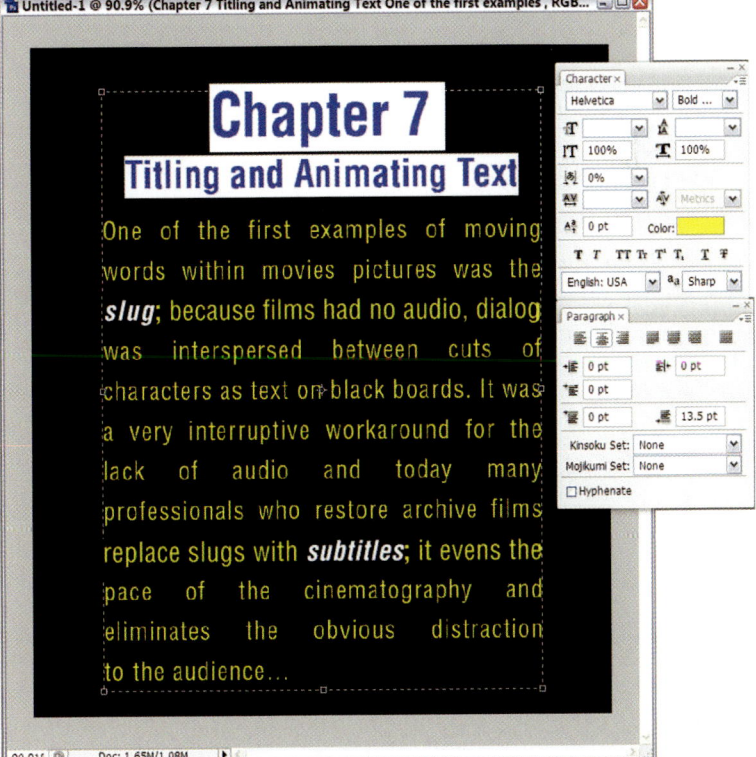

Figure 7.11
Because all text contains different content, you must shape up paragraph text manually.

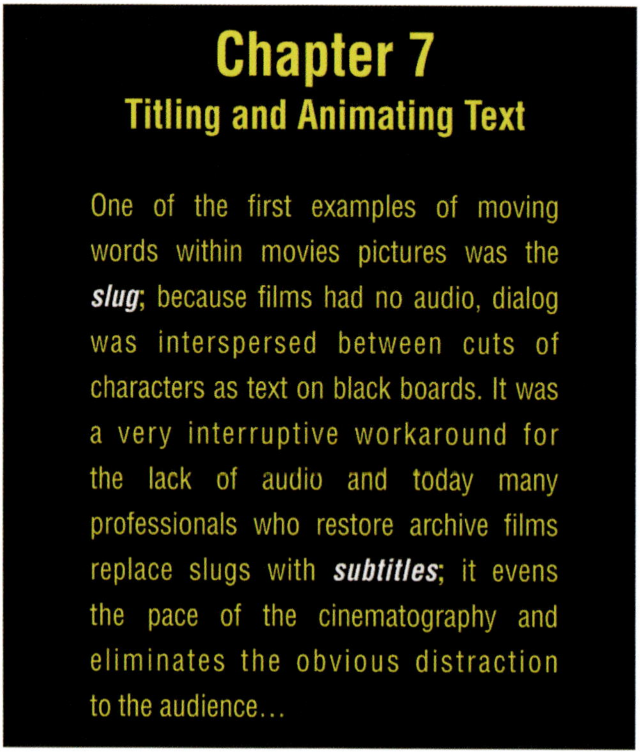

Figure 7.12
The completed text.

Creating Your First Animation Pass

I've got a treat for you—I created a starfield to put behind the crawling text you'll use to make my meager prose a sci-fi epic. However, to create this 3D crawl, you'll need to write the animation out as a movie and then perform 3D distortion (perspective) on the imported movie as a Photoshop Smart Object. Occasionally you'll need to do several passes to build a stunning and sophisticated video clip, but fortunately, as long as you don't compress the exported movie, it's digital, and there is no loss of image quality.

Therefore, you follow these steps to build a QuickTime movie with alpha transparency that makes it effortless to put the resulting movie on top of a starfield or any other background:

1. Evaluate how long the playtime for the footage should be, based on the comprehension rate of the audience. Earlier I said that reading for comprehension is between 200–400 words per minute (wpm). In a plain text editor or word processor it's easy to discern the document word count—the Chapter 7.txt file contains about 75 words (Acrobat cannot give you a word count, nor can Photoshop). Therefore, a 30-second crawl will enable the audience to read this message with room to spare.

2. Open the Animation palette and then click the flyout menu icon and choose Document Settings. Set the frame rate to 29.97 fps (this is broadcast standard frame rate, because this epic will surely play on Saturday mornings) and the duration to 0;00;35;00 just to leave yourself a little wiggle room, and then click OK to apply.

3. At the head of the animation, first make certain your text is horizontally centered. Then with the Move tool chosen, hold Shift and drag down until about half the height of the Chapter 7 text is visible in the document window. Holding Shift constrains your Move tool movement to the direction in which you begin a drag. You'll soon see that by making the text start the crawl with part of it visible, when you distort it and then animate it, the text will begin approximately at the beginning of the compiled animation. Now click the position stopwatch for the text layer on the Animation palette; doing this sets a key.

4. Set the timeline indicator to the end of the Work Area. Then with the Move tool, hold Shift and drag upwards until only the last three or four lines of text are visible; this might take two editing moves, depending on where you first placed the Move tool in the document window. In Figure 7.13 you can see the document window at the head of the video, at the middle, and then at the end. Press Ctrl/Cmd+S now.

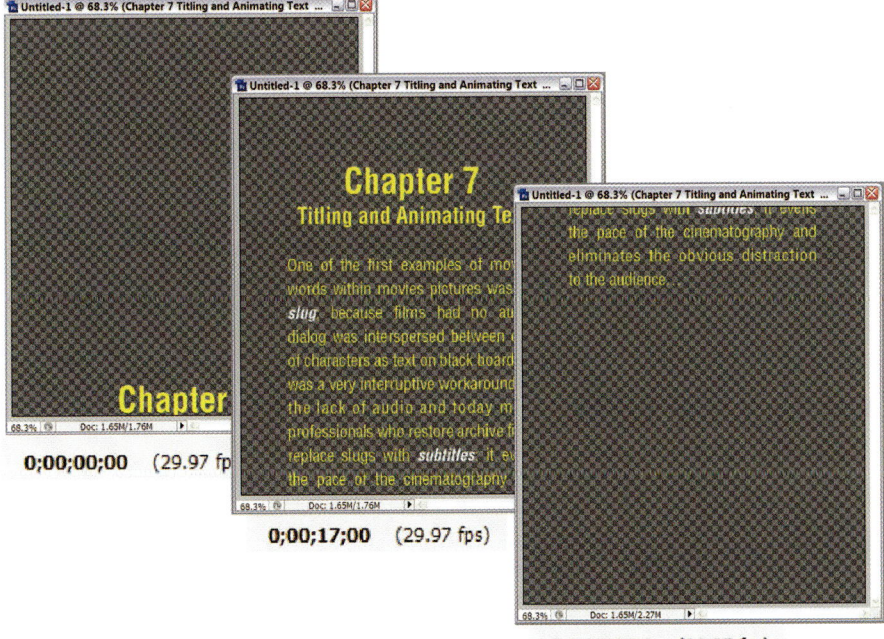

Figure 7.13
Animate the text by pushing it on its layer relative to the document window.

5. Hide the black Background layer and make sure the Text layer is chosen on the Layers palette.

6. Choose File > Export > Render Video.

7. Choose QuickTime Movie from the drop-down list, click Settings, click Settings in the Movie Settings dialog box, and then choose None from the drop-down list of codecs; also choose Millions of Colors+ to write the transparency into the movie. The result will be a huge QuickTime file, almost a gigabyte, but you're aiming for no loss of quality, and you can delete the file later after it's been repurposed. Click OK to apply and then click OK to get back to the Render Video box.

8. In the Render Options field, choose Alpha Channel: Straight-Unmatted. I mentioned that you'll be adding this video in front of a starfield animation, so ostensibly Premultiplied with Black would be a better matting choice. But…no: The premultiplied anti-aliasing against black would create a black edge, obscuring some of the white stars in the starfield, spoiling the effect of the text floating in space.

9. Choose the filename and location and then click Render.

10. After Photoshop has written the video, minimize the text document window, then open Starfield.mov, and then open the text crawl QuickTime you rendered in Step 9.

11. On the Layers palette, right-click over the layer title (not the thumbnail) and then choose Convert to Smart Object from the contextual menu. Now some but not all filters on the Filter menu are available to apply.

12. Chances are you have Transparency set up for display on layers in the default mode of white and light gray checkers. This makes it very difficult to see the yellow text, particularly in the Lens Correction preview window. Press Ctrl/Cmd+K to go to the Transparency & Gamut page.

13. Click the Grid Color Swatches and give them a color that contrasts against the bright yellow text, such as deep blue. Click OK and return to the workspace.

14. Choose Filter > Distort > Lens Correction.

15. Drag the Transform, Vertical Perspective slider all the way to the right, as shown in Figure 7.14, and then click OK to apply.

16. Although the effect looks okay, it can benefit from a second application of Lens Correction to really make the text dramatic—there is obviously a limit to the Perspective feature. Return to Lens Correction and drag the Vertical Perspective slider all the way to the right again; then click OK.

Figure 7.14
Lens Correction can be used to uncorrect an image.

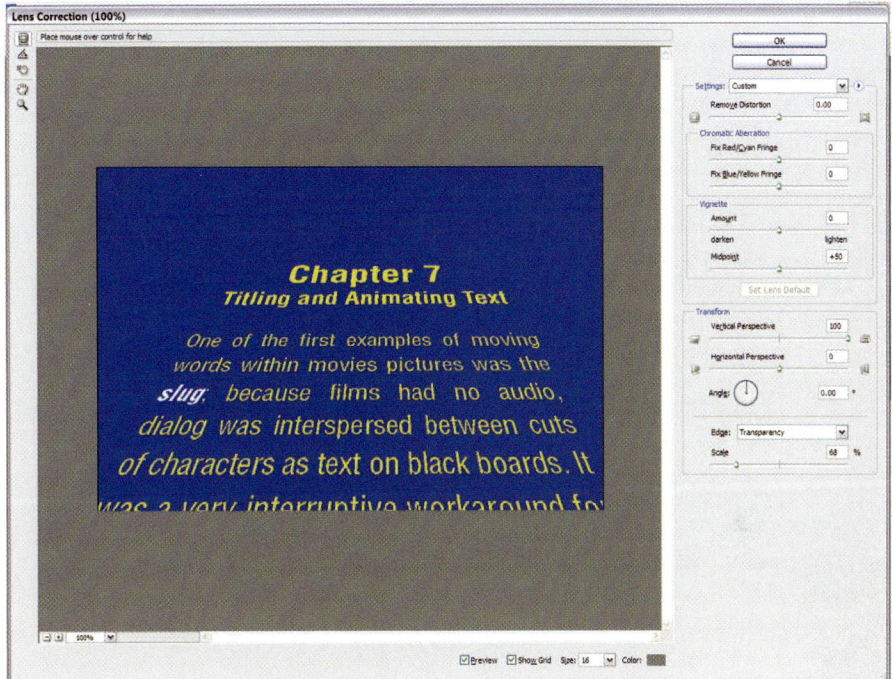

Building the Animated Crawl

Here's the fun part. In the following steps you compile the video, fine-tune it, and then add some audio I created for this assignment. Real fanfare hokum!

1. Drag the Text layer thumbnail into the starfield document window. Choose the Move tool.

2. Drag the timeline indicator to a point in the video where you can see the clipping at the bottom of the text, and then with the Move tool, move the layer down so it touches the bottom of the starfield document frame.

3. Let's make the text appear more as though it fades to infinity in the distance instead of merely disappearing at the top edge of the layer. With the text layer active, click the Layer Mask icon on the bottom of the Layers palette.

4. If necessary, press D for the default colors (black should be the foreground color). Choose the Gradient tool from the Tools palette. Set the gradient type to linear on the Options bar and then choose Foreground to Transparent from the presets in the right-click contextual menu (you need to right-click in the document window). Press Enter to dismiss the Gradient Options dialog box.

5. Start your drag at about one screen inch from the top of the document, hold the Shift key, and drag down and release at about the halfway point in the document window. Holding the Shift key constrains the gradient drag to a perfect vertical line.

6. Play back the video. You'll notice that the text plays shorter than the background starfield because the Lens Correction filter scooted the text upward. No problem; the playlength is okay at 30 instead of 35 seconds—drag the Work Area end marker at right to the point where the last line of text is gone from the screen, at about 30 seconds.

7. Add my epic music by choosing File > Open As (Mac: choose to open as a QuickTime movie), and then (Windows users) choose Epic Music.mp3 and choose QuickTime Movie from the Open As drop-down list in the box.

8. Drag the Layers palette's title for the new audio layer into the starfield document window. Adjust the track for the audio on the Animation palette by dragging it to the head of the animation workspace—see Figure 7.15 where I've labeled the layers. When working with multiple layers, especially with video, I recommend that you take a minute to label layers—you double-click the default name on the Layers palette and then just type.

9. Rock and roll: Choose File > Export > Render Video. Because this production has audio, you have to choose QuickTime as the file format. As far as codecs go, you're okay with H:264, Medium Quality, because this video has

Figure 7.15
Your compiled video should look like this.

very few unique colors, and the compressor tends to brighten tones and dull colors. Click OK.

10. Make sure the size is Document Size (H:264 doesn't support alpha channels, so this option is dimmed), pick a hard disk location and name, and then click Render.

Text Warp and Animated Text

Photoshop's Text Warp feature has been extended in this Extended version to enable you to animate text in attractive and attention-getting ways. Everything you could do with the Text Warp feature in previous versions you can do in Extended, but you can also change the appearance of warped words across time. This capability presents a lot of interesting and creative possibilities you'll explore in the following sections.

Creating Wavy Text

A friend and I took a dip with some dolphins a few years ago at a marine institute in Key West, and I thought I'd surprise my friend by adding a subtitle to what Kona, one of the more loquacious dolphins, was saying to us. This is a special event that calls for special text treatment. In the following steps I'll walk you through a method for making a short phrase wave up and down, more or less like Kona's flippers were animating in the Kona, Laur & Button.mov file. Open the movie in Photoshop, think of a fun but legible typeface you can use, and follow along here:

1. Even though you'd expect Helvetica at 72 point to be the same height as say Garamond, every typeface has a different size because the typeface's creator has chosen to let characters occupy a given area of an imaginary grid used to compose typefaces. In this example I'm showing Croissant URW at 72 points; use any fun font you like, but adjust its size accordingly. Begin by clicking an insertion point with your font and font color, center justification, and about 72 points in size specified on the Options bar. Type "I'm not a fish!" because this is what Kona is saying in the video.

2. Add a Layer style: open the Styles palette, click Chiseled Sky, and you'll add an effect to make the text stand off the background video some more. If the Styles palette doesn't display the default style options, click the Styles palette flyout menu and choose Reset Styles, then click OK to replace current styles or click Append to add the default styles to the currently displayed styles. Use the Move tool to move the text into the image by at least 10% of the document size away from the bottom edge (see the previous section on titling safety zones). See Figure 7.16.

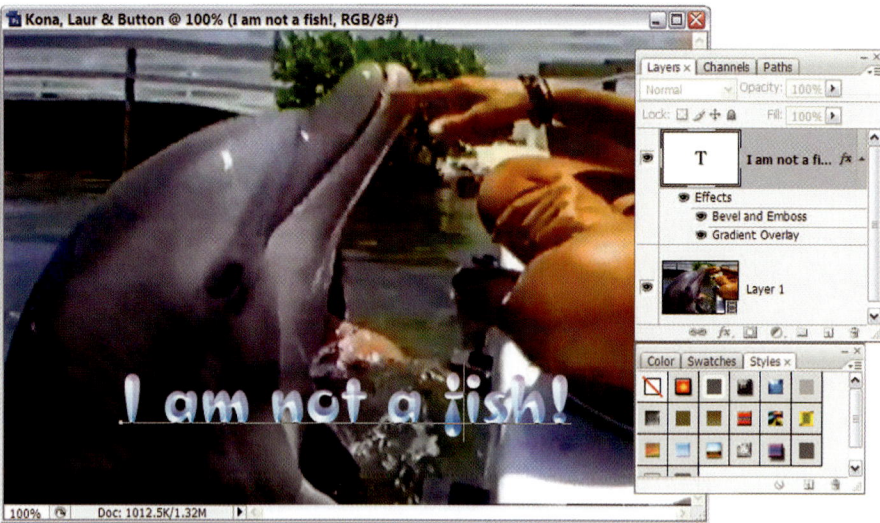

Figure 7.16
Add a style to the text that reflects the fun of the occasion and the gentle humor of the typeface and message.

3. Click the fx icon on the Layers palette and then choose Outer Glow from the menu.

4. Choose Multiply mode and a dark blue for the color. Then try Opacity: 100%, Spread: 12%, and Size: 16 pixels. I think the text reads a lot more clearly now, and the blue color is compatible with the water in the scene.

5. Scrub the timeline to see where Kona pops out of the water to greet the trainer and to see how long this sequence lasts. I put Kona's entrance at 7;05 and her exit at about 10;00, which leaves three seconds of titling, more than enough to read the silly subtitle. Move the timeline indicator to the middle of this sequence, at about 8;15.

6. Click the Text Warp stopwatch icon on the Animation palette and then click the Text Warp button on the Options bar.

7. Choose Wave, but put the Bend amount at 0%. Your screen should now look like Figure 7.17.

8. Put the timeline indicator at the beginning of the sequence, about 7;05, and then click the Text Warp button on the Options bar. There's a trick to animating text using Text Warp—you *do not* highlight the text to create keyframes; the cursor doesn't even have to be in the document window. You just click the button and then drag the Bend slider to about –95, as shown in Figure 7.18, and then click OK. A new keyframe marker appears on the track.

9. Move to the end of the sequence (10;00 or so), and then click the Warp Text button. Drag the Bend slider all the way to the right and then click OK. I found through experimenting that, yes, you can make the text wave more frenetically by placing more keyframes and adjusting the Wave Bend amount,

Figure 7.17
The Bend Text Warp is at 0 in the middle of the sequence where the text will wave up at the beginning and then down at the end.

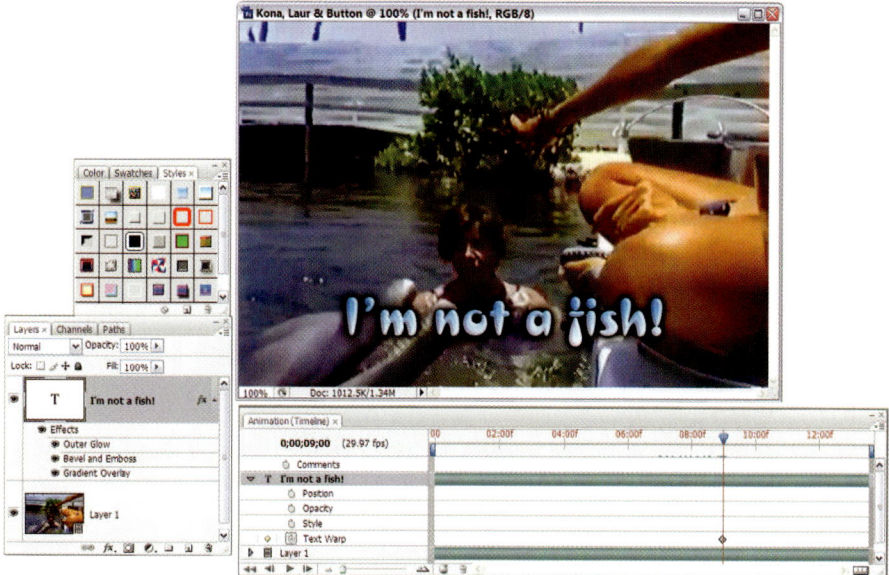

Figure 7.18
Keyframes for Warp Text are created simply by clicking the Text Warp button and then specifying a different value.

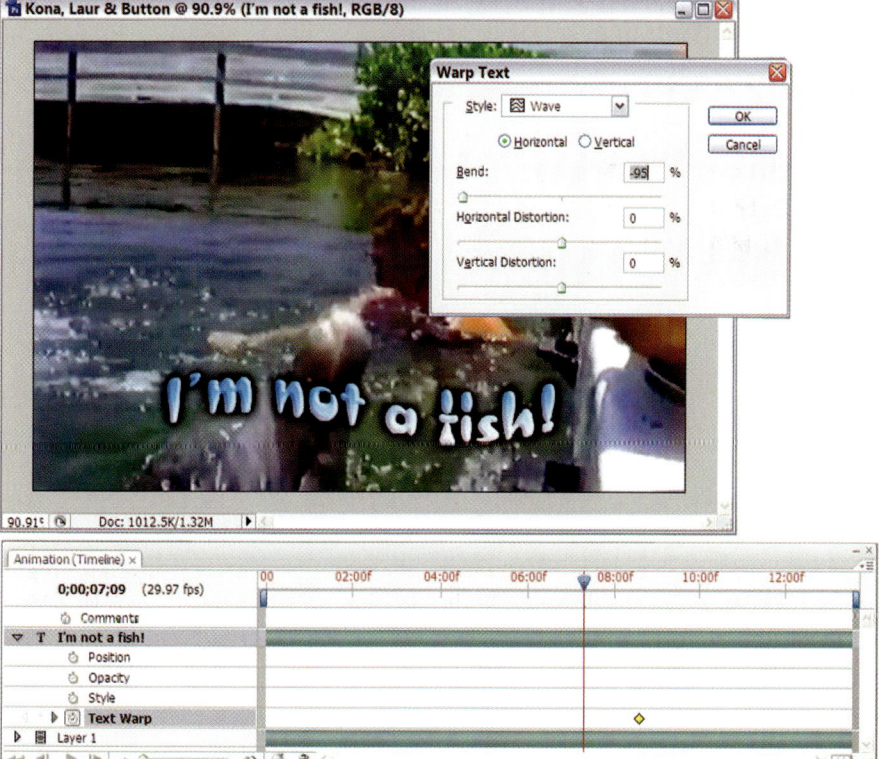

but doing this proves to be real annoying to the audience; they can't read the subtitle, the animation competes with the underlying video and wins, and all the text waving about splashes water into the camera lens.

10. What you want to do next is fade up the text and then fade it out. To do this, click the Opacity stopwatch and then create four Linear Interpolation points: 0% opacity (on the Layers palette) just after the keyframe for the Text Warp's beginning; 100% about 15 frames afterward; 100% at about 9;20; and then 0% just a touch before the end of the Text Warp at 10;00. What you've done is make the text fade up *while* it's animating—it is *always visible* moving. Your animated text will look awkward if it stops waving while visible. See Figure 7.19; I've zoomed the timeline so you can clearly see where the keyframes go.

11. Preview the animation (click the Play button while holding the Alt/Opt key to hear real dolphin sounds!), adjust the Warp and/or Opacity key if you feel the subtitle appears onscreen too long, and then export to QuickTime. Alternatively, you can lose the sound—after all, the clip now has a subtitle—and export to AVI. I recommend QuickTime in this instance, however, because you can export using the Sorenson 3 codec, which comes with QuickTime. Unfortunately, Microsoft is not up to speed with offering a lot of different codecs, and Sorenson provides moderately good compression and virtually no tone shifting or loss of saturation, as can happen with codecs such as H:264.

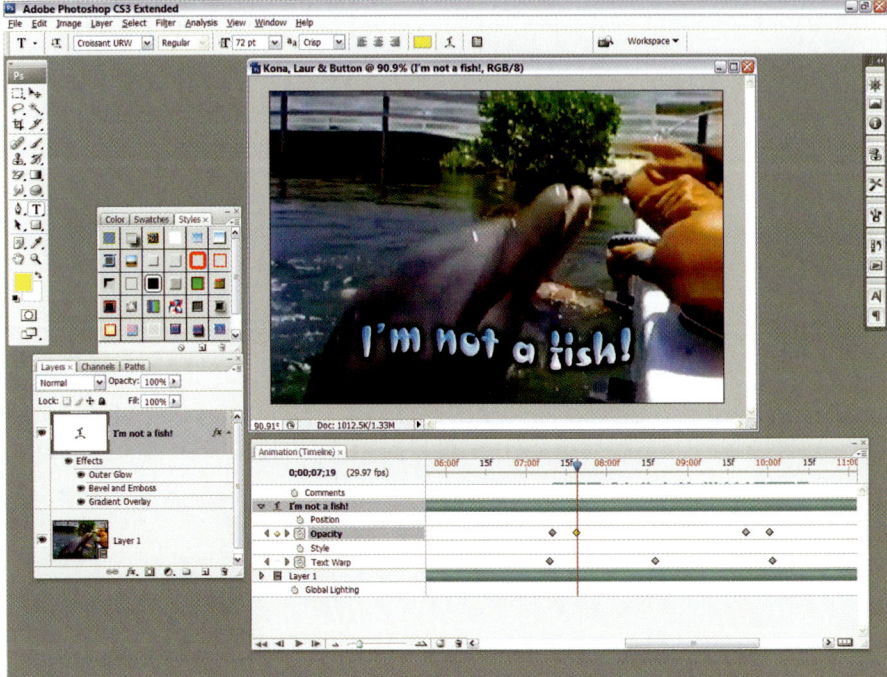

Figure 7.19
Keep the text animating while it's visible.

Animating a Logo Using Text Warp

With your new animation skills, you are bound to get a client who wants an animated logo. Sadly, Photoshop will not use Shapes and other vector-based objects with Text Warp. However, let's ponder this one for a second: What's a typeface? It's a runtime whose only visual attribute is that it puts little symbols onscreen with the assistance of your operating system that drives the runtime. A font can have any path-based info in it, and that's why symbol (Pi) fonts abound on the Web—it's a lot easier to draw a little symbol than a perfectly kerned and designed text typeface such as Galliard and Hoefler Text.

So the solution to pleasing your client is to build their logo into a font and then use Text Warp in Photoshop to animate the character (the glyph) using a typeface you build and then install on your system. If you know how to draw, there are several economical applications that can be used to make a logo typeface. Pyrus Software virtually owns the font creation program market today: They offer FontLab Studio for $900, Fontographer (formerly Macromedia Fontographer) for $400, and have a nice, bare bones applet called Type Tool for under $100. The UI feels like Illustrator, so Mac and Windows users can feel right at home, and in about an hour's worth of learning and working, you'll have your client's logo in a typeface.

Windows users, if they don't already own a copy, can use CorelDraw (any version since version 3.0) to make a TrueType of Type 1 fonts with a client's logo. I have seen ads on the Web for versions 5 through 10 for as little as $79 from reputable dealers. In Figure 7.20 you can see I'm exporting a single character to TrueType. To make it easier on myself when I eventually use the font in Photoshop, I assign the character to multiple slots in the typeface, including lowercase "a," making finding and typing the logo character painless.

To follow along in the next steps, install Geotype SE.otf, a font I cobbled a while ago and to which I added the nautilus shape that you saw in Figure 7.20. Here's the plot: The owner of an exclusive (fictitious) club and day spa wants an ad with his logo for Club Ned. He provides you with a video clip for the background he was able to create by reading Chapter 2. The following steps are very simple; here's how to animate a logo when the logo is part of a font:

1. In Photoshop, open cocktail timelapse.mov that you downloaded with this chapter's media files. Alternatively, you can use any still photograph as a background, but it won't be as fun, and you'll need to set the Animation palette's document properties to 10 seconds duration at the frame rate of 29.97fps (for television).

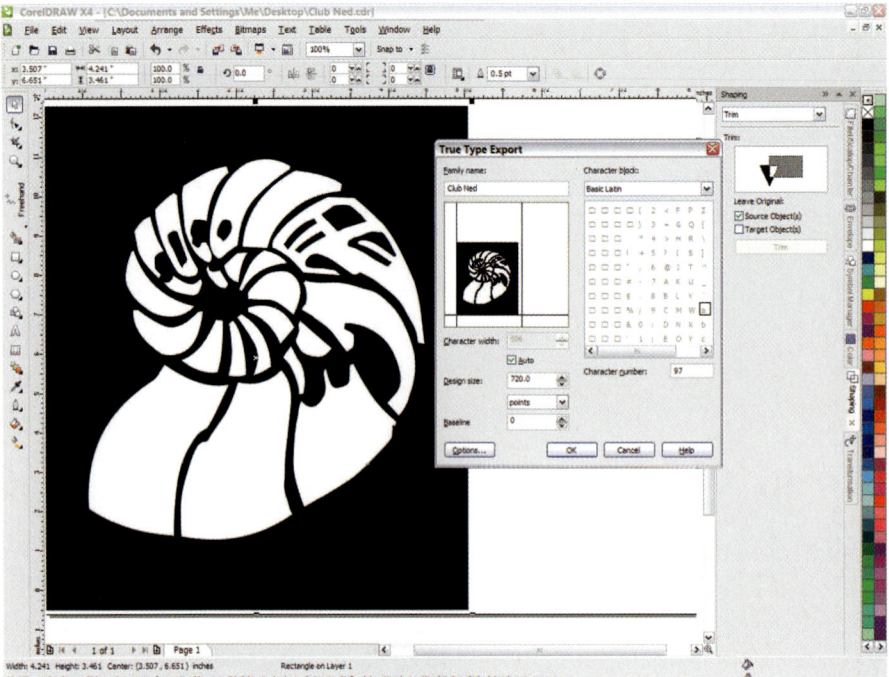

Figure 7.20
Create a logo and put it in a typeface you can use in Photoshop.

2. With the Type tool, type "a" using the Geotype SE font you installed. Use any color you like for the text, and because it's a graphic, ignore my type size guidelines I mentioned in previous sections and set the height to 72–200 points. See Figure 7.21.

3. Apply a style to the character. I'm using the Raised Coffee Stain from the Text Effects 2 collection, accessed from the Styles palette's flyout menu.

4. Just as you did in the previous tutorial, you set keys for the Text Warp effect. To have some fun with this logo, I suggest experimenting with Squeeze. Set the Bend amount to 0 at the beginning of the animation, change the values once or twice through the duration of the animation, and then end the animation with 0% Bend. You do this so the clip begins and ends with an undistorted logo (clients appreciate this). In Figure 7.22, I'm fine-tuning the Squeeze values early in the duration of the clip.

5. Optionally, you can add some "normal" text; perhaps your client has a specific typeface. You can animate this, too, but exercise restraint, particularly with short durations. You want the audience to focus on the message and let the animation be subordinate, as entertainment.

6. Export the movie to your client's specs; collect big bucks.

Chapter 7 ■ Titling and Animating Text 211

Figure 7.21
Add a design as an editable vector object when you use a picture font in Photoshop.

Figure 7.22
Use one or more of the options in Text Warp to get creative with an animating logo.

In Figure 7.23, you can see four stills I pulled from the animated logo. When you want to pull a still from a composition but haven't yet rendered it to video, you can press Ctrl/Cmd+A to Select All, and then choose Copy Merged from the Edit menu. Then paste into a new document window. The paste includes no animation data. The scene is fun, but it's also of production quality. You could easily render this composition out to a 2K or 4K file for broadcast.

Figure 7.23
Animating a logo will please and astound a client, and it takes only four or five steps.

> **Note**
>
> You'll notice that the layer style in the nautilus logo didn't animate as it was stretched and warped. This is because the layer style is a *mask* for the non-transparent areas on a layer, and the style itself is consistent although the shape of the nautilus clearly changes. Check out Chapter 8; you can indeed animate a style, but to create an animation such as the one you just learned with animating text and texture, you need to create the animation in two passes—you animate text with no layer style, export it as video, and then bring it in for style application, when you can then animate the style over time.

Animating Text Manually

So far I've shown you how to move text, make it wiggle, and fade in and out of a scene, but there are plenty of other animation treatments for text and shapes if you take the manual approach to animating text. The following section verges on full-frame animation, and it's a good segue into future chapters where I concentrate on character animation and rotoscoping. The rewards, however, easily offset the effort, and you'll soon know how to create short sequences that other professionals might assume you used After Effects to achieve. This section covers the steps needed to make a single text phrase spin toward the camera. You can use this technique for TV commercials or just to liven up a video sequence that calls for a titling "event."

Creating Handsome Text for Animating

The clip to which you'll add animated text, Knightly entertainment.mov, has a very short and simple plot, proportional to the length of the clip—a knight is on a battlefield, the castle he's supposed to be defending is firebombed, and he reacts. Because the Middle Ages didn't have videos with audio, you need to create a subtitle for the knight when he reacts. If you're a good lip-reader, you might discern that the knight is exclaiming, "Yoiks!"

However, this is a very rich and highly detailed computer animation that deserves a special subtitle. I'm remembering back to the *Batman* television series, when the production had the budget to hand-animate and then superimpose "Bam" and "Bang" spinning toward the camera during the fight scenes. They dropped the clever, comic-bookish treatment and went to slugs when the budget waned—this was expensive stuff at the time but can be easily done today with Photoshop, the Actions palette, and some working knowledge of the Animation palette and Frames mode.

To begin, I feel as though the text "Yoiks" should be medieval in appearance and should be textured as richly as the animated scene. You don't need to follow steps here, but I'd like to show you a third-party plug-in that is used commercially on nine out of ten packages you find in the supermarket and retail stores. Path Styler Pro by Shineycore produces glossy, dimensional text and has so many parameters you're unlikely to see the same look on retail goods twice—hence its popularity with graphics professionals.

> **Tip**
>
> You can download a fully functional time-out demo of Path Styler Pro for Photoshop and Illustrator (Mac or Windows) at www.shinycore.com/products/tryouts/.

You begin with a path in Photoshop. In Figure 7.24 you can see I've got a new document set up using the Film & Video preset to add safety guides. What I did here was use a font called Becker, which has that Goth look but is much more legible than Bible Script, and then chose Create Work Path by right-clicking over the text layer. This creates a work path you can see and access on the Paths palette and does not destroy the text layer, so if you made a typo you can go back and correct it at any time. Path Styler Pro needs a path (or several joined paths) to do its thing. You then hide the text layer, create a new blank layer, and choose Filter > Shinycore > Path Styler Pro.

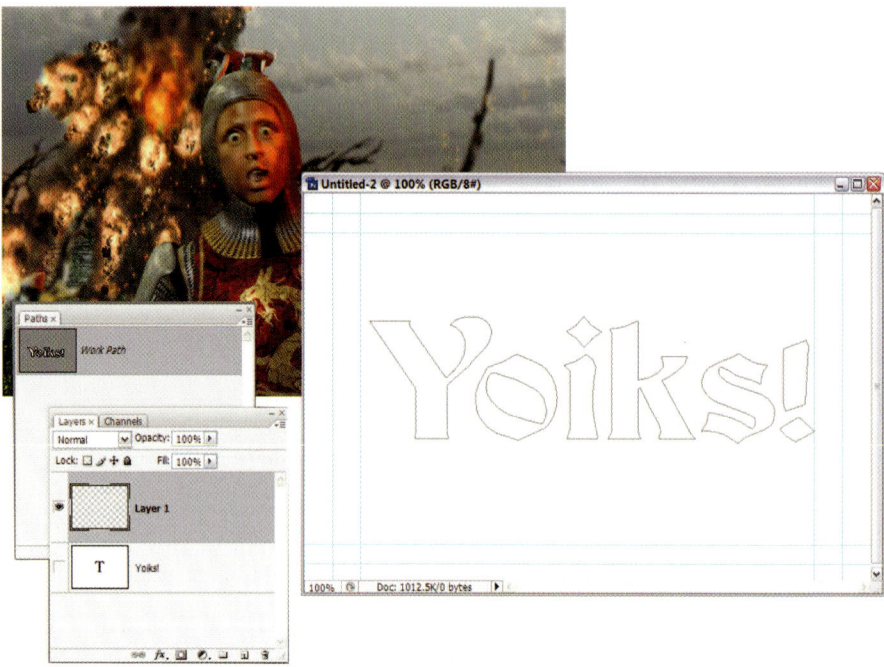

Figure 7.24
Create a series of paths based on font outlines.

Next, you can choose a preset to apply to the layer within the paths or double-click a preset to build a custom look. In Figure 7.25 I've played with the basic Glass preset, changing the color and then adding a layer to create a dull pewter collar around the text. This is an effect not easily achieved by mixing Photoshop styles, and like anything, it takes a little time to learn to earn Path Styler Pro's rewards.

Figure 7.25
Path Styler Pro offers scores of variations for authentic, attractive, embossed looks.

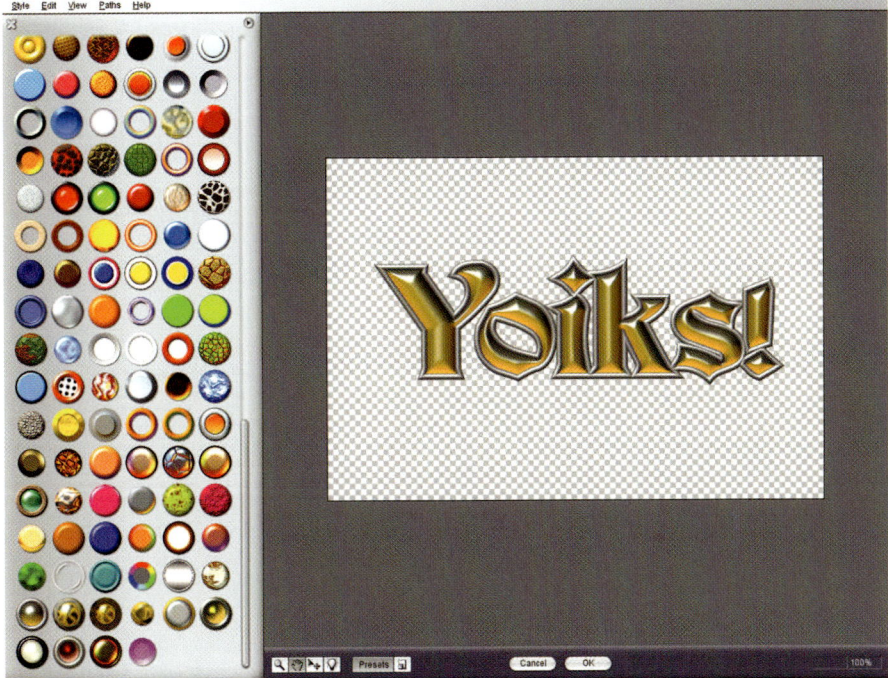

Writing an Action to Animate Objects

I've created Yoiks.png for you to use in this section. It's okay that the text is not editable as text (I spelled "Yoiks!" correctly)—in fact, you can make objects other than text spin toward the screen, such as a logo or debris, after you learn the steps.

Here's how to create a video clip from the Yoiks.png still image:

1. Gauge the dimensions of the spinning text effect based on the dimensions of the video into which you'll superimpose it. The Knightly entertainment.mov file you'll use as the target is 720 by 480. So Ctrl/Cmd+double-click the workspace and then choose Film & Video from the Presets drop-down menu in the New dialog box; then turn off Pixel Aspect Ration Correction in the View main menu. On the Animation palette, toggle to Frames mode instead of Timeline.

2. Open Yoiks.png and then drag its layer title on the Layers palette into the new document window and with the Move tool, center it.

3. Open the Actions palette. Create a new Actions folder (you'll want to store all your animation actions in one handy place) by clicking the flyout menu and choosing New Set.

4. With your new Actions set selected, click the flyout menu and then choose New Action. In the dialog box, name the action Spin and Shrink. Click the Record button.

5. Press Ctrl/Cmd+A to Select All and then press Ctrl/Cmd+C to copy the "Yoiks!" text to the clipboard.

6. On the Layers palette, hide the layer.

7. Press Ctrl/Cmd+V to paste the clipboard copy to a new layer.

8. Click the layer title on the Layers palette to make it the current editing layer and then *un*check Propagate Frame 1 so the animation will *not* be created with all the layers visible.

9. Press Ctrl/Cmd+T to put the "Yoiks!" text in Free Transform mode.

10. Although you'd usually manipulate a Free Transform object using the cursor, you need precise transformations here to make the action for the animation work: On the Options bar, click the link button between the Width and Height scales so scaling the object is done without distortion. Now, type **90** in either W or H field.

11. In the Rotation field, type **3**.

12. Click the checkmark icon on the Options bar to apply the transformations and then click the stop recording button on the Actions palette.

Believe it or not, you're done and now have an action to remove 90% of the rote tedium out of animating this text. Now on to building the animation…

Building a Frame-Based Animation

You use the Frames mode of the Animation palette because the animation truly is a digital equivalent of the traditional cel animation—every frame can be thought of as a keyframe; every frame contains different data than its neighbors. You'll also get hands-on experience with an invaluable feature on the Animation palette's flyout menu, the Make Frames from Layers command. This is simple, so entertain the scores of creative variations on this spin and grow effect as you work through it.

1. Let's think about this spinning animation. It should probably do its thing in one second and then hold onscreen for an additional second before disappearing. So you need to run the action 29 times (you already have the first frame). Either click the Play button on the Actions palette 29 times or, if you

feel this repetitive task might invite error because the Play button is so small, click the flyout menu icon and choose Button Mode. The button is clearly labeled with the name of your Action script. If you like, in List mode you can select an action and then choose Action Options on the flyout menu and choose a unique color for the action when it's in Button mode.

2. On the Animation palette in Frames mode, click the flyout menu and then choose Make Frames from Layers. Bang, zoom, the Animation palette is populated with successive frames from the layers the action generated.

3. Hold Shift and then click on all the thumbnails on the Animation palette. Click the triangle next to the play time on any thumbnail on the Animation palette, choose Other, and then type .03 in the field. So, roughly, you're going to build a 30 fps animation. In Figure 7.26 you can see the Animation palette before the Make Frames from Layers command has been chosen and then at the bottom what the palette should look like after you've specified a duration of 0.03 for all the frames.

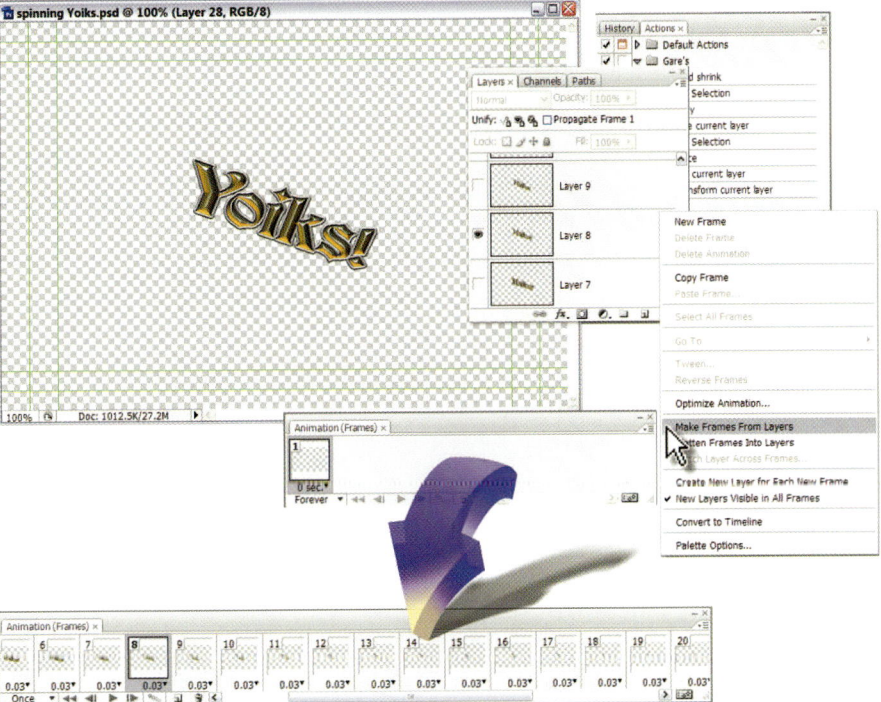

Figure 7.26
Let an action create layers, then let the Animation palette create frames from the layers.

4. You want the "Yoiks!" text to spin toward and not away from the screen. The reason why I asked you to build the action this way is because objects shrink better than they grow. It's mathematically very hard to enlarge a digital image without losing focus. Bitmaps are resolution-dependent. So on the Animation palette choose Reverse Frames from the flyout menu. See Figure 7.27, and try playing the animation now. *Yoiks!*

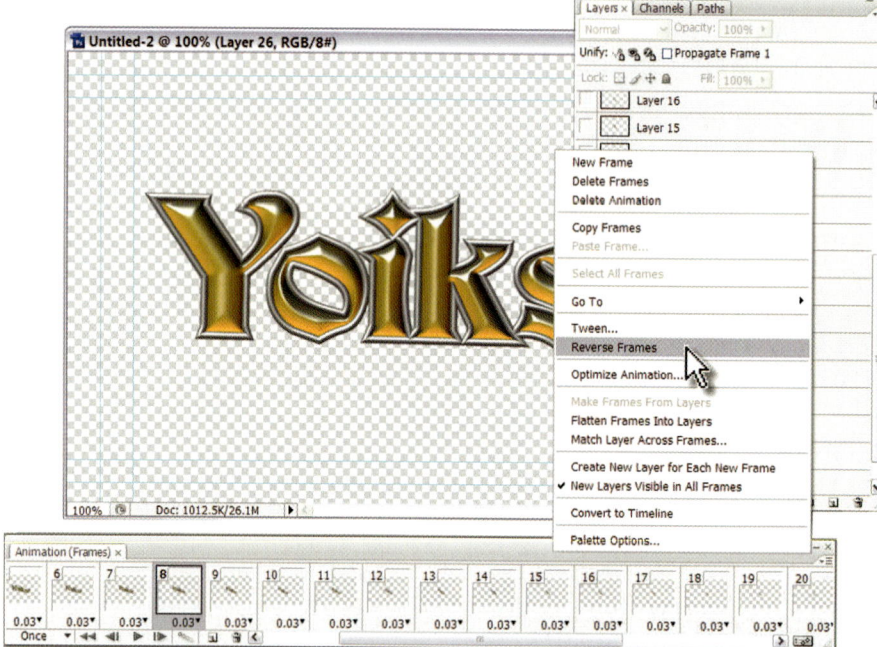

Figure 7.27
The Frames mode of the Animation palette is where you can reverse an animation.

5. The animation needs a one-second hold on the last frame, so click Frame 31's duration drop-down triangle and set the frame to 1 second. Everything else preceding it is traveling at 30 fps.

6. If you clicked the toggle and switched to Timeline mode, you'd see an absolute mess of complexity as the layers switch on and off through the play length. Fortunately, you can write the video now and not concern yourself with the machinations of turning layers into a *structure* that's ready to render to video. Choose File > Export > Render to Video. Write the movie out to QuickTime using No Compression, Millions of Colors+, 29.97 fps and make sure the alpha channel in the Render Options field is set to Straight-Unmatted (and not None). Click Render.

Compositing and Timing the Spinning Text

Compositing the animated text follows the same basic procedure as when you added the wavy text to Kona the dolphin earlier in this chapter. Follow these steps to put the "Yoiks!" text into the Knightly entertainment.mov scene, line up the exclamation with the actor's lips, and then bring up and fade out the text effect.

1. Open Knightly entertainment.mov and the spinning text movie you just exported. Then with the spinning text in the foreground in the workspace, on the Layers palette Shift+drag the title into the Knightly document window to keep it centered relative to the window.

2. Find the point in time where the knight begins to say "Yoiks." I put the beginning at about 3 seconds in. With your cursor placed on the Yoiks track on the Animation palette, drag it so the head is at about 3 seconds.

3. Do a quick fade up and a quick fade out for the Yoiks track; see Figure 7.28 for the keyframe points. The first is opacity: 0% for this layer on the Layers palette, the second is 100% opacity, the third is 100% opacity, and the last is 0% opacity. You also might want to move the text down a little using the Move tool so it doesn't totally obscure the knight's face.

Figure 7.28
The hard work is done; your main concern now is timing of the fade up and out and the entry point for the text.

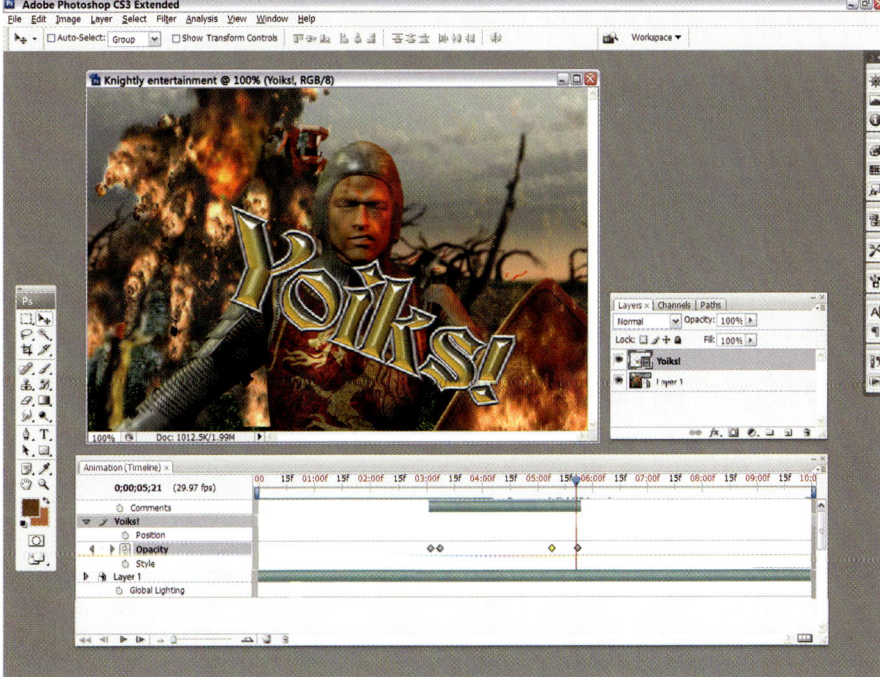

4. Write the video out to QuickTime or AVI (AVI has no sound export capability in Photoshop, but the video has no audio). I recommend Sorenson compression for QuickTime. The video has a lot of activity going on, and it won't compress as well as using other lossy codecs, but Sorenson preserves colors, all the subtleties, better than many other codecs.

Creating Typewriter Text

One of the build-type animations that has been used quite effectively through the years has been the "typewriter" effect—so lasting in popularity that it's included as a preset in Flash and other animation programs.

The following tutorial was inspired by a comment my father used to make on Saturdays when he'd drive me to my dreaded weekly accordion lessons. He'd say, "This is Mission: Impolkable," referring of course to the popular television show during the 1960s. This, by coincidence, had opening titles that sported the typewriter effect. To build a typewriter effect, the easier way is to cast your text and then do a reveal, character by character, using Hold Interpolation on the Animation palette. Open fuse.mov and I'll show you how to make text pop onscreen, character by successive character.

1. With the Type tool chosen, select a typewriter-style font from your installed fonts (I'm using ITC American Typewriter in these figures, which should really be a part of your stable of typefaces), white color, and about 72 points in size.

2. Toward the top of the document window, type **Mission:**.

3. On the Layers palette, create a new layer, press D (default colors) so black is the current foreground color, and then choose the Rectangular Marquee tool.

4. Drag a bounding box over the word Mission:. Then press Alt/Opt+Backspace to fill the marquee selection. Press Ctrl/Cmd+D to deselect.

5. Decide when you want to begin revealing the text. I recommend 1 second into the video, when the guy is about to light the fuse. Put the timeline indicator at 1 second on the Animation palette (in Timeline mode).

6. Click the position stopwatch for the black layer (it should be labeled Layer 2) to put a keyframe marker at 1 second.

7. Move the timeline indicator over to 1 second, 15 frames, and then with the Move tool, move the black rectangle so the first character is visible in the document window.

8. Move the timeline indicator to 2 seconds and then drag the black rectangle to the right to expose the second character. This moves the rectangle in a linear fashion across time, and although this can be used as a look, it's not the look for this tutorial.

9. Right-click over any of the keyframe markers and then choose Hold Interpolation, as shown in Figure 7.29. I'm up to the third character in this figure—you should complete the keyframes for all the characters and then set all the keys to Hold Interpolation; this is the way to pop an element onscreen. Alternatively, you can pop an element into any point in time by using Hold Interpolation in combination with the Opacity setting for a layer. Set a key for 0% opacity, set one for 100% a second or so later, and make both keys the Hold Interpolation type, and elements pop into frame.

10. My recommendation for half-second pop-ups for the characters is a gross estimate; you need to work on precise timing for the text appearance or the typewriter effect won't work for the audience. How fast can someone type? I discovered the sweet spot for timing through trial and error; I played back the video a few times (allowing Photoshop to cache the animation in memory for real-time playback) and came up with about seven characters per second, which translates to a keyframe about every four frames (at 30 fps). So click the flyout menu and choose Palette Options, and set the timeline to Frame Number.

Figure 7.29
Hold Interpolation creates an abrupt change in the attribute of layers.

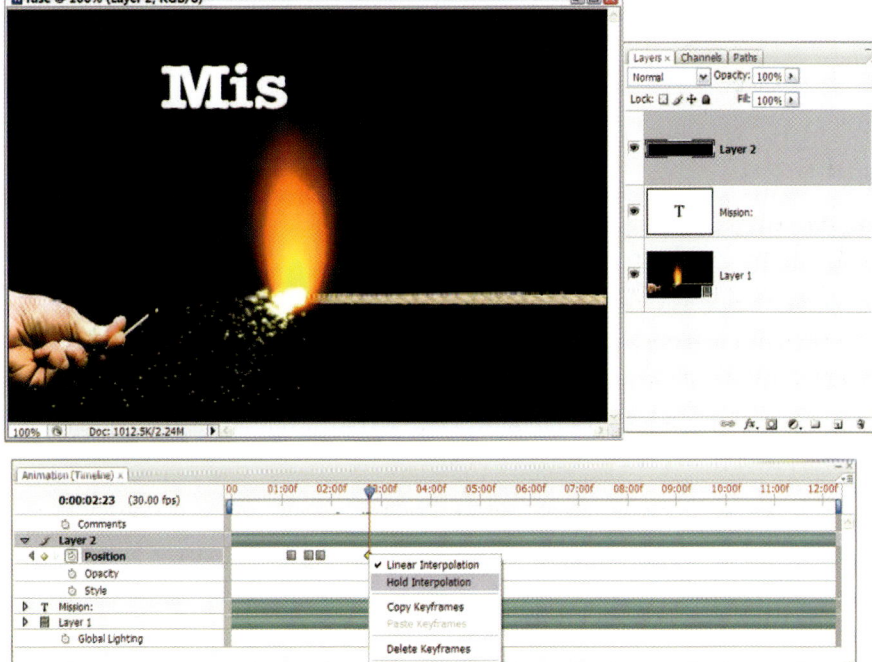

11. Space the keyframes at four frame distance from one another. This is best accomplished by zooming the timeline by dragging the slider at the bottom of the palette to the right. In Figure 7.30 you can see the keyframes evenly spaced. If you do this and then play back the video, it'll look authentic and as attention-getting as back when Mr. Phelps learned to play accordion.

Figure 7.30
The best way to evenly time multiple events is by displaying the Animation palette in Frame Numbers instead of Timecode.

12. This is optional, but it'll hone your animation chops. As you might recall, this TV show had its second name fade in and spin to make the show's logo. You already know how to spin a logo or text, so you might want to find a condensed stencil-type font and use the Yoiks! steps to spin the word "Impolkable" onto the screen. You then write the file out to video with transparency, bring the movie into Photoshop, add it to this project, and then do a fade-in for the text. In Figure 7.31 you can see the progression. I added audio to the fuse.mov file that's appropriate to the theme; hold Alt/Opt and click the Play button on the Animation palette to see and hear the finished piece.

Figure 7.31
Combine animation treatments with text objects to make elaborate presentations for titles, logos, and other slogans.

3D Animated Text (with a Helper Application)

To conclude the survey of text animation and titling, I'd like to show you a little helper application called Xara 3D, because there is no third-party plug-in I know of for Photoshop that can render extruded text *and* animate it. For about $35, Xara 3D could easily be your one-stop shop for dimensional text for video.

Xara 3D does not write to Microsoft's specs for alpha channels in AVI films, so I chose Xara 3D in this section as an opportunity to demonstrate another invaluable action you can write to separate and remove the background from an AVI file to make text float within transparency. In Figure 7.32 I'm using Xara 3D to make a conclusion to a video clip reminiscent of the 1950s mystery movies and bad sci-fi flicks. The preset I've chosen for the text is Pulsate 2, set to only Grow—which makes each 3D character come toward the camera from infinity. I've cast the lights upward to create the "emanations from hell" lighting typical of Boris Karloff and other "verrrry scary" budget films.

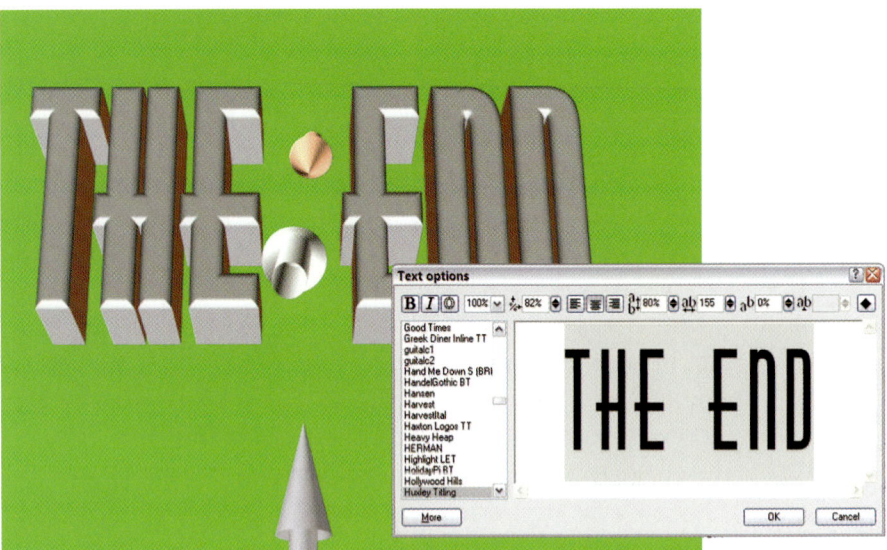

Figure 7.32
Xara 3D comes with several presets you can use to auto-animate 3D text.

Background Removal via Actions

Here's the trick to making Xara 3D video or any other application that cannot write alpha masking information usable as an element in a Photoshop video composition: You define the background color in Xara 3D as a color that contrasts against the text color. By doing this, you're more or less creating a green screen. In the steps to follow, I show you how to perform some jiffy masking using a hand-cobbled action.

Here's how to write the action for removing a solid background color:

1. Open THE END.mov and then turn off Pixel Aspect Correct.

2. Create a new layer and then put it beneath the video layer. Fill it with red so you can better see when you have the green background thoroughly removed. Click on Layer 1 to make sure this is the active layer.

3. On the Actions palette, click the flyout menu and create a new action called Background Removal in the folder you created in the previous tutorial for your video actions. You're recording now.

4. Choose Select > Color Range. In the Color Range box, use the eyedropper to click over the green in the image and then turn the Fuzziness up to maximum. Click OK, and you now have a marquee outside the text.

5. Press Delete and then Ctrl/Cmd+D to deselect the selection marquee. You'll notice that the edges around the text contain some green due to the anti-aliasing in the movie.

6. Choose Layer > Matting > Defringe. Defringe by one pixel, and click OK.

7. Click the next frame button on the Animation palette and then hit the Stop button on the Actions palette. You're done writing the action.

8. On the Actions palette, click on the Background Removal title to make sure the action plays from the beginning. Play the action by clicking the Play button until you get an error message, which means you've run out of frames to edit and the clip is now ready for export. Play back the movie just to make sure every frame has had the background deleted, as shown in Figure 7.33. Understand that this action works only for this clip; the Select > Color Range will not apply to other clips because of the color and the area where you selected the target color. If you want to reuse this action, you edit the Color Range Step with your target video in the workspace; you double-click the step on the Actions palette list to bring up the command, redefine your target color, and your script is ready to use on a different piece of footage.

9. To add drama and a little hokum to the video, right-click the video layer and then choose Convert to Smart Object. Now you can add a filter before writing the file out with transparency to video.

10. Click the fx button on the bottom of the Layers palette and then choose Drop Shadow. Drag in the document window to set the direction of the shadow. As you can see in Figure 7.34, casting the shadow upward emphasizes the ghoulish lighting on the extruded text. Perfect!

Figure 7.33
Run the action you created to remove the background of the video to transparency.

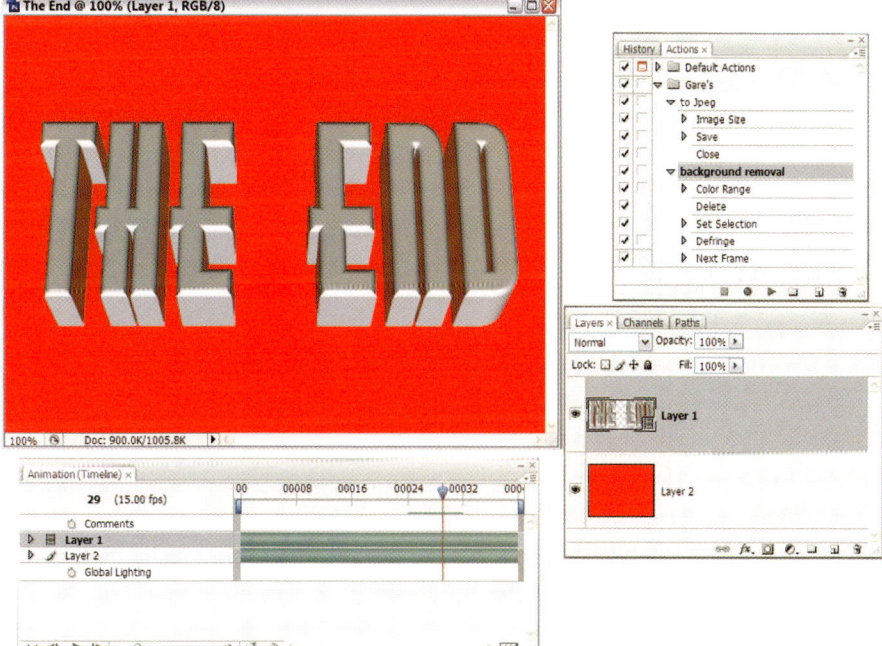

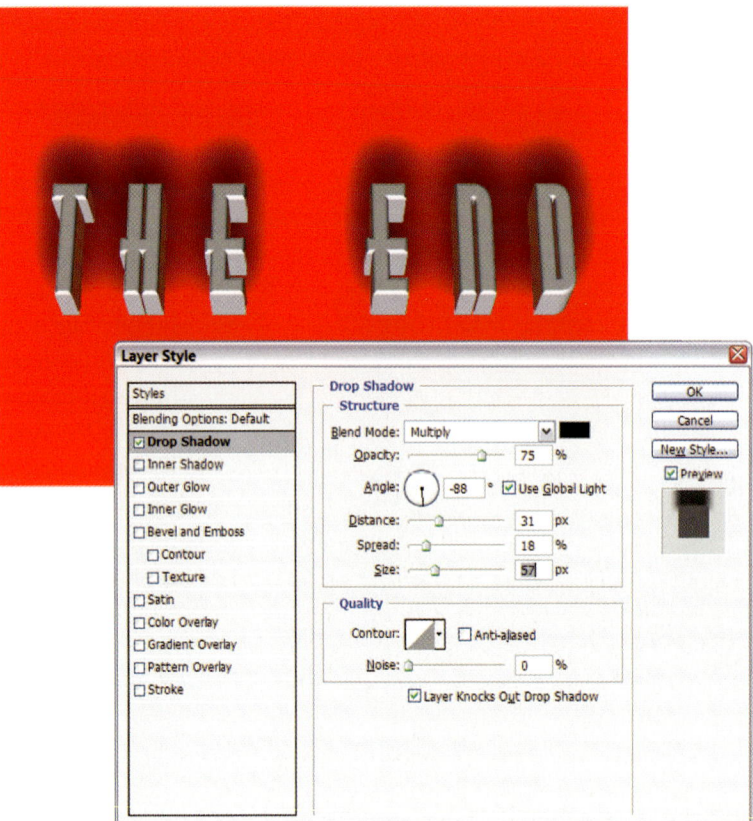

Figure 7.34
Add a drop shadow. You can remove it later if you save the PSD file for re-use with a different look in a different video.

11. Delete the red layer (Layer 2), which is no longer needed. Then select File > Export > Render Video. Write the file with an alpha, no compression, and original document size. The file will be huge, but you can archive it or delete it after you've used it as titling in a different video. No compression means no corruption from codecs.

Adding a Hold to an Animated Title

I'd like to show you one more trick relating to titling. This THE END clip is one animation cycle, and so it doesn't hold onscreen; it just ends the animation cycle using the same keyframe timing as all the frames in the video. Therefore, to make this title fit into a video clip, I'll show you in the following steps how to fade up and then hold the animated text. Load Suspense Theatre Special.mov and follow along.

1. Load THE END.mov and then copy it to the Suspense Theatre Special.mov document window. You can close THE END now without saving.

2. Move the head of the title track to about 10;20 (Frame 330 if you have the palette set to Frame Number increments). See Figure 7.35. Play the video; I think you'll enjoy the titling effect you worked on.

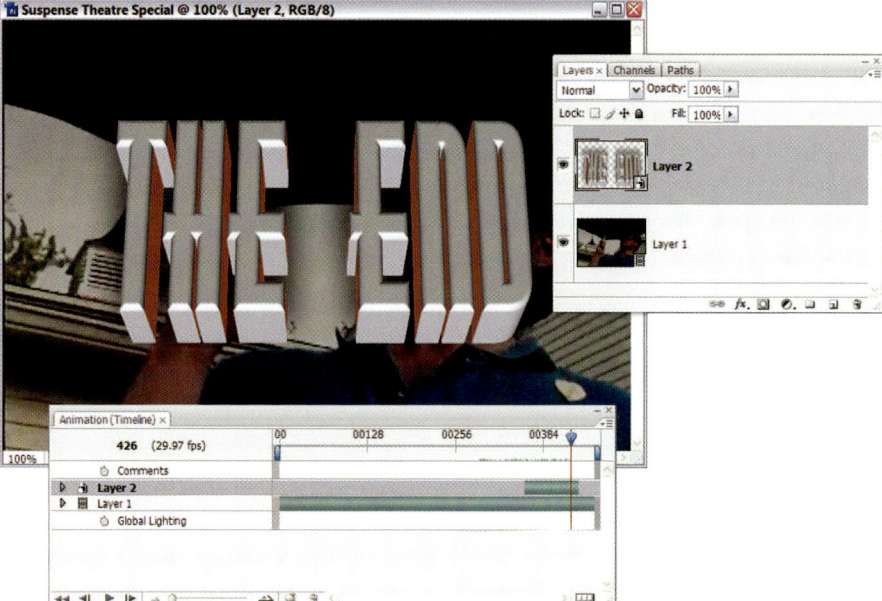

Figure 7.35
Put THE END close to the end of the video clip.

3. Move the timeline indicator to the end of the frames for the text.

4. Hide the bottom video layer.

5. Press Ctrl/Cmd+A and then choose Edit > Copy Merged. What you've just done is to copy the last frame of the text, with transparency and without any video attribute, to the clipboard.

6. Press Ctrl/Cmd+V to paste the clipboard still image to a new layer. With the Move tool, align the text to the text video on the layer underneath.

7. What you want to do now is scoot the beginning of the still image's track to just about the end of the track for the animation text. Now you have the leisure of fading the text, which now appears to hold in its final size and position because the still image picks up where the animation leaves off. I suggest you put a keyframe for opacity for the still image layer at the point where it takes over from the Animation track and then do a slow fade to black by setting a keyframe near the end of the overall video, as shown in Figure 7.36, and then set it to 0% Opacity on the Layers palette.

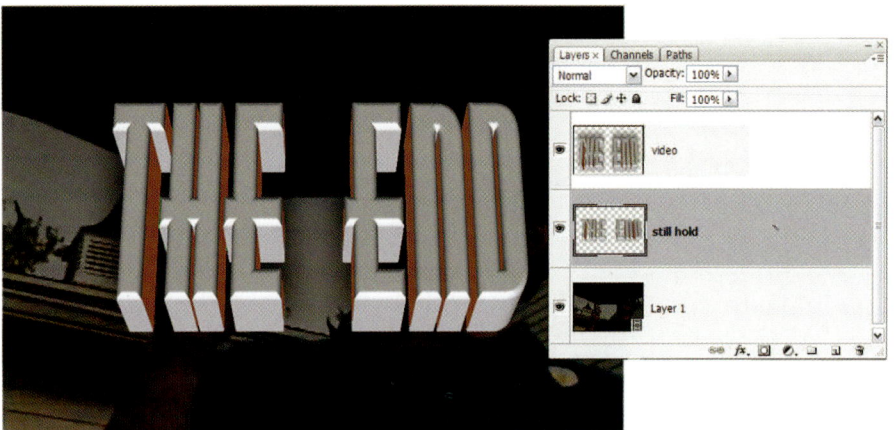

Figure 7.36
Create a hold and fade by copying the last frame of animated text.

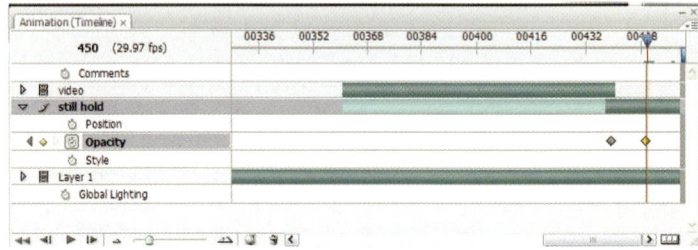

You have a slew of variations you can create based on the numerous effects shown in this chapter; for example, you can not only rotate text but also make it stretch, shrink while gliding into the frame, you name it.

It is you who owns the effect people see when they watch your video. Techniques are to be shared; what you do with the techniques is the feather you earn for your own cap.

Part III
Animation and Rotoscoping

8

Basic Animation and Rotoscoping

Hand animation and animation that looks as though it was hand-crafted is enjoying a renaissance through the vehicle of digital production techniques, and Photoshop Extended is soon to become another player in this medium. A brief explanation of rotoscoping is in order here—its physical roots and what rotoscoping accomplishes.

Traditionally, rotoscoping has been performed using an expensive piece of photo-mechanical hardware called an Oxberry animation stand and was created to get away from stereotypical cartoon animation. The stand consists of a movie projector and a movie camera. Live action footage is shot, developed, and then loaded into the projector, which displays one frame at a time on the animation stand where the animator places a sheet of acetate with registration holes and then traces the action, be it a drawing of a human or an interpretation (usually a cartoon character). The animator then snaps a frame of the finished cell by triggering the movie camera mounted above the stand, advances the movie projector, puts a new blank cell on the stand, and repeats the process. The finished footage contains very realistic movement because essentially the movement has been distilled from real action footage. This is why Snow White in the Disney classic looks so stunningly real and the dwarves look like, well...*cartoons*.

If this sounds tedious, it *is*! But so is hand-crafting a piece of furniture or finely tailoring a suit. Fortunately, the personal computer and programs such as

Photoshop have eliminated much of the rote, boring work from rotoscoped animation, and this chapter takes you into some of the basics for creating fresh and original animated work. Additionally, I show you a little about cartoon physics (how to build elastic, whimsical content) and how to integrate animation with live footage, all using the new features in Photoshop.

Rotoscoping a Walk Cycle

Almost synchronously with the development of animation came solutions for short-cutting the months and years necessary for making feature-length attractions. One shortcut is called the *animation cycle*. For example, suppose the director wants you, the animator, to build a scene of a character taking a dozen eggs from a basket. It would be folly to spend a day hand-drawing a repetitive motion when the sequence could be effectively conveyed by creating a cycle of the hand taking one egg out, and then shooting the cycle a dozen times (eggs often come in dozens). If you're up early on Saturdays, you can still see Fred Flintstone running in place for five seconds; what you're really seeing is 12 frames repeated five times (I'll discuss frames per second further later in this chapter).

Therefore, in the following example, to rotoscope a complete walk cycle you need to photograph someone making this cycle. I've provided a small animation of a walk cycle for you to use that I created in e-frontier's Poser instead of photographing someone walking, for reasons of practicality. You'd need a treadmill to keep the subject framed consistently, and the Poser animation not only looks natural, but every frame is in perfect focus.

Building the First Rotoscope Frame

There's a caveat when building an animation cycle that has to do with matching the first frame to the last to complete the cycle. That is: The last frame does not complete the action, but rather it needs to serve as the frame "before" the first frame. So suppose your cycle takes 1 second to complete at 30 frames per second. You have 30 frames; however, the cycle *does not complete itself* at the end. This is a difficult idea to grasp: Frame 1 is *not* the same as Frame 30, not in a seamless cycle.

In fact, for me it makes more head sense to label a 30-frame cycle 0 through 29. Photoshop's Animation palette starts at Frame 0, and it makes following clips easier to sort. For example, the following second of animation would then run from Frame 30 to Frame 60, and the increments to follow can be quickly and easily calculated by adding one to the end of the previous clip. Here's a table to make more visual sense of how cycles follow one another when you use 30-frame clips:

Clips	Start Frame Number	End Frame Number
First	0	29
Second	30	59
Third	60	89
Fourth	90	119
Fifth	120	149
Sixth	150	179

As you can see, it's not obvious how you find a frame in different animation cycles, but there's a pattern you simply need to get used to. This is also why you'll want to switch from Timecode to Frame Number display under Palette Options for the Animation palette; measuring an animation in seconds removes the ambiguity of frame counting.

It would be time consuming and not to the point to design a walk cycle of a detailed human or other character, so you'll only design a video of an uncomplicated skeletal stick figure. Here's how to begin the design of a walking stick figure cycle:

1. Open the Walk cycle.mov file in Photoshop. Then choose Layer > Video Layers > New Blank Video Layer. Think of the walk cycle video layer as your Oxberry stand movie projector and the new blank video layer as your prepared acetate cell(s). (Your movie camera will be File > Export > Render Video when you're finished.) See Figure 8.1.

2. Consistency between frames is critical for a smooth animation, and therefore even a simple stick figure requires several of Photoshop's tools to draw. Choose the Elliptical Lasso tool and then on the Options bar, choose Fixed Size Style and specify 90 pixels Width and Height to create the stick figure's head (the same size for every frame).

3. Click over the kid's head area and then press D (default colors). Choose Edit > Fill and then choose Contents, Use: White, and then click OK.

4. Choose Edit > Stroke, and then type **3** in the Width field (the foreground color should be black as you specified in Step 3), click OK, and then press Ctrl/Cmd+D to deselect.

5. Choose the Brush tool and then right-click in the document window and set the brush size to 5 pixels, hard tip. Press Enter to dismiss the palette and make sure Brush settings are at 100% Opacity and Flow. Draw the torso and arms using single even strokes.

234 Adobe Photoshop CS3 Extended: Retouching Motion Pictures

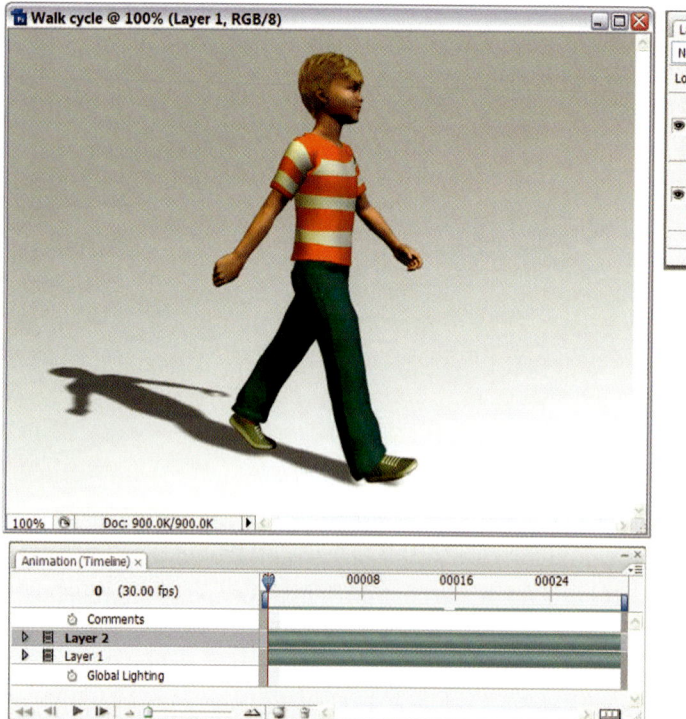

Figure 8.1
To perform rotoscoping, you need a source video beneath the video layer upon which you draw.

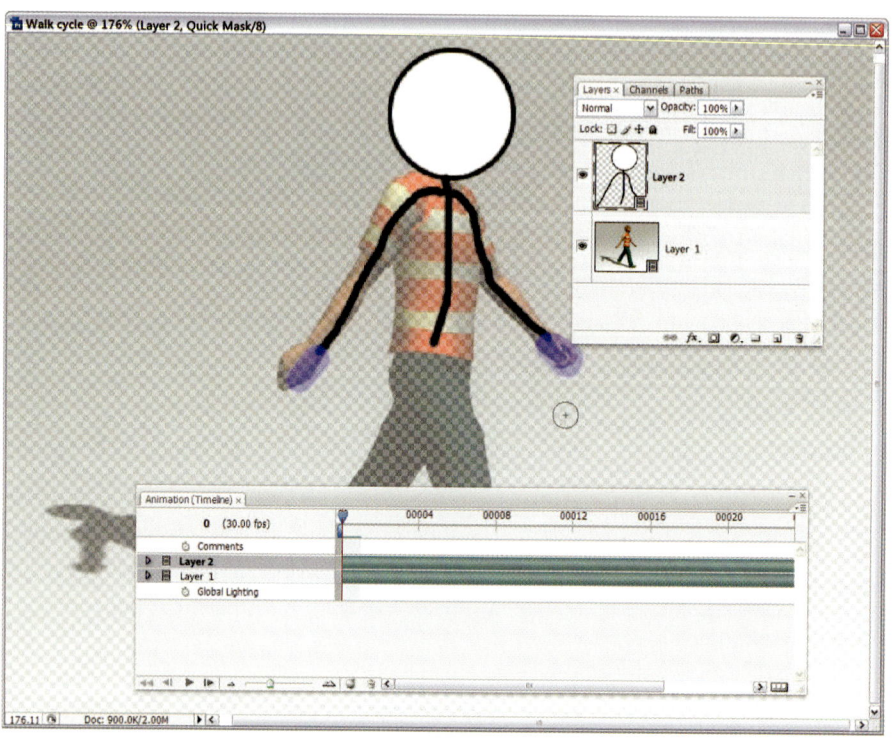

Figure 8.2
Use these same steps when you create additional frames to ensure stroke and fill consistency in the animation.

6. Click the Quick Mask icon on the Tools palette. Draw ovals for hands at the ends of the arms and then switch back to Standard Editing mode. It helps for the moment while you're creating to reduce the opacity of the video layer to better see what you're doing. See Figure 8.2.

7. Repeat methods used in Steps 3 and 4 to stroke and fill the hand areas.

8. Create stick legs and ovals for feet using the steps you used for the arms and hands.

You've designed Frame 1 (Frame 0 as indicated on the Animation palette). Now stop, and read on for the details on automation techniques, frame consistency and smooth transitions, and fps rates used in traditional animation.

Designing an Animation Using Twos

Animation was originally created using physical movie cameras that captured motion at 24 frames per second (fps). For the sake of expediency, animators soon discovered that each frame could be duplicated in a second's worth of time, and the resulting animation would still look reasonably smooth at a playback of 24 fps, even though there were only 12 frames of content per second. With the advent of broadcast television, the fps rate has increased to 29.97 fps, and today's digital displays play back with increased fidelity at 30 fps (non-dropframe is acceptable for Web animation and video because the necessity to reconcile black and white and color transmission using dropframe is not necessary).

However, the amount of content in a second's worth of animation has absolutely *nothing to do with* the speed of the playback, and traditional animators called this cheat *animating in twos*. Animating this walk cycle in twos therefore requires only 15, not 30, frames of content. However, due to the fact that each frame in the underlying walk cycle is unique (it was not designed in twos), you'll need to average out the motion through the use of Photoshop's onion skin features to draw the 14 remaining frames in the cycle. This process is called *tweening,* but it is not the same as the Animation palette's Frames mode Tweening feature.

Play along with me and follow these steps:

1. If you haven't done so already, create a shortcut key combo for duplicating the current video frame. Choose Edit > Keyboard Shortcuts, choose Shortcuts for Application menus, and then find Layer > Video Layers > Duplicate Frame. I recommend pressing Ctrl/Cmd+Shift+D and accepting the conflict, but use anything you're comfortable with. Click OK to apply and return to the workspace.

2. Press Ctrl/Cmd+Shift+D to duplicate your first frame. Now you need to create a second frame whose content is an average of the pose between Frames 3 and 4 on the underlying rotoscope reference video of the kid.

3. Go to Frame 3 on the Animation palette.

4. Click the Animation palette flyout menu and then choose Onion Skin Settings.

5. You want to look behind by one frame and probably have no use for looking ahead, so type **1** in the Frames Before field and **0** in the Frames After field. Because you're animating in twos, type **2** in the Frame Spacing field as shown in Figure 8.3 and then click OK. What you will see in the document window might be a tad disorienting because Onion Skin applies to all layers, both the animation layer and your rotoscope reference layer, but the view will serve you well once you get used to it, and you can hide a layer's visibility at any time. Also, put a layer between your design and the rotoscope layer and fill it with white and then hide the layer. This is a quick way to check the progress of your animation.

Figure 8.3
Set up the Onion Skin feature like this.

6. Use the steps described earlier to create your next frame using the same stroke widths and fill colors. The head of the stick figure will remain pretty much in the same position throughout the animation, but when drawing the arms and legs, make your strokes an average of the distance between the Onion Skin positions you see, as shown in Figure 8.4. This is the "tweening" technique: designing frames whose content is in-between the frames you see in the Onion Skin display.

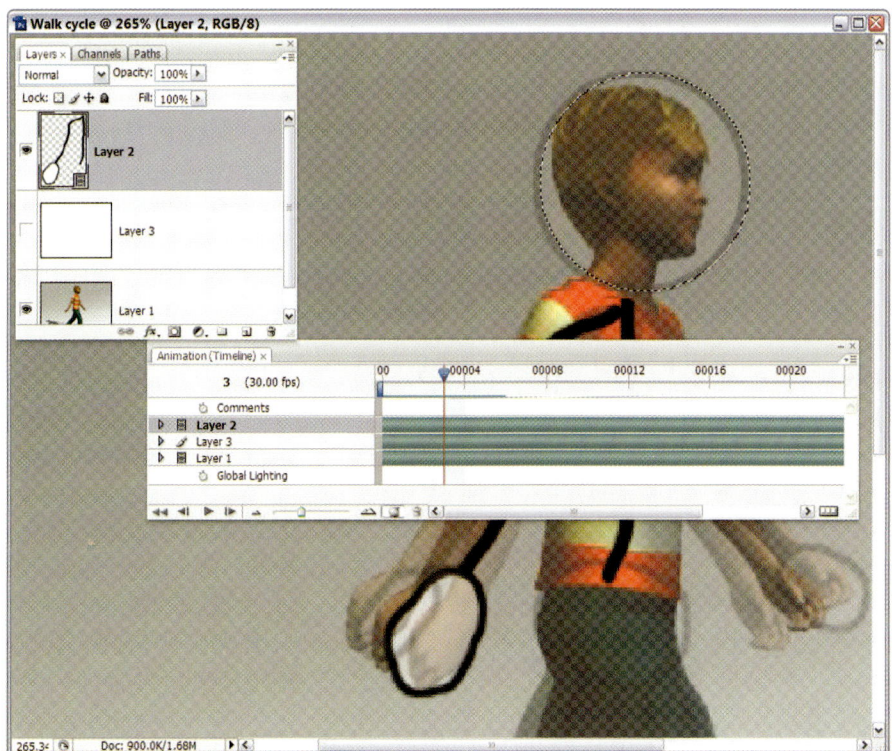

Figure 8.4
Tweening is necessary when your rotoscope source is on ones and your animation is on twos.

7. Once you're done with a frame, remember to duplicate it on the timeline.

That's the story. All that remains is to exercise your manual dexterity to create 13 more frames. Hand animation is a chore, pure and simple, but it's a lot less of a chore today than traditional rotoscoping, and it looks unlike the dearth of 3D animation out there, so you have a distinctive look when plying your trade. Play back the animation when you're done (hide or delete the rotoscope reference layer). In Figure 8.5 you can see that I also have a perspective shadow going on in a final composition.

Figure 8.5
A perspective (cast) shadow can help put a 2D character *in* a scene, not simply *on* a scene.

To create a perspective shadow what you need to do is the following:

1. Make the animation a movie: Delete the white background layer, and since you don't need the walk cycle bottom layer any longer, delete that, too. Choose File > Export > Render Video. Click Settings and then choose Animation as the compression type for QuickTime, which allows alpha masking to be retained.

2. Open the rendered video, and then duplicate the video layer. With the bottom layer selected on the Layers palette frame by frame, Ctrl/Cmd+click the layer thumbnail to load the nontransparent areas as a selection and then fill it with black.

3. Frame by frame, use Gaussian blur to make each frame a soft shadow.

4. Right-click the layer title and create a Smart Object from the video.

5. Frame by frame, press Ctrl/Cmd+T to put each frame into Free Transform, and then (first) right-click and choose Scale and scale down the height to 25% or so. Then right-click and choose Skew from the context menu. Skew the object to the left by dragging the top center bounding box handle left until the head of the shadow is about one screen inch from the left edge of the document window, or until it just looks right. Click the check icon on the

Options bar or press Enter to apply. It's critical not to move the position as you progress from frame to frame or change the skew and scale values or the Gaussian blur amount.

6. Write the animation out with an alpha channel just like you did in Step 1. Open the animation now; I'm going to show you how to animate a background in the following section.

This seems like a chore, but it ensures consistency from frame to frame. You don't have a rotoscope reference for your stick figure shadow, and I tried hand-painting a shadow from frame to frame, only to result in a twittering shadow that spoils the animation.

Fleshing Out Your Animation

You now have a walk cycle, which looks great but is hardly an animation sequence. You'll certainly want to repeat the cycle so it plays for at least 4 or 5 seconds. Additionally, in the sections to follow I show you how to add simple but effective embellishments such as shading and a background for your character.

Backgrounds 101 and Repeat Cycles

If you have less than a half hour to deliver a completed Mr. Stickman animation to your client, follow the steps below. If you have more time, I'll show you how to build more visual detail into your scenes later in this chapter.

1. Render your existing video with alpha transparency if you haven't done so already (File > Export > Render Video). Then choose File > Open and bring the video into the workspace. You can save and close your original animation now.

2. Click the menu icon on the Animation palette and then choose Document Settings. Increase the play length to 4 seconds; in Frame increments your first frame will be 0 and the last will be 119.

3. Duplicate the video layer three times by pressing Ctrl/Cmd+J or dragging its thumbnail on the Layers palette list into the Create a New Layer icon at the bottom.

4. On the Animation palette, stage the start and end points for the video layers by dragging the green bars so heads and tails align.

5. On the Layers palette, create a new layer and move it to the bottom of the stack.

6. To keep the background simple and copacetic with the stick figure, choose the rectangular Marquee tool and then drag a selection for some ground in

the background. Fill the selection on the bottom layer with medium green, and then press Shift+F7 to invert the selection.

7. Choose light blue as your foreground color on the Tools palette and then choose very pale blue, almost white, as the background color.

8. Choose Filter > Render > Clouds. Press Ctrl/Cmd+F to trigger the last-used filter if you're not pleased with the random cloud pattern; the filter creates different fractal clouds every time you reissue the command. Stop when you're happy with the clouds and then Ctrl/Cmd+D to deselect.

Run your animation! The simple animation has a lot of high production values such a fluidity of motion, the shadow anchors the stick figure, and rotoscoping the character truly adds a sense of humanity to an unlifelike object. The visual contrast between smooth animation and primitive shading and character development becomes an art form of its own. By the way, I cheated the Poser kid toward the camera deliberately. He's not exactly three-quarter view, but by rotating him just a little, your rotoscoped animation has more depth, and the stick figure indeed still looks like it is traveling toward camera right. That's one thing I've never liked about the production line cartoon animations of the late 1950s—animators felt compelled to show a perfect profile of their characters walking, but this flattens the scene. See Figure 8.6 and always think about your camera view even when you're not using a camera.

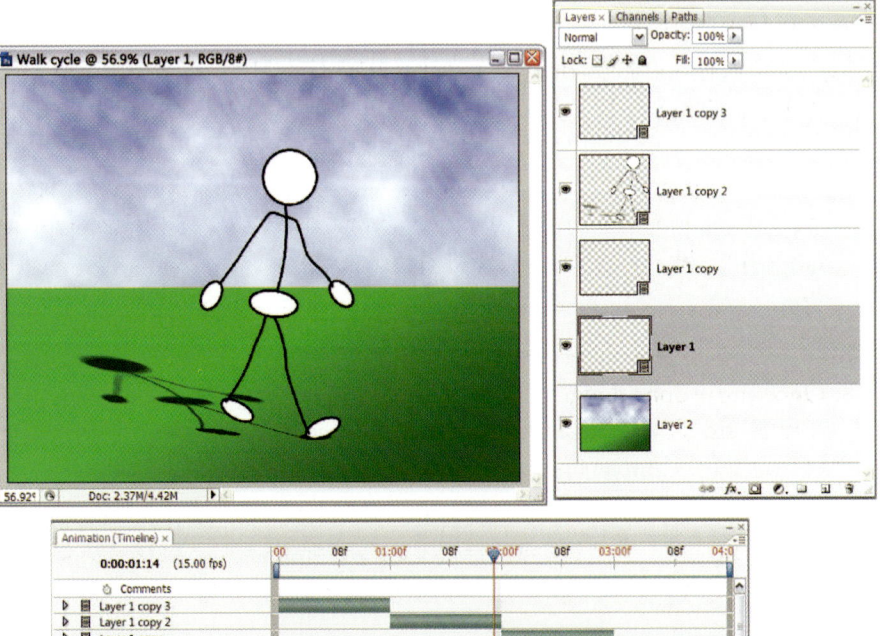

Figure 8.6
Flesh out your cycle into a whole video clip by duplicating layers.

Quick Character Shading

In the following example, you'll assemble a 28-frame animation in Photoshop that I've created. That it's not 30 frames, or 15, is irrelevant to the fps playback rate as I described earlier (I hit a technical snag and skipped a frame). Compressed animations that contain alpha information are exponentially larger than non-alpha animations, so this is why I'm asking you to open an image sequence to build the animation: to save download time.

My character Dexter is a more detailed character than the stick figure; it took more time to illustrate but I basically rotoscoped him using the Poser kid clip exactly like the stick figure tutorial. In the steps to follow I show you a quick shading technique that will bring out the depth of an animated character and add visual quality to this video or any you design yourself.

1. Unpack the Dexter.zip file and then in Photoshop choose File > Open, click on any of the PNG files, check the Image Sequence box, and then click Open. Choose 30fps as the frame rate. Choose Multiply blending mode for the video (on the Layers palette).

2. Choose Layer > Video Layers > New Blank Video Layer and then move the new layer underneath the animation layer.

3. Fill the bottom video layer with a neutral (try 40%) gray.

4. At Frame 0, use your shortcut key combo to duplicate this filled frame for the duration of the Work Area.

5. Go back to Frame 0. Choose the Dodge tool from the Tools palette. Choose the 27-pixel diameter soft tip from the Options bar and set the Range to Highlights and the Exposure to about 17%.

6. Frame by frame, "paint" using the Dodge tool to create highlight areas. Here's the deal: Frame 0 is your reference for future frame dodging; Onion Skin will guide the consistency of your strokes. See Figure 8.7.

7. Choose Onion Skin Options from the Animation palette's flyout menu and choose one frame before and no frames afterwards.

8. Once you're done dodging, choose the Burn tool, keep the tool diameter and softness from the Dodge tool, and set the Range to Shadows with about 17% exposure.

9. Stroke to burn areas, creating shading on the character, as shown in Figure 8.8. I already did a little shading, but the body of the character could use more dimensionalizing through toning the gray layer.

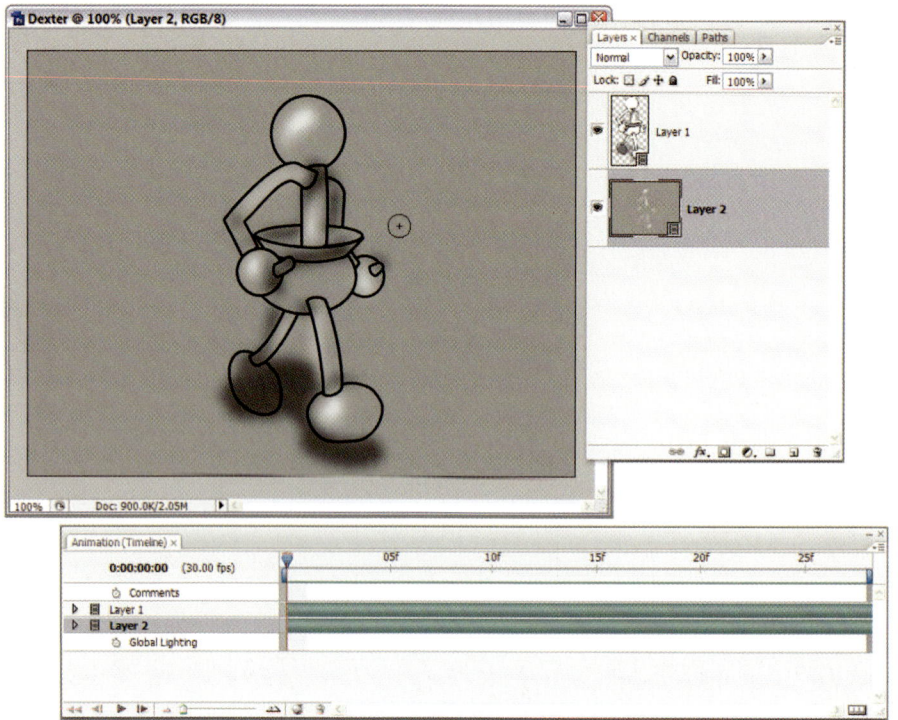

Figure 8.7
Use the Dodge tool as you would a painting tool to create character highlights.

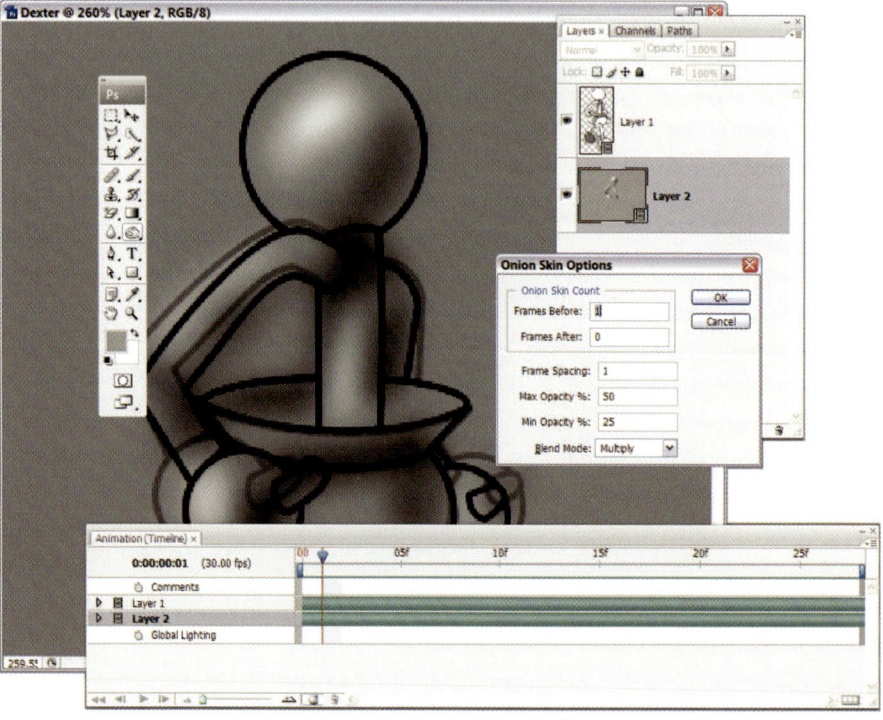

Figure 8.8
Use Onion Skin to keep your shading fluid and consistent from frame to frame.

> **Working Between Illustrator and Photoshop**
>
> If you own Illustrator CS3, you can work between Photoshop and Illustrator to create an animation whose elements are always consistent and perfectly aligned; some artists work more quickly with vector objects than paint strokes. You create your character in Illustrator and then save it to Illustrator (AI) file format. Then you choose File > Open As Smart Object in Photoshop, choose the Illustrator file, and you now have a linked design. You duplicate the (Smart Object) layer on the Layers palette and then double-click the duplicate's thumbnail to call Illustrator. You move the objects in Illustrator to advance the animation to the following frame, then close the design in Illustrator; when you return to Photoshop, your duplicate frame is updated.
>
> This might seem like the long way about things, but if your client insists on precision and crispness (such as an animated logo), this procedure is your ticket. After all the frames have been created, you choose Make Frames from Layers on the Animation palette flyout menu, and you're ready to render your video.

Adding a Static Background and Hierarchal Motion

The background you added to the stick figure earlier is serviceable, but Dexter is a more detailed character who deserves a more detailed background. Additionally, Dexter looks a little awkward walking in place, so you're going to address this problem in the following steps by adding what is commonly called hierarchal (nested) motion to the video.

Here's an example of hierarchal nesting that's used in 3D modeling animations and in traditional animation: You have a character scratching his nose. That's a motion (probably a cycle) that is *local* to the character. But to breathe more life into the character, he's scratching his nose while walking across the stage. The walking is animation that is *global* to the scene, and his local nose scratching is subordinate to the global walking scene. It's nested; to expand on this, if you designed the animation so the camera appears to pull back, the pull back is now global, and the nesting goes as nose scratching < walking < pull back. Hierarchal nesting helps communicate a complete scene to fellow animators; it helps break down a scene to various animators' responsibilities, and the result can be a complex and visually rich animation.

So now that Dexter is walking, let's make him walk somewhere in a scene. You can lose the background layer from the previous tutorial to better concentrate on the subject at hand:

1. Open the Backdrop.png file and then while holding Shift, drag its thumbnail on the Layers palette into the Dexter animation document window. Then move the layer to behind the animation video layer. Keep the file open for later, but you can minimize its window for the moment.

2. Create two duplicates of the video layer.

3. Click the menu icon on the Animation palette, choose Document Settings, and let the document Work Area take up about four seconds. You can trim it later; the excess time gives you room to play with Dexter walking across the stage. You have no real way of knowing how long it takes the character to cross the stage because his walking motion doesn't really tell you the scale of the area onstage he's traversing.

4. Stage the three walk cycles so that the heads and tails meet on the Animation palette; use the cursor to drag the green video layer bars.

5. Start with the bottom Dexter layer (I've labeled it "first" in the screen figures). Click the stopwatch button for Position, then move the keyframe marker to the end of the layer's track and move to this point in time by dragging the thumb on the timeline.

6. With the Move tool chosen, nudge the position of Dexter so he's about one-third of the way across the scene from the left side of the document. You don't want to simply drag the object in the document window because this could inadvertently introduce vertical movement into the animation. In general, nudge using the keyboard arrow keys when you want fluid, steady position changes.

7. Move the current time to Frame 0, and then with the keyboard keys, nudge Dexter so he's completely offstage to the left. Doing this creates a new keyframe marker at the 0 frame.

8. Perform Steps 5-7 with the second and third video layers, except start Dexter one-third into the scene with the second layer and then put him at two-thirds across the screen at the end of his track. The third video layer should start Dexter two-thirds heading right offstage and the end of the track should position him offstage at right. See Figure 8.9 for the keyframe markers and the overall staging of the animation. A total playlength of three seconds seems to

put Dexter at a comfortable walking pace, but if you feel he needs to slow down, you can adjust all the track position markers, add a fourth video layer, and let the animation play for four seconds. I personally felt three seconds running across the scene was fine and pulled the end of the Work Area to three seconds before rendering to video.

When you're done, duplicate the document, save and close the original, and keep the duplicate window open for the tutorial in the following section. Delete the first and third Dexter video animations and the background layer, then position Dexter in the center of the document and remove the Position keyframes by clicking its stopwatch icon so it doesn't have a hairline highlight around it. Be sure to change the layer blending mode back to Normal for all Dexters concerned.

Render the video (no alpha channel; just about any compression scheme is suitable). QuickTime player has an option to loop the video under the View menu if you render to QuickTime, and Windows Media Player loops automatically with AVI and other formats it supports.

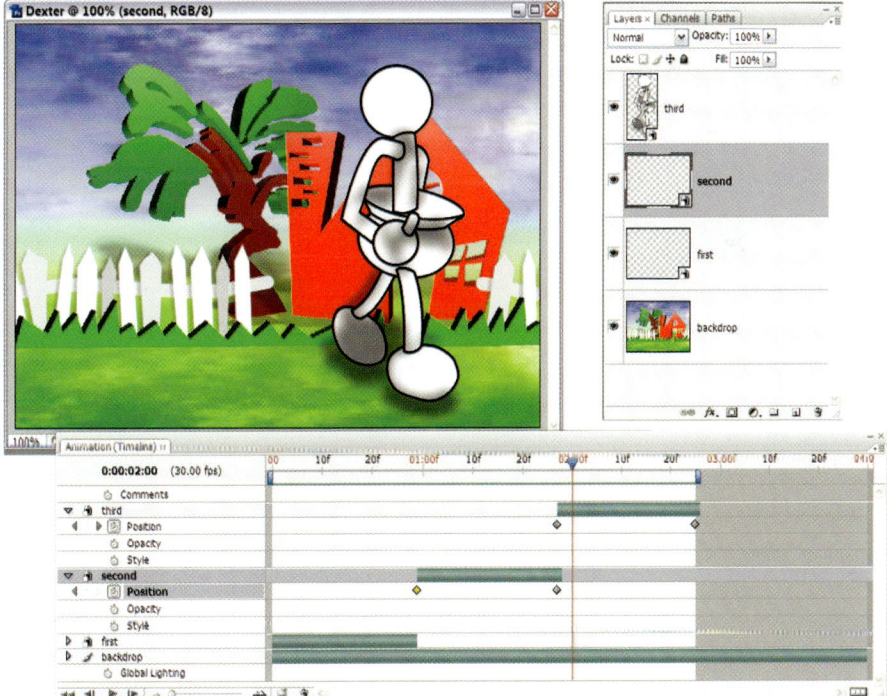

Figure 8.9
Make sure the end position of each layer matches the beginning position of the following layer. Use the keyboard arrows with the Move tool selected to nudge the character.

Simulating a Camera Tracking the Character

I get a kick out of some of the 1950s Hollywood B movies where the budget didn't allow a camera to go on location and track the hero running around. Usually, a painted backdrop, a very wide one, was rigged on two poles and scrolled behind the hero running in place. Hokey stuff for sure, but a scrolling background can be a very effective way to enhance a scene of a walking character in a cartoon such as Dexter. To do the effect so that it cycles, you need to make the backdrop seamlessly tile horizontally. Follow these steps to make Dexter run in place, make the background move, and simulate a camera tracking Dexter as he walks:

1. Open the Backdrop.png document. Choose Filter > Other > Offset.

2. Type **380** in the Horizontal field as shown in Figure 8.10 and click the Wrap Around button to wrap the image to the right so you can clearly see where the right edge of my drawing does not seamlessly align with its left. Click OK.

3. With the Clone Stamp tool and a brush setting on the Options bar of 17 soft edge, Alt/Opt+click to the right of the seam in the drawing, release Alt/Opt after you've defined the sample point for the tool, and then stroke over the seam, as shown in Figure 8.11. In your own work, use precision and get the seam totally, artistically hidden. For this example, one or two strokes will hide the seam, and because the background will animate, precision is not of paramount importance.

4. The speed at which the background scrolls is of some importance, plus how long the duration of the animation should be to qualify as mild entertainment. I feel that Dexter should pass by the background three times, so the background needs to scroll three times (and begin where it ends so the finished clip will loop). Double-click the thumbnail on the Layers palette and then accept the default name for the layer to turn the ordinary bitmap image into a layer-type image.

5. Right-click over the title bar of the document and then choose Canvas Size.

6. Click the chicklet at the 9 o'clock position to make the canvas grow to the right and then choose Percent for the units from the drop-down box. Then type **300** in the Width value field as shown in Figure 8.12. Click OK to apply the resizing.

7. On the Layers palette Ctrl/Cmd+click on the layer thumbnail to load the image as a selection.

Figure 8.10
The Offset filter wraps an image within its document window.

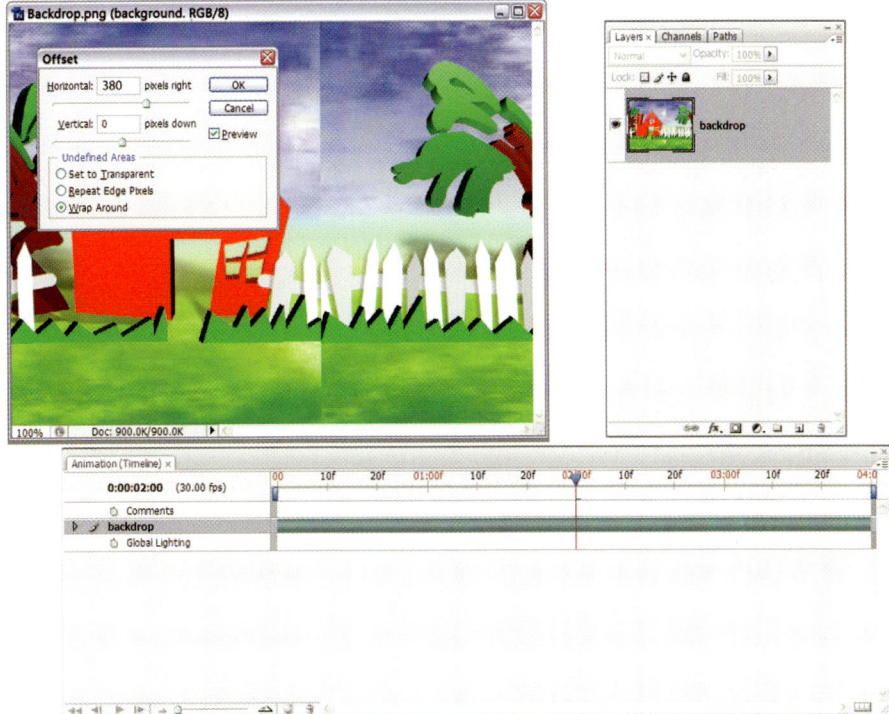

Figure 8.11
Clone over the seam to make the background design wrap.

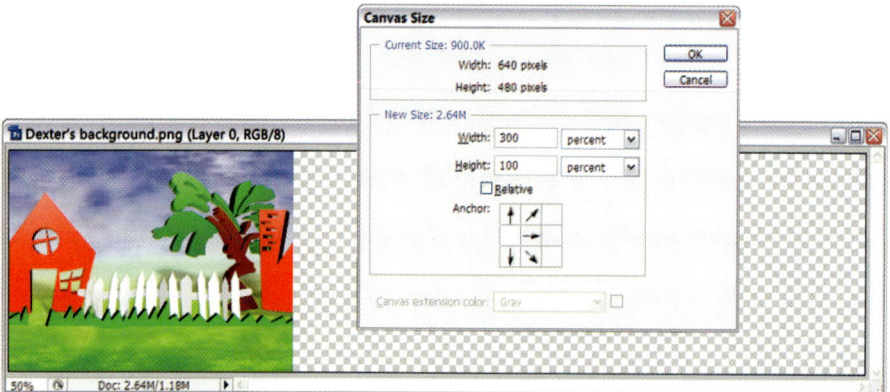

Figure 8.12
Create three times the current vertical space in the document via Canvas Size.

8. Go to Edit > Define Pattern, and name the pattern or leave the default name; click OK. Press Ctrl/Cmd+D to deselect the selection.

9. Choose Edit > Fill and choose the Pattern option in the Fill dialog box, with the custom pattern you saved in Step 8 defined as the chosen pattern. Click OK. You should now have an image that looks like Figure 8.13.

Figure 8.13
Create a very wide seamless background by using a saved pattern that's seamless.

10. Shift+drag the thumbnail into the Dexter video window to center it. Put this layer on the bottom of the stack on the Layers palette.

11. With the Move tool chosen, nudge (using the left keyboard arrow key) the background so its left edge just touches the left edge of the document window. Photoshop uses a feature called Big Data, which holds all the content of an image you duplicate into a window of smaller size without cropping it.

12. Click the Position stopwatch icon for this track on the Animation palette to create a keyframe. Then move the timeline indicator to 3 seconds (the end of the Animation palette Work Area) and use the right keyboard arrow key to nudge the layer contents to meet the right edge of the background with the right edge of the document window. Holding Shift while you keystroke power-nudges by 10 pixels instead of one to speed up this step.

13. Create two duplicates of the Dexter video layer and then arrange the tracks on the Animation palette so that the tail of one meets the head of the following one, as shown in Figure 8.14. Drag the end Work Area marker to the end of the last Dexter animation track and then on the Animation palette menu, choose Trim Document Duration to Work Area. Your animation is done; when the Work Area has completed playing, the background returns to the beginning, which perfectly matches the end frame. Render the file to video; if you choose the Loop option in QuickTime rendered video, the animation will play back seamlessly. Tutorial completed.

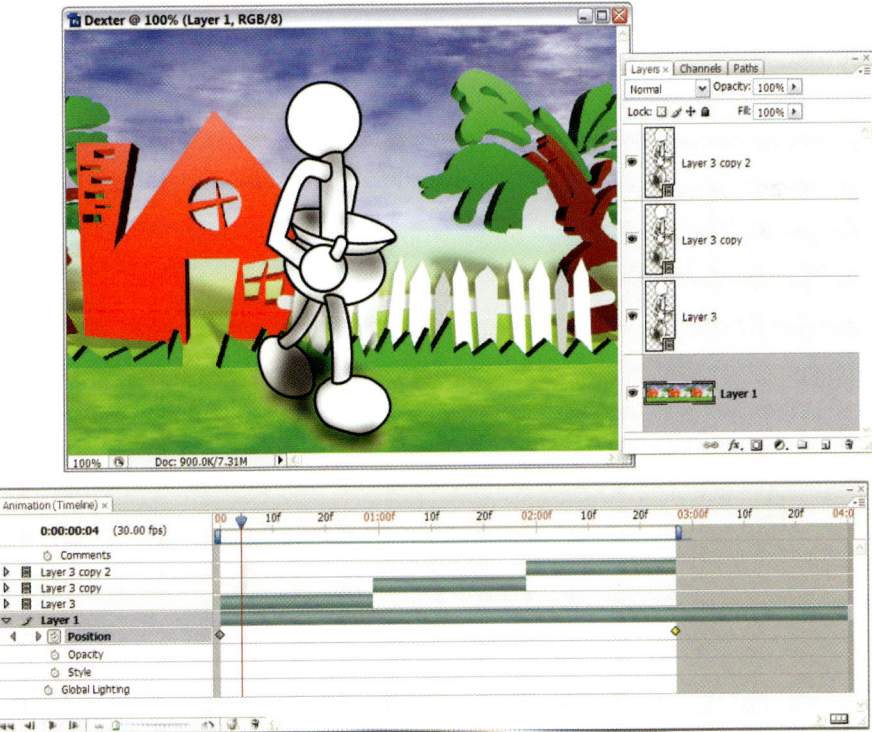

Figure 8.14
A character running in place can be made to cover ground by scrolling a seamless background.

Cartoon Physics

You'll surely want to venture out without a net on occasion, working without a rotoscope reference, and the following section takes you through creating a cycle of a bouncing ball that features something called *cartoon physics*, the unnatural laws of gravity and other forces that make everything from falling Acme safes to squashy barnyard characters so entertaining to watch.

Creating a Squash and Stretch Bouncing Ball

When designing a humorous cartoon animation, you'll want to fracture reality, including the laws of physics, to add the element of plasticity to a motion's fluidity. You bend, overstretch, and add the playfulness of time and space distortion to the animation as an entertainment element to the video without letting it overwhelm the character you develop. There are many rules (okay, let's call them *guidelines*) to cartoon physics, the most common being:

1. Gravity is suspended indefinitely until the character who walks off the cliff looks down and realizes it.

2. There is no momentum. Characters can accelerate to warp speed without start-up time and halt on a dime.

3. Characters and objects usually don't have skeletons, and their exteriors can stretch and squash without limit, *but there is a conservation of mass.*

This last rule applies to the bouncing ball you'll animate shortly. Notice what happens to the mass of a cartoon elephant when a cartoon mouse (3 inches tall) produces a 4-foot tent stake mallet from behind its back and proceeds to do the predictable thing. When struck over the head, the cartoon elephant's sides usually stretch out laterally by a few hundred percent of their original dimensions while its head squashes the same few hundred percent. Mass is conserved when you perform squash and stretch cartoon physics. And then, naturally, the elephant or other victim eventually returns to its original dimensions after a few cycles of squash and stretching. Optionally, cartoon characters appear to return to normal proportions after shaking their head vigorously a few times.

To build a squash and stretch bouncing ball requires only a few keyframes to describe the cycle's motion. In Figure 8.15 I've mapped it all out in an illustration you might want to use as a reference.

1. The ball is undistorted and hangs in the air. Its shadow is placed appropriately.

2. The ball descends, and in this frame a little squashing can be applied. The ball is closer to the ground, reflected by its position and proximity to its shadow, which is now a little larger.

3. The ball impacts with a surface. Its horizontal axis is greater than its vertical axis, and this is your opportunity to exaggerate the dimensions of the ball. It's now touching and overlapping its shadow.

4. The ball rebounds back into the air, releasing an unrealistic amount of energy, and is distorted so that its vertical axis is stretched. Note the corresponding position and size of the shadow.

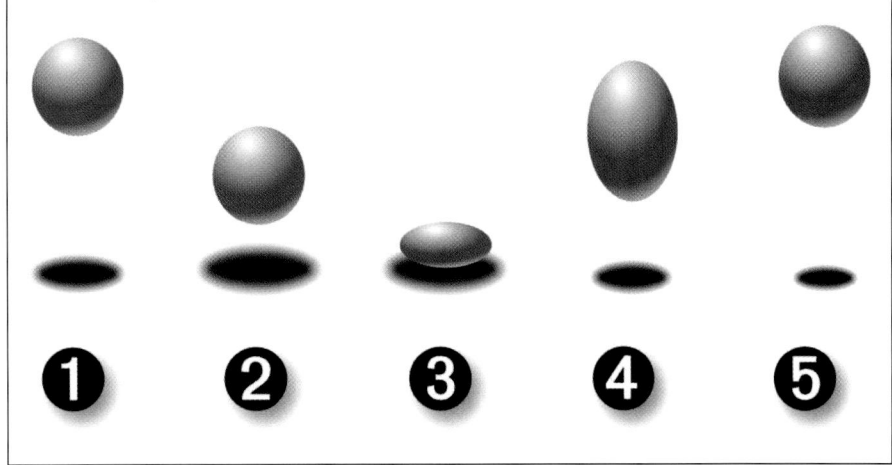

Figure 8.15
A ball that exhibits cartoon physics looks like this in successive frames.

5. The ball reaches its apogee and is prepared for the descent, which plays right back to Frame 1. Its shape is mostly restored, and the shadow is smaller as the ball is farther away from the ground.

Bouncing ball.psd is in the ZIP archive and ready for you to use in the steps to follow if you don't care to illustrate but would prefer to cut to the chase and animate. There are two approaches I can think of for illustrating the frames: You can paint a ball in Photoshop and then stretch and squash duplicates of it, thus keeping patterns and other embellishments to the ball perfectly aligned. Alternatively, you could use Illustrator or other drawing programs (I used Xara Xtreme to build Bouncing ball.psd). The advantage to illustrating over painting the frames is that vector art can be stretched and squashed without losing focus. By the nature of pixel-based art, when you Free Transform it, either you acquire jagged edges as the pixel colors are reassigned to different areas or you lose focus, as is the case with Photoshop's anti-aliasing filters, which mostly negate the blurring effect, although never entirely.

Here are the steps to animating the bounce cycle:

1. On the Layers palette, if using your own file creation, arrange the layers so that your first frame is on the bottom and frames to follow are arranged in sequence to the top. This is for convenience's sake when animating.

2. On the Animation palette, if necessary, click the toggle button at bottom right to switch to Frames mode.

3. Hide all layers except the first frame. On the Animation palette, give the first frame a 0.1 second duration and make the scene loop forever by choosing this option from the drop-down list. Ten frames per second is a little raw for a smooth animation, but you'll smooth out the animation's appearance a little later using Photoshop's tweening feature.

4. Click the Duplicates Selected Frame icon on the Animation palette and then hide the visibility of the first layer and make the second layer visible.

5. Repeat Step 4 until you have five frame thumbnails on the Animation palette as shown in Figure 8.16. Play the animation to see how it runs. Save the file to PSD format and keep it open in the workspace.

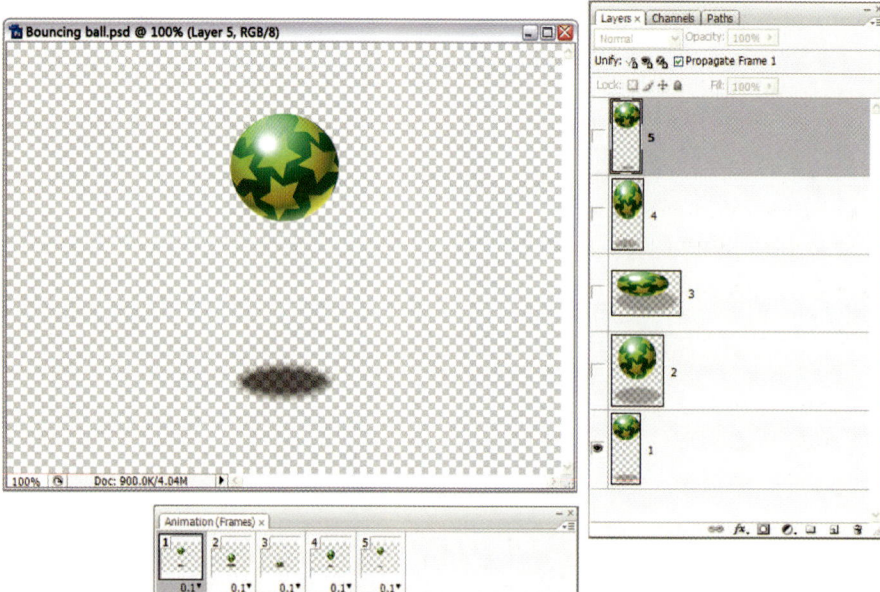

Figure 8.16
Create the animation using the Frames mode of the Animation palette.

Adding a Background and Tweening

The bouncing ball needs a background to contextualize the animation and to give the ball's shadow a ground…literally. My illustration is fairly detailed, and therefore I thought an interesting backdrop would be something photorealistic, so you can use Bouncing ball backdrop.png, which I rendered out of Vue d'Esprit based on a Vue example file. You'll see that there's something visually interesting going on: The ball is not quite photorealistic, but less so than the Vue render. There's harmony yet a little dissonance, and I find this quality to be of entertainment value; consider realism and how you can play with it in the animations you build.

Tweening in Photoshop can be more accurately called *averaging*. Earlier in this chapter I discussed traditional tweening, which requires human input and artistic sensitivity to draw areas that are in between areas shown in Onion Skin mode derived from neighboring frames. In contrast, when you use the tweening feature in Frames mode on the Animation palette, what Photoshop does is create a new frame that is an average of all the image content from the two neighboring frames you choose. For example, if two frames have a ball in different positions, Photoshop does *not* create a ball between these different areas but instead shows you the first and last frame blended together at 50% opacity each.

This *can* be a good feature as you'll soon see, because when you tween frames in the bouncing ball animation Photoshop-style, the resulting video takes on a slow-motion, almost Sam Peckinpah-like quality. Here's how to slow the frenetic bouncing a little, while smoothing out the animation *and* giving it a classic film treatment:

1. If you used my PSD file in the previous steps, the image dimensions are fine to proceed. If you designed the animation frames yourself, the document needs to be 640 by 480 pixels. Use the Canvas Size command, available by right-clicking the document title bar, to adjust the current proportions.

2. Open Bouncing ball backdrop.png and then on the Layers palette, hold Shift and then drag the thumbnail into the animation document window to duplicate and center the background image. Then move it to the bottom of the layer stack. See Figure 8.17. Close the original backdrop image without saving changes.

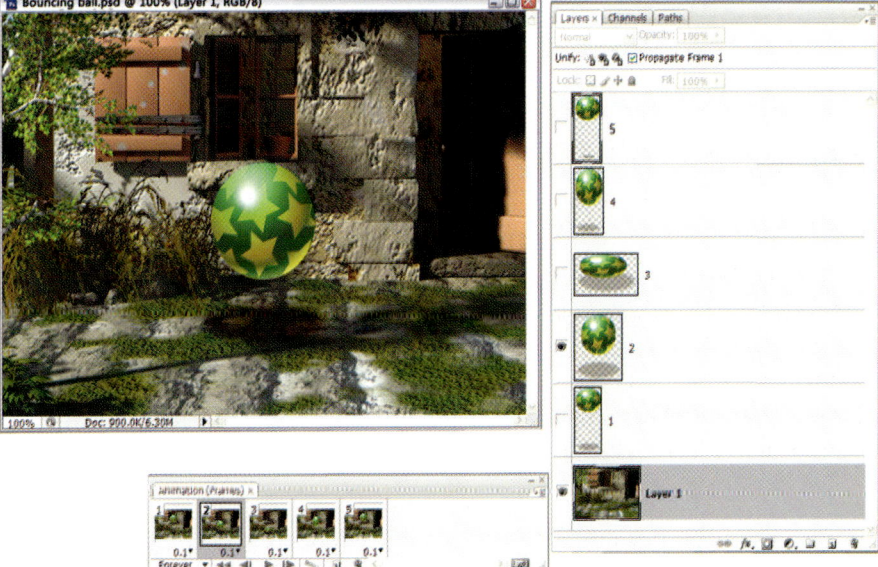

Figure 8.17
Duplicate the background image and center it behind the animation frames.

3. Shift+click to select the first and second thumbnails on the Animation palette. Click the Tweens Animation Frames icon on the bottom of the palette. In the dialog box, type **3** in the Frames to Add field as shown in Figure 8.18, and then click OK. Your original Frame 2 is now Frame 5.

Figure 8.18
Tweening on the Animation palette creates intermediate frames from those selected, which contain a composite percentage of the selected frames.

4. Perform Step 3 with the second and third frames (currently Frames 5 and 6 on the Animation palette because you added three frames), and repeat this process until all frames have three tween frames between them. When you get to the last frame, you hold Ctrl/Cmd and click the last frame thumbnail and then the first frame thumbnail to tween three frames between them (they'll fall at the end of the animation).

5. In the following section I show you how to perform a little integration of the ball with the background scene, and to do this you will eventually add a blank video layer to the composition. And to add a blank video layer, the frame-based video should become a timeline-type layer. Click the flyout menu and choose Convert to Timeline. Your screen should now look like Figure 8.19.

Play the animation. I think you'll be pleasantly surprised with the tweening effect. Keep the file open.

Figure 8.19
Convert the frame-based animation to a timeline-based one.

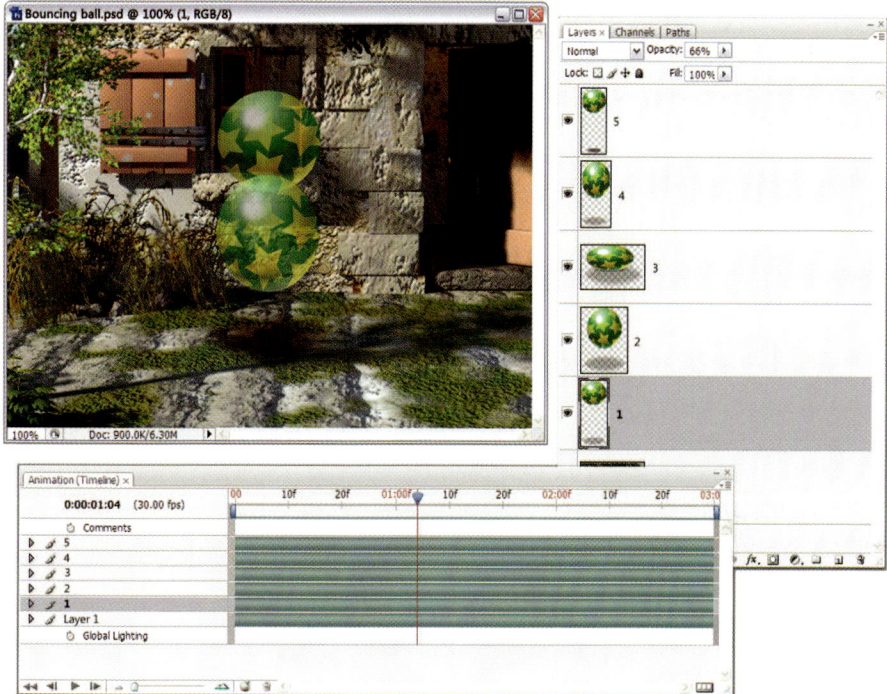

Adding an Appropriate Shadow

One thing I noticed when building the scene is that the bouncing ball hasn't a trace of integrating into the background because they're separate elements. The ball's shadow helps somewhat as an anchoring element, but you can do better. When the ball approaches its apogee, in reality it should receive a little shadow from the tree branch at camera left. As I've mentioned frequently in this book, the accurate *shape* of a shadow isn't nearly as important in moving pictures as the fact that there *is* a shadow—it's what the audience expects and looks for.

In the following steps you'll use a special brush tip on a blank video layer to suggest a shadow periodically when the ball reaches a specific height in the video. Here's how to finish the animation video:

1. You might want to move the ball up in the frame so it's compositionally more eye-catching and also closer to the tree at camera right. To do this, Shift+click all the entries (the layer titles for the ball) on the Layers palette, and then with the Move tool, move them. Because the Position stopwatch is inactive on the Animation palette, you haven't messed up the animation at all.

2. Choose Layer > Video Layers > New Blank Video Layer and make sure this new layer is at the top of the layer stack on the Layers palette.

3. Choose the Brush tool, and then open the Brushes palette from the docking strip (or press F5 if it's not on the strip). Pick the Splatter 59-pixel diameter tip as shown in Figure 8.20. It's easiest to create a credible shadow cast from the leaves on the tree if you increase the spacing to 75% and distort the tip as shown in this figure. Then you put the video layer in Multiply blending mode on the Layers palette, decrease the opacity to about 40%, and choose a deep brown as the foreground color (shadows are rarely pure black). Advance the timeline to where the ball approaches the leaves, and then make your shadow strokes using brisk cursor movements or just click without dragging to apply the shadow.

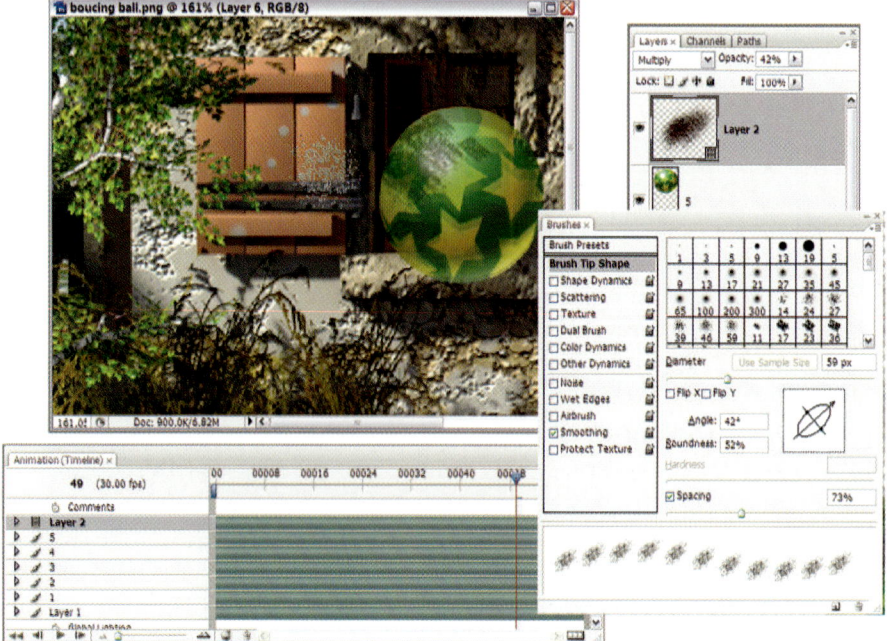

Figure 8.20
Create a detailed, natural-looking leaves shadow by using a Splatter brush tip.

4. Because the action is fairly slow in the video (because you added the tweened frames), you have the leisure to duplicate the frame you just shaded in Step 2. Press Ctrl/Cmd+Shift+D or whatever key combination you set up earlier in the chapter for duplicating the current frame (the long way is Layer > Video Layers > Duplicate Frame).

5. Switch to Frame Number display of the time ruler via the Animation palette menu, Palette Options. You can keep duplicating frames from what I see as Frame 49 to 59 (the last frame if you tweened as I listed the steps earlier). Then it's back to Frame 1 through about Frame 9. At frame 1, create the shadow and then duplicate the frame out to Frame 9.

6. If you're not picky, the shadow can remain in Frame 9 as is, because it's more or less hidden by the shaded window frame. But if you're nit-picky like me, the simple remedy to removing unwanted shadow areas you painted is to switch to Clear painting mode on the Options bar as shown in Figure 8.21 and stroke over the unwanted, inappropriate shadow areas. You don't have to switch brush tips or anything.

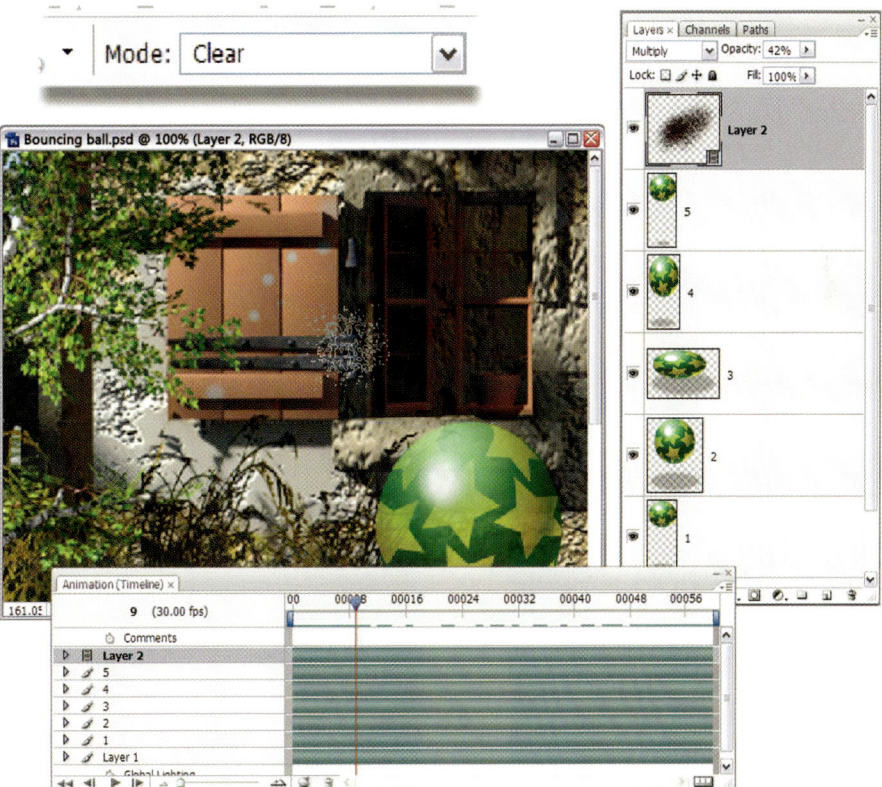

Figure 8.21
Clear painting mode works exactly like the Eraser tool but you don't have to switch tools from your current painting tool.

Embellishing the Animation

Although the bouncing ball cycle animates, it's not a video, and it would be a chore to make it repeat cycles by duplicating layers. Let's say that this cycle (approximately two seconds long) could stand as entertainment if the finished video plays for three cycles. Additionally, and especially with cartoon animation, without audio, the video fails to draw interest. There's a very simple remedy for this: You use the ball hit.mp3 file in the ZIP archive you downloaded for this chapter. I recorded a basketball striking a driveway and then filtered it to sound a little deeper, a sort of audio caricature of a normal ball hitting the ground. I show you how to cue the audio and where to place it in the following steps:

1. Choose File > Export > Render Video. Render the video to QuickTime file format using H.264 compression at a frame rate of 30 fps. Save and close the animation you created in the previous steps and then open the rendered MOV file in Photoshop.

2. With Animation palette options set to Timecode, click the flyout menu on the Animation palette, choose Document Settings, and then increase the duration to 6 seconds.

3. Drag the video layer into the Create a New Layer icon on the Layers palette twice to make two duplicates (or alternatively, press Ctrl/Cmd+J twice).

4. Stage the clips on the Animation palette so the heads and tails of the clips meet and the total of the Work Area is filled.

5. Import the Ball hit.mp3 file. Windows users need to use File > Open As and then open the file as a QuickTime movie. Macintosh users can simply specify that the file's a QuickTime movie when you choose to open it.

6. Drag the thumbnail of the MP3 audio from the Layers palette into the composition. To avoid confusion, it might be a good idea to rename this layer "ball hit," and then with this layer as the active layer, press Ctrl/Cmd+J twice to duplicate it twice.

7. Scrub the timeline until the moment the ball clearly hits the ground in the composition. Here's the deal with synching audio: You generally cue an effect slightly before the corresponding action onscreen for two reasons. First, digital audio has a nasty tendency to lag during playback, which is far less of a problem when playback is from a DVD player hooked up to a TV set. Also, although sound travels slower than light, the human nervous system is more sensitive to a sudden burst of sound than a sudden burst of light (think of your reaction during a lightning storm). The audio sound effect is trimmed very close to the head for ease of placement; drag the green bar that represents the audio layer's duration so the head meets the current time.

8. Perform Step 7 with the other two layers, and then hold Alt/Opt and click the Play button on the Animation palette to preview your video. See Figure 8.22 for the proper staging of the clips.

9. Render the document out to video. Because the enhancements are so simple, there's no real need to keep the current document—you can set it up again to re-render at any time if ever needed in a jiffy.

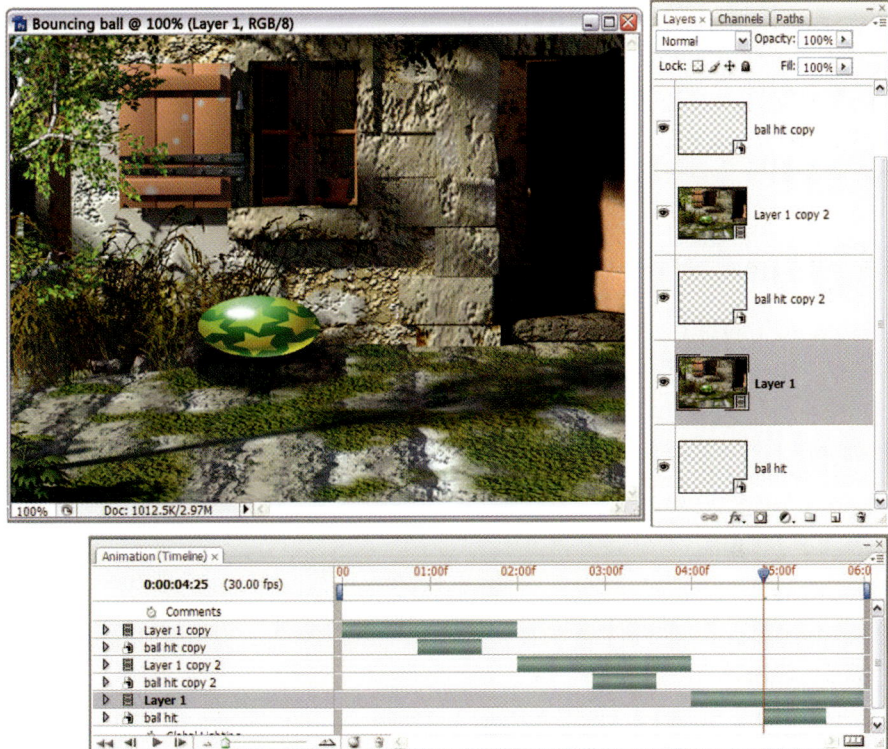

Figure 8.22
For sound effects, let the audio slightly lead the event.

Creating Cycles from Non-Cycling Videos

A motion cycle is more than a time-saving device, as you've seen so far. It can be used as filler to pad out a visual idea that just happens too quickly to be appreciated, or distributed as a feature-length film! In Poser I created a very short idea, sort of abstract: A concrete guy walks toward camera, and a huge block of concrete falls on him midway. Not to be deterred, he walks *through* the concrete block, something that would be hard to film. I thought this would make a nice short, a complete idea expressed in about five seconds. But the audience will want to see it more than once, and there isn't a clean extension to the video (the guy approaches the camera until his face fills the frame).

The solution for both me and for you and future projects is to build some connective tissue to the video so it can repeat without hammering the audience over the head that the five seconds is cycling. You'll shortly see that you don't have to brute-force a clip into cycling, and the result of looping a clip can sometimes *add* a cinematic dimension to the finished presentation.

Creating Continuity with a Background

The theme of the movie is surreal, so I thought a quickly panning sky (borrowing from surrealist Renee Magritte) would be good as a background. Sky.jpg is a very narrow and tall image file that I used the Clone Stamp tool on to get it to seamlessly tile height wise. In the following steps you'll add the background to the animation, and the film's background will then loop as the movie plays over and over again. Then we'll move on to the thornier problem of getting both the foreground *and* the background to play as a loop.

1. Load Determinator.avi. Load Sky.jpg, hold Shift and then drag the thumbnail on the Layers palette into the Determinator document window to center it.

2. On the Layers palette with the Determinator document in the foreground, drag the sky layer to beneath the video layer.

3. Power-nudge (hold Shift and press the keyboard down arrow key) until the top edge of the sky layer touches the top of the document window.

4. On the Animation palette (in Timeline mode), click the Position stopwatch icon at time zero.

5. Hide the video layer and then move the current time on the Animation palette to the end. Power-nudge the sky layer until the bottom edge of the sky image touches the bottom of the document window. Then restore the visibility of the concrete guy layer. With the guy's face filling almost the whole frame at the end of the movie it might be hard for the audience to tell that the sky is seamlessly looping, but don't count on it. See Figure 8.23. Save the document to PSD file format and keep it open.

Building a Static Frame into a Seamless Image

My idea to get the movie to loop seamlessly is an expedient yet artistically effective one: The sky image can fade up at the end to reappear and fade out at the beginning of the movie. However, unlike a simple seamless scroll, when you want your beginning frame to fade up in exactly the same place as it fades out at the end of the video, you need to do something special to a seamless tiling image such as Sky.jpg. In a nutshell, you need to duplicate the area where the video will end and copy it to the area where the first frame of the video begins. This makes the image no longer tile seamlessly, but it makes the *video* loop seamlessly. Fortunately, this is easy to do using Photoshop (you just have to realize you need to do it!). The following steps take you through the method to make the scene come out of the clouds and re-enter at the conclusion.

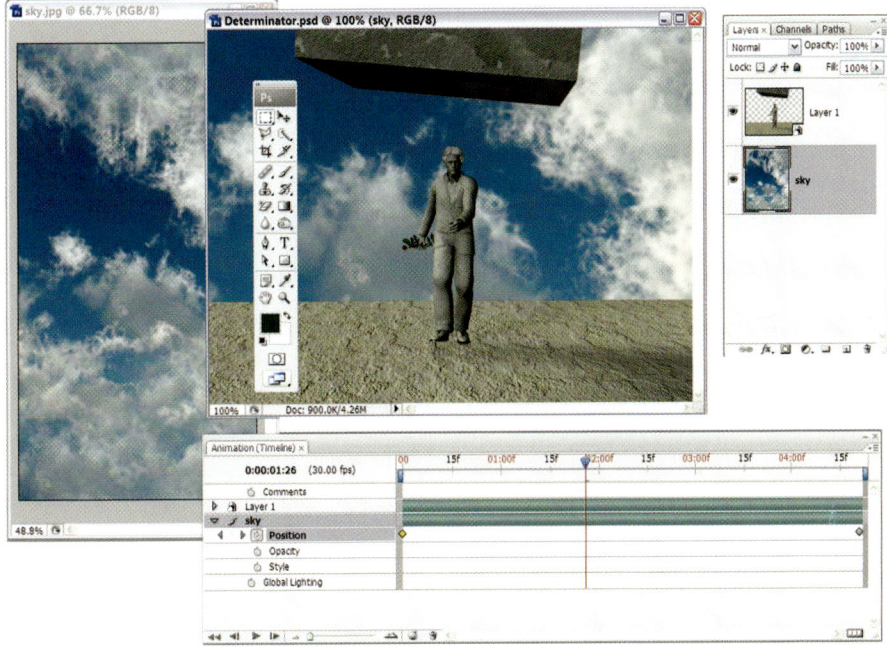

Figure 8.23
Like the Dexter background, the background to Determinator seamlessly scrolls from beginning to end and back again.

1. The Determinator video is 400 by 300 pixels, so with the rectangular Marquee tool selected, choose Fixed Size Style on the Options bar and then highlight everything in the Width value box and type **400**. When you do this, Photoshop assumes you mean 400 pixels and adds the increment label automatically. Do the same with the Height field; enter **300** and you're all set.

2. With Sky.jpg in the foreground of the workspace, click the bottom of the Sky.jpg image. Then right-click and choose Layer via Copy from the contextual menu, as shown in Figure 8.24 (or alternatively, press Ctrl/Cmd+J).

3. Right-click over the title bar to the sky image and then choose Canvas Size.

4. You need to add 300 pixels to the height of the document, specifically to the top, so click the bottom center anchor chicklet and then type **1500** in the Height field (the present height is 1200, plus the height of the new layer); click OK.

5. Hold Shift and then click both layer titles on the Layers palette. With the Move tool chosen, click the Align Top Edges icon on the Options bar as shown in Figure 8.25. Then right-click over either layer and choose Flatten Image from the context menu.

6. Hold Shift and drag the thumbnail on the Layers palette into the Determinator document window. Make sure it's the top layer in the stack.

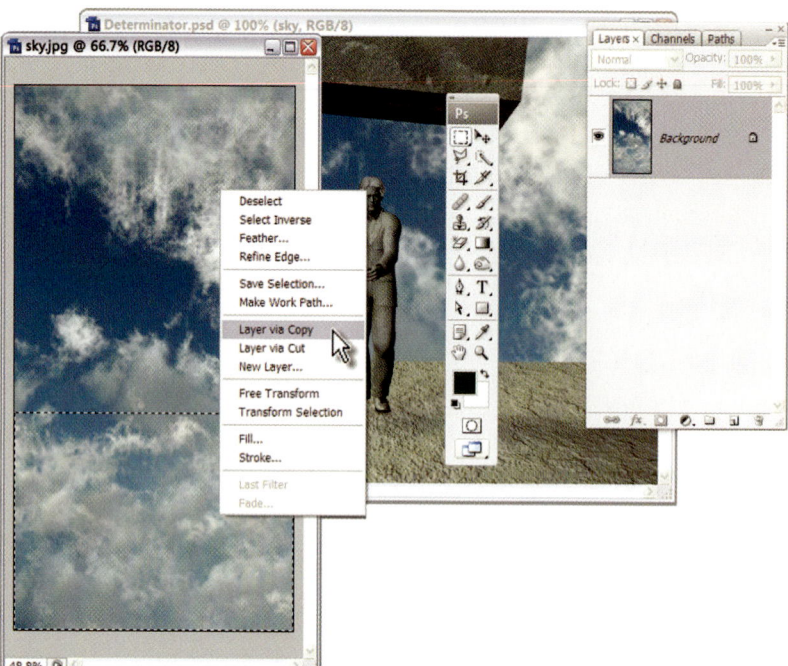

Figure 8.24
Copy the bottom of the image to a new layer.

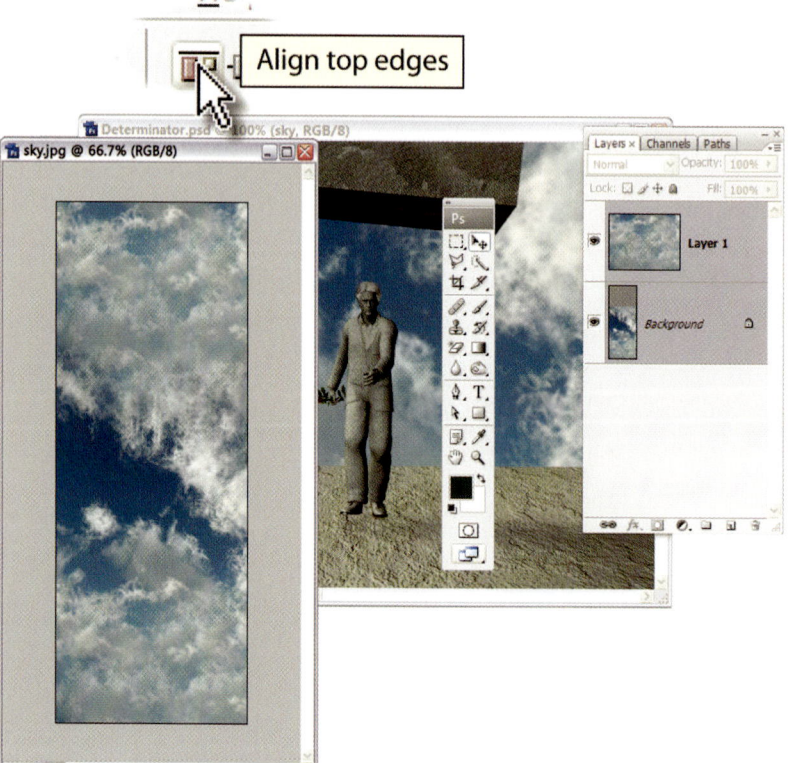

Figure 8.25
Align the tops of the two layers.

7. As you did with the background layer, use the Position stopwatch to start the sky at the top edge of the document at Frame 0, and end it at the bottom edge at the end of the animation timeline. By the way, if your preference of surrealism is to make the sky travel upward, you reverse the keyframe positions, but don't make the background and foreground clouds travel in opposite directions. That would be confusing and mildly irritating to your audience. Interestingly, because the background and foreground cloud layers are of different heights, the foreground clouds will travel at a slightly slower speed, giving an added depth to the final animation.

8. Start the foreground opacity at 100% and then fade it to 0% at about one-half second into the playtime using the Opacity stopwatch for the foreground layer. Then set the opacity to 0% at about 4;07, then back up to 100% at the end of the playtime duration. A quick way to generate keys on the Animation palette is to set the timeline indicator at a specific time and then *create a change* in the position, opacity, or other attribute—and then *readjust* the percentage to your need.

9. Play the animation a few times (mostly to get the buffer going in Photoshop to play the animation in real time). You might feel as though you want a longer or shorter fade in and out of the clouds. Try dragging the 100% opacity keyframes in from the ends of the Work Area as shown in Figure 8.26. When you're satisfied, render the video out and consider your work well done.

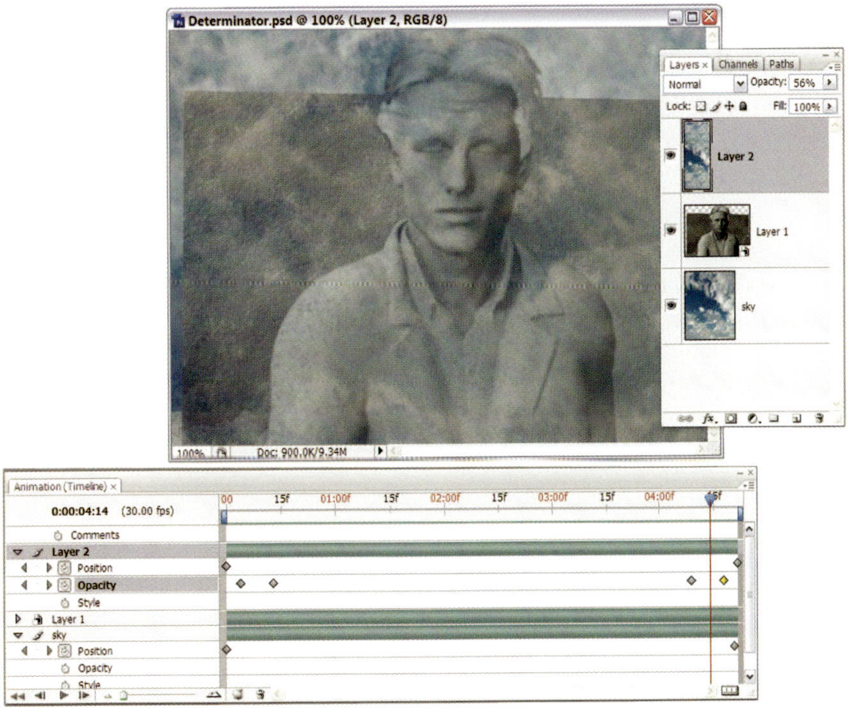

Figure 8.26
The clouds fading in and out help complete a story and mask the reality that the man's walking is not a cycle animation.

If you check out the Gallery folder, I added an abstract synthesizer music track to the video, played it out to run three times, but kept the music continuous—another method of binding the three looping clips together. I also punctuated the fall of the concrete block with a sound effect, slightly preceding the event onscreen, as I discussed earlier.

My artistic decision to loop my finished Gallery animation three times was a call on the overall length of the final animation and the "meaning" added to it by playing it repeatedly. Fifteen seconds is mild entertainment; any less and the audience won't really get to see the work, and more times would be boring. At three times looping, I feel the concrete guy is more determined than walking through his obstacle only once, sort of saying, "Whatever life tosses down on me, I'm *determined* to get this rose to my concrete girlfriend!"

Mixing Animation with Photography

The next tutorial shows how to combine rotoscoped animation with a still photograph, the next logical step up from pure animation. You could certainly use the following techniques to add rotoscoped animation to live footage, but the theme of this animation did not call for video footage. It's a toy circus seal; the game is to toss rings over the seal's head, and the animation in this section will spin the ring before its descent around the seal's body. The seal is not a moving toy, and the perk to using a photo instead of cinematography is that the image (the seal in this example) shows sharper and with better color with my digital camera than my digital movie camera.

The rotoscope footage was more of a challenge than you might realize. I spun one of the toy rings on my index finger, but if you do something like this, consider how the pivot point (your finger) needs to move to put energy into the ring to make it spin. That's right—your finger moves, but the seal in the image used for the composite does not. The way I reconciled this was to stabilize the footage of the finger spinning the ring so the finger always appears to be centered. I show motion matching in Chapter 15. Figure 8.27 shows the media you need to use in the following sections; open Ring spin.mov and Seal.png now.

Rotoscoping a Simple, Fast-Paced Video

Play the Ring spin movie a few times to understand the motion of the ring. Clearly, the ring maintains a local shape of an ellipse, with more of the variation in its orientation (its degree of rotation relative to the global scene) and its position relative to the scene, which is also a global characteristic.

Figure 8.27
Add Photoshop Extended to a still photo and a little rotoscope reference and you'll get an interesting movie out of the deal.

It would be daunting and unnecessary to paint every video frame you need to spin the ring in the finished animation; a vector path can serve as the skeleton for the ring shape, and then you can stroke the path. A good question to ask at this point is how many frames you want to rotoscope. In the Gallery folder, my own finished animation runs eight seconds: 240 frames at 30 fps. No, I'm not going to ask you to hand-render 240 frames; I only mention this to give you a scope of what is needed to produce an entertaining piece of footage, and I only cover the techniques in the following section. However, the reason why I felt so many frames were necessary and did not depend on creating an animation cycle for the ring is because there is an additional attribute of the rotoscope footage that's visually interesting. The ring speeds up and slows down in reaction to how hard I spun it, and I feel this is a natural motion and an important one to include in a hybrid piece of still photography and rotoscope.

Follow these steps to set up a path and to create a custom brush to stroke the path:

1. Zoom way into Ring spin.mov, the first frame on the Animation palette (300% is good).

2. Choose Layer > Video Layers > New Blank Video Layer.

3. Choose the Pen tool and then draw an ellipse that falls on the centerline of the hoop in the video, as shown in Figure 8.28.

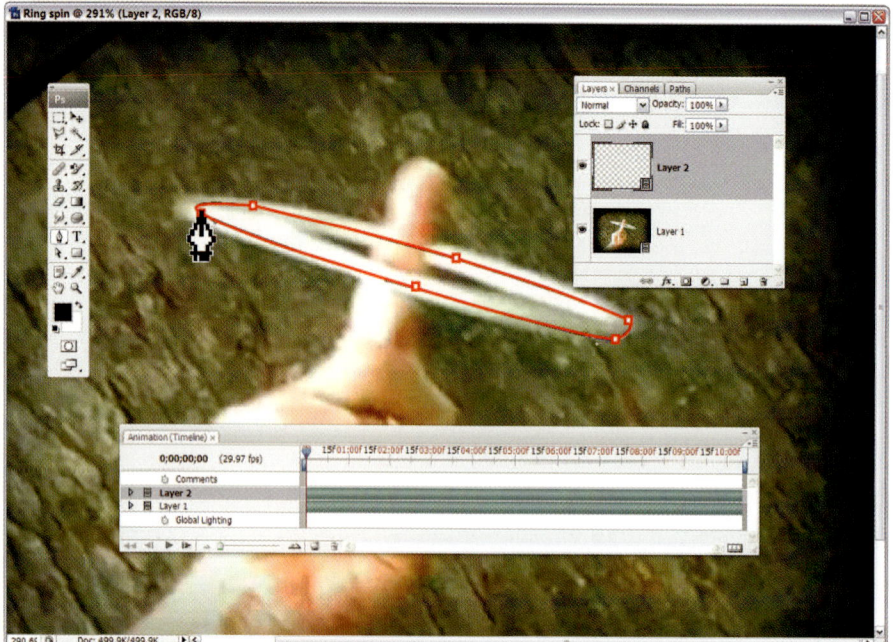

Figure 8.28
Use the Pen tool to trace the shape you'll stroke.

4. You'll need to move the path, rotate it a little, and occasionally reshape it because video layers do not animate Photoshop paths; they're placeholders and need to be stroked or filled to make content in a video frame. Open the Brushes palette (F5).

5. If you stroke the path using black foreground color, you then open the possibility later of recoloring to anything you like using the Styles palette. However, you should be precise and elegant with the shape of the stroke; it should be elliptical to match the dimensionality of the ring on the rotoscope layer. Choose the Brush tool. Choose the 5-pixel hard tip and then click the Brush Tip Shape tab. Using the cursor, squeeze and rotate the tip in the proxy window to about 48% Roundness and a 53 degree angle.

6. Click the Stroke Path with Brush icon on the bottom of the Paths palette, as shown in Figure 8.29.

7. Occasionally, you'll notice no real movement of the ring in the video layer. What you do (as is the case with Frames 2 and 3) is duplicate the frame (Layer > Video Layers > Duplicate Frame or use a shortcut key combo you've defined).

Figure 8.29
An elliptical brush tip creates a dimensional ring shape.

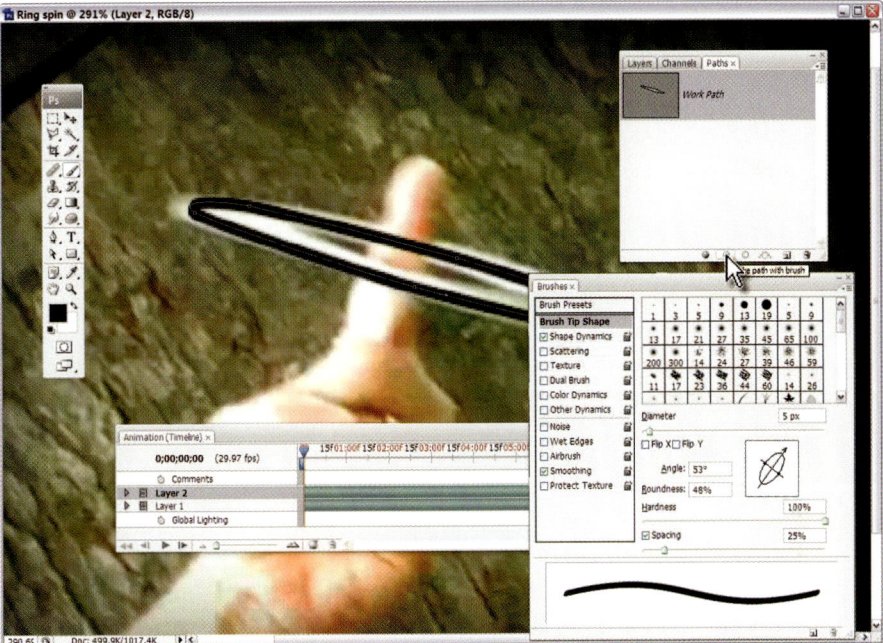

8. It will help your workflow if you memorize the hotkeys, A for the Path Selection tool and B for the Brush tool, because you'll alternate between these as you create additional video frames. Because the Selection tool is part of a group, first choose the Path Selection tool and not the Direct Selection tool on the Tools palette, so the hotkey A toggles to the Path Selection tool. Frame 4 shows a clear rotational change as well as a change in position. With the Path Selection tool, move the path to correspond to the center point of the ring you're rotoscoping. Then press Ctrl/Cmd+T to put the path into Free Transform mode. Paths can be transformed exactly as you do with nontransparent layer pixels, and reshaping the path is more quickly achieved with better overall video transition smoothness than using the Direct Selection tool for hours on end. Rotate and scale the path by dragging the bounding box handles and then press Enter when the transformation matches the underlying ring, as shown in Figure 8.30. Then press B and click the Stroke Path with Brush icon on the Paths palette.

That's the technique. All you need to do now is invest the time in building a few seconds of video animation. The overall effect of the spinning hoop isn't finished; I cover the finessing techniques in the following sections. If you'd like to cut to the chase, the Ring animation.mov file in the ZIP archive is an eight-second rendition of the previous steps I created for you to use.

Figure 8.30
Move and reshape the path frame by frame using the Path Selection tool in combination with Free Transform mode.

Adding a Style to the Video Layer

Photoshop styles affect all the nontransparent regions of a layer, including video layers, so to embellish the simple black ring shape is largely a matter of choosing the most appropriate style or customizing an existing one. An additional perk to applying a style is that you can modify the style over time in the video, which I'll show shortly.

Here's how to make the black hoop into a splendid, dimensional silver hoop:

1. Drag your finished rotoscope layer (or use my Ring animation movie) from the Layers palette into the Seal.png image window. Note that the rotoscope movie and my animation file both scale properly to the seal image. If they didn't, you would convert the video layer to a Smart Object and then scale it.

2. Earlier I discussed local and global movement. I think the completed video would be much more interesting if the ring began spinning around the seal's nose and then made a gradual descent. You'll need to be careful to align the descended ring to the seal's torso, which doesn't align with the ball on its nose, and you might have to create several Position keyframes, but here goes: At Frame 0, put the ring around the pivot point of the seal's nose and ball. You'll need to scrub the timeline to see the rotational center of this off-centered rotoscope animation.

3. Click the Position stopwatch for this layer on the Animation palette. Then move the timeline to the end of the Work Area and, with the Move tool, move the ring toward the seal's belly as shown in Figure 8.31. I needed to create additional keyframes to keep the hoop around (and not outside of) the seal's torso, and you probably will, too.

Figure 8.31
Create keyframes to move the spinning hoop, thus creating more interesting action.

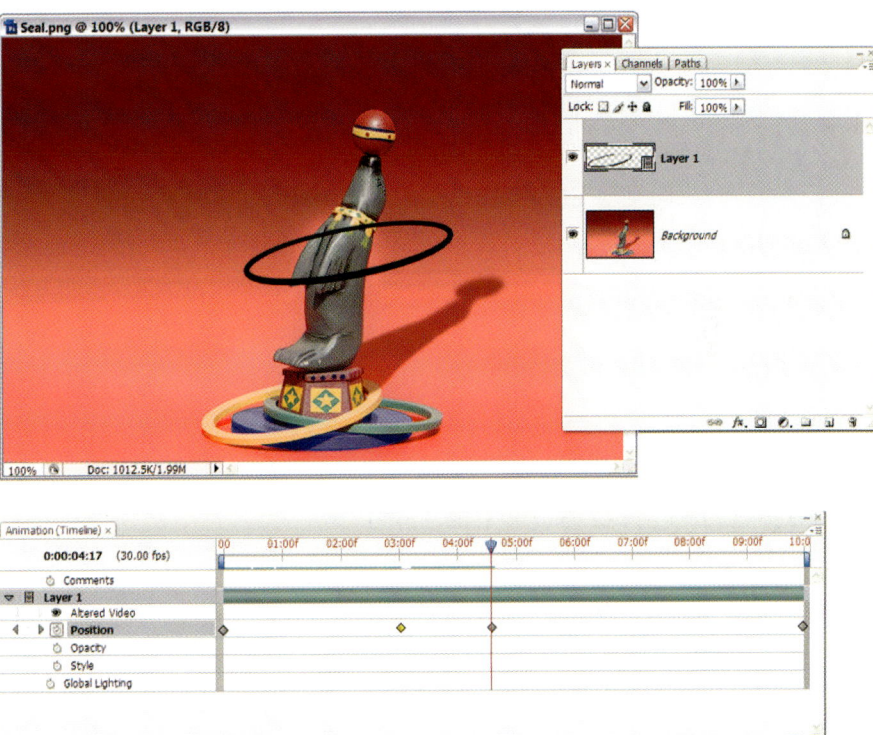

4. The Styles palette is by default attached to color, so pressing F6 will display it if it's not docked on the strip. Choose Web Styles from the flyout menu and then with the animation layer highlighted on the Layers palette, click Chrome.

5. Chrome has a default offset for the drop shadow that doesn't work for this video, so you need to correct this. Double-click the Drop Shadow entry under Effects on the Layers palette, and the Layer Style dialog box opens.

6. Manipulate the shadow from directly within the document window by dragging it to the appropriate area above the seal's shadow. Also, you might want to lower Opacity to 45%, Size to about five pixels, and then click the color swatch and then change the shadow color to a dark reddish-brown; see Figure 8.32.

Figure 8.32
By dragging the shadow over, it will remain aligned to the correct area of the animation throughout.

7. There's not a lot of interesting style changes you can define for Chrome for this video, but you can certainly add a style attribute that can later be changed over time. While the Drop Shadow dialog box is open, click the Outer Glow option title to display the options for this attribute and also activate the checkbox for the Outer Glow option.

8. Click the color swatch below Noise to display the Color Picker. Choose a pale red as shown in Figure 8.33 and then increase the Screen mode opacity to 100%. As you'll see in the document window, the red glow around the chrome hoop looks terrific and blends well thematically with the seal background. Click OK.

9. Go to the head of the video on the Animation palette and then click the Style stopwatch for this layer, creating a keyframe.

10. Go to about halfway through the playlength of the video and then double-click the Outer Glow entry on the Layers palette.

11. Try changing the color to green and upping Size to 32 pixels or so. Actually, knock yourself out here and use any values you, the artist, think would play well. Click OK and a keyframe is made on the timeline. See Figure 8.34.

12. Put the timeline indicator (the current time) at the end of the Work Area on the Animation palette, double-click Outer Glow, and then set the color to anything you like. The video might have more inner consistency when played repeatedly if you went back to a red glow.

By all means, preview the video. The hoop is in front of the seal and not around it, and this is the final edit you need to make in the following section.

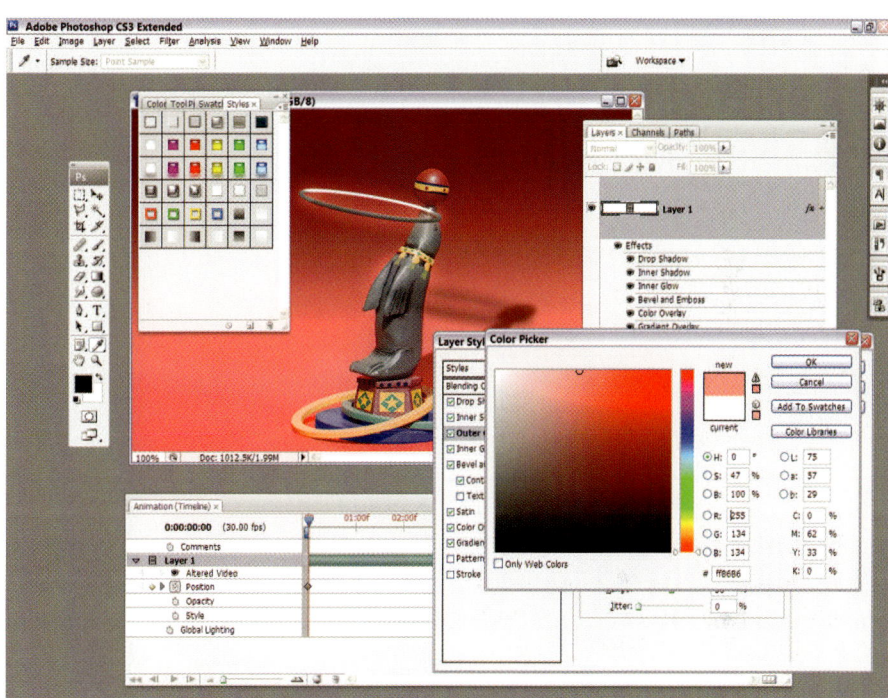

Figure 8.33 Add to the style to customize it. Your custom style can then be modified over time.

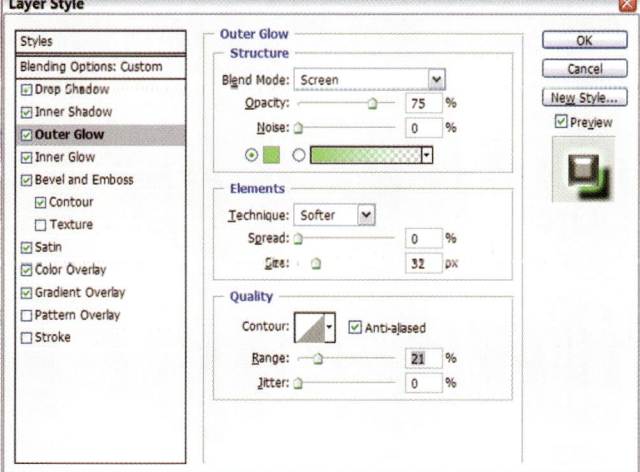

Figure 8.34 Change the color and intensity of the glowing ring through time.

Using the Clone Source Tool

To hide the back of the hoop when it's behind the seal requires that you use the Clone Source palette along with the Clone Stamp tool. It might seem like it would be easier to erase the back of the hoop frame by frame, but if you did that, you'd also erase the corresponding area of the Layer Style Drop Shadow.

1. Choose Layer > Video Layers > New Blank Video Layer.

2. Open the Clone Source palette from the docking strip or the Window menu and then choose the Clone Stamp tool from the Tools palette. On the Options bar, choose the 9-pixel hard tip for the tool (because the hoop was painted using the smaller 5-pixel diameter brush).

3. With the bottom layer of the seal highlighted on the Layers palette, Alt/Opt+click over the area at Frame 0 where the hoop is on top of the ball or nose and should be hidden. Release Alt/Opt after you've defined the sampling point.

4. On the Clone Source palette, make sure the Offset and Frame Offset values are all at 0 before you click+drag. Also, make sure you're working on the new blank video layer (check the Layers palette). Finally, make sure Aligned is checked on the Options bar.

5. Stroke over the areas that should be hidden for the hoop and hoop shadow. It's that simple; see Figure 8.35 and continue frame by frame until you're done.

Optionally, before you render the video, I wrote a 10-second audio based on John Phillip Sousa's (public domain) "Liberty Bell March," which works well with this circus theme animation. (I don't believe anyone has used this music commercially.) Open Liberty Bell March-JP Sousa.mp3 as a QuickTime movie, drag its thumbnail from the Layers palette into the document window, align the track to play from the head of the video, and then render the video. You need to use QuickTime file format whenever you want to save audio.

You've learned to perform rotoscoping using round objects and other simple shapes in this chapter. On your own, I recommend practicing your skill with irregularly shaped items such as spinning cereal boxes and corporate logos (which can help pay the bills). You're almost always working with the silhouette of an object regardless of its shape, so practicing with the Pen tool (particularly if you're not well versed with a vector drawing program) can only help speed you along with personal and commercial gigs.

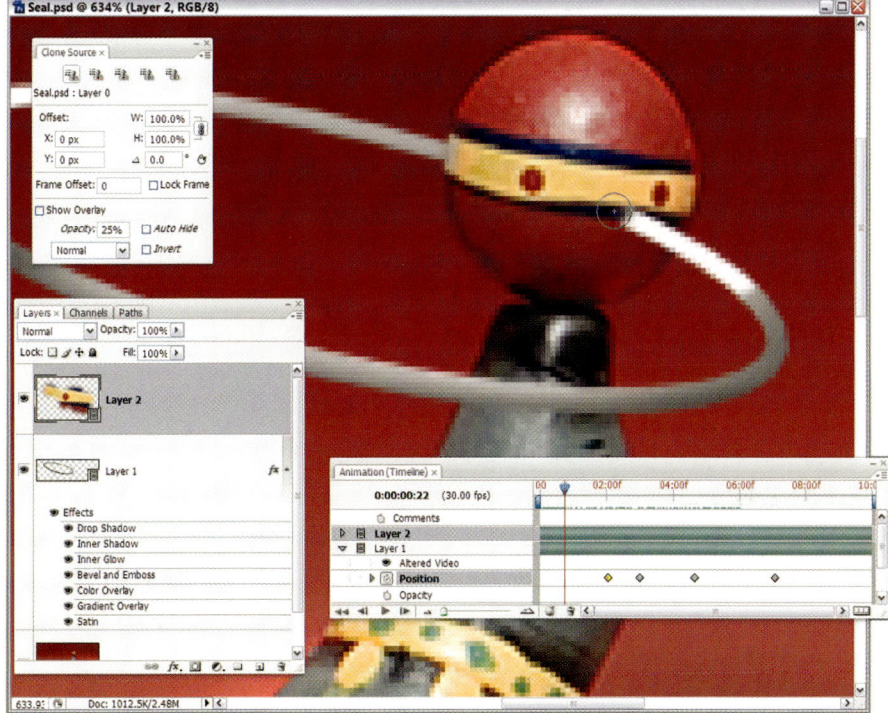

Figure 8.35
The Clone Stamp tool "hides" unwanted areas on layers below, frame by frame.

Rotoscoping is but one talent of many you'll develop for enhancing and correcting videos. And like Photoshop, tools and skills integrate. You use a little of one and a little of another to pull together a polished piece of video.

9

Advanced Rotoscoping and Wire Removal

Chapter 8 is a guided tour to simple rotoscoping with an emphasis on animation. However, as you will discover out in the work force, the bulk of rotoscope work is performed on video footage to create illusions, to clean up sloppy compositing work, and to remove unwanted objects from a scene. I recommend that you review Chapter 8 before beginning this chapter because there are several Photoshop techniques used in animation that relate directly to rotoscoping and live footage.

In this chapter, I take you through some methods for cleaning up some footage where some unwanted background spoils the scene. Then you'll work with some green-screen footage in an unusual and inspired way—you'll use the foreground figure as a silhouette, compositing an animation within the profile of an actress. Later in this chapter I show you some simple, effective compositing techniques for creating surreal, special effects footage. I also show you how to perform wire removal; there is a high calling for experts who can, for example, retouch the wires out of footage of a magician levitating an object. Finally, I show you a technique for correcting a few frames that rendered poorly in a 3D animation video. If you're not familiar with 3D animation, it takes a lot of time to set up, days to render to video, and it's absolutely heartbreaking to discover after hours and hours of rendering time that a few seconds came out wrong. You don't have to re-render the entire animation; all you need to do is read this chapter on retouching video footage via rotoscoping!

Rotoscoping Away Unwanted Scene Areas

In Chapter 1 I familiarized you with the Animation palette using a short clip of a Main Coon cat threatening a house of cards; you saw that it's unrealistic to expect a housecat to take direction, but more importantly the scene is quite hindered because we ran out of seamless for the cat, and he was uncooperative in staying on his mark.

Unless you work at a major studio, you're likely to run into a problem similar to the Black & white & red all over.mov file. Practically, you never have enough backdrop, and frequently there will be areas you need to mask in the final video clip. The following sections take you through a worst-case scenario and show you the steps needed to rotoscope away scene areas that don't belong in a video for its final presentation.

Creating a Garbage Matte

A *garbage matte* is a misnomer—it is not garbage and is actually instrumental in masking scene areas you hope to complete in a lifetime. A garbage matte is a crude generalized mask in footage that is used to hold (mask) large, static areas in a scene.

Open Black & white & red all over.mov in Photoshop and turn off the View > Pixel Aspect Ratio Correction. In Figure 9.1, I've outlined in yellow areas in this video where the background needs to be painted over, and for the most part, these areas remain constant throughout the play of the video.

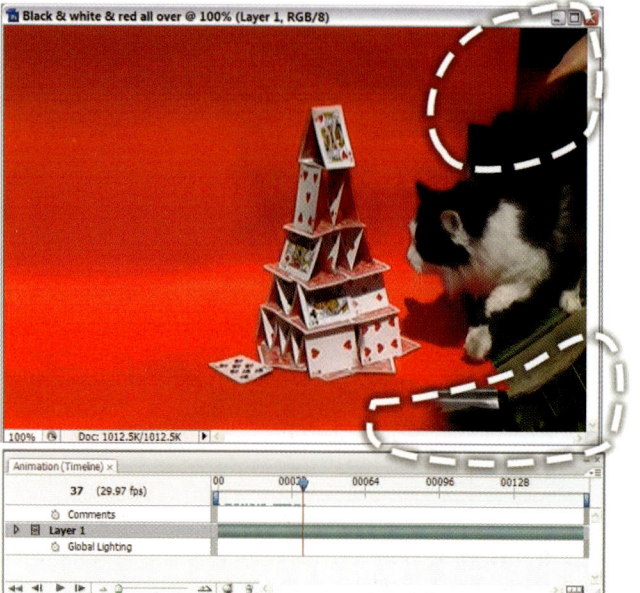
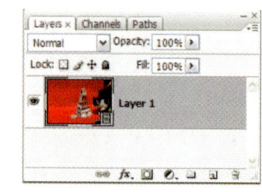

Figure 9.1

Scene areas you want to hide that remain stationary throughout the video can be masked using a garbage matte.

> **Tip**
>
> A *travelling matte* is often simply a garbage matte that is moved relative to a moving actor or object in a scene. A garbage matte (or any matte) can be turned into a travelling matte by moving its position in time using the Position stopwatch on the Animation palette. See Chapter 15 on motion matching for more details on relocating mattes and objects over time.

Follow these steps to create a garbage matte to hide the upper and lower right of the frame:

1. Choose Layer > Video Layers > New Blank Video Layer. Rename the layer "garbage matte."

2. Scrub the timeline to see the location of the areas across time that can be masked over. If you like, display rulers (Ctrl/Cmd+R) and then drag guides out of the rulers to mark the areas. Occasionally, I use paths to mark areas; they're precise and they don't animate over time. Before you proceed, make sure the current time is at the head of the video composition.

3. If you look closely, the red backdrop has lighting falloff and as a consequence is uneven in the red tones. What you need to do to ensure consistency throughout the duration of the clip is to match the colors. Select the areas that need to be hidden on the bottom video layer (use the rectangular Marquee tool). With the Clone Stamp tool, choose All Layers from the Sample drop-down list, uncheck Aligned on the Options bar, and then Alt/Opt+click a sample point close to the area that needs to be covered.

4. Stroke over the areas as shown in Figure 9.2. Hide the marquee by pressing Ctrl/Cmd+H. If you need to blend the areas a little to better match the bottom video layer, I suggest you use the Brush tool at partial opacity; Alt/Opt+click to sample a color area and then use brisk strokes.

5. Duplicate the first frame on this new video layer as many times as needed. In previous chapters I recommended that you set up a keyboard shortcut for duplicating video frames. You do this in Edit > Keyboard Shortcuts > Application Menus > Layer > Video Layers. (Ctrl/Cmd+Shift+D is a comfortable configuration for the left hand and easy to remember.) It's okay if you overshoot the timeline when you duplicate frames and consequently mask areas of the cat's front paw by a few frames in excess.

6. For the frames you just need to be mostly masked with the same duplicate frame, but Domino the cat is moving over part of the garbage matte area (and is thus partially hidden). Switch to the Brush tool, choose Clear painting mode, and then stroke away the areas covering Domino's paw, as shown in Figure 9.3.

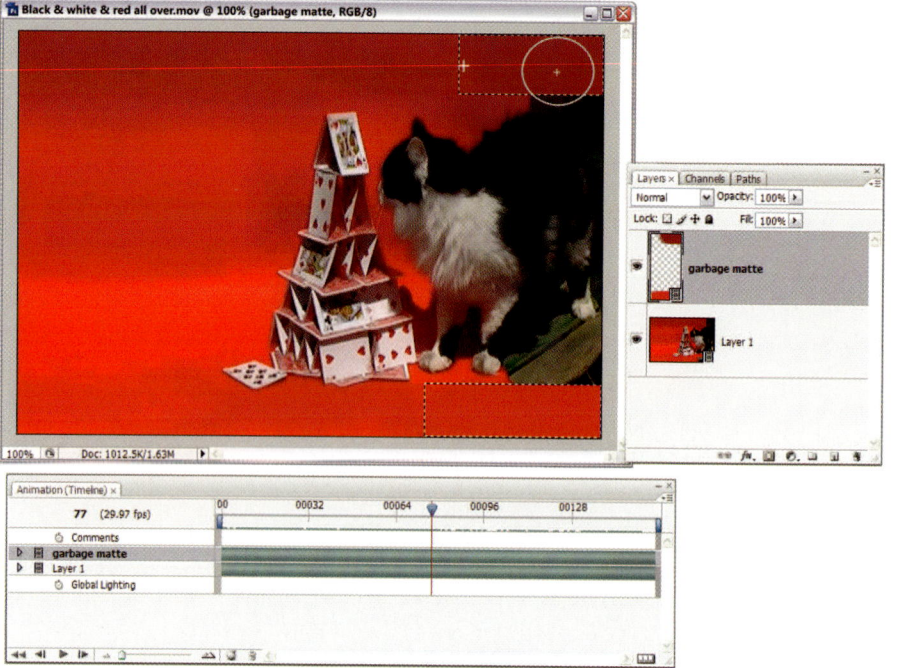

Figure 9.2
Fill the video layer areas with shades that blend into and complete the backdrop.

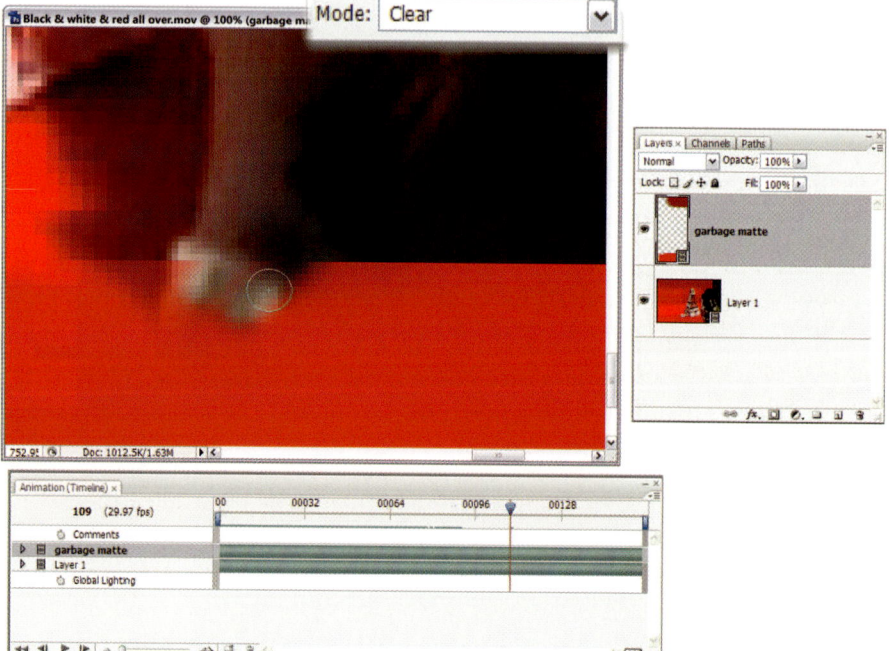

Figure 9.3
Use Clear painting mode to erase areas on the video layer where the garbage matte shouldn't exist.

A garbage matte is meant to save you time and work, and from a workflow perspective, it's quicker to duplicate frames whose content might be a *little* wrong (and then erase using Clear mode) than to hand-paint entire frames. You ensure consistency when you duplicate frames, and you reduce the chance of video twittering from frame to frame.

7. Save your work and keep it open.

I recommend that you get used to shortcut keys when you rotoscope; this means memorizing a few keystrokes such as B for Brush tool, H for Hand tool, and S for Clone Stamp. You *will* need to alternate between tools as you work from frame to frame.

Caution

Although holding the Spacebar is a very convenient way to toggle to the Hand tool for panning a document window, *don't* use it when working with the Animation palette; press H instead. Photoshop Extended is hard-coded to play a video when you hit the Spacebar, and you'll get unexpected results when you use the Spacebar to toggle to the Hand tool.

Working with Duplicate Frames

A garbage matte can be as simple or as elegant as the need arises, but you don't have to merely create one frame, duplicate it, and then cope with an excess of retouching where the garbage matte covers areas you want to show.

Procedurally, you work from the general to the specific: find areas that can take a garbage matte and then duplicate frames where needed. Then rewind the video and scrub the timeline for other areas that need a stationary matte, but only for a portion of the duration of the video. Create garbage mattes for that duration, and then repeat the process so your edgework is at a minimum. The only thing you need to remember is to start from the head of the video as you create additional mattes because the Duplicate Frame command only applies in a forward direction for video. Consider creating new blank video layers for different garbage mattes to ensure you don't inadvertently mask areas you want to show. Photoshop has a hypothetically unlimited capacity for layers, limited only by your system resources.

Hand-Rotoscoping the Edgework

The garbage matte is great for coarse composition previsualization, but naturally the assignment isn't complete. Here's the deal: You don't want retouched areas to twitter as the video plays, so just as the garbage matte solved this problem by providing a constant mask, your edgework should also be masking work and not painting work, to expose a constant background area. Notice that Domino is casting a shadow when he's on the red seamless; the seamless area you add via rotoscoping should feature an identical and consistent shadow. Working back to front, then, in this tutorial, you rotoscope the shadow, then you rotoscope the cat.

If you want to use your own garbage matte, write your file from the previous tutorial to video (File > Export > Render Video) and then import it so you can start fresh with the edgework. Or if you want to simply get down to the edgework business, you can use my garbage matte work; open Domino with garbage matte.mov. Additionally, you'll notice that Domino and the area where he isn't on the backdrop seamless are quite close in tone in certain areas, making finding his edge difficult. I address both problems as follows:

1. Create a new blank video layer on top of the rendered video layer. Name it "shadow mask."

2. With the bottom video layer chosen on the Layers palette, click the Adjustment Layer icon on the bottom of the Layers palette and then choose Levels.

3. In the Levels box, drag the midrange slider to the left until you can clearly see Domino's shadow cast on the wooden slats. Then click OK to apply this non-permanent adjustment. See Figure 9.4. Note that because the Adjustment layer is beneath the new Shadow Mask video layer, your view of this layer is unaffected by the mask; only layers under an Adjustment layer are altered.

4. The best tool for detecting and selecting areas in the underlying video is the Magnetic Lasso tool. Unlike other selection tools, the Magnetic Lasso is not layer specific; you can be on any layer and select edges in the composite of the layers in the document window. Choose the Magnetic Lasso from the Tools palette and then on the Options bar use 1 pixel Feather, enable Anti-aliasing, use a low detection width (the distance of an image area from your cursor) such as 2 to 4, use a very low Contrast setting such as 1% to make edge detection very sensitive, and choose about 10 for Frequency. Frequency sets how fast the tool sets fastening points—sharp changes in direction for the selection. Also, choose the Adds to Selection button of the Options bar to save time, because Domino is casting multiple shadow areas in discontinuous areas.

Figure 9.4
Use an Adjustment layer so you can see the hidden details in the underlying video.

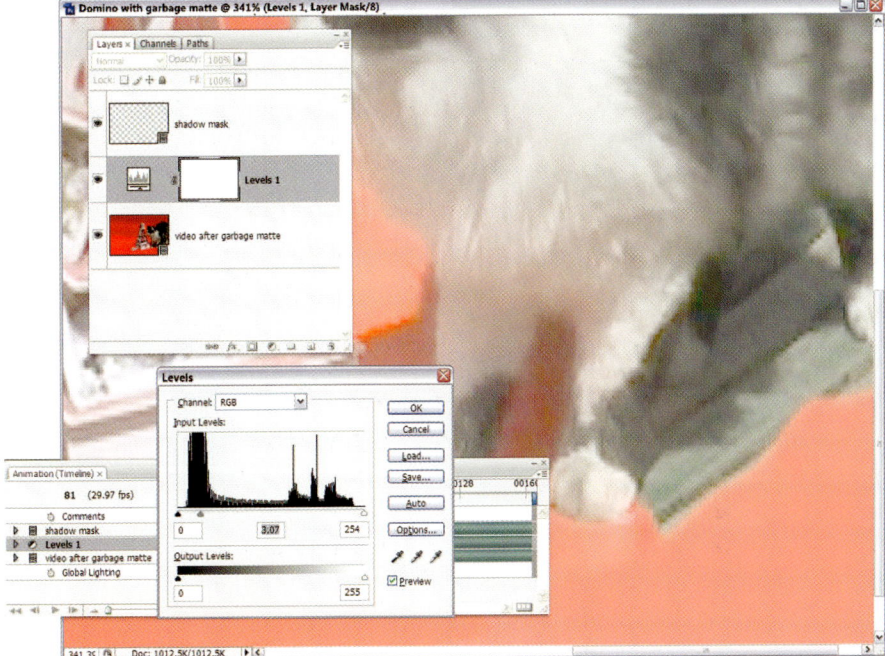

5. Begin at the head of the video; use the Magnetic Lasso by making an initial click over an edge of the shadow, then hover your cursor (don't click) and guide it along the edge of the shadow. If the tool travels in a direction you don't want it to, you remove anchors by pressing Backspace (or Delete). Additionally, you can click to manually set a fastening point (they look like Pen tool anchors but they are not; they're temporary).

> **Tip**
>
> If you want to see the detection width onscreen for the Magnetic Lasso tool, press Caps Lock. Just don't write books with this option enabled, or they'll READ LIKE THIS!

6. Once you've defined all the shadow areas for a single video frame, press Alt/Opt+Backspace to fill it with foreground color and then press Ctrl/Cmd+D to deselect. You can use any foreground color you like because this mask will eventually be evaluated by Photoshop based on layer opacity for the pixels and not color. I'm using black in these figures so you can see what you should do more readily; check out Figure 9.5 to see what a filled selection should look like as you progress.

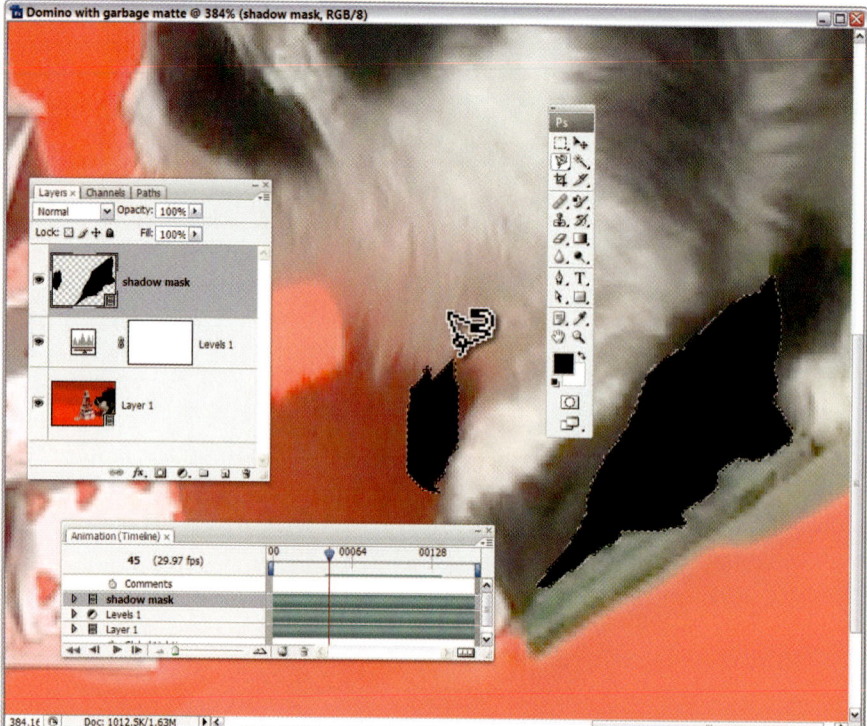

Figure 9.5

Fill selections made with the Magnetic Lasso tool to create a video mask for the shadow areas.

7. Turn off the Levels layer for a moment so you can get an accurate color sample. With the Eyedropper tool set to 3 by 3 Average, click over an area of existing shadow on the red seamless to sample the color; the color varies from place to place, and so an average works in this example. Now turn the Levels layer on again.

8. Create a new static, normal layer on top of the video layer.

9. Alt/Opt+click on the edge between the layers on the Layers palette list. Doing this makes the top layer clip to the video layer underneath as a mask (or press Ctrl/Cmd+Alt/Opt+G).

10. On the top layer, make sure the Brush tool is set to Normal on the Options bar and paint in the shadow area, as shown in Figure 9.6. Make the area large, because Domino and his shadow will move throughout the duration of the clip. You can hide the Adjustment layer at any time to better see what your rotoscope work looks like.

Play the video and check to see that all the areas that should be showing a shadow off of the seamless do and that the color matches the shadow color of Domino on the red seamless. The hardest area to reconcile is right on the edge where your clipping mask shadow eventually meets the cat's real shadow. Don't be afraid to extend

Figure 9.6
Create a clipping mask from the video layer with the shadow matte.

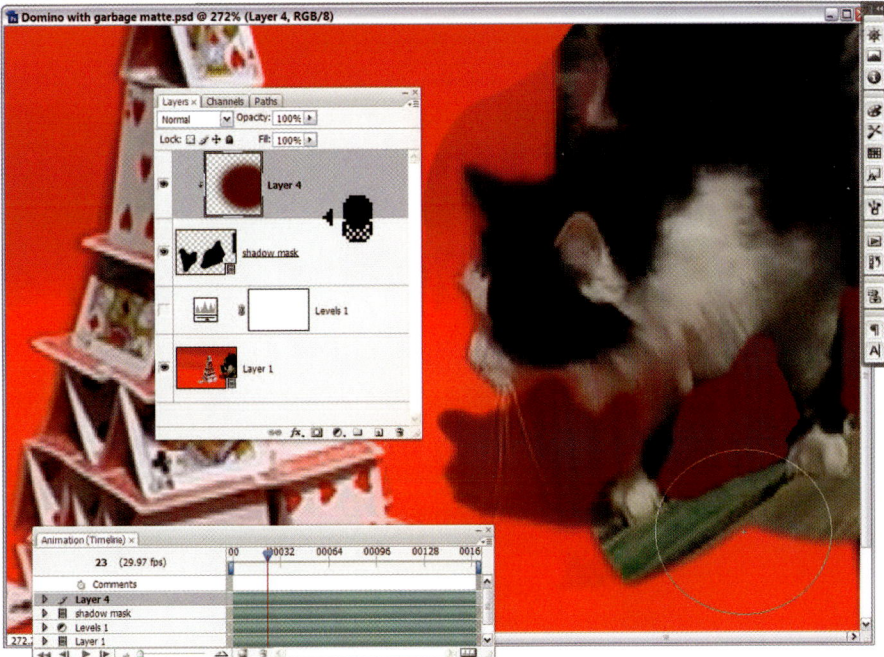

your clipping mask; play the video, scrub the timeline back and forth and, if for a frame or two there's a nasty seam, paint over it for these frames.

At the risk of sounding anticlimatic, there's really nothing new to masking the areas around Domino once you've worked through the previous tutorial. Again, to prevent the background from bopping around during the length of the video, you use a clipping mask of the exterior of Domino and clip a layer area that looks like the red seamless. I've created Backdrop.png (it's in the ZIP archive), and you can either clone from it to a new layer in the composition or just copy the upper right corner. Here's a brief list of steps you take to get rid of the off-seamless background in the video:

1. Create a new blank video layer under the shadow (normal) layer on the Layers palette. Name it "Dom mask" so I can refer to it during this tutorial.

2. With the Adjustment layer visible so you can see the edges in the video, choose the Magnetic Lasso tool and, from the beginning of the video, guide the cursor around the outside of Domino; use Add to Selection mode on the Options bar.

3. Press Alt/Opt+Backspace to fill the selection with black and then Ctrl/Cmd+D to deselect, as shown in Figure 9.7. You'll work more quickly and with fewer errors if you hide the shadow mask layer; you hide the clipping mask, and the layer it's clipping will hide as well. Do this for all frames.

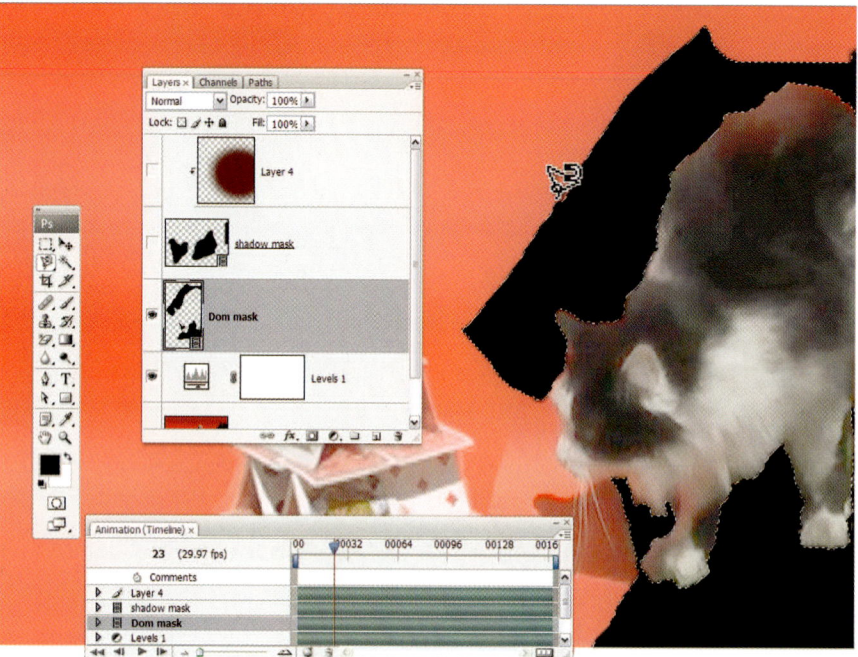

Figure 9.7
Use the Magnetic Lasso tool to select outside the edge of Domino.

> **Note**
>
> The Magnetic Lasso won't go completely to the right edge or any other edge of a document window; certain frames will need to be manually masked after using the Magnetic Lasso tool.

4. Put some of my Background.png file on a layer on top of the masking video layer for Domino and then use Alt/Opt+click between the layer titles to clip the red background layer to the mask you've created. As a final pass for the shadow layer I suggest that you soften the somewhat hard edge by applying Gaussian blur to each frame of the shadow mask; you go to the beginning of the Work Area, blur by about 1.2 pixels, advance the video, and then press Ctrl/Cmd+F to apply the last-used filter. Also, decrease the opacity of the shadow to better match the real shadows in the video; use your eye, 90% should do the trick. In Figure 9.8, you can see a frame from the nearly completed composition, with the Adjustment layer turned off. You could, in theory, delete the Adjustment layer when you think the video is completed; I discourage this—the layer adds only nominally to the saved file, and you know what happens two minutes after you delete something. Play back the video; if there is any fringing around Domino, the culprit is the Dom mask layer—paint more black around the edges in frames that clearly show fringing.

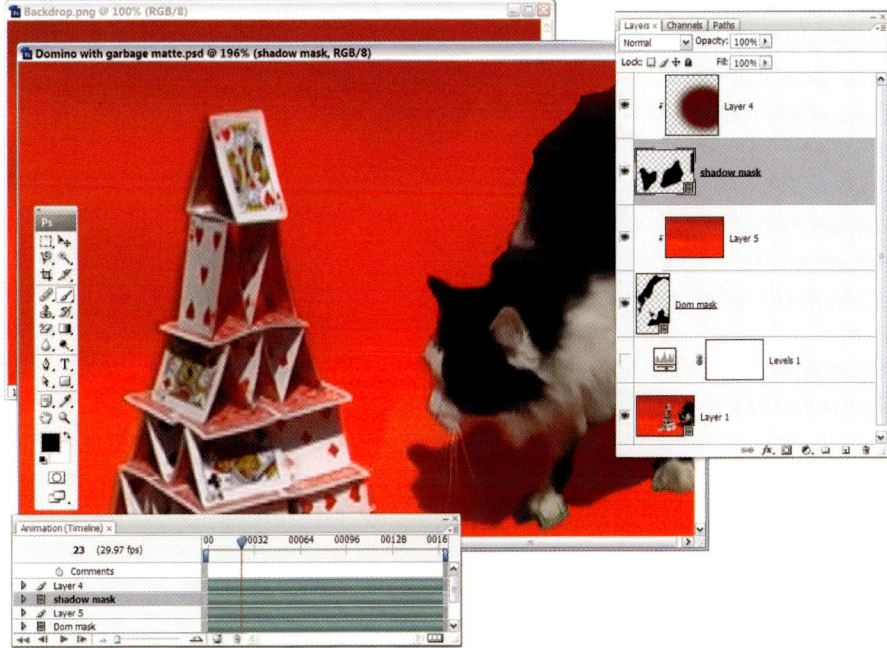

Figure 9.8
Clip the backdrop image layer to the outside silhouette of the Domino video layer.

Working with Irregular Outlines

You might not be happy if you wrote the file out to video right now because even though you used feathering to define the Magnetic Lasso tool options, Domino's outline will look like a 1960s "helmet-do." Hair is the most difficult aspect of film and still photography to isolate, and with video it is more so because it moves from frame to frame.

My solution to this hairy problem is to roughen the edge of Domino, ever so slightly, in different areas of the video. Practice consistency from frame to frame: if you roughen an area, for example, in Frame 23, Frames 24–34 (roughly a second) should have that rough area move as Domino moves. You should also ease the rough area out for at least five frames, gradually letting it return to a smooth outline to prevent a jarring effect when played back. Remember, this is a moving picture: You can get away with only roughening certain areas for only part of the playlength, and the audience's perception will usually sustain the illusion.

Here's how to mess up Domino's fur a little:

1. Choose a part of the video where the mask around Domino is obvious and unappealing.
2. Choose the Dom mask layer on the Layers palette.

3. Choose the Brush tool and then choose the 14-pixel Splatter brush from the Options bar. Reduce its size to about eight pixels (right-click to bring up the Brush palette).

4. Any color will do, as I mentioned earlier regarding clipping masks. Zoom in to an area and then make a few brisk strokes as shown in Figure 9.9. Then proceed to the next frame—you probably want to enable Onion Skin from the Animation palette's menu—and then repeat the process. Remember some of the technique I showed in Chapter 8 on cell animation. You're quite literally illustrating over time when you rotoscope.

5. Save to PSD and then choose File > Export > Render Video. Because this video has an extremely limited number of unique colors and they are all intense and saturated, you can use almost any codec you like for compressing the video.

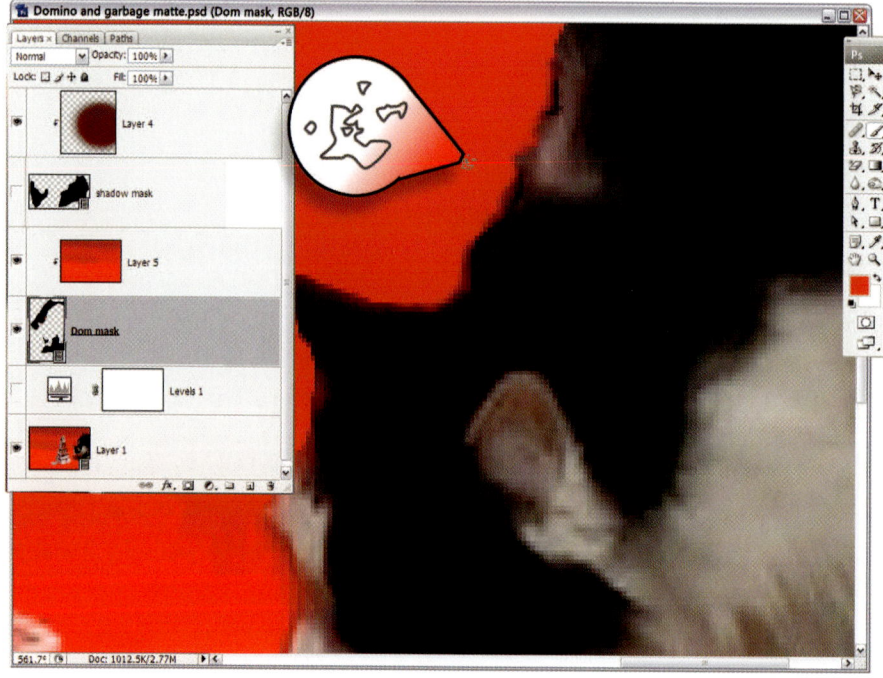

Figure 9.9
Roughen the edges of the clipping mask layer to simulate the uneven appearance of the cat's fur.

Using Live Action as a Rotoscope

I had a lot of fun with the tutorial in this section; it gave me the opportunity to experiment with green screening and to work with an outstanding local talent. Here's the concept: I wanted to use the motion, but not the actual picture, of a karate black belt going through some forms. I wanted to make a silhouette animate—using a live actor is certainly a legitimate approach—and then fill the silhouette with a movie, specifically, a raging fire. A green screen helped but was not absolutely necessary; I show you all about green screening in Chapter 14. All I needed was a background that color contrasted with Melissa and her *gi* (the uniform worn in sparring). Spill (green screen reflectance onto the subject) and fringing were not a large problem because the day was overcast, and additionally, none of Melissa's details show in the finished video.

I've provided all the materials you'll need to work through the following section in the ZIP archive.

Writing an Action, Hacking a JavaScript

The length of the video is 890 frames (just short of 30 seconds at 29.97 fps); this means you have 890 frames in which Melissa needs to be separated from our green screen. You let Photoshop do this for you by creating an action and then modifying a JavaScript that ships with Photoshop. I explain how to hack (your Photoshop folder)\Scripting Guide\Sample Scripts\JavaScript\ ExecuteMoltenLead.jsx in the "Scripting" section of Chapter 4, right next to Figure 4.8, to execute a Photoshop action any number of times. Here's a brief recap:

1. Open ExecuteMoltenLead.jsx in a plain text editor.

2. Change the phrase `MoltenLead=MoltenLead` to `x=x`.

3. Hit Enter (Return) after the semicolon on this line and on the new line type `var i=0`.

4. Push `try{` down to create a new line; on the new line above, type `for (i=0;i<=890;i++)`.

5. Make absolutely certain you haven't done anything else; then save the file as ExecuteX.jsx to your (Photoshop)\Presets\Scripts folder. You now have a JavaScript that will execute a Photoshop action named X 890 times, and it's available from the File > Scripts menu. See Figure 9.10 for a visual guide to this little operation; at left is the original text to be modified in red, and at right is what your saved JavaScript should look like with modifications marked in green.

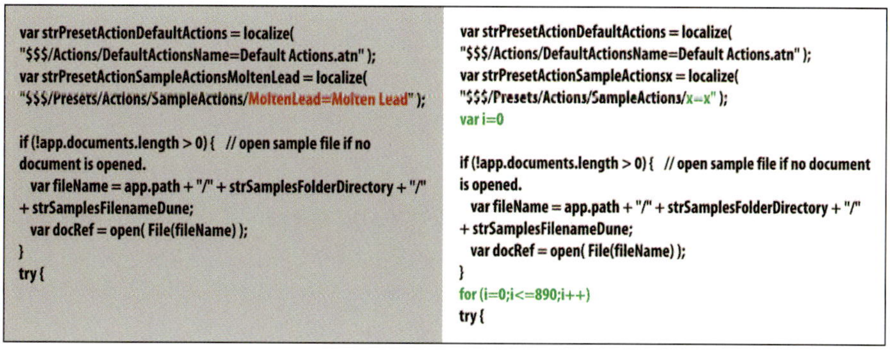

Figure 9.10
Modify a Photoshop JavaScript to make an action run as many times as you need.

```
var strPresetActionDefaultActions = localize(
"$$$/Actions/DefaultActionsName=Default Actions.atn" );
var strPresetActionSampleActionsMoltenLead = localize(
"$$$/Presets/Actions/SampleActions/MoltenLead=Molten Lead" );

if (!app.documents.length > 0) {   // open sample file if no
document is opened.
    var fileName = app.path + "/" + strSamplesFolderDirectory + "/"
+ strSamplesFilenameDune;
    var docRef = open( File(fileName) );
}
try {
```

```
var strPresetActionDefaultActions = localize(
"$$$/Actions/DefaultActionsName=Default Actions.atn" );
var strPresetActionSampleActionsx = localize(
"$$$/Presets/Actions/SampleActions/x=x" );
var i=0

if (!app.documents.length > 0) {   // open sample file if no document
is opened.
    var fileName = app.path + "/" + strSamplesFolderDirectory + "/"
+ strSamplesFilenameDune;
    var docRef = open( File(fileName) );
}
for (i=0;i<=890;i++)
try {
```

> **Tip**
>
> Executing an action 890 times is sort of an odd script, and you might want to change it to an even 30 seconds (900 frames) in the future. The reason why you want to specify exactly 890 times in this example is that there's no practical way to halt a script once it's been executed. Let's say you run the action to follow in this tutorial 900 times on a video clip that's only 890 frames. The result would be that the script would apply the same action to the last frame an unnecessary and unwanted 10 times, ruining the content of the last frame.

Apply the Script to Create a Video Transparency

You've got your custom script, so it's time now to separate Melissa from the green screen background. Follow these steps to create transparency wherever there's green for the duration of the clip:

1. With the Melissa.mov file loaded, open the Actions palette. Under Default Actions, create a new action by clicking the menu and choosing New Action. Name the action "x"; you're recording now.

2. Choose Select > Color Range. In the Color Range dialog box, it's helpful to choose the Quick Mask option for the Selection Preview so the document window displays your current Quick Mask tint. Click your cursor over the green background in the document window, and then drag the Fuzziness slider until the document window shows a nice, tight mask around Melissa, as shown in Figure 9.11. If necessary, use your mouse scroll wheel to zoom into the document window to better see the selection. Click OK when you're satisfied with the selection.

3. Press Backspace to delete the background and then Ctrl/Cmd+D to deselect.

4. Click the Selects Next Frame button on the Animation palette, then click the Stop Record button on the Actions palette.

5. Run the Execute 890 times script. It's under File > Scripts. If you didn't put the JavaScript in the Presets > Scripts folder, click Browse and then navigate to the script you created in the previous section.

It's more than likely that the script and your action will not produce a flawless transparency around her; outdoor green screens are very difficult to light, and it's equally difficult to prevent a breeze from catching areas and producing slight shadows. What you want to do now is put a normal static layer underneath the video layer, fill it with bright red to detect areas that weren't selected and erased, and

Figure 9.11
Color Range is the first step in the x action.

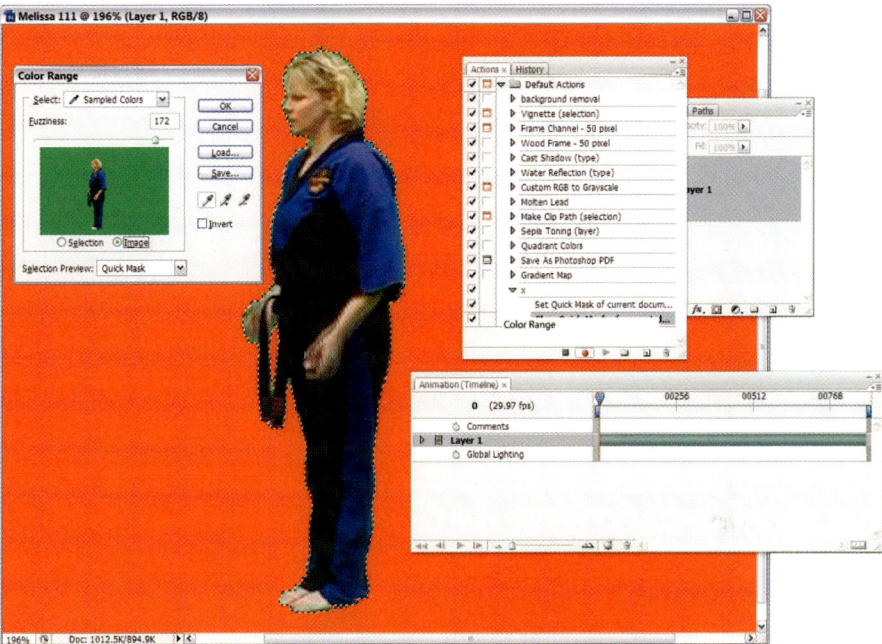

then scrub the timeline to detect flawed frames. Then use the Eraser tool or the Brush tool in 100% Clear painting mode to address these frames. Then when you do your own green-screen videos, pick a day with no breeze or shoot indoors!

Integrating the Subject with a New Background

I thought Melissa's performance deserved an elaborate but visually subordinate background, so I created the video Sparring arena.mov; it's in the ZIP archive, and I designed it in Cinema 4D. A still image could work in this example, but I wanted to gild the lily a little by adding a background whose banners subtly waft around.

1. Open the Sparring arena.mov file and then Shift+drag its thumbnail from the Layers palette into the Melissa document, then put the layer on the bottom of the stack.

2. The background video is 10 frames longer than that of Melissa; just let the additional frames fall out of the Work Area on the Animation palette at the tail.

3. I found that Melissa isn't positioned very well in the composite; use the Move tool to drag her to center stage. Because the Position stopwatch isn't active on the Animation palette, your move is persistent throughout the composition, and Melissa will not perform any user-introduced movement—see Figure 9.12.

Figure 9.12
Reposition the actress relative to the background video.

Creating a Fiery Performance via a Clipping Mask

Here's where you perform some magic; open the fire 900.mov file in Photoshop. You're going to clip the fire video to the Melissa video layer and then embellish the surreal performance with a Layer Style, which also helps separate the black areas of the fire video from the dim sparring area.

1. Shift+drag the fire thumbnail from the Layers palette into the Melissa composition; you can close the fire movie without saving now.

2. Put the fire video layer on top on the Layers palette if it didn't land there.

3. Hold Alt/Opt and then click between the fire and the Melissa layers as shown in Figure 9.13. You will want to adjust the area of fire showing through Melissa's nontransparent areas; do this by choosing the Move tool and then dragging in the document window with the fire layer highlighted on the Layers palette. It helps to scrub the timeline and see the extent of Melissa's motion in her virtual sparring arena.

4. Choose the Melissa layer on the Layers palette. Click the Layer Style icon on the bottom of the palette (it's the fx icon), and then choose Outer Glow.

5. The default color for Outer Glow happens to work in this example. Increase Opacity to about 84%, however, and increase Size to about 35 pixels or whatever looks good to you. See Figure 9.14.

Figure 9.13
Clip the fire layer to the Melissa layer.

Figure 9.14
Use a Layer Style to help separate the fiery woman from the dim background.

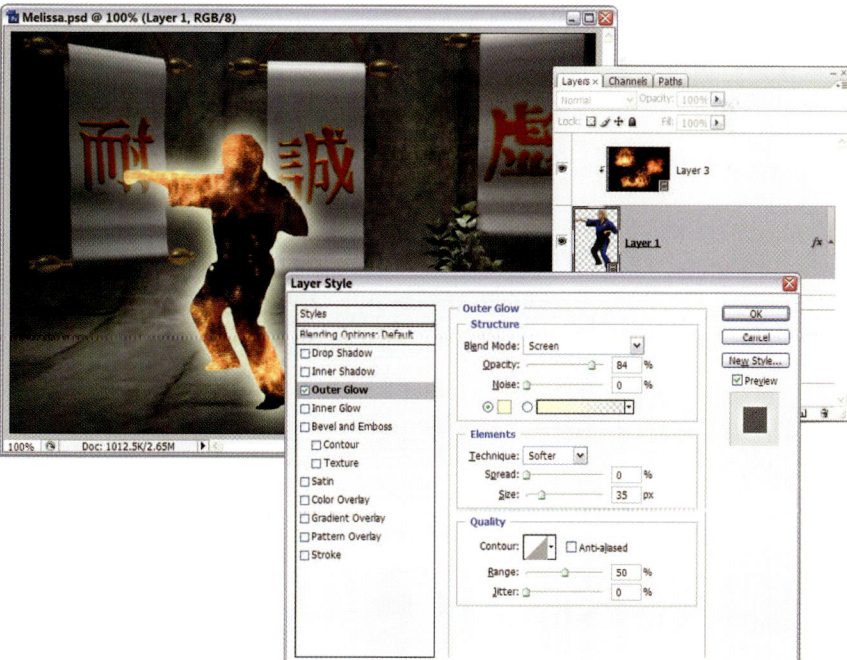

> **Tip**
>
> This is optional: If you feel ambitious, you can alter the Outer Glow over time to create, for example, a sudden flash or dimming of the glow, or change its color over time. To do this, you click the Style stopwatch for this layer on the Animation palette to set a keyframe, move the thumb on the timeline, and then alter an attribute of the style by double-clicking its icon on the Layers palette.
>
> You could make Melissa's glow heat up to bright red during a kick or increase the size of the Outer Glow over time. I feel there's enough action going on with the composition as is, and this is only a suggestion for future assignments of your own.

Creating a Perspective Shadow

A perspective shadow isn't a drop shadow; it appears to recede into the background from the object casting the shadow and is a visual cue to the audience that the subject is standing in a scene, not simply floating on top of it.

To create the cast, perspective shadow, you'll need to first create an action, name it x to save some time, and then run the script you hacked earlier when separating Melissa from the green screen.

1. Duplicate the Melissa video layer and rename the top copy layer as Melissa. Rename the original Melissa layer underneath as shadow. Delete the Outer Glow effect attached to the shadow layer.

2. On the Actions palette, rename the x action you created earlier to "x2."

3. Move the timeline indicator (the thumb) to the head of the composition.

4. Click the Actions menu and choose New Action. Name it x; you're recording now.

5. Ctrl/Cmd+click the duplicate video layer thumbnail on the Layers palette to load the nontransparent areas as a selection.

6. Fill the selection with black; Alt/Opt+Backspace with black defined as the current foreground color is a quick and easy method.

7. Ctrl/Cmd+D to deselect.

8. Choose Filter > Blur > Gaussian Blur. A value of about 3.3 pixels is good. Click OK to apply.

9. Press Ctrl/Cmd+T to put the nontransparent areas of the video layer into Free Transform; accept any attention box that might pop up to tell you that Photoshop needs to convert the layer to a Smart Object, because this is your

intention. This is why you needed to fill the layer first; Smart Objects can't easily be directly edited (you have to right-click the layer title, choose Edit Contents, respond to two dialog boxes…it's a cumbersome process for this example).

10. Zoom out if necessary to see the top center bounding box handle and then drag down until the H field on the Options bar reads about 30%, and then press Enter to apply the scaling. I arrived at this part of a "formula" by trial and error. The shadow is smushed but not correct looking; bear with me and proceed to Step 11.

11. Choose Filter > Distort > Shear. Drag the top dot in the proxy box all the way to the right and then drag the bottom one all the way to the left. Click OK to apply, and the shadow should look good in the document window; it just needs to be moved a little to the right (do this after running the script).

12. Advance the timeline to the next frame and then stop the Actions palette recorder. Your action should look like Figure 9.15. Run the script previously tweaked for the action x.

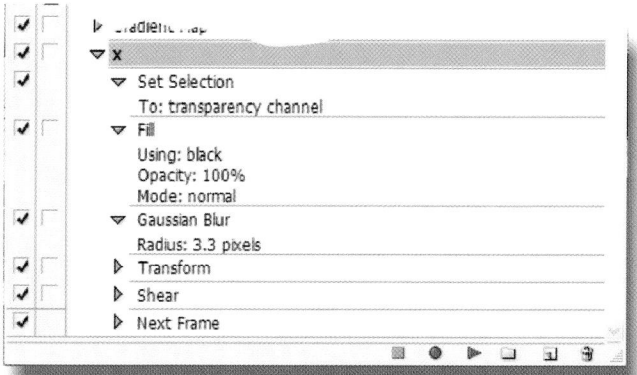

Figure 9.15
Your custom action will drive the script to make a video shadow for Melissa.

Because Melissa went through her forms in three dimensions, she appears to move up and down as she moves away from and toward the green screen (because 2D video flattens 3D visual data). This will make the cast shadow depart from her feet at certain points in the total video. There are a number of remedies: First, as a director I found the awkward phenomenon to be acceptable because of the intense visual interest in Melissa on fire. However, a quick fix is to reduce the opacity to about 40% for the cast shadow on the Layers palette, thus calling less attention to it. The more thorough fix is to open the Position attribute on the Animation palette for the shadow layer, click the stopwatch icon, and then move the thumb on the timeline to areas where the shadow leaves Melissa's feet. You then use the Move tool to reposition the shadow wherever it looks wrong in the overall video.

Fading In a Second Video to Enhance the Performance

First of all, I love this little animation but feel it's a little too long to sustain an audience's interest without any cuts. Take a look at today's movies and you barely get 10 seconds worth of hold on a character before the editor and director move to a different scene.

As it happens, there's a perfect break in Melissa's action in the video where a fade-up can be introduced and then faded out. Because my knowledge of karate is about the same as my knowledge of particle accelerators, I did not direct Melissa. I asked her to do "some visually impressive stuff," and my real task was keeping her on the green screen. Karate forms (katas) really need a larger area than a 20' by 10' green screen, and at Frames 400 though about 450 or so, Melissa needed to break her action and move to reset for a different form.

Hands 4 sec.mov is a blow-up from a different piece of footage I did of Melissa, featuring some chops and a roundhouse kick through an imaginary target. The footage is a little pixilated because I didn't dare move my camera closer to a 4th-degree black belt in action and decided after the shoot to simply blow up four seconds of footage and reposition it using the same techniques as I cover earlier in this section. However, the clip will work as a fade-in cut; I did some minor smoothing and other editing (that's why the green screen is a different shade than the Melissa footage) and with fire and a glow added, the audience will watch the action and not the rough edges.

In the composition, mark the in and out points with comments: Click the Comment stopwatch icon at 400 frames on the timeline (use the Palette Options to change to Frame Number if you haven't done so already) and type anything you like in the Timeline Comment box; click OK. Right-click over the key marker and then choose Copy Keyframe. Then advance to about Frame 450; right-click over the 400 frame key and then choose Paste Keyframe—as strange as this seems, the duplicate keyframe appears at the current time indicator point and not over the original key marker. Now you have your coarse fade in and fade out points marked, as shown in Figure 9.16.

Follow these steps to add a little more than two seconds of fade in and out to the static area of the composition:

1. Open a plain text editor, and then open your execute X 890 times JavaScript. Save it as execute 101 times. Then replace the value 890 in the script with 101 and it to your Photoshop > Presets > Scripts folder. The new script is perfectly mated now to the hands movie and will be available to use in the File > Scripts list.

Figure 9.16
Use comments as a handy tool to mark transitions in a composition.

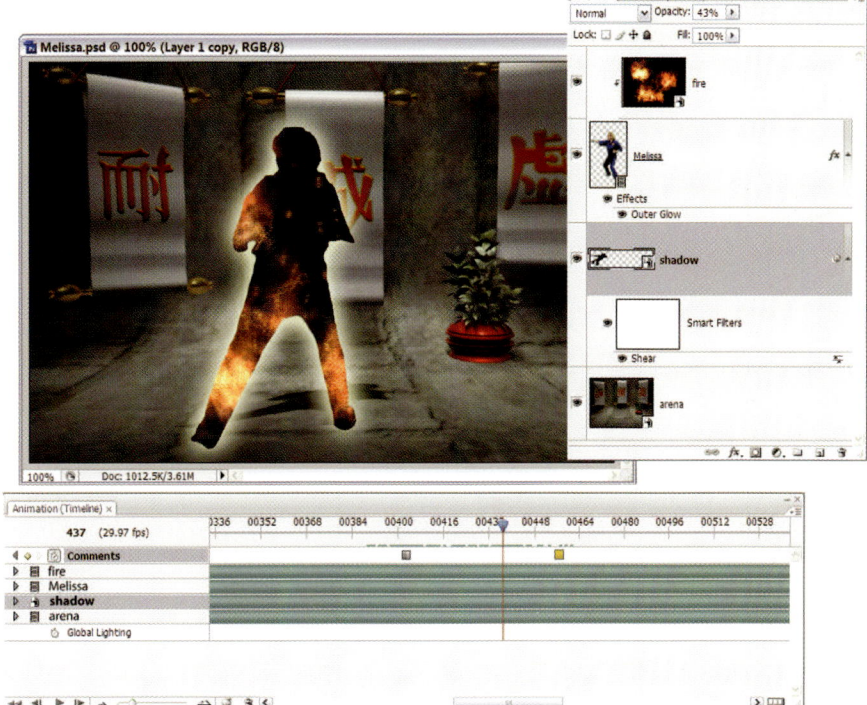

2. Open Hands 4 sec.mov in Photoshop and turn off Pixel Aspect Ratio Correction if prompted. On the Actions palette, rename the x action by double-clicking its title and typing **Cast Shadow**.

3. Rename the X2 script back to x, and then choose File > Scripts and choose the execute 101 times JavaScript.

4. Add a copy of the fire layer to the footage and hold down the Alt/Opt key and click between the two layers to add a clipping mask to the main layer. Add the Outer Glow to the main layer, exactly as you did with the Melissa layer earlier (Hint: Right-click the Melissa layer and choose Copy Layer Style, then right-click Layer 1 in the Hands 4 sec.mov file and choose Paste Layer Style). You also should check for any remaining green screen and erase it in a few frames. In Figure 9.17 you can see a before and after; clearly the rough edges remain, but the interior fire will prove to sufficiently take the audience's mind off it during the clip's short appearance.

5. In the Melissa composition, for the sake of tidiness, create a new group on the Layers palette by clicking the Create a New Group icon on the bottom of the palette and then drag all the layers into the folder title. Rename the group and any layers to meaningful titles; I used a title of Main Group for the folder.

Figure 9.17
Create the same fire effect you did with the Melissa layer through the use of a clipping mask.

Then click the Group folder to select it. Click the Hands title bar to make it the foreground document in the workspace, and the layers appear on the Layers palette.

6. Hold Shift and then click both the Hands layer and the Fire layer, and then Shift+drag both layer titles into the Melissa composition to duplicate them. You can close the Hands movie without saving it at any time now.

7. Move the hands 4 sec track on the Animation palette between the Comment keys established earlier.

8. Click the hands 4 sec layer on the Layers palette and then click the Opacity stopwatch for this layer on the Animation palette.

9. Using the Layers palette's Opacity value field and slider, set the opacity to 0% at about Frame 390 and then to about 75% at Frame 400. Then at Frame 430 or so, make the layer 75% and 0% at Frame 448 or so, as shown in Figure 9.18.

Let's talk about video editing for a moment. The overall pace of the video composition is quite frenetic, and because of this, a short insert as you just did acceptably fits the overall pace. Usually, durations for cuts are way too brief at 4 to 5 seconds, but this fade up never reaches 100% opacity and therefore becomes part of a continuous montage, and the brief fade in works.

Also there's a sound track: Melissa went through her moves to a recording on a boom box; it's copyrighted music so I had to dump the Audio track to be able to share the clip with you. What I did was figure out the tempo of the music and then recorded a different public domain piece, Bach's "Toccata and Fugue in Dm," at the same tempo using a digital audio workspace. You can add JSBach-Toccata in Dm.mp3 to the composition before rendering the video by choosing File > Open As and then opening the file as a QuickTime movie; you then drag the layer

Figure 9.18
Fade the clip in and out when Melissa pauses in her routine.

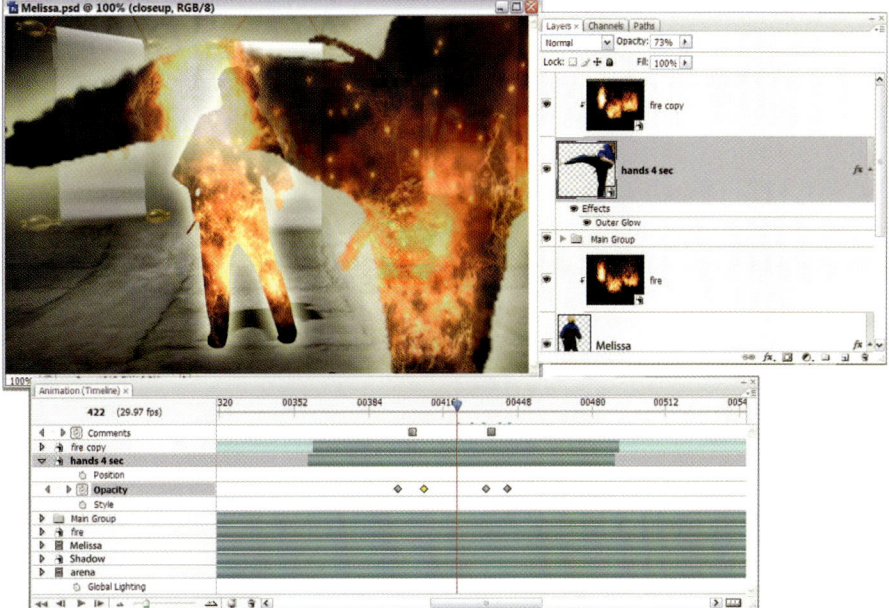

title on the Layers palette into the composition. Its duration matches the video, and as you'll see and hear, the tempo of the music does *not* precisely synch with Melissa's moves, and yet it works. This is because Melissa is not dancing; she is not strictly adhering, body-wise, to a tempo. The tempo of the music instead *supports* the video; it makes a contribution to the overall aesthetics of the clip—and my apologies to classical music buffs for Disco-izing the fugue! Additionally, the tempo of the tune is 135 beats per minute, and it's mostly eighth notes, so the odds are high that randomly placed, the music will synch to the action.

The lack of complete motion and tempo synchronization also allows you to plop the fade-in clip without the labor of matching the tempo to key moves—you would need an audio editor such as Audition or Premiere to precisely match the music to Melissa's moves.

An Exercise in Fantasy Composition

Playing with the scale of objects in a video has been a popular special effect for decades. The good news is that my example in this section didn't require greenscreen work to build the illusion, but at the same time your rotoscope work will be minor. The trick lies in planning.

Here's the setup: I wanted someone treading water in one of the turtle ponds you used to be able to buy in department stores along with those 69¢ pet turtles—kidney shaped clear plastic with a diving board and a tiny coconut palm. First, such a prop is nearly impossible to buy today; instead, I modeled it using Cinema 4D, and the movie is in the ZIP archive you downloaded. One of the unobvious advantages of modeling the scene is that I could define the water in the turtle pond as a movie, thus making the integration of the synthetic 3D footage and the live footage of a guy treading water a lot easier to accomplish. In Figure 9.19 you can see that C4D will load a movie as a 3D texture on an object (the water in the pool); at upper left is the movie I created by cropping the lower area of the Guy treading water.mov file you'll use shortly.

Figure 9.19

Using a movie for a 3D texture can ensure that the 3D movie's colors match the video to which you add the synthetic scene.

Creating the Garbage Matte

To save you a little time and to get to the heart of the techniques and steps, I've created a mask around the guy treading water in the QuickTime movie using the same steps you used to mask Domino's background earlier. There are clearly nonessential areas in the movie; they are persistent and unmoving; therefore the following steps take you through the method for creating an in-place layer mask to better seat the guy in the turtle pond. You can use but not apply a layer mask to a video layer, which is different than the properties of a regular image layer, but this is fine, and in the following steps you'll define partial transparency on the mask to better blend the guy's water with the 3D rendered water in the turtle pond video.

1. Open the Turtle pond.mov file and then the Guy treading water.mov video.

2. Drag the thumbnail of the guy from the Layers palette into the turtle pond video and close the Guy treading water file without saving changes; then with the Move tool, situate the guy toward the left of the pond, as shown in Figure 9.20, so he doesn't bother the sunbathing turtle.

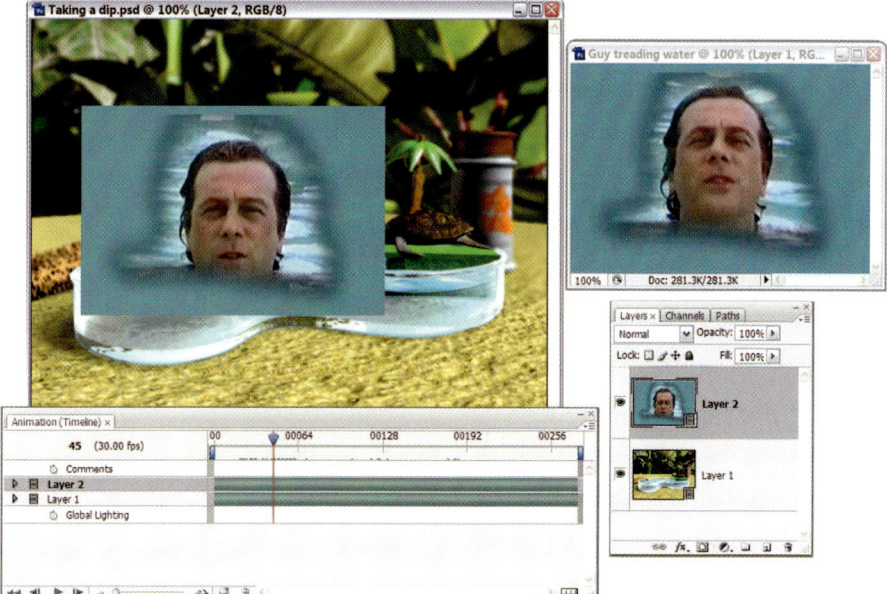

Figure 9.20
Add a duplicate of the guy video layer to the turtle pond video.

3. Ctrl/Cmd+click the guy's thumbnail on the Layers palette to load it as a selection.

4. Choose black as the current foreground color on the Tools palette, and then click the Layer Mask icon to mask everything outside the guy.

5. Choose the Polygon Lasso or the regular Lasso tool, whichever you're more comfortable with, and then drag around the darker blue halo around the guy; I did this deliberately to show the outside edge of the action in the video frame.

6. Right-click in the selection and choose Select Inverse, press Alt/Opt+ Backspace to fill the current selection, and then press Ctrl/Cmd+D to deselect. You now have your garbage matte more or less completed, as shown in Figure 9.21.

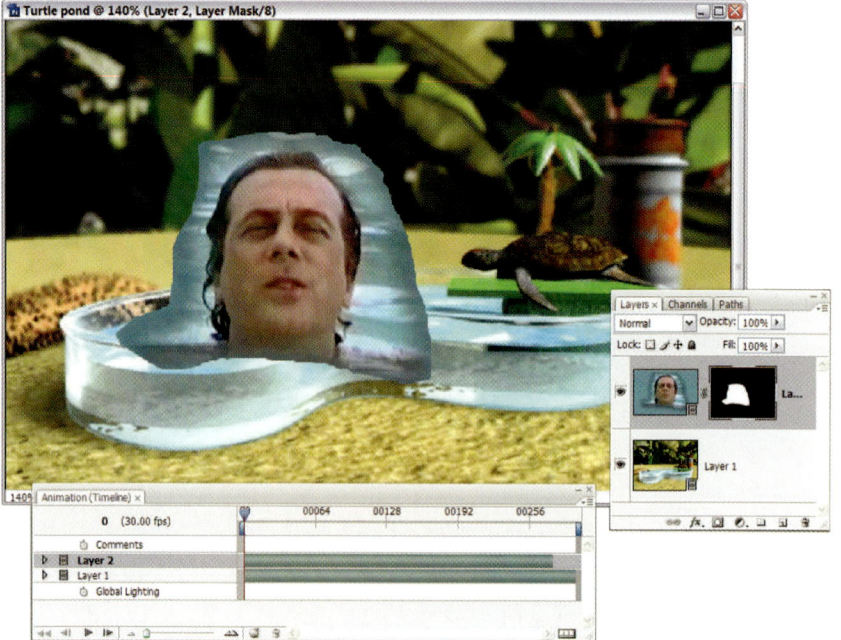

Figure 9.21
Create a coarse garbage matte to eliminate most areas outside of the guy.

Using Partial Opacity for Easier Blending

If you're guessing ahead, then, yep, the area around the guy's hair will need to be masked frame by frame; that's what rotoscoping is all about. But where the guy's chest should be submerged in the pond and only partially opaque can be a persistent attribute you can define by using the Brush tool on the layer mask and a Pen tool path as a guide. You'll notice that the lip of the pool should be a hard demarcation between full opacity and reduced, as you'd see a person peeking out of a halfway rolled-down car window.

Follow along here to refine the layer mask and get a lot of the rotoscoping accomplished in a few easy steps:

1. Hide the guy layer on the Layers palette and then choose the Pen tool. You have a good idea where the guy is located, but while visible he hides the lip of the pool.

2. Drag a closed path whose top edge is right on the lip of the pool (zoom in if needed), and whose other sides fall outside of the guy on the top layer. Restore the guy's visibility and if necessary adjust the sides of the path using the Direct Selection tool.

3. On the Paths palette, Ctrl/Cmd+click the Working Path thumbnail to load it as a selection.

4. Choose the Brush tool, and then on the Options bar set the opacity to about 60% and choose the 100-pixel diameter tip.

5. Stroke briskly around the guy's neck and chest areas and then apply more strokes to the outskirts of the selection, as shown in Figure 9.22, to blend the guy's water with the rendered water on the bottom layer. I've activated the Layer Mask display in this figure so you can better see the areas that need partial masking. Layer Mask display and Quick Mask look the same but are called from two different areas in Photoshop. You hold Shift+Alt/Opt and then click the Layer Mask thumbnail on the Layers palette to show the overlay and then do this key combo a second time to hide the display. Options for opacity of the display and color are accessed by right-clicking over a layer mask.

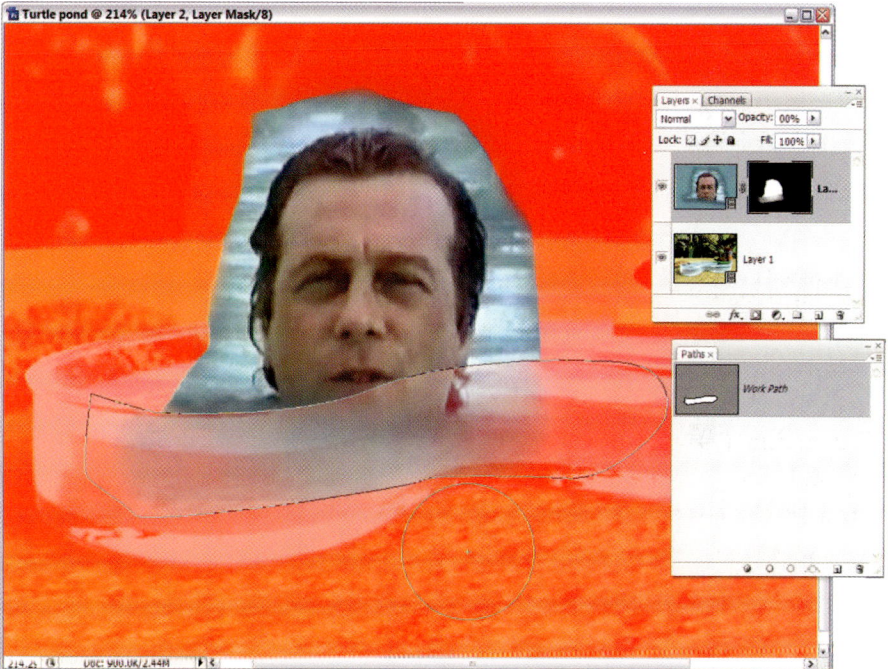

Figure 9.22
A layer mask using partial opacity serves well for blending areas between video layers.

Working with Clone Source for Rotoscoping

As I've mentioned and described in several tutorials in this book, the easiest way to hide a video area is not to erase it but instead to cover it up with a duplicate of the corresponding background video layer. The Clone Stamp tool is ideal for this task, and you also avoid twittering between video frames, so common when you retouch individual frames.

The following steps show how to set up the Clone Stamp tool and the Clone Source palette to complete the video illusion in this section. Beyond these steps is simply a lot of repetition as you retouch fames; there's really no automation to a problem that requires an artist's hands and eye, no shortcuts I can think of. The professionals at Hollywood studios do rotoscoping the same way as I show here; they might use different software, but practice the same manual labor.

1. Choose Layer > Video Layers > New Blank Video Layer.

2. Choose the Clone Stamp tool from the Tools palette and then open the Clone Source palette. If it's not on the docking strip, you can open it from the Window menu. Set the X and Y Offset values both to zero if necessary.

3. Right-click in the document window to bring up the brush sizes for the Clone Stamp tool. Set the Master Diameter to about 21 pixels and the Hardness to about 60% for a clean edge that has a touch of softness for better blending.

4. Click the bottom layer on the Layers palette; choose Current Layer from the Sample drop-down menu on the Options bar, check Aligned, and then Alt/Opt+click on an edge of the sand in the image, just outside the guy to the document's left side to set the traveling sample point.

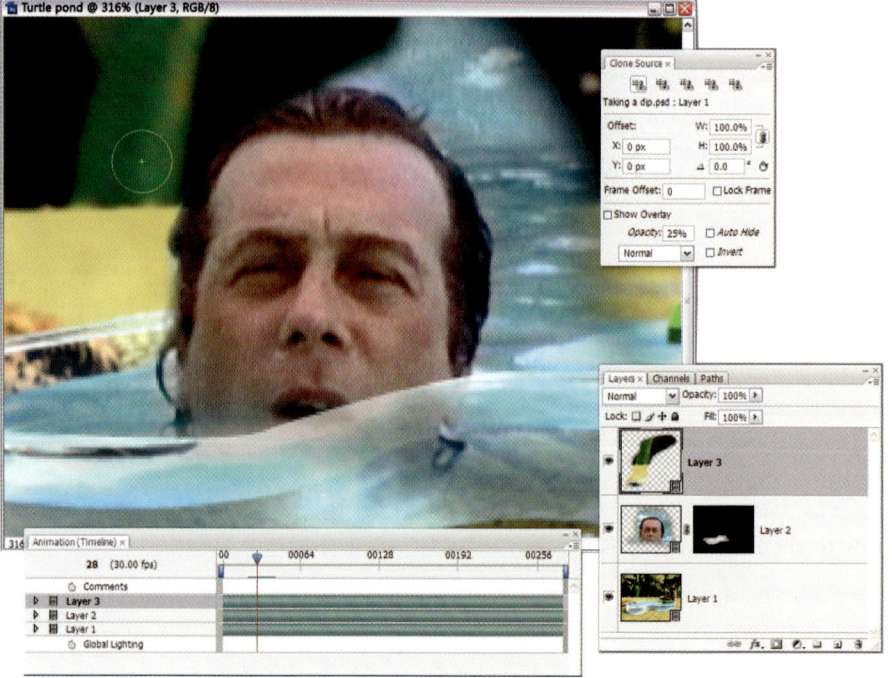

Figure 9.23
Clone over the unwanted areas using the Clone Source feature with the background layer as the target.

5. Choose the new blank video layer, and then start cloning at the point where you Alt/Opt+clicked in Step 4 to set the sampling point. It's okay if you intrude on the guy's hair a little to remove the blue; his hair is wet, and the audience won't examine the varying volume of his hair (but they will detect any blue edge). Also, the guy has a curly lock below his right ear, creating a closed area that needs cloning over, and it's a difficult spot because it's in the turtle pond. I recommend that you go through the entire clip using the 21-pixel brush tip and then go back to the first frame, set the brush size to about 4 pixels and address this area. If you have a pressure-sensitive stylus, you might want to set it up on the Brushes palette to respond to Pen Pressure or the Stylus Wheel to increase the size of the tip, thus rotoscoping away the unwanted background areas in one swoop. My point here is that it's a nuisance and can introduce errors if you redefine the brush size every frame—it's a much smarter workflow to make two separate passes. See Figure 9.23.

Saving Time by Retouching Rendered Videos

The following tutorial is a brief one and intended for any Photoshop user who renders videos in 3D applications such as Maya, modo, Cinema 4D, and so on. There's nothing more frustrating and heartbreaking than carefully setting up an animation only to view it three days later after the application has been rendering away to find a few bum frames.

Depending on the severity of the video problem, you don't necessarily have to go back and render the frames again. Instead, you can rotoscope away the problem in Photoshop Extended.

Open Sophie with elbow injury.mov in Photoshop and then scrub the timeline and you'll see the problem. The little character I animated moved in an unexpected way, beyond the bounds of her 3D mesh, and as a consequence her right elbow (at stage left) shows hard polygons instead of a smooth surface. I used the Animation palette's Work Area markers to isolate the problem footage (it's only a few frames) and then rendered the video so I'd only have to deal with a small file in Photoshop instead of the whole video.

Here's how to massage a few frames in a rendered video that had an accident, and how to then slip the corrected frames back into the animation:

1. Choose the Color Sampler tool from the Tools palette. Press F8 to display the Info palette. If you're lucky enough as I was to have an uncorrupt area from which to clone, there's no point in guessing the sampling point, but rather you use the Color Sample to make an approximation, an educated guess as to where you want to sample.

2. Set the Info palette to read HSB values by clicking the top right eyedropper icon in the Info palette to reveal your options and then choose HSB.

3. Hover around the elbow area that needs repair and then click a marker. It appears on the Info palette as RGB values, and they should be in the ballpark of R: 137, G: 118, B: 90.

4. Go down to Sophie's belly area, hover, and then when you see the values as close to your first marker at the upper left (as shown in Figure 9.24), click a marker. You can reposition a marker by dragging the marker when the tool is active.

Figure 9.24
The sampling points marked in the image will help you define cloning points.

5. One of the things I do when retouching is open a duplicate window so I have a perspective of my Work Area plus a view of the whole composition. Choose Window > Arrange > New Window for Sophie with elbow injury.

6. Zoom one of the windows to include a good view of Sophie's problem elbow and zoom the other window out to 100%.

7. Choose Layer > Video Layers > New Blank Video Layer.

8. Choose the Clone Stamp tool (a soft 13-pixel tip is good) and then with the bottom layer selected and active on the Layers palette, Alt/Opt+click over the second marker in the image, the one on Sophie's belly. Release Alt/Opt.

9. Choose the top blank layer on the Layers palette. A few times in this book I've mentioned to "brute force" the Clone Source palette to clone directly over the sample point by typing **0** in both Offset fields, but not in this example. You want to clone from the belly onto the elbow; see Figure 9.25.

Figure 9.25
Set the Clone Stamp tool's sample point and then change the current layer to the new blank one.

10. Clone away on the first problem frame and then move on to other problem frames and clone away the bumpy elbow. As you can see in Figure 9.26, this really works. When you're finished, play the short clip back and you will indeed see nothing! The replacement texture moves and integrates with the "good frames" perfectly.

11. Markers don't print; you can leave them in the document or hold Alt/Opt with the Color Sampler tool active and then click on them to delete them. They're only visible when the Eyedropper or painting tools are chosen; your client might balk at seeing them, so Alt/Opt is your key to keeping the document tidy.

12. To put this or any other clip you've isolated from footage and wish to put back in, replacing the bum frames, you first take the original video, pull the Work Area markers to around the problem frames, and then choose Lift Work Area from the Animation palette's menu. Then you copy your edited footage to the document and put it on the timeline to match the lifted (removed) area, as shown in Figure 9.27. Alternatively, you could simply place the rotoscoped video after rendering it to file on top of the original damaged footage (use Layer > Video Layers > New Video Layer from File), line the segment up with the bad original segment, and then re-render.

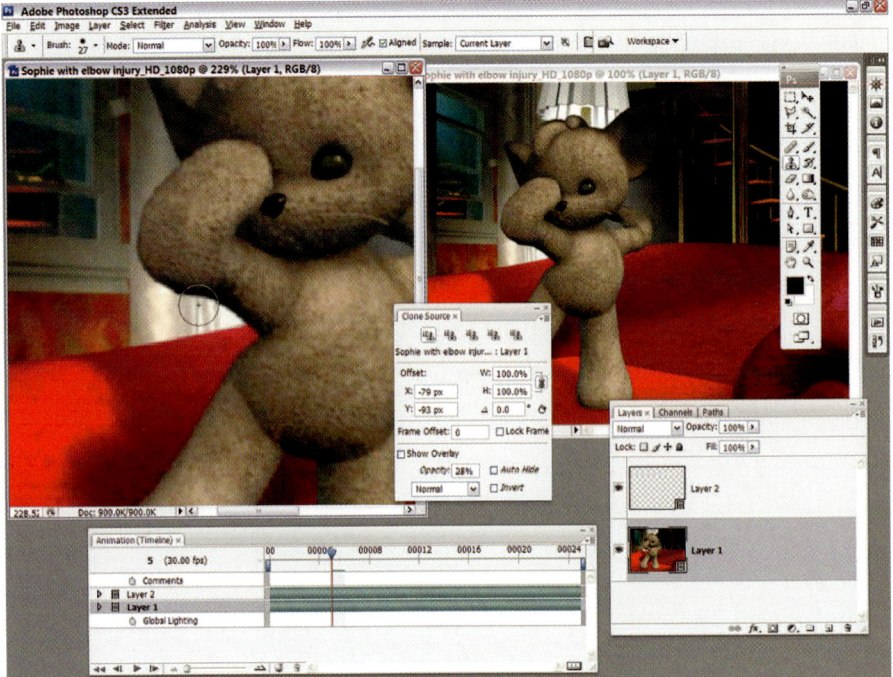

Figure 9.26
Use the Color Sampler tool's markers to initially set your sampling point. You can ignore them later because Aligned is turned on (on the Options bar).

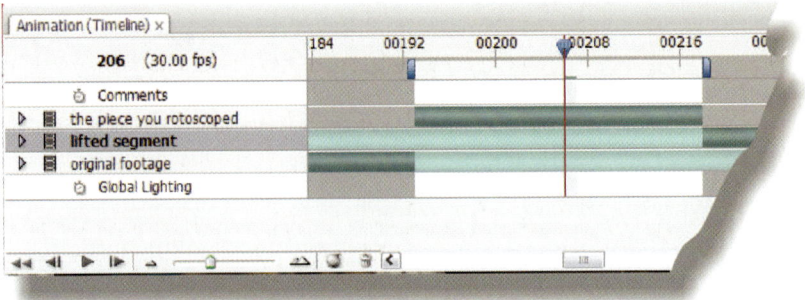

Figure 9.27
Lift the area you want to replace and then duplicate your repaired footage into this Work Area. File > Export > Render Video, and you're done.

Wire Removal

Although a lot of special effects such as a wicked wizard levitating a crystal ball are accomplished today by CG, there is still call for experienced marionette folks guiding objects across a scene using wires or poles. You might notice in a lot of 1960s television shows (*Bewitched* in particular) that the director had the set designer put a mottled backdrop behind the scene area where the "wire work" would occur, which the director thought would solve any post production retouching work. Sometimes it worked, sometimes it didn't; unless you dust a monofilament wire with dulling spray, it will catch a stage light, and the special effects scene will look like the Saturday afternoon specials with flying pie plates dangling from highlights on the wires.

As with any special effect, the more planning you do before shooting, the less Photoshop work will be required at the back end of production. If you want to do a remake of the remake of *Bewitched* in the future, I recommend:

1. Indeed use a patterned background to hide most of the wire work. And use dulling spray on your wires.

2. Find an accomplished marionette professional to do the wire work. He'll most likely want to bring along an assistant because you almost never accomplish a levitation using one wire. You need lateral control in addition to the primary wires so objects don't wobble and careen in unexpected directions.

3. Use a pole for objects that weigh more than a few ounces to stabilize the object. "Wire work" is a euphemism; stunt people are elevated using steel cables the diameter of your thumb, and even marionette artists use poles in addition to wires.

The Magic Nutcraker.mov is an example of a worst-case wire work removal challenge; I deliberately used a plant stake to work the nutcracker toy that shows visibly against the backdrop. Additionally, I arranged shadows from trees to fall on the backdrop, making it impractical to simply airbrush a solid color over the plant stake. In the following sections I show you how to remove an extremely difficult piece of wire work from a video to make a charming, fun bit of levitation video actually work.

Scoping Out an Area to Copy

The first thing you do when asked to rotoscope something out of a scene is to assess the damage; you scrub the timeline to see the extent of that which needs to be corrected. Open The Magic Nutcracker.mov now, and then on the Animation palette, scrub the timeline. Look at how large an area the pole guiding the nutcracker toy moves. Also note that the plant stake casts a shadow. You probably don't want to remove the stake and leave its shadow; check out Figure 9.28.

You've also seen now that the yellow backdrop has shadows on it; the shadows don't really move. This tells you that if you can find a part of the video with no plant stake, you can copy it to a new layer to effectively hide—or rather cover up—the plant stake. No animation is necessary; you'll find a segment at the end of the clip that can be used. And this leads me to rule #4 when doing wire work:

Always cover your shot. Leave some head and tail in your video clip where there's *no* action and *no* props and *no* wires.

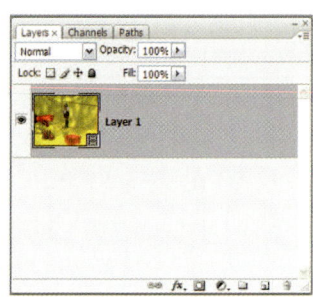

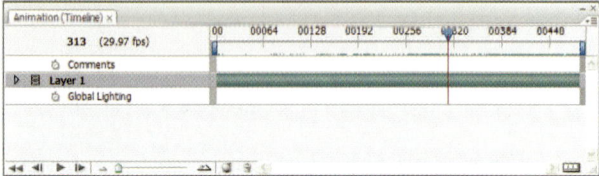

Figure 9.28
Always look at a project before choosing your tools. Doing this also helps you to prepare the estimate for your client!

Duplicating a Selected Area

Here's where you begin. In the following steps you'll select and then copy a scene area from the tail of the video to a new layer. When you make a selection and then perform Layer via Copy with a video layer, the result is a still image and not a duplicate of the original video carved out in some weird shape or something. And, for our purposes, this is ideal.

1. Go to Frame 0 on the Animation palette, the head of the video.

2. Click the Quick Mask mode button on the Tools palette. Choose the Brush tool and a fairly large brush tip. Make the current foreground color black and, if necessary, make sure the Opacity and Flow settings on the Options bar are at 100%. Usually in art, it's wise to work from the *general* to the *specific*, so you'll rough out the area that needs hiding and later on perform some fine edge work.

3. Paint Quick Mask over the areas that need hiding. Use Figure 9.29 as a reference; the Quick Mask color isn't default red in this figure only because I wanted to make the area you need to mask very evident. Why did I cover Mr. Nutcracker's head with Quick Mask? Because I scrubbed the timeline and saw that the toy moves up and down, and *all* areas the stake travels into need to be hidden.

Figure 9.29
Use Quick Mask mode as a means to create a non-saved selection.

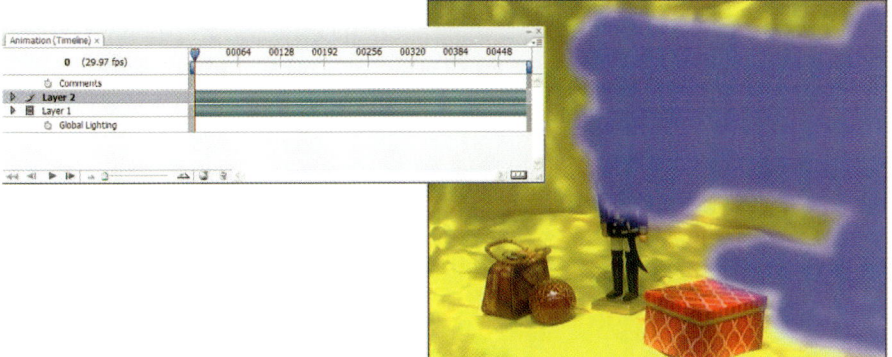

4. Switch back to Standard Selection mode on the Tools palette, and then move to the end of the timeline where there's no nutcracker and no pole.

5. Press Ctrl/Cmd+J to make a Layer via Copy. You'll see that the new layer is not tagged with a video icon at the lower right of the layer thumbnail.

Cleaning Up the Wire Work Removal

All of the preceding was more or less garbage matte work; now it's time for the real magic and the finessing of the video to make the nutcracker appear lighter than air. To do this, you resort to a new video layer and the Clone Source palette once again, alternating between the Clone Stamp and the Brush tool in Clear painting mode.

1. Choose Layer > Video Layers > New Blank Video Layer.

2. Choose the Clone Stamp tool and set the size to 21 pixels, soft tip.

3. Open the Clone Source palette and make sure the X and Y offset is set to 0 pixels, then choose the bottom layer on the Layers palette. You've seen so far that you don't actually have to see the sample point on a layer to choose a location. When Sample Destination is set to Current Layer, the same as the sample point, the sample point can indeed be hidden by layers on top of it.

4. Alt/Opt+click a point near the top area of the nutcracker and then click the blank video layer title on the top of the Layers palette list.

5. Begin at the head of the video; clone in any areas of the nutcracker that remain invisible from the middle static background layer.. Don't worry if you accidentally clone in part of the rod at the top of the helmet. This is fixed in the next step. See Figure 9.30.

Figure 9.30
Clone background layer areas to refine the edges around the nutcracker.

6. Set the Brush tool to about 13 pixels, Clear painting mode (on the Options bar). Go back to the beginning of the video and go through each frame and paint away any unwanted rod that accidentally got cloned onto the top layer. This is an intelligent workflow, and because manual labor is part of rotoscoping (the unpleasant part), you do everything you can to make the manual labor progress with aplomb and alacrity. Render the finished video and surprise your friends. It's really an interesting clip and costs less than $15 to set up.

I think you will have found in this chapter that, unlike Chapter 8, rotoscoping is not confined to creating funny little moving cartoons. (I *like* cartoons, but that's not my point.) Rotoscoping lends a professional touch to photorealistic illusions, and one look out in the market reveals that there's an abundance of special effects. So it follows that there's an abundance of work for a skilled rotoscoper; all you need to hang your shingle is some practice and the ability to convince nonprofessionals that "rotoscoping" is not a procedure for timing a car's engine.

Part IV

3D and 3D Animation

10

3D and CS3: An Introduction

I'll assume that as a Photoshop professional you have some but not a lot of experience working with 3D files. It's a rewarding sport, and the real reason I'm discussing it here is that in addition to video editing, Photoshop Extended offers 3D editing tools. The tools aren't as full featured as a genuine modeling/rendering/animation program such as Cinema 4D, modo, or Maya. However, there are a lot of tricks I'll show you in this chapter to do things with 3D data that'll enhance your worth as a videographer *and* a previsualization specialist.

Two good jump-off points to cover here lie in defining somewhat new phrases for traditional artists. *What is 3D as it relates to Photoshop and computer graphics?* 3D is a catch-all phrase that describes a virtual object or objects in a virtual scene that you build or manipulate in a simulation of 3D space in an application. Objects consist of various data sets, depending on the application, but in general they're a lot of 2D polygons arranged in 3D space to represent a surface or volume. Depending on the application, the polygons can have flat (diffuse), specular (shiny highlights), and self-illumination (glows or self-lighting) properties. Additionally—and the features usually increase as the software's price increases—polygons can display bumps, transparency, and reflection, and usually you can wrap an object with a bitmap image that makes the model look quite photorealistic.

Photoshop can import 3D objects but does not have the tools to build an elaborate model or export it. However, in this chapter I'll show you how to manipulate a couple of 3D models using a trial copy of Luxology's modo and how to "pull a render" that looks extremely photorealistic. Then I'll show you how to animate a series of renders.

As for *pre-visualization*, it's an overly erudite phrase that simply means *visualization*. Often, manufacturers and architects are required to show an example of a product or a structure before it's built. In this chapter I'll show you how to perform *pre-viz* using Photoshop and outside applications.

And the best news is learning all this 3D stuff will *not* make your head hurt afterward. I promise!

Understanding the 3D Tools

The tools for working with 3D objects in Photoshop do not appear until you load a 3D file; they're not on any palette, but rather they pop up on the Options bar after double-clicking a 3D layer thumbnail (not the title) on the Layers palette. Photoshop can import 3D data in:

- 3D Studio file format (files with the 3DS extension, not MAX, which is a scene file and includes cameras and lighting, and Photoshop cannot import it).
- Google Earth 4 (KMZ files) but only version 4, and you must have installed the *Google3D.8LI import filter (available for free at Adobe Labs' site) into Adobe Photoshop CS3 > Plug-Ins > File Formats.
- The Alias|Wavefront OBJ file format (but not Maya's MB files, which are scene information like MAX files).
- The Universal 3D file format (U3D, which is at this time very young, and you probably won't find models on the Web for free download yet).
- If any of your business associates got clever, you can open a PSB (Photoshop "large" file) that has a 3D layer embedded in it.

The following chart is intended to familiarize you with navigating 3D space. As a convention in modeling, a camera is generally presumed in a file containing one or more objects, and as in the real world, you can alter the orientation of an object relative to your camera or reorient the camera relative to the scene (or object). Therefore, the chart in Figure 10.1 shows both views of navigation: camera and object.

Many of the tools are used interactively: You click the tool to select it and then perform an operation by dragging in the document window. Here's the legend for Figure 10.1:

> *b* Clicking the Home icon resets the view of the imported data. If you downloaded a model and have experimented with different views, for example, clicking the Home icon takes you to the default view defined by the creator of the file.

Figure 10.1
The options for navigating and editing a 3D object.

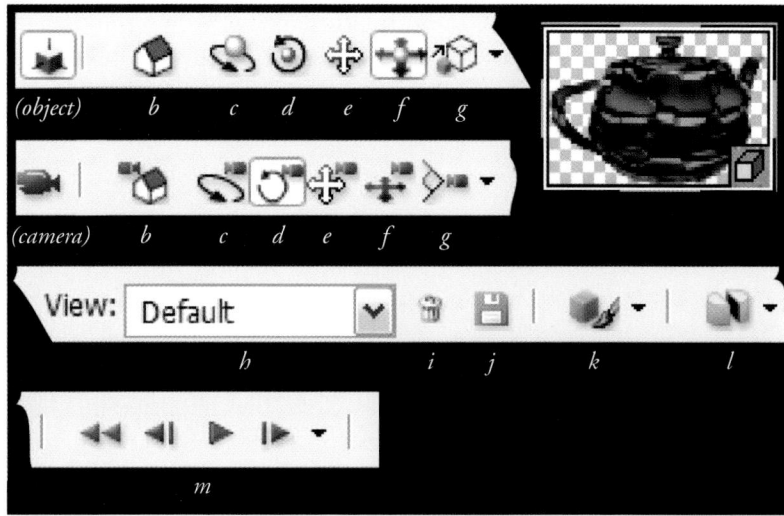

c Rotate (the object). You'll use this icon most often for matching the perspective of an object compared to a photo that might be on a layer underneath. Dragging right rotates the object counterclockwise (to the left), dragging left performs the opposite function, dragging up enables you to see the bottom of an object, while dragging down will provide you with a roof's view of the object. Often you'll need to drag diagonally (or left then down, for example) to position an object the way you want it seen. If you hold Ctrl/Cmd while dragging, you remove the 2D rotate constraints and can rotate the object freely in 3D in space. I recommend that you play with Rotate with objects to better hone your 3D navigation skills. Remember that *you rotate an object in the direction in which you drag*, which is the opposite effect in some 3D modeling applications.

> **Tip**
>
> Modeling is not the same as Computer Assisted Design (CAD), although both professions require the skill to navigate virtual 3D space. CAD requires extreme accuracy—you probably would want this with your house design or a hip replacement part! Modeling, on the other hand, is a sport for artists, and although accuracy is a goal, modeling is more closely akin to painting with a 3D brush—the quality of the render is of the most importance.
>
> In modeling, we usually use the X axis to describe movement and rotation from left to right, the Y axis represents up and down (height), and the Z axis represents depth. However, in CAD, where a schematic is usually rendered from a top view, Y is depth and Z is height.

d Roll. This icon can be used to straighten an object when its vanishing point (or horizon) is crooked or doesn't match the underlying scene. Roll rotates clockwise and counterclockwise parallel to your view. In the modeling community, this is called rotating across the Z axis (X is width and Y is height).

e Drag. Actually, it's a Move tool. You use this tool to move an object up, down, and across relative to your current view of the scene.

f Slide. Actually, think of moving an object along its Z axis. Dragging upward in the document window moves an object away from you, and dragging down moves it closer to your current view. If you download the free models from Google Earth, you'll be moving the objects away from you (drag upward) most of the time. For reasons unclear to me, KMZ files import with a very close, tight view of the wonderful buildings and other objects contributors have been kind enough to post.

g Object Position. This is quite a useful statistics field that pops up. From this data, you can match an object's position from within Photoshop and use the data in a modeling program, as I'll show you later in this chapter.

Along the second strip in Figure 10.1 you see the same a–g callouts. You'd don't need me to rehash what the Camera icons do; they function identically to the Object icons when you choose this mode, except they change your view of an object instead of relocating the object. Most of the time, because you're literally working on a 2D space that virtually represents 3D space, what you do to an object nets out to the equivalent of what you do to your camera view. Modelers frequently move a camera instead of an object, particularly when the object consists of a number of ungroups subcomponents. The real difference is that G in the Camera 3D mode shows you camera data, and this, too, can be used in modeling programs to match a view between a Photoshop composition and in the modeler.

The views are positioned relative to each other according to either of two schemes: first-angle or third-angle projection. In each, the appearances of views may be thought of as being projected onto planes that form a six-sided box around the object.

H This is a Views list. Photoshop has presets for front, left, bottom, and so on. Additionally, if the creator of a 3D file has added explicit camera locations, you'll find these, too, in the drop-down list.

I&J These icons are used to delete and save views, which is very handy for paring down the list of unwanted views and for adding your own after you navigate around and find a view you really like. New views are auto-named Custom View #.

K Light and Appearance Settings. Photoshop is not a rendering program, and it is able to display 3D objects through the use of Open GL, which is fast but only supports shading parameters (light and material properties) for diffuse and specular colors and bitmap textures as I described earlier. You have a number of lighting presets from which to choose from this drop-down field, and if the creator of the file added lights (and named them), you can choose to use their lights. CAD Optimized Lights and Hard Lights are my favorites because although they make the model look unphotorealistic, they provide a good, clear view of all aspects of the model. Appearance settings are presets that include Wireframe and Transparency so you can provide a client with a more technical, less appealing view of a proposed building or product. I choose to use Default in most of my work, but I'll show you some worthwhile alternate choices later in this chapter.

L The cross-section options. This is a valuable option when you want to show a client the inside and outside of an object at the same time, and it's also fun and semitherapeutic after a long day's work. I show you how to use the option shortly.

M As far as I know, an animated object can only be created in AutoDesk products such as 3D Studio—these are the controls for playing back an animation if one exists in an imported 3D file (they work just like a VCR). Competing products such as Cinema 4D and others cannot export animation tracks to 3DS or OBJ file formats. If an imported object has no animation, the controls are dimmed for this layer. Note that animations in 3D files cannot be rendered to a video file—a 3D layer is not a video layer in Photoshop, and the Animation palette will show no animation tracks. However, Chapter 11 takes you through animations using modeling applications, and videos you render out of modeling programs can indeed be used as video tracks in a Photoshop composition.

Getting Some Perspective

The term *perspective* is something we casually toss about day in and day out, but relative to Photoshop and modeling programs, perspective has a very specific meaning and use.

Perspective is a quality of all objects we see in the real world. When you look at an object straight-on, you see one plane perspective (no points). If you move a little to the left or right, you achieve a two-plane perspective (1-point); add a move up or down, and you see the object in two-point perspective with three planes, as shown in Figure 10.2.

Notice in Figure 10.2 that the depth and height of the cube diminish in perspective. This is a function of the eye and camera lens, and if you were to draw lines across the edges of the second and third perspective points, the lines would converge. This convergence point is called the *vanishing point*. In art, we generally try to use a vanishing point and 2-point perspective to make scenes look natural; Leonardo DaVinci was one of the first artists to not only discover but also to document the phenomenon of the vanishing point. My simple drawing in Figure 10.3 shows the vanishing point of a 2-point perspective view of a long house.

The Zoom for the Camera tool (in Figure 10.1) exposes fields on a drop-down box in which you can specify the camera position and orientation (degree of rotation along the three axes) as well as an Orthographic View option. Orthographic views are not natural views but rather "flattened" views of objects in scenes based on math calculations. An orthographic view is sometimes called *forced perspective*; the vanishing point is removed from the scene, and as a consequence all perspectives on the scene are more or less parallel to the camera lens. Orthographic views are also occasionally called isometric.

The purpose of orthographic views is not really for aesthetics but instead to provide architects and professionals who need to examine the perspective of an object such as a product with one or two points of perspective, all of which have equal emphasis and do not suffer the distortion inherent to the human eye. In Figure 10.4 I rendered a cottage using orthographic perspective in Cinema 4D and then pulled a second render using a (normal) 55mm lens. You can clearly see a drawback to using orthogonal views: The scale of objects is not realistic because everything is brought to a single depth plane parallel to the camera. However, it's very easy to tell in orthogonal view that the two trees are of equal size; in normal view you can't even see the second tree behind the cottage.

The red lines overlaid at the bottom of this figure emphasize the properties of orthogonal views: Notice that orthogonal perspective edges run parallel while normal perspectives have edge lines that will eventually converge. This is important stuff not only for product design but also to gain more experience in the world of 3D modeling. An orthogonal view of a no-point perspective on a scene is critical to ensure objects line up correctly—normal perspectives shift the apparent spatial relationship between objects as you move the camera.

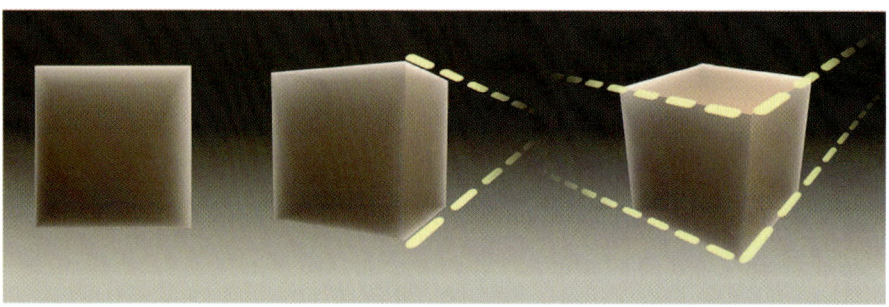

Figure 10.2
Examples of a cube viewed in 0, 1, and 2 point perspective.

0-point perspective
(1 plane)

1-point perspective
(2 planes)

2-point perspective
(3 planes)

Figure 10.3
Vanishing points in photographs and art usually lie somewhere around a scene's horizon.

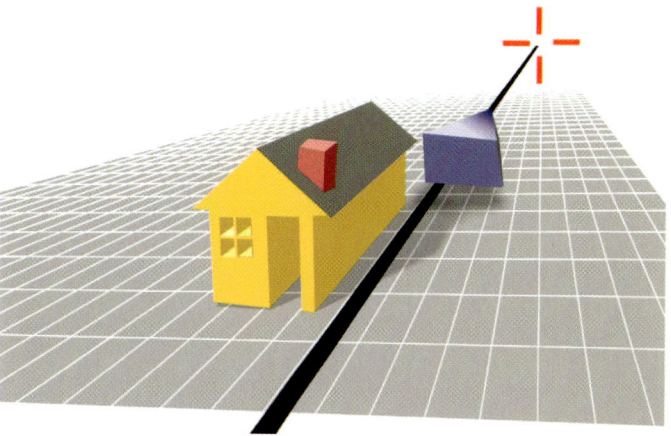

Figure 10.4
Normal perspective (left) and orthogonal (right).

Hands-On 3D: Experiment 1

In Figure 10.5 you can see an extremely simple scene done in 3D Studio—the tea kettle is a preset shape. All I really did was rotate the kettle for a duration of 60 seconds and put the unusual texture on the model. There is no ground in the scene, and therefore it imports to Photoshop surrounded by transparency. At upper left you can see a finished render window; when the file comes into Photoshop, the display quality will be somewhere between the finished render and

Figure 10.5
Primitive shapes are usually included on palettes in most 3D modeling applications.

the flat shaded scene in the lower right preview window. You're going to work with the saved file in the steps to follow to get a handle on navigating and editing in Photoshop's 3D space.

In the next steps, there's no "right" or "wrong"; I'm only going to suggest things you can do with the imported 3D object—creative things you might want to try out on your future (paying) 3D assignments. I suggest that before you begin, you turn off color management: Photoshop will pop you a Profile Mismatch attention box for each and every texture map on a 3D object because most modeling programs don't export texture maps with color profiles, and some of the models you'll work with have almost a dozen different bitmap image texture files. Double-click the workspace and then choose the tea kettle.psb you downloaded earlier. The 3D object is embedded in the file; later, I'll show you how easy it is to simply bring in an object and then save it to PSB.

1. Double-click the thumbnail on Layer 1 to access the animation controls that appear on the Options bar. Play the animation; first click the Selects First Frame (far left VCR) button (you need to rewind because of the way Photoshop reads 3DS animation), then click the Stop button—the Play button then replaces the Stop button, and you can then play the 3D "movie." It's just fun to see something you've never seen in earlier versions of Photoshop. Click the Stop button after the amusement wears thin.

2. Try the Camera navigations; click an icon on the Options bar and then drag in the document window. Try to pose the tea kettle at an interesting viewpoint.

3. Press Enter or click on the checkmark icon on the Options bar to commit any 3D transform changes made. Add a layer to the document from the Layers palette below the 3D layer by holding Ctrl/Cmd while clicking the Create a New Layer icon. Fill the layer with a pleasing gradient or pattern.

4. Even a virtual camera has lens options. Double-click the thumbnail of Layer 1 to access the 3D controls again. Let's create a fisheye perspective of the tea kettle; click the 3D Camera Settings drop-down and then type **18** in the Field of View value box. The tea kettle will zoom away from you only because of virtual camera optics. Here's the trick: Now, use the Walk with the 3D Camera icon (it's a Zoom tool for 3D) and then drag upward in the window to zoom in. In Figure 10.6 you can see the original perspective on the tea kettle and then a wide-angle view. Therefore, in addition to all of your standard filters in Photoshop for distorting things, you can now distort a 3D object. This is terrific for exaggerations to make an artistic point and for suggesting that a box of Product X contains more cereal or detergent than it really does. It's an

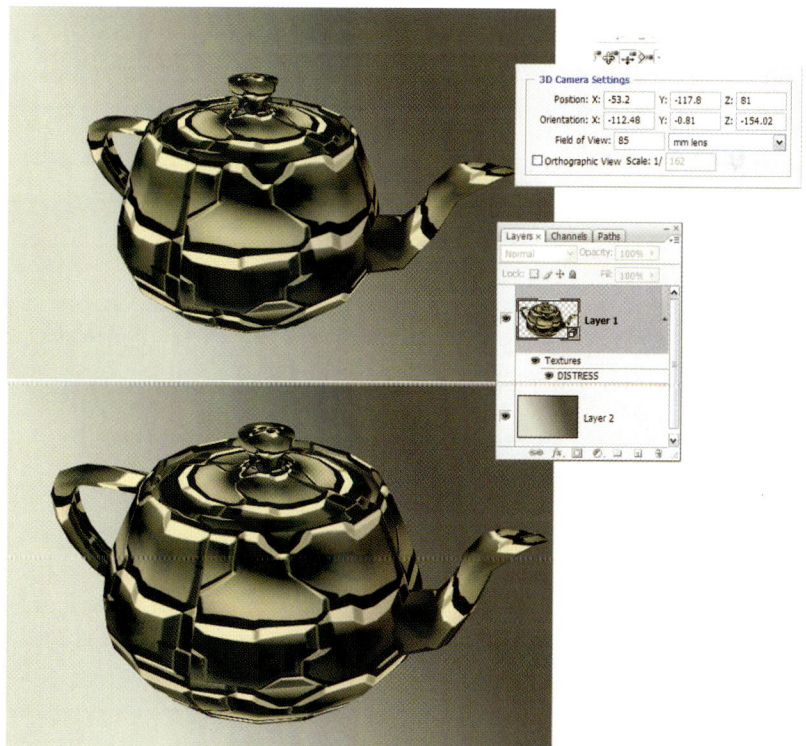

Figure 10.6
Use Photoshop's 3D camera controls as you would the features on a physical camera.

old advertising trick with a twenty-first century spin, and I'm seriously questioning my business ethics while writing this....

5. You'll get requests from clients to explain visually a scene or object very clearly, unambiguously, and at the price of realism and aesthetics. Try this: Click the Light and Appearance Setting icon, choose Hard Lights, and then choose Transparent from the Render Mode drop-down list. Then drag on the label Opacity (the text is actually a cleverly disguised slider) until you hit 50% or so. Your client can now see straight through the tea kettle and examine where the spout meets the body…on both the front and back side at the same time. This is invaluable when demonstrating machine parts and other technical equipment.

   The Line and Face color options are available but don't do anything unless you choose Transparent Wireframe, and the Crease Threshold determines how many lines in a wireframe view are displayed. The lower the value, the more edges you'll see, which is good for technical pieces that have a lot of different plane angles such as gears.

6. Try Transparent Wireframe. At lower left in Figure 10.7, I put a checker pattern behind the Transparent Wireframe because there was no good line color for the warm gradient added in Step 3. I also chose a pale cyan for the line color by clicking the Line Color swatch box (which takes you to the Color Picker), and clearly the model is more geometrically explicit and a tad less photogenic—textures hide from view when you use most of the custom appearances.

> **Tip**
>
> Unfortunately, the Save and Delete Views icons pertain to only object and camera views and not to the lighting and appearance settings. If you have several particular appearances you want to save to show to a client, you do this: Convert the single layer document to a Smart Object layer. Then double-click the thumbnail (not the layer title), click OK in the Edit Contents dialog box, and Photoshop spawns a new PSB document whose layer is a 3D layer; converting a 3D layer to a Smart Object layer destroys the 3D editability. Do what you like in the new PSB document and then when you're done, right-click the layer title on the Layers palette and choose Rasterize 3D. Get yourself three or four different views using different angles, lighting, and appearances, and then copy the layers to a single document; then use the Window > Layer Comps feature to make a document you can quickly toggle through to impress your client.

Figure 10.7
Lighting and appearance settings are terrific when you want a schematic treatment of an imported 3D object.

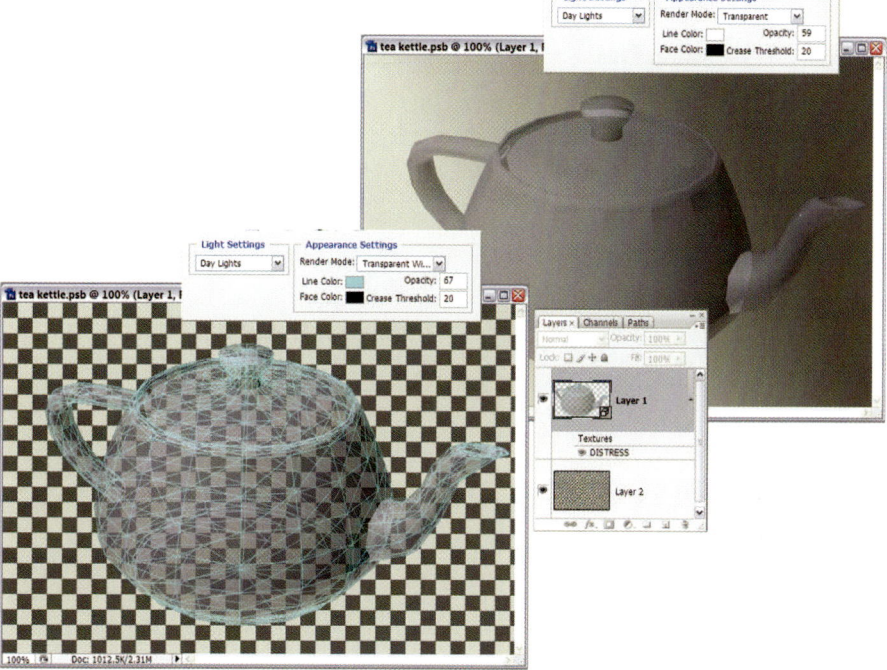

7. Click the Cross-section icon. In the drop-down box, click the Enable Cross-section checkbox. The Flip checkbox inverts the volume that's hidden on the model, and the Show Intersections checkbox makes the cut visible with any color line you like (but you cannot set a line width). Choose the X checkbox to make the cross-section facing your current view, choose Y to make the cut on the left or right, and choose Z to cut from top to bottom. In the area at right, the Offset slider sets how much you remove: Higher values expose more object. Tilt 1 and 2 set an angle to the cross-section so your cuts don't have to be 90 degrees parallel to your view. Cross-section serves a valuable industry purpose: Not too many years ago, small fortunes were spent hacking and taking a cutting torch to autos and other expensive goods to show interior views of products. In Figure 10.8 you can see that there's nothing of interest inside my tea kettle. But there *could* have been a genie, and you'd never have known were it not for the Cross-section feature. Or you could use the Rotate Object tool, turn it upside down, and give it a shake. (I'm kidding.)

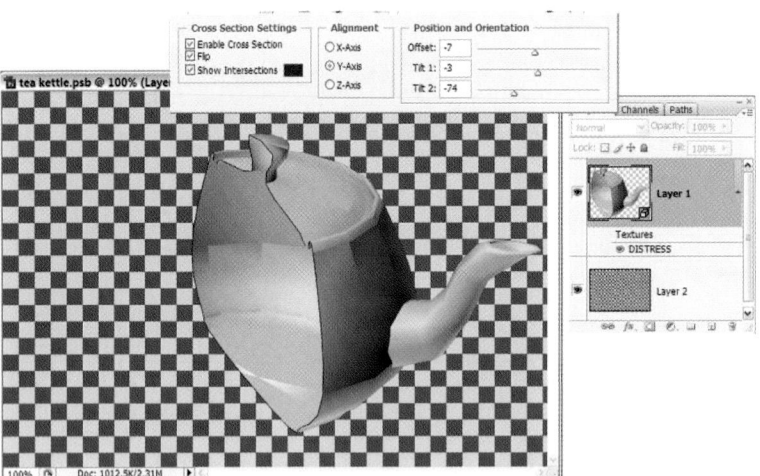

Figure 10.8
Use Cross-section to expose the interior of an imported 3D object.

Retexturing a 3D Model

It's beyond the scope of this book to thoroughly document UV mapping. In a nutshell, scenes created in 3D modeling programs are measured in 3D space along X, Y, and Z axes. However, when you want to put a bitmap on a model, different measurements are used; they're coordinates local to the object and not the whole scene, and they're called UV mapping coordinates (U is width and V is height, and there is no third coordinate most of the time).

I used a "generic" UV mapping definition to put the armor texture on the tea kettle in 3D Studio, but there are a lot of fancy tricks you can do with UV mapping to make a model look positively photoreal. Cubic, spherical, cylindrical, and other *projections* are available in most modeling programs, and advanced programs such as modo and Cinema 4D enable you to adjust the UV map *in situ* to flawlessly tailor your bitmaps to the surface of complex models. I'll show this and how to edit textures to use in modeling apps later in this chapter.

Additionally, I used a repeating texture on the tea kettle to conserve saved file space; it's a relatively small JPG, and 3D Studio offers the option to bind the bitmap into the 3DS model file so there's no way to misplace it on hard disk. This means that you can import the model in native 3DS file format and open the texture in a child window and edit it—and even replace it. In the following steps you'll get creative with the Type tool, and in the tradition of full disclosure you'll put a typical warning on the tea kettle. Here's how:

1. Open the Tea Kettle.3DS file in Photoshop. You just use File > Open (or double-click the workspace). Choose 1024 by 1024 pixels as the document size.

2. Double-click the DISTRESS title on the Layers palette list. This is the texture name of the bitmap image I used to map across the kettle in 3DS. Double-clicking a subgroup item of a 3D layer opens the texture in a new window; you can also hide a texture by clicking its eye icon on the Layers palette.

3. As I mentioned, this bitmap, embedded in the 3DS file, repeats across the surface of the tea kettle. Without a UV map to follow in Photoshop, you really cannot accurately adjust the tiling or location of image content, but you can resize the canvas of the PSB file you now have on screen and alter it in any way you choose. Right-click over the title bar and choose Canvas Size.

4. Extend the canvas to 1024 by 1024 pixels. Choose any background color you like; you'll replace it soon with a texture. Resizing the canvas results in fewer repeats of the design you'll create across the surface. Through trial and error, you can make a canvas size that doesn't appear to repeat at all; the larger the canvas, the fewer repeats. See Figure 10.9.

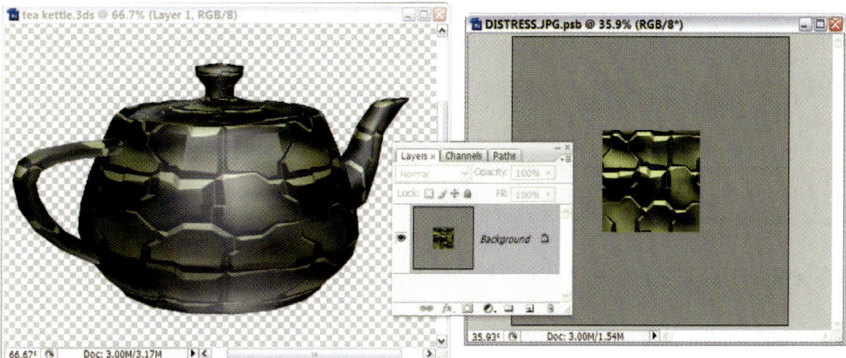

Figure 10.9 Extend the canvas of the bitmap embedded in the 3DS file.

5. Use the foreground/background color swatches on the Tools palette to define a dark warm gray and a light warm gray.

6. Choose Filter > Render > Clouds. This is an easy, quick way to texture the tea kettle. Because the Clouds filter creates seamless tiles at 128 pixels and multiples of this, the 1024 by 1024 canvas now repeats seamlessly. If you have a different stratagem for making the canvas seamless, feel free to experiment here. Press Ctrl/Cmd+F to reapply the last-used filter (Clouds) to play with variations; no two renders are the same. Stop when you've arrived at a pattern you like.

7. Click the Type tool and then get the Character and Paragraph palettes from the Options bar.

8. Choose an authoritative font such as Helvetica or Arial Condensed (bold). On the Paragraph palette, set the justification to Justify All, and then set the font size to about 40 pts. Use a bright yellow color. Drag a marquee using the Type tool on the center of the document about 300 pixels in width and then type **CAUTION: <cr>Contents are <cr> understandably <cr> HOT**. Then highlight lines of text and use the Character palette to scale the text into an official-looking message. See Figure 10.10, and if you're not experienced with Paragraph text check out Chapter 7.

9. Right-click the background layer title and then choose Merge Visible from the context menu. Close the document window and reply Yes in the Save Changes box.

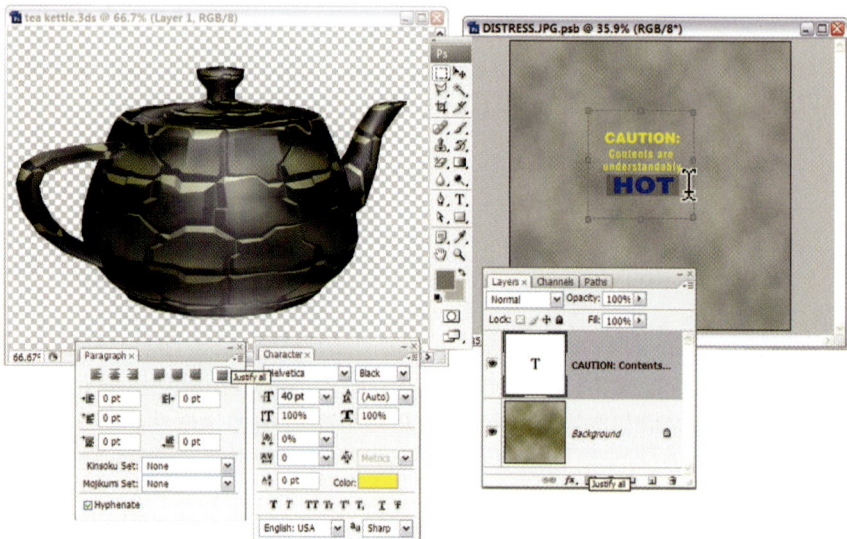

Figure 10.10
The text is small compared to the canvas; this means the warning will appear infrequently on the tea kettle.

Done! As you can see in Figure 10.11, the tea kettle now has ample warnings all over it. Double-click the layer thumbnail to get the 3D options visible on the Options bar and then rotate the kettle to admire your work. If you save the file as a PSB now, you can return at any point in the future and resurface the tea kettle. The handy thing about PSB files is that as a 3D content creator, you can share the 3D data in a format that others cannot extract the model and repurpose it. PSB is a good means of copy protecting your investment in 3D models you might have purchased or built yourself.

Figure 10.11
Add a custom texture to a 3D object you import to a Photoshop document.

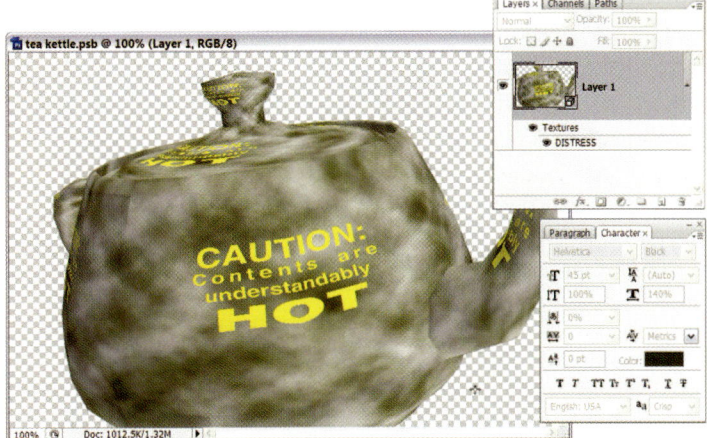

Google Earth and 3D Architecture

Shortly after Google acquired SketchUp, an entry-level architecture design application, they capitalized on the fascination with visiting real landmarks…virtually. Google Earth consists of several online components that enable visitors to see structures in geographically correct Earth coordinates. But the fun part for Photoshoppists is the free version of SketchUp we can download at http://sketchup.google.com/download.html and the free plug-in for PS Extended at http://labs.adobe.com/wiki/index.php/Photoshop_CS3_Extended_Plug-In_for_Google_3D_Warehouse. With the plug-in installed, you can then download KMZ files at Google's 3D Warehouse and open the architecture (or models of anything anyone has posted) in Photoshop (http://sketchup.google.com/3dwarehouse/cldetails?mid=c016fdc42d23ccb579d64ab0158ff971). And with SketchUp (and a few hours working through tutorials) you can create and save your own structures and then bring them into Photoshop.

Resurfacing a Google Earth Structure

Download the plug-in and go find a model that appeals to you. I recommend Romeo's Times Square coffee shoppe (the file I show in the tutorial and following figures) at http://sketchup.google.com/3dwarehouse/details?mid=4e7d1379101972dd2e4bbb0f9acb8421, handsomely replicated by TomL. You'll need SketchUp installed because the file is not available online in KMZ, and Photoshop can only load Google Earth 4 files in the KMZ format, not SketchUp native SKP files. In SketchUp, you choose File > Export 3D model and then choose Google Earth 4 from the Export Type drop-down list. I'm going to show you how to edit TomL's wonderful model to better show you how materials are applied to a SketchUp model; the original model uses very nice colors that you'll make ghastly yellow and hideous red for a constructive purpose. First, Photoshop cannot resurface a material on a model if it's just a stated color value in the file's code; the material *must* be a bitmap, even if the bitmap is a solid color. Second, in the tutorial to follow I'll show you how to change the color scheme of an ugly building so it meets the codes and taste of the local authorities who approve proposed building sites.

Download and open Romeo's or a similar building from the 3D Warehouse. Then follow these steps in Photoshop:

1. Create a new image 50 pixels by 50 pixels. Fill it with red and then save the file as a JPEG; name it red.jpg. Then fill it with yellow and choose File > Save As, and name the file yellow.jpg. You're done in Photoshop for the moment; load SketchUp and open the SKP file you downloaded.

2. Right-click over the color you want to replace and then choose Entity Info. I'm going to replace the medium gray on the front of Romeo's.

3. Click the color (or texture) in the Entity Info box.

4. A new box pops up; click Edit.

5. In the Texture field, check the Use texture image checkbox and then click the folder icon to search for the yellow JPEG file you saved in Step 1. Choose it from the folder window and then click OK. Rename the textures "hideous yellow" for the yellow file and "nauseating red" for the red file; see the pale blue circle in Figure 10.12.

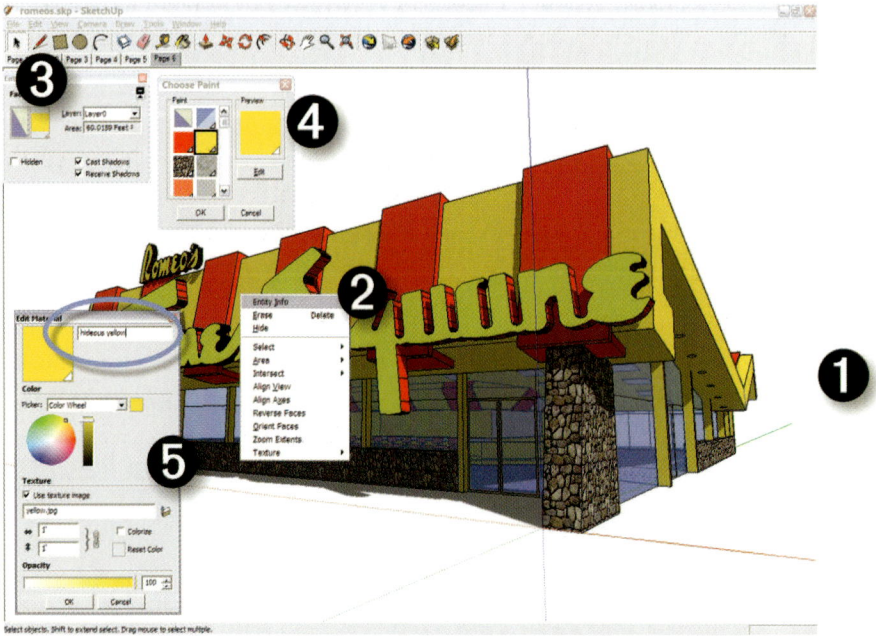

Figure 10.12
Follow Steps 2–5 to uglify the building.

6. Replace the black front part of the coffee shop by repeating Steps 2–5; use the red JPEG image. In Figure 10.12 I've put large numbered bullets that correspond to the previous steps; it's simpler than it looks.

7. Save the file in SketchUp's SKP format (to validate your changes in the file) and then choose File > Export.3D Model and then save the file to Google Earth 4, KMZ file format.

Using Photoshop to Pre-Visualize KMZ Architecture

It's time to return to Photoshop and clean up the color scheme for the zoning commission, and then it's on to providing a pre-viz image of the coffee shop on a downtown corner in Hollywood, Florida (you downloaded the image earlier).

1. Open the KMZ file in Photoshop—choose 1700 × 1700 pixels as the document size so it will scale properly against the Florida photograph. Use your newfound navigation skills to pose the building so your current view shows the whole structure.

2. Double-click the entry below the 3D thumbnail on the Layers palette list that you marked nauseating red (or whatever).

3. Choose a medium deep green as the foreground color swatch on the Tools palette. Hunter Green is popular for modern commercial architecture; it's 33, 94, 33 using the RGB color fields in the Color Picker.

4. Press Alt+Backspace.

5. Close the PSB and click Yes in the following dialog box to save changes. In Figure 10.13, I've divided the screen to show you a before and after. Clearly the building is shaping up; next let's interlace the top front of the building's handsome Hunter Green with some brick.

6. Open the Brick.jpg image you downloaded in the ZIP file. You'll notice it's miniscule; this is the scale of textures Google Earth uses to conserve bandwidth. I created the seamless image from a much larger one, using the Offset and Clone Stamp tool trick Photoshop users have been using since version 3.

7. Press Ctrl/Cmd+A and then Ctrl/Cmd+C. You can close the file now but don't copy anything else to the clipboard!

8. Double-click the texture on the Layers palette list that you used the hideous yellow JPEG image for to open in a new window as a PSB file.

9. Press Ctrl/Cmd+V to paste the brick texture from the clipboard and then press Ctrl/Cmd+E, the shortcut to Merge Down, close the file, and answer Yes to save changes. Actually, you can save layers in a PSB file; you can keep a whole collection of textures in the saved model file so you can show variations to a client. I'm just asking you to flatten files to simplify housekeeping as you work. In Figure 10.14 you can see a significant improvement to the coffee shop's edifice. I think it'll pass zoning codes, and so it's time to put the model into a photograph. Save the file as a PSB file but don't close it.

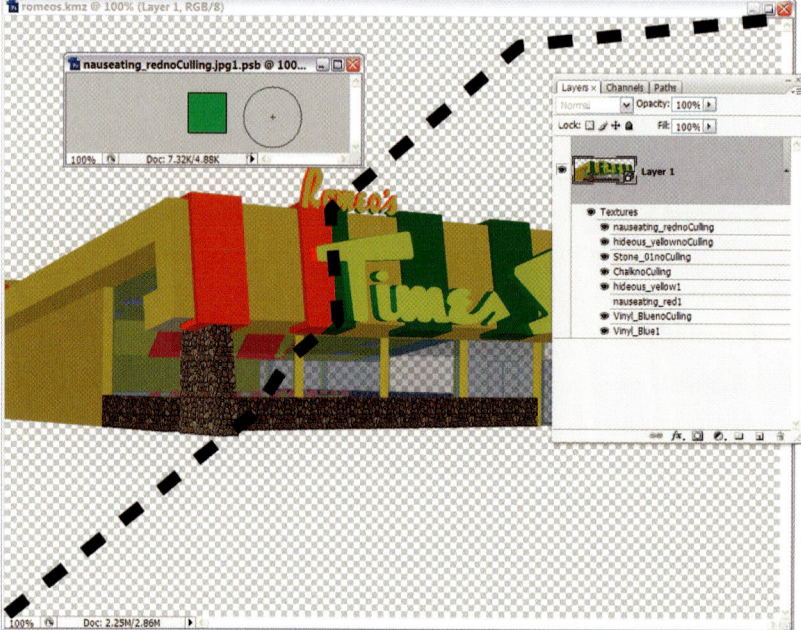

Figure 10.13
You can recolor a material only if it's a bitmap image embedded in the Google Earth file.

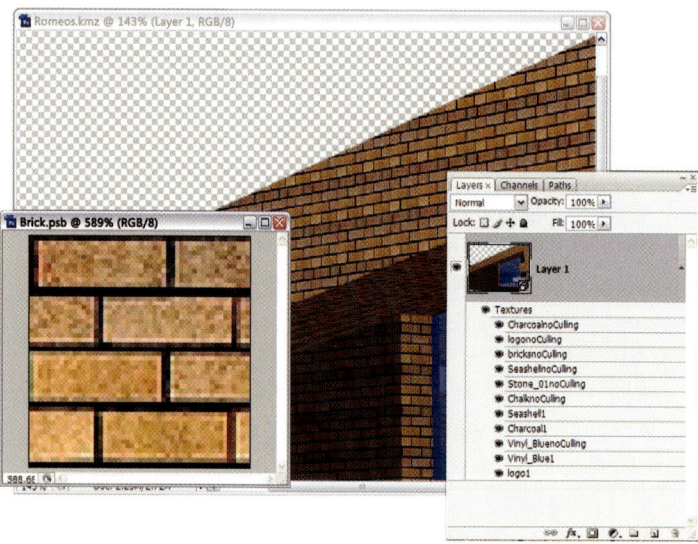

Figure 10.14
Change the base texture of the object by pasting a new image into the PSB container document.

Basic Contextualizing of Pre-Viz in a Photograph

Pre-visualization is not complete until you actually put the pre-viz model into a scene so the folks who need to approve construction can see it, evaluate it, and get a feel for how it blends or clashes with a community's surroundings. Open Downtown Hollywood 5272.jpg now. You'll notice that there's already a building on the corner of the proposed construction of the coffee shop. No problem; I'll guide you through airbrushing away the building if you don't already know how to use the Clone Stamp tool. Additionally, it'd be a shame to waste the bench, lamppost, and other foreground objects. I've created a saved path in the JPEG file so you can load it as a selection and duplicate the foreground stuff; JPEGs and TIFFs can retain saved paths—Adobe Systems has leveraged a lot of previously undiscovered possibilities in these file formats.

1. Drag to copy the Times Square coffee shop 3D layer to the Downtown Hollywood file and then save the file in PSB file format.

2. Hide the 3D layer and then choose the Background image layer.

3. On the Paths palette, Ctrl/Cmd+click the thumbnail of the path on the list to load the geometry as a selection.

4. Return to the Layers palette, and press Ctrl/Cmd+J to Layer via Copy.

5. Move this new layer to the top of the stack on the Layers palette, and then unhide the coffee shop layer.

6. Double-click the 3D layer thumbnail to expose the navigation controls on the Options bar.

7. Pose the model so it faces camera right, with its corner lined up approximately with the corner of the sidewalk. I found that in the Lighting and Appearances panel that CAD Optimized lighting works very well for this file, and you should eyeball the scale of the building by evaluating the size of the front door against the current structure in the photograph.

8. The bottom of the coffee shop will not look tidy contrasted against the architecture in the scene, so I recommend you hide the very bottom edge of the coffee shop by clicking the Add Layer Mask icon at the bottom of the Layers palette, choose black as your foreground Tools palette color, and then paint over the bottom to hide it. Alternatively, you can use the Polygon Lasso tool (with the coffee shop layer hidden) to precisely mark the area where the coffee house shouldn't show, click the Add Layer Mask icon, and then press Ctrl/Cmd+I (Invert colors) to auto-hide the interior of the selection. This is what I did in Figure 10.15, and overall, the pre-viz looks almost all set to show to the commission.

Figure 10.15

Integrate a model into a photo by placing objects in front of and behind it.

9. Create a new layer on top of the photograph: click the Background layer to make this the active layer and then click the Create a New Layer icon to create one directly above the Background.

10. Choose the Clone Stamp tool; on the Options bar, choose Normal mode and choose Sample: Current & Below. Use about a 100-pixel soft brush tip and uncheck the Aligned option.

11. Alt/Opt+click to set the sample point at the upper right of the photo, near some clouds. Try setting the Flow option on the Options bar to about 20% to create subtle shading changes. Then make short strokes over the building the coffee shop is unsuccessfully hiding. Before your sampling point travels into some of the buildings, release the mouse button and then continue to stroke. In Unaligned mode, the sampling point snaps back to the original point after releasing. Then continue. You also might want to try straight Brush tool strokes. First set the Eyedropper tool to 5 by 5 Average, sample a sky blue close to the white building, and then use the Brush tool. In Figure 10.16 I've got the pre-viz 99% finished.

It is at this point we arrive at a perceptual crossroads. You're an accomplished artist, and therefore it's hard to believe that this job will please the keenest of eyes because it probably doesn't please *you*. Without advanced rendering attributes such as reflections, highlights, refraction (the bending of light) on glass surfaces, bumps, and other real-world material properties, an imported Google Earth model looks somewhat unrealistic when contrasted against a photograph.

Figure 10.16
Remove what used to be there, and your pre-visualization is complete.

But believe it or not, the final image in the previous tutorial *does indeed* suit the needs of professionals in different areas such as construction and engineering: They are looking at properties in the image other than photorealism. What you can do to please *yourself* a little more and really impress the client is to rasterize the model after it's been positioned correctly in the scene; you right-click over the layer title (not the thumbnail) and then choose Rasterize 3D. The 3D layer becomes a standard layer containing only pixels; you can then use the Dodge and Burn tools to emphasize lighting and create areas of lighting falloff. You can also add layers and create shadows, copy areas of the Background image to new layers, horizontally or vertically flip them, and then put the layers in partially transparent mode to simulate reflections in windows. Essentially, you use your still image retouching skills in Photoshop to make the rasterized model look more photographic.

Alternatively, you can read the following section on exporting camera data and SketchUp models to a genuine, advanced modeling/rendering application.

From Pre-Visualization to Photorealism

In this section I demonstrate a trick or two for copying the virtual, 3D camera data from Photoshop, along with real camera data embedded in the Hollywood JPEG photo. Why? Because many modeling/rendering applications, notably Cinema 4D, can receive this data and use it to render a structure such as Romeo's coffee shop with accuracy, fidelity, and state-of-the-art photorealism. The goal is to provide town planners with a visualization that is complete and as easy to assimilate as an actual photograph.

Although the details on modeling, from building polygon 1 through to a final render, would fill a book (a book other than this), the sections to follow illustrate basic principles that are familiar to experienced modelers and will prove interesting to novices. Additionally, and most importantly, a rendered model is often not a finished product; nine out of ten skilled modelers perform post work in Photoshop. Therefore, the rendering setup I'll show you isn't the end of the Romeo's coffee shop visualization. In this section I show you some procedures for heightening the realism of the rendered model and flawlessly integrating it into the Hollywood photo.

> **Tip**
>
> A book *has* been written on photorealistic modeling, by Dan Ablan: the *Official Luxology modo Guide* (Thomson Course Technology). Dan is a skilled veteran modeler and an excellent guide to modo.

Here's how to begin the process of getting the data you need into a modeling program:

1. Open the 3D tools on the Options bar once the model is posed in the correct aspect relative to the Hollywood photo layer by double-clicking the 3D layer thumbnail on the Layers palette.

2. Click the Camera Mode icon on the Options bar and then click Zoom the 3D Camera panel to reveal the 3D Camera settings.

3. Copy the Position and Orientation values by double-clicking in a field to select all the values, and then press Ctrl/Cmd+C to put a copy of the values on the clipboard.

4. Switch to a plain text editor. Open a new document and then paste the data. Additionally, copy the Field of View value. Save the text document to your desktop. Press the Enter key to exit the 3D Controls.

5. From the previous tutorial, because the Downtown Hollywood picture is the Background layer, camera info is available even though you might save a photo with a 3D layer to PSD or PFB format. Choose File > File Info and then click the Camera Data 1 field. As you can see in Figure 10.17, the day, date, and year were recorded by my wife's Nikon digital camera. Write this data down in the text file you saved in Step 4: May 8, 2004, at about ten past five (17:09 Military Time).

Figure 10.17
Save all the data you can find in a 3D file and photographs; it'll serve you well in a modeling program.

6. Go to keyhole.com, the originators of the technology behind Google's KMZ format structure and part of Google Earth. Or you could type Hollywood Florida longitude and latitude in the Google search box (most people have it installed in Internet Explorer and Firefox), and the search results will be displayed as part of a KML search on the results page. Longitude: 80'16"; Latitude 26'03". You now have the longitude and latitude of Hollywood, the time of day and season when the photo was taken, and the coordinates of the Google Earth KMZ file's camera, as it looks correct against the photograph. With the model itself, you can now construct a scene of the coffee shop that's optically accurate for a finished visualization.

7. Now you start from square one. Forget about the model in Photoshop; forget the fancy texturing you performed in the previous tutorial. You're starting with the original coffee shop geometry, its original textures, and a better rendering engine. Go back to SketchUp and export the coffee shop file to Alias|Wavefront's OBJ file format.

8. Here's the hypothetical area: If you own Cinema 4D or other modeling program that accepts camera and light conditions at a specific time, follow along here. If not, sit back for a moment; I've provided the finished render you'll work with in the ZIP file you downloaded.

9. In Cinema 4D, in a new blank document, choose File > Merge and then open the coffee shop.Obj file. Because SketchUp is sensitive to positioning of objects, the object should land on the working plane in the new document.

10. Cinema 4D imports the textures defined in the original SKP file, but now's your chance to *re*define them. For example, you click a material thumbnail (the spheres listed in the Material panel), and then on the Attributes panel, you can use a color or an imported bitmap to govern the appearance of basic texture color, shininess (specularity), transparency, reflection, and other properties you see on real-world objects. TomL neatly labeled all the materials he defined in the coffee house structure, C4D reads them, and when you modify the attributes of one of TomL's materials, the surface to which the material is applied changes in the document window.

11. Choose Objects > Scene > Camera to add a camera to the scene. Then click Cameras on the document window menu bar (not the main menu) and choose Scene Camera > Camera. Now you're looking at the scene through the virtual camera.

12. Choose Objects > Scene > Sun light.

13. With the Sun light object highlighted, click the Sun tab in the Attributes panel at the bottom right of the workspace. Uncheck Interpolate Time and Set Light Color. You're free to redefine these attributes now.

14. Copy, one value at a time, the longitude, latitude, and date and time from the plain text file and then paste them into the appropriate fields in the Tag Properties fields in the Attributes panel. Here's one more detail you unfortunately cannot know: The photo was taken from the south and west of the downtown Hollywood street intersection; you therefore choose North and East from the button drop-down list in Attributes, and your light should be set up correctly.

15. Click the Camera title on the Objects panel. Down on the Attributes panel, click the Coord. (inates) tab and then enter the position and orientation (rotation values) from the text file you saved.

16. You massage the camera and light data by directly dragging objects in the scene window or by typing slightly different values in the Attributes panel and then press Enter. All of this empirical data is fine and dandy, but it doesn't compare to the final results you achieve by using your artist's eye. Figure 10.18 shows enlargements of the Attributes panel when the Camera and then the Sun light objects are selected. Above the panels, the coffee shop looks correct relative to the Hollywood photograph. I deliberately show a preview mode render in this figure; this is the view you work in within modeling programs; you'd have a processor meltdown if you were working in full render view (massive calculations) all the time, if this was possible.

Figure 10.18
You enter camera and light data into Cinema 4D, and the application more or less does the rest.

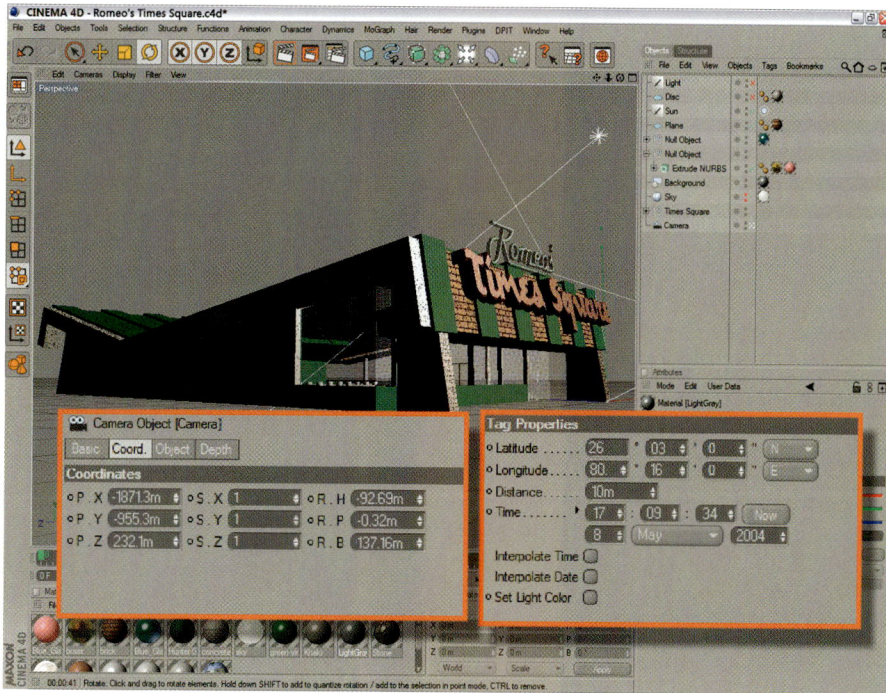

If by some slim chance the coffee shop is facing the wrong direction, you Shift+click to select all the component objects on the Objects panel and then click the Rotate tool below the main menu. You would only need to rotate the objects along the Y axis, which is the green hoop in the preview window that turns deep yellow when you have your cursor in the correct position to drag.

> **Note**
>
> I did a few clever things in addition to the previous steps before rendering the scene. First, I replaced the signage on the building; TomL's text was fine, but SketchUp only extrudes text and I wanted a fancier, neon tubing treatment. I also added a ground plane and colored it similar to the pinkish pavement in from of the corner building in the Hollywood photo. By doing this, the coffee shop now casts a shadow on the pavement, and you'll mask away the C4D pavement areas that were rendered to make the coffee shop integrate perfectly into the Photoshop composition shortly.
>
> I also put mild reflections in the glass on the coffee shop. I added a front door and made tiny credit card stickers on the glass; small details help realism, regardless of the clarity or size of the added details. I used the Bricks.jpg image as a displacement map (displacing is like bumping a texture in Photoshop using Lighting Effects or

> Texturizer but more photorealistic), and to cap it off, I added a sky object to add realistic ambient lighting and made the diffuse attribute an HDR image.
>
> High Dynamic Range images provide fantastic clarity; they're 32-bit and higher, and you can create them in Photoshop. In addition to pretty pictures, HDR images can also be used as *probes* in advanced modeling programs. The rendering engine calculates where some light should fall or be hidden in the scene based on the HDR image's visual data, and to make short of it, injecting an HDR image into the environment in a modeled scene makes a realistic render look ultrarealistic.

17. Click the far right clapboard icon below the main menu to specify Render Settings; choose an image size that compares to the Hollywood photo (about 2000 by 1500 pixels), choose the Photoshop PSD file format with alpha channel, set the name and path for the render, exit Render Settings, and then click the Render icon to the left of Render Settings.

On a Core Duo 2 machine, the finished render took about half an hour; this is with all the fancy atmosphere, calculating image "grit" through the use of Ambient Occlusion (some ambient light in scenes doesn't bounce back to the camera lens—it's occluded), and realistic shadows. Thirty minutes isn't bad for a large, photorealistic scene; it gives you time to make a sandwich.

Photo-Realizing a Building in a Scene

In the following tutorial I'll walk you through a few CG tricks to make the rendered coffee shop fit perfectly into the scene. The first trick is an old magician's trick—the art of misdirection. After you get the rendered model into the scene, you'll add a pedestrian and a passing car to the scene to put the audience into the scene. They'll have their attention divided between the hero—the coffee shop—and the "business" going on in the scene. The more you give a client to look at, the less time he has to concentrate and subsequently nit-pick on the hard work you put into realizing the scene.

1. Open the Romeo's from C4D.png image. In the Hollywood composition, you can hide or delete the 3D layer.

2. Click the Layer 3 title in the Hollywood composition (on the Layers palette), and then press Ctrl/Cmd+Tab to toggle to the Cinema 4D rendered image. On the Layers palette, drag the layer thumbnail into the Hollywood composition to duplicate it and then close the C4D render without saving.

3. Reduce the opacity of the C4D render layer on the Layers palette so you can see how to align the bottom of the coffee shop to the base of the existing building you're replacing. Then with the Move tool (V), drag the coffee shop

to where the bottom meets the bottom of the existing building. Press 0 on the keypad to return the coffee shop to 100% opacity (this trick only works when the Move tool or selection tools are active).

4. Click the Add Layer Mask icon on the Layers palette and then press D to ensure you're painting with default black. Choose the Brush tool.

5. Right-click in the document window to display the current tool's characteristics on the context menu (it's actually a palette in this instance). Set the Brush size to about 200 pixels in diameter and set the Hardness to 50%. Then press Enter twice to commit the Hardness setting and dismiss the palette.

6. Stroke over the areas that need to be deleted eventually, as shown in Figure 10.19. If you remove too much of my synthetic pavement, then press x to swap foreground/background colors and then paint with white to unhide the pavement area you may have unintentionally hidden while masking.

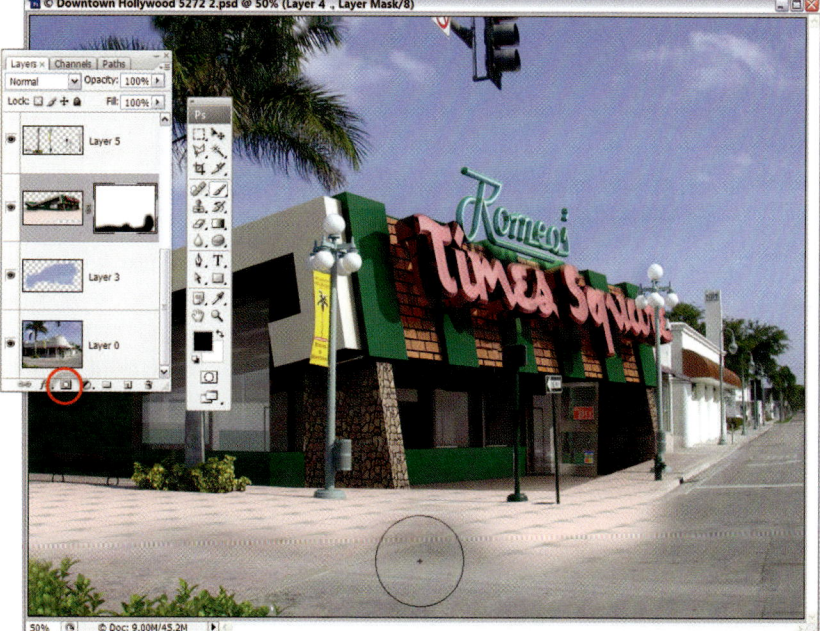

Figure 10.19
Use the layer mask to hide the pavement areas that don't belong in the final image.

7. At this point if you want to conserve on system RAM and saved file size, you can perform Merge Visible on the layers by pressing Ctrl/Cmd+Shift+E; doing this auto-applies the layer mask, removing hidden areas, and it does this without popping you an attention box (so be alert when using this command). Press Ctrl/Cmd+S.

8. Open the Girl in Hollywood.png file; it's a carefully lit Poser render with transparency. Copy the layer into the Hollywood composition and then with

the Move tool, put the model just to the left of the front corner of the coffee shop. By doing this, the model isn't intruding on the coffee shop you want the client to focus on, and the model visually leads the eye in the composition toward the new proposed building. In general, artistic compositions should contain elements that cause the audience to travel around the piece. As an artist, it is you who knows where you want the audience's eyes to go and eventually land. Therefore, you use compositional elements not only as ornamentation, but also guides to take the audience through your piece, still or video.

9. Open the bugatti.png image. I didn't model this piece, but only rendered it out of C4D. The model was created by the talented and generous Valery Gus'ev. If you'd like to download the model and experiment, it's at http://dmi.chez.tiscali.fr/models1.html along with other accurate and intricate automobile models. Copy the layer to the Hollywood composition, put it near the top of the Layers stack (below the Girl layer) and then use Free Transform to scale the Bugatti Veyron down to about 60%. Press Ctrl/Cmd+T and then hold Shift (to scale proportionately) and drag toward the car until the Options bar reads about 60%; then press Enter. Place the auto coming into frame at left (on the street!) using the Move tool.

10. Add some motion to the auto. Choose Filter > Blur > Motion Blur. Use your eye to evaluate how much blur distance you want, and set the Angle to –4, just a little south of perfectly horizontal. Refer to Figure 10.20 for the location of the car; click OK to apply the blur.

11. The girl apparently is moving toward the coffee shop and not left to right, so although she could use a little blurring, Motion Blur is the wrong choice. Click on the Girl layer to make it the active layer. Choose Filter > Blur > Box Blur. You blur the girl a little to suggest motion while the camera's shutter was open, but also to disguise the fact that it's a rendered model. Box Blur is great for this because it blurs across both the X and Y axes (creating an imaginary box), intimating motion far more sophisticated than Motion Blur and in a more visually appropriate way than Gaussian Blur. A value of four is fine for this example; it blurs the girl significantly, but the audience can still make out that it's a person jogging toward Romeo's.

12. Save the piece as a PSD file. You have the option now of hiding the girl and the auto to show only the proposed coffee shop to the client. All in all, I think you'd agree that although it's more work, the visualization using a modeling program provides a much more realistic composition than even the finest retouching of the SketchUp imported file. Figure 10.21 shows my completed piece.

Chapter 10 ■ 3D and CS3: An Introduction 341

Figure 10.20
Add Motion Blur to an object on a layer to suggest that something moved faster than the camera shutter could close.

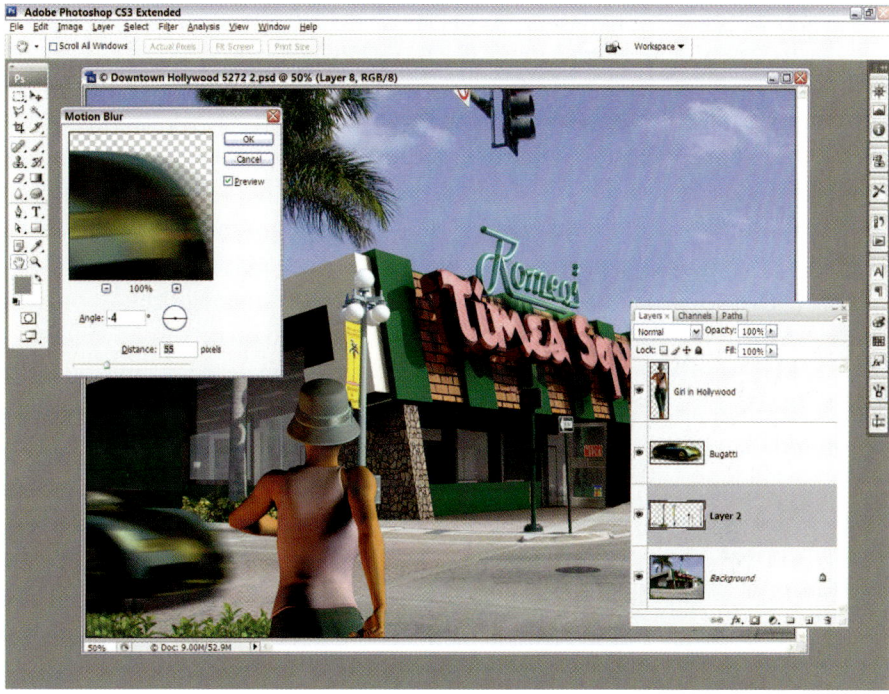

Figure 10.21
Photoshop is the hub for compositions that require all sorts of different types of media.

Texture Replacements and Basic 3D Animation

I have a mock assignment for you in this section to show you how to size up an existing label on a product, replace it, and then render the scene. Additionally, I show you how to create a simple video animation using variations on the rendered model scene. Please don't run away screaming when I lay this on you: Whether you have some or absolutely no skills in 3D modeling, you're going to get hands-on experience in modo 203; download the 30-day trial version from http://www.luxology.com/trymodo/. It's about a 40MB download, and the registration process to receive the download takes about 5 minutes. A modo scene you downloaded in the ZIP file contains all the 3D models and textures you need to complete what might seem like a daunting assignment; it's not, really. You don't need modeling skills for the following tutorial—all you need to do is hide and unhide objects in the scene, follow the commands I list, and then render the scene. Thirty days with modo (the trial version has no limitations beyond the time-out) is ample time to experiment with the modeling/rendering program, and after you see the photo-realistic quality of a render, you might indeed add modo to your creative toolbox.

Here's the fictitious assignment: Look at Figure 10.22. Something is clearly *wrong*. It's a product of these steps, which might sound very familiar to you as a professional:

1. A fellow runs a growing family business.
2. The fellow's nephew wants to be a part of the family business.

Figure 10.22
Artistic licenses should sometimes be revoked.

3. The nephew claims to be interested in art, and his sister tells him her son is quite talented.

4. The fellow calls you to bail him out of this inappropriate and amateurish label design on his new product.

Exploring modo and Sizing Up the Label

Invent a much better label for the bottle; keep the design in mind and shortly you'll discover the proper dimensions for replacing the smiley label. You should know that grappa is fairly nasty stuff, similar in strength to brandy, and the goblets I have in the scene are much too large for this potent after-meal digestive. But they're classier looking than traditional squat and square grappa glasses, and your mission here is to make a classy label (it sells more product). Install the trial (or retail) version of modo, and follow along here:

1. Launch modo and choose File > Open, and then select Testadura scene.lxo from your hard drive. If by any chance you receive a message that a bitmap file can't be located, direct this attention box to the folder where you unzipped the example files. If modo continues to complain and the file(s) referenced doesn't look relevant to a wine advertisement, ignore the message and continue.

2. Choose Layout > Layouts > Render from the main menu. The palettes change, as does your view in the main document window. Choose Camera from the Document menu bar. I put a Camera object in the scene so it's all set up to render.

3. You have a palette at top left in this modo layout that lists all the "objects" that will render in the scene. An object can be 3D geometry, the environment, or an image used as a texture. Click the triangle to the left of Object: Amateurish Label entry in the list to expand this entry, and then click on the Image: Smiley Label entry.

4. This is simply an exploration step: Choose Texture > Open UV Editor. As you can see in Figure 10.23, the UV editor displays the bitmap image using 2D coordinates. Yep, there is some distortion; I did this deliberately because the area on the grappa bottle defined as this label texture stretches the display of the bitmap image a little. It all works out in the finished render; if you want to define a material that takes up only part of an object's overall surface (such as a label), you click the Polygons button below the main menu and then highlight the target area using the cursor. The selected area turns orange in preview mode (you add to a selection by holding Shift, and you subtract by holding Ctrl/Cmd) and then you press M to save a default material to this surface selection. From there you modify the default material; I explain how to do this in a moment.

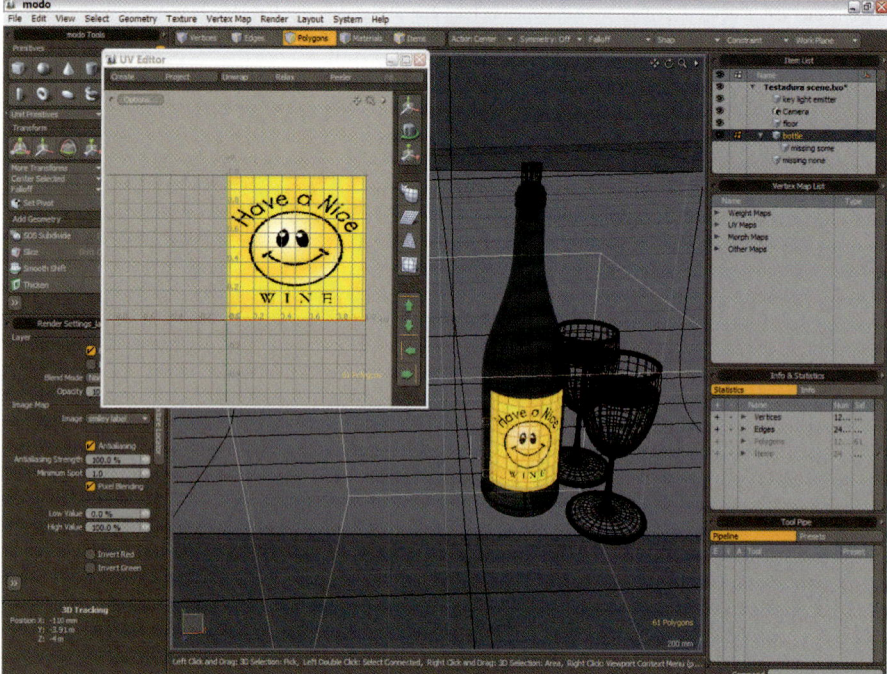

Figure 10.23
You can access bitmap components of modo textures through the UV editor.

Now, what I've done is *not* proper UV mapping, but rather to define a selection, apply a unique material (the bottle itself has a green glass material), and then edit the material to tell modo, "Go out and display smiley label.png on the material area I defined."

5. Minimize modo, switch to Photoshop, and then load the smiley lable.png image included in the ZIP file you downloaded. It's time to work in Photoshop a little.

Creating a Replacement Label

You'll return to modo shortly and replace the smiley label with a more handsome label of your own design (or use my Testadura label.png file in the ZIP volume). As with the coffee shop model textures, it's easiest in Photoshop to just overwrite the original smiley texture with your own label—you design on a layer or two above the original image layer and then merge down. By doing this you ensure the dimensions of the new label in the scene correspond to the old one, sparing you learning all about UV mapping.

1. Open smiley label.png.
2. Create a new layer on the Layers palette above the smiley design.

3. I recommend filling this layer using the Filter > Render > Clouds plug-in, as you did with the tea kettle example using light and dark beige colors as the foreground and background color swatches. It gives the label itself some texture, similar to expensive parchment. Also, the light in the LXO scene uses a "gel" to cast mottling in the scene, so a mottled parchment is thematically in keeping with the design.

4. Then get going with some text. I decided to go over the top in this tutorial; "Testadura" is an Italian expression that means "hard head," and the Calabria reference on my label points at a region in Italy renowned for stubbornness. My father-in-law's family hails from Calabria and somewhat stubbornly clings to the regional trait. I used Mona Lisa and Charlemagne for the main fonts (available online from the ITC catalog and a lot of other sites that sell "knock-offs" of popular digital typefaces), and for smaller text I used Adobe Myriad. I think the combination works harmoniously.

5. To give the text in the finished render a 3D, embossed appearance—as you find on expensive liquor labels—you can apply a style to the text, as shown in Figure 10.24. I used a modified preset from the Web Styles collection; it's Chrome, and I changed the color Overlay property from gray to a warm bronze. You could also use a third-party plug-in such as Shinycore Path Styler Pro to achieve a very refined metallic look for the text.

Figure 10.24
Create an elegant label for the bottle. Use picture fonts of lion's heads and castles; it increases the perceived value of a product.

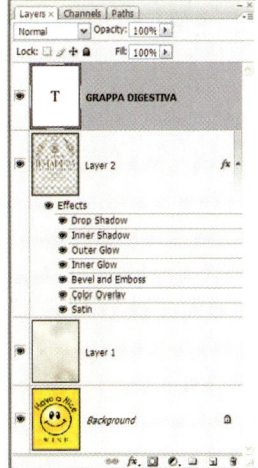
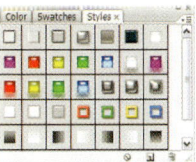

6. Flatten the image and then save it to PNG file format (modo accepts JPEGS, PNGs, and several other formats). Use any name you like; modo imports bitmaps to use as a material component instead of embedding bitmaps in the saved scene file. This means you can swap out textures for scenes very easily for revision work.

Placing a Texture and Rendering a Scene

To replace the label in the modo scene is very simple; I walk you through this in the steps to follow and also explain how to get three different renders from the scene to edit into a video in Photoshop. I've clearly labeled all object on modo's Items list and created several levels of grappa in the bottle. Additionally I put grappa in the glasses; one of the glasses is an *instance*—a clone of the glass that conserves an application's resources. There are two corks in the scene: one in the bottle and one lying in the foreground. By hiding and revealing items on the list (you click the Eye icon, exactly as you do on Photoshop's Layers palette), you'll create three scenes that can cross-fade on Photoshop's Animation palette, thus making a short timelapse of the bottle being emptied and the glasses filled.

Here's how to replace the bottle label and render the three scenes needed for the animation:

1. In modo, at upper left on the Shader Tree palette (the palette that lists all the materials that make up the scene), click the Image: Smiley Label entry.

2. Just below the Shader Tree palette is the Render palette that contextually displays the parameters you can change, depending on the entity chosen on the Shader Tree palette. Click the Texture Layer tab in the Render palette, and then click smiley label in the Image Map field to reveal a drop-down list.

3. Choose Load Image and then scout down the Testadura label file you created earlier in Photoshop in the Folder window. Choose it and then click OK to load it.

4. On the Item list at top right, prepare for the first of three renders: The bottle is nearly full, the cork's on top, and the glasses are empty. Make sure the following items are hidden: cork on floor, missing most, missing some, grappa in front goblet, and grappa in back goblet.

5. Before you render, make sure of two things: Click the Render Shader Tree entry and make sure the Camera Frame dimensions are what you want. The video you'll create in Photoshop needs 720 by 480 pixels in dimensions; enter these values if they aren't in there already. Also, do a preview render (it takes less time than a full render)—click the triangle to the right of the Zoom tool at upper right of the document window and then choose Application > Preview.

6. All set? Choose Render > Render Visible from the main menu. This command renders only non-hidden scene items. Although the shortcut key combo of Ctrl/Cmd+F9 is clearly listed on the menu, modo, Photoshop, and certain other applications are thwarted from executing the key combo if you have other applications running that use the same hot keys. I have SnagIt running a lot of the time, so this shortcut doesn't work for me; also, some of the fancy Microsoft keyboards reserve function keys for e-mail and printing, so it's usually best to hand-pick the command.

7. The render should take less than 10 minutes and happens in a child window. Once the render is complete, click the Save Image button and then save the image to hard disk in PNG or TIFF file format.

8. Here's the setup for the second scene render: Hide the cork on top item and reveal the cork on floor item. Then unhide the grappa in back goblet, hide the missing none item, and reveal the missing some item. Sorry; I couldn't think of a more explicit title for the diminishing volumes of grappa than my "missing none, missing most…" entries! Render > Render Visible again; save the file to hard disk.

9. The last scene: Hide missing some, unhide missing most, and then unhide grappa in front goblet. Render > Render Visible; save the image to hard disk. Save the LXO file; you have 30 days to pull a larger render if you like. As you'll see in Photoshop, modo's renders are exquisite and rival commercial photography for product photography. modo dominates the product design field because of its photorealistic renders, and chances are the last package you saw in a magazine ad wasn't photography at all.

It's time to animate the still frames and get back to the core of this book: video editing in Photoshop Extended. If you had problems rendering from modo, your trial version timed out, or modeling in general appeals to you like a kettle of fish, I've provided the renders in Testadura 3 frames.psd in the ZIP archive.

Creating a 10-Second Commercial via Stills

In Chapter 2 I showed you how to create a timelapse sequence from still photos, and I recommend you review this chapter before beginning the next tutorial. Unlike actual photography where an object can blow over in the wind during a day's worth of timelapse still image captures, the grappa scene is locked down, and the transitions between the renders will be perfect.

Follow these steps to make a cross-fade transition between the three renders. Along the way, I talk a little about timing: It would be too simplistic and "bad theater" to simply assign each render one-third of the play time and make the transitions of equal length (this becomes math instead of storytelling!):

1. Copy two of the rendered image files to the third and then drag the entries on the Layers palette so that the first render is on the top layer and the final render is on the bottom. Double-click on the layer titles, one at a time, to open the layer name and then label the layers 1, 2, and 3 for convenient reference as you edit; the thumbnail images on the Layers palette look pretty much identical with this scene.

2. By default, the duration of all videos is 10 seconds, which is fine for this example, and you don't need to change anything. Begin by opening the layer labeled 1 on the Animation palette. Drag the thumb on the timeline to one-third into the duration, click the opacity stopwatch and then drag the Opacity on the Layers palette for this layer to 0%. Then go to about one second before the keyframe with the thumb (the timeline indicator) and set the layer opacity to 100%. You now have a 1-second transition from Layer 1 to Layer 2 beneath Layer 1 at about one-third the time duration from the head of the video.

3. Perform Step 2 with Layer 2, but create the opacity transition at about 6:15f.

4. Play the animation twice—the first time to let Photoshop cache the video in non-realtime. You'll see that the video is boring; the transitions are predictable. Now, you'll do some fine-tuning in the following section because I'll introduce two additional characters to the finished video. But for now, move the keyframes for Layer 1 so they bracket the two-second point on the timeline. By doing this, you're introducing motion to the video earlier. Then try this: Move the 0% opacity keyframe for Layer 2 out by about a second so the transition to Layer 3 is two seconds long. Then play back the video. By offsetting the "symmetrical" events in the video, it looks more visually interesting as video. This will be a 10-second TV commercial and not a PowerPoint slide show! Check out the Animation palette in Figure 10.25 for reference.

Creating an Animated Overlay

TV commercial and motion picture cinematic clichés *become* clichés due to overuse. However, this doesn't *invalidate* the use of clichés: Clichés such as the camera slowly panning to a fireplace from a couple embracing on the bear rug make a good artistic suggestion. The *point* of a cliché is immediately absorbed by the audience, and the good news for directors is that clichés fall in and out of fad. Okay, you've seen a partially transparent bottle gradually fade into a scene and rotate; it's a good way to register name brands on TV, particularly to audiences who own small screens, and this is what you'll create in the following tutorial, cleverly repurposing the label you designed for the bottle in modo. It's a cliché that's not being used these days, and so you'll use it—it's that simple.

Figure 10.25
A transition between three images requires natural timing to look natural.

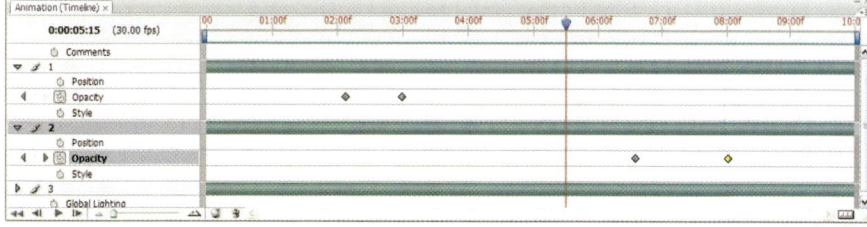

Follow along to build a rotating grappa bottle label, export it to video format, and then add it to the transition scene you built in the previous tutorial.

1. Open a new document that's 720 by 480 pixels in dimensions. By default, Photoshop will display the document play length as 10 seconds on the Animation palette. Make the Background layer black.

2. Click the menu icon on the Animation palette, choose Document Settings, and then choose 30 fps as the frame rate. You don't want or need the default drop-frame rate of 29.97 for this example. Click OK to apply.

3. Open the grappa label image window Testadura label.png and then on the Layers palette while holding Shift to keep duplicates centered, drag the layer into the new document window. You can close the grappa image without saving now.

4. With the Move tool chosen, open the layer tracks on the Animation palette and click the Position stopwatch.

5. At time 0, power nudge the label horizontally to the right so its left edge lines up with approximately the horizontal halfway point in the document window.

6. Go to six seconds in the Animation palette workspace and then nudge the label to the left until its left edge is flush with the left edge of the document window.

7. Create a new layer. Choose the Gradient tool, make sure your current foreground color is black, and then choose the second preset from the current catalog at left on the Options bar (Foreground to Transparent), and then hold Shift and drag from about 25% the horizontal measure of the document window, ending the drag a little inside the grappa label.

8. Repeat the gradient to the right side of the layer so the appearance is that the label is peeking through soft-edged curtains.

9. Create a new layer. Choose pale yellow as your current foreground color, choose the rectangular Marquee tool, and then create a marquee that runs vertically through the left side of the label. Fill the marquee, and then give the layer 50% and put it in Screen blending mode. This is a bright spot on the label and adds more photorealistic credence to flat digital artwork.

10. The cliché shouldn't run the length of the 10-second commercial; six seconds is ample time, including a fade up and fade out. Move the workspace end marker to six seconds on the timeline; this will crop the duration before you write it to video.

11. Try out the animation by playing it; in Figure 10.26, by playing it back I realized that the highlight shouldn't move, but it does need to appear and disappear so it doesn't overlap the gradients on the layer below. Step 12 fixes this problem.

Figure 10.26
Play your animation at regular intervals to spot problems before you write it out to video.

12. For the Highlight layer, open the track on the Animation palette and then click the Opacity stopwatch at three seconds or so out from the head. Then move back to about two seconds on the timeline and set the opacity to 0% on the Layers palette. Your fade in and fade out points are completely dependent on where you put the highlight to avoid the highlight shining over the Gradient layer. At about 4:15f set the opacity for the highlight to about 30% and then make another key at 5:15f and set the opacity to 0%. Open rotating label.psd and see the events and the location of the highlight to use this as a reference; in Figure 10.27 you can see the tracks. You really have to play back the animation to see where the fade keys should be; you move them if the animation looks wrong, and the keys are *Linear* interpolation, even though one would think Hold interpolation would work, popping the highlight in and out.

13. Save and then choose File > Export > Render Video. Render the video to original dimensions with no compression; AVI or MOV is fine.

Now, you could have copied these layers to your grappa bottle transition animation and had one tidy PSD file. I didn't ask you to do this because I want you to do some filtering on the now rendered video. The label travels to suggest clockwise rotation (because Westerners read from left to right), but it looks flat. An actual bottle label that a property master clocks for a movie camera would show

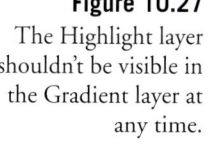

Figure 10.27
The Highlight layer shouldn't be visible in the Gradient layer at any time.

some vertical distortion as the center of the label bulges toward the camera. Therefore, you'll bring the rendered video into Photoshop next as a Smart Object and then use a filter that adds some photorealistic lens distortion.

Finishing the Video

After you've opened the rotating label MOV file as a Smart Object, it can be duplicated to the transition scene, where it retains its effects, and you can fade it up and out. Additionally, the layout of the Testadura bottle and glasses was deliberately staged asymmetrically, leaving room at the left so the rotating label only partially obscures the scene (asymmetrical compositions are usually more visually interesting than objects neatly aligned). We also need to add a text tag line to the end of the commercial.

Oh, yes: You can add a much-needed audio track by copying Testadura 10s.mp3 as a QuickTime layer to the composition. When you have 10 seconds to sell a product, giving up the audio opportunity to hammer home a message just isn't cost effective.

Here's how to finish the 10-second commercial:

1. Open the MOV file you rendered in the previous steps as a Smart Object (File > Open as Smart Object). Now you have choices on the Filter menu.

2. Choose Filter > Distort > Spherize. This plug-in is misnamed because you can bulge a Smart Object or regular layer across a single X or Y axis. On the Mode drop-down menu, choose Horizontal Only and then crank up the Amount to 100% (see Figure 10.28). Click OK to apply. To review a little, Smart Objects can be video layers, and you can open a video and then turn a video into a Smart Object (layer) by right-clicking the layer title and choosing the conversion from the context menu. If you apply a filter to a video layer, you've filtered a single frame, producing an interesting but often unwanted effect. However, filters applied to Smart Objects are Smart also; the effect is persistent and plays through the length of the Smart Object video layer. You can also apply multiple filters to a Smart Object, and you have the option of turning a Smart Filter on or off by clicking its eye icon on the Layers palette.

3. Duplicate the Smart Object (its Smart Filter will come along) to the bottle transition scene and move this layer to the top of the layer stack in the Layers palette. You can then close the Smart Object file without saving.

4. With the Move tool, position the Smart Object to the left in the scene, and then choose Lighter Color for the blend mode of the object (on the Layers palette). You can now see why I recommended framing the label with black—in Lighter Color mode the black drops out to expose a gently feathered label.

5. Use your director's judgment as to when to fade the label into and out of the scene. I calculated after playing back the video several times that right after the scene dissolves from render 1 to 2 is a good event; it doesn't conflict with the transition event, and the audience might become distracted after watching more than two seconds of a beautiful but static render of a bottle scene. Fade the label out at about eight seconds, between the Layer 2 and Layer 3 transition, leaving almost two seconds to flash a slogan. See Figure 10.29 to refer to the Animation palette.

Figure 10.28
A Smart Object video layer that is filtered becomes a Smart filtered Smart Object.

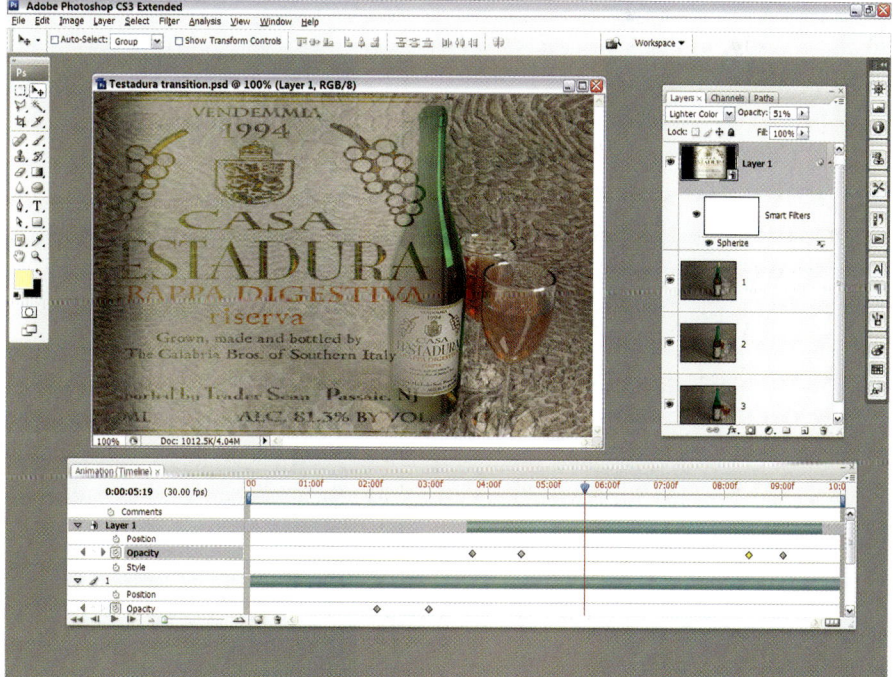

Figure 10.29
Keep your events isolated; if you have two things happening at the same time in 10 seconds, you confuse your potential customer.

6. Add a snappy slogan using the Type tool in the empty space the label leaves in the scene after eight seconds on the timeline. In Figure 10.30 you can see I've sneaked a fade in for the slogan just stepping on the tail of the rotating label's disappearance. It works; check out the finished video in the Gallery folder. Don't be hesitant about fine-tuning any video element's appearance; that's what the keys are for.

Figure 10.30
Scheduling the right moment for the appearance and disappearance of characters in videos is called *choreography*.

7. Add the MP3 audio track by opening the file as a QuickTime file and then duplicate it to the composition. The audio times well against the video because I composed it after a test render to video was done. Sony Sound Forge, Adobe Audition, Premier, and the new Adobe Soundbooth are all good tools for synching audio events you buy or create to existing video. In future chapters, I show how to work the other way and compose video to an existing audio track. Since the 1940s, animators have made it a practice to record audio before creating animation. Imagine how difficult it would be to ask Mike Myers to read his lines perfectly in sync with the Shrek character already rendered.

8. Choose File > Export > Render Video. For this composition, color fidelity is very important, so I recommend the Sorenson 3 codec used on QuickTime (Sorenson 3 under Standard Video Compression Settings supports audio while standard Sorenson does not). Click Render.

Integrating 3D elements into a photograph and video footage is certainly not a new sport; professionals have been doing this since the late 1970s, but Photoshop and modeling programs bring this power to the desktop. I have to chuckle when my 12-year-old nephew dismisses a great motion picture special effect with the broad stroke, "Aw, that was done digitally!" Computer generated images (CGI) don't by their nature alone make a photorealistic scene, but rather it's up to the *artist's skills* to bring that suspension of disbelief to the audience. Quality tools in Photoshop, Cinema 4D, modo, and other programs simply increase the number of calculations your machine can perform, and our processors and drives can handle enough data in 2008 that the resolution of digital images looks photographic.

High-resolution imaging is the great-grandchild of the practice of using a really small brush tip and then painting into every nook on a canvas. The world is a visually complex place, and the more detail you put into a render, the more complexity it displays, hence the more realistic it can look.

Clearly there's a convergence going on between photorealistic retouching capability, 3D scene simulation, and digital video. As an artist I'm very pleased to be able to dip my brush in all the new "colors" that blend together so well. As you progress and experiment, you'll also discover some visualization *synergy* happening. A model grafted into a photograph can be a more interesting composition than the photo by itself, and digital video frequently captures the audience's imagination more thoroughly than still imaging alone.

11

Basic CGI Compositing into Video

There was a time, specifically in *my* lifetime, when a fantasy sequence or a special effect added to an original clip was performed by:

1. Rotoscoping an illustration into the scene. The suspense of reality was directly proportional to the talent of the animator; lightning and even the laser blasts in the original *Star Wars* were painstakingly motion-matched frame by frame. If reality was of no concern, the illustrator was still obliged to rotoscope. Two classic examples of full-animation compositing are *Anchors Aweigh* (1945), in which Gene Kelly dances with Hanna and Barbera's Jerry the Mouse, and the cavorting waiter penguins catering Dick Van Dyke and Julie Andrews in *Mary Poppins* (1964).

2. Blue-screening an object or, in more ambitious endeavors, a stop-motion figurine, from King Kong to the Pillsbury Doughboy.

Fast-forward to today and the hair-trigger response to a screenplay's need for a fantasy event or character is CGI (computer generated image). It is another Golden Age for Hollywood special effects; not only do computer-generated image sequences hold up to the critical scrutiny of sophisticated audiences, but creating CGI has become quite a common sport with 3D animation software that has become affordable and muscle machines that can render the frames within a lifetime (usually overnight for short sequences).

This chapter takes you behind the scenes to demonstrate how to create a few visually interesting CGIs and then whisks you back to Photoshop for the compositing work that makes an average film clip into something captivating, fantastic, and impossible.

Everything's Coming Up Lilies

The first scene in this chapter that you'll work with is a fairly suburban one: a woman mowing the lawn. It was her *performance* that caught my eye and gave me an inspired idea. You know how when you're wearing earphones and get immersed in your music? This was evidently what happened with the woman; I felt certain she was listening to opera or other classical music while mowing; she was positively gavotting the mower across the lawn with stage-worthy flourishes!

The woman's performance seemed spoiled in that she was mowing and not *sowing* something. Hey, how about this: as she mows, a beautiful garden grows in her wake? This is do-able, and I'll show you what software you'd use shortly. Figure 11.1 shows a frame from the original clip.

Figure 11.1
Look for a visual opportunity to create a fantasy scene out of a hum-drum one.

Cinema 4D was my choice of 3D animation programs in which to create growing flowers. There are several botanical modeling plug-ins for modelers such as C4D, including xFrog and DPIT Nature Spirit. With enough patience, you can also model a flower by hand; the real trick is getting the underlying splines (paths), which are the "skeleton" of a flower, to animate across time. A little preplanning was in order to build a virtual garden of day lilies to be composited behind the woman, growing in sequence. Camera angle, lighting, film speed (fps), and frame size were a given—they necessarily had to match the video clip. Fortunately, C4D has a Background layer that can take a video clip as a texture and always remain behind objects in the scene; this made the lighting and camera angle go in a snap.

Additionally, anything you add to a scene where there's light must cast a shadow. Examining the video clip, the shadows seen in the clip are uneven in their silhouettes because they are casting on uneven grass blades. A module you can get from Maxon for Cinema 4D 10 and later is called HAIR. What I did (and this did not require a lot of brainpower or talent) was create a plane beneath the lilies and then add hair. By default, hair is hair-colored, but if you change the gradient colors of the default texture to shades of green, you have instant grass. In Figure 11.2, you can see the scene as it's set up for rendering.

Figure 11.2
Cinema 4D offers modules and supports plug-ins for creating time-lapse animations of flowers growing.

It's not necessary to create a bunch of flowers growing when you want to animate a whole garden; you create one flawless animation, and then most modeling programs enable you to copy and paste the model with its animation. Then you move the duplicates around, and when you want the scene to feature different growth times, you offset the keyframes for the duplicates. This is how I created the video clips for you to use of the flowers sprouting in a line, one after the other, reverse dominos-style. Figure 11.3 shows the Timeline palette in Cinema 4D. The top entry is the first day lily growing, and as you can see, the animations of the duplicates follow. To create a little randomness to disguise the fact that this is a bunch of duplicates, I rotated the duplicates relative to the scene's camera and created minor time offsets within each duplicate for the keyframes—the points at which they shoot up, blossom, and spread their leaves and petals.

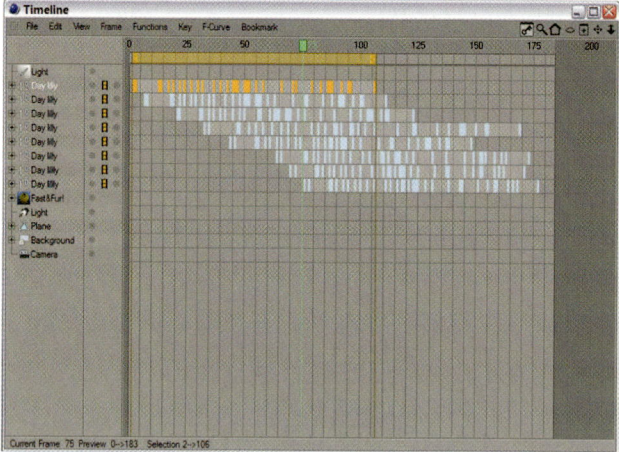

Figure 11.3
Create an animation, and then duplicates of the animated object can be offset in time to create an illusion of uniqueness and independent behavior.

Before rendering a video, I had a few things to consider to make compositing easier in Photoshop, and you should be mindful of these, too, if you get into CG animation. First, two passes are required; two different videos need to be generated in order to keep the grass that's receiving the shadows separate from the lilies. I don't want the grass in the finished video, but I *do* want the shadows that are on the grass. In Cinema 4D, in Render Settings, you can specify a video to be rendered in addition to the main video (see Figure 11.4); I specify that shadows shall be rendered as a separate video, I render the video, dump the primary render, and then render a second time with the grass object hidden in the scene. By using QuickTime export file format, the lilies are surrounded by transparency (alpha masking), and the result is that I have a video of only the lilies and one of only the shadows.

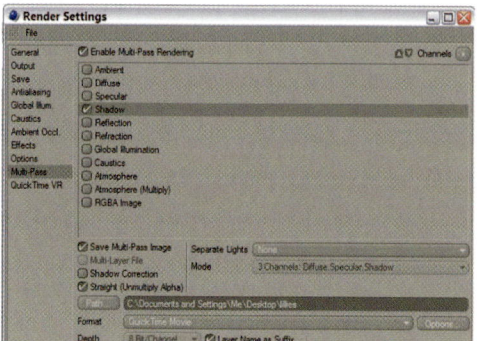

Figure 11.4
Cinema 4D writes videos that contain only the elements you need for compositing later.

Before exiting this section and Cinema 4D, I should point out that timing of the lilies blossoming was important; I created keyframes by looking at the position of the woman in the Background video, so she's not standing at any moment where a lily is bursting from the ground. The number of lilies I animated will not fill the frame as the woman mows; it's not necessary. In Photoshop, you'll duplicate the growth sequence and then reposition it and offset it in time so the scene will feature the lilies blossoming from edge to edge.

Also, you'll see that in the video clip the woman makes a transit from right to left and then from left to right. The second row of lilies you'll composite into the piece grows from left to right, and to accomplish this I just moved the lilies in C4D so their direction (and their animation timing) flip-flops, or mirrors.

A Trick for Reducing Compositing File Sizes

In other chapters I mention that QuickTime (and AVI) videos that contain alpha channels do not compress well. Occasionally I've provided very small and short clips for you to download and work with, but not the lilies animation—it proved to be too large for a speedy download, and this led me to a trick I'll show that you might want to use when working on a collaboration using the Internet.

Lilies Right to Left.mov is a regular video clip and has no masking; the lilies are composited against a green solid background (I chose green to lessen fringing in the composite video). Lilies Right to Left alpha.mov is a black and white video that perfectly corresponds to the visible content of the lilies movie; it shows white where the lilies movie contains flowers and black in areas where there is no content. Together, at good video quality (not a lot of compression), the two movies total a little more than 5MB in file size. In comparison, the lilies movie surrounded with alpha masking, with lousy quality (high compression) came out to more than 12MB.

Before you begin, check into Chapter 4 if you haven't done so already. It contains the recipe for cobbling a JavaScript from one of the scripts that shipped with Photoshop that will repeat an action any number of times, and you'll need this to avoid repetitive keystroking and/or mouse clicking. Check out Figure 4.8; set the number of times to 220 for this example.

In the steps to follow I show you how to strip the background from the lilies movie using the alpha movie, to make the video of the flowers sprouting a breeze to composite.

1. Open Lilies Right to Left.mov and Lilies Right to Left alpha.mov in Photoshop's workspace from the archive you downloaded.

2. With the alpha movie in the foreground, right-click on its layer on the Layers palette and then choose Duplicate Layer. Choose the other movie as the destination document, click OK, and then you can close the alpha movie without saving.

3. On the Layers palette, click the bottom layer, the one of the lilies, to make it the current editing layer, even though it's hidden from view by the alpha video.

4. Build the following action in the Default Actions folder: choose New Action from the Actions palette's menu, and then name it "x."

5. Choose Select > Color Range. In the Color Range box, set the Fuzziness to the maximum of 200. Then click with the cursor over the black area in the document window. Click OK to select this area.

6. Press Backspace and then Ctrl/Cmd+D to deselect. Although the document window shows no change, you've deleted all the areas outside of the lilies on the bottom layer. You can often perform a Photoshop operation on an active layer you can't see due to other visible layers on top of it.

7. Click the Selects Next Frame button on the Animation palette.

8. Stop the Actions Palette Recorder. You're done, and the process looks like Figure 11.5.

9. Choose File > Scripts and then choose your JavaScript you created earlier to run x 220 times. If you didn't put the script into the Scripts folder, choose File > Scripts > Browse. Then wait a few moments for the script to execute.

10. Hide the top layer, the alpha layer you used to strip the background from the lilies layer on the bottom. Choose File > Export > Render Video. Choose QuickTime, don't use any compression, choose Millions of Colors + in the

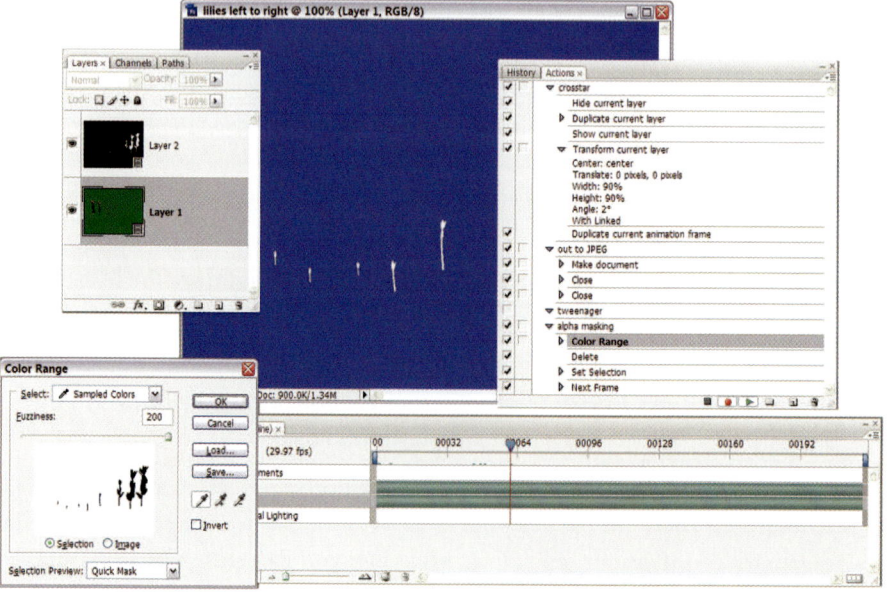

Figure 11.5
Create an action that removes the background from one layer, based on a selection from a different layer.

File Options > Movie Settings box, and before you click Render make sure the Alpha Channel option is set to Straight-Unmatted in the Render Options area.

11. Bring the movie into Photoshop and play it. If it looks okay and has a transparent background, minimize it (but don't close it), and you can safely close the document in the workspace from which you rendered the video without saving it.

Setting Up the CGI Composite

First stop is getting the lilies positioned and timed correctly in the composition. Then you'll add a shadow layer I provide; without it, the lilies won't properly integrate into the fantasy composition. This new document you'll create is not the final composition but rather a workbench for sizing up and prepping the lilies animation for the final video.

1. Open OperaMower.mov and then duplicate the lilies animation to the movie. You can close the lilies animation now without saving changes.

2. On the Animation palette, choose Frame Number in the Palette Options box, available from the palette's flyout menu. Slide the Lilies track on the Animation palette to begin at about 200.

3. With the Move tool, move the lilies into position at frame right. You'll see that the lilies are on the large side. You'll correct this in a moment; actually, the lilies play better to your audience a little oversized—I rendered them larger than life to afford you some creative latitude. You can decrease the size of pixel-based images, but enlarging them tends to ruin focus. See Figure 11.6.

Figure 11.6
Duplicate the CGI to the movie; position it and then put it at the correct entrance time on the timeline.

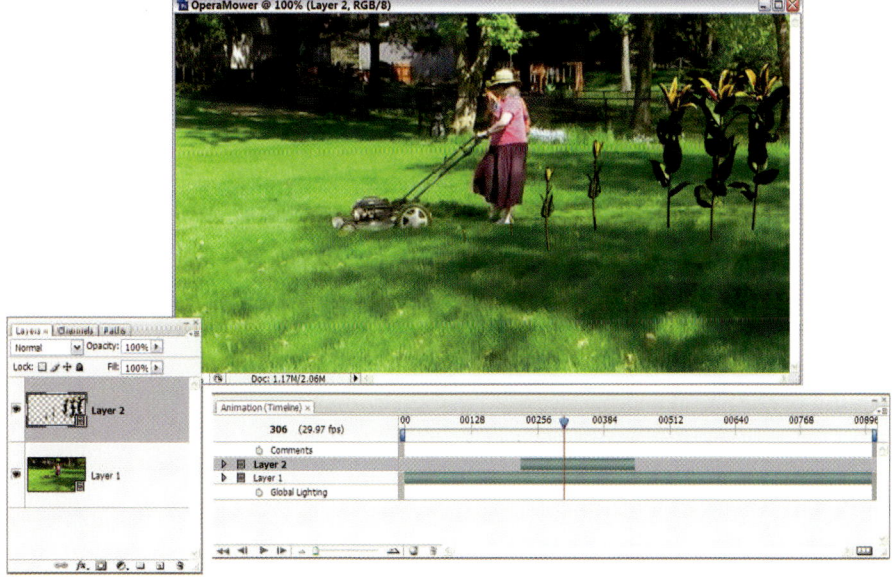

4. Load Lilies Right to Left Shadows.mov. Duplicate it to the main composition and then close it without saving.

5. Hide the Background video on the Layers palette and hide the top lilies layer.

6. Click on the Shadow layer to make it the active layer. Create an action in the Default Actions folder, name it "x" (delete the previous "x" action), and then run the action similarly to how you built the action in the previous section: choose Select > Color Range, choose the white areas on the Shadows layer, press Backspace to delete the selected areas, deselect, and then move on to the following frame.

7. Make sure you click on the Default Actions folder to make this the active folder and then run the Execute X 220 times JavaScript you built earlier. Your setup for the action should look like that in Figure 11.8.

8. Put the Shadows Layer below the lilies layer on the Layers palette and then put this layer into Multiply blending mode at about 40% opacity.

9. Align the Shadows layer with the Lilies layer and put its entrance on the Animation palette timeline at the identical point as the Lilies layer.

10. Shift+click to select both layers on the Layers palette and then press Ctrl/Cmd+T to put both layers, synchronously, into Free Transform. This will result in a warning dialog box to convert the video layers to a Smart Object layer. Click the Convert button.

11. On the Options bar, you can click the link button (Maintain Aspect Ratio) to scale both the layers proportionately and then type about 70% in either the Width or Height box and then press Enter to apply the scaling. Alternatively, you can hold Shift to constrain proportions and then manually scale down the lilies and their shadows by dragging on a corner of the Free Transform bounding box. Your screen should look like Figure 11.7 now.

12. What you want to do is create your hold frame for the Shadows and Lilies layers right now, and this calls for a little thought so you can plan. The woman traverses from right to left in about 15 seconds, the lilies animation is 8 seconds, but the lilies need to remain onscreen after they blossom for 30 seconds. Go to the last frame, duplicate the lilies and shadows, and then right-click them on the Layers palette one at a time and rasterize the duplicates, which now occupy the full 30;07 duration the bottom video layer defines. One at a time, drag the beginning of the timeline for the rasterized layers to meet the tail of the original video layers.

Figure 11.7
Shoulder height for full-grown lilies is a stretch, but generally both TV and hand-held device presentations are a medium of close-ups.

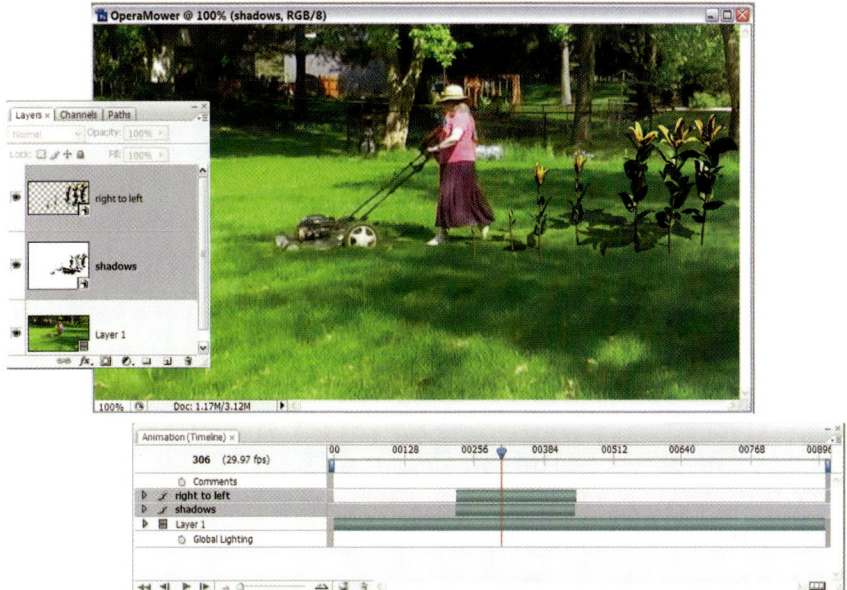

Editing and Exporting the CGI

As I've mentioned in other chapters, a Smart Object cannot be edited directly. However, the background on the Shadows layer needs to be removed; if you try to render the CGI without the background, the white will show on the Shadows layer. The next steps show how to remove the white from the Shadows layer and then export the lilies video, the still hold layer, and the retouched shadows video and still layers.

1. Choose the original Shadows layer and then right-click it on the Layers palette; choose Edit Contents. You'll get an attention box that essentially says, "After you edit the layer in a new document window, you have to File > Save it to the default directory." This is okay, and it generates a large PSB file that actually contains the video. You can delete it after you've compiled the video. Click OK and a new window opens with only the original, unscaled Shadows layer in it.

2. Create an action in the Default Actions folder, name it "x" (delete the previous "x" action), and then run the action similarly to how you built the action in the previous section: choose Select > Color Range, choose the white areas on the Shadows layer, press Backspace to delete the selected areas, deselect, and then move on to the following frame. See Figure 11.8.

3. Make sure the Animation palette is set to the beginning mark. Also make sure you click on the Default Actions folder to make this the active folder and then run the Execute X 220 times JavaScript you built earlier.

Figure 11.8
Use Color Range as part of the x action to remove the white in the PSB document window (the extracted contents of the Shadows layer).

4. After the JavaScript has run, save the shadows.psb file (or whatever you named the layer) and then you can safely close the file. You'll see that the shadows on the layer have no white around them. However, the action of converting the videos to Smart Objects automatically resets the Multiply blending mode's opacity back to 100%; turn it back down to about 40% or whatever value looks best to your artist's eye.

5. Hide or delete the bottom video on the Layers palette and File > Export > Render Video. Use the same settings as you used earlier: QuickTime, alpha export enabled, no compression. When you're sure the video rendered correctly (by watching it), you can safely delete the current composition. Close without saving.

Congratulations: The hard part is *over*! You now have exported and saved what you need to put the lilies GC effect into the Operamower.mov clip. You've also gained hands-on experience doing something in Photoshop Extended that very few people who didn't read this book will know how to accomplish, and this trick *did* take me several hours to solve and cobble, so we might want to keep this a Magician's Secret between you and me.

Creating the Final Right-to-Left CGI Pass

As you probably guessed, the lilies CGI you edited in the previous section will be reused across 15 seconds, and to stage the growth requires a little timing expertise so the lilies appear to grow in a logical and natural sequence. Also, you must pay attention to the order of layers when you duplicate and reposition the CGI, because from right to left, the layers must progress in ascending order to keep the shadows behind the new lilies. Follow these steps to complete half the total video; the other half uses steps you now know to build a left-to-right sprouting sequence:

1. Open OperaMower.mov.

2. Choose Layer > Video Layers > New Video Layer from File. Choose the video you rendered in the previous section. By my calculations, if you align the layer flush with the right edge of the document window, it should begin playing at about Frame 208; make sure the Palette Options is set to Frame Number before continuing.

3. Duplicate the Lilies layer by dragging its thumbnail into the Create a New Layer icon on the bottom of the Layers palette.

4. Move the timeline ahead to about Frame 320 or so. This is where I see the entrance of the duplicate layer. However, please don't simply plug my recommended values into this tutorial to complete it, because you won't learn, hands-on, the relationship between time and position in a document using CGI (or real footage, for that matter). Experiment for yourself with position in frame and entrance times.

5. With the Move tool, move the position of the duplicate layer in the document window so it's about in the horizontal center of the document; this should be the top layer in the stack, and it'll look like artificial flowers if the original layer cast shadows in front of newly created flowers. Try overlapping the duplicate with the original to create a random, clumpy sort of growth with the final composite. Also, notice that the camera angle is slightly off, and the path the woman is mowing runs slightly downhill at left. Position the duplicate lilies to follow the path along which she's mowing.

6. Scrub the timeline to ensure this staging of the CGI looks correct; it worked for me, but you're the artist here. In Figure 11.9 you can see the finished comp at top, and at bottom I've put a green tint around the video layers so you can see a relative positioning I'd suggest.

7. Try duplicating the duplicate, offsetting its time and position if you chose to make smaller lilies earlier and the duplicate from Step 4 doesn't complete a horizontal row of lilies.

Figure 11.9
Augment the row of lilies by using a repositioned duplicate of the video you placed.

Setting Up a Second Pass for the Mowing

I've mentioned a few times that the woman makes a left to right pass with the mower after about 15 seconds into the video. Herein lies a problem and a solution to the problem: The woman's second pass is in *front* of the first, from the camera's POV (point of view). You could clip the video before she makes the second pass and call it a day, and you could put her behind the row of lilies making the second pass: The path of the mown grass is faint, and you could indeed cheat the effect this way.

Nahhhh; let's put the woman *in front* of the row of lilies, creating a second row. Your friends are going to seriously wonder how you did the effect without using a green screen or hand-rotoscoping.

The trick lies in Dr. Brown's Background Remover, a JavaScript you can download for free at http://www.russellbrown.com/tips_tech.html. You want to save your work in PSD file format now, close Photoshop, download the file, and put the JavaScript in your (Photoshop)\Presets\Scripts folder. Then restart Photoshop, and the script will be in File > Scripts. Russell Brown's script can be used to remove any background color; it calls the Select > Color Range command at the beginning, where in this example you'll choose the green grass in a duplicate of the bottom video, using a low Fuzziness value, and then a little hand-editing to effectively isolate the woman and the mower from the background. This a "Just Left of Orthodox" use of the script, and a little bit of a kludge (proper green screening would produce a cleaner silhouette of the woman), but in this example it works. One thing you have going for you by using a trick such as this is that the audience is not really directed at the woman but instead at the CGI. A magician's livelihood thrives on the art of misdirection, and by following these steps you'll see that misdirection can also work in video:

1. Duplicate the bottom lawnmower video layer and then put it on the top of the stack on the Layers palette.

2. Set the current time on the Animation palette to about Frame 512. Dr. Brown's Background Remover doesn't need to remove anything for the first half of the video where the woman is in the clear "sowing" the CGI lilies. The script runs only from the current time until it runs out of frames in the Animation palette's Work Area.

3. Choose File > Scripts > Dr. Brown's Background Remover.

4. The Color Range command box pops up. Set Fuzziness to about 60; doing this helps make a clean edge around the woman and mower. *Spill* is an inevitable consequence of shooting outdoors. If you took the Eyedropper tool in your spare time and sampled areas of the woman and particularly the nearly green housing of the lawnmower, you'd discover some grass-green color spilled into these areas.

5. Set the Selection Preview to Quick Mask in the Color Range box.

6. Click on the brightest area of the grass. When I ran this tutorial I found I needed an additional sample; click the Eyedropper + (Add to Sample icon) in Color Range and then click in an unselected area, as shown in Figure 11.10. When your screen looks like this figure, click OK and then sit back for a while.

7. Notice that the house at the right in the background remained on the duplicate layer, not being remotely similar to grass-green color. Advance the timeline to about Frame 700 (or earlier, depending on how you composed the lily layers) and then with the Lasso tool, select the remaining house area and any other areas that are hiding the lilies at frame right.

8. Delete the selection (press Backspace), advance the composition by one frame, and then repeat. The selection remains in the document when you advance frames; to clean up the background areas that Dr. Brown's script left, you click the Selects Next Frame button on the Animation palette and then press Backspace a few dozen times. Be careful and make sure you reselect areas when the woman moves far enough to the right, closer to the flowers. I saw no reason to script this repetition; it's straightforward and shouldn't cause arm cramping. In Figure 11.11 I've put the document into Quick Mask mode to better illustrate the unwanted area on the duplicate layer.

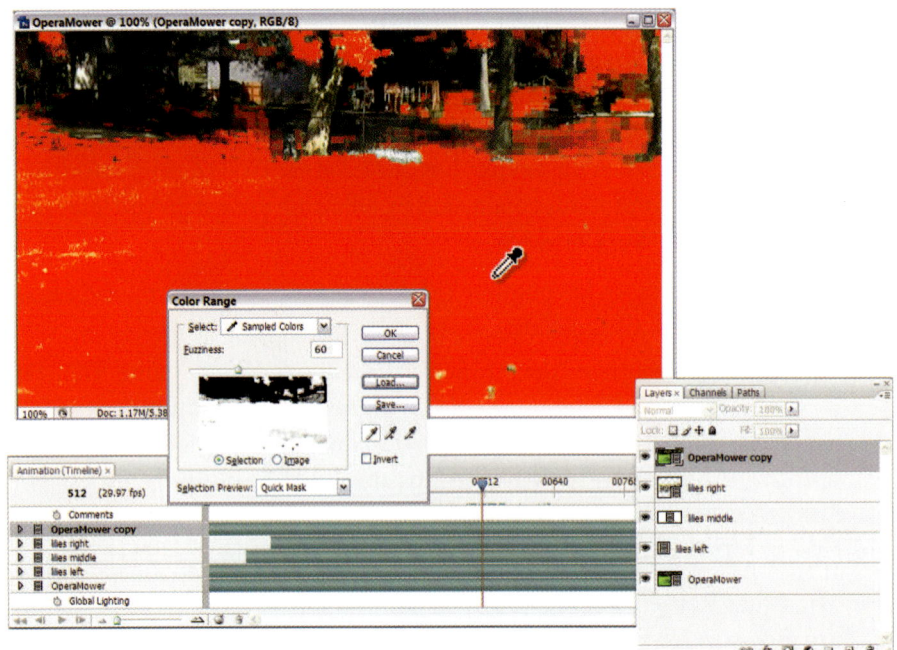

Figure 11.10
Choose a moderately narrow color range (Fuzziness) to select a fairly clean edge outside of the woman and mower.

Figure 11.11
Select, delete, and then advance to the next frame.

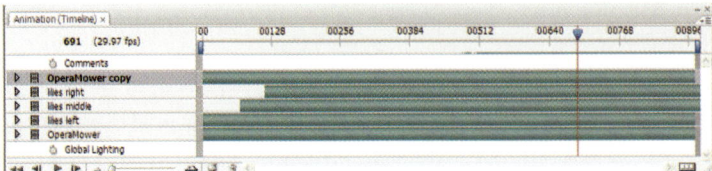

Adding a Second Row of Lilies

There's nothing new to teach in order to complete the composition. There's Left to Right Lilies.mov, Left to Right Lilies alpha.mov, and Left to Right Lilies Shadows.mov in the ZIP archive you downloaded. To shorthand the finale to this CGI composite:

1. Use Color Range as part of an action to select the alpha movie on top of the pink lilies layer to then delete the areas outside the bottom layer (of the pink lilies).
2. Scale the shadows video along with the Lilies layer to the size you feel is good for the video.
3. Remove the white outside of the Shadows layer using Color Range and the JavaScript you built for executing the "x" action several times.
4. Create a hold for the end of the pink lilies animation. Render the composite video.
5. Add two or three duplicates to the composition you saved to PSD earlier.

Figure 11.12 shows a frame from the finished composition. Render the video using any compression (codec) for QuickTime you like, without alpha channel support. The reason I recommend QuickTime is that the original footage has music. I used part of the Overture to Rossini's *The Thieving Magpie* (it's public domain music) along with a tuned sound sample of a lawnmower. Sound samples can be played like a piano using a digital audio workspace (DAW).

Figure 11.12
Add the second row of flowers using the steps you've already learned earlier in this chapter.

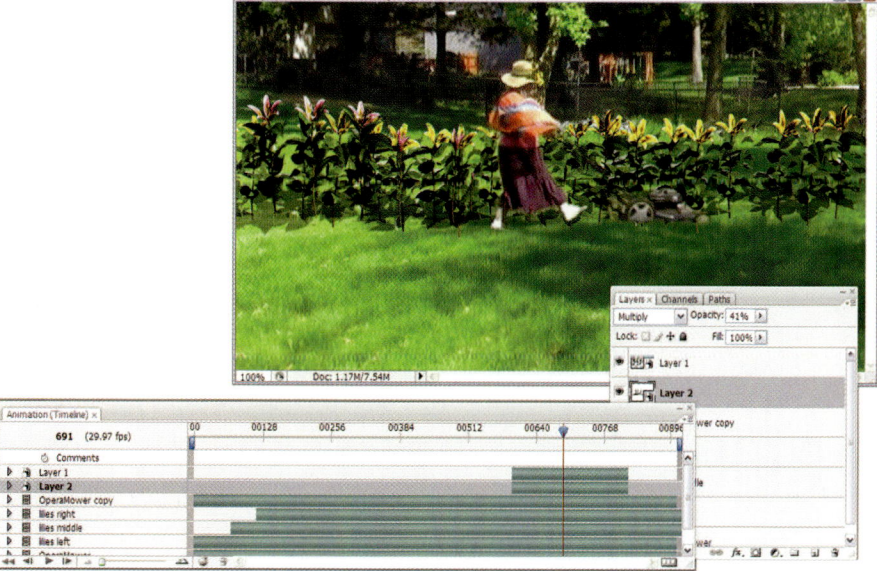

An Example of Simple 3D Character Animation

The example to follow relies a lot on the setup of the CGI in a modeling program as well as the concept and setup of the location shot. I review the compositing techniques as performed in Photoshop, but I just want to meander into areas of good story-telling as it relates to a finished CGI sequence.

My idea was derived from *The Ernie Kovacs Show*, aired on NBC from about 1952 to 1956 with reruns abounding through the early 1960s. Aside from stock issue comedic skits, the show also helped popularize the TV convention known as the *blackout*. A blackout is typically a visual idea that takes very little time to explain and run its course (usually under 30 seconds). The visual idea is presented, and then the camera fades or cuts to black. Mr. Kovacs probably didn't invent the sight gag, but he certainly popularized the bizarre visual shtick of paintings in a museum or in a house coming to life. A family portrait would scarf a drink from a nearby table while the main character's back is turned, or remove his toupee. This "While the cat's away…" treatment is good for a chuckle by the uninitiated. It's a variation on the moving eyes in gothic movies, and it's lasted right up to the *Harry Potter* movies.

Wanting to bring something to the party instead of merely annexing it, my variation on the unexpected object coming to life is a stand of vegetables in a supermarket. They're jumping up and down, partying, but the moment before an unsuspecting shopper passes by, they shush up and quickly return to their static places. Then the moment she passes by, the vegetables start leaping around again.

When you create a CGI sequence, getting the lighting the way you want it in the video clip into which you insert the CGI is not critically important. In the example to follow, we were restricted to the supermarket's default lighting, which was fine, and would've been pushing a favor to ask the management to change it. The camera angle was a cheat between showing our shopper at the best angle and getting the real vegetables in the bins at an angle that clearly showed them. The shot was composed as interestingly as possible, clearly providing a view that telegraphs that it's a supermarket to the audience; the shot was set up in almost perfect profile to the action to eliminate hassles animating the vegetables. A three-quarter view might look more interesting, but then the CGI would have to animate across three dimensions, and the perspective would have taken a lot longer to choreograph. Figure 11.13 shows the midpoint of the video you'll use, where the CGI will not be seen in the finished video.

Then it was on to creating the vegetables. A cucumber and a tomato are the scallywags in the video, and because of their final size on the CGI composite video, their shapes were relatively simple to build. Basically, a tomato is a squashed sphere with a few dimples and possibly a stem (the base video clip actually shows only a

Figure 11.13
Plan your video so the CGI can "star" in position, in the finished special effects video.

4-pixel dot or two as the stem). I created the cucumber by creating several soft-corner hexagons of different sizes and then did something called *lofting* in Cinema 4D. You position the paths in space the way that describes the cucumber in this example and then tell the program to build a surface be connecting the 2D paths in 3D space.

What presented the most challenge was defining a texture for the vegetables. Digital artists, myself included, sometimes rely on empirical data about color, bumps, reflections, and other object attributes; we occasionally think it's clever to eyedropper sample colors for accuracy—and fail. When creating textures and defining colors, you can get a ballpark idea from sampling photos and video frames, but in the end, if it looks right to your own eye, then it *is* right, at least for the purposes of matching a CGI to a video.

In Figure 11.14 I show close-ups of the modeled vegetables used to create the CGI clips. Yep, they look dull, but this CGI isn't a "beauty shot" but instead is intended to match the actual vegetables in the bins. Materials on the skin of 3D models react to the light in the scene, so the first thing I did after importing the video as a scene background was to try and match the somewhat cold fluorescent overhead lights in the video. This made previewing different colors on the modeled vegetables easier and, because the cucumbers in the supermarket are wrapped in cellophane, part of my texture for the fake cuke is a reflective transparent material that gives off noticeable specular highlights. At times you'll see more highlight than cucumber in the CGI you'll work with, but look at the video clip; art has to imitate life to pull off an effect. You're going to create something surreal and outrageous; therefore you need as much realism as possible to help "ground" the audience while the fantasy plays.

A fair question to ask yourself when animating the implausible, in this case, would be: How do vegetables look when they're partying? Part of the answer is, "Yeah,

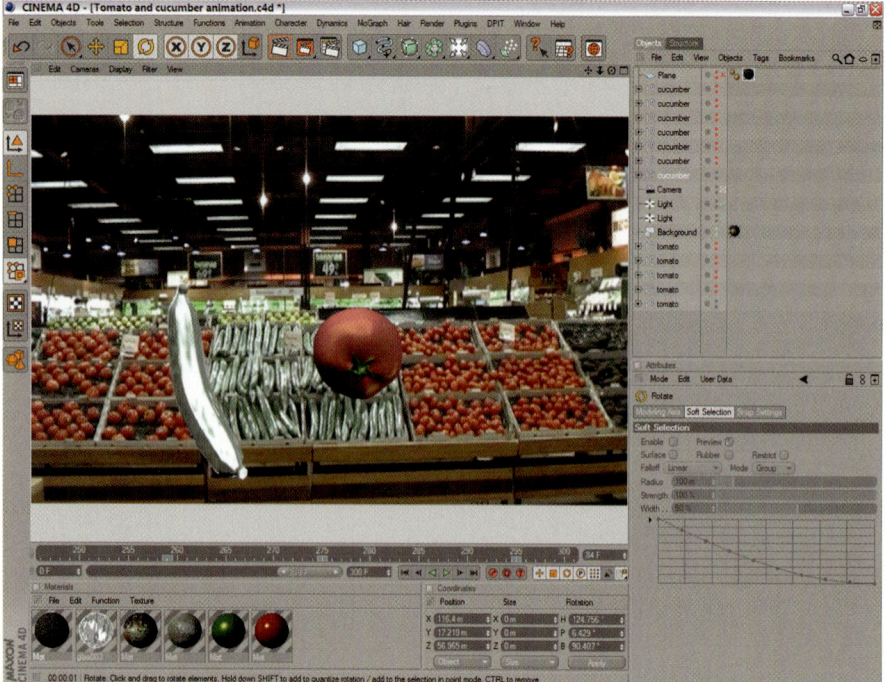

Figure 11.14
Real objects can be duller than you imagine when filmed. Trust your artist's eye.

they jump up and down a lot because they don't have appendages or faces." My approach was to make the veggies jump all over the place, but with realistic dynamics and timing. Suppose you wanted to do this scene with wire work and real vegetables? The laws of physics would apply, and that's what I did when animating the modeled vegetables. I first took out a stopwatch and timed some objects I tossed lightly into the air: about 1.4 seconds for an 8-ounce object to travel from my hand, up about two feet and then down again. So the CGI clip you'll be using features vegetables animating at no longer than two seconds for a transit up and then down.

Something I avoided, unlike the earlier example of CGI lilies, was any similarity of movement. I began with one tomato and one cucumber model, duplicated them several times, and then animated each one with a fresh keyframe track. This took some time, but it gave me the feeling and the responsibility of a choreographer/director. Directing CGI and directing video might seem like different disciplines, but they are converging. Figure 11.15 shows the animation path of one of the cucumbers.

I timed the duration of the dancing vegetables to come to an abrupt end a few frames before our actress entered frame pushing her cart. It's 300 frames, and in Figure 11.16 you can see the timeline for all 12 of the objects. There is similar yet not identical movement at the beginning, the "setup" of the scene, and because the tracks are not unfolded in this figure you can't see the rotation values of the depth of movement for the objects, which gives them a slightly different appearance animating, although *en masse* the vegetables are doing a dance as sort of a group. Just before the actress enters scene, I wanted a frantic scramble back to the bin, and this is why you can see dramatic, tightly paced key frame changes just before the Frame 300 mark.

Also unseen in the figures in this section, but visible in the animation itself, is a little *easing-in* and *easing-out* at keyframes, which is an animation technique that

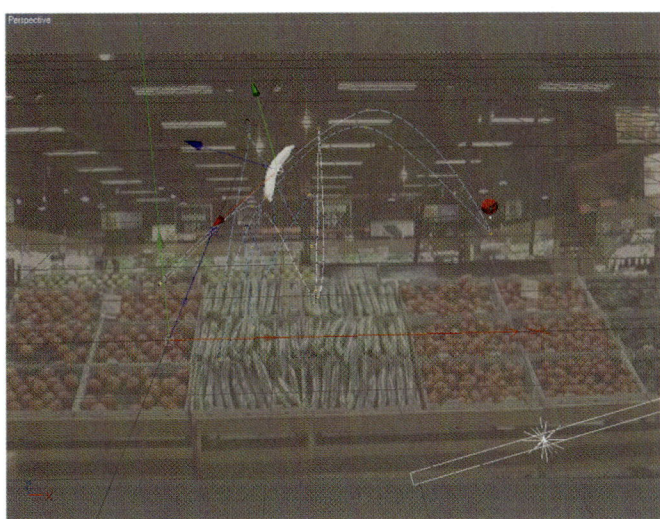

Figure 11.15
Animation paths in most advanced modeling application uses keyframes. The application then performs the tweening.

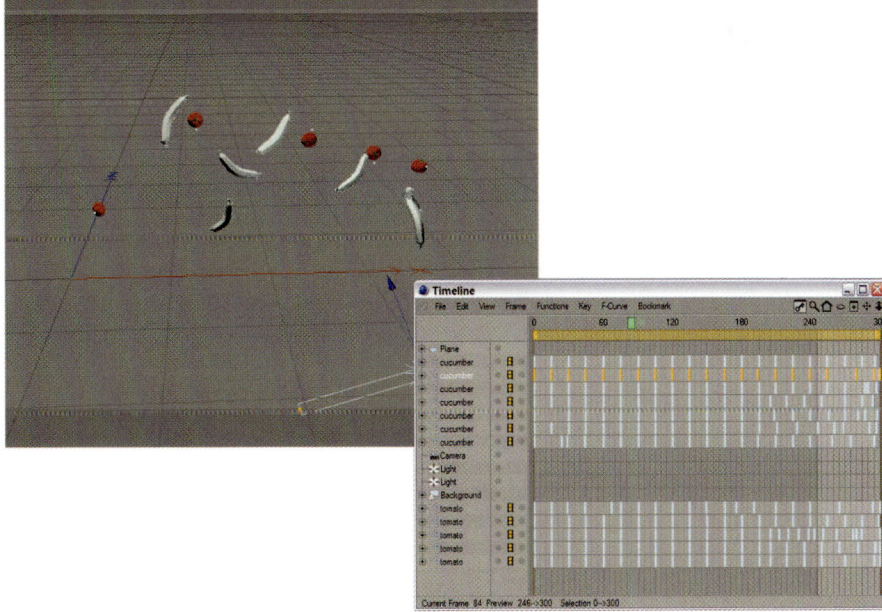

Figure 11.16
Keyframes in 3D animation programs are similar to Photoshop's Animation palette in Frames mode. You set a key, and then tell the palette to perform tweening.

used to have to be calculated manually. With every real life action, there is acceleration; a baseball player steps into a swing, accelerating, and then after hitting the ball out of the park, the follow-through decelerates. This is often an automated routine in advanced modeling programs; the vegetables appear to have real weight because they slow down between the keyframes I defined, and their movement slows down as they complete the motion between keys. If you were to graph the motion, it wouldn't look like a straight line, but rather like a curve, bowing at each end, denoting easing into the motion and easing out of it. The more art imitates life, the better you hook the audience into the fantasy.

Positioning is also critical when you want to swap a real object in and out for a CG one. I spent a great deal of time matching the position of all the CG vegetables to fit over existing ones in the background video at the first and last keyframes. You might think that as long as the CG objects' textures are compatible with the underlying video, you're home free. Not so: When our shopper enters the scene, the vegetables stop moving. Necessarily, without manual rotoscoping, the vegetables have to be quite similar in shading and fairly accurate in matching the positions of existing veggies in the video. If they don't, when the CG clip ends, the audience will see a jerky transition, spoiling the effect.

> **Tip**
>
> Before I wrote the CG animation out of Cinema 4D, I played back a rough render and found that not only are my CG tomatoes as dull as the real-life ones, but they were *too* dull to provide a clean read as they frolic in the air against the dark supermarket ceiling. To compensate, I added a light with *falloff* toward the top of the scene. If you're familiar with real-life stage lights, falloff is the confinement of illumination to a specified area, and it's quite tough to be precise with real lights. However, in the virtual world of CG, lights can be defined and directed so they intensely illuminate an area in 3D space, with any degree of falloff as an object travels in and out of the defined space, steep or gradual. In this example, when the tomatoes jump up, they fall within the falloff virtual light and pick up just enough illumination to separate well in the finished composite. However, when they travel back to the bins, they gradually fall out of the "sphere of influence" of the light with the falloff attribute and therefore will return to their dull, photorealistically accurate illumination as they reach the supermarket bins.

Creating Alpha Channels for the CGI

In the following steps you can rely on the action you created earlier to strip the background from the lilies CGI. If you skipped over to this section, I'll briefly recap; again, I created the video clips this way deliberately to conserve on download time, but you might anticipate that a client would receive CGI segments this same way. Not all animation programs can write alpha information directly into a video; Vue 6 and Poser for Windows require that a separate video is rendered for alpha information.

1. Open Partying Vegetables.mov and Partying Vegetables alpha.mov and turn off Pixel Aspect Ratio Correction.

2. With Partying Vegetables alpha.mov in the foreground in the workspace, on the Layers palette first hold Shift and then drag the thumbnail into the Partying Vegetables.mov document window. Holding Shift centers the duplicated video layer relative to the current document window. The result is that the two layers are perfectly aligned. You can close the alpha movie file now without saving changes.

3. Click the bottom layer on the Layers palette—the color image of the animated vegetables.

4. Similar to the action you created earlier: create an action named "x" in the Default Actions folder and, with the bottom layer still active, select the top layer's black areas using Color Range, press Backspace to delete the selected area on the bottom layer (which is chosen but you can't see it in the document window), and then press Ctrl/Cmd+D to deselect and advance to the next frame. Stop recording the action. This is the list for the action in case you skipped over the previous tutorial. See Figure 11.17, which shows the Color Range command, the first step in the action.

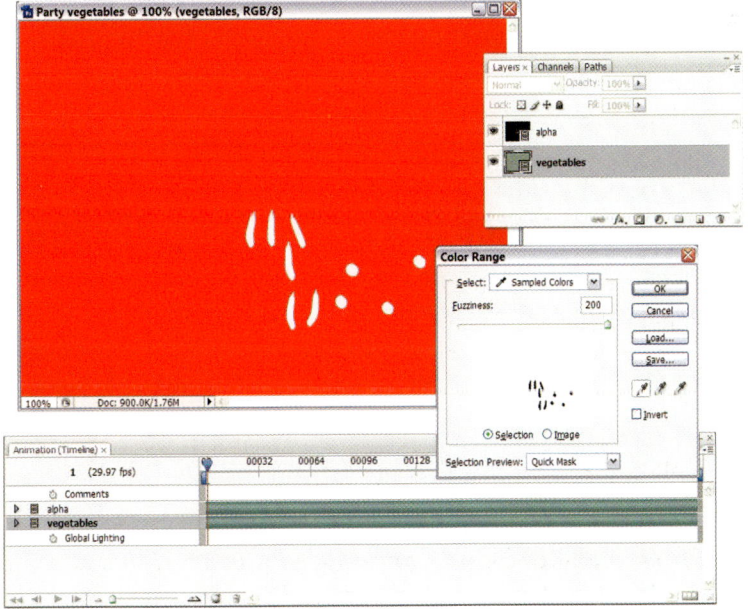

Figure 11.17
Use an action to select areas on the top layer to then delete areas on the bottom (current editing) layer.

5. On the Actions palette, make sure to click on the Default Actions folder to make this the active folder. You need to run the action 300 times. As I mentioned earlier, the Execute X (any number of times) JavaScript is great for repeating actions. You can minimize Photoshop, open a folder window on your desktop, choose the JavaScript file from Photoshop's Scripts folder, edit the script, save it to a different name (same file extension), and then restore Photoshop. Choose File > Scripts, Browse to load your new custom script without exiting Photoshop.

6. You can delete the Alpha top layer now. Keep the document open for the steps in the next section. You don't necessarily have to save to PSD unless you plan a system crash; you'll copy the bottom layer to the video clip in the next section, and what you have is what Adobe calls *altered video* in the document window. Saving altered video creates huge PSD files, so I'm simply trying to save your hard disk and save you some effort here.

> **Note**
>
> Any video you import to Photoshop and then edit directly, such as cutting an area out of a frame, turns the video layer into a Smart Object layer. One perk to making a video into a Smart Object is that filters can be applied across the duration of the clip. Video layers per se cannot be filtered (Gaussian Blur, Watercolor, and so on) as video; only single frames can be filtered. The not-so-good news about video Smart Objects is that adjustments such as Levels and Hue/Saturation are unavailable. You can adjust Levels for a Smart Object by right-clicking the object's thumbnail on the Layers palette and then choosing Edit Contents. This is a roundabout and cumbersome way to adjust a video Smart Object's lightness or hue. It's much easier and equally accurate to use an Adjustment layer on Smart Object videos, available on the bottom of the Layers palette as a pull-down menu.

Compositing, Reusing the Clip, and Fading Shadows

Compositing the vegetables into the scene is fairly straightforward; it uses some simple steps covered earlier in the lilies example, with one or two minor differences. I'm trying to give you a feel for what a special effects artist or a client might hand you for compositing. This one will be easier than the lilies example because there's no hold frame to cobble, and because I placed the vegetables accurately relative to the underlying video, there is no scaling or repositioning to perform. Therefore your "client" was a thoughtful one for a change!

I also created a shadow layer for the CG by creating a plane in my C4D scene faithful in position and angle of rotation to the bins of vegetables in the supermarket. The audience will not see that the shadows aren't perfectly placed or faithful with respect to the bins of vegetables, but they *will* notice an *absence* of shadows. The tricky thing about the shadow animation is that it has to fade to 0% over a few frames at the end of the vegetable CG; if the shadows come to a halt abruptly when the veggies return to their bins, the audience will see a glitch in the finished video.

Here's how to composite the video you currently have in the workspace with the Cleanup In Aisle 9 movie:

1. Open Cleanup In Aisle 9.mov and turn off Pixel Aspect Ratio Correction.

2. With the altered video document in the foreground, on the Layers palette, hold Shift and then drag the layer thumbnail into the cleanup document window.

3. Scrub the timeline. As you can see on your monitor and in Figure 11.18, when you duplicate a video layer to a different video document window, it starts at the start of the Work Area on the Animation palette. There is no track sliding needed for now.

Figure 11.18
Duplicate the edited video layer to its place in the document in which you're creating the CG composite.

4. Choose Layer > Video Layers > New Video Layer from File. Choose Partying Vegetables shadows.mov. It, too, plops into place starting at the head of the Work Area.

5. Drag the layer on the Layers palette so that the shadow layer is under the vegetables and then put the layer into Multiply blending mode at about 40% opacity.

6. Shift+click to select the Vegetables and the Shadows layers on the Layers palette. Then drag the thumbnails into the Create a New Layer icon on the Layers palette.

7. While the two layers are still selected, put them below the original Vegetables and Shadows layers and slide their tracks on the Animation palette to about Frame 533. This point in the video is where our shopper exits frame after inspecting the apparently ho-hum vegetables, so the veggies see that it's okay to resume partying. Reusing this clip is okay; the vegetables in the CG display so much random behavior that it's quite impossible for the audience to tell that you've repeated the CG. As a rule, however, don't do this: Hollywood B movies abound in reused car chase scenes and effects that were too expensive to create more than once. And they look as phony and as awkward as you might expect, dampening if not crippling the storytelling.

8. Go to Frame 288 or so on the Animation palette. The original shadow layer needs to be tweaked to make the veggies return smoothly to the bins.

9. Click the Opacity stopwatch icon on the Animation palette for the original Shadows layer. A keyframe is auto-created.

10. Drag the timeline indicator (the *thumb*) on the Animation palette to Frame 300; or more simply double-click the Current Time indicator (the bold number at top left on the palette) and then type **300** in the Set Current Time box. Large videos and video compositions with a lot of layers are hard to scrub through using the thumb, even on high-performance computers; double-clicking to scoot to a specific point in time avoids the "drag" of scrubbing for a point in time you need.

11. On the Layers palette, drag the Opacity from 40% to 0% for the shadow layer. Your screen should now look like Figure 11.19.

12. After viewing the video, I found it was not necessary to fade the shadow layer up on the duplicate, which starts at about Frame 533. As designers, we often tend toward symmetry in design work, but video is a different playing ground. There is not always an equal and opposite reaction to an action; the shadow popping into existence at Frame 533 looks quite natural (as fantasy CG goes). Call it an experiment well done and write your composition out to QuickTime; there's a humorous audio track in the supermarket video that can only be exported from Photoshop using QuickTime file format. I felt an audience will expect the vegetables to be partying with squeaky little "Yay" and "Hoo, hoo—whee!"; besides, audio definitely comes to the rescue of CG effects to complete a character, even one with seeds. I'd recommend Sorenson 3 as your codec (it provides better color than H.264 for this particular video), and do not export with alpha channel support.

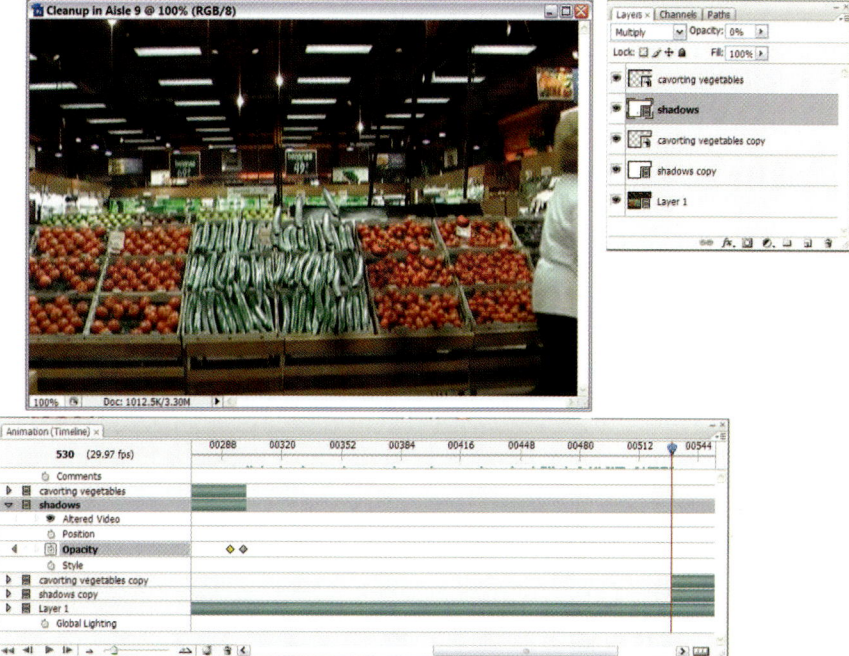

Figure 11.19
Decreasing the opacity of the Shadows layer helps the CG vegetables blend almost seamlessly with the real supermarket footage underneath.

If you are familiar with modeling/animation software and know how to define alpha transparency, you've got it licked for hanging your shingle out as a Photoshop CG compositing specialist. If you have zero interest in learning and owning such software, by working through these examples you now know how to composite just about anything a client or co-worker might toss your way. In any event, computer generated images are mature enough in desktop technology to pass the test of today's "been there, seen that" audiences. CGI requires less effort for compositing than rotoscoping and green screening, and a bunch of moving pixels combined with your growing skills and artistic vision will continue to make the stuff that practically everyone with a television has seen hundreds of times continue to be an eye-catching novelty.

Retouching motion pictures isn't about special effects. It's about the best visual trappings to tell a story.

12

Creating 3D Scene Props

One of the characteristics that makes Adobe Photoshop the preferred tool for imaging work is that it's a terrific integrator of media from different source into a seamless composition. For this reason you open Photoshop with a goal in mind and then pick and choose from different areas of the UI for tools and features best suited to arrive at your goal. Along this train of thought, this chapter takes you through accomplishing a goal—putting a prop into a scene—through the use of two unrelated Photoshop features: Vanishing Point and the Clone Source palette.

I show you how to create a 3D cube and then get more practical and design a 3D arch for a street scene. You can then export it to a modeling program for reference for designing an elaborate and photorealistic arch. Then I show you how to integrate the arch into a video clip so a car passes *beneath* the arch in three dimensions, so it looks plausible and completely believable to the audience.

Also in this chapter I demonstrate how to animate a neon sign and put it in perspective on a building. Finally, you'll work with lighting and an animation clip to put a seven-foot marble tuna statue in the back yard of a neighbor's house, whether he likes it or not. It's not all fun and silliness: Digital arts have advanced the quality of backstage props and painted seamlesses to the point where they're often undetectable in movies. Less than 15 years ago, this was Indigo workstation territory, but as you'll soon see, Photoshop Extended has brought unbelievable motion picture tools to the desktop.

Working with Vanishing Point

Vanishing Point is in version 2.0 with CS3, and it has a lot of unobvious features that are great to use on video. You can find it under the Filter menu; its "standard" use is for matching the perspective of, for example, architecture in a photo so you can then match perspective with a different image, text, or painted work. However, Vanishing Point can also be used to create 3D objects in a PSD document that you can retexture and rotate (see Chapter 10), and you can export a painted creation to 3D Studio and DXF file formats through the Vanishing Point UI.

Let's start with something simple in the next section so I can better demonstrate the features before getting to the creative uses of Vanishing Point.

Designing a Child's Building Block

I'm asking you to design a kid's building block in this section not to be cutesy, but because if you put letters of the alphabet on each side it's much easier to visually grasp the orientation of the faces of the cube when you make a 3D layer from a copy of it and rotate it around. Here's the scoop of building a 3D object in Photoshop with Vanishing Point: Although you can design as many faces as you like in Vanishing Point, designing all six sides of a cube will give you a headache aligning all the faces properly, so I'll walk you through designing only a top, the right, and front sides. In a 2D image or video, you can only see three of the perspective points of an object at a single instance, and if you really need a 3D cube for an assignment, a modeling program is much easier to use than trying to do this in Vanishing Point; it's the wrong tool for the job.

Therefore, what you need to do is begin with a new document with transparency and then design an "unfolded" cube: The top is above the front, and the right side joins the front to the direct right of the front. If you'd like to check out and/or use the cube I built, open Kid's block.png. Then create a new blank layer on top of the design so when you work with Vanishing Point you're messing with a fresh layer and not your original design. When you have something that looks like Figure 12.1, follow the steps below.

1. With your design visible and Layer 0 selected as the active layer on the Layers palette, press Ctrl/Cmd+A to copy it to the clipboard and then Ctrl/Cmd+D to deselect.

2. Hide the design layer and then click Layer 1 to make the new layer active.

3. Choose Filter > Vanishing Point (Ctrl/Cmd+Alt/Opt+V is the shortcut). Note that Vanishing Point is a "special" filter; there's a divider between the special filters and the normal and third-party filters on the Filter menu. Unlike other filters, the "special" filters cannot be invoked twice or several times by the Ctrl/Cmd+F and Ctrl/Cmd+Alt/Opt+F (last-used filter without applying it) keyboard commands.

Figure 12.1
The three faces should be located as you see here so that Vanishing Point can map the faces correctly to 3D space.

4. Your cursor is loaded and ready to use to design the three front faces of a 3D cube. Begin by drawing the front face in perspective by clicking four points. By perspective, I mean a shape that looks skewed: The left and right sides should be perfectly vertical, but the top and bottom sides should be parallel, but converging toward 3:00 o'clock for the right side or 9:00 o'clock for the left side in this example. If your front face is not perfect, you can move the corner bounding box handles to finesse the shape. You can also try again from scratch by pressing Backspace to delete the current perspective box.

5. To create the opposite side, you hold the Ctrl/Cmd key and then drag the middle bounding box handle to the right or left as needed. Vanishing Point should extend the front face to the needed side at a 90 degree angle. If it doesn't, adjust the angle in the Angle field at the top of the UI; see Figure 12.2. Alternatively, hold the Alt/Option key down and drag on the middle bounding box handle to adjust the angle of the plane.

Figure 12.2
Extend a plane by dragging while holding Ctrl/Cmd.

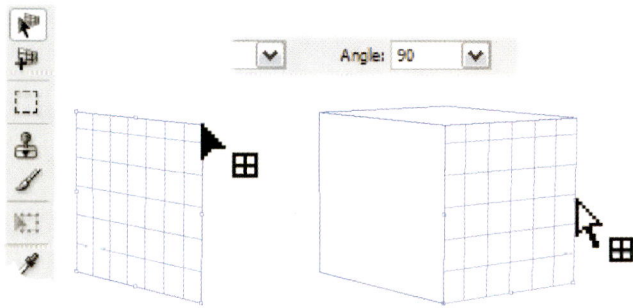

> **Caution**
>
> There is no option in Photoshop to change the color of the perspective grids in Vanishing Point from the light blue. If the interior of a plane does not have the light blue grid inside, you've created a perspective that Vanishing Point believes is geometrically impossible (the angle is too steep), the grids appear as yellow, and the outline of the box turns red. To correct this, move a corner bounding box handle around until you see the blue grid and then continue.

6. From either the top of the front side or the top of the right side, hold Ctrl/Cmd and then drag a middle bounding box handle to extend the plane to create the top of the cube. You might need to zoom in to perfectly align the top plane to meet the other two sides (use the Zoom tool on the Vanishing Point toolbox).

7. Press Ctrl/Cmd+V to paste the clipboard copy of your cube design into Vanishing Point. Then drag it into the perspective planes you created, as shown in Figure 12.3. No, it's not that simple, and your design might not fit perfectly into the perspective planes; you might need to use the Transform tool, covered in Step 8.

Figure 12.3
Paste the design into Vanishing Point and then drag it into the perspective planes.

8. If the design doesn't align with the Vanishing Point planes (it took me three tries), press T or click the Transform tool shown in Figure 12.3 and then drag a bounding box handle to scale the design within the perspective planes. If you back the cursor slightly away from a bounding box handle, you get the rotate cursor to rotate a design. You cannot reproportion a perspective plane after it's been defined (drawn). Dragging on a plane's bounding box handles only extends the face; it doesn't change its perspective, and mistakes have to be corrected by deleting the plane and starting over. Note that the first plane you define is the parent plane, and 90 degree extensions are child planes. You can delete a child plane (by highlighting it and then pressing Backspace), but if you delete a parent plane, you also delete its children.

9. Click the round button with the flyout triangle symbol on it at the top and to the right of the toolbox; this is a flyout menu in Vanishing Point. Choose Return 3D Layer to Photoshop, and then click OK at the right of the UI. 3D layers are made up of textures that have no color profiling, so if you're using color management you'll get three successive dialogs asking you about color conversions—just click OK and seriously consider turning off color management warnings when working with video and 3D layers.

10. You've done it! Double-click the 3D layer thumbnail on the Layers palette and then use the tools on the Options bar to rotate and zoom your child's building block. In Figure 12.4 you can see that I've rotated my cube to the extent that you can see the back side, and the letters face forward regardless of whether you view them from the front or the back. This is because Photoshop is mapping the design to both sides of a 3D object with the same image and doesn't have a backside image with which to work. Also note that 3D files in Photoshop have surfaces but no volume; in effect, they're like empty eggshells. This is because many modeling programs dismiss volume and only render a surface because no one can see a volume obstructed by the surface, and surface modeling is more economical than rendering, processing, and saving file-size perspectives. This is also why you can see the "eggshell" treatment instead of a closed volume when using the Cross-section feature on the Options bar when in 3D manipulation mode.

Figure 12.4

It's easy to paint a 3D object in Photoshop.

Putting a Neon Sign in a Video

Frequently a screenplay requests a structure that either doesn't exist or a shooting schedule prohibits. The traditional workaround has been to paste the appropriate sign on a building the cinematographer then uses. You know: an ordinary panel van made up to look like a bank truck or an abandoned warehouse that instantly becomes a nightclub with the correct signage and a few extras tossed in.

Okay, to put a sign on a building, you'd use Vanishing Point on a sign you created and then match the perspective to the perspective of the building, as shown in the previous cube example. But what if the director wants a glowing animated sign?

You only use Vanishing Point to generate a grid and then rely on Layer Sets and the Free Transform mode to make the sign dimensional with perspective that matches the video clip; *building the animation* is a whole new set of steps I cover in this section. In Figure 12.5, a friend of ours (a realtor) allowed us to use a vacant building to shoot a simple scene; the guy looks at the sign and at his watch and then exits frame. This is a fairly boring scene! However, by using the steps in this section you'll transform the scene and the "meaning" of the video clip to make it a guy waiting outside of a bowling alley. It's Stone Soup; you're going to make something out of nothing, using Photoshop.

If you'd like to cut to the chase and skip ahead to just work on the compositing of this special effect, Neon Bowling Frames.psd is in the ZIP archive you downloaded for this chapter (but you'll learn much more through building your own Neon Bowling Frames file!).

Figure 12.5

This doesn't look like much of a scene, but give it about half an hour's worth of Photoshop work.

Creating the Neon Sign

The animation of the neon sign you'll build is a simple three frame "plot": Frame 1 shows a glowing ball and some pins, in Frame 2 the ball moves closer to the pins, and in Frame 3 the ball strikes the pins. The cycle repeats, as is the custom of animated neon signs.

Open the League Night.mov file now. I've already removed the sign in the video using Clone Source, which I cover later in this chapter. The reason you can't simply clone or paste over the sign area is that over time the lighting on the building changes ever so slightly as to jinx this idea. Follow these steps to create the neon sign animation:

1. Create a new blank document that's about 900 pixels wide by 425 pixels tall. This is larger than you'll need for the video clip, but you'll scale it after you've completed it. You lose clarity when you resize graphics, but you don't really lose "business," the visual complexity you ultimately add to a scene. For example, if you scale 12 point text down to 2 points, obviously it's going to look blurry and illegible. However, this 2 point text reads as typing on a piece of paper on a scene even though the audience can't read the text.

2. Use the Pen tool to build multiple paths of the shape of a bowling ball and a bowling pin. Artistically, you don't close the paths; neon tubing needs to have a start and end point to look authentic. You can save the paths to a single path (layer) on the Paths palette by double-clicking the Work Path title on the Paths palette after completing your first path. The path is then permanently saved as the default name Path 1, and all subsequent paths you draw belong to this same multiple path entry on the Paths palette.

3. Create a new blank layer on the Layers palette.

4. Choose the Path Selection tool from the Tools palette, the black arrow cursor. Choose a path in the document window; try the bowling ball for this example.

5. Switch to the Brush tool. On the Options bar, set the size to 5 pixels, hard tip. Set the foreground color on the Tools palette to a purple-blue; neon signs are colored using a combination of argon, mercury and phosphor gasses, and this color is your typical blue neon, R: 82, G:30, and B: 252.

6. Click the Stroke Path with Brush button on the Paths palette.

7. Set the brush size to 3 pixels (hard) and a lighter shade of the purple-blue; the easiest way to do this is to drag the cursor up and to the left in the color field in the Color Picker.

8. Click the Stroke Path with Brush button again. Now you have a decent simulation of neon.

9. To make the neon glow, Ctrl/Cmd+click the layer thumbnail on the Layers palette, and then choose Select > Modify > Expand Selection. Set the amount to about 8 pixels.

10. Ctrl+click on the Create a New Layer icon to put the new layer behind the bowling ball layer on the Layers palette.

11. Fill the layer with the lighter color you specified in Step 7 by pressing Alt/Opt+Backspace, then Ctrl/Cmd+D to deselect.

12. Choose Filter > Blur > Gaussian Blur. Set the value to about 6 pixels; click OK. Then reduce the opacity of the layer to about 65%. In Figure 12.6 you can see the neon creation process; I've applied a glow to the bowling pin, and you can see all the paths.

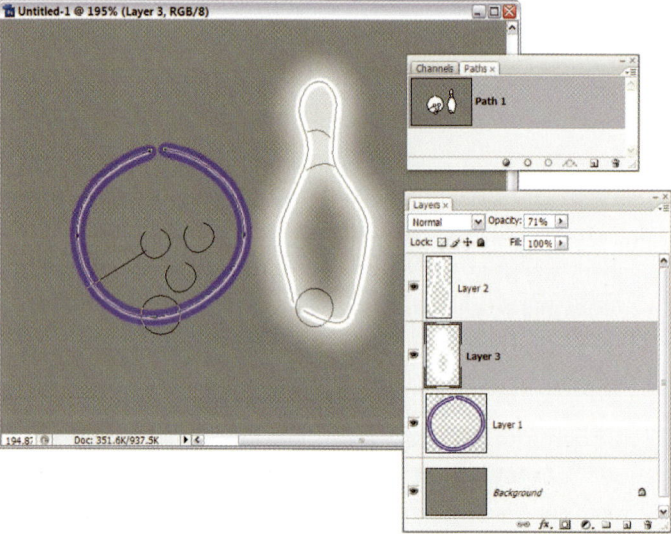

Figure 12.6
Stroking a path is the simplest and fastest way to simulate neon in a composition.

Figure 12.7 shows the finished art I want you to create. From an art standpoint, all I really did was use the Dodge and Burn tools on a copy of the neon (not the glow) to add dimension and then added little details. Adding verisimilitude to an illustration makes it hold up better against live video footage; you want to create unlit tubing to connect an area of neon or two and a base that connects the neon sign to power and the building. Also, the ball is rolling toward the pins, so rotating the holes in the ball clockwise helps complete the little animation's story.

The numbers in this figure are the layers you need to create, to turn them on and off at points in the animation. So create copies of the pin and position the copies,

Figure 12.7
The four frames you need to design for the neon sign progression.

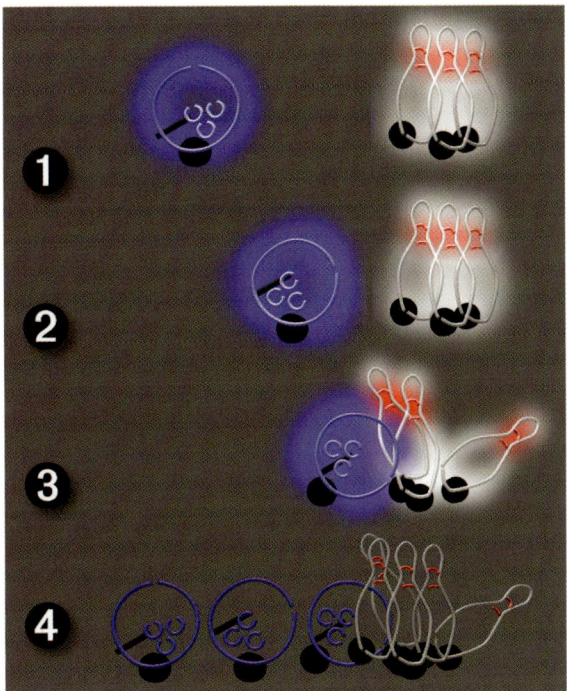

use Merge Down, and label the layers for easy reference as you work with the Animation palette next. Here's how to build the animation:

1. To make life easy setting a lot of keyframes, set up a shortcut key combo for copying and pasting keyframes to eliminate the need to click the flyout menu and choose the Paste command. Choose Edit > Keyboard Shortcuts and then choose Palette Menus.

2. Open the Animation (Timeline) entry and find Copy Keyframe(s). Press Ctrl/Cmd+Alt/Opt+C on your keyboard. This conflicts with Photoshop's default shortcut for Image Size > Canvas, which I personally don't use. Choose any keyboard combo you like; this one is simply easy to remember. Do similar steps with the Paste Keyframe(s) entry; Ctrl/Cmd+Alt/Opt+P is a good one. In Keyboard Shortcuts and Menus you can save and load sets, and also restore Photoshop's default keyboard shortcuts.

> **Tip**
>
> You can choose Paste Keyframe(s) from the right-click menu over a video track, but only if the timeline is over an existing keyframe; the keyframe is overwritten and replaced with one or more keyframe markers you previously copied.

3. The video clip the animation will go into is 247 frames. On the Animation palette, click the flyout menu and choose Palette Options. Choose Frame Number; click OK.

4. Click the flyout menu and choose Document Settings. Type **247** in the Duration field and then choose 29.97 fps from the Frame Rate drop-down list, because you usually don't want a higher frame rate resolution than is necessary, and the video clip you'll add the animation to is 29.97 fps, standard for a DV camera.

5. Through trial and error I discovered that an animation cycle for the neon sign is comfortable (not too frenetic) at a second and a half, approximately 90 frames. The first frame (with the bowling ball furthest to the left) should be highlighted on the Layers palette. On the Animation palette, click the Opacity stopwatch at Frame 0.

6. Move the timeline thumb to Frame 30 and drag the Opacity slider for this layer on the Layers palette to zero. What you have now is a layer in the animation that fades away, but neon flashes on and off, so you need to Shift+click the keyframes on this layer's track and then right-click and choose Hold Interpolation.

7. As a timesaver, you can right-click while the keys are still selected and then choose Copy Keyframes. This layer shouldn't reappear until Frame 90; double-click the Current Time indicator number (it's actually a slider) to display the Set Current Time dialog box and then type **90** in the box; click OK.

8. Use the keyboard shortcut you set up in Step 2 to paste the keyframes.

9. Repeat the process at 120 frames, and then finally at 180.

10. You'll notice that the pasted keyframes have the Linear Interpolation property; this is just the way Photoshop defaults to the keyframe pasting action. Shift+click all the diamond-shaped keyframes and then right-click and choose Hold Interpolation. See Figure 12.8.

11. Switch the second frame layer on at 30-frame intervals after the first frame layer, and then switch it off after 30 frames. Then perform this with the final third frame layers, offsetting the time by 30 frames. Use the copy and paste keyframe technique, and this task will take you less than 5 minutes.

12. Because the playlength of the video is 247 frames, obviously you can't play the whole 90-frame animation cycle completely, but this is okay. In Figure 12.9 you can see the setup for all the frames; the unlit frame is behind the glowing layers, and it's on all the time and not animated with respect to opacity at all. I also have a black layer I need to delete before compiling the animation just so I can see what I'm doing. The final frame layer can go on at Frame 240 when the second frame turns off, and as a Hold Interpolation it'll just remain on to the end of the duration of the animation.

Chapter 12 ■ Creating 3D Scene Props   393

Figure 12.8
Once you have a keyframe sequence set up, you can repeat it by copying and pasting keyframe markers.

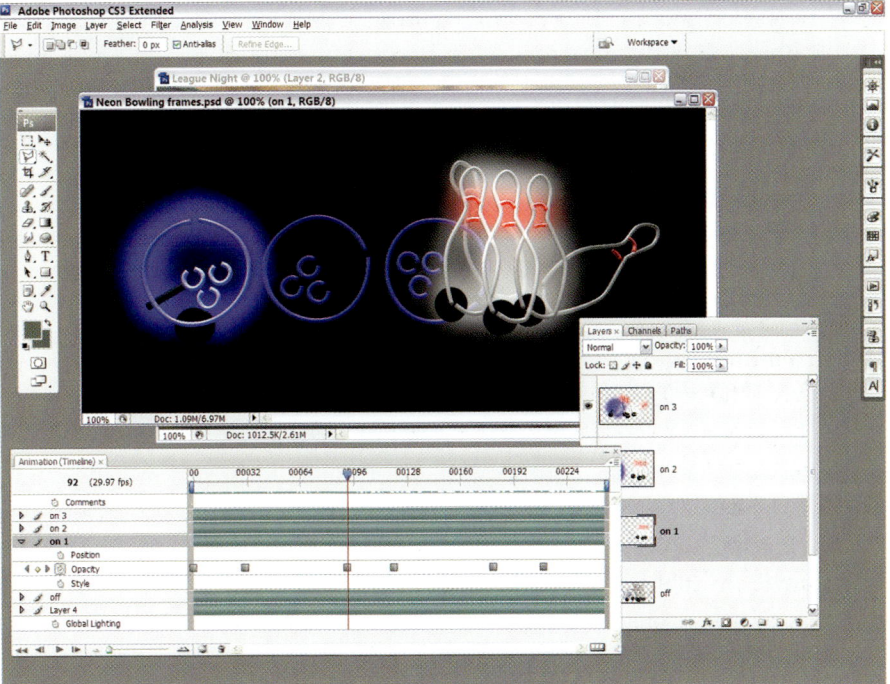

Figure 12.9
The attributes for the tracks in the animation, expressed as keyframes.

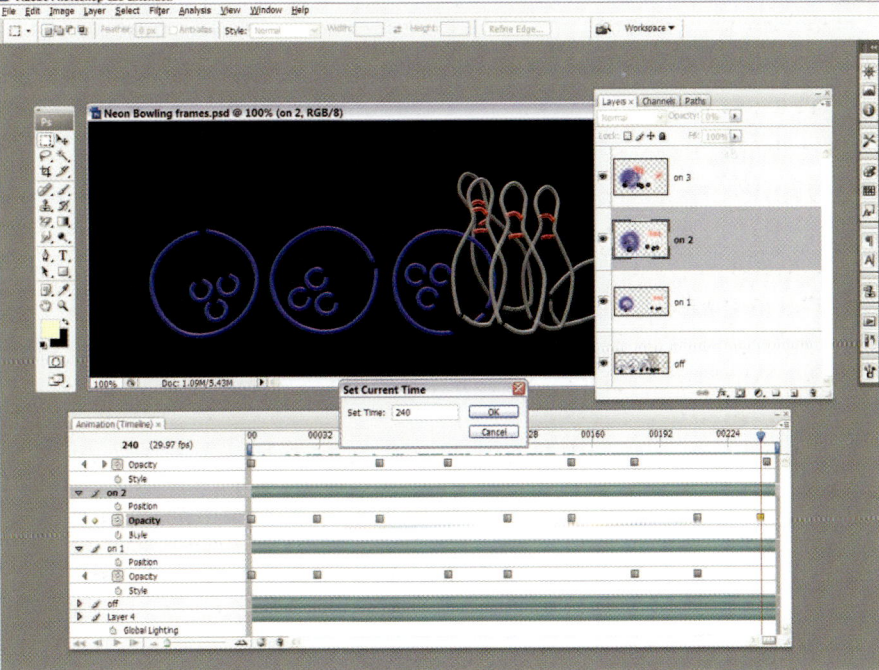

> **Tip**
>
> You might ask, "Shouldn't Frame 1 go off at 90 and Frame 2 go on at Frame 91?" Well, yes, you could do this, but it would create more work to remove overlaps on three tracks when visually it's not necessary. At 29.97 fps, there is no real visual difference if two frames are on for a thirtieth of a second, and if they don't overlap in time. The only time (as you'll see later in this chapter) when tracks shouldn't overlap is when there is noticeable action going on that absolutely has to be fluid with no stutter or jerks.

Sizing Up the Animation Proportions

It's time to open the video and size up the area where the neon sign will be animating. I'm showing you how to use the Free Transform feature here because the Vanishing Point command is unavailable with layer groups, so you use a VP grid as a *reference*. In your own work you might or might not need a Vanishing Point grid as a reference to align Free Transform distortions; I'm showing it here in case you have a number of objects to which you need to add perspective, and they must be aligned in a precise and specific fashion. Follow these steps to learn how to use Vanishing Point to create a grid that makes creating the correct perspective of the sign a snap:

1. Create a new layer group for the neon sign layers by clicking the folder button on the Layers palette. If you put a blank layer to use as a background in your PSD file, you can delete it at any time now.

2. Shift+click the neon layer titles, all four of them, and then drag them into the layer group entry on the Layers palette. A group is a nondestructive entity, so your animation has not changed in any way.

3. Load League Night.mov.

4. Drag the Layer Group icon from the Layers palette of your Neon Bowling frames file into the League Night document window. You can close the neon sign document after saving.

5. Create a layer below the neon layer group, and then hide the neon group.

6. With the Brush tool, white foreground color, and the 5-pixel diameter hard tip, click four dots on the new layer that describe the distorted rectangular perspective of where the neon sign will go; see Figure 12.10 for a reference. It's easier than it looks—use the undistorted vertical parallels of the slats on the building as your guide and you own eye for the horizontal placement of the dots.

Figure 12.10
Create an area using four points that describes the shape of the edifice of the building as it's viewed in perspective.

7. With the new layer selected, choose Filter > Vanishing Point.

8. In Vanishing Point, click points around the edges of the polygon shape you created in Step 6.

9. Choose Render Grids to Photoshop from the flyout menu, as shown in Figure 12.11. Then click OK to return to the workspace and apply the grid.

10. With the neon sign layer group selected, press Ctrl/Cmd+T to put the contents of this group folder—all four animation layers—into Free Transform mode.

11. With the Move tool (V), right-click over the Free Transform bounding box and then choose Distort from the context menu.

12. Zoom in if you need to, and then align the four corners of the group to the corresponding corners of the grid Vanishing Point created in Step 9; if you have Smart Guides visible, you're guided by the magenta lines when you're directly over the dots. In Figure 12.12 you can see the process, and I edited this figure so the grid is easy to see as white lines. When your alignment is perfect, press Enter or click the check button on the Options bar to apply the transformation.

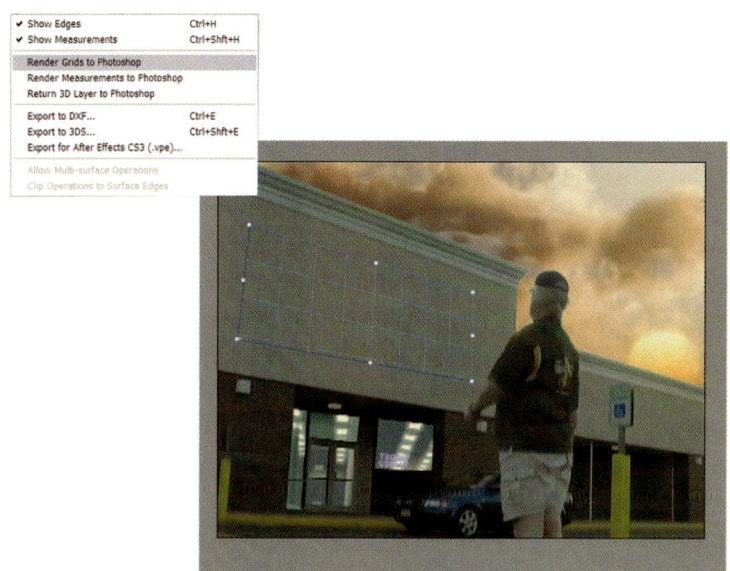

Figure 12.11
Vanishing Point can draw a grid for you at the perspective of your choice.

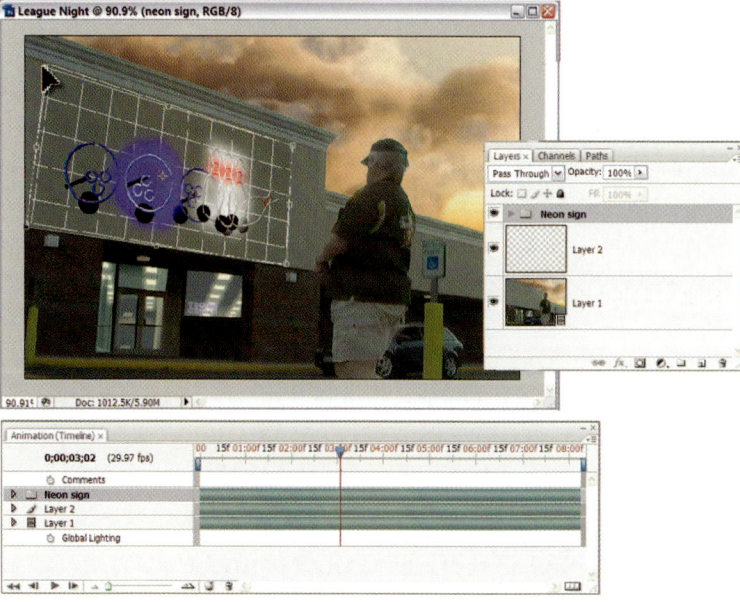

Figure 12.12
Use Vanishing Point's power in combination with Free Transform.

13. You're almost done. When I created this tutorial, I found I could improve the believability of the sign by adding a subtle drop shadow traveling to about 7 o'clock, in the opposite direction of the setting sun in the video. Open the layer group and choose the unlit animation layer. Click the fx button and then choose Drop Shadow, as shown in Figure 12.13. Crank Size up to about 10 pixels and lower the opacity of the effect to about 46%. You can then drag in the document window to set the position of the drop shadow or use the

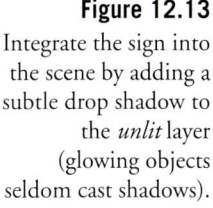

Figure 12.13
Integrate the sign into the scene by adding a subtle drop shadow to the *unlit* layer (glowing objects seldom cast shadows).

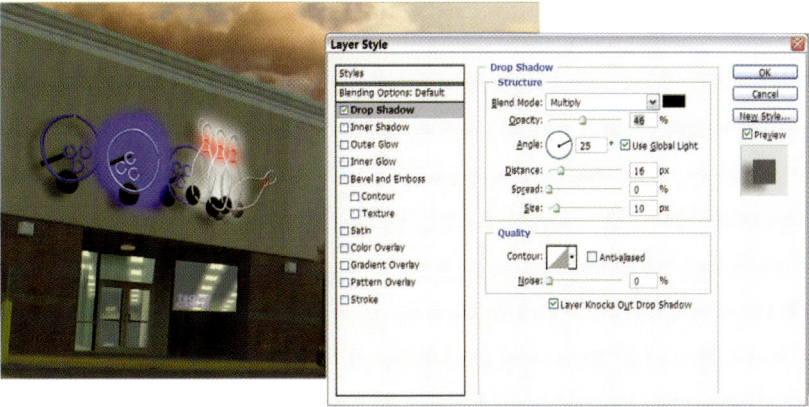

settings shown in Figure 12.13. You can also fine-tune the opacity of individual layers by digging into the layer group; layer groups are merely organizers for large numbers of layers, and it's a terrific feature for hiding scores of layers without changing a layer in any way. You can delete the layer with the grid at this point.

14. I created some ambient sounds for this video, and I think they really help the overall finished clip. Windows users, choose File > Open As and then choose the LeagueNight.mp3 file in the archive you unzipped, using QuickTime as the Open As drop-down list in this dialog box. Mac users need to open the MP3 as a QuickTime, too, but the Mac OS is not often concerned with file extensions, so there's no file type pull-down to bother with.

15. Drag the layer entry from the Layers palette into the movie file. I timed the clip so there's no timeline shifting to do.

16. File > Export > Render Video. Choose QuickTime as the file format, use H.264 compression to conserve file size, deselect the alpha channel option if you used it in a previous session, render the video to a convenient place on your hard drive, and hope the guy in the video breaks 100 tonight.

Putting a 3D Prop Into a Scene

When compositing elements into a video, traditionally film producers have resorted to what I call *The Patty Duke Effect*, used a lot to portray twins using the same actor. Scene markers were placed, and the actor was instructed not to come close to the marker. Then the camera was sandbagged, and both needed parts were acted out. I think perhaps 2% of audiences 40 years ago were actually amazed at the trick photography.

Fast-forward to today, and Photoshop, After Effects, and other photo and video compositing can be used to integrate an actor playing multiple parts and to put a prop into a scene with no constraints—the actor can move freely about the scene, and then it's up to skilled editors to make a composite that looks believable.

Let's walk before we learn to run and begin with a simple setup that uses the Vanish Point filter to create a sign in a scene that is masked and can go in front of a video clip. Because the sign doesn't move and it's in the foreground, the scene behind it doesn't violate any of the sign's space, and all will look natural in the edited clip. Then you'll get into foreground/midground/background compositing work, more challenging, but quite effective as a workaround to having to shoot a short scene on location.

Adding a One-Way Sign the Right Way

In the ZIP archive is an Illustrator drawing, One Way sign.ai, is the art I used in the following tutorial; you can use it or cobble a sign of your own, using this file as a reference. My file is functional but not as elaborate as it should be for integrating into a video, so the process I describe in the following steps deals with placing the Illustrator file first and then things you can do with the drawing as a pixel-based graphic to make it blend into the scene more thoroughly.

The sign is a persistent compositional element throughout the play time of the video, so all you need to do is correct the perspective of the sign to match the video and then use your photo retouching skills to add some character to the artwork. Here's how:

1. With Welcome to The Shades.mov loaded in the workspace, choose File > Place and then choose One Way sign.ai from the directory window.

2. The drawing is placed but its size and location can be adjusted now. Hold Shift and then drag a corner bounding box handle toward the center of the bounding box to proportionally scale the sign down. When it looks like the right size for a foreground scene object, press Enter or click the checkmark button on the Options bar to apply the transformation. In Figure 12.14 you can see the process. In addition to control and precision, using a vector drawing app to make the sign also means that it can be scaled without losing focus or image detail as a placed design on a layer.

> **Caution**
>
> If you don't own Illustrator, *don't* double-click an Illustrator layer placed thumbnail on the Layers palette, because this is an action that tells Photoshop to call Illustrator to enable you to edit the drawing. You could halt your system or halt Photoshop by doing this; it's looking for an executable file you don't have on your system. The layer is "placed," which is an Adobe term for "linked."

Figure 12.14
Place an Illustrator file to achieve good detail and crisp text.

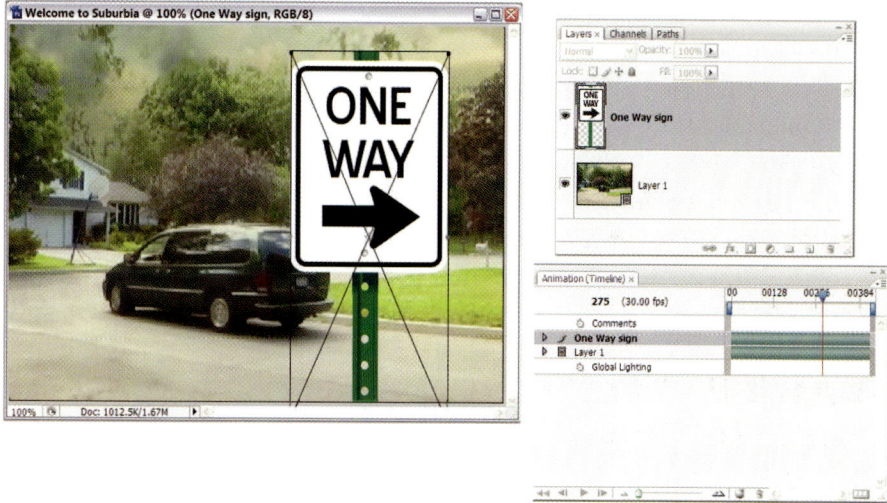

3. Use the Move tool to position the sign where it's compositionally appealing.

4. The placed file has to be turned into a pixel-based layer to perform future edits. Right-click over the drawing layer's title (not the thumbnail) and choose Rasterize Layer.

5. Choose Filter > Vanishing Point, and then with the cursor click four points to make a rectangle around the sign. Then choose Return 3D Layer to Photoshop, as shown in Figure 12.15. Then click OK to return to the workspace with a new 3D layer on the Layers palette.

Figure 12.15
For flat artwork, a simple rectangle, face-forward perspective works to make a 3D object from it.

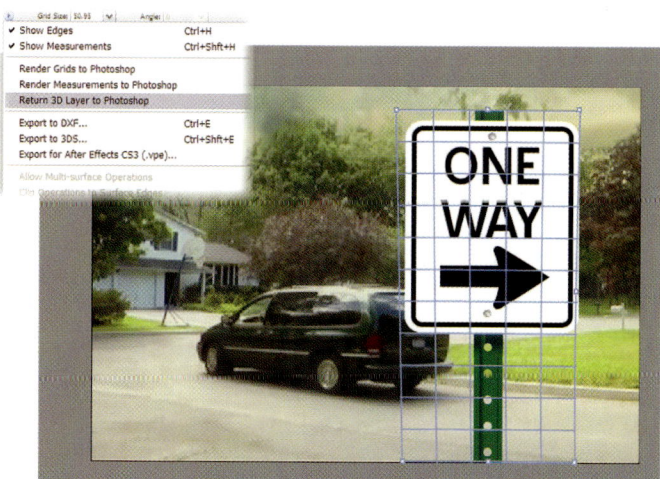

6. Regardless of whether other layers are visible, Photoshop renders a background into a layer that's been through Vanishing Point and then sent back as a 3D layer copy of the original. Therefore, you have a copy of the video layer surrounding your 3D sign…or a white background if you hid the layers (which is worse, because the white background is difficult to remove from a white sign). Double-click the temp0 material layer entry grouped beneath the 3D layer to open it for editing.

7. Choose the rectangular Marquee tool and make a rectangle selection around the green post for the sign to protect this part of the sign. Press Ctrl/Cmd+Shift+I to invert the selection. Choose the Magic Eraser tool, set the Tolerance to about 64 on the Options bar, and then click as necessary outside of the sign's profile until the unwanted areas are removed to transparency as shown in Figure 12.16. If the Magic Eraser wanders from the greenery in the background to the green of the sign post, open the History palette and then use the History brush to restore parts of the sign post. Then click the close box on the document window and reply Yes in the following attention box. The material is named temp because when you open a material on a 3D object on a layer, the bitmap info is in an unsaved document that is not embedded in the file yet but instead is written to a temporary PSB file in the same location as where the last-opened or current file you're working on is located.

Figure 12.16

Remove the unwanted background areas in your 3D layer by using the Magic Eraser tool.

8. Turn off the original One Way Sign layer and double-click the 3D layer thumbnail on the Layers palette to expose the 3D editing tools on the Options bar, and then rotate the sign so its perspective matches the video underneath. Use the curb in the video as a visual guide for the proper perspective; see Figure 12.17.

Figure 12.17
Getting the right perspective relative to a video clip is easy when you use a 3D layer.

9. The drawing was once an embedded Illustrator file that needed to be rasterized to be pixel edited, and now it's a 3D layer…that needs to be rasterized before you can retouch it as a pixel image. Right-click over the layer title on the Layers palette and then choose Rasterize 3D. To the credit of Adobe engineers, this Illustrator file has been transformed significantly, and yet the edges are clean and there's no visible pixellation.

10. Ctrl/Cmd+click the layer thumbnail to select the sign. Press Ctrl/Cmd+C to copy the layer to the clipboard and then on the Channels palette, click the Create New Channel button and then paste the clipboard copy of the sign in. Press Ctrl/Cmd+D to deselect after pasting into the new channel if necessary. It's retouching time.

11. Choose Filter > Render > Lighting Effects. The video clip displays a lot of haze, but if you look at the car's shadow, the sun is casting into the scene at about 9 o'clock. Adjust the spotlight in the Lighting Effects proxy window so it's casting on the sign from 9 o'clock.

12. Increase Ambience to about 28 so the shading on the sign is subtle.

13. Choose your alpha channel you created in Step 10 as the Texture channel. Make the height about 20 to slightly emboss and add a metallic look to the sign. Click OK to apply Lighting Effects. You can delete the alpha channel now (it might impact on your rendered video if you forget to turn alpha export off). You can also delete the original One Way Sign layer below the

temp layer. In Figure 12.18 you can see the finished scene. I used the Dodge and Burn tools a little to visually emphasize areas of the sign. In general, if you want to add contrast to specific areas of a layer, the quickest way is to set Dodge to Highlights on the Options bar and Burn to Shadows.

14. Keep this file open, save it as Sign.psd or something similar, and then delete the 3D sign. Choose File > Save As and then save the document as Welcome to The Shades.psd. By doing this, you're all set for the tutorial in the following section.

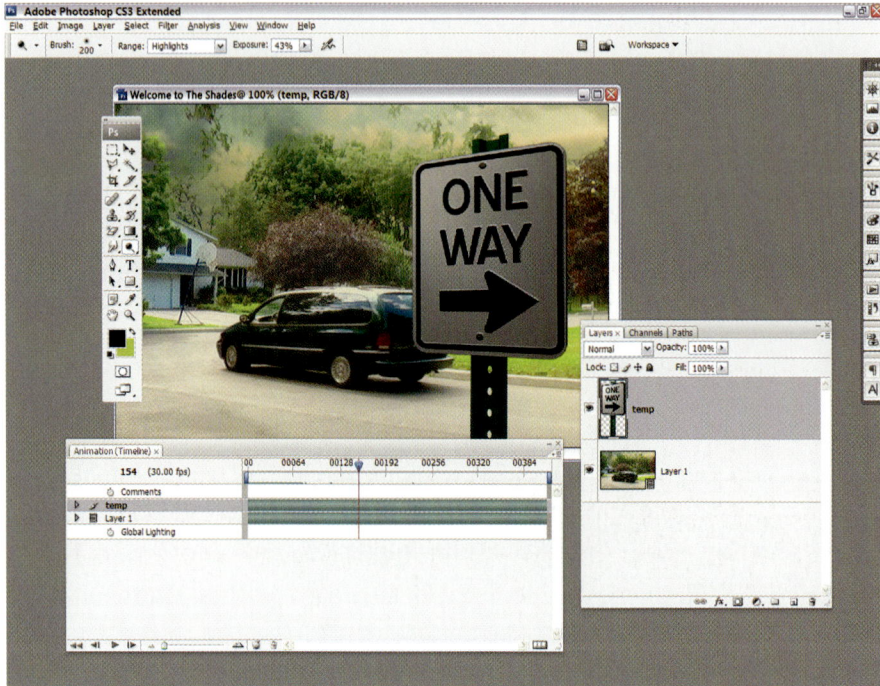

Figure 12.18
Lighting Effects doesn't change lighting in a scene but instead renders shading that can be useful to heighten the depth and photorealism of drawn objects.

Pre-Viz for Adding a Prop to Video

In Chapter 10 I walked through some pre-visualization techniques for architecture, and it's time now to use Vanishing Point to pre-viz some architecture—an arch—by drawing it in Photoshop and then exporting it as a 3D object.

Here's the story for this section: Welcome to The Shades.mov is not visually interesting without an effect; I see this as an establishing shot for a longer video—"The Shades" is a suburban development, for example, and the cut to follow moves into a story that takes place in The Shades. To make the clip an establishing shot therefore, you need an arch that has a "Welcome to" title on it. I've created a rendered 3D file for you to use, but I'd like to spend a moment showing how artists with just a little experience with modeling and rendering apps (3D programs) can leverage the power of Vanishing Point to create a crude 3D object in Photoshop to use for proportions in the modeling program for a finished model. Here are the steps:

1. Because I'm a hack at heart, I skimped on a location shoot where an arch could comfortably rest on appropriate areas of public property. Therefore, play along with me and imagine town ordinances would allow an arch's pillars resting on people's front lawns, straddling the street. Create a new layer, and then paint an arch on it, as shown in Figure 12.19. Don't paint it in perspective; you'll add the perspective in Vanishing Point. Note in this figure that I painted the arch in green, the pillars in red, and the side of the right pillar in blue. This color-coding makes it a lot easier to reference objects when the painting is exported to a modeling application. Create a blank layer on top of your painting.

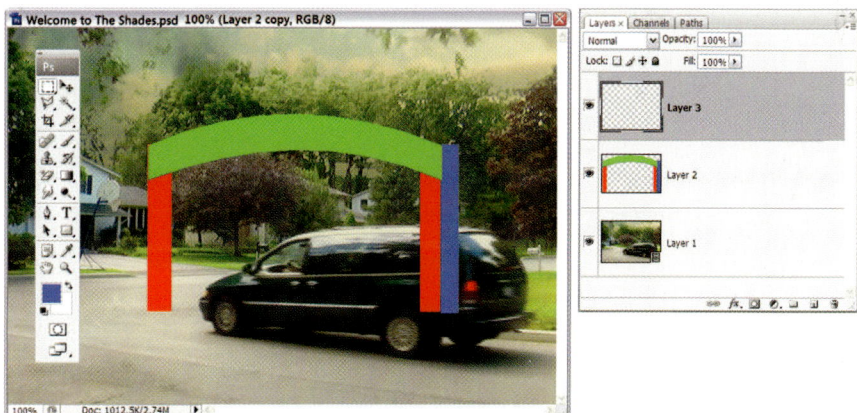

Figure 12.19
Can you paint a 3D object? Yes, with some help from Vanishing Point.

2. Copy the painting of the arch to the clipboard, hide this layer, and then highlight the blank layer on the Layers palette.

3. Choose Filter > Vanishing Point.

4. Create your first plane so it's in the correct perspective for the underlying video layer; look ahead to Figure 12.20. This task is very similar to the cube you created earlier in this chapter.

5. Extend the right side of the first plane, as shown in Figure 12.20.

6. Press Ctrl/Cmd+V to paste the arch into the perspective planes. Then, just as you did with the kid's block earlier, drag the pasted bitmap into the perspective planes and then move it around until the colored sides are in the right places. Now, you *could* command Vanishing Point to Return 3D Layer to Photoshop, but you can see the results in the preview window so there's no need to make two trips to Vanishing Point.

Figure 12.20
Essentially, the camera's view in this special effects scene will only reveal two perspective planes of the arch you design.

7. Here's where this assignment gets hypothetical; if you have a modeling program that can import 3D Studio files (or DXFs), read on. If you have no modeler and no modeling experience, please read on anyway; this Photoshop feature might pique your interest enough to buy or download a demo of a modeling/rendering program. Choose Export to 3DS or DXF (see your modeler's documentations) and then put the saved file in a folder you can easily find later; see Figure 12.21. Name the file Arch.3ds or Arch.dxf so I can reference some corresponding files in the following steps.

Photoshop automatically generates textures for the exported model into the same folder as the 3D model, but the PNG files (you don't get to choose a different file format) contain unwanted background layer pixels. I'll show you a quick fix in the following steps. Don't click OK after exporting the model; click Cancel and return to the workspace.

Figure 12.21
You've just created a 3D model.

8. Double-click the workspace to bring up the Open dialog. You're going to have two PNG files in the model folder, but you only need to edit Arch0.png; scout it down and open it. See the sidebar for the low-down on texture mapping, the 3D objects Vanishing Point creates, and why you want to edit the PNG images Photoshop creates.

2D Objects in 3D Space and Transparency

Earlier I'd described 3D objects Photoshop creates as "eggshells"; they have no true depth, however, they exist in three dimensions. This is fine for simple planes such as building architecture fronts and cereal packages. This is also not a problem when importing 3D objects into modeling programs from Photoshop; however, the associated PNG images become a problem if you try to use them unedited in a modeling program because areas of your textures that should be transparent are not. The underlying pixel areas on other layers (or pure white when layers are all hidden) obscure your pre-visualization in the modeling program. This is why you'll often want to edit the PNG files before loading a 3D object into a modeling program. If you don't, you only see flat shaded planes in your modeling app with no holes cut out, for example, for windows you might have on a model of a store.

9. You can use the plain Eraser tool, the Brush tool in Clear painting mode, or if you want precision, you can put the PNG file in Layer Mask mode and then remove the unwanted layer areas so only the arch and the front of the pillars (the red and the green areas) remain and then save the file. See Figure 12.22.

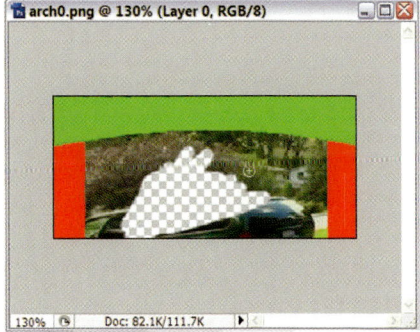

Figure 12.22
Edit away the areas you want to show through in a modeling application.

Building a Model Based on an Exported Model

I'll make this section brief and only an education point because this isn't a book on modeling. What you want to do in a modeling application to create the synthetic arch for the video clip is open or import the model—different modelers have different terms for placing, merging... essentially bringing the Photoshop model into the modeling program. You then build over the imported Photoshop model; the proportions are correct because they were correct in Photoshop. You'll want to match the camera angle to the video scene, and often this can be done by eye; check out Chapter 10 on exporting camera views for complex scenes where angle matching is critical.

In Figure 12.23, I've used File > Open in Luxology modo, and after 30 seconds of twiddling with camera views, the mockup (the pre-viz) looks good—this camera pose will work fine for the video integration. Also note that the render window at bottom right of this figure clearly shows the transparency of the PNG file as mapped to the planes that Vanishing Point exported. In your own work, you can use this transparency attribute to quickly set up objects that go through arches or are behind one another.

In even the least expensive modeling programs, an Extrude feature is included; I used modo's extrusion feature extensively to build the arch you can see in Figure 12.24. Extruding is accomplished by taking a 2D wireframe shape (sometimes called a *profile*) and then telling the application to create surfaces that extend in a direct line behind or in front of the profile to create depth for the width and height of the 2D profile. If you look at a lot of common objects in the real world, their geometry can be described as a 2D profile projected into a third dimension:

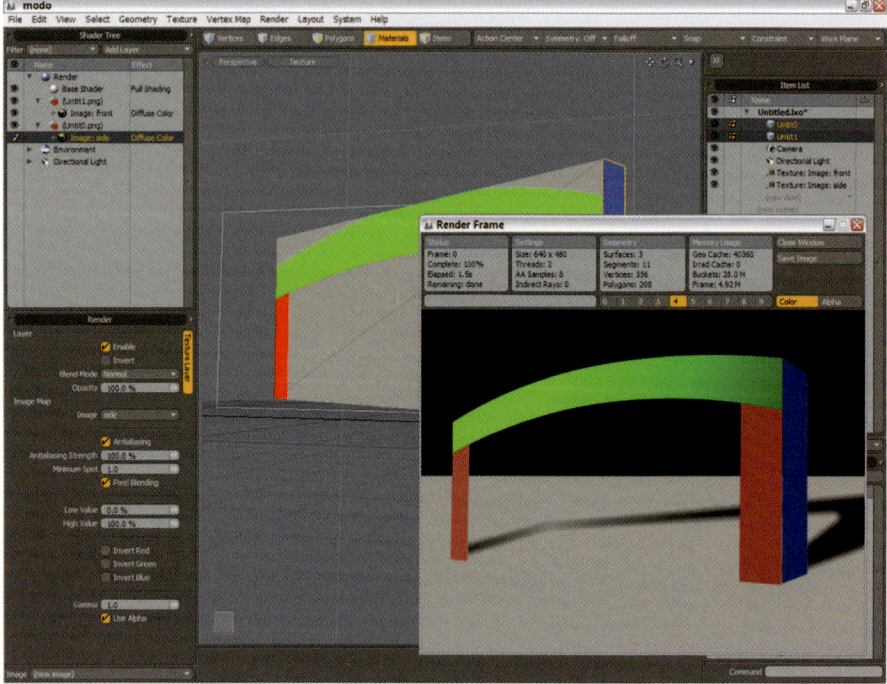

Figure 12.23
Bring the model Photoshop exported into your favorite modeling program.

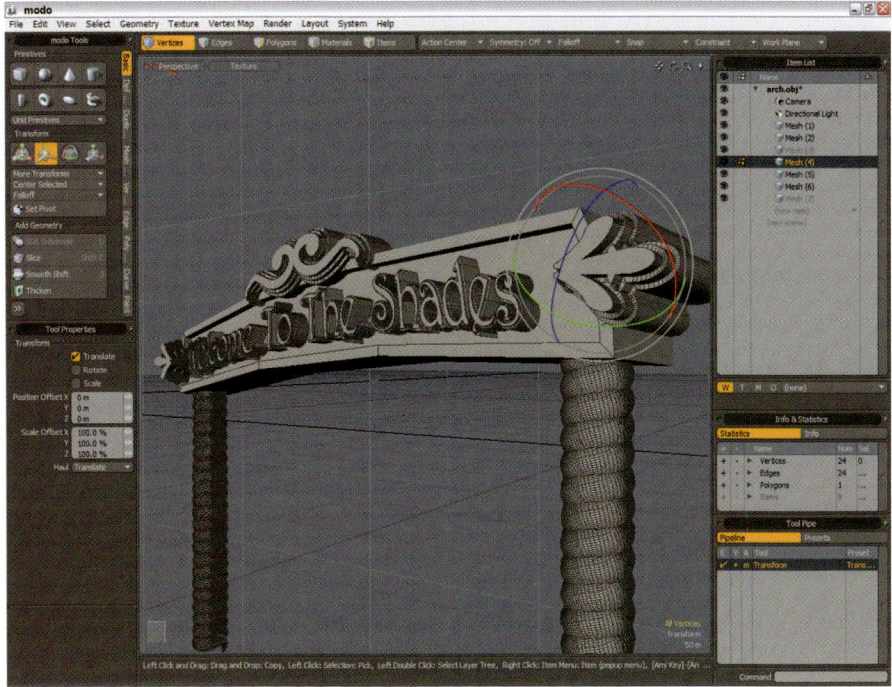

Figure 12.24
Modeling often consists of projecting a 2D shape along a path to make the third dimension.

Building blocks are squares projected into a depth dimension, cookie cutters project dough to make gingerbread men, and so on.

The pillars in Figure 12.24 were built similarly: I designed a helix (a coily cord shape) and then swept a large 2D circle along the path the helix describes.

Finally, I used a dull marble texture to cover the arch model and then lit the scene to match the video clip.

Clone Source and Hiding Moving Image Areas

We move on now that the model arch has been rendered to image file format; in arch.png, modo rendered transparency around the arch, and then I did a little finessing. Specifically, I erased little areas at the base of the pillars to create the final illusion that the grass in the video is growing around the pillars: Sometimes you need to think "back to front" when compositing with transparency. Additionally, I hand-painted a faint perspective shadow to "root" the arch in the scene. I did not extend the shadow into the area that falls on the street, because it would create much more work removing it when the car passes across the street. This is artistically acceptable because the shading in the video is diffuse, and a suggestion of a shadow often does the trick. Audiences don't examine the *correctness* of a shadow so much as they balk when there's an *absence* of one.

Begin by opening the arch.png file, and then with Welcome to The Shades.psd in the workspace:

1. Drag the layer entry on the Layers palette for the arch into the video document window to duplicate it, and then position it as you see in Figure 12.25. Close the arch.png file without saving changes.

Figure 12.25
Duplicating a layer to a different document window is as simple as drag and drop.

2. Choose Layer > Video Layers > New Blank Video Layer. A blank video layer appears on the Layers palette, and it's marked with a special icon. Unlike normal layers, video layers change over time, and when you paint and clone on them, your painting disappears in the following video frame. This is because you only painted in one moment in time in the video; I show you how to make a painting that changes and *extends across time* in this tutorial.

3. Move the thumb on the Animation palette to the point in time when the arch clearly violates the green van: Frame 31 is a good one. From a workflow standpoint, you'd eliminate the overlapping arch starting at the first point that it shouldn't cross the green van. However, you're just getting your feet wet with Clone Source here, so Frame 31 provides the best beginning point to gain experience with a technique.

4. Zoom into about 500% resolution. Choose the Clone Stamp tool from the Tools palette, set the Clone Stamp brush size to 9 pixels diameter, and then get the Clone Source palette. If it's not docked, choose Window > Clone Source.

5. Click the bottom video layer on the Layers palette; this is the layer from which you'll clone.

6. Alt/Opt+click on an area where the pillar intrudes on the green van. It's okay that you can't see the target sampling point on the van. Photoshop can clone from one layer to a different one, even when you can't clearly see the content of the source layer. Notice on the Clone Source palette that it says Layer 1 below the stamp icons.

7. On the Layers palette, click the top video layer title to make it the current editing layer. On the Options bar, make sure Current Layer is the Sample drop-down choice. The Clone Source is sort of overriding the Current Layer setting.

8. Hover your cursor before stoking and make sure on the Clone Source palette that X and Y Offset and Frame Offset are all at 0. You want to clone the green van, matching position and frame number, throughout the video where the arch intrudes over it. If you wanted to create a special effect such as several of the same person moving around in a scene, you'd want to use (X and Y) Offset. Similarly, if you wanted to create copies of an object in a scene moving around at different times, you'd use Frame Offset. But not in this example.

9. You have the option on the Clone Source palette to Show Overlay, which is a little like putting tracing vellum over the area you're cloning from; in this example it apparently dims the pillars so you can more clearly see the clone of the van. I'm not showing it in this tutorial but do indeed try it out.

10. Carefully stroke over the pillar area, hiding it with the sampled van area, as shown in Figure 12.26. The most critical area is the edge where the van meets the pillar. Try to keep your stroke smooth and follow the slight slope of the top of the van. Time is literally on your side, however; because the van is moving from frame to frame, continuity between cloned frames to prevent a fluttering effect is a challenge, but certainly not impossible to achieve.

11. You can move on to the next frame once you're done with Frame 31 by clicking the Selects Next Frame button on the Animation palette. However, let's approach this like a pro and complete the sequence where the van passes in front of the pillar by going to Frame 22 on the timeline. Also, consider setting up a keyboard shortcut for Selects Next Frame, like you did earlier with Paste Keyframe(s). This is a smart move from a workflow point of view because it's quicker to keystroke to the next frame than moving your cursor to the Animation palette and then repeatedly back to the document window. Ctrl/Cmd+Alt/Opt+A (a good mnemonic for "advance") is a comfortable keyboard gesture, and I just overwrote Photoshop's default shortcut for Select All Layers. To me it's expendable.

Figure 12.26
Instead of erasing areas of the pillar, you clone over it with background video areas to hide it.

That's it; there's nothing more to teach about hiding the arch areas for both autos from Frame 22 to Frame 275. Consider the half hour or so you spend cloning as refining a technique you didn't previously own (*no one* did, because Clone Source is a new feature to Photoshop). However, the video isn't finished; the next section deals with a thorny problem—how to prevent jitter when masking an object that is only moving a little from frame to frame.

Moving a Static Layer's Contents Across Time

I'm sure you've seen clumsy masks in some of the cheaper films from past decades. The girl's hair has fringing against an obviously painted matte, you're distracted by the matte outline of a person to the extent that you ignore the performance; you get the idea.

A similar problem exists in this composition. The green van comes to what traffic cops call a "rolling stop" at the intersection; if you examine Frames 103–127 or so (it depends on exactly where you placed the arch), the van's decelerating mass makes it bob and even move backwards ever so slightly. It's this "ever so slightly" stuff that will mess up an otherwise convincing illusion, because unless you own After Effects and its motion tracking and vector masking features, Clone Source will not get you where you want to go for half a second's worth of frames where an object jiggles. Inevitably (and I tried this) you'll introduce distracting jitter if you try to clone over these frames.

The solution lies in copying the tail of the van to a static layer and then moving its position on the Animation palette frame by frame. You can get away with this trick because the van is visible moving in 2D during this sequence; there's no noticeable perspective change until it turns the corner. Follow these steps:

1. At Frame 103, with the Pen tool, carefully drag a selection around the tail of the van, the area where it crosses the arch's pillar.

2. On the Paths palette, Ctrl/Cmd+click the Work Path thumbnail to load the path as a selection.

3. Press L to toggle to the current Lasso tool, and then on the Layers palette with the bottom video layer chosen as the current editing layer, choose Edit > Copy Merged. The copied area is copied as a still and not a video object. Don't deselect the marquee yet.

4. Create a new layer on the top of the Layers palette's stack and then choose Edit > Paste Into. The copied still object is pasted in its proper place, surrounded by an unnecessary mask. Right-click over the mask thumbnail on the Layers palette and choose to either apply or delete the layer mask; either choice works in this example.

5. Advance to Frame 104. Clearly the tail of the van is not aligned to the underlying video.

6. For this layer (it should be Layer 4) on the Animation palette, click the stopwatch icon for Position and then with the keyboard arrows, nudge Layer 4's contents into position.

7. Repeat Step 6 until the van starts moving again.

8. On the Animation palette, click the Opacity stopwatch at Frame 102, and then on the Layers palette set the Opacity to 0%. Right-click over the new keyframe the Animation palette created and choose Hold Interpolation.

9. Repeat Step 8 with Frame 128 or whatever frame is one after your last position change. Now you have a clean Hold entrance for your little masking trick and a clean exit. See Figure 12.27, where I've highlighted the path just to show the area you want to copy. You can delete this path at any time now.

Figure 12.27
A little hand animation can smooth out video areas the audience would surely spot as artificial.

Adding Finishing Touches

I have a friend in Hollywood who examines my work with a microscope; he'll look at my matte work frame by frame and then critique the minutest details. This is helpful but irksome because I don't *solicit* his critique. This exposition clip isn't finished because you edited out the arch pillars where they crossed the vehicles in entirety; the pillars should be partially opaque as viewed through the windshield of the passing van.

You could have edited in partial opacity as you use Clone Source by reducing the opacity of the Clone Stamp tool, but this would have created a lousy, painful workflow, adjusting the opacity back and forth for every frame. Instead, you'll now set up a second Clone Source, one of the arch layer; Clone Source offers four Clone Source targets, and you can even clone across different documents. This addition of verisimilitude is not difficult because you don't need an entrance or exit for the new video layer you clone onto; you just begin and finish. Because new video layers are 100% transparent when you add them, there will be no need to change opacity on the layer as you did with the tail of the van. Follow along here:

1. With the top layer as your current editing layer, choose Layer > Video Layers > New Blank Video Layer.

2. Choose the static arch layer on the Layers palette, and then on the Clone Source palette, click the second Clone Source button; you've been using the default (first of four) Clone Source.

3. Starting at about Frame 34 (depending on where you located the arch) with the Clone Stamp tool, Alt/Opt+click over the arch and then switch to the new video editing layer (it should be titled Layer 5 on the Layers palette).

4. Set Opacity on the Options bar to about 50%, clone the arch into the windshield, and then move on to the next frame.

That's it; see Figure 12.28. Also check out Adobe's Help Viewer on the topic of Clone Source (press F1 or choose Help from the Help menu). Adobe has some useful shortcuts keys and additional info on using Clone Source. You can use the Spot Healing brush instead of the Clone Stamp, and you can invert an overlay to show gray instead of the clone target frame by frame, which really shows you when your target cloning is perfectly aligned to a video clip.

To get super-picky (again), the leaves wafting from branches in the video at screen right are a compositionally important element to the film, but they really should go in the foreground, in front of the arch because their scale is clearly wrong. I tried the cloning trick described in this chapter, and it's an exercise in futility. Although the leaves visibly move around, they're interlaced and composed of very few pixels—too few to labor over cloning in front of the arch.

Figure 12.28
Clone at partial opacity to add scene areas viewed through windows and also to add highlights and reflections that appear to move in a video.

So when you have movement but the objects moving are too small to effectively clone, you get creative. I animated a model of a branch waving around using Cinema 4D, Cinema 4D wrote the animation sequence out to MOV file format with transparency, and I placed the movie as a layer on top of the composition. Ninety-nine percent of the effectiveness of this trick is that as a foreground object in a shaded video, by carefully lighting the modeled branch, it reads quite realistically, and the audience looks at the movement and not the object's detail. The Branches wafting.mov file is in the ZIP archive you downloaded, and in the fol-

Compression and Alpha Masking

This book would be an incomplete resource if I didn't talk a little about video compression; you'll at some point want to exhibit your work on any number of online video parlors such as YouTube and MTV and want the best quality for the smallest file size.

The Branches wafting.mov is a perfect example of how I spent five minutes building and rendering an animation, and then several hours devising the best scheme for getting it to you in the smallest possible download size. QuickTime does support compression on movies that contain alpha masks; in Photoshop you choose Animation under Compression Settings. However, compression on movies with masking is not nearly as good as straight compression on a 24-bit movie. Part of the trick to achieve greater compression is to set a low keyframe rate. You have to artistically judge, through trial and error, how few keyframes you can get away with, but the Branches Wafting movie contains very little visual data; it's essentially a silhouette of waving leaves. By specifying a keyframe every 15 frames, I was able to save the compressed movie at slightly over 6MB as compared to Auto keyframing, which yielded an 11MB file.

The fewer keyframes you specify, the jerkier the motion, which works on some videos but not on others. Simply put, a keyframe is rendered to file with the greatest fidelity while transitional frames take the greatest compression (hence least quality). So the fewer keyframes, the greater compression you achieve.

Later in this chapter I needed to deliver to you another animation that needed masking; I wrote the animation out to a PNG sequence of still images using SuperPNG. You should add SuperPNG to your toolkit (www.fnordware.com/superpng); it's a free plug-in that crunches PNGs with transparency more effectively than Photoshop's default PNG filter, it can retain metadata about file resolution, and it can color tag a PNG to Adobe RGB color space. The animation compressed better than compressing a movie as a movie. The reason why the still image sequence is in a ZIP archive is for organization's sake; you don't squeeze a PNG any better than its native compression when you put it in a ZIP, StuffIt, or other archive format. In fact, you increase the sum saved file size slightly because zipping an archive adds header info to the archive, usually several KB.

lowing steps you'll add three copies of it to the composition. It's a short clip that ping-pongs: The first frame is the same as the last; by offsetting three copies along time, the branches wave throughout the 427 frame video clip perfectly. I created the ping-pong short file to demonstrate a technique and also to save on download file size and time.

1. Open the Branches wafting.mov file in Photoshop. Then drag its entry on the Layers palette into the Shades movie composition. Arrange it so it crops out of frame at upper right, obscuring the leaves in the background video, and make sure it's the top layer. You can close the Branches wafting.mov file without saving changes.

2. On the Animation palette, scoot this track's position to start at the head of the video.

3. Duplicate this layer twice by dragging its title into the Create a New Layer icon on the Layers palette. Alternatively, press Ctrl/Cmd+J twice.

4. On the Animation palette, butt the duplicate sequences so their in points match each other's end point. The last duplicate will finish outside of the Work Area and this is okay; actually, if this branch bounced around exactly the same way three complete times, the audience would smell something. Like a good magician, you don't call attention to a deception—three cycles is usually the maximum you can get out of an animation before it appears staged and phony. See Figure 12.29.

Figure 12.29
Small details often can make or break a special effects scene.

5. I stress the use of audio as a sweetener for video work, and this example is no exception. Add Welcome to The Shades.mp3 to the video before rendering the composition, just as you did with the League Night composition.

The MP3 clip has a little tune in it, but more importantly some ambient outdoors sound and car engines. There is something "not quite right" about a video without ambient sound; the lack of any sound whatsoever is a distraction to the audience, but adding ambient sound actually takes some of the attention *away* from artificial elements in your video. I recommend starting a sound effects collection for your video work; begin by recording different room tones, and check out online resources for free special effects clips such as glass shattering, sneezes, general crowd mummers, and so on. www.wavsource.com/ has a nice collection, as does www.grsites.com/sounds.

Combining Animation with Models and Videos

I wanted to share a fairly easy and relaxing tutorial with you after all this heady 3D stuff you've worked so hard on in the rest of this chapter. This is a little "what if" pre-visualization work; what if my backyard neighbor decided to install a large and truly ghastly fountain?

Integrating a Still-Rendered Image with the Video

The fountain in the following tutorial was modeled and rendered out of Luxology modo using a lot of modo's sculpting features, but overall it's a render with an alpha channel just like the Shades arch. The water for the fountain was built using particles in Wondertouch ParticleIllusion (see Chapter 16 for links to this invaluable program and others), and the background video is simply a guy instructed to gawk at a visual placeholder, shake his head, and leave frame. On your own, you have the technique down now to make the fellow actually cross in front of the fountain (you use Clone Source), but I staged the video so he doesn't *need* to cross into the fake fountain to make the whimsical clip work. I'll show you in the following steps some integration techniques (drawing from your Photoshop still image editing skills) and how to offset time tracks for duplicates of the gushing water. You can therefore effectively use a single clip several times; offsetting two tracks in time is even today a popular animation technique for distracting an audience from realizing they're seeing the same animation twice or several times at once onscreen.

1. Open Neighbors.mov. Scrub the timeline at around Frame 133. This is where the fellow gets closest to the left of the scene, where you'll add the stone tuna.

2. Press Ctrl/Cmd+R to display rulers around the document, and then drag a vertical guide out of the ruler at left and put it at the fellow's left as an editor's marker for the right-most edge where you can position the rendered fountain

Chapter 12 ■ Creating 3D Scene Props   417

image. Then press Ctrl/Cmd+R to hide the rulers—Photoshop rulers have the disagreeable tendency to pop up in all subsequent documents you open unless you hide rulers in the current open document window. See Figure 12.30 for the setup.

3. Open Big Fish.png. Turn off Pixel Aspect Ratio Correction from the View menu. Duplicate its layer to the video document window and then with the Move tool position it to the left of the guide you dragged in Step 2. Then hide the guide by pressing Ctrl/Cmd+; (View > Show > Guides) and see Figure 12.31.

Figure 12.30
Leave a marker for the closest "safe" position of the image you'll add.

Figure 12.31
Now the guy will come very close to but never cross the fountain image area.

> **Tip**
>
> I did use Vanishing Point a little to reproportion the fountain sculpture after rendering it. Its top-to bottom-axis of rotation (the X axis) wasn't quite perfect for the scene, so I exaggerated the top of the sculpture, in place in the video document, by defining a perspective plane whose top is larger than its bottom. This trick leaves almost no visible distortion on objects that are not planar (cubes and buildings are planar). No, the fish fountain could be best described as a cylinder, not a cube or a plane, and therefore X axis distortion isn't really visible. If I had to modify its perspective front left to right (the Y axis), then I would have encountered trouble; squishing the fish would have been fairly obvious to the audience.

4. The sun in the video is casting a shadow at about 8 o'clock into the scene. I correctly lit the model, but wrote it out to image file format without a shadow. Create a layer on top of the video (beneath the fish), put it in Multiply mode on the Layers palette at about 75% opacity, and then with the Brush tool hold Alt/Opt and then click over a deeply shaded area at image right to sample a good color for the fish shadow you'll paint. Shadows are seldom pure black, especially shadows outdoors cast on green lawns that reflect some blue in the sky. As a rule, I always sample colors to paint into photos and videos. Doing this take the peril of introducing an eye-chosen, non-real color into the composition.

5. Paint a shape that looks appropriate for the fountain to be casting, as shown in Figure 12.32. Then adjust the opacity for this layer until the shadow looks proper for the video. Again, shadows are funny things: They don't necessarily have to be optically correct, but the *lack* of one tips off an audience all the time. Shadows (and highlights) put an object into a scene instead of on top of one.

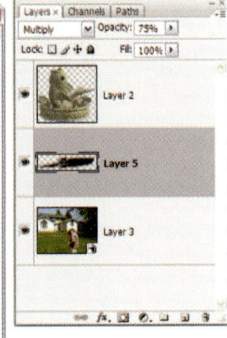

Figure 12.32

The audience won't be examining the *shape* of the shadow. But they'd become wary if the fountain didn't *have* a shadow.

> **Tip**
>
> A good, quick, and effective way to make a perspective shadow (one that casts into a scene, as opposed to a scene-flattening drop-shadow) is to load an object surrounded by layer transparency as a selection (Ctrl/Cmd+click its layer thumbnail), create a new layer underneath, and then with this layer chosen fill the marquee with a deep shadow color. Put the shadow object into Free Transform mode and then specify Skew by right-clicking inside the Free Transform bounding box to access the context menu. Skew the object in the direction opposite the sun in the scene and then switch to Scale mode from the context menu and make the object much shorter than it is wide.

6. Create a new layer on top of all the others.

7. Logically and realistically, after a few days grass would be sprouting around the base of the fountain. Zoom into the base of the fountain, Choose the Brush tool and then choose the Brushes palette from the docking strip (or press F5 if it's not on the docking strip).

8. Find Grass on the default palette; it's clearly marked as a little sprouting silhouette with 134 beneath it. One hundred thirty-four pixels is way too large a diameter for use in the video, but you'll soon change that.

9. Choose the Expanded view from the Brush palette menu. Uncheck Color Dynamics because although the color scattering this preset provides is nice, it's inappropriate for use in this composition. Also, try reducing Spacing to 10% in the Brush Tip Shape entry on the palette (click an entry to open it; they're sort of like tabs). With small spacing you'll have much greater control over the placement of the grass blades.

10. Hold Alt/Opt to toggle to the Eyedropper tool, sample a good grass color, release Alt/Opt, and then right-click in the document to display the context menu. Set the size to about 22 pixels. When the Brushes palette and your screen look like Figure 12.33, *click* a few times, don't drag the cursor, over the base of the fountain.

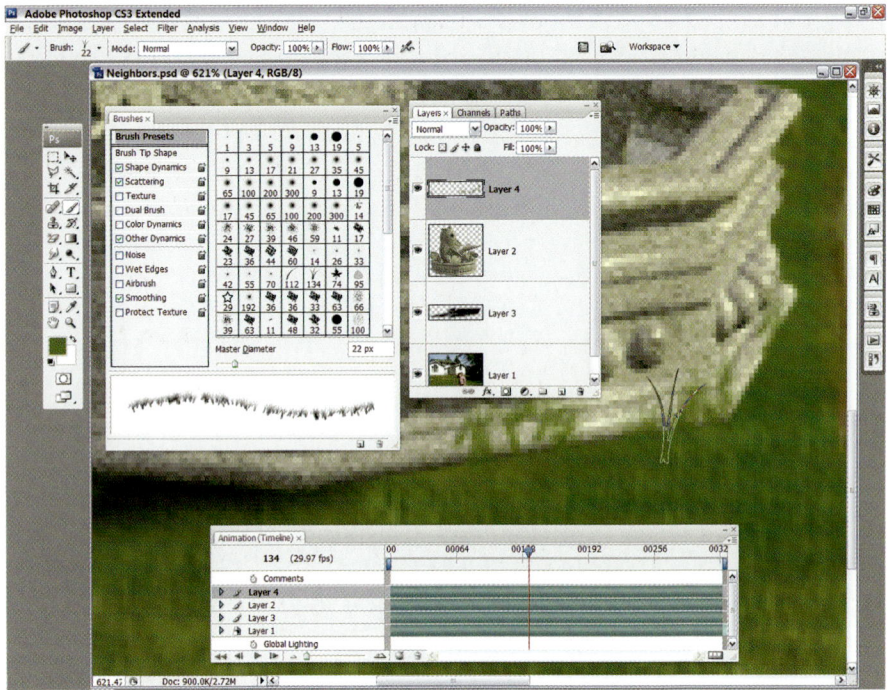

Figure 12.33
Blades of grass will look realistic even though they're a painting because of the small resolution of the blades.

Adding Water to the Fountain

It's time to bring in the water. Make sure you popped the Fountain.zip archive and can easily find the folder. Then you begin by compiling the stills as an animation:

1. Choose File > Open (or double-click the workspace) and then choose any of the files in the Fountain folder you created. Check the Image Sequence checkbox and when queried about frame rate, choose 29.97fps because this is the resolution of the Neighbors.mov file. Turn off Pixel Aspect Ratio Correction from the View menu when prompted to do so.

2. Duplicate the video layer over to the Neighbors document window and as the top layer, position it using the Move tool in an appropriate place such as in the water in the base to the right.

3. The water looks phony, even when animated (but the animation *itself* is good). Fortunately, the animation can be enhanced to near-believability by first decreasing the opacity of the layer to about 70% and by putting it in Lighter Color blending mode on the Layers palette.

4. As a video layer, without converting it to a Smart Object, you can access Image > Adjustments > Shadows/Highlights. In Shadows/Highlights, drag the Shadows slider down to 0 and the Highlights slider up to about 23% as shown

in Figure 12.34. What you've done is left the deeper regions of the water alone and darkened the highlights, making the water look more realistic. Notice that Shadows/Highlights is appended beneath the video layer on the Layers palette as a Smart Filter. The layer is not a Smart Object, however, and you can change the nondestructive settings for the Shadows/Highlights Smart Filter at any time by double-clicking its title on the Layers palette.

Figure 12.34

Water is so simple! It's three atoms, but getting *fake* water to look real is *not* quite so simple.

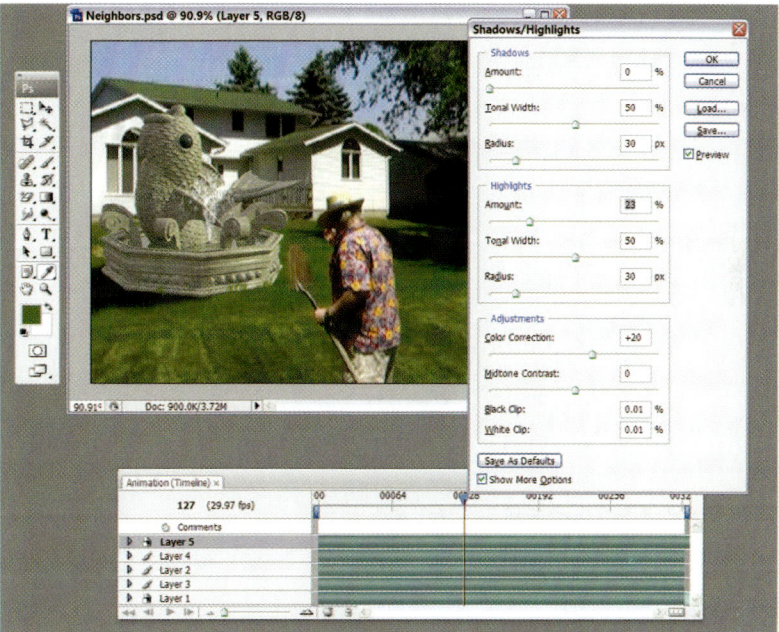

Caution

Smart Objects are terrific. So is chocolate. And indulging in either isn't good for you. A video layer converted to a Smart Object can noticeably slow down loading the file and plump up the saved file size. In general, if you need to make a video correction via a filter, try the filters available to video layers, try some of the Scripts (File > Scripts), and only as a last resort (Free Transformations, for example) do you make a video layer into a Smart Object, an irreversible process.

5. Now that the single water animation is tonally correct, duplicate it and put it around the fountain. The first thing you'll want to do is put at least one gusher behind the fish layer to make the composition more dimensional; the other can go in front of the fountain layer if you like; use your artistic taste.

6. Shape at least one of the water duplicate videos differently. Without converting the water video to a Smart Object, you can perform a minor Free Transform on it. Press Ctrl/Cmd+T and then scale a duplicate water so it's tall and narrow, then press Enter to apply the transformation (which is permanent, a destructive change unlike many other Photoshop operations).

7. I've given you a little more water animation footage than the playlength of the guy on the bottom layer. This is so you can offset the times of the water duplicate videos so they don't all dance in unison. Animated water looks phony when the choreography is timed; only real timed fountains look real, if somewhat cloying. On the Animation palette drag one of the tracks for a water video so its start point meets the start of the composition (the Work Area). Its tail will go off the Work Area, and this is okay.

8. Offset another water track. In Figure 12.35 I've provided a close-up inset image of the right side of the Animation palette. As you can see, the tracks don't line up, and this is what you want to do.

9. There's one final nit-pickism to perform. Depending on the position of the water, one or two might not look like they're anchored in the fountain but floating a little above them. Create a new layer on top of the layers stack, zoom way in to the bottom of a water video, choose the Brush tool with a 3-pixel tip, hold Alt/Opt, and click near the water to sample its surrounding color,

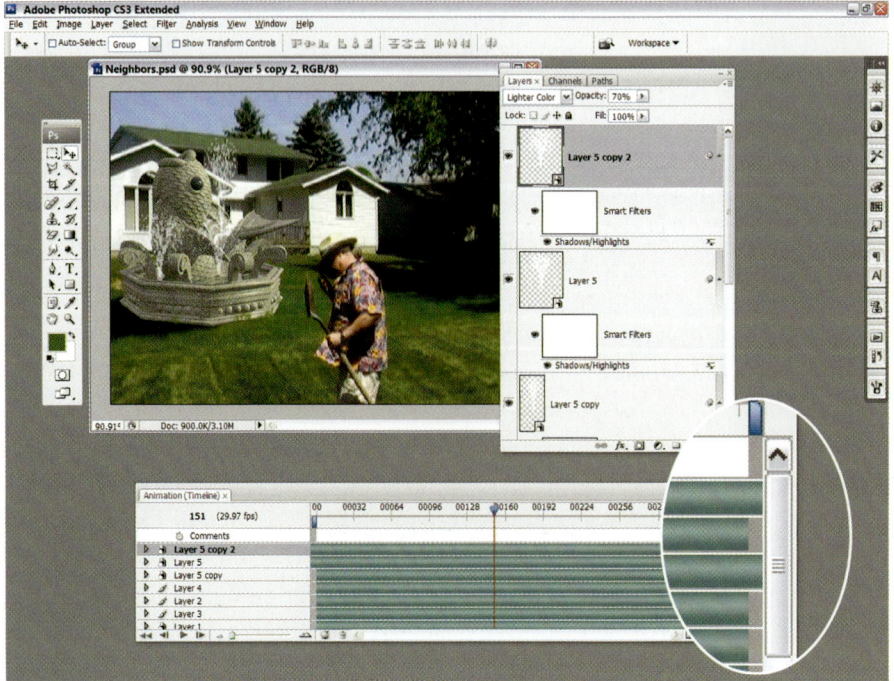

Figure 12.35
Offsetting time among tracks (layers) in a video composition prevents the animations from looking staged and static.

release Alt/Opt, and then paint a very small "V" to taper the appearance of the base of the water.

10. Reduce the opacity of the Brush tool to about 50% and then stroke above the "V" shape. What you've done is to make it *unclear* at 100% viewing distance where the water connects to a submerged pipe in the fountain. You haven't actually hidden the bottom of the video, you've just visually introduced some ambiguity, and this is a terrific trick used in digital special effects to reconcile visually impossible stuff. In *Total Recall*, Arnold Schwarzenegger's woman's mask was physically impossible to take off; After Effects was used to fudge the scene. In *Transformers*, much ambiguity was added to reconcile the reality that there's too much mass for a three-story tall robot to collapse into a four-foot tall Camero. See Figure 12.36.

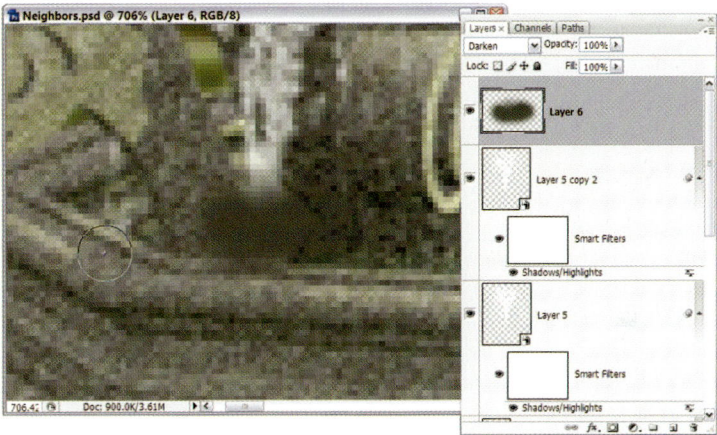

Figure 12.36
Make the area where the water is supposed to connect to the pool or a pipe a little fuzzy to the audience.

11. Add the audio Neighbors.mp3 to the composition before rendering it to video. I have nothing but a few robins chirping, some ambient microphone wind, and a few gurgles the audience will presume are coming from the fountain. If you like and you have access to audio equipment, you could in fact add some monologue to the fellow. Note that for several seconds you can't see his face; try the simple, classic, "*Honnnnnn-ey!*," or "Well, at least it's not a Boy of Brussels…" Otherwise, consider this a job well done.

Seriously consider the career possibilities you can now approach with some of the info in this chapter. Digital matte painting is performed quite similarly to steps in these tutorials; the resolution of movies is greater, so you use a bigger Brush tool diameter (!) and render larger models, but you get the point. All of this is piecemeal work for larger bodies of work called *movies*; you can now build interesting opening credits for podcasts, make nice establishing shots for home DVD movies, and wetten a dry PowerPoint presentation, but props are parts of storytelling and not the whole story.

I'm personally and professionally delighted that digital tools such as Photoshop can be used for special effects today. A lot of classic films, Alfred Hitchcock's in particular, would withstand the trial of time a lot more if someone went in and replaced 1950s "state of the art" effects shots with digital ones. Overall, the less an audience focuses on your video trickery, the more they can get into the *story*, the whole point of enjoying a film.

Video editing, just like Photoshop still image editing, is often best performed when the viewer is unaware of the work.

Part V

sfx and Compositing Techniques

13

Creating Fun, Simple, Effective fx

Learning to walk before you run doesn't necessarily take the fun out of walking; this chapter gets you up and running with special effects—and then I quicken the pace and complexity of fx in future chapters.

You begin by cobbling an animated sparkle, a pointy highlight, very popular in today's cosmetic commercials. I'll then show you how to fade it up and out and to match the moving position in an underlying video layer. I move on to creating a bolt of lightning in a scene—quite useful for Goth castle scenes, a punctuation to prophetic statements in commercials, and a must for Ben Franklin clips. You'll also simulate a camera jitter, which can help out an earthquake scene, and then I show you how to build a split-screen scene. Finally, I cover time distortion; how to speed time up, slow it down, and even how to reverse time.

If all of this sounds interesting, great. If it sounds hard or overly ambitious, don't worry; it's not. It helps to read Chapter 4 on transitions before beginning, and Chapter 8 on animation and rotoscoping is a useful precursor, too. However, I'll walk you through all the steps in the sections to follow, and by the end of this chapter you'll be able to add sparkle as well as shakes and other effects to perk up any clip you're handed.

Adding a Cross-Star Sparkle to a Clip

Actually, cinematographers have tried to *avoid* specular glares in film for decades, but recent times have rediscovered the aesthetics of a highlight (it's good for calling attention to an area in a movie without using an arrow!) and iconized a sparkle in cartoons and TV commercials. Before we begin, let me point out that a sparkle, a highlight with spokes on it, is *not* the same camera lens reflex as a lens flare. I took a look at a number of pieces of bum footage that contain an unwanted highlight bouncing from shiny metal into the lens and concluded a number of things:

1. A glare has no ring around it as lens flares do; therefore, using Photoshop's Filter > Render > Lens Flare effect is out of the question.

2. The sparkle's spokes depend on the coating of the camera lens. My budget DV camera produces four highlight spokes at about 45, 135, 225, and 315 degrees. However, I'll show you how to get fancy and suggest a double-coated lens that produces twin spokes at these approximate degree angles in this chapter, so the traditionally unwanted artifact looks elegant and expensive.

3. A glare usually is not persistent; it happens in about a second when the subject or camera is moving, so building an animation of a sparkle takes less than 30 frames.

4. It's a Hollywood fantasy that a highlight's spokes rotate, but it's a fantasy so ingrained in the audience's mind they expect it, and we'll deliver this.

Figure 13.1 shows a frame from Pirate movie.mov. As you'll see, the plastic cutlass catches some occasional highlights but without the classic spokes because it's a cheap Halloween prop coated in an equally cheap metallic paint.

Figure 13.1
You can enhance the appearance of inexpensive props using inventive special effects.

Creating the Sparkle

Although a sparkle can be created in Photoshop, I prefer the control and precision of vector drawings. Here are the steps for building a single frame sparkle, which you'll later animate in Photoshop, using Photoshop, and also any vector drawing application:

1. In Photoshop, create a new document; the Film & Video preset is fine, and you build the sparkle larger than necessary to ensure clarity in the finished fx clip. Accept the prompt to turn off Pixel Aspect Ratio Correction.

2. On the Layers palette, create a new layer.

3. Choose the Brush tool, about a 9-pixel, hard tip and any foreground color you like.

4. Click toward the top of the document, then hold Shift and click a second point toward the bottom of the document, thus connecting the first and second points.

5. Press Ctrl/Cmd+T to put the layer's nontransparent contents into Free Transform and then right-click and choose Warp from the context menu.

6. Use the bounding box handles to put a bulge in the center of the line, tapering it at each end. Click the check button on the Options bar to apply the transformation.

7. Duplicate the layer and then with Free Transform scale the duplicate vertically so it's a little taller than the original. Offset the position slightly so you have twin spokes (peek ahead to Figure 13.2) and then merge the duplicate down to the original.

8. Duplicate the layer and then with Free Transform rotate the layer's contents by 90 degrees.

9. Press Ctrl/Cmd+E to merge the duplicate layer down.

10. With the elliptical Marquee tool drag a circle at the vertex of the star. Then press Alt/Opt+Backspace to fill the circle; deselect now.

11. Delete the Background layer. With white as the foreground color, press Alt/Opt+Shift+Backspace. Adding the Shift key to the shortcut will fill only the nontransparent pixels.

12. Apply a Gaussian Blur of about two pixels to soften the sparkle a little. Save the document.

If you have a copy of Xara, just about any version, the steps are a lot simpler:

1. Draw two lines that intersect at right angles. Thirty-six point width is good.

2. Use the Line Gallery's Stroke Shapes collection to apply Ellipse or Slim Blip to the lines.

3. Duplicate the lines (right-click, then drag and drop).

4. Select All and then apply about 15 pixels of Feathering using the slider on the Options bar.

5. Put a circle in the center and then feather it. See Figure 13.2.

6. Select All, then press Ctrl+Shift+E. Export the selected to PNG with alpha (transparency).

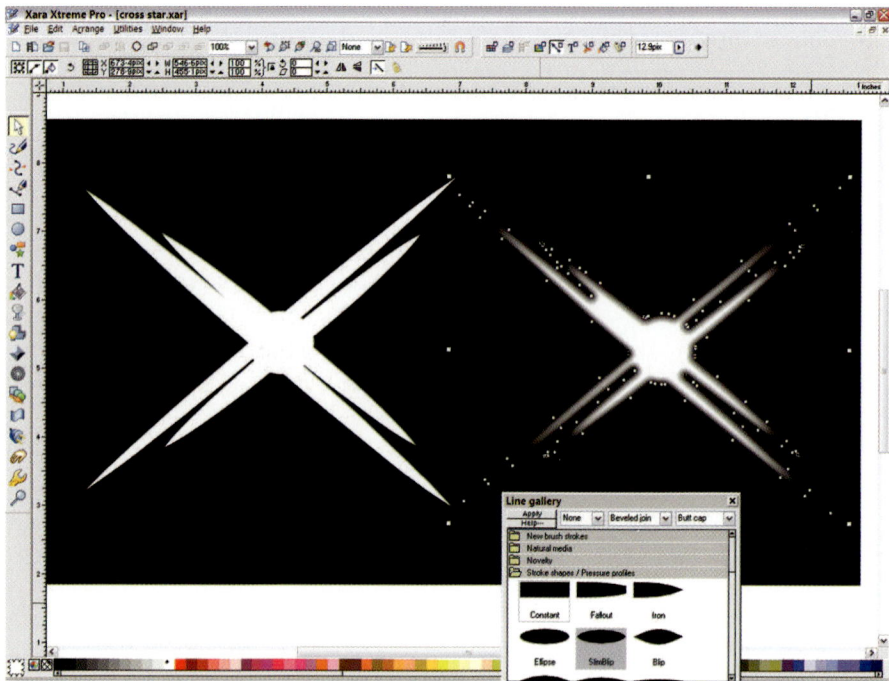

Figure 13.2
Vector drawing programs can export to bitmaps; making a cross-star sparkle takes only a few steps.

Illustrator has become the *de facto* drawing app on both platforms in recent years; the steps to creating the cross star sparkle are similar in all advanced vector applications:

1. Create a cross using the Line Segment tool.

2. On the Brushes palette, find a good tapering stroke and then apply it by double-clicking the thumbnail.

3. Increase the width on the Options bar for the stroke to about 24 to 36 points.

4. Duplicate the strokes and offset them to make twin spokes for the cross star sparkle.

5. Put a circle in the center and then File > Export to PSD or PNG file format.

6. Bring the file into Photoshop; recolor it if necessary to white and blur it slightly.

Driving the Sparkle Animation with an Action

I asked you to make the cross star drawing larger than needed because now you're going to animate the sparkle, making it grow and shrink and spin slightly. Because pixel-based images are resolution dependent, you necessarily lose detail and smoothness when enlarging a pixel image. You therefore start large, progressively shrink the pixel image (which loses detail as well, but less perceptibly than enlarging bitmaps), and then reverse the animation.

To do all this stuff is most easily accomplished by an action, so with your image in Photoshop's workspace, follow this recipe:

1. Set the Animation palette to Frames mode by clicking the icon at the lower right of the palette.

2. In theory, you should set the first and all subsequent frames to have an onscreen duration of 0.029 because the pirate video runs at 29.97 fps, but the Animation palette does rounding of fractions below a tenth of a second, so just set the first frame to No Delay and life will be fine.

3. Put a layer behind the sparkle layer and fill it with black so you can see what you're doing.

4. Make sure the sparkle layer is the current active layer on the Layers palette and then open the Actions palette.

5. Click the flyout menu icon and choose New Action. Name the Action "Sparkle" or "Cross Star" or something similar, and after you click OK you're recording.

6. Hide the current layer.

7. Duplicate the current layer; do this by dragging its title on the Layers palette list into the Creates New Layer icon on the bottom of the palette (it's quicker than Layer > Duplicate Layer or other methods).

8. Unhide the current layer.

9. Press Ctrl/Cmd+T. Scale the selection proportionately to 90%; this is most easily done by clicking the Link icon on the Options bar and then typing **90** in either the W or H field. Pressing Enter is not necessary.

10. On the Options bar, type two in the Rotation field (rotations are clockwise in Photoshop). Click the check icon to apply the transformation or press Enter.

11. On the Animation palette, click the Duplicates Selected Frame icon, and then click the Stop button on the Action palette. Your action is complete.

12. Run the action about 12 times; see Figure 13.3. You're not finished yet because you only have half of the one-second sparkle animation.

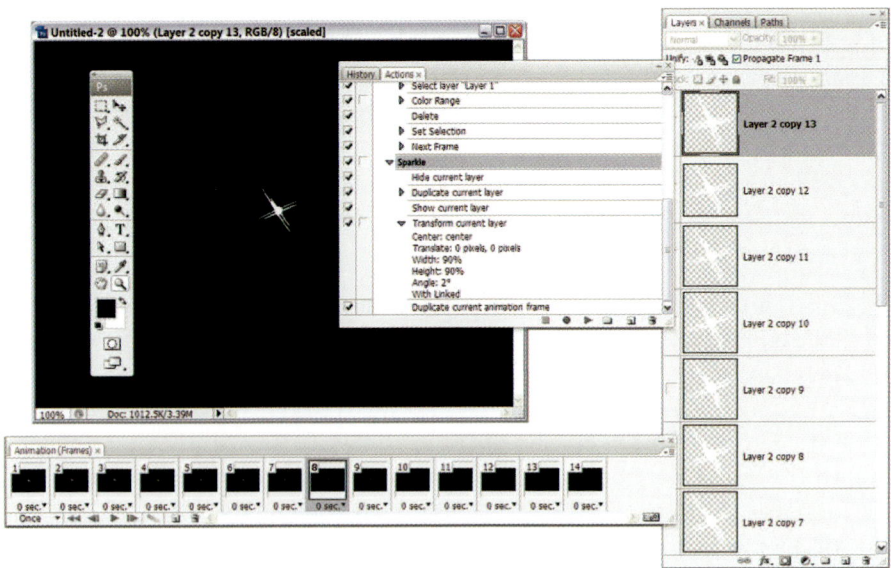

Figure 13.3
The cross star sparkle now shrinks and spins and is halfway completed.

Here's how to complete the cross star sparkle animation:

1. Assuming you have 14 frames on the Animation palette now, hold Shift and select Frames 1 and 14 to additively select all.
2. Click the menu button on the palette and then choose Reverse Frames. The largest sparkle is at Frame 14 now.
3. Hold Shift and then select Frames 1-13; then drag them into the Duplicates Selected Frames icon on the bottom of the Animation palette. The new frames are highlighted. *Don't* deselect them.
4. Hide, or better still, delete the black background layer.
5. Click the flyout menu button and then choose Reverse Frames.
6. Click the flyout menu button and then choose Convert to Timeline.

    In Figure 13.4 I've changed the transparency preference so you can see a still frame in the document window, and this is not a necessary step. It's an animation, and you can play it now. The document is also fairly a mess with 27 frames and 27 layers; the best thing to do with the animation is to write it to video now.

> **Caution**
>
> Do *not* mistake the Convert to Timeline command with switching modes on the Animation palette from Frames to Timeline. When you toggle views of the Animation palette, you destroy timeline keyframes; the Convert option from the Animation palette menu is the goof-proof procedure.

Figure 13.4
At 29.97 fps, the sparkle animation runs less than a second and is ideal for a noticeable but underplayed special effect.

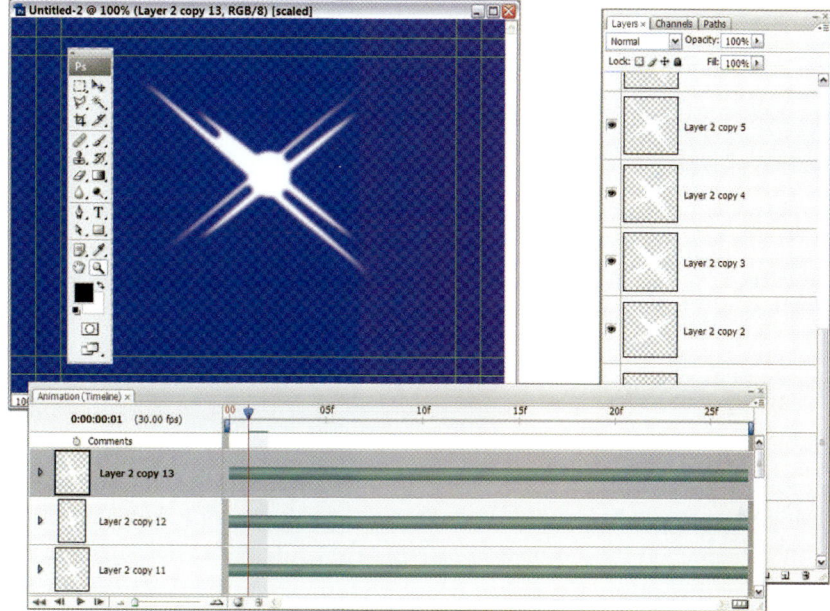

7. Choose File > Export > Render Video. Write the file to QuickTime file format, no compression, with alpha transparency support (Millions of Colors+; the Render options, alpha channel should read Straight-Unmatted). You can close the file after saving, but you won't have a further need for it after you're certain the video rendered correctly.

Comp'ing and Motion Matching

Chapter 15 is devoted to motion matching; for right now, there's just a little to teach, seeing as the sparkle animation covers less than 30 frames (and therefore the motion matching is not a significant task).

You begin by compositing the sparkle into the pirate movie as a new video layer, and then I show you how to match the sparkle to the relatively minor movement of the cutlass, then I'll get into a little scene integration and enhancement to make the cross star look perfectly natural.

1. Open the Pirate movie.mov file. Then choose Layer > Video Layers > New Video Layer from File. Choose the sparkle animation you rendered as a video in the previous section.

2. The sparkle is way too large, approximately 400% too large, so press Ctrl/Cmd+T to call up Free Transform and convert the video layer to a Smart Object when prompted.

3. Proportionately scale the sparkle to fit the scene; my own example worked with a scale down to 25%. Press Enter to apply the transformation.

> **Tip**
>
> This conversion is of no consequence in this tutorial, but the only disadvantage to working with Smart Objects is that they are not directly editable—most of the Tools palette and most Image > Adjustments are disabled. The only way to edit a Smart Object is by right-clicking the layer on the Layers palette and choosing Edit Contents from the context menu.

4. Find a good location on the timeline for the sparkle to do its thing; if you set the Animation palette document options to Frame Number, you can easily locate Frame 167, a good midpoint for the one-second sparkle. Move the layer on the timeline on the Animation palette so it strides Frame 167, as shown in Figure 13.5, and then with the Move tool, move the sparkle to perch on the edge of the cutlass.

5. Use the Zoom control on the Animation palette to zoom way into the duration of the sparkle layer. If you put the thumb (the timeline indicator, the current time) right at the center of the layer track, when you click the mountain icon at the right of the Zoom slider, your view of the track zooms toward the current

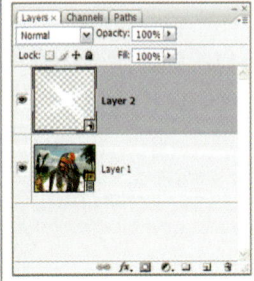
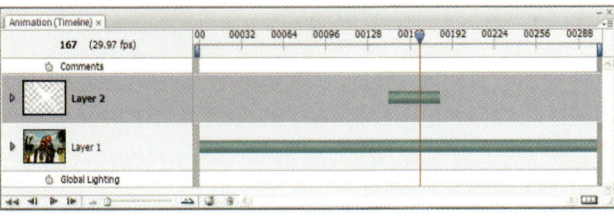

Figure 13.5
Move the position of the sparkle in time and then its position in the document window.

time, saving you from scrolling all over the place to find the track. I've marked the zoom controls with a big, fat arrow in Figure 13.6 for your reference.

6. Click the Position stopwatch for the sparkle layer on the Animation palette to set a keyframe.

7. Advance the current time to the end of the layer track. Then with the Move tool chosen, use the keyboard arrow keys to nudge the sparkle layer to the appropriate position and set a new key. I prefer nudging over direct dragging to prevent erratic motion across the timeline.

8. Set the current time to the beginning of the track and then nudge the sparkle layer's contents into position against the cutlass.

9. Drag the start and end markers for the Work Area on the Animation palette in so they bracket the sparkle layer's track fairly tightly, and then click the Play button on the palette to see how the motion matching looks. It's not perfect but that's okay; because you've narrowed the Work Area, Photoshop has less video buffering to do, and by the second playback all the frames you're working with should be in cache, and the playback will be in real time (29.97 fps).

10. Noodle with creating keys where the sparkle drifts off the cutlass. Go to a point in time where the sparkle drifts, and then nudge it into position, thus creating another key. In Figure 13.6, you can see that about 10 key changes are needed to match the sparkle with this particular video segment beneath the sparkle layer.

Figure 13.6
Create keys where the sparkle animation strays from the corresponding edge of the cutlass.

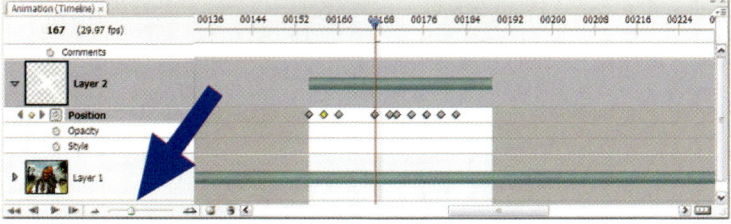

Polishing Off the Sparkle fx

In essence, you've just mastered the sparkle effect, but in the following section I riff on the effect and elaborate on it to enhance the presentation of the video in its entirety. First of all, the sparkle could use a little directional blurring to add verisimilitude and also to disguise the reality that it's a drawing. Then I show you how to reuse the sparkle clip, shortening it and relocating the duplicate on the timeline so the cutlass shows a second, briefer highlight later in the overall video composition.

> **Tip**
>
> Digital Anarchy offers a Photoshop plug-in called *Knoll Light Factory* (as in John Knoll, one of the principal architects of Photoshop and head of ILM's special effects department today) if you plan to make sparkles and other photorealistic optical effects your trade. It's about $150, and although it processes still images, you can easily write a script (covered in Chapter 9) to run any filter across as many frames as you need. With scripts and actions, just about anything you can filter, you can animate.

1. Choose Filter > Blur > Motion Blur. Because the proxy box in this filter displays transparency as the default checkerboard, it's easiest to see its effect live in the document window, so move the box away before you proceed so you can see what you're doing.

2. Set the angle to about 34 degrees if your sparkle shape has spokes at 45 degree angles starting at about 45 degrees, as mine does in these figures. What this does is significantly blur the 5 and 11 o'clock spokes and blurs the 2 and 8 o'clock spokes only a little, as you can see in Figure 13.7. To me, this is a fairly credible look, and you'll see that it looks good as it animates. Set Distance to about 6 pixels and then click OK to apply the filter.

Figure 13.7

Use motion blur to selectively blur the spikes on the cross star sparkle.

3. Create a duplicate of the sparkle video layer by dragging it into the Creates New Layer icon on the Layers palette. Note that the Smart Filter (the Motion Blur) is duplicated, too, and for our purposes this is good.

4. Move the current time to about Frame 200. Scoot the duplicate track over to this as a midpoint.

5. Let's try some augmenting instead of outright fabrication; the cutlass already displays a highlight or two at this time so let's enhance the highlight with this duplicate cross star. First, move the sparkle so it's on the cutlass (using the Move tool). Click the Position stopwatch for this track on the Animation palette to set a keyframe.

6. Click the Opacity stopwatch for this track on the Animation palette to set a keyframe.

7. Move the current time indicator (the thumb) to about Frame 190 and then set the opacity to 0% on the Layers palette. Then move the thumb to the end of the track and set the opacity to 0%. What I'm helping you create here is a shorter sparkle burst, and the beauty of this is that the audience will see it as a different effect and not simply a reused one.

8. Move to Frame 215 or so and then match the position of the sparkle to the cutlass.

9. Drag the opacity keys on the Animation palette so the position keys fall within the opacity range, as shown in Figure 13.8. From 200 to 215, the

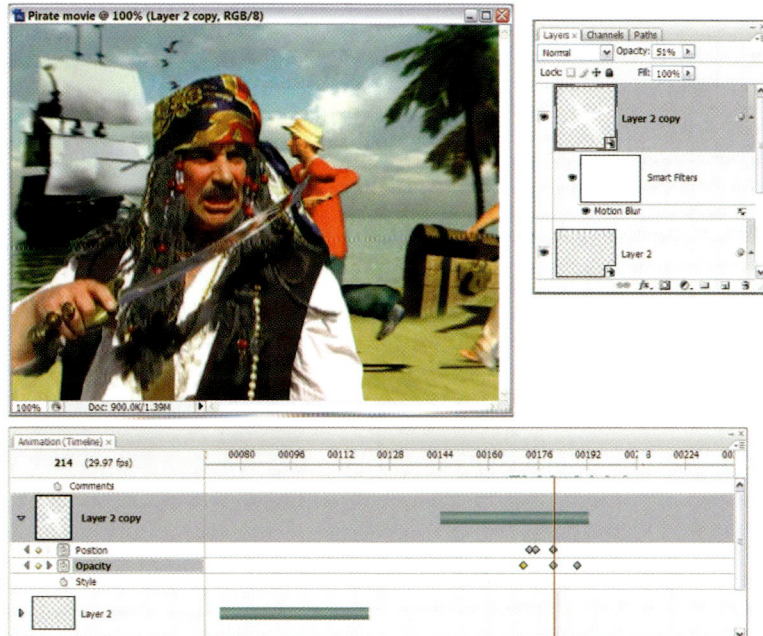

Figure 13.8
Create a different look from the same video clip by abbreviating its length.

cutlass doesn't move very much, and you can probably get away with only three or four position key changes. The cutlass shows off a sparkle for half a second, long enough to register as a recognizable event in the human mind, but conveniently brief enough to avoid scrutiny and the subsequent flagging as a fake special effect.

10. Render to video using any QuickTime compression (codec) you like, with no alpha channel support. QuickTime out of Photoshop, unlike AVI, supports audio, and the clips does contain music.

Creating a Lightning Strike

Admittedly, this chapter migrates into "video hokum," a brand of unsophisticated light special effects touches that audiences eat up nevertheless. My concept for the example in the following sections is essentially puerile slapstick: A woman who is clearly lying to a fellow swears that if she's (caught) lying, may she be struck by…you guessed it. And the sight gag is the simple irony that the *guy* gets blown to oblivion by lightning and not the woman. Mother Nature evidently has astigmatism.

So you'll need to draw some frames of lightning or use the ones I've provided in the PSD file in the ZIP archive for this chapter. Interestingly, I found it quite difficult to examine a real lightning strike on film because Hollywood has leaned toward synthesizing the event for several decades. This actually works toward your advantage as a special effects animator because if you draw a lightning strike that looks stylized, audiences educated by moviegoing (who might not get out very often during actual storms) will register your hand-drawn lightning as the real thing!

Okay, lightning happens as fast as, er—therefore you don't need a lot of frames, less than a second's worth, for sure. Lightning displays a fairly random, chaotic non-pattern, and the simulation you'll build consists of changing the layers every frame to imitate the erratic behavior. Additionally, lightning lights up the sky in a fairly blinding fashion, so part of the simulation involves putting a white strobe frame or two into the finished fx video. There is a thunderclap in the audio track of Crumbs and Punishment.mov, and I've also included a visual denouement to the guy getting hit; there should be some smoke where the guy totally vanishes, and I'll also show you how to fade in some scorched earth.

Figure 13.9 shows the individual frames as you'll find them as layers in the PSD file. I used Xara Xtreme, which is simply quick to use and renders bitmap versions of vector designs that Photoshop reads accurately.

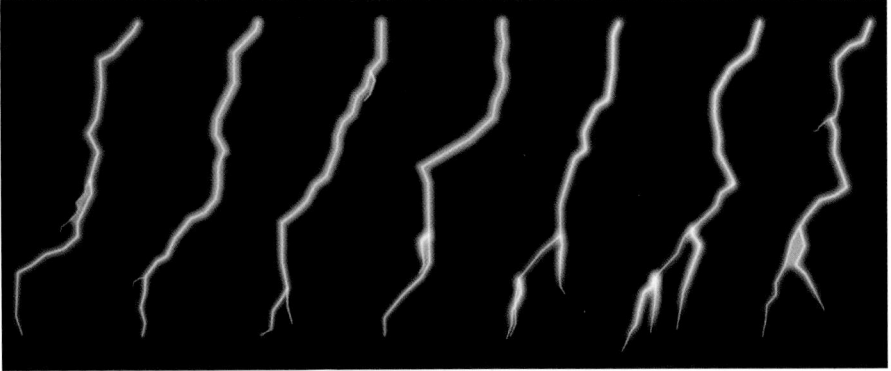

Figure 13.9
By alternating frames, you can simulate a bolt of lightning touching down.

Prepping the Original Video

Getting a person toasted by lightning requires split-second editing, and the first step in this example is to get the fellow to vanish from the scene a few frames after the lightning is introduced. You'll duplicate the video to a new layer in the document and then use Photoshop's clipping mask layer feature to hide the fellow. This is feasible because of the setup of the scene while shooting it, and whenever you do special effects you should plan your camera work to make your Photoshop work later unmarred by needless *coping* work. It's real simple: I asked the guy to step out of frame at a certain point, right after the woman says, "…may I be struck by…" That's all you need to cover now with footage on the duplicate layer that is time-shifted to reveal empty space through the clipping mask. It's only 115 frames, a little more than three seconds you need to mask. Here's how:

1. Open Crumbs and Punishment.mov and then turn off View > Pixel Aspect Ratio Corretion. Set the Animation palette to display Frame Number and not Timecode.

2. It's good practice for you to pinpoint a frame and mark it with a comment. Here's the general location: Drag the Work Area start and end markers to surround Frame 282. How would you know this is the general location where the clipping mask needs to be added? You'd scrub the timeline and hone in on where the fellow makes a retreat stage left.

3. Hold Alt/Opt to enable audio during playback and then hit the Play button on the Animation palette. Let the Work Area play through a few times as Photoshop caches the Work Area because the audio will not synch up until all the Work Area is in cache.

4. Look at the current time indicator on the Animation palette; look carefully and listen for, "…may I be struck by…" I get Frame 282 as a good place to vanish the fellow.

5. Move the thumb to Frame 282 and then click the Comments stopwatch icon. In the box that appears, type your remark ("lightning" is fine) and then click OK to shut the text box and put a key marker where the lightning will eventually enter and more importantly where you need to hide the guy. See Figure 13.10.

Figure 13.10
Create a Comment key in the composition as a reference point for editing.

6. Duplicate the video layer by dragging its thumbnail on the Layers palette into the Creates New Layer icon.

7. Create a normal blank layer on top.

8. With the Brush tool, set to black foreground color and about a 100 pixel diameter soft tip, stroke over the guy and to the left of the guy as shown in Figure 13.11. This layer will be the clipping mask, and you want to fill all areas where the guy is standing plus the area where he exits. Scrub the timeline a little at around Frame 282 to get an idea of the exact area. Be careful to keep the woman's arm and leg free and clear of the mask; this is why it's important to scrub regularly.

Figure 13.11
Stroke over the layer wherever the guy stands and makes his exit.

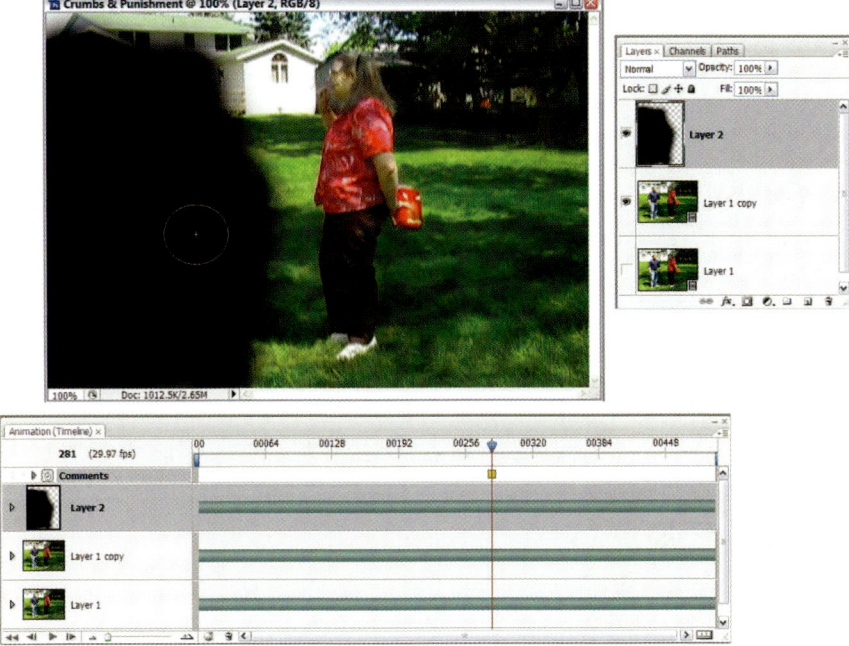

9. Move the layer to beneath the duplicate video layer and then hold Alt/Opt and click between the top video layer and the layer you painted on in Step 8. Doing this clips the top video layer to the mask beneath.

10. Shift the track for the top video layer on the Animation palette so that its timeline falls at Frame 324 at the point where the bottom layer is at Frame 282. The fellow now apparently vanishes at Frame 282.

11. Because the clipping mask is not animated, it occupies the duration of the composition, but it shouldn't. As you'll notice, the lighting changes toward the end of the video, and therefore the top layer will mismatch the end of the video unless you hide it after it's served its purpose (to hide the guy from Frame 282 until he has exited at about Frame 323). The good news is that when you trim a clipping mask's duration, the layer it clips also is trimmed to that duration. Drag the start and end points for the clipping mask layer on the Animation palette timeline so it appears at 282 and ends at 323, as shown in Figure 13.12.

12. Save the composition to PSD file format; keep the document open.

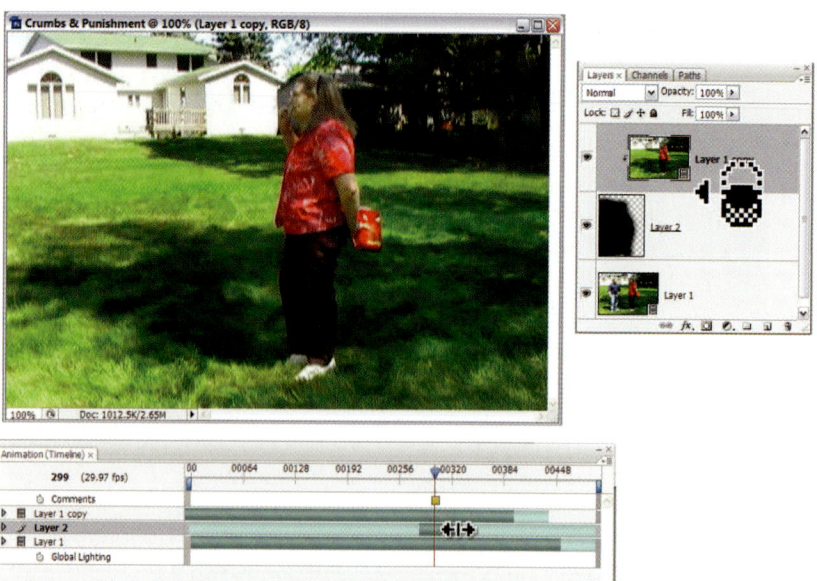

Figure 13.12
Make someone disappear from a scene; use coverage of the scene's background and a clipping mask.

Animating Lightning

When I first experimented with a lightning bolt animation, I discovered that the shape of the bolt can flutter about every which way, and it still retains the semblance of lightning as long as the main stem remains fairly static in position. Also, an animated lightning bolt doesn't really need to enter the scene from the sky and then exit; it can simply appear and then disappear, and the effect effectively plays to the audience. In the following steps, you can open my Lightning Frames.psd document and animate it, or if you want to design your own frames, go for it—you'll need six or seven frames and can certainly use my document as a reference.

Here's how to animate the bolt over a little less than a second's worth of time:

1. Open the multilayer Lightning frames.psd file and then switch to Frames mode on the Animation palette; this exercise is going to be similar to building the cross star sparkle.

2. The first frame should have a duration of No Delay. Choose any layer you like to be visible, and then hide all the rest except the background (so you can see what you're doing) on the Layers palette.

3. Click the Duplicates Selected Frames icon on the Animation palette and then hide the current layer on the Layers palette and unhide a different one. Repeat this step five times.

4. You can select multiple frames and then click the Duplicates Selected Frames icon, or more easily and with more control, hold Shift+Alt/Opt now, select a frame of two and then drag them to the end of the keyframes. Release the mouse button and then Shift and Alt/Opt when your cursor turns into a twin arrow, as shown in Figure 13.13. Just about everything in Photoshop has a key combo shortcut if you click, drag, and drop in the right places. When you have about 25 frames, you're done; mix the frames up, don't let them fall in a predictable order.

Figure 13.13
Drag and drop frames in any location between or at the end of a keyframe sequence to duplicate them.

5. Delete the black background layer, and then choose Convert to Timeline from the Animation palette's flyout menu.

6. Choose File > Export > Render Video. Use QuickTime file format, no compression, Millions of Colors+ and before you click Render, make sure the Render Options field says Alpha Channel: Straight-Unmatted. In this example, Unmatted and Premultiplied make no difference—I just want you to be sure an alpha channel is being written out.

Building the Lightning Strike Scene, Part I

In the following steps you'll add the lightning strike video to the video with the guy conveniently disappearing at Frame 282. Additionally, you'll add global flashes to the scene to reinforce the lightning effect. And you'll do a little tweaking as well.

A problematic thing with artificial lightning coming out of the sky during a broad daylight scene is that it's a tough read. On the other hand, an overcast day would show the lightning strike better, but would spoil the scene's setup: The audience could anticipate lightning on a cloudy day, but not on a sunny one. So we work with what we have; a neat foreshadowing trick is to make the scene darken a little just before and partially during the lightning strike. If timed correctly, it reinforces the woman's lines, "oh, no…impending doom!," you know?

Here's how to add the lightning, time its introduction, and then use layers to add faux drama to the clip:

1. With the Crumbs and Punishment document in the workspace's foreground, click on the top layer to make it the active layer and choose Layer > Video Layers > New Video Layer from File. Choose the lightning animation, which should now appear at the top of the stack on the Layers palette. If the bolt appears to be on the large side, you can scale and/or rotate it using Free Transform (Ctrl/Cmd+T). Doing this converts the clip to a Smart Object, which is acceptable because no further editing of the clip's visual data is necessary.

2. Drag the video track on the Animation palette so the lightning begins a few frames before the guy disappears.

3. Create a new layer just beneath the lightning animation. Choose a deep blue for your foreground color on the Tools palette and then fill the new layer.

4. Put the layer in Multiply mode on the Layers palette and decrease its opacity while the current time is at about 290 so it's about 30% or whatever looks good and creepy to your own eye.

5. Click the Opacity stopwatch on the Layers palette to set a key. Then set the current time to about Frame 210, where the woman is waving her index finger and getting very strident about not taking the cookies (that she's clearly holding behind her back). Set the opacity on the Layers palette to 0% and just for the sake of palette tidiness, drag the duration start on the blue layer in to just before the 0% opacity key. It's easy to quickly reference the impending doom blue shading when the unused part of a layer track is hidden.

6. Move the current time to about Frame 308 and then decrease the opacity of the blue layer to 0. As you can see in Figure 13.14, the blue layer really helps the lightning read for the audience. I suggest blue because it's a sky color;

Figure 13.14
Darken the sky before and partially during the lightning strike to add cliché foreshadowing and help the lightning read against a sunny, clear day.

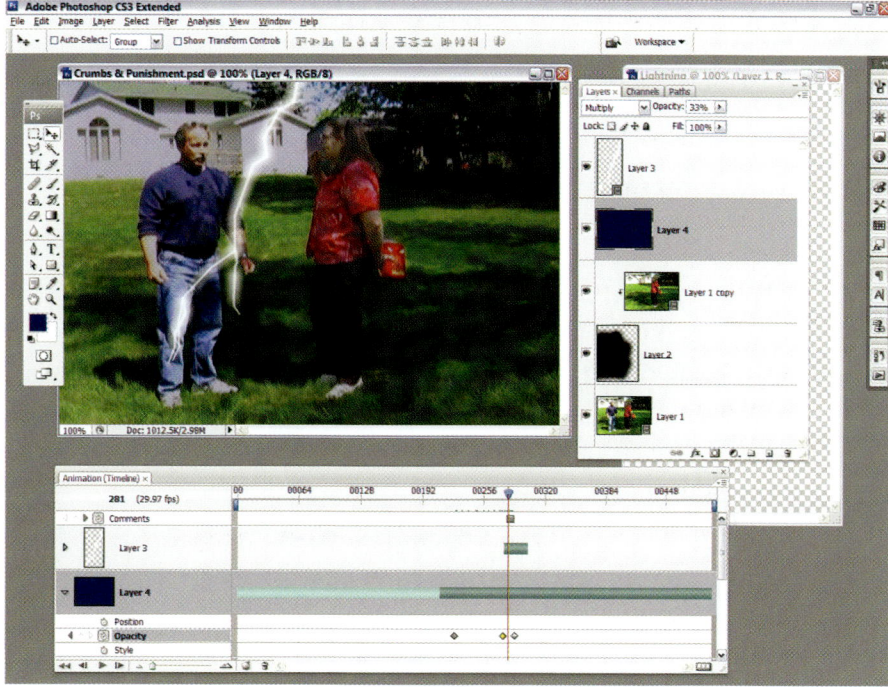

editors frequently use blue to fake day-for-night shots. So the effect is already accepted by audiences, and it simply works.

7. Add a new layer on top of the blue layer on the Layers palette and then fill it with white.

8. Drag the start and end of this track on the Animation palette so it's more brief than the lightning strike.

9. Zoom way in on the timeline to the white layer, and then use the Opacity stopwatch in combination with the Layers palette to turn the layer on, off, on, and then quickly fade to 0% opacity. I calculate the maximum opacity between the two 0% Opacity keys to be about 50%, but use your own artistic eye. This represents the strobes one sees during lightning strikes, as shown in Figure 13.15. Optionally, you can specify a Hold Interpolation for the flash's opacity keys. You right-click over a key and then choose Hold Interpolation. The two strobes happen very fast, in only a few frames, and using Hold Interpolation removes any tweening between keys that Photoshop does by default with Linear Interpolation. The result is a little more punch with the strobes, and it also allows the audience to see a few more frames of your lightning. All of this stuff is on a barely perceivable level, but you're imitating a real-world event, and if done correctly, you'll get the appropriate audience reaction.

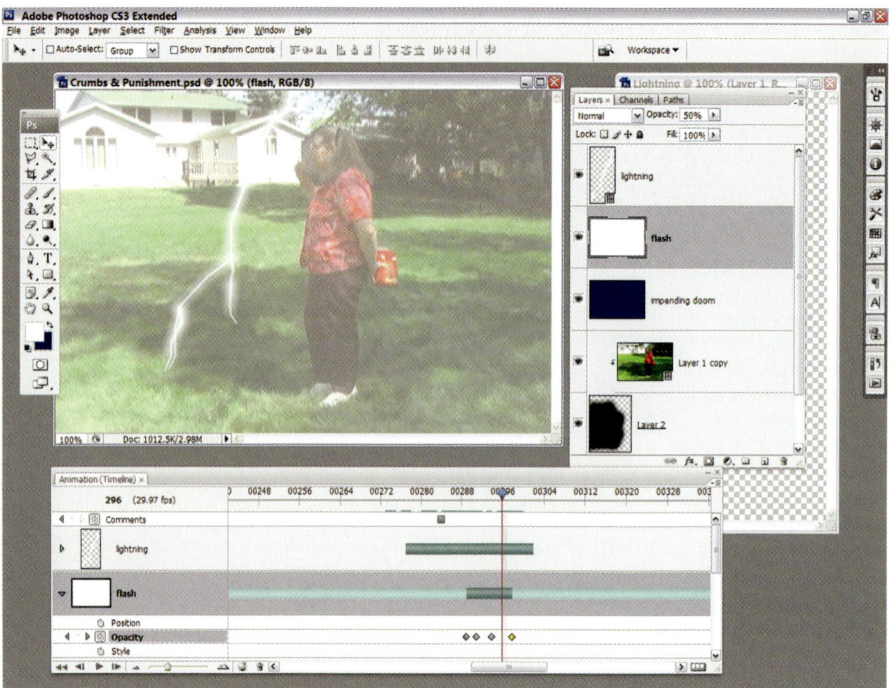

Figure 13.15
Add a strobe of white to support the flash of lightning.

Adding Scorched Earth and Some Smoke

Anything worth doing is worth *over*doing when you're entertaining. It's not good cinema to let the scene play out with a lightning bolt hitting the undeserving guy…and that's it. The woman smarmily waltzed out of frame, and I believe we should "remember" the guy, even in a clip this brief. Therefore, in the spirit of "an action calls for a reaction," in the following steps you'll introduce a little crispy earth where the guy was standing and then a wisp of smoke rising. I created the smoke wisp with particleIllusion (see Chapter 16); it's got an alpha channel, but you'll need to tweak the video a little to work in the composition because the smoke is not light or visually intense enough as rendered (it was rendered against black) to be visible in the composition as is.

Here's how to add a little toasted earth and the smoke footage to complete the composition:

1. Add a new layer on the Layers palette to beneath the white strobing flash layer.
2. Choose the Brush tool, black foreground color, 100-pixel tip and then choose Dissolve painting mode and about 40% opacity on the Options bar.
3. Stroke over the stroke point of the lightning in the composition.
4. Put the layer in Multiply blending mode on the Layers palette to heighten the effect.

5. Optionally, use the Blur tool here and there on the painted areas.

6. The scorched earth should happen as a response to the lightning and remain onscreen to the end of the clip, but it needs to be introduced after the lightning has concluded. On the Animation palette, drag the start and end handles for this track close in (to be tidy and for easy future reference) and then alter the opacity across time, from 0% at about Frame 310 to the final 40% at Frame 320, as shown in Figure 13.16.

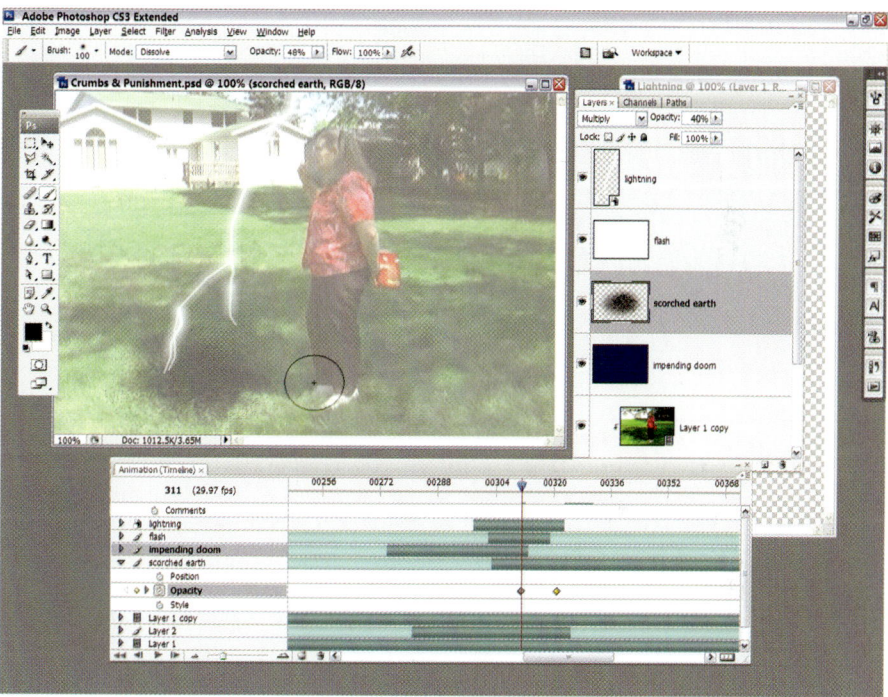

Figure 13.16
Bring the scorched earth layer up quickly and only to partial opacity to keep the event subordinate to all the other stuff going on.

7. Choose Layer > Video Layers > New Video Layer from File, and then choose Smoke.mov.

8. Put the head of this layer at about Frame 320 of the composition's Work Area. With the Move tool, put it in position in the composition, where the guy used to be standing.

9. Turn this video layer into a Smart Object by right-clicking over its title on the Layers palette and choosing this command. Now the layer can be tuned across the playlength of the clip, and not just a single frame.

10. Image > Adjustments > Shadows/Highlights. Notice the difficult-to-see smoke instantly pops into visibility; too much so, in fact.

11. You can gain experience by playing with the parameters in this box now, but we can also cut to the chase by entering these values: Check Show More

Options and in the Shadows > Amount > 29%, Tonal Width 40, Radius: 30 pixels. In the Highlights > Amount: 100%, Tonal Width: 47%, and Radius: 3 pixels. In a nutshell, the lower the values for a tone range, the less correction, the less change. Finally, set the Color Correction to +4 as shown in Figure 13.17. If the smoke is visible but doesn't steal the scene, you're in business; click OK.

Figure 13.17

Use Shadows/Highlights almost as you would Levels to correct exposure (Levels cannot be directly applied to a Smart Object).

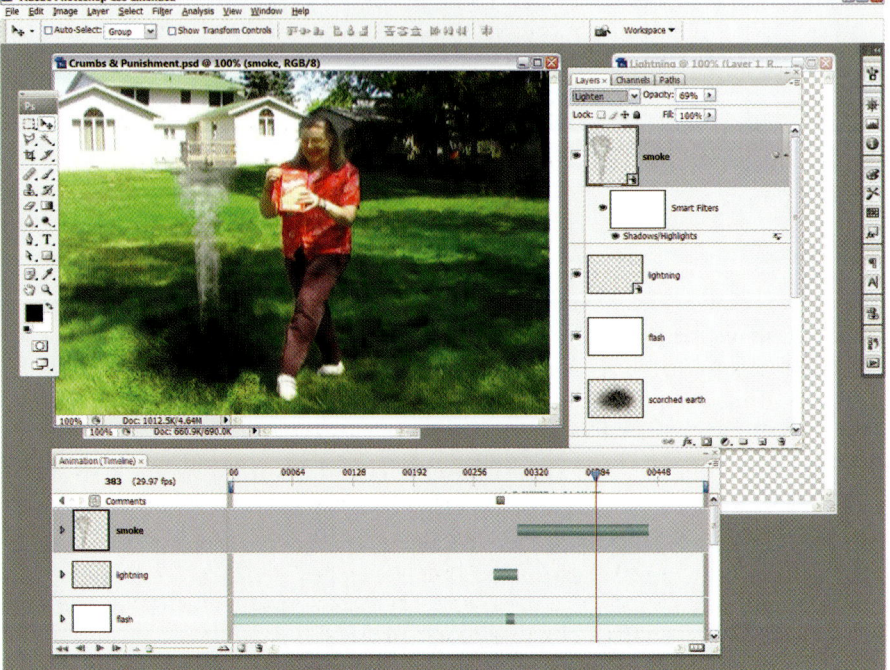

Figure 13.18

Lightning, strobes, a little foreshadowing, scorched earth, and some smoke are a recipe for making a special effect into a full-blown event.

12. Figure 13.18 is for reference; play the composition; hold Alt/Opt to play the audio and make sure your lightning happens around the time of the thunderclap. If you're happy, choose File > Export > Render Video. Don't render with an alpha channel, and H.264 or Sorenson 3 codecs will compress the video while holding good quality and again, only QuickTime out of Photoshop supports audio.

What's It All About, Alpha?

When Alvy Smith, one of the founders of Pixar, first invented the digital image alpha channel, it was naturally a boon to artists who want some flexibility in compositing work, but it was only the first step toward the type of compositing artists perform today. An alpha channel is an additional channel of information in a multi-channel image; you're used to, for example, an RGB image that has three channels, and an image with an alpha is occasionally called an RGBa(lpha) image.

However, there is a somewhat blurry distinction between an alpha channel-enabled image and an image that holds transparency. Dr. Smith's original specification for alpha channels was that the alpha is an additional information channel, and that information can be anything the host application and the user wants it to represent. For the most part, we use alpha channels to strip background content from a foreground object in an image, but if you've ever used the Lighting Effects filter in Photoshop you know that any light and dark areas in an image's alpha channel can also be used as a bump map (a Texture channel, in Photoshop-speak).

For the most part Photoshop users don't have to be concerned with the technical difference between alpha channels and transparency, the feature of layers in Photoshop, and also an attribute held in PNG files. If an alpha channel is written correctly by an application, Photoshop won't even display an alpha channel in, for example, a TIFF file, but instead simply open it with transparency mapped to a layer as dictated by the alpha information.

As all of this relates to video; QuickTime supports alpha channels as does Microsoft's AVI file format, but the alphas are not read into Photoshop; rather, Photoshop displays the video with objects surrounded by transparency wherever the alpha channel (by default) has specified dark or black areas. You should exercise a little caution, therefore, if you use modeling applications such as Cinema 4D, when requesting that foreground animated objects are held with a transparency mask. Cinema 4D, Maya, and other applications are capable of writing several different alpha channels as animation footage, including maps for lights, shadows, depth of field, and other real-world simulations. Make sure you define an alpha channel to hold object opacity when writing an animation to composite in Photoshop. Other attributes such as shadows are composited in Photoshop as footage that goes on a layer in Multiply blending mode; they do not hold transparency; keep the distinction between alpha channel information and transparency in mind, and your project will always go smoothly and as anticipated.

Simulating an Earthquake

Increasingly in Hollywood, a camera shake to suggest an earthquake or other event that causes camera unsteadiness is accomplished in post-production, using a technique very similar to that shown in this section. As recently as the 1980s, cameras were mounted on something called a shaker box to simulate camera unsteadiness for Hollywood disasters, and as you might expect, something marginally more sophisticated than a hand-held belt sander tended to decrease the life span of a $100,000 camera.

In the following example, I motion-matched a CG render of a cartoonish but still menacing safe falling out of the blue and just missing the same hapless guy who was struck by lightning earlier. It's a good clip, but it is problematic that the safe needed to fall a little more slowly than an actual safe would so the audience can see the fall. What the clip needs is for the "camera" to bounce a little after the safe falls and then gradually settle to stability. Doing this, given that the playtime of the clip is short, helps guide the audience through a mental reaction that takes some of the phoniness off the cartoon safe. If you want to rig and shoot something like this on your own, I recommend that you set up your frame and then back out a little, to give your camera frame shake somewhere to travel out of frame without revealing unwanted background. The clip you'll work with, Dave's safe.mov, was not cropped with any wiggle room, specifically so you can learn a technique for turning *any* footage you receive as an assignment into a disaster film.

Creating a Matte to Hide Frame Motion

The solution to giving the clip some wiggle room is a pedestrian but effective one; you put a border on top of the video layer to hide the edges when the video layer travels. A 16-pixel wide border will allow the video clip to travel 16 pixels in any direction without showing blank background, and this is quite enough for a camera bounce simulation. Follow these steps in preparation for the Big Event:

1. Open Dave's safe.mov, turn off Pixel Aspect Ratio Correction, and then create a new layer on top.
2. Fill the layer with black.
3. Ctrl/Cmd+click the layer thumbnail to load it as a selection.
4. Choose Select > Modify > Contract. Put **16** in the field and then click OK.
5. Press Backspace and then Ctrl/Cmd+D to deselect. Done, and the border is both centered and proportional on all sides. Save the comp as a PSD file and keep it open. See Figure 13.19.

Figure 13.19
Put a border on top of the video so you can move the video without revealing any blank background areas.

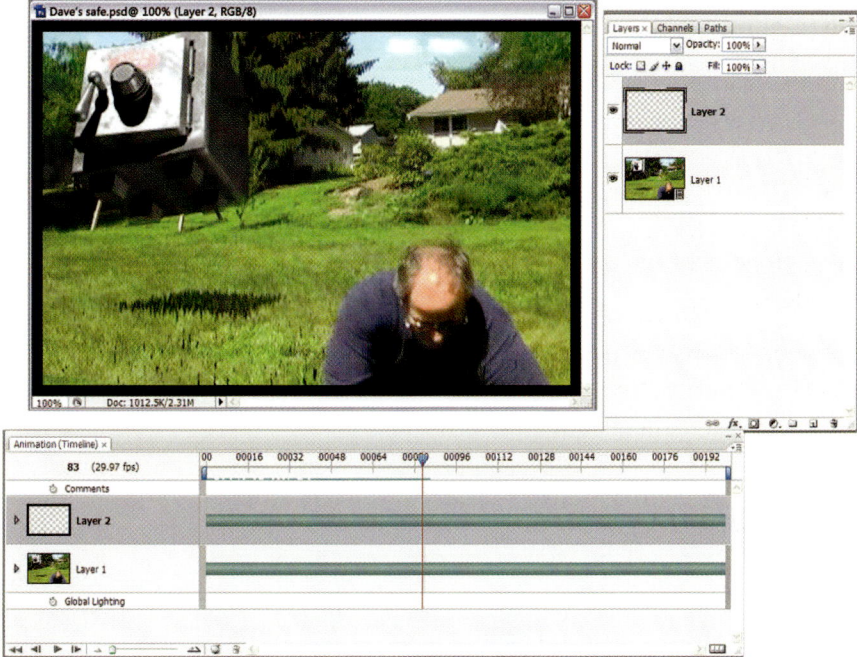

Motion Expressed as a Waveform

To get a camera bounce as a reaction to the safe dropping onto the ground is not as simple as moving the video clip up and down; it requires some choreography and a little understanding of the loss of energy after something suddenly transmits energy.

Take a ping-pong ball and drop it. After the initial bounce, it loses energy exponentially and gradually comes to a stop. In real life, a 500 pound safe falling on the ground would probably make an impact once or twice, and as a result the event would hold little visual interest. Therefore, making good film here doesn't necessarily mean being 100% faithful to real life physics, but instead you rely a little on cartoon physics and give the camera's reaction to the safe a little more of a ping-pong ball bounce rather than a boring "drop, bounce once, end of story" motion.

Today's entertainment in the cinematography arena is a blend of the real and the unreal. As the master chef of special effects and film editor, it's up to your experience and creativity to decide on how much of one ingredient goes into the recipe and how the final entertainment sits with the audience. My feeling in this example is that the safe is fairly photorealistic, the fellow is clearly real, and therefore, the camera bounce can border on the whimsical side to spice up the small idea of the clip without going over the top.

1. The safe hits at about Frame 89; it's a good idea to mark the frame with a Comment.

2. Let's get pseudo-scientific and decide that it would take a few frames for the ground shock to arrive at the camera. Go to Frame 89 and then on the Animation palette with Layer 1 (the video layer) as the active layer, click the Position stopwatch to set a key.

3. Go to Frame 95 and then use the keyboard up arrow while the Move tool is chosen to nudge the bottom video layer down by 10 pixels or so, to remain within the 16-pixel border. Why down? You'll see when you're done that it looks right because of a see-saw effect; the safe goes *down* to make the impact, you the cinematographer would theoretically be bounced *up*, therefore the frame needs to travel *down*.

4. Go to Frame 98 and then nudge the video layer up by 10 pixels. Optionally, you might want to nudge the frame left or right by 5 pixels or so to add a little exaggeration for the audience's benefit.

5. The safe stops its vertical motion at Frame 107 or so, but you can cheat the motion by a few frames out to Frame 110 without the audience seeing or sensing the incorrectness. Create about 7 keys between 89 and 110, each key moving the video layer less as you progress. Take a look at Figure 13.20 where I've drawn a little squiggle that looks like an audio sinewave. This is more or less the course of a ping-pong ball when dropped. The distance is initially large and then tapers off as the ball loses energy. Additionally, time-wise, the ball would traverse up and down much faster as it comes to a stop, so I've chosen greater spans of frames to make keys near the safe initially hitting the ground, with decreasing durations as it comes to rest.

Figure 13.20

Decrease the distance by which you move the video layer, while increasing the frequency of the keyframes.

Adding Motion Blur

There's something wrong with the hit and the camera's bounce in reaction to the hit, and it has more to do with physical camera optics than any correctness or enhancing you might do to the scene. Cameras write and/or pass media at 29.97 frames/second, and quite often you'll note that an event happened in less than a 29th of a second, and the result is that the frame is blurred.

So why don't we blur a few frames? Because the whole visual premise is that the camera was bounced, it's perfectly okay to blur the whole scene instead of just the safe, which is not traveling at a blurring speed anyhow. Follow these steps to add a touch of photo-optics to the event:

1. Duplicate the video layer and put it on top of the original.
2. Convert the duplicate to a Smart Object.
3. Choose Filter > Blur > Motion Blur.
4. Choose 90 degrees as the angle; actually, an "off" integer helps mess up the video a little more believably, so set the angle to 88 or 89 degrees to create a smidgeon of lateral motion blurring along with the significant vertical blurring.
5. Set the distance to about 14 pixels; click OK to apply.

As you can see in Figure 13.21, you now have all the footage blurred; the blur looks good, but it's inappropriate for it to happen before the safe lands.

Figure 13.21
Motion blur can only be applied at a single strength.

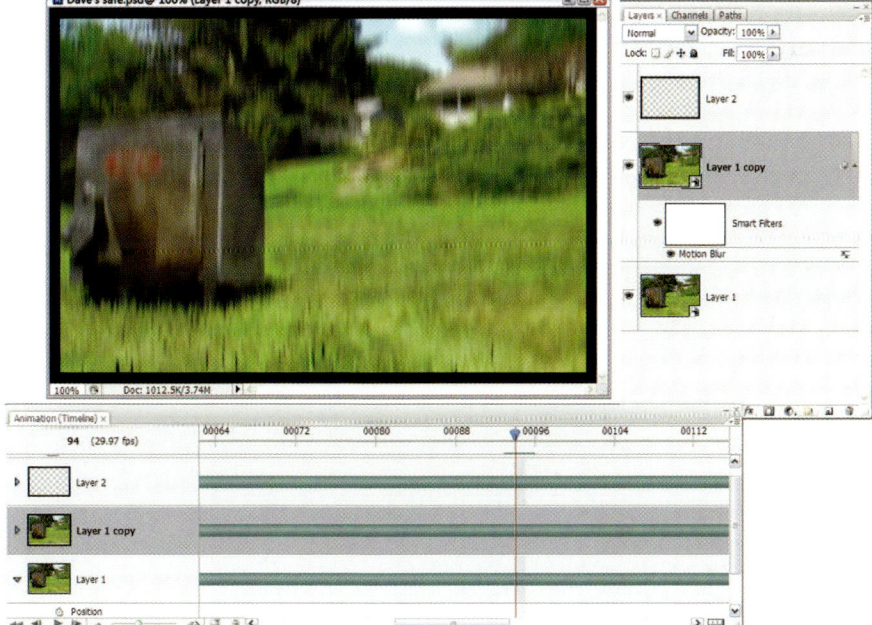

Therefore, because you can't alter any parameter of a Photoshop filter over time (styles, yes, filters, no), you fade the blurry layer up and then out, like so:

1. At Frame 89, click the Opacity stopwatch for the duplicate layer. On the Layers palette, set the opacity for the layer to 0.

2. At Frame 92 or so, set the opacity to 100%, and then at Frame 100 or so, set the opacity to 0, as shown in Figure 13.22. It works; the blur is noticeable, but it happens for too short a duration for the audience to examine the quick fade up and out. File > Export > Render Video. Use Sorenson 3 as your codec and do not render an alpha channel.

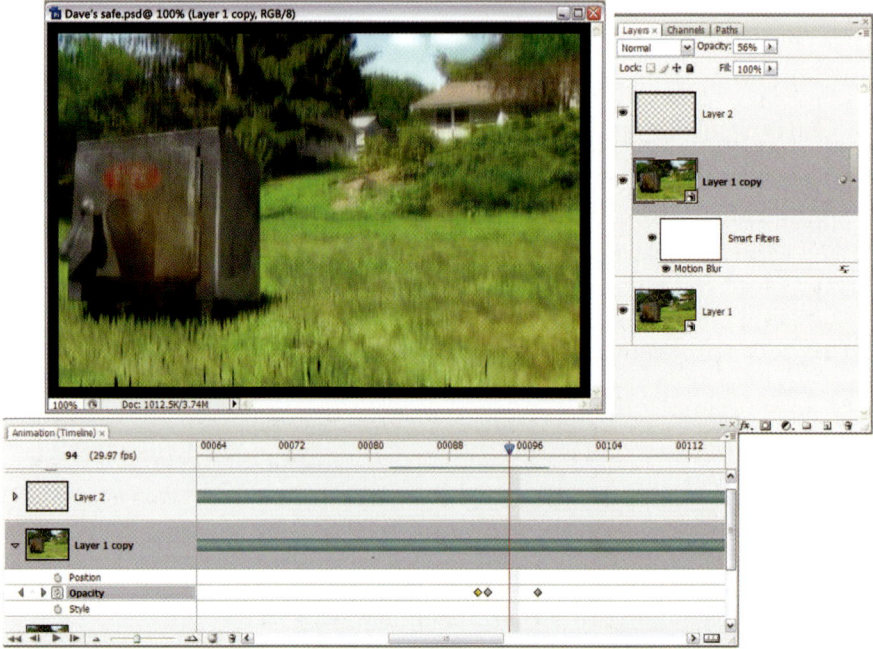

Figure 13.22

Fading a blur up for a few frames actually adds a suggestion of camera blur the audience will believe was caused by camera motion.

> **Tip**
>
> It would take some time, but you *could* actually blur the scene at the time of the hit and then reduce the blurring to zero after a few frames. Video layers can take any filter, even third-party filters, and what you'd do in this example is to apply the motion blur to a video layer that has *not* been converted to a Smart Object. The editing would be a lot of trial and error and guesswork, and Photoshop is not the ideal tool for creating the effect because this is destructive editing. You'd do something like this:
>
> 1. Set up a keyboard shortcut for advancing to the next frame in a video through Edit > Keyboard Shortcuts.

2. Choose filter > Blur > Motion Blur.

3. Blur the first frame you want blurred, Frame 89 in this example, at about 14 pixels in distance.

4. Keyboard to the next frame and then press Ctrl/Cmd+Alt/Opt+F to call the last-used filter without actually applying it.

5. Decrease the distance a little; press OK.

6. Repeat Steps 5 and 6 until the distance is zero.

Again, to me this is unacceptably experimental, but it can be done.

Adventures in Split-Screen

I believe that every sitcom in the 1960s and even part of the 70s featured *The Evil Twin* of one of the stars, from (I Dream of) Jeannie to James T. Kirk. And it was accomplished via split-screen post production, a big-time advancement from doing this sort of thing in the camera through masking and two separate passes; if you'd like a headache, consider how the timing of lines used to have to go. Okay, split-screen doesn't have to be wrought out of a Hollywood writer's desperation to get the last of the season's episodes out. And split-screen cinematography suffers no degeneration using today's digital technology; you can perform as many passes as you like, and the composite shows all elements with crystal clarity. Digital special effects actually help push the believability of the tricked-up scene, and in the sections to follow I walk you through the shooting setup and then the compositing of a very silly but effective composite.

Gathering Your Split-Screen Elements

First, split-screen cinematography more or less demands controlled lighting; indoor shooting is best, while a totally sunny day (or a completely clouded-over day) can provide acceptable raw footage. Then you need a total lock-down camera situation; sandbagging your tripod is a good idea, as is really tightening all your mount's joints.

Begin your shoot by overshooting the background with no actors in the scene; if your concept is a 60-second movie, then shoot at least four or five minutes of empty background. Then call in your actor, do a few rehearsals with the camera running; unlike film, digital media can be reused, or at very least it's substantially less expensive than traditional film, and my experience has been that the good stuff always happens during rehearsals. When doing an Evil Twin movie, get your actor to react to a stand-in or to the empty area of the scene where you'll add the twin. Interaction helps the final movie, and I think we can all recall how embarrassingly stiff split-screen scenes looked a few decades ago when it was still in its experiment, phase.

Creating a Multiple Split-Screen with a Bonus

The files in The Hat Tree folder in the ZIP archive contain all the elements you'll need in this tutorial, which is basically a lot of mugging, not a very strong story, but you'll get the technique down for doing something more mature than I filmed. I simply asked my wife to film me poking my head out from behind a tree and wave my hat at the camera four different times, posed at different heights behind the tree. As you might expect, it's fun eye candy to have four of the same person interacting, but more so because this example shows you how to have four guys appearing from behind a tree that's clearly too narrow to hide behind! So this is actually two techniques rolled into one in this section, and you can perform many different variations on it, real Keystone Cops material, such as:

- The two dozen clowns emerging from a European subcompact.
- A guy carrying a ladder past a tree, both at the beginning and the tail of the ladder.
- Someone tossing an object behind a tree and having a different object appearing from the other side.

The divider for your scene in split-screen effects can be anything, and the object doesn't have to be impossibly narrow to produce a good effect and get a laugh. Trees are particularly well-suited as a divider; they have texture that blends well from one side to the other, and when you need to slightly feather the divider (and you might), organic textures tend to hide the division from clip to clip.

Here's how to set up the first part of the illusion, a guy peeking out from behind a tree that couldn't possibly hide his back half:

1. Open Background.mov and turn off Pixel Aspect Ratio Correction, and then choose Layer > Video Layers > New Video Layer from File. Choose the lower right guy.mov file, and it's then added to a new layer on top of the background. In Figure 13.23 you can see the setup, and nothing is unusual yet. Note that because the lower right guy was filmed (staged) in such a way that he appears first in the finished composite, the duration of the film equals the duration of the background video layer. The clips you'll add shortly are only as long as they need to be for this composition and to save you download time.

2. Finessing can come at any point in the future; for now, create a layer between the top and bottom ones, choose the top video layer, choose the Brush tool in Normal painting mode, 100% Opacity (in case you didn't reset it from the

Figure 13.23

So guess what happens if you put a clipping mask on the right side of the top layer?

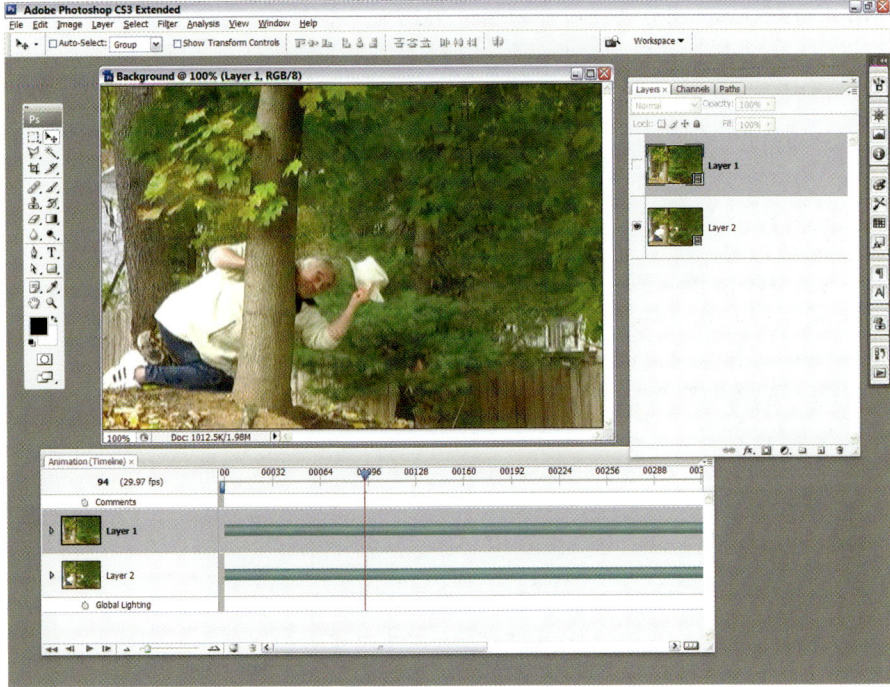

previous tutorial), and then click the Quick Mask Mode button (or press Q) on the bottom of the Tools palette.

3. Paint all over the guy, with plenty to spare at the right of the document, because I lean out of the tree at some point in the clip. At the left where you stop painting, create sort of a random edge along the vertical of the tree trunk; by making it uneven and including some but not all of the leaves, your split-screen work is better hidden.

4. Press Q to toggle back to Standard Editing mode. There should be a marquee selection around the right of the composition, but occasionally users set up Quick Mask for Masked and not Selected Areas. If the mask is not on the right side, press Ctrl/Cmd+Shift+I.

5. Click the title for the still image layer between the video layers on the Layers palette list.

6. With any foreground color, press Alt/Opt+Backspace to fill the selected area and then deselect. Clipping masks are evaluated by layer opacity and not color.

7. Alt/Opt+click on the edge between the top video and the still image layer, and you now have a clipping mask that hides the bottom of my sweater, my sneaks and jeans and would hide my socks if I'd been wearing any, as shown in Figure 13.24. The dashed line shows approximately where the clipping mask begins and ends in the composition.

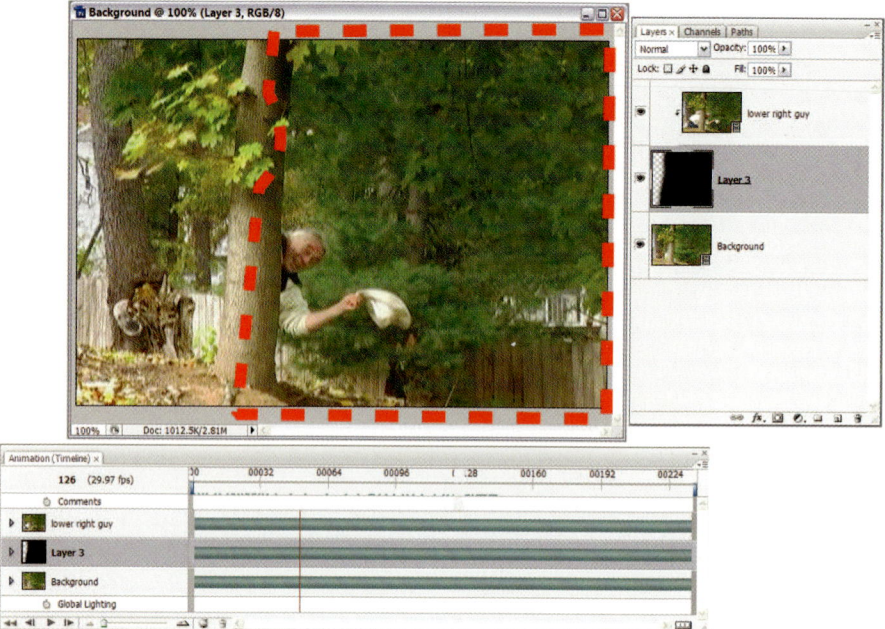

Figure 13.24
Hide all of the guy to the left of the tree, but include about half of the vertical of the tree trunk.

Adding the Second Guy

The upper right guy clip has the same duration as the two existing clips in the composition so there's no need to slide entrance points or anything. And like the previous set of steps, the compositing magic is done with clipping masks. After finishing the next set of steps I'd like you to work on your own for a while, scrubbing the timeline to check for anything that's showing on the layers that shouldn't be, and vice versa. I staged this scene with some but not an excess of wiggle room between the multiple characters, mostly because I detest split-screens that have too much air between characters. It looks staged, unnatural, and spoils the effect.

If lower right guy or any of his surroundings hide upper right guy, what you do after detecting the problem area is use the Brush tool in clear mode to erase areas on the clipping mask layer. Conversely, if any part of the guy or scene is missing, you increase the masked areas by painting with foreground color in Normal painting mode. It's actually quite magical looking in Photoshop and therefore a little amusing to counter any tedium to paint on the clipping mask and see the results on the video layer.

1. Before you do anything, make sure the very top video layer is the current editing layer on the Layers palette. If it's not, when you import a new video layer it'll mess up your clipping mask layer. Choose Layer > Video Layers > New Video Layer from File. Choose upper-right guy.mov.

2. The timing is right in this second clip compared to the overall story; bottom right guy looks up when upper right guy enters and I confess that this was a happy shooting coincidence. Create a new layer, paint a clipping area, and then create a clipping mask layer for the second guy, as seen in Figure 13.25.

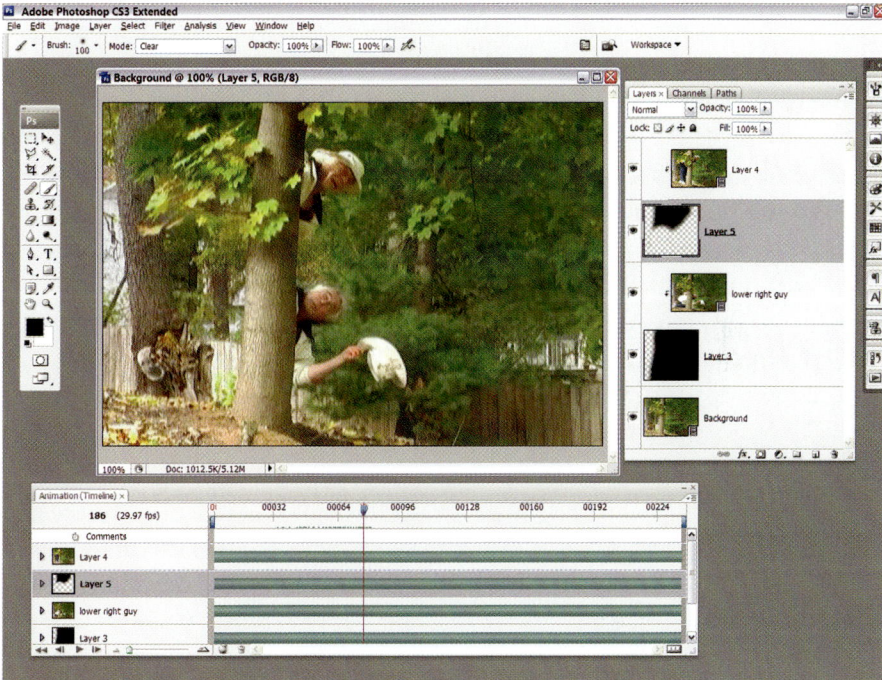

Figure 13.25
Add a layer, paint a mask, and then clip the new top video to the mask. Instant twins!

Trimming Durations for Clipping Masks

This leaves the upper and lower left guys to add to the composition. Because these characters are introduced later in the video, the duration of these clips doesn't fill the Work Area, and this is good and bad news at the same time. The good news is that you have the flexibility of introducing the two extra fellows at any point in the Work Area you like; use your creative chops and I'll sit back and kibbutz. The not-so-good news is that although clipping masks are terrific, they are also persistent; by default, because they're created using normal, static layers, their duration is the duration of the Work Area, and when the video they are masking runs out, you'll get the mask itself remaining.

Follow these brief final steps to add the two more guys and to trim (hide) the clipping masks at times in the composition when they are unwanted:

1. Click on the top layer of the stack and add lower left guy.mov to the composition through Layer > Video Layers > New Video Layer from File, and then mask him exactly as you did with the first two guys.

2. Find a good location in the composition for the guy to make his entrance. I think Frame 207 on the Animation palette's timeline is good, but again, I'm just kibbutzing on creativity in these steps. Drag the track on the Animation palette so the head of this video layer is where you like it.

3. On the Animation palette, drag the head and tail of the clipping layer to just a few frames inside of the video layer's length (with which the clipping mask is associated). Doing this makes the clipping mask and the video layer it clips appear and disappear according to the clipping mask's position in time relative to the Work Area. No clipping mask at a given time, and there's no video above it to see. If you need to move the video layer in time after trimming the clipping mask, you hold Shift, select both the clipping mask layer and the video layer on the Layers palette, and then shift both tracks simultaneously on the Animation palette.

4. Repeat Steps 1–3 with upper left guy.mov, and then render the composition to video. I recommend using the Sorenson Video 3 codec because the leaves moving in the composition are visually complex, codecs lose detail in a video when they compress, and my first render to the H.264 codec (usually fairly good) made mud out of the background leaves. See Figure 13.26. The Background layer features an audio track; none of the other videos have sound because you can't mute audio when exporting multiple clips to a single video composition, and if they had sound, the composition would sound quite dreadful.

Figure 13.26
Split-screen effects can be amusing and also cut down on your talent bills.

Warping Time

I've mentioned a few times in other chapters that the fps value of video has nothing to do with the speed of the video content. For example, importing a 30 fps video and then rendering it to 15 fps doesn't make the video play real fast. Feet per second is an expression, a fractional value that denotes the resolution of a video, the quality of playback, much like pixels per inch denotes the resolution (the quality) of a bitmap image. As an example, if you look at the astronomical videos that NASA releases, they appear choppy because they are filmed at 12 to 15 frames per second, to save on relay time down to Earth. Many of the videos on YouTube are 12 frames a second, again to save on download time, as are a lot of Adobe Flash Shockwave files. Think of fps as a method for compression, not as a changing of playback speed for a video.

Great. So how do you change time in a video? The following sections show you how to slow down time, speed it up, and even how to reverse it. Before you begin, set aside about 2GB of empty hard drive space; although the videos are only a few MBs that you'll experiment with, you'll need to decompile one or two into still frames without compromising image quality, and the result is going to be a lot of files taking up a lot of hard drive space while you work.

Fast Times, Slow Times

A caveat before beginning this section: slow-motion cinematography (SloMo) is usually captured in the camera, and only minor sweetening is performed in post. Slow motion cinematography calls for refitting a camera with a special motor drive, it's expensive, and just to give you a ballpark idea, to get a *Six Million Dollar Man* look, a "swimming underwater" type effect, the camera needs to crank at 800 frames per second, called *overcranking* a camera. Then when played back at 29.97 fps, the resolution value changes, and you get your effect. Ignoring this truth, I boldly went out and shot some footage for this chapter of three or four darts hitting a dartboard. Surprise: there wasn't enough *visual content* to slow the film down in Photoshop. My 29.97 fps DV camera caught the event of a dart hitting the board, and there were perhaps three frames, two of which were blurred beyond recognition. You *cannot* drag three frames of video out to video that lasts longer than a sneeze; you have interesting still images, but you don't get fx video!

My point is that when you want to make time-warping special effects videos, you choose your video content wisely; you choose something that's already slow that you can make a little slower, or something that happens fast that you think would look interesting if played a little faster. The first example in this section stars a tin of dominos. We rolled, set up the dominos, and then did the predictable thing. It works out nicely as source footage as you'll shortly see, not only for the film's geometric interest, but also as a tiny piece of story-telling. Consider this: It is a long, boring, challenging, and tedious process to line up a few dozen dominos, and the thrill of watching them topple in a cascade is over in only a moment or two. Therefore, we're going to redistribute the film's interest: set up the dominos a lot quicker and then show them falling down at a tempo that would make a snail yawn.

Splitting and Creating Still Image Layers

I should point out that the following set of steps more or less demands a muscle machine; read the section, but don't try it unless you have a Core Duo (a Quad core is better) machine with at least 2GB of RAM (4 is better). This is video editing, not making JPEG images, all of this stuff requires serious processing horsepower, so don't run other apps such as a Web browser or an MP3 player, and yes, this is Hollywood on a small scale so there's a corresponding price tag.

The first thing you need to do is split the video into two parts: the setup and the knockdown. Because the setup takes approximately 40 seconds (about 1,250 frames) while the knockdown takes a little less than two seconds, I'll show you the processor-demanding part first: taking the setup sequence apart into 1,250 frames. This is the deal: To change time in videos, the most effective way is to deal with the video as still frames. You can then delete frames to speed up action, and to slow film down, you can use the Frames mode of the Animation palette to assign every frame a key whose duration is as long or as brief as you like. Let's begin:

1. Open Dominos.mov, turn off the Pixel Aspect Ratio Correction on the View menu, and then save the file as Setup.psd.

2. To save you time scrubbing the timeline to determine where to make the cut, double-click the current time indicator and then type **1250** in the box; click OK.

3. Now that the thumb is at the cut point, choose Split Layer from the palette's menu. The Animation palette should look like that in Figure 13.27 now. Save; in fact, save after you do anything intensive in this section; it's a pain to have to reconstruct this example if Photoshop picks a fight with your OS and wins.

4. I see no point in keeping the layers in one document, so right-click on the top layer (the setup sequence) on the Layers palette, choose Duplicate Layer from the context menu, and then choose New to duplicate the layer over to a new document window. In the As field, type **Knockdown** and in the Destination Document field, type **Knockdown.psd**, then click OK to create the duplicate. Because Photoshop can perform nondestructive editing, the entire movie is still held in knockdown.psd—the setup sequence is just hidden, it's the light green area on the Animation palette. I ask you to do this just for good digital bookkeeping (tidiness) in this tutorial, and you'll see that dumping the bottom sequence doesn't affect the saved file size for the document. See Figure 13. 28. Close knockdown.psd ; you re-open and work with it later in this chapter.

Chapter 13 ■ Creating Fun, Simple, Effective fx 463

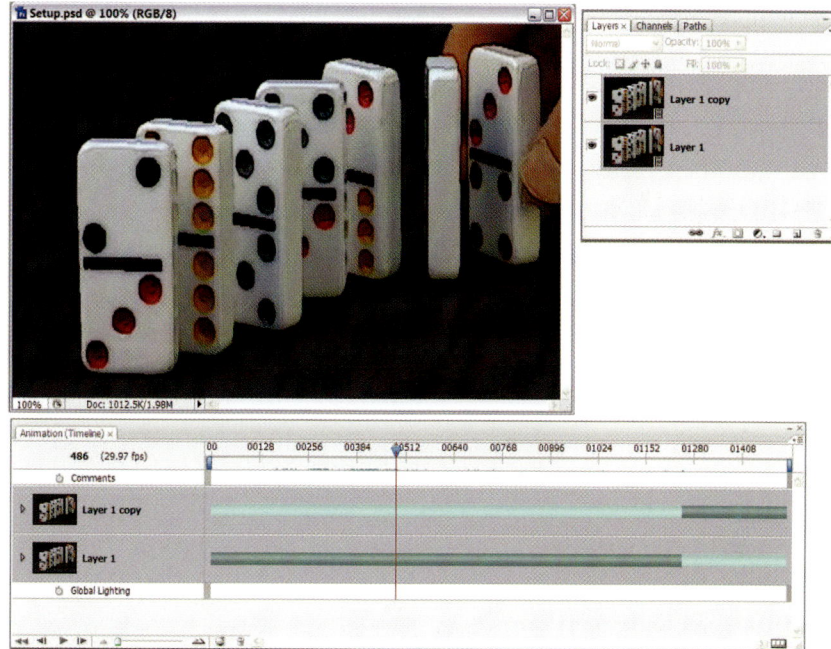

Figure 13.27
Split the video into two layers at the event point.

Figure 13.28
Split the movie, and then create two separate documents.

5. The setup sequence now needs to be simplified (and the file size will increase dramatically) to prepare it for a Photoshop script called Export Layers to Files. Choose Flatten Frames into Layers on the Animation palette's flyout menu and then go get a sandwich; 1,250 frames will take a few minutes.

6. Scroll down to the bottom of the Layers palette, find and then delete the hidden video layer. Again, Photoshop hides the trims from videos; it doesn't delete them, and this video layer will mess up the script you'll use in a moment.

7. Choose File > Scripts > Export Layers to Files. In the Export Layers to Files box, choose a location for the saved files; you'll need at least 300MB of free disk space, and I recommend JPG as the saved file format with the 8 Quality setting. I shy away from JPEGs for exhibiting art and for printing because JPEG is lossy file compression, but the native video file was already compressed right out of the camera using DV-AVI, and I found the JPG loss is nominal for images that will soon become a video. Use Setup as the filename prefix so I can better guide you through this technique, and then click Run. Sit back for a while; in Figure 13.29 I've drawn a red circle around the video layer you need to delete before running the script. Once the script has executed and you're certain the JPEG images were rendered, you can safely delete the PSD file. It's three-quarters of a GB, it's outlived its purpose, and I believe the JPEGs total about one-third that figure.

You're more than halfway finished. Read on.

Figure 13.29

Have Photoshop write individual files from the layers in the converted video document.

Reordering, Sifting, and Renaming Your Files

Adobe Bridge can be of great assistance in the time warping of the setup sequence of the video. You can also use a batch renaming utility and your system's folder view of the JPEG files, but essentially you want to do the same thing. Here's how it goes: Setting up the dominos took the good part of a minute, most of which is not good entertainment. I figure the sequence could be speeded up by three times without the sequence taking on a comedic look; this is not supposed to be a funny video. Additionally, just as audio editors take the breaths out of a commercial announcer's spiel (thus allowing more words in a 30 second radio commercial even though it's uncertain people *understand* all the words), there are video "breaths" in the setup, where the hand goes out of frame to fetch another domino.

Here's how to remove two thirds of the saved JPEG files so you can import them as footage in Photoshop:

1. In Bridge, point the application to the folder where Photoshop wrote all the JPEG files.

2. Arrange the sorting tray in the center of the UI so that the files are displayed as thumbnails three across.

3. Put your cursor on the first thumbnail in the left column and then drag down to add every third frame to the currently selected frames. Windows users should bear in mind that Bridge's paradigm for selecting is Illustrator-style; *if an edge of a neighboring thumbnail is touched by the cursor,* it's included in the selection. Avoid mishaps and follow this step with precision.

4. Once you reach the bottom of the sorting tray area, right-click and then choose to move the selected files to a new folder. In Figure 13.30 you can see the Bridge selection process, and at right the same deal in a Windows folder window; you choose View > Icons, reshape the folder window to display the icons three across, and then drag down the first column; right-click when you're done and then move or copy the selected JPEGs. Bridge does not offer an icon view of media files (that's not why it was created, it's a viewing app), but with an icon view in a folder window, you can more quickly select the files you want to copy.

5. In Bridge, open the folder to which you copied every third frame. You can delete the other two thirds of the JPEGs at any time to pick up free HD space.

6. By eye, go through the images and delete every frame that doesn't have a hand in it. Believe it or not, the audience will not find anything peculiar about a speeded up sequence that has no pauses; most people under the age of 40 have seen this stuff in commercials all their lives. They are just mostly unaware of the editing or how the video was edited!

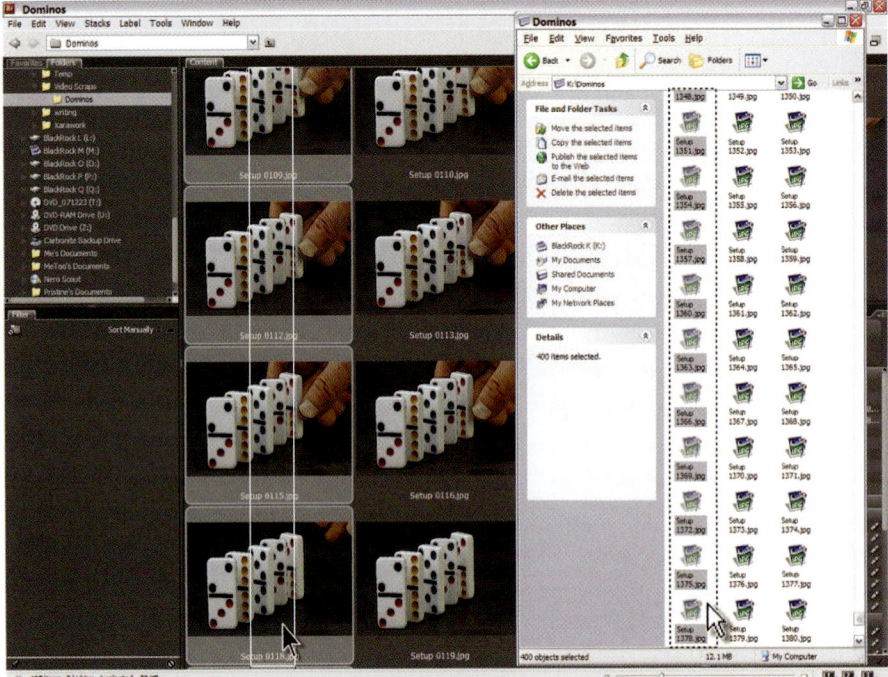

Figure 13.30
Sort and then select every third frame in the files Photoshop wrote out from the video.

7. Select All (Ctrl/Cmd+A, the same as in Photoshop), and then choose Tools > Batch Rename.

8. In the Batch Rename box, Rename in Same Folder will save hard drive space, so choose it. In the New Filenames field, "Setup" is fine, the Sequence Number should probably begin with 1, and without looking in the folder window to see how many files you copied, you already know the sequence ran to about 1250 frames, so you'd want four digits appending the sequence name. In reality there are only hundreds of frames, so three digits would do here, but better safe than sorry. Photoshop will balk on importing files to animation frames unless all of the sequence is named the way it's supposed to be named. In the preview field you can see an example name to confirm that the changes you've commanded are correct (see Figure 13.31); if all looks okay, then click Rename.

Done, and it's time to return to Photoshop.

Compiling Frames and Creating Slow Motion

There's more of a procedure than an artistic technique to tear the video into frames and then reassemble them. Also, I'm a fiend for organization; this is why I always tell you when it's okay to delete scrap files and why you write animations out to

Figure 13.31
Batch rename your files using Adobe Bridge.

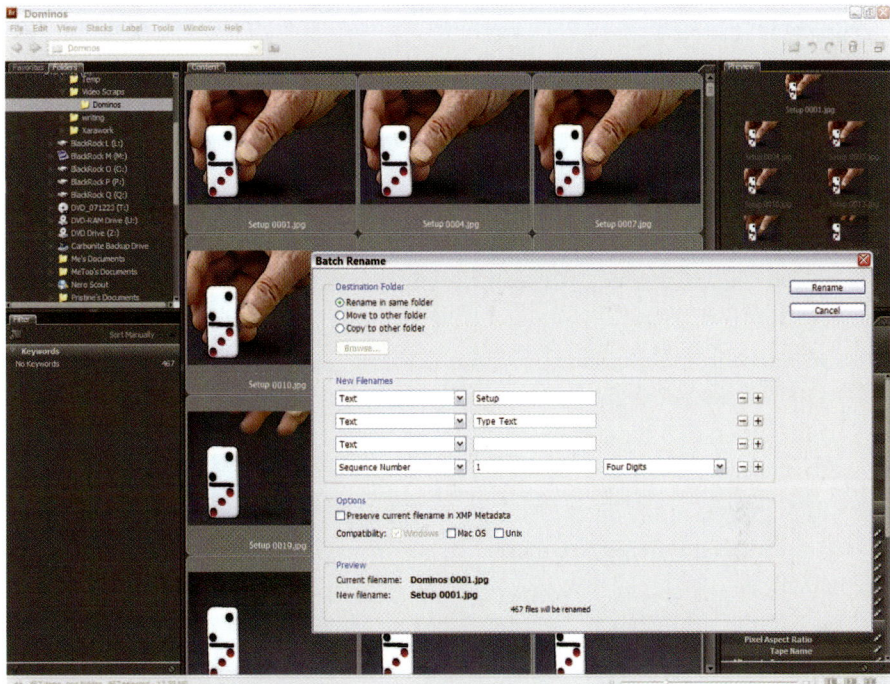

video instead of creating a grand document with dozens of snippets that's excessively large and a pain to scroll through. So the next step is a simple one: You import the renamed frames as a video, render the video to disk, move on to this section's topic—creating SloMo footage—and finally stitch the front and back videos into one seamless fx composition.

To create the accelerated setup sequence:

1. In Photoshop, double-click the workspace to display the Open box. Go to the folder that contains the renamed files, click any of the files to select it, click the Image Sequence checkbox, and then click Open.

2. You're importing frames as an unsaved, unrendered video, and Photoshop needs to know the fps for this proposed video. Choose 29.97 in the box, and then click OK.

3. Choose File > Export > Render Video. Render the video with no compression to QuickTime, no alpha transparency. There's no particular reason for QuickTime in this step over AVI, but the important thing is not to use compression. You don't want to needlessly lose more image quality by using a codec at this point in the work.

4. Open the knockdown.psd file you saved earlier.

5. Drag the start and end Work Area markers to begin at Frame 1392 and end at Frame 1431; this is where the action takes place when the dominos fall and is easily discovered on your own by scrubbing the timeline. Then choose Trim Document (the video) Duration to Work Area to make the following steps easier.

6. Choose Flatten Frames into Layers from the Animation palette menu. Then scroll to the bottom of the Layers palette and delete the copy of the video (it's labeled "Layer" instead of "Frame") so there are only static image layers in the document.

7. Delete the frames that don't contribute to the fall itself if necessary; however, the 39 frames you converted should do the trick. I suggest that you keep some of the very tail of the sequence because it'll make an interesting conclusion to the finished clip to have the back domino wobble a little.

8. Go to Frames mode on the Animation palette and then choose Make Frames from Layers on the palette menu.

9. Here's where the slow-motion effect is created. Hold Shift and then select the first and then the last frame thumbnail on the palette to select all, and then click any of the duration triangles below a thumbnail and then choose .2 seconds from the pop-up menu. Let's see here; the original video played the knockdown sequence at 29.97 fps, so if you make the duration .2 seconds, you've time-stretched the sequence by 600 percent, almost the same as the slow motion sequence I discussed earlier with the overcranking camera drive. I'll explain shortly why you're not going for 800 percent. See Figure 13.32.

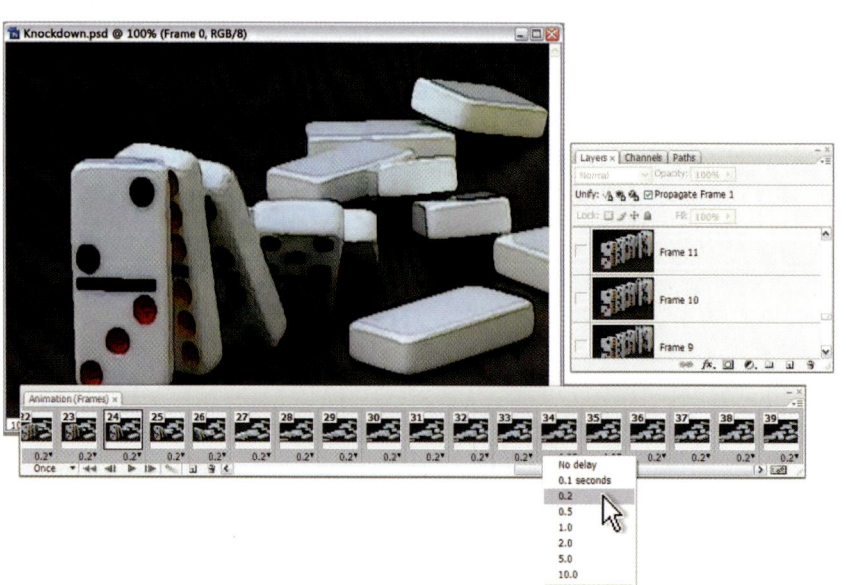

Figure 13.32
Lengthen the duration of each frame to make it play back in slow motion.

The next steps are optional, but definitely worth demonstrating because the effect enhances the slow motion, which can look stultifying and jerky sometimes. A popular video effect that accompanies SloMo is *time echoing*. That is, frames contain traces of in-between times derived from other neighboring points in the clip. You can imitate this effect with a little manual labor, and although what I show you here is not a true video echo, it works and makes the slow motion sequence visually sumptuous. Note that the frames as shown of the Layers palette begin at 0, but the frames displayed on the Animation palette begin at 1: You click on Frame 24, for example, on the Animation palette, and you'll see on the Layers palette if you scroll it that Frame 23 is visible at this point in time. You need to mentally shift the relationship between frame number and layer name to perform the next steps successfully.

1. One at a time (there's no practical automation you can do here), hold Shift+Alt/Opt and then drag the first frame thumbnail on the Animation palette to on top of the second one. This duplicates the frame and puts it right after the original and before the next frame. You visual signal that you did it right is that your cursor changes to a twin head black and white arrowhead as you drop the frame onto the following one, and a vertical bar appears to the right of the following frame to indicate the position in time where you're duplicating.

2. Click on the duplicate frame and then locate it on the Layers palette; the duplicate should be the only visible layer in the layer stack; for example, Frame 24 on the Animation palette calls for the layer titled Frame 23 to be visible, and the frame you just duplicated also calls for the visibility of layer Frame 23. Look at Figure 13.33; I'm pulling this frame because there's suggested action in it, whereas the first few frames don't show a temporal difference.

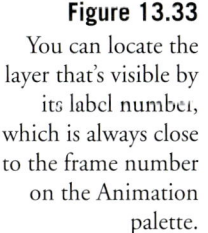

Figure 13.33
You can locate the layer that's visible by its label number, which is always close to the frame number on the Animation palette.

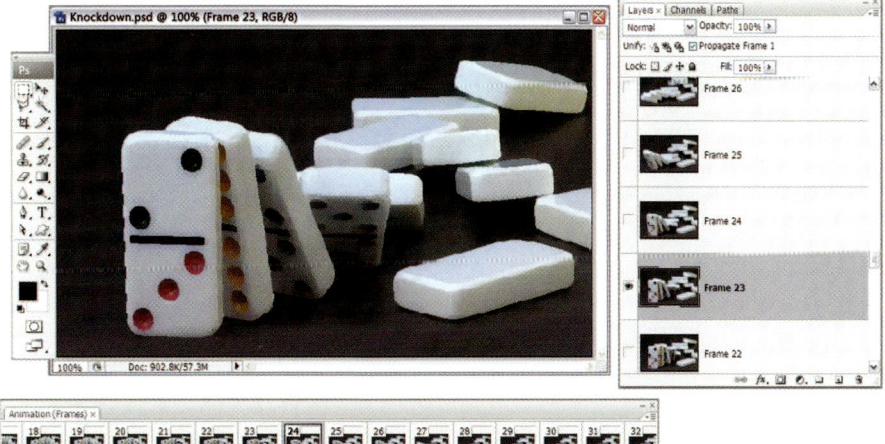

There's always a correlation between frame number and the number Photoshop auto-creates for layers pulled from a video. It might not be an exact correlation, but the *progression* is 1:1.

3. One layer up on the Layers palette, continuing my example in Step 2, is the layer labeled Frame 24, the layer that's visible at Frame 25 on the Animation palette. Make the layer *above the current frame* on the Animation palette 50% visible.

4. If you culled 65 frames for the slow-motion sequence, you need to repeat Step 2 64 times. It takes patience, but I guarantee that the effect is worthwhile. In Figure 13.34 you can see my edited duplicate of Frame 24, now called Frame 25 on the Animation palette. Because renumbering takes place when you duplicate a frame, I urge you to perform this optional time echo technique beginning at Frame 1, or you'll easily lose your place in the segment while you edit. But the SloMo is going to look really *cool* as your creative payoff for the work.

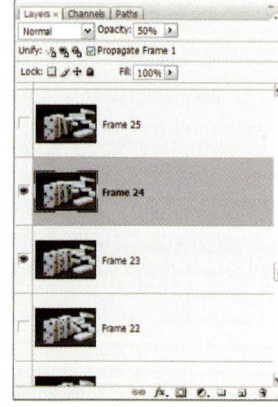

Figure 13.34
Think of video echoing as "time blurring."

5. Because every frame is a keyframe in Frames mode on the Animation palette, and because this animation is not exactly a true video yet, it's safe to simply click the toggle at bottom right to now switch to Timeline mode. You'll see a massive number of layer tracks, and they all appear to run the duration of the animation. This is because Photoshop has used Hold Interpolation every 1/30 of a second to turn each layer's visibility on and off; the layers exist on the timeline, but only for a faction of a second. This is also the reason why you can't use the Tween feature in Frames mode to automate the time echo effect. The Animation palette can't successfully tween between layers that are

hidden and unhidden; if all layers were visible then you could automate opacity changes to create time echoes, but this is not the way Photoshop converts video to still frame animation.

6. Choose File > Export > Render video. Don't use compression, make sure your fps rate is 29.97, and then click Render. After watching the exported video, and it looks good, do some hard drive housecleaning and delete the still frames and the PSD file.

Assembling the Time-Warping Domino Movie

I covered earlier how to stitch video clips into a single composition, and this is all you really need to do to complete the composition now. Here are the steps:

1. Open the video of the setup in Photoshop.

2. Choose Layer > Video Layers > New Video Layer from File, and then choose the SloMo sequence you wrote in the previous section.

3. There's not enough Work Area for both clips because when you import a video, the Work Area only runs from head to tail. So click the Palette menu and then choose Document Settings.

4. Set the duration to 25 seconds or so. Always define more Work Area than you need to save a trip to this setting. If the Work Area of a composition is too long, you can always drag the tail of the Work Area in to match the playlength of the composition.

5. Shift the SloMo layer's track on the Animation palette so its head butts with the bottom layer's tail, as shown in Figure 13.35.

6. I'm big on audio tracks accompanying video, and this movie has no audio; I removed it because it only had spoke stage and camera directions with a household appliance or two kicking in. Here's my philosophy with audio to accompany a video whose time shifts: A consistent audio track, one with a steady tempo, helps bind the two events in the audience's mind. Load Ring Around the Rosie.mp3 in Photoshop; Windows users need to use File > Open As and then choose QuickTime movie from the Open drop-down list or Photoshop won't recognize the music.

7. Add the audio to the composition by dragging its thumbnail from the Layers palette into the dominos document window.

8. The music runs for approximately 23 seconds. If this is too short for your composition, your best bet is to center the track in the Work Area on the Animation palette. It will then take a moment to begin, which is fine because the audience is paying attention to the video, and the end of the music fades, so a fade to silence at the end of the composition is perfectly natural.

Figure 13.35
Match the head to the tail of the bottom video to create a seamless transition between fast and slow motion.

9. Render the video to QuickTime, using either the H.264 or Sorenson 3 codec. Because the video has few unique colors, you can probably get better compression using H.264, while I've found that Sorenson codes better color for brilliant, lively scenes.

> **Tip**
>
> The Ring Around the Rosie music is public domain so I can share my arrangement with you with no financial or legal encumbrance. The reason I arranged the children's song as a marching drum and bagpipe score was not to be silly, but instead to provoke a little thought on the audience's part. When I played the finished file back for my wife, she (and I'm sure most other people) started humming and singing the "…all fall down" part. Hey, this is called engaging the audience, and the music has a certain appropriateness, adding an entertainment element to the video—marching drums call to mind soldiers all lining up for a military review. The dominos substitute for marching soldiers just fine, I felt.

Reversing Time

To conclude this chapter, I thought showing how to make videos run backwards is a good one. It's simple to perform, and all you really need is a good piece of footage whose content clearly demonstrates linear progression forward, to then catch the audience off-balance and usually amuse them. By the way, the sequence of the dominos falling can be reversed just like the video I show in the following section, if you'd care to practice later.

Cracking Up the Audience with Revered Eggs

The scene that immediately came to mind before writing this tutorial is to crack a couple of eggs and then make them return to their shells using Photoshop. I'm sure you can think of other creative pieces of video: a bicyclist traveling backwards, leaves returning to their tree in the autumn, even a couple of eggs unfrying in a stove pan.

Open 2 eggs.mov now in Photoshop and follow these steps to learn how to reverse footage:

1. Click the menu button on the Animation palette and then choose Flatten Frames into Layers. This might take a few moments to process; be patient.

2. Delete the hidden video layer at the bottom of the Layers palette. Photoshop does nondestructive editing, so the video is safely hidden but unnecessary for this example, and its presence will actually trigger an attention box later if you don't trash it right now.

3. Choose Convert to Frame Animation from the palette menu.

4. Choose Make Frames from Layers.

5. Select all 242 frames on the Animation palette by hold Shift while you click the first frame and then the last frame.

6. Choose No Delay from the duration pop-up below the thumbnail image of any frame on the Animation palette. You change one duration value, and all selected frames fall into the same duration. This delay jazz is covered later in this book; basically it's for timing an animation you want to write out as a GIF, but it has other creative purposes. At No Delay, the frames will fall back into a video format (29.97 fps) perfectly.

7. Choose Reverse Frames while they're all still selected; the command's on the flyout menu on the palette, as shown in Figure 13.36.

8. Choose Convert to Timeline from the Animation palette's menu. As you can see in Figure 13.37, the palette is a mess, holding 242 frames, hiding and showing them in reverse succession at 29.97 fps. Once you're sure the video version of the composition has been correctly rendered, you can lose this document.

9. Render the document to video using any codec you like. If you look in the Gallery folder, I added music to my own finished video. And you might expect the audio I did; it features reversed cymbals and drums and is quite reminiscent of one of The Beatles' experimental tunes during the Rubber Soul and Sgt. Pepper's era. Again, video without any audio these days can creatively undermine what you're cobbling as entertainment.

Figure 13.36
When a video has been converted to frames, it's a simple matter to reorder the frames.

Figure 13.37
Convert the reversed frames to Timeline mode.

That's the story for a potpourri of basic special effects. Do they tell a story? Not really, but rather they can be used to help tell a larger story. I'm confident with the clues in this chapter you'll find a wealth of variations that will suit dozens of needs and rescue scores of assignments from the doldrums of "set 'em up and shoot" video clips.

As always, you just need to fit your talents and your work into a story. Stories are what video is all about.

14

Advanced Compositing: Green Screening

From flying superheroes to the Little People who are dwarfed by teacups and housecats that have graced the silver screen for three-quarters of a century, it has all been achieved through clever compositing. Today, you can perform compositing and make fantasy tales come true using Photoshop, in very much the same way you composite a still photograph foreground object into a new background—it's all done with layers and transparency. With video layers, it just takes a little more time and scripts, and actions are an essential part of the recipe.

We refer to the whole process of removing the background (and in this chapter a foreground element, too) from video as *green-screening*, but the screen is only the first step in the process. Think of the screen and your video camera as the hardware and Photoshop Extended as the software component that performs the actual masking. In this chapter I'm going to catapult your skills into a new, pro-league arena with an example of creating an entire television newsroom, complete with flashy graphics and a correspondent who is composited against the classic metropolitan skyline. I also show you how to work with *green garment* to build a clip where an actor's body apparently vanishes in the tradition of Claude Rains (1933, *The Invisible Man*).

Lighting and Why We Use Green for Screening

Before you begin *cutting keys*, it would be good to know what cutting a key means (!), and it all begins with lighting a green screen before you even think of launching Photoshop.

A *key* is slang for chroma key and *color key*; it's the color that cinematographers want to assign (key) to scene objects so that the specialist processing the film could mask the areas, making them transparent so the film could be sandwiched with background footage or a special effect. Traditionally, blue was used for keying because physical motion picture film—we're talking RGB—has the least noise in the Blue channel. Thus, cutting a blue key from a blue screen or other object was less cumbersome and produced the most refined edges with the fewest holes. Naturally, as a director, you didn't want anything else in a scene that was the same shade of blue or it would drop out as well.

Flash forward to the present, and we use green for keying because digital film responds the most to green in the visible spectrum, whether it's the affordable 4.1.1 or the more expensive professional 4.2.2 format (4 is the number of luminance passes, and the following numbers refer to chromacity passes).

A natural question is this: What color green do I use for green screening? There is no answer to that one; I've purchased a large green screen and several smaller ones from Hollywood suppliers, and none of them is a precise match (I've therefore taken to shopping locally at fabric stores for future keying needs). To work, your green screen simply has to have a lot of pure green in it (avoid bluish casts) and absorb light but not reflect highlights. Consistency is important: Your green screen should be tight on its mount to minimize creases and folds that cast self-shadows and as evenly lit as possible within your budget. Hollywood folks such as George Lucas sometimes resort to having a rig built with fluorescent tubing inside so that the green or blue object holding miniatures is self-illuminating, almost completely eliminating shading and falloff.

In Figure 14.1 you can see the preliminary setup for the green screen shoot you'll work with in the following sections, from the camera mount's point of view. Clearly the setup is not finished; the wrinkles in the green screen were massaged to acceptability with gaffer's and duct tape at the edges, out of frame.

Keying things out of a video composition can result in very fun stuff, but the process itself needs meticulous attention paid to lighting and a lot of dry runs, and it helps to think of it as fun that just happens to involve hard work! If you care to take up green-screening as a trade, here's a basic checklist to review before you hang your cottage industry's shingle out:

1. Outdoor green screening I've found is easier than domestic indoor shooting. Your talent, your lights, and your camera have more freedom of movement. If you have a budget for location, try to rent a local TV studio set during off-hours; chances are good they will already have a green screen set up with default lights. If you go the outdoor route, choose an overcast day and then use studio lights. By doing this, you have more control over lighting and lighting consistency. I've found that sunny days are awful for cinematography

Figure 14.1

The green screen is 20' by 10', positioned against a house wall, hung on a 1" PVC tube from a loop on one end, and mounted using household curtain mounts.

where you need to cut a key; highlights are practically unavoidable on brilliant days. Additionally, the sky will cast into your green screen, tinting it more than you'd think, and this will make the green screen less green and harder to cut out in Photoshop.

2. Keep shadows off the green screen at almost all cost. If you're shooting full figure, buy a screen that is long enough to put behind your actors, scooping below them, and estimate enough floor coverage (depth from the wall) so your actor can stand at least four feet in front of the screen. By positioning your actor like this, shadows will (ideally) not fall on the wall. It's artistically acceptable to allow a shadow cast by the actor on the floor to be included with the actor you're keying, but you will find a drop shadow on the green wall difficult to work with in a composite.

3. Out of your total stage lights, dedicate at least one, perhaps two, to lighting the green screen. This is another reason you want to keep your actor away from the screen. As you can see in Figure 14.1, I'm on a budget, and we bought work lights instead of proper stage lights that come with barn doors so you can focus the lights. But I outfitted the lights with properly color-balanced bulbs, and as a result I was able to buy several lights on varying height mounts, resulting in less professionalism (no one will see the lights) and more coverage and options for lighting.

4. Have a can of dulling spray handy to dust areas where you might get highlights off the screen or indirect reflections from the screen onto objects you don't want to vanish. Read the label before you apply it to any surface, but you're generally okay with art supply store dulling spray that says it can be

used to knock down reflections on photographing silverware. Color key that ekes into unwanted scene areas is called *spill*, and Photoshop doesn't have a utility for spill suppression (but After Effects does).

5. Consider what you're replacing in your green screen work—what's the lighting in the background replacement footage? Take a good look at the key (main) light and any fill and spot lights in the scene that'll replace the green screen and then strive to match your subject lighting to it in your green screen shoot. This might seem like an obvious one, but take a look at the unintentionally laughable blue screen work in 1950's B movies. The pilot in the fake cockpit who is lovingly key lit while the sky background is all blown out with ambient lighting—you want your composite work to be successful, and you match elements as you would in a still composition.

6. Find a stand-in for your talent, and run the scene a day or two before the shoot; actually film it and review it for any potential problems. Use identical lighting, props, and clothing as you will for the live shoot. Actors appreciate this as a courtesy, as will you unless you're the gutsy type and don't mind recalling talent after a blown session.

Cutting Your First Key

I think you'll find the project I've created for you to work through will be exciting, and the techniques you'll learn can be applied to spruce up any Talking Head video a client might bring to you. You'll be able to put stunning set designs behind the actor, and later in this chapter I'll show you how to integrate crawling and fade-up graphics and text to achieve the same effect used on news shows (and especially fake news shows such as *The Colbert Report*).

Before beginning, however, I need to introduce you to a script you can download from Russell Brown's site (a fun teacher and one of Adobe's top graphic designers) and point out a few things you'll want to do to prep Photoshop's memory handling and other options to make your work go without a hitch.

Killing the Clipboard and Saving a Snapshot

Unlike video editors such as After Effects, Photoshop treats video you import a little differently when it comes to masking and other effects; it also saves video editing to PSD file format differently than After Effects, specifically to save file sizes, which I discuss a little later in this chapter. Realistically, there are certain things you can do in Photoshop with video you can't do in After Effects, but for the most part, After Effects is designed for video, whereas Photoshop is designed to integrate media from many different sources, and video editing is more of a perk than a specialty. The reason I'm bothering to mention the differences between these Adobe products is for the benefit of After Effects users who want to test the waters and begin to ply their trade using Photoshop Extended.

In After Effects, you're always working with proxy footage, and the saved project files are typically small. In contrast, when you alter an imported video clip in Photoshop, you're not altering the source file on your hard drive, but you are indeed generating a large chunk of data for Photoshop to save later. Additionally, when you run Dr. Brown's script, there are some things you'll want to do before, during, and after the script event.

First, go to http://www.russellbrown.com/tips_tech.html. At the time of this writing, you can download a bundle of Dr. Brown's scripts if you search or scroll down to the section marked "Dr. Brown's Adobe Photoshop CS3 Scripts." Look for the "Dr. Brown's Background Remover" script; it comes in a bundle, and they're all good scripts. I recommend that you don't download the installer package but instead the archive or scripts. It's very easy to manually install them: You unpack the archive and then—while Photoshop is not running—put all the JavaScript files (Windows users look for the .jsx file extension) in Adobe Photoshop CS3\Presets\Scripts. I'll explain what this JavaScript does in a moment; you access it from Photoshop's File > Scripts menu.

This script will make green screen removal, which is a permanent event unlike green screen keying in After Effects, very easy and fairly automated, but it uses the clipboard. Ordinarily I keep the Export Clipboard option activated in General Preferences, but for green screening, turn it off by pressing Ctrl/Cmd+K and unchecking this option on the General page of Preferences. Most of us have other programs and processes going on while Photoshop is running, and I've found that my apps really don't like what Dr. Brown's script will send to the system clipboard.

Caveat #2: After opening the Jackie.mov file, open the History palette, click the flyout menu icon, and choose New Snapshot—name it something you'll remember. I recommend you do this as a practice, and it has very little to do with the tutorial to follow but it will have a lot to do with your own assignments. Here's the deal: Dr. Brown's Background Removal script runs a whole lot of steps, probably more than your History States is set up for in Preferences > Performance. After the History palette hits the max, it starts deleting states, beginning with the first one of your maximum number, to continue to add to the History events. With a saved snapshot, the original state of your video—or *any* point in your critical editing work—is saved regardless of the number of history steps you (or a script) runs through. Use the Snapshot feature before running a script. and you ensure that a point in your editing never falls off the History palette list—you can always return to a needed Undo point.

Finally, after running a script, it's usually best to Purge Undos and History via the Edit command. Histories can take up RAM and temp space on your hard disks. Simply put, you dump what you don't need anymore. Figure 14.2 has three bulleted numbers: You do the first one before you open a video file, you do the second before running a script, and you do the third to purge all the steps a script might have run.

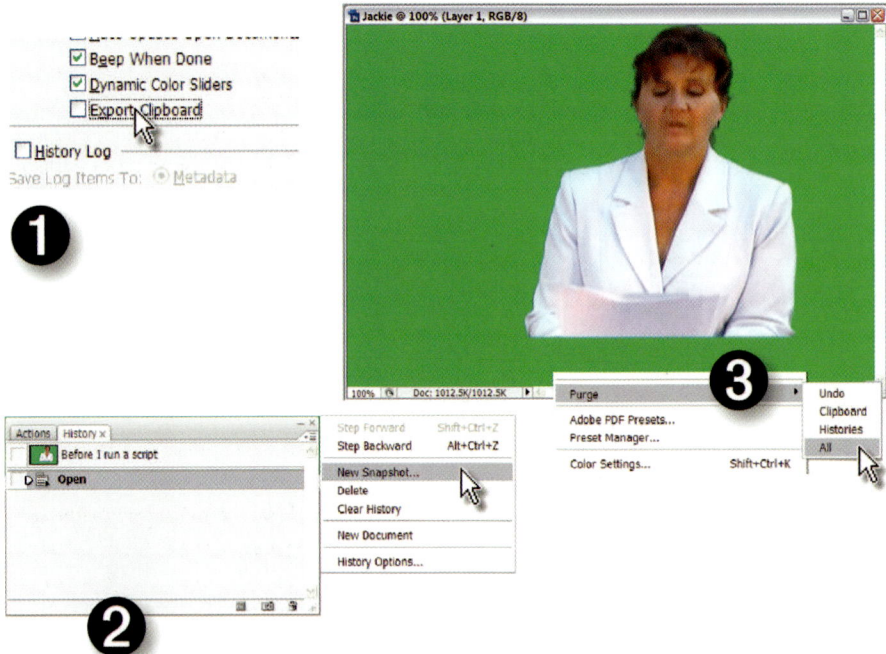

Figure 14.2
Video editing requires a lot of resources; keep your work fast and slim by saving what you need and releasing things that are no longer needed.

Running the Background Removal Script

What Russell Brown and the programmers at Adobe have done is very clever, and I'd be hard pressed to say you could write something as elegant yourself; I certainly can't. But it might be useful to you in the future to understand what the script does. The Select > Color Range is called after launching the script, and you're then prompted to choose the color you want erased in the active video layer. What then happens under the hood is that Hue/Saturation is called, and the green channel (or whatever color you've chosen in color Range; you can perform blue screen keying, too) is increased to maximum saturation to make choosing the color key more precise with less edge fringing.

The selected areas are then deleted, and the video is advanced to the next frame; the process is repeated to the end of the Work Area, where you'll then get a box that tells you the script can't continue. Therefore, it's important before running the JavaScript that the thumb on the Animation palette is at the beginning of the

> **Video Quality and Your Success at Cutting Keys**
>
> In the interest of full disclosure, no script on Earth is going to cut a key flawlessly unless the footage you use is high quality. My definition of "high quality" is video taken with a DV Pro camera (which start at $2,000 used) and not a prosumer cam like I use, that can capture frames that are at least 1K (1,000 pixels by 1,000 pixels; the frame proportion is unimportant in measuring frame size). Additionally, more color is better; a 4.2.2 capture is better than the prosumer 4.1.1 color information.
>
> Before you consider plunking down the approximate cost of a good used car for a professional camera, consider this: The line between prosumer and pro is blurring with respect to features and price and will continue to do so. Steven Soderbergh directed *Full Frontal* starring Julia Roberts for $3 million in 2002 using a mini DV camera that at the time went for $3,500 and was considered a prosumer model, which can be bought on eBay for about $2,000 today. In contrast and in comparison, *Revenge of the Sith* was the first feature-length all-digital film, done using a Sony camera modified for Panavision, whose current incarnation is $85,000, with rentals beginning at $1,500 a day with camera and lens only. I point to this film because at the time the digital camera wrote to 3.1.1 color sampling, in a certain respect returning lower quality color than my $500 Panasonic Palmcorder.
>
> The reason why green screen keying is cleaner with professional video data is that there's more data to work with. Russell Brown achieved spectacular results in his video tutorials online, and aside from his talent, he used "good data"; a professional camera yields professional footage with which to work. In comparison, the tutorial videos for this book you've downloaded vary in quality because I used a lot of compression to save you download time. For example, the Jackie.mov file was originally 1.2GB in its native DV-AVI file format. The inevitable interlacing of frames as recorded with a prosumer camera also thwarts green screen keying using scripts to a certain extent.
>
> The bottom line is that I encourage you to work through the tutorials, expect acceptable results, and know that your own green screen work using native DV-AVI video will come out cleaner—and even better if you purchase a pro digital camera.

Work Area and that your Work Area is defined to include all the frames whose background needs to be erased.

The finished composite video will feature animated text, and let's presume this news program will be broadcast—you therefore should use guides to mark action and title safety. This takes a few steps because there's no convenient way to copy guides from document to document:

1. Ctrl/Cmd+double-click the workspace to open the New dialog box. Choose Film & Video from the Preset drop-down, and you might as well specify Transparent background because you only need this document for the guides

included with the preset. If necessary, press Ctrl/Cmd+; (semicolon key) to toggle the guides on if they aren't currently visible.

2. Choose Layer > Video Layers > New Video Layer from File and then choose Jackie.mov, the video you downloaded earlier in the ZIP archive. You can delete the bottom layer now, and the safety guides will remain. Never merge a video layer down or you'll destroy its video properties.

3. If you haven't done so already, choose View and then turn off Pixel Aspect Ratio Correction. The advantage, always, of turning off the view (but not changing the actual video data) is that you have a correct view of the video content. The disadvantage is that painting tool brush tips look squashed, not nice and round. This is a trivial inconvenience; see Figure 14.3 for a comparison of pixel aspect ratios and what the guides look like now in the document window. The outer guides are for action safety, and the inner ones are title safety. You want to do this because standard definition TV sets tend to overscan by about 10%, I've never seen any compensation for it on my TV, and you don't want your audience to miss all the fun stuff I show you how to add to the video.

Figure 14.3
A comparison of pixel aspect ratios.

4. By default, the new Film & Video preset is 300 frames. The Jackie.mov file you copied in is 820 frames, so the Work Area is presently clipping most of the video. This is bad for the script you'll run; choose Document Settings from the flyout menu on the Animation palette and type either **30;00;00** or **900** in the Duration field, depending on how you have Palette Options defined (Frame Number or timecode).

5. I suggest you zoom into an edge where Jackie meets the green screen in the document window. After you launch the script, it will be hard to detect exactly the right shade of green to have the script erase.

6. Make sure the Jackie video layer is actively selected on the Layers palette by clicking its title. Choose File > Scripts and Dr. Brown's Background Remover.

7. You're presented with the Select > Color Range box, as shown in Figure 14.4. I recommend that you click very near the edge of Jackie against the green screen as a beginning sample using a low Fuzziness setting such as 50 and then choose the Add to Sample eyedropper from the box and click on the mostly solid green screen color; try adding a selection area within the gaps in the strands of hair. As you add to the selected color range, increase the Fuzziness value, and then back it down when the proxy window shows some of Jackie's blouse is included. Your final Fuzziness setting depends on the areas you eye-dropper sampled; a value between 95 and 100 worked best for me.

By doing this you're eliminating some possible fringing. *Do not* hold Alt/Opt to reset the box if you make a mistake; doing this will baffle and error the JavaScript. Instead, you're best cancelling the whole operation and trying again. After you click OK, the process is automated, and even with a fast machine, you'll have enough time to wait to go get a fresh coffee.

8. Save the file to PSD file format somewhere where you have at least 100MB of free hard drive space. This action will take approximately three minutes on a Quad Core, five minutes on a Core Duo machine, and six to seven years on an iPod (I'm kidding). So make a sandwich to go with your coffee from Step 7 while you wait.

Figure 14.4
Run Dr. Brown's Background Removal script to automatically cut a key based on your selection of color.

> **Caution**
>
> Also notice for future reference the blow-up I've created in this figure of the Animation palette's track for this video layer with the parameters opened to reveal Altered Video, which shows up in purple on the Work Area. Yep, every frame of this video is being altered. This means that the saved file is going to be very large, anywhere from 20 to 50MB, even though the Jackie.mov file is only 5MB and the document sizes area of the document window cheerfully tells you the document is less than 2MB (this is a Photoshop programming error). I'll get to managing huge PSD files shortly.

Finessing the Key the Script Cut

In addition to interlacing, you can't cut a flawless key from prosumer video data because of the native compression with DV AVI; it's too noisy for Dr. Brown or anyone else's script to cut the key perfectly. The workaround is to finesse the key you now have using any of a number of different methods, depending on the background you want to use as a replacement.

Obviously if you wanted to put The Emerald City behind Jackie now, the edgework would be hidden pretty well due to hue similarities. It's important to add the background at this stage to better examine how the edges look; you might need a little work, or you might need none at all—you have to evaluate with a background image in place.

In Figure 14.5 you can see a close-up of an edge to Jackie's blouse contrasting against the skyline you'll add in a moment. You can zoom in while reviewing the video at 100% resolution (the way the audience will see it), by choosing Window > Arrange > New Window for (whatever the filename is). This opens a new view of the same document. Upon some careful examination, it's Jackie's blouse and not her hair or any other edge area that needs refining.

Here's how to write your own action and reuse a script you created in Chapter 9 as one of several different ways to clean up the fringing:

1. Open Skyline.mov and turn off Pixel Aspect Ratio Correction. On the Layers palette, right-click over the layer and then choose Rasterize Layer. It's a still image now, still good for your reference work, and it no longer carries the overhead of working with a video layer.

2. Right-click over the layer title and then choose Duplicate Layer. Shift+drag the layer to the Jackie.psd document and then arrange it so it's on the bottom. Close the Skyline.mov file without saving changes.

Figure 14.5
When only certain areas need refining across hundreds of frames, you can write an action to automate the task.

3. Click on the Jackie layer to make sure this is the active layer. With the rectangular Marquee tool, select only the area of Jackie's blouse where the fringing needs to be hidden. Removing the color pixels that make up the fringing is not a good idea because it would change the shape of Jackie's outline. Instead, you'll *deemphasize* the fringe color to better blend with the background. *This is an* el primo *trick to add to your repertoire.* It's retouching, not butchery an audience will spot in a second. You're selecting before creating an action to keep the Action "clean"; the selecting process will not be part of the action and so you can reuse the action with any selection area in the future.

4. Open the Actions palette and rename any action you created in previous tutorials named x in the Default Actions folder. Then create a new action, name it x (lowercase is critical, as is creating it in the Default Actions folder), and you're recording now.

5. Press Ctrl/Cmd+U for the Hue/Saturation adjustment.

6. You'd think that you need to reduce the saturation in the greens, but that's not the case here. If you were to sample the edge fringe with the Eyedropper tool and then use the Color Picker to look up the color, you'd see that the fringing is closest to cyan. This is because we shot outdoors, and Jackie's blouse caught some ambient light from the sky, the blue additively mixed with the background green screen, and cyan is the result. Choose Cyans from the Edit drop-down list and then drag the Saturation slider all the way to the left. Optionally, try dragging Lightness up a little. Look at your document; it looks pretty darned clean in Figure 14.6. Click OK to apply, advance the current time by one frame on the Animation palette, and then stop the Actions palette from recording any further.

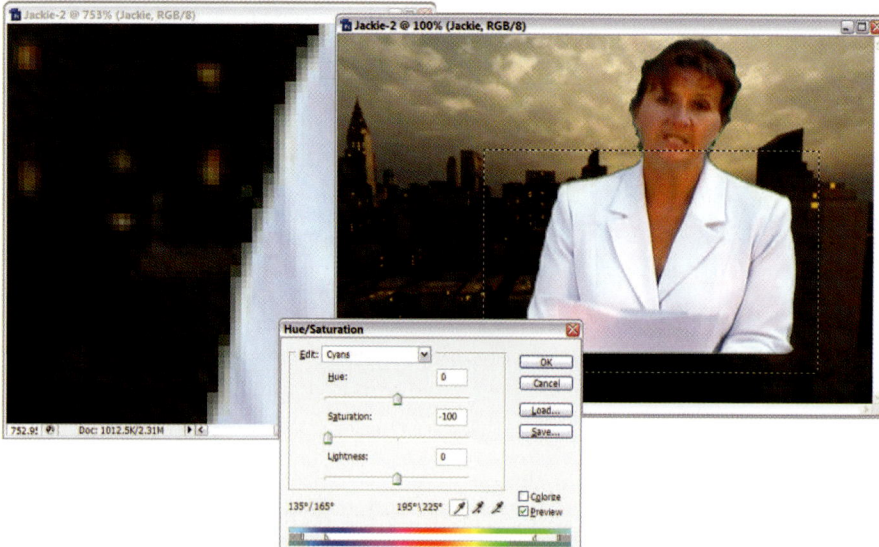

Figure 14.6
You don't need to alter the geometry of a composite piece to defringe a green screen cut. Often you can blend the fringe with the background by desaturating it.

Cutting a Key Around Hair

Keeping loose strands of flowing hair clean and free of fringing without breaking up and causing twittering is the problem of video special effects people of *all* skill levels, not just mortals like you and me.

There are many proprietary and extremely expensive software programs designed to keep loose strands of hair composited properly in green screen work, but I still see hard edges in multimillion-dollar theatrical releases.

For Photoshop Extended users, I recommend getting it right in the camera as completely as possible, so you have less of your *own* hair to remove when trying to get it right in Photoshop. Ask yourself how often you really need wafting hair in a composite scene. If you're doing a shampoo commercial or special effects for a metal band, you probably have the budget for compositing software and something such as After Effects. However, let's stick to Photoshop.

Getting it right in the camera can engender asking your talent to put their hair up, as I did with Jackie. Alternatives include a hat, some really cheap hair spray, and as an extreme option a really close crop haircut. In any event, the more evenly you light your screen, the better your chances are of cutting a good key.

Digital Anarchy offers one of the best tools I've ever seen called Primatte (like the ape) v3.0 for about $300. It is a specialty tool not intended for general chroma keying, but instead to seek and mask difficult areas such as hair, when staged against a color contrasting background. If you plan on making keying your bread and butter, you should consider Primatte.

7. Run a script that will execute Action x 820 times or so. The ExecuteMoltenLead.jsx that ships with Photoshop in the Sample Scripts folder requires three lines of text to be modified to make it work with your X action. If you followed along with instructions on how to do this in Chapter 4 and Chapter 9, then you should be able to use the ExecuteX.jsx script, which has already been modified with the necessary line changes in place. All that is needed now is a minor change to the script for the number of times the script will need to run. Open the script in Notepad and make the minor change and save changes.

8. After the JavaScript runs your action x, delete the bottom skyline layer and render the video; it'll be easier and faster to work with than the altered video you have saved as a PSD now. Choose File > Export > Render Video.

9. In the Render Video box, choose a hard drive location that has a lot of open space. You could in practice write this video out using QuickTime Animation compression to save the alpha channel the script created, but you won't be happy with the fidelity of the resulting file. So write it out with no compression, Millions of Colors+ in the (Movie) Settings box, choose Straight-Unmatted in the Render Output field, and then click Render. QuickTime is the only file format that preserves audio, and if you played the clip by holding Alt/Opt while clicking the Animation palette Play button, you'll hear that there is audio in this clip. You can close the file without saving now.

Compositing and Adding Graphics Elements

Now you can composite the Skyline movie with the saved Jackie version with the alpha transparency. In the steps to follow, you'll also add one of those text crawls that contribute to the over-information we see on the daily news. This is a simple effect I covered in Chapter 7 and will breeze through here.

1. Sadly, Photoshop guides are not written to exported videos, so Ctrl/Cmd+ double-click the workspace to display the New dialog box and then choose the Film & Video preset.

2. Use the View menu to hide Pixel Aspect Ratio Correction for the file, then choose Layer > Video Layers > New Video Layer from File and then choose Skyline.mov, the file you created a still frame from in the previous section. Delete the bottom empty layer that was generated from the Film & Video preset. And as mentioned before, the Film & Video preset defaults to 300 frames, so again, go to the Animation palette menu and choose Document Settings and adjust the settings to approximately the number of frames in the background skyline video.

3. Choose Layer > Video Layers > New Video Layer from File and then choose the Jackie movie you rendered out in the previous tutorial. Using the Layer menu is a good and fast shortcut to opening a video and duplicating the layer to a different document window. If necessary, use the Move tool to move Jackie to the right of the document a little so she's positioned in the window, similar to the position shown in Figure 14.6.

4. With the rectangular Marquee tool chosen, create a new, normal static layer on top of the document layer stack and then drag a rectangle approximately 30 pixels high that runs edge to edge horizontally just below Jackie.

5. Choose a deep gray, almost but not quite black as your foreground color and then press Alt/Opt+Backspace to fill the rectangle, then Ctrl/Cmd+D to deselect. This is your background for the crawling text, and my reason for deep gray is that it's frequently used for crawls on news programs.

6. Think of some good news to run across the screen. The duration of the clip is almost 30 seconds; at a moderate pace, you have the opportunity to run about six or seven short phrases.

7. Choose the Type tool and on the Options bar choose left justification. To be legible on a television set as well as on a user's computer screen, you can get away with about 20 pt. text. I recommend Helvetica Bold condensed or Bold Condensed Arial for legibility and also to imitate the text commonly used on news shows. Choose a medium purplish-blue as the font color; make sure it's legible against your deep gray background.

8. Click an insertion point at the left of the document window in the deep gray rectangle, at the first frame of the timeline, and then continue typing, even when the text has run off the document window at right. Photoshop doesn't clip the out of bounds text; it'll become visible after you animate it, and if you made a typing error it can be corrected after it appears (after you scrub the timeline). In Figure 14.7, I typed some "headlines" in keeping with Jackie's mock news report about world peace. "Don't run with the scissors," "Pigs can fly," "the check is in the mail"…fantasy stuff and urban legends. Think of "that'll be the day" headlines and put ellipses after each "news brief" to imitate the ticker tape look.

9. On the Animation palette, open the attributes area for the text track and then choose the Move tool.

10. Jackie doesn't begin to address the camera until Frame 55 or so. It will not look right if the text starts crawling before she starts the report, so set the thumb on the Animation palette to Frame 55.

11. Using the keyboard arrows (alternatively, hold down the Shift key when dragging with the Move tool) to prevent accidental vertical position changes,

nudge the text out of frame to the right so it makes an entrance outside of title safety. Then click the stopwatch button for Position on the Animation palette to set a key.

12. Go to the end of the Work Area with the thumb (the timeline current time indicator), and then nudge the text until it has traveled to the left up until the last word in your headlines is just outside to the right of title safety. A second key has been automatically generated at the end of the clip, and your screen will look like Figure 14.8.

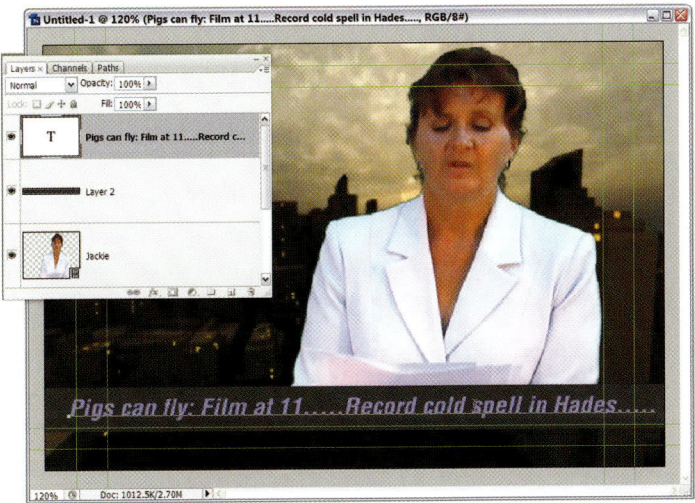

Figure 14.7
Create the text for the crawling banner.

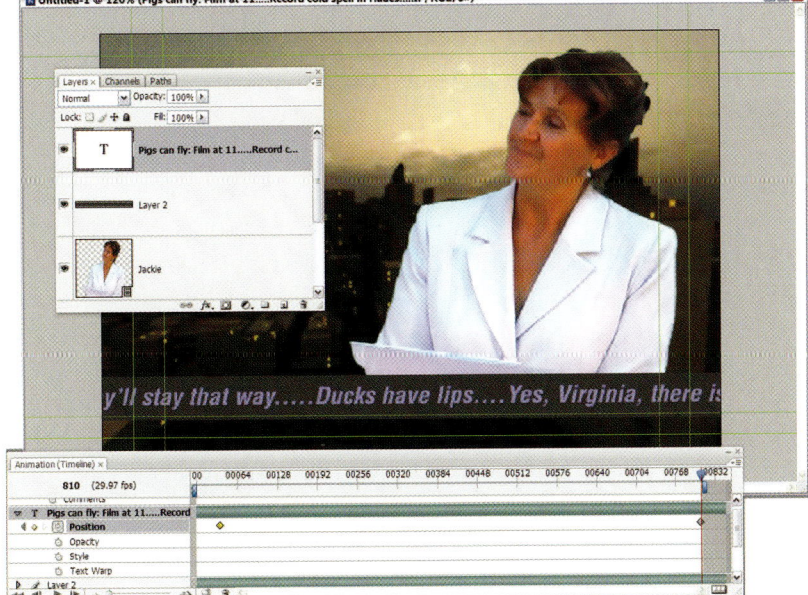

Figure 14.8
To create a crawl, you create a beginning key and an end key while changing the horizontal position of the text.

Adding Other Screen Elements

"Overdoing it" is the stock and trade of broadcast graphics folks; if you're like me, you're overwhelmed by the onscreen info before the reporter utters a word! So to better clutter up the scene (thus taking the viewer's mind off the usually depressing news), you'll now add some static graphics that can be faded up at various points in the news report. I created the graphics in a drawing program and saved them as PNGs with transparency, so putting them on top of the video layers will be a snap.

1. Open sunny forecast icons.png, USB logo for screen.png, peace epidemic.png, and Rainbow.png.

2. Duplicate the files over to the video composition and then you can close the originals. Rename the new layers for easy reference in the video document, and then arrange them using the Move tool so they look like Figure 14.9, or if you have a better layout idea, go for it, but keep the text within title safety. The rainbow isn't visible in this figure, but if you peek ahead to Figure 14.11, have it arc behind Jackie's head, landing around where the Tuesday sunny icon is located.

3. Let's get creative in the staged appearance of the elements. At about Frame 150, Jackie tells the audience that peace has broken out worldwide. This is a good opportunity to fade up the Peace Epidemic headline. Click open the

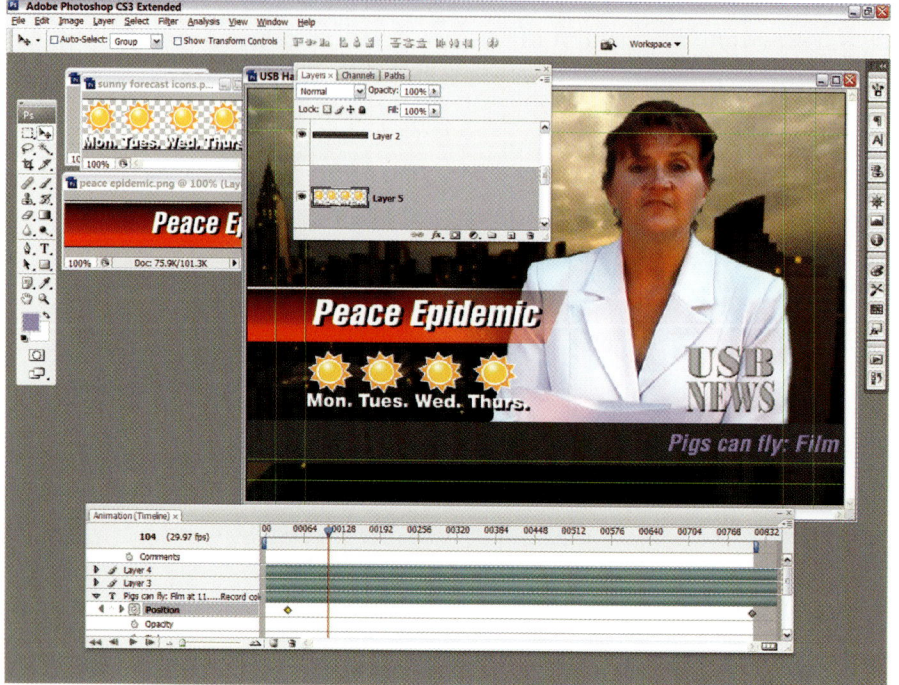

Figure 14.9

Lay the frame out like you would a bleed advertisement, keeping text within safety (*trim* or *live size* in magazine layouts).

Peace Epidemic area on the Animation palette track, scrub the timeline to about Frame 135, set the opacity on the Layers palette for this layer to 0%, and then click the Opacity stopwatch to set the entrance key. Then go to Frame 150 and increase the opacity of the headline to 100%. You've created a half-second fadeup, impactful without totally disorienting the viewer.

4. The four-day weather forecast can come up a little later; I leave the exact point up to your judgment. A slower, two-second fade up at about 10 seconds into the report, when Jackie flashes a smile at the camera, seems to be appropriate. Remember, a graphic's entrance should not be upstaged; it's confusing and looks unpolished to introduce elements too closely spaced together in time. See Figure 14.10.

5. The USB news logo should be persistent; no fades, just position it to clip Jackie's shoulder, within title safety. I built transparency into the exported PNG file, so there's really nothing to do in this step. In fact, ignore this step and move onto Step 6.

6. Finally, the rainbow can appear very gradually over a relatively long duration for a touch of subtle sarcasm. A fade up from 10 seconds to final opacity of about 80% in Screen mode is good. Also, as an exported vector graphic, it's a little too clean, so apply about a 5-pixel Gaussian blur to it, make sure it's positioned on the Layers palette above the skyline but behind Jackie, and you're in business to render the video, as shown in Figure 14.11.

Figure 14.10
Stage the appearance of graphics so each has some breathing room in time from its neighbor.

Figure 14.11
The rainbow is a good but subordinate element to the other graphics, so give it partial opacity and let it fade up for about one-third the duration of the entire clip.

7. Choose File > Export > Render Video. Write the video out without an alpha channel to QuickTime, and I suggest no compression, because you're going to put a short intro clip before this video in the following section. There's no sense in compressing (and thus degrading) your exported work twice. However, after you're certain the clip exported okay, you can delete the Jackie.psd file and the alpha channel export from earlier in this chapter to pick up hard drive space.

Adding Polish to a Production

Every news special and broadcast has a program identifier, usually no more than five to six seconds. I created USB opening graphic.mov using Luxology modo 301 and a few particle effects, and it's much simpler than it might look to rotate a ball toward the camera with extruded text. Additionally, I cobbled USB News intro.mp3 as a separate file so the music track can dovetail the opening graphic and Jackie's report. To put this piece together takes only a few steps, as follows:

1. Open your compiled news report and then add seven seconds to it by choosing Document Settings from the Animation palette's menu and doing the addition in the Duration field.

2. Slide the Jackie track so it begins at seven seconds on the timeline and butts to the end of the Work Area.

3. Choose Layer > Video Layers > New Video Layer from File. Choose USB opening graphic.mov and then drag its track so it overlaps the Jackie video layer track by a little less than a second (20 frames is good).

4. Drag the head and tail of the Work Area in to crop to the video in the document without leaving the padding I've recommended when setting up the timeline in this chapter. It's easier to crop to the action in a composition than to visit the Document Settings again when your video exceeds the Work Area.

5. Give the intro a half-second fade out to reveal Jackie. In real reporting, reporters arc aware of the fade out and make sure they're not primping when the intro has faded out. This is why I left some air at the beginning of the original Jackie.mov file, and true to the spirit of news reporting, she was looking off-camera for a few seconds.

6. Open the USB News intro.mp3 file; Windows users need to specify File > Open As and set the file type to QuickTime movie.

7. Drag the MP3's thumbnail from the Layers palette into the video document window and then close the file without saving.

8. Move the audio layer to the head of the Work Area on the Animation palette. In Figure 14.12 you can see the whole setup. I've included a screen capture of the audio track as viewed in an audio editor. GoldWAVE, Sony SoundForge, and Adobe audition are common examples of audio editors that display sound

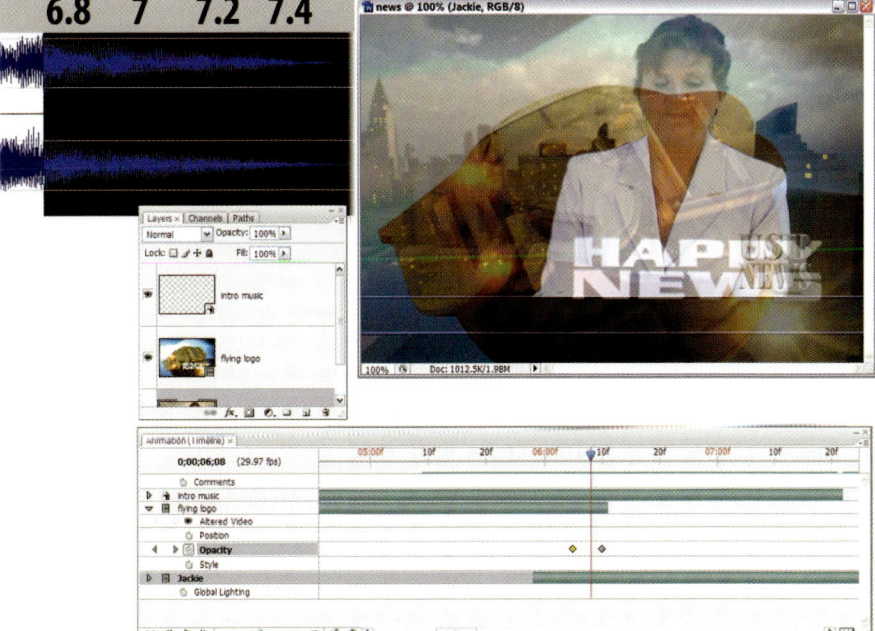

Figure 14.12
Join two pieces of video using an audio clip.

analytically as a waveform or spectrograph readout, making it easy to detect specific passages. The audio works perfectly in the composition because I faded out the music at the exact point where Jackie begins her report, leaving a little xylophone trail into her speech. If you own a digital audio workstation such as Cakewalk or Cubase, all you need is a tympani, a xylophone, a few strings, and some trumpets (and a twisted sort of humor) to make your own news intro.

Unfortunately, there is no way to adjust volume on an audio track using Photoshop; you need an audio editor.

9. File > Export > Render Video. I suggest QuickTime using either H.264 or Sorenson for the best quality if you want to compress the file.

An Extracurricular Tutorial: Adding an Inset Video

In the spirit of news, this section is the OpEd page: Optional Education! Notice that in the film you just composited and exported, Jackie turns to a vacant area of the screen and introduces a foreign correspondent. There's actually more to that video. It plays for 59 seconds and has about a 25-second pause in it while Jackie pretends to react to an inset image of the foreign correspondent. It's green screening on green screening that you'll learn next, and I've taken the repetition out of the following tutorial by doing the composite work for you of a foreign correspondent against an animated background.

In the next set of steps you'll work on timing, how to fade Nicholas Bivalve in and out of the upper left of the screen. The reason this composition will work is because the correspondent ran his lines off-screen with Jackie; the timing is therefore very good and tight.

1. Create a new file from the Film & Video preset. You don't need the preset's guides for title safety, but you do need them for action safety, to keep Nick within bounds in the video.

2. Choose Layer > Video Layers > New Video Layer from File and then choose 59 secs needs Nick.mov. Delete the bottom empty layer now, and turn off View > Pixel Aspect Ratio Correction.

3. Choose Layer > Video Layers > New Video Layer from File, and then choose Nicholas Bivalve.mov.

4. In Document Settings off the Animation palette menu, set the duration to 1773 frames (or 59;03 if your palette is set up for timecode).

5. Nick needs to appear at about Frame 952; move the track in the Work Area on the Animation palette so the head of the clip is at 952, as shown in Figure 14.13. Better still, to give yourself a little practice in timing, drag the Work

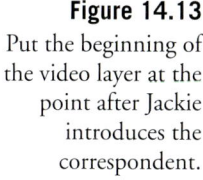

Figure 14.13
Put the beginning of the video layer at the point after Jackie introduces the correspondent.

Area into about 900 start and 1644 end to save Photoshop from buffering the whole composition. Then hold Alt/Opt and click the Play button on the Animation palette. Watch the timeline carefully for Jackie's introduction of Nick, and then set a comment at this point by clicking the Comment stopwatch on the Animation palette. Then you decide for yourself when Nick should appear.

6. With the Move tool, position Nick as shown in Figure 14. 13. Keep him within action safety, the outer guidelines.

7. A pop-up inset would look unprofessional. So give Nick's box a half second fade up and fade out by adjusting the layer's opacity, like you did with the graphics earlier. A half-second fade up is sort of a soft cut; it's not really visually a fade; see Figure 14.14.

8. Export the file to QuickTime and use H.264 or Sorenson as a codec.

You're done. I admit I had some fun spoofing the news, but you just learned a wealth of production and compositing techniques that will put you on your way toward walking into just about any indie studio and get a freelance gig, serious Talking Head shows, or lampoons in the vein of *SNL*. Play the video for friends and family and see what the reaction is. Interestingly, the video in the Gallery folder appeared to be so authentic my own family ignored the dialog, mistaking it for just another 60-second news bulletin!

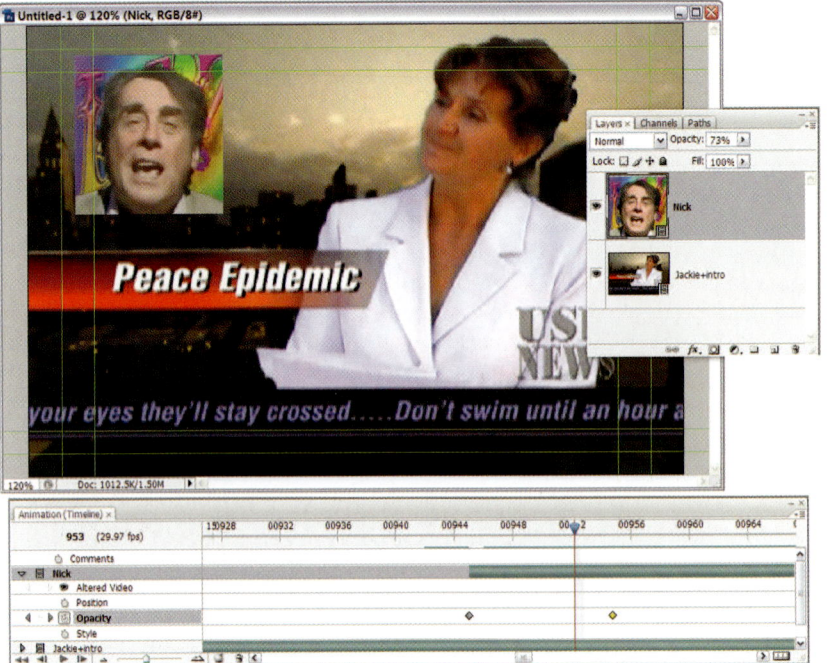

Figure 14.14
Fade the inset video in and out. Doing this is not only professional, but it also spares the audience from Nick's off-camera glances at the head and tail of the clip.

Green Suiting on the Cheap

Hollywood uses chroma keying in more than just background matting; blue garments have been worn by every stunt person to drop out the hands of prop handlers and entire anatomies of invisible folks for many, many years. In fact, blue cloth was used as Harry Potter's invisibility cloak in the first of the movie series (because it was shot on film and not DV). Also, one of the most inventive uses for green costuming was done by Special Effects supervisor John Knoll at ILM in *Star Wars Episode I: The Phantom Menace*. The character C3PO is introduced as an unfinished skeletal version of the prissy golden droid, and George Lucas and Knoll had to decide whether or not to do this with CG. They both had seen Japanese *bunraku* theater where actors and stagehands are entirely clad in black against a black stage to suggest invisibility. ILM decided then to dress puppeteer Michael Lynch up in a green suit (green for digital video keying) and walked the skeletal C3PO rig around in front of him for a most convincing illusion. American audiences might be more familiar with the performing troupe *Mummenschanz*, who use the same sort of masking disguise as in bunraku theater and performed on Broadway in the late 1970s with a reunion tour in 1995.

I'm not going to present you with a tutorial that is as ambitious as any Hollywood trickery, but the following sections will indeed clue you in to the creative possibilities of green garments as color keys and perhaps inspire you to invent creative variations of your own.

Here's the tutorial's plot: I got a performer to move around as though he's actually playing the flute he holds. He was performing to a soundtrack I'd arranged, and I later stripped out the raw audio and synched it with the original audio track. It's a short sequence of Bach's *Boureé in Em* (public domain music), delivered in the classic Jethro Tull jazz style. I thought it would be visually interesting to drop the actor's torso out and replace it with the music notation of the melody, the sheet music. This required a little ingenuity: What I did was write the piece in a music composition program and then print it to Adobe PDF. I then took the PDF file into Photoshop, cropped it, and saved it as the Music.png file you'll open shortly. This might sound like the long way about things, but a music aficionado might see the finished clip, and I wanted the notes to be right!

Figure 14.15 shows the lighting setup. We used a key light for the actor that also served to fill the background, a light dedicated to illuminating the green shirt, and then a carefully placed household lamp outfitted with halogen bulbs to match our work lights for color temperature to "paint" the scene where incidental light could fill and even out the shirt. Lighting took over an hour to test and get an acceptable overall exposure and even lighting on the shirt. You'll see that the actor casts shadows on the shirt, but for this example that was acceptable. The hardest part was keeping illumination off the background so it wouldn't look like flood lighting but at the same time keeping the green shirt evenly illuminated.

Note that in the "Cheap but it works" Lighting Department we used a windshield reflector over the key light, not to direct the light, but instead to reflect a little

Figure 14.15
Work on your lights and do a lot of test footage before attempting green costume keying.

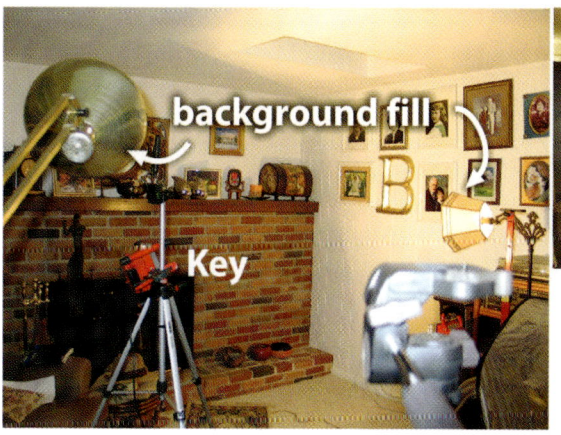

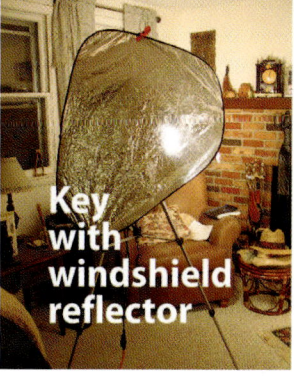

> **Buying Green: St. Patty Is Your Friend!**
>
> I was lucky to find a closeout store that still had St. Patrick's Day novelty shirts available in late August. If you want to outfit an actor or actress in green, I suggest you go shopping in late February. You'll find green T-shirts, green plastic bowlers you can use to drop out an actor's hair, gloves for moving props invisibly, and other apparel in what's usually a perfect green for keying.
>
> I don't recommend tailoring your own green shirt; we tried this, and actually the tighter the shirt, the less apt it is to crease and display shadows. If the shirt has *O'Malley's Pub* or some other signage on it, you just wear the shirt backwards (which is what our actor did) or turn it inside out.
>
> I also found a lime green pair of women's tights at the closeout store. You don't necessarily want or need them to create the illusion of a legless phantom—you can cut off a leg and put it over your actor's head (and then please *don't* film in a financial institution), and you can do a Headless Horseman scene. The actor can breathe and has some vision through the stocking, and you have yourself quite a startling fantasy composition.

indirect lighting while cutting down the transmission of light from the key light. A cheese cloth sort of diffusion was achieved, while picking up bounced light from other sources was had for less than $5. It worked, as you'll see.

Dr. Brown's Foreground Remover Script

I'm kidding with the header; you use Dr. Brown's *Background* Remover JavaScript in the steps to follow; you simply pick the green on the shirt instead of a background green screen. In Figure 14.16 you can see that the video clip is DV widescreen, not your typical 4:3 but instead double-wide 16:9 in aspect because we felt a video of a flute lent itself to an exceptionally wide document treatment. Open Boureé.mov now from the archive you unzipped and, because I never intended the video to be played back on a TV set, the pixel aspect ratio is square, 852 by 480 pixels, and you should not need to change the pixel correction in the View menu.

Follow these steps (they are very similar to masking Jackie's green screen) to take the actor's shirt off and still maintain a PG rating:

1. Choose File > Scripts > Dr. Brown's Background Remover.

2. When the Color Range box pops up, click on the actor's T-shirt. You might want to use the Eyedropper + tool to pick up more of the green areas, and I found that a Fuzziness of 200 works well with this example; refer to the

previous tutorial on cutting a key around Jackie for a good technique using the Eyedropper in combination with the Fuzziness slider. In Figure 14.17 I've chosen to preview the unselected areas using a white matte, an option from the drop-down list. Doing this better helps you see the selected color range without the distraction of the background; click OK to launch the script.

Figure 14.16
Video frame aspect isn't really important if your target playback is for computers.

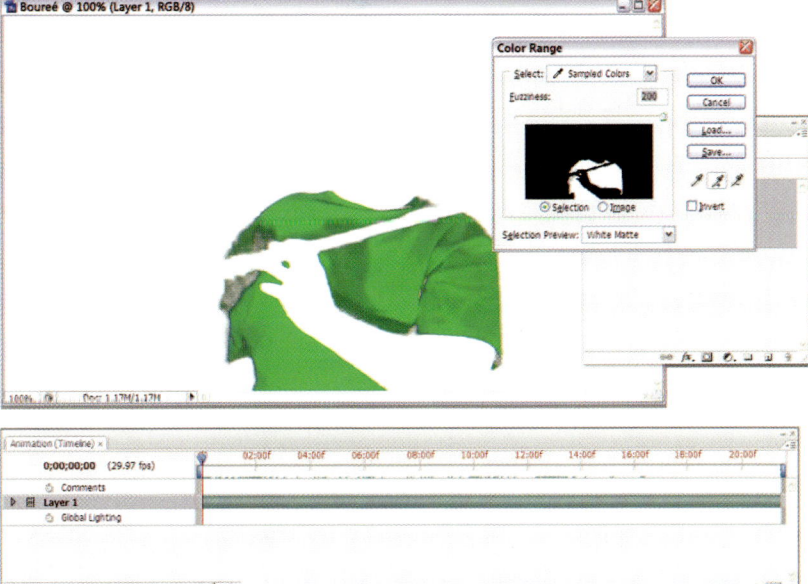

Figure 14.17
In Color Range you can choose from several different preview options.

3. Once the script has run, your document should look like Figure 14.18. Hey, the guy looks good in checkers. There's no real reason in this example to save the document as a PSD, which will simply slow the composition creating process down. Instead, choose File > Export > Render Video, and then render the composition out to QuickTime file format, no compression, with a Straight-Unmatted alpha channel. Then close without saving. Open the movie you just created with the alpha channel in preparation for the fancy stuff to come.

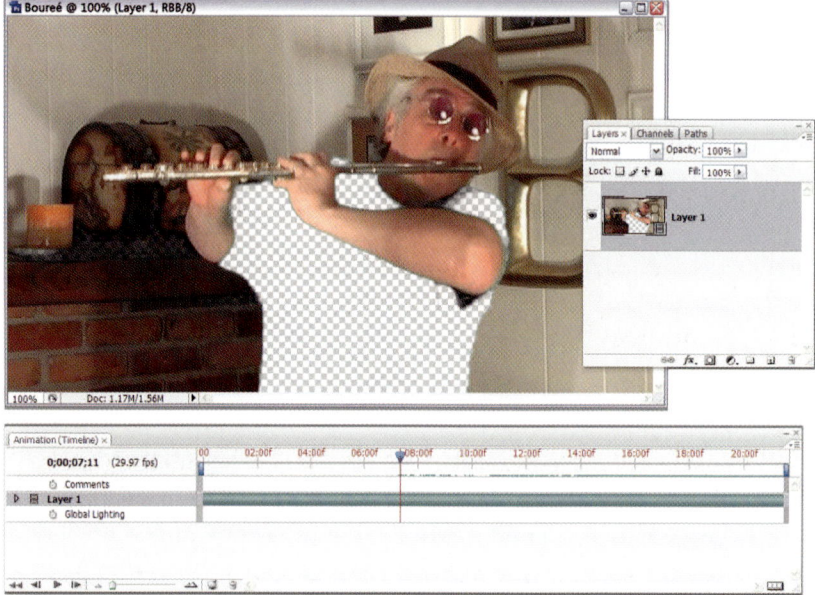

Figure 14.18
As long as the areas aren't green, some of the remaining interior shading (the shadows cast by the actor onto the shirt) is fine for this particular assignment.

I Got the Music in Me

On to the fun part: adding animated music to the actor's shirt. To do this, you'll need to open Music.png—the background is transparent so you can use any color background you wish.

1. Drag the PNG file's thumbnail from the Layers palette into the video document window, then close it without saving. Save the file to Photoshop PSD file format before continuing to ensure you don't accidentally lose your work.

2. Put the music layer underneath the video and then, with the Move tool, position it so it's centered on the actor's shirt.

3. Take a look at Figure 14.19. You want to stage the music notes so they're more or less in tempo with the actor playing the notes. There's a pause before he begins; with the Move tool, drag the music notes so that the G clef and the rest are centered on the shirt.

Figure 14.19
Begin to synch to appearance of the notes with the video.

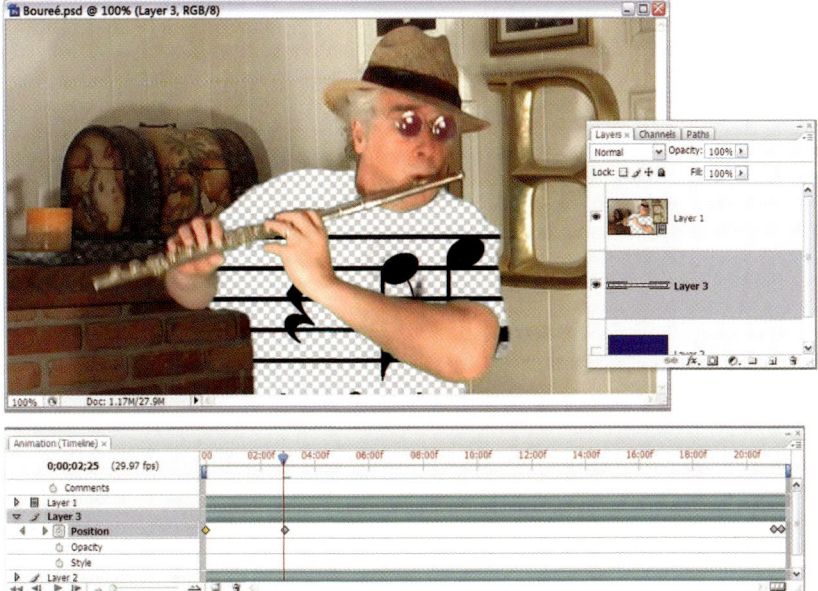

4. Click the Position stopwatch now for this track on the Animation palette to set a key.

5. Scrub the timeline ahead to where you see the actor begin to play the first note. To avoid unintentional vertical position changes, use the keyboard arrows to nudge the music to the left until the first note of the music is in the center of the actor's shirt.

6. Go to the end of the Work Area on the Animation palette and then use the Move tool to nudge the music layer so the rest in the music notation lands on the shirt's center after the actor is finished playing. The tempo might seem a little frantic when you play it back; it's your artistic call as to whether you want to slow it down, but it's fairly accurate right now, regardless of how it animates. The notes more or less appear on the center of the shirt when the actor "plays" them.

7. Create a Background layer for the shirt on the Layers palette. Then fill it with deep blue, which will obscure the music notes. This is okay; you're going to dress up the notes.

8. Open the Layer Styles palette, choose Web Buttons from the palette's menu, and then with the music notes layer as the current editing layer, click the Blue Gel with Drop Shadow icon. Your screen should look like Figure 14.20; my rationale for this style choice is that jazz is related to blues.

9. I'm not happy with defaults in general, and the Blue Gel could do with some tweaking for this composition. On the Layers palette, double-click the Outer Glow item under the Effects entry. The Layer Style box appears; choose near-white (with a hint of blue) by clicking the color swatch and then make the opacity 72% (or a little higher), then decrease the size to about 21 pixels. You're previewing your changes live in the document window as shown in Figure 14.21, so use your own creative input to make the notes the hero of the composition.

Figure 14.20
Add a Layer style to separate the music from the dark blue background and also to gussy up the notes.

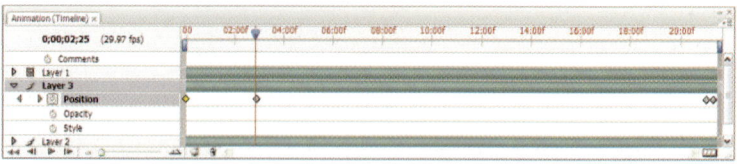

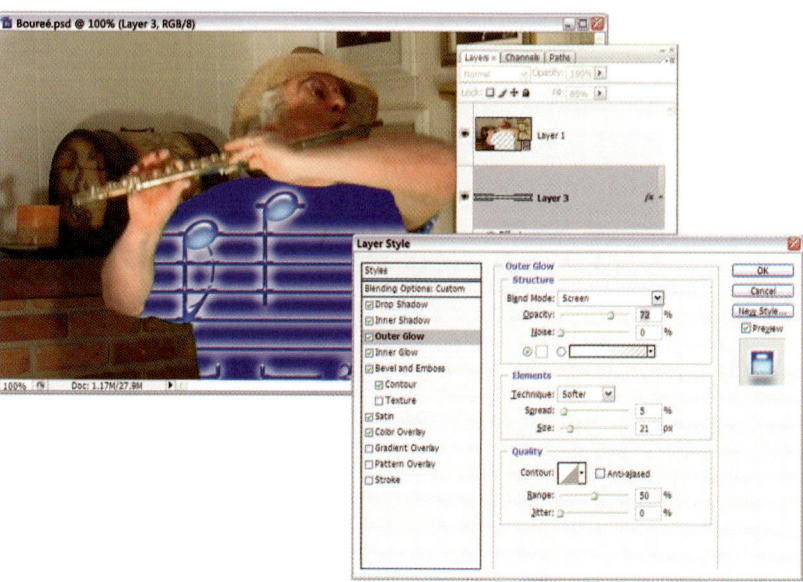

Figure 14.21
Modify the Layer style to add some punch to the music notes.

In several other tutorials I shun saving to PSD because all the video frames are altered, and the resulting PSD file is ungainly. However, none of the video you have in the document has been changed in any way, and Photoshop will only add animation info to the saved PSD, which is nominal in file size as well as the speed with which you work on the file.

Finessing the Video

Although it's a visually interesting video and in theory you could call it quits now, let's not and work on polishing the effect and then the presentation. When you work with green screen compositing, you can turn out several, not only one, variations on the geometry, the motion, and even the meaning of the video composition.

First, it looks as though the notes are superimposed on the shirt and not actually on or *in* the actor. A very simple, effective fix is to shade the blue background. The actor doesn't move significantly throughout the video with respect to camera left or right (although he bops up and down once or twice), so you can get away with persistent, unanimated shading to help the composition along a little, like so:

1. Choose the bottom layer on the Layers palette.

2. Choose the Dodge tool from the Tools palette. Give it about a a 65-pixel tip and choose Midtones with an exposure of about 30% on the Options bar. At 30% you have more control over the nuances of your shading, and by choosing midtones on a deep blue background, the resulting highlight areas will be pale blue instead of intense chroma key blue (as you'd get by using Highlights as the Range choice).

3. Pick a good segment of the clip in which to work, a frame where the actor is located most of the time throughout the clip, like about 12 seconds into the video.

4. Take a look at the source of lighting in the scene; it's predominantly from the left, so stroke a few times on the camera left (document left) side of the blue background, inside the shirt. Stop when you have a subtle increase in lighting; don't bludgeon the audience with it, thus drawing attention to the illusion and not the composition.

5. Do the converse; with the Burn tool set to Midtones with 20% Exposure or less, stroke over the right side of the background, where the torso to the shirt should be. The result should look like Figure 14.22. Just think of how you'd shade a cylinder and then add a little shading for the arms.

6. Save, don't close.

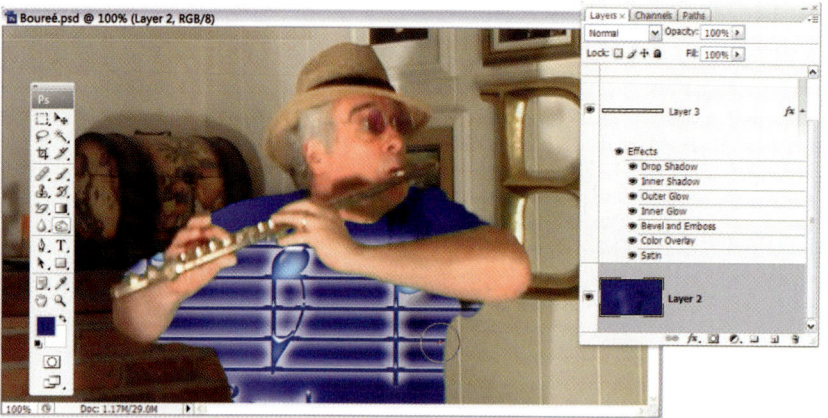

Figure 14.22
Add a little non-moving shading that will enhance the dimensional quality of the background (the shirt that features the animated notes).

Distorting the Music

As a further measure to make the music appear as though it's in the shirt, it would be good to make it look more like a projection on a cylinder. You can do this in Photoshop, but not with an animated layer—it bears no Smart Object properties, and because it's not a video layer, you cannot transform it for a duration of time.

The good news is that you can simply hide the actor layer, write the document out to video, and then import the result to the document.

Follow these steps to convert the animation and then apply a little distortion to it:

1. Hide the top video layer, leaving the blue background and the dancing notes visible.

2. Choose File > Export > Render Video. Use no compression; you should export to QuickTime because, although the animation has no audio, exporting a non 4:3 document to AVI occasionally results in a failed render containing severe image skewing and general color loss. Don't use any alpha channel export (choose None from the Alpha Channel drop-down, and the QuickTime Export options automatically adjust). Click Render.

3. Hide or better still delete the background and dancing notes layer from the document, then choose Layer > Video Layers > New Video Layer from File and choose the document you rendered in Step 2. Put this layer behind the actor layer on the Layers palette.

4. Reduce the opacity of the actor layer so you can see the extent of the animated notes underneath. As you can see, a lot of the action falls on wasted space.

5. Press Ctrl/Cmd+T to put the music note layer into Free Transform mode, accept the warning that the object will now become a Smart Object, and then drag the edges of the layer toward the actor, but make sure the shirt is completely covered with music. See Figure 14.23; click the check icon on the

Options bar to apply the transformation, or more simply press Enter when you're ready. You can return the opacity for the actor layer back to 100% when you're done.

6. Photoshop has now converted the video layer to a Smart Object, and as such, you can apply any of a number of filters to it. First, Ctrl/Cmd+click the Smart Object thumbnail on the Layers palette to select only the nontransparent regions. Doing this directs and focuses certain Photoshop filters, thus concentrating the effect and not wasting space and time requesting Photoshop to calculate and the transparent areas that are unaffected in any event.

7. Choose Filter > Distort > Spherize. In the Spherize Filter box, choose Horizontal Only Mode and then drag the Amount slider to +100, as shown in Figure 14.24. Click OK to apply, and I think you'll agree that the notes now look more visually interesting and dimensional.

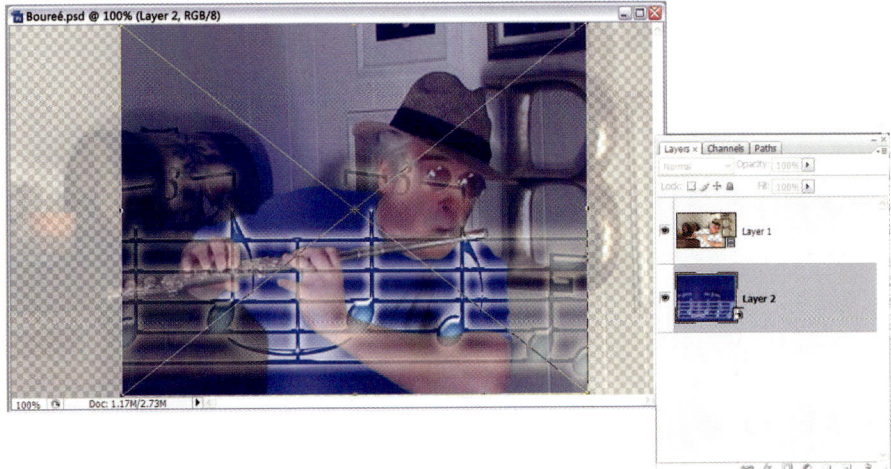

Figure 14.23
Narrow the music notes video so it's more like shirt music instead of sheet music.

Figure 14.24
Use Spherize along only one axis to bend a layer's contents into something resembling a tube.

Jazzing Up the Foreground Actor

You'll see when you play the composition at this stage that the star of the film, the animated notes, is a little upstaged by the actor. Sometimes the best way to dress up a composition is to tone down an element. In the steps to follow I show you several variations of the composition, each expressing different "texture," a different treatment, and all of them help cast the spotlight on the music. Incidentally, you should save the PSD at regular intervals as you work, and unfortunately you've altered the video layers so the PSD file (which you can delete after you've finished the tutorials and rendered a final composite) is large and a little ungainly to work with on machines with less the 1GB of RAM and a single processor.

1. The notes are blue, so perhaps the actor should be, too. Right-click the actor video layer on the Layers palette and choose Convert to Smart Object.

2. Choose Filter > Render > Lighting Effects.

3. In Lighting Effects, choose a Spotlight, and then drag the points in the proxy window so the spotlight is casting in the same direction as the key light in the scene (refer to Figure 14.25).

4. Choose a rich, Superman blue for the light color, choose a paler blue for the Surface property of the layer, and then fiddle with the ambience and intensity of the light until your scene looks like Figure 14.25.

5. The effect is interesting, but let's play some more. You don't have to undo and return to the Lighting Effects filter if the effect is too heavy. Instead, because Smart Objects make filters Smart Filters, you now have a layer mask in place on the Layers palette, and at any time you can paint onto the mask with black to hide areas of this or any other filter. For example, if you click the layer mask thumbnail, you are now editing the mask in the document window and not

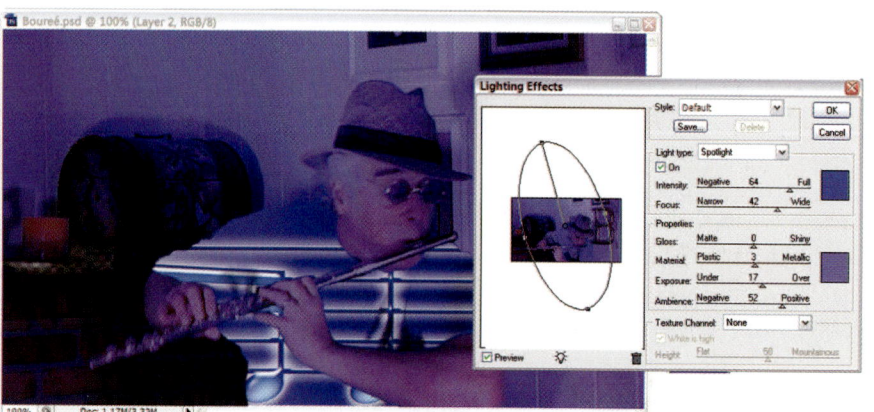

Figure 14.25
Lighting Effects simulates a light in a scene but doesn't actually change the illumination native to objects in a photo or video.

the Smart Object (the video); fill the mask with a shade of gray, and the Lighting Effect in this example is partially removed.

6. You'll note that because the actor is now tinted blue, the highlights and shading you applied to the original background deep blue might not be reading as intensely as you'd like. Here's an ambitious technique: Create a new layer in Screen mode at about 50–60%, put it beneath the actor but on top of the notes, and paint pale blue (R:186, G: 190, B: 255 worked for me) on it in areas you want to emphasize. Then create another layer, put it in Multiply mode at about 35%, and then paint deep blue (try RJ, G:12, B: 148) at partial opacity in areas where you want some shading.

7. Create keys for change in position for the Screen and Multiply layers, so the shading and highlights actually move with the actor. Motion matching is covered in detail in Chapter 15, but this technique is a simple, pseudo-rotoscoping effort that is effective and takes little time to rig. See Figure 14.26.

Figure 14.26
Lighting and highlighting areas can help integrate the two video layers.

8. Finally in this section, the animated notes are moving two dimensionally, but you can make them appear to move more dramatically, apparently in three dimensions, if you simply apply the Warp Free Transform to this Smart Object. Choose the Notes video layer on the Layers palette.

9. Zoom out and drag the document window away from the composition so you can see beyond the edges. If you have a scroll wheel on your pointing device, drag inward to see the (default gray) document background.

10. Press Ctrl/Cmd+T to put the nontransparent areas of the notes video into Free Transform mode; accept that the layer's contents need to be converted to a Smart Object when the attention box pops up. Then right-click in the document and choose Warp from the context menu.

11. Create an upward-facing arc with the Warp box, as shown in Figure 14.27. This will take several editing moves, and to make the notes cascade dramatically, scooping down into the actor's chest area, you need to drag outside of the document, and that's why I told you to zoom out in Step 9. Click the Commit Transform icon (the checkmark on the Options bar) to apply the transformation.

Figure 14.27
Warping the video notes can make them appear to move in three dimensions.

Reducing the Actor but Not His Performance

To make the animated notes even more heroic than they presently are would point to reducing the importance of the actor in the composition. This can be done quite easily without reducing the actor's *contribution* to the movie. Here's the deal: What is the actor contributing? Yes, he's holding the flute, wearing shades and a hat, and he moves around. If you alter the colors more drastically than you did using Lighting Effects and simplify the actor's shape to its essential outline, you still have his motion and his performance, but without the distraction of elements that might steal from the music notes.

Does this mean stylizing the video layer and fantasizing the meaning, the content of the composition? Yes!

Why not?

Here are the steps to yielding a third variation of the animated notes video, and I confess it's my favorite:

1. Choose the actor video layer on the Layers palette and then choose Filter > Filter Galley. Here's the place where you can stack filter effects.

2. Choose Cutout from the Artistic folder and then drag Edge Simplicity to 0 (not at all simple). Then drag Edge Fidelity to the maximum.

3. Click the new filter icon (the dog-eared page) at the bottom of the right panel. It creates a duplicate of the cutout filter, but you don't want this. Click the Stylize folder to open it and then choose Glowing Edges. Click OK to apply.

4. This is effect #1; you now have the outline of a blue flutist with blue notes inside of him, playing jazzed-up Bach. But it might be more visually interesting to heighten the actor's interest a little more by retaining the original colors when filtering. All you need to do is hide the Lighting Effects filter on the Layers palette; it's under the Smart Filters thumbnail. In Figure 14.28 you can see the version I prefer. Render the video out to QuickTime and choose a compression if this is not a personal keeper; in either case, don't use alpha channels when you render the file, and you can delete the PSD file to save on hard disk space now.

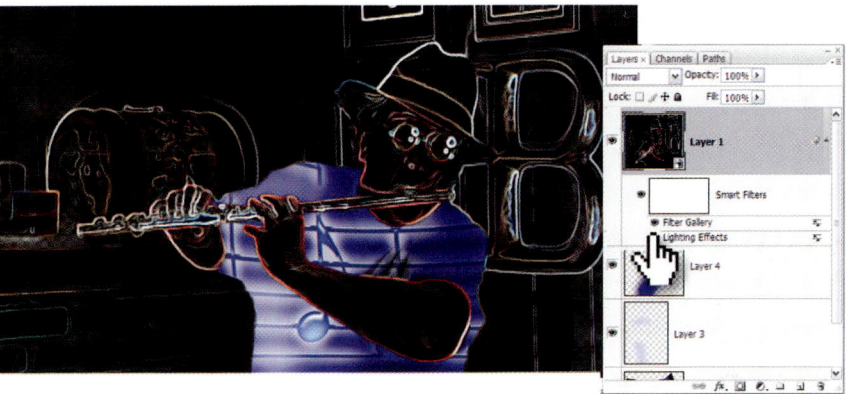

Figure 14.28
The actor moves like a human, but reduced to an outline in appearance, the animating notes are clearly the point of interest in the finished video.

Green screen compositing is also shown in other chapters as an unspoken part of an example file and as an instrument to discuss other compositing and special effects techniques. As you'll see, compositing is an important part of today's motion picture arena, but green screening is only one method by which part of a video is separated to then be sandwiched with other elements.

15

Compositing and Motion Matching

In previous chapters I covered how to mask and rotoscope an element from a video into a different video. This was comparatively easy because the scenes were locked—a locked element on top of a locked background equals a flawless composite. However, more work and a little more learning are required to motion match a composite video when the camera or characters move, and that is the topic of this chapter.

You'll learn shortly how to move a static video element in synch with a panning background. Then to up the stakes I show you how to track the movement of a basketball one of our neighbors graciously dribbled for us. For the grand finale, you'll see how to create a 30-second situation comedy starring talking lawn ornaments; it takes skill to move a video clip in perfect synch with the background clip. I also take you through the ropes on cuts, the appropriate timings, and how to polish the mini-sitcom with an audience laugh track.

Adding Elements to a Camera Pan

Get out the Niagara Mohawk video you created in Chapter 2 now. If you didn't hit this tutorial yet, open NiMo pan with barreling.mov, a video I created using the steps in Chapter 2. As you can see, the pan is visually interesting and everything, but I think we can do better—the neon sign isn't lit, which is good for conserving energy during daylight hours, but not very exciting. In the sections to follow you'll trace over the neon sign in the video, apply a custom style to it to make it glow, toggle the neon on and off so it's a flashing neon sign, and then align the sign layer to the underlying video as it pans.

Tracing and Styling the Sign

When designing the following tutorial, my instincts initially pointed me toward using the Pen tool to draw the centerline of the NIAGARA MOHAWK neon sign. Then I remembered that when you click, hold Shift, and then click elsewhere in the composition, a straight line between points is auto-drawn. So I recommend *you* recall this feature, too, because the sign is composed mostly of straight strokes.

After the strokes have been made, you'll apply a custom style to the strokes and then remove the strokes by killing the Fill attribute on the Layers palette.

1. In the NiMo pan with barreling document, click the Create New Layer icon on the Layers palette. Although this layer will move, it's an animation move recorded by the Animation palette's Position attribute, so a new video layer is not necessary.

2. Choose the Brush tool, choose any foreground color you like (I chose black in the screen figures), advance the video to about Frame 584 so the neon sign is onscreen, choose the 3-pixel hard brush tip, and then draw the centerline to the neon sign as shown in Figure 15.1.

3. Click the fx icon on the Layers palette and then choose Outer Glow.

Figure 15.1
Click a starting point and then hold Shift and click another point to create a straight line between the points to finish the stroke.

4. In the Layer Style box, increase the opacity of the style to 100% and then change the color of the glow to a bluish purple, which is easier to read than the default yellow and adds a little class and more impact to the video.

5. Make the size about 7 pixels and adjust Blend Mode to Lighten and Technique to Precise. This is an attribute you'll modify across time to add realism to a neon sign powering up then turning off. See Figure 15.2.

6. On the Layers palette, set Fill for the layer anywhere between 2% and 0%; 2% adds a subliminal "heft" to the neon sign, improving the clarity of the lettering a little. When your screen looks like Figure 15.3, you're ready to rock and roll and animate the neon in the next section.

Motion Matching and Animating the Glow

Scrub the timeline and you'll see that the sign makes an entrance at the bottom of the document at about Frame 493 and exits at about Frame 679, giving about six seconds of visibility. I point this out so you can judge how often the neon sign flashes on and off—too many times will make the sign look frenetic and broken—not a good "sign" for an electric company. I figure we can make the visual point if the sign turns on and off in two-second intervals, three times.

In the following steps you'll change the position of the layer over time to match the movement of the background video, then you'll alter the opacity and layer style to make the sign flash on and off.

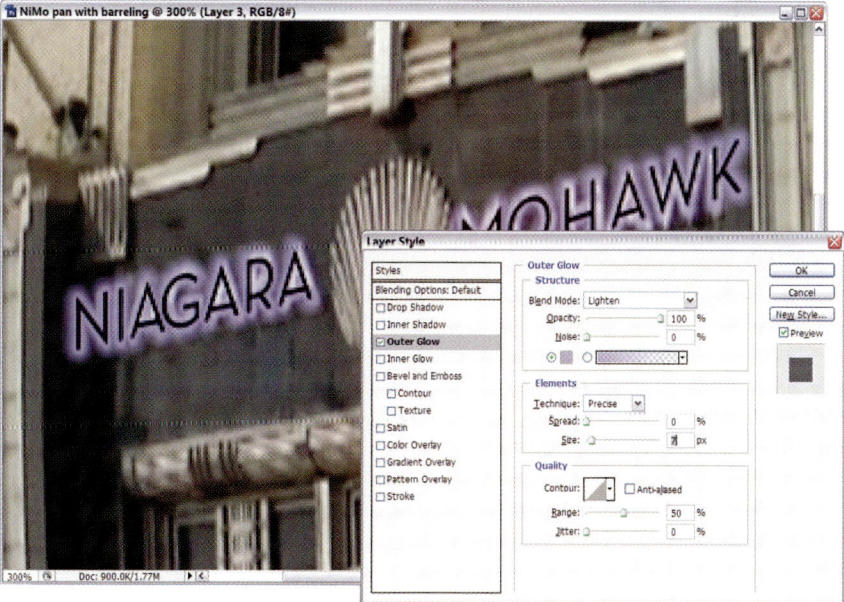

Figure 15.2
Modify the Outer Glow Layer Style to add drama and additional visibility.

Figure 15.3
Remove the fill but not the style using the Layers palette.

1. Scrub the timeline to about Frame 523, the first change the sign on the video layer is in the clear.

2. With the Move tool, move the neon on the top layer to fit over the overlying video sign. Then click the Position stopwatch icon on the Animation palette to set a keyframe. Although the glow will not precisely match the fisheye building pan (because the center of the distortion remains constant while the glow moves), I found this to be acceptable because the film is panning the building, and it's difficult for the audience to detect the slight mismatch in a moving sequence.

3. Scrub to Frame 647, the last frame where the sign on the video layer is in the clear as it exits frame.

4. Choose the Move tool. With the keyboard arrow key, nudge the top glow layer to match the position of the sign on the underlying layer. This sets a key at Frame 647 for Position.

5. Advance to Frame 680 where the sign has traveled completely offscreen. Then keyboard-arrow nudge the glow layer up and offscreen. It makes no difference for a little more than one second if the glow layer accelerates offscreen at the same tempo as the video. Scrub the timeline between 647 and 680, and if the glow layer looks unaligned at any point, set a new key automatically by nudging the layer at the frame where it's not aligned.

6. The very entrance of the glowing sign falls between 488 and 523, a little more than a second in duration. Repeat Steps 3–5 to make the neon layer enter the scene aligned to the underlying video. Your Animation palette should now look like Figure 15.4.

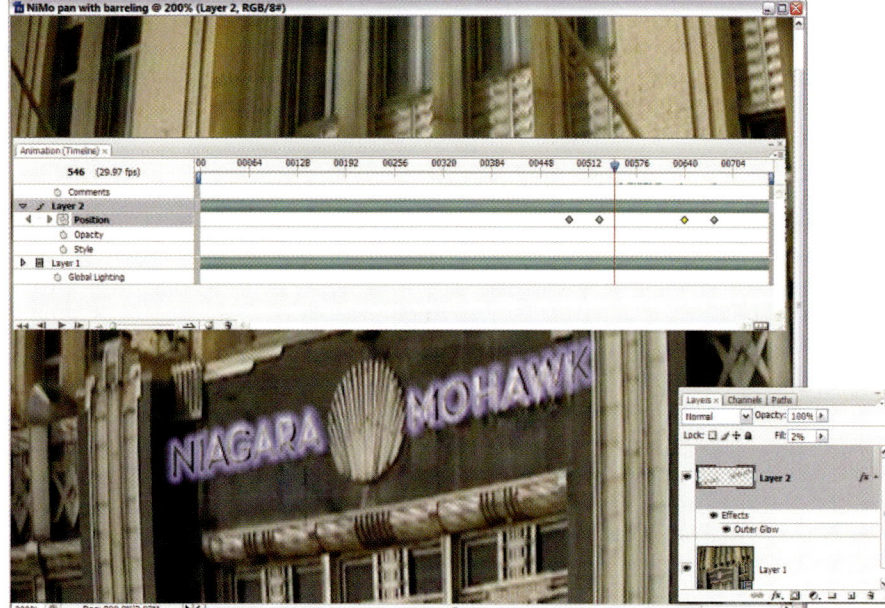

Figure 15.4
Use the keyboard arrows to nudge a layer's contents to prevent accidental lateral moves.

7. You don't want the neon to blink but instead to fade up and down (a fade produces a glow, neon signs do not blink); therefore, you use Linear and not Hold Interpolation for changes in Opacity now. You're in luck because Linear is the default interpolation method, so all you need to do now is set keys. Scrub to Frame 488, click the Opacity stopwatch, and then on the Layers palette set Opacity to 0% for the glow layer.

8. It's important to proceed at regular intervals restoring and reducing the opacity; you don't want the sign to flicker like *cheap* neon signs do. You have six keys to set while the neon is in frame; I suggest you set them at 30-frame intervals.

9. To add a little pulsation to the glow, change the style at the same frames and identical intervals as you did with Opacity in Step 8. Begin by toggling to Frame 488 (click the arrow icon, the Go to Previous Keyframe, at the left of the layer track on the Animation palette), then click the stopwatch for Style just to set the current style.

10. Got to the next keyframe for Opacity, then *click the Style track* on the Animation palette (*not* the Opacity track). Double-click the Outer Glow entry on the

Layers palette list to display the dialog box. Increase Size to 18 to 24 pixels; use your own artistic eye to judge how intensely you want the neon to glow.

11. Either copy and paste the keyframes to locations on the Style track to match the key times on the Opacity track or manually modulate the Size setting for the glow. You can copy a key by right-clicking over it, but you can't paste at a new time (you can only paste over an existing key) directly on the Animation palette. Instead, you choose Paste Keyframe(s) from the Animation palette flyout menu. See Figure 15.5.

12. Save the document to Photoshop's PSD file format and keep it open.

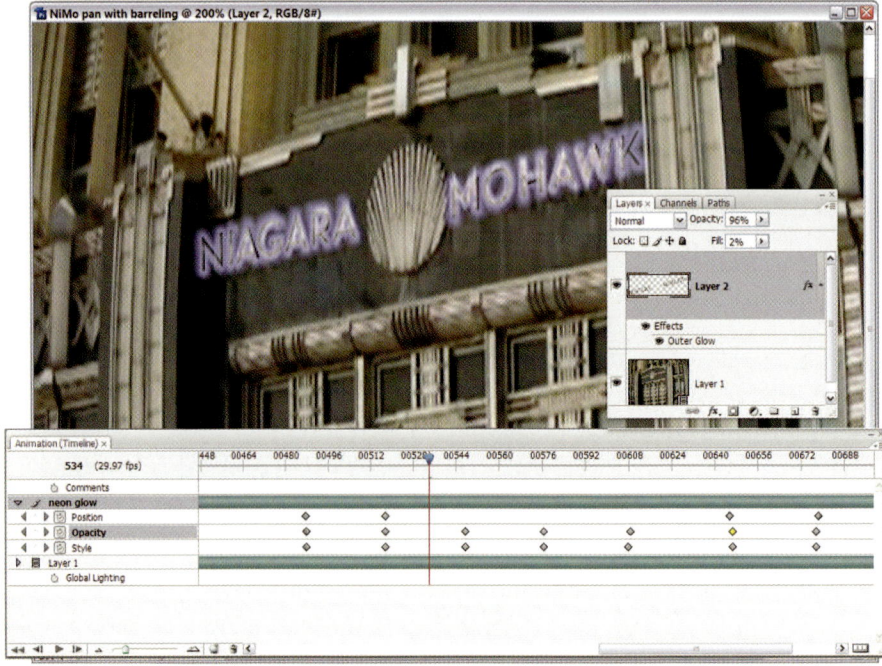

Figure 15.5
Make the neon glow spread as it becomes visible by keying the size of the Outer Glow Style.

Motion Matching a Video Clip

When we took the still photos used to make the panning footage in Chapter 2, we *did* notice that there would be a problem with the opening. The American flag, although it's onscreen for less than two seconds, doesn't wave. Additionally, the Niagara Mohawk building didn't have any flags hanging on this day, so we have a lovely neon sign now framed by bare flagpoles in the video. I asked the management to put up flags for us, but they politely told me that I was lucky enough to get a Property Release signed.

No problems in this book, only solutions. One clever way to add flags that move is to use a modeling application to match lighting and camera angle and then make some objects wave around like flags in the breeze, then composite them into the video. It's clever, and modeling is also not the topic of this book.

I've created the resource videos for you to use in the following tutorials. Just for your future reference, the flags were created using Luxology modo; in Figure 15.6 you can see modo 301's interface. What I did was create an American flag texture (a bitmap) and an Art Deco design (in keeping with the architecture) and more or less pasted the materials onto a mesh that's a plane of proportions to suggest a flag. I then set a few keys in modo, distorted the flag mesh at various points, then told modo to render the in-between frames out to QuickTime with alpha channel support. I'd estimate it took about six months to learn the application adequately to pull off this stunt. It works in the scene because the special effects flags appear dimly lit and very briefly. If you need sequences such as this, you can learn to use a modeling program or contact the application's online community and arrange some sort of talent barter.

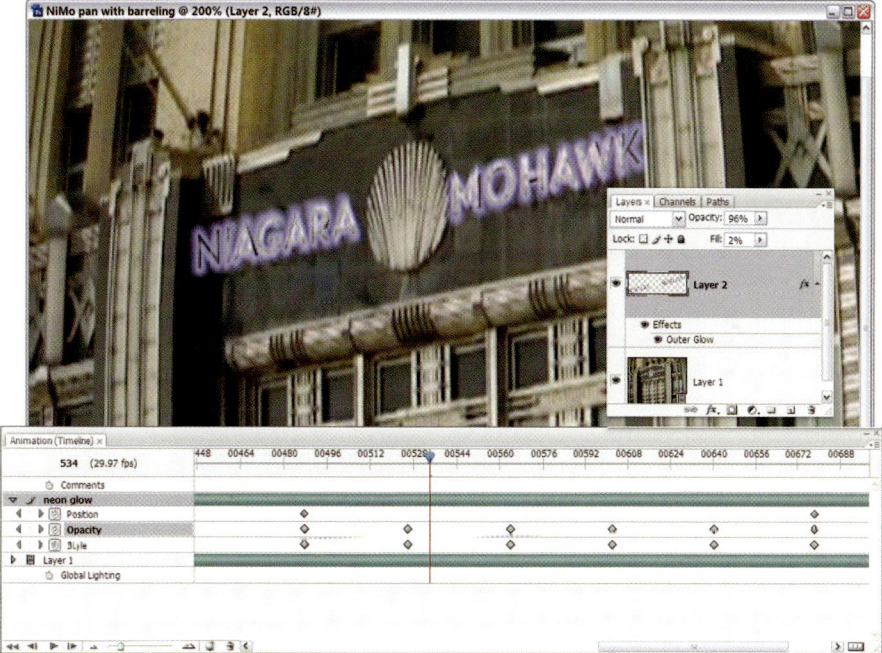

Figure 15.6
You animate a model in modo by setting up keyframes and then letting modo "morph" the positions and the geometry.

Follow these steps (which are even less complex than adding the animating neon) to add flags to the video:

1. Open the Right Art Deco Flag.mov file and then drag its thumbnail on the Layers palette into the Niagara Mohawk video. I wrote only enough footage to cover the sequence in the movie and forgive the quality—I used Animation

compression to keep a movie with an alpha channel small in size for you to download, and this setting tends to whack the daylights out of video quality.

2. Scoot the track on the Animation palette for the flag to the area where the neon sign appears.

3. With the Move tool, align the flag to the flagpole at right in the document.

4. Set keyframes for the position of the flag, as shown in Figure 15.7. Notice also that this video layer is now considered an altered video layer, and as such your PSD file is going to plump up in file size significantly. I recommend that you back off this file to DVD as an archive after you've run and fully understand this chapter's tutorials or delete it.

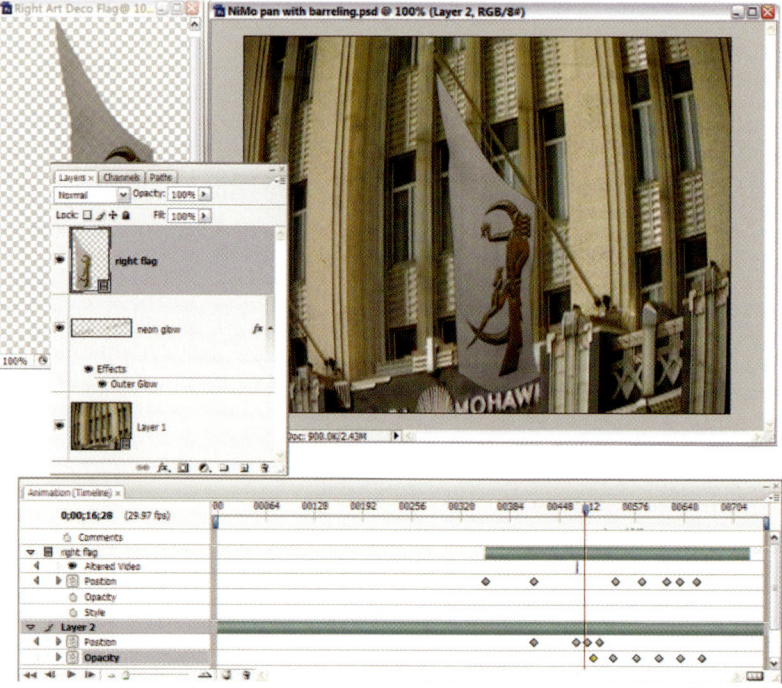

Figure 15.7
Move the flag's position over time to match the flagpole.

5. If you're game and want to bring this video completely to life, open Left Art Deco flag.mov and then repeat Steps 2–4.

6. Add the American flag. Open US flag.mov and then drag it into the composition. It will "stick" to the head of the Work Area (as do all duplicated movie clips), so there should be no need to adjust the time of its appearance in the composition.

7. Create a new normal layer and then put it beneath the US flag layer; you need to create a traveling matte to hide the static flag in the original video.

8. With the Clone Stamp tool set to about 65 pixels, soft tip, Aligned turned off, and Sample set to All Layers on the Options bar, first hide the US flag video layer and then Alt/Opt+click to set a sample point near the original flag.

9. Release Alt/Opt and then make brisk strokes over the original flag area to hide it, as shown in Figure 15.8. Optionally, you might want to blur the cloned area using Gaussian blur when you're done, perhaps two pixels in radius. The reason I suggest this is because there's vignetting in the original video, a slight falloff in light around the edges of the video that might cause a color mismatch unless the painted areas has very soft edges.

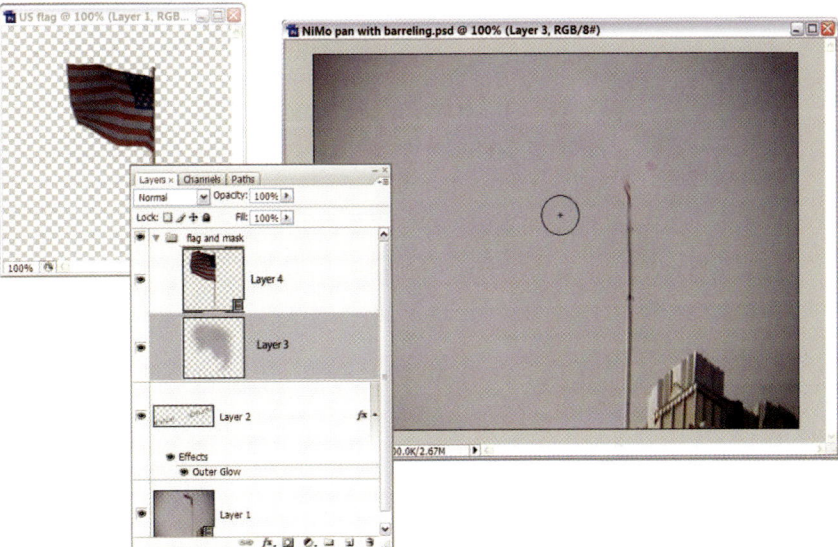

Figure 15.8
Cover the flag with identical color and texture using the Clone Stamp tool.

10. Unhide the flag video. First align its position so it matches up with the pole in the underlying video, and then click the Position stopwatch for this track on the Animation palette to set a key at Frame 0.

11. Set a key position for the mask layer beneath it.

12. Here's a neat trick: To keep the mask traveling upward in synch with the flag video, choose the Move tool, Shift+click the flag and the mask layer titles on the Layers palette to select them both, move the timeline indicator to the out position for the flag (about Frame 72), and then keyboard arrow nudge both layers up and out of frame. You might need to create an intermediate key when the top of the flagpole on the flag video layer just touches the top of the frame (the document window), but basically you're home free and clear, as shown in Figure 15.9.

13. Render to video (File > Export). Choose any compression scheme of Quick-Time's you like; H.264 will produce a fairly clean video and a pretty small size.

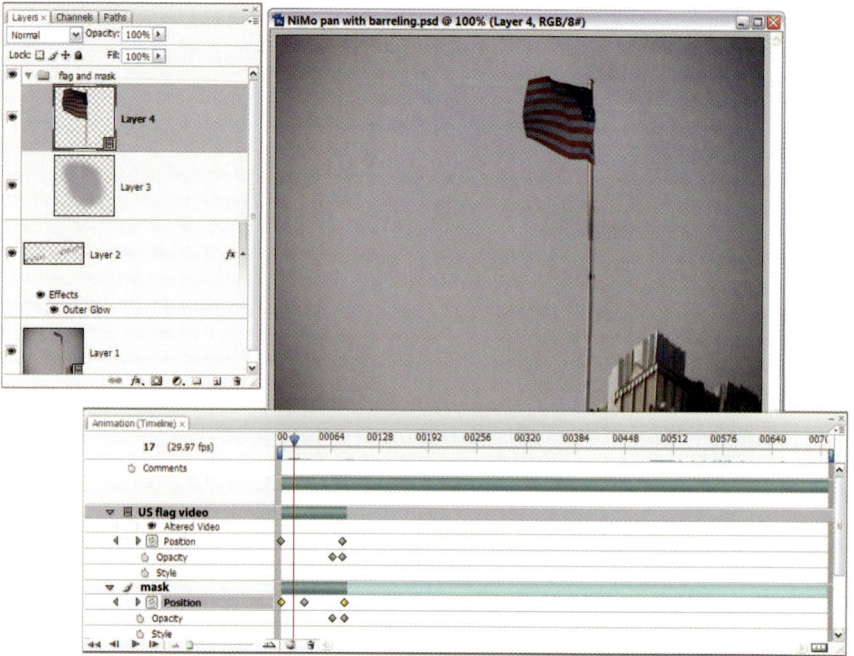

Figure 15.9
Nudge multiple layers in tandem by selecting them on the Layers palette before nudging the layers' contents.

Complex Motion Matching

The following tutorials will take some time to work through; shut off the TV and close the door to your den. Here's the plot: We asked our next-door neighbor Hector to perform some fancy basketball moves on the family's driveway. I thought it would be fun through the course of time to fade in a different ball for Hector to be dribbling and passing between his knees, perhaps several different balls, all relating to sports.

So we need source videos of balls that then need to be keyed at positions corresponding to and overlapping the basketball in the original video. To do this, just about any modeling program that supports animation will do; although you'll be animating the position of the ball, it would still be visually interesting to rotate the ball over time, seeing as the basketball in the original video has a spin on it. I used Cinema 4D to light and render videos of three different balls, at lengths that summed up will cover most of the 22 seconds of Hector.mov. I also thought it would be good film to fade the different balls in and out of the head and tail of the clip to better anchor reality before distorting it!

From Basketball to Baseball

Let me explain *Linear Interpolation* for a moment, as it applies to all attributes you can key using Photoshop's Animation palette. In film, there are two meanings to the term *linear*: how the position changes, and how motion *eases* in and out of an action. *Easing* is an animation term that also applies to special effects—it describes acceleration and deceleration in an action. For example, if someone rushes into frame and then halts, the action is not linear; the person is actually easing out of a motion as he (or it) comes to a halt. Unfortunately, Photoshop Extended does not offer spline curves as a video editor does to "put a curve" on the position and the acceleration of movements, but this is okay in the following example. Although Hector dribbles the basketball with visually *non*linear acceleration and as a consequence position of the ball, it's bright orange and easy to track and simply requires a lot of keyframes.

Let's begin by introducing a baseball to replace the basketball:

1. Open Hector.mov, then open Hector's baseball.mov and drag its thumbnail into the Hector movie document. Close the baseball movie file without saving changes.

2. Look at the timeline on the Animation palette. You can see you've got coverage for about one-third of the total length of the finished composition. Give the entrance of the baseball about 4.5 seconds; set the head of this video layer on the Animation palette to about 4;15 (see Figure 15.10).

3. Press Ctrl/Cmd+T to put the baseball video layer into Free Transform mode. If an attention dialog box appears, click the Convert button. Doing this converts the video layer into a Smart Object, as a tag on its thumbnail confirms on the Layers palette.

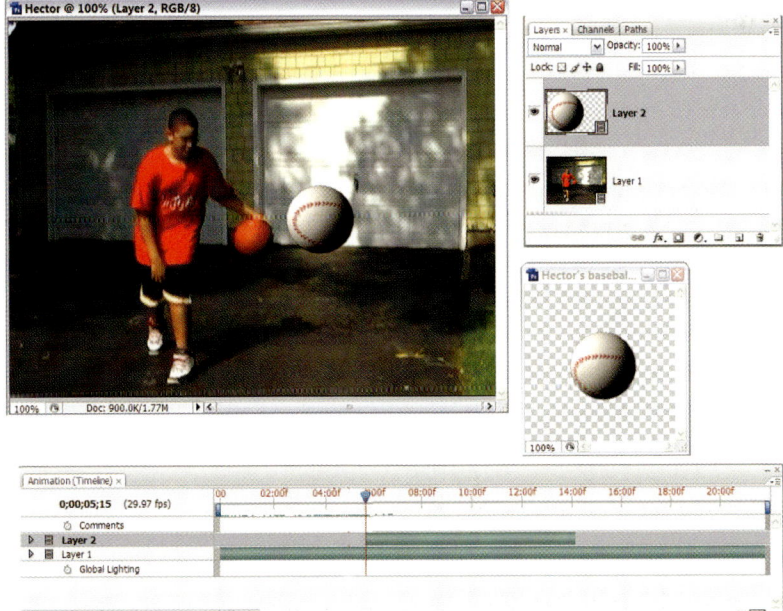

Figure 15.10
Begin the appearance of the baseball at about 4s;15f to better establish the real basketball.

4. Scale the ball down proportionately to about 66, just enough to completely hide the basketball during all frames where the baseball replaces it (Hint: Scrub the timeline and use rulers to see the largest size for the replacement ball). Click the check icon on the Options bar or hit Enter to then apply the transformation. I created the ball a little too large so you can use it in assignments of your own at larger sizes; it's a fun little clip. Zoom into the document for precision placement in Step 5, and then zoom the timeline on the Animation palette—you'll be setting keyframes for Position at nearly every frame and want to be able to see them. See Figure 15.11.

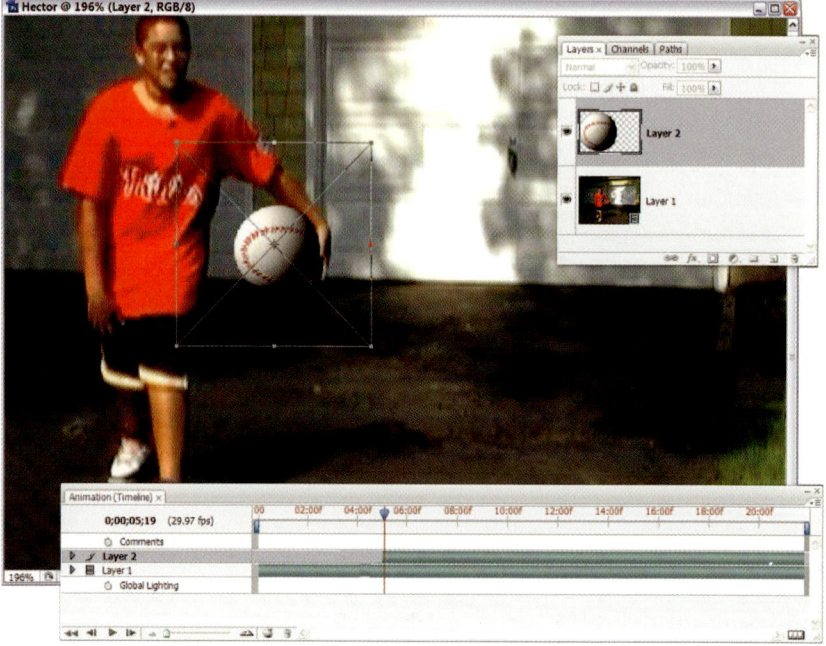

Figure 15.11
Scale the ball so that it completely covers Hector's basketball.

5. At the head of this video layer, with the Move tool move the ball to fit over the basketball. Then click the Position stopwatch on the Animation palette to set your first key.

6. Start keying, exactly as you did with the flags and glowing neon earlier in this chapter, but start frame by frame; this is why I asked you to zoom the timeline in. There will be occasions when Hector sends the ball in a linear direction for perhaps three or four frames, in which case you set a beginning and an end position four frames apart. But mostly you'll need to alter the position of the ball every frame or every other frame. Yep, it's tedious, but I can promise a spectacular, visually intriguing finished CG composition for the effort. Eventually, you'll need to hide parts of the baseball because they'll hide Hector's fingers; this is covered in following sections. But to minimize your

post-motion matching work, try to keep the baseball right on the edge of the underlying basketball, the edge closest to Hector's fingers. At 1:1 viewing resolution, the audience might not see that his fingers aren't touching the artificial baseball for a few frames, thus saving some work later in this example. See Figure 15.12.

Figure 15.12
Move the ball's position where needed with the Move tool.

Before continuing, fade the baseball layer up using a half-second duration at the head of the layer in the Work Area on the Animation palette. At the head, click the Opacity stopwatch on the Animation palette to set a key, turn Opacity down to 0% for this layer on the Layers palette, advance half a second on the timeline, and then turn Opacity up to 100%. That's a neat and effective introduction of the baseball, almost like morphing.

Cloning Away Unwanted Baseball Areas

As I mentioned earlier, much of the footage has Hector's hands in the clear or his dribbling hand behind the basketball—which means no retouching. The areas where his hand violates the basketball, however, need to be present in front of the baseball, so using the Clone Source feature is the natural remedy.

1. Choose the Clone Stamp tool and open the Clone Source palette (from the Window menu if it's not on the docking strip).

2. Choose Layer > Video Layers > New Blank Video Layer.

3. Let me begin by showing you a significant edit at about 6;10 into the clip where Hector passes the basketball behind his torso. Choose Sample Current Layer, the 19-pixel hard brush, and check Aligned on the Options bar.

4. Choose the bottom video layer on the Layers palette. Then Alt/Opt+click right on the star dotting the "i" in *Phillies* on Hector's shirt to set the sampling point. It's a very easy point to align to your work after releasing Alt/Opt. See Figure 15.13.

5. Click the new video layer title on the Layers palette and then in the Clone Source palette type **0, 0** pixels for the Offset x and y positions.

6. Stroke over the basketball only where the baseball is in front of his shirt, as shown in Figure 15.14. Then continue, advancing frame by frame, until the baseball "pass" behind Hector has been edited to hide the appropriate baseball areas. Remember, you're not erasing anything—rather, you're cloning from the bottom layer to the top to hide the baseball. I've highlighted the brush in blue in these figures to make the cursor easier for you to see.

Exposing Hector's Hands

There are additional areas of the baseball footage that need hiding and a little shading (which I cover in pages to follow). As I mentioned earlier, Hector occasionally holds the ball with his fingers facing the camera and are presently hidden by the baseball video layer. In the following steps, you'll use the same technique as hiding the ball when it's supposed to be behind Hector; you basically use a smaller Clone Stamp brush and then clear areas on the top video layer if you've overshot the goal (which is something I did numerous times cobbling the Gallery finished video).

> **Tip**
>
> The techniques covered in the examples in this section aren't actually the sequence you want to use in your own retouching of 60 or more frames. To make your workflow an easy one, you retouch at the beginning of a clip, not the midpoint, and you work through. If you retouch a time segment here and there, even though it might relieve tedium, you'll lose your place quite easily; even by adding Comment fields and keys, it's more convenient and will cause fewer inconsistencies in the finished clip if you work from Frame A to Frame Z.

Chapter 15 ■ Compositing and Motion Matching

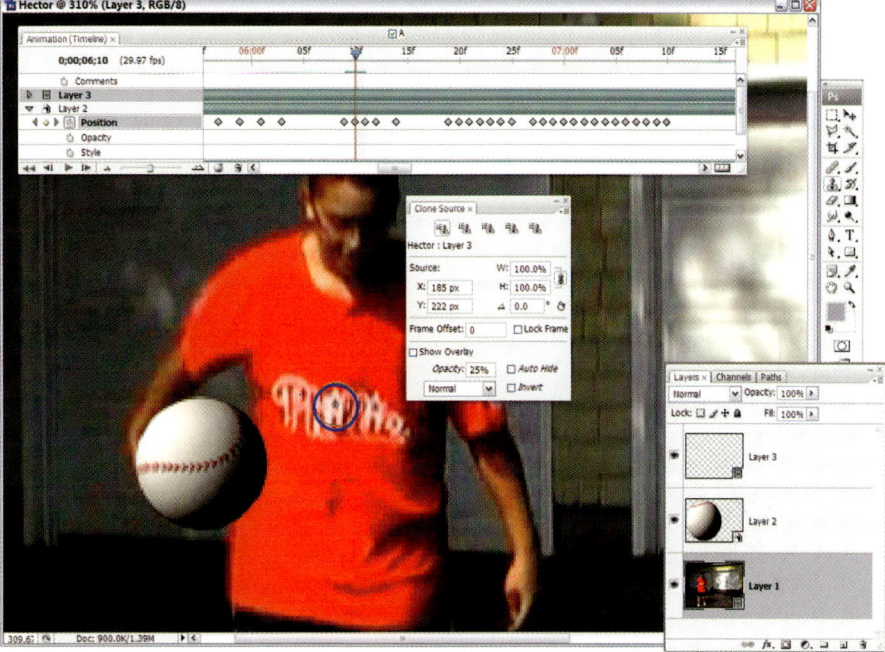

Figure 15.13
Set a sampling point that's easy to track on the Clone Source palette.

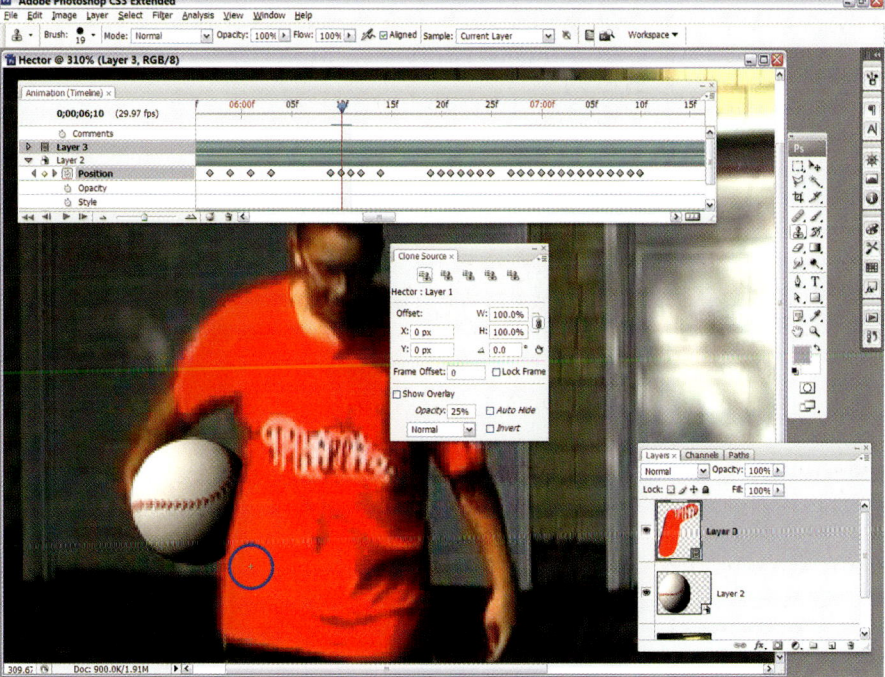

Figure 15.14
Hide the unwanted baseball areas using the Clone Stamp tool.

Here's how to put Hector's hand in front of the baseball where needed:

1. The Clone Stamp is aligned so that although you'll clone in different areas, the source point is synched to the bottom video layer—you don't need to redefine the sampling point. Move the time line to about 5;20.

2. Hide the baseball layer, and then using the 5-pixel diameter brush tip, stroke over Hector's hand. After a few frames, you'll intuit where the hand is and won't need to hide the baseball layer. Save the document to PSD file format now. Return the layer to visibility and check out your handiwork, as shown in Figure 15.15.

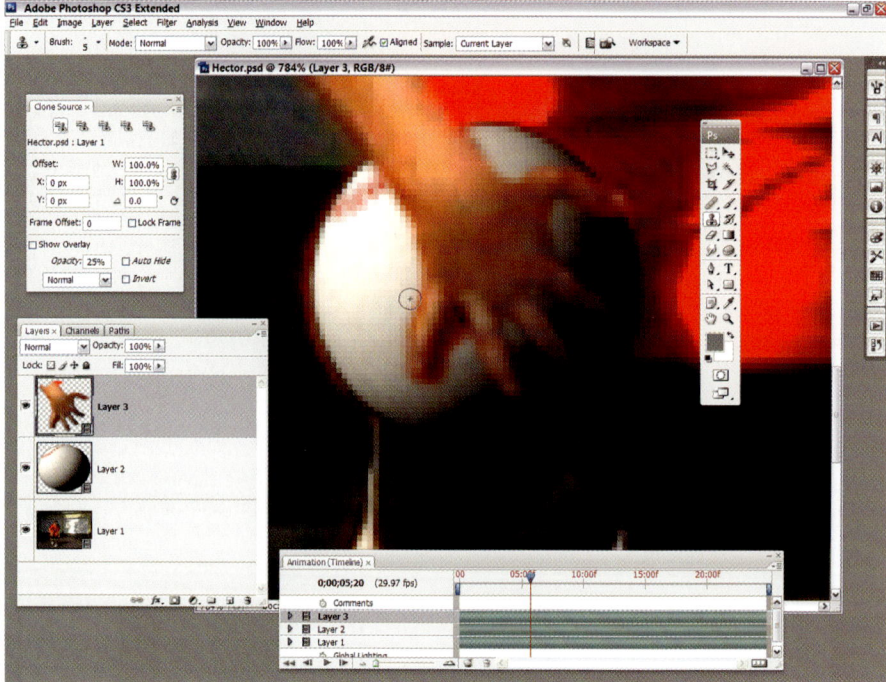

Figure 15.15
Clone from the bottom layer to a new video layer to put his hand in front of the ball.

3. Here's the addendum to the technique: I recommend you go through an entire sequence where Hector's hand should be in front of the baseball, stroking new content onto the top layer using the Clone Stamp. Then I recommend for continuing work that you memorize the keyboard shortcuts S for Clone Stamp, H for Hand tool (pressing the Spacebar causes the video to play unless you're really fast holding the Spacebar), and B for Brush tool. You set the Brush tool up on the Options bar for clear painting mode and then toggle between cloning and erasing (that's what Clear painting mode does, regardless of the current foreground color).

Choose the Brush tool and go back and clean up any areas that hide the baseball but shouldn't. Problematic areas will be between Hector's fingers; see Figure 15.16.

4. Save to PSD file format and keep the document open. Because you altered a video layer, the PSD file will be larger than you'd expect, but you can safely delete this file after you're confident a final render came out okay.

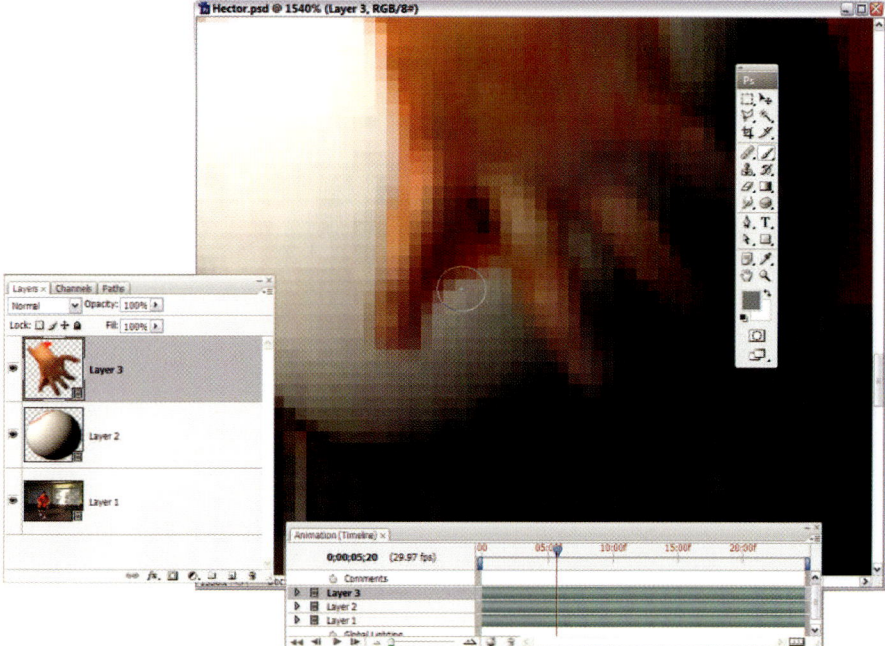

Figure 15.16
Unhide areas on the top layer where you might have performed too much cloning.

Working with Shadows in the Composite Video

The light in the original video at the bottom of the layers is hard light, cast from about 10 o'clock into the scene. As a result, shadows on the original basketball are crisp and somewhat opaque. For many areas of the finished composition, you can fake the shadows cast by Hector's palm and fingers by including these areas in your cloning work…and of course, they'll be orange-ish instead of off-white as you'd expect on a baseball. The quick and effective fix is to use the Sponge tool in Desaturate mode (on the Options bar) for every frame where the shadow is the wrong color—no color is acceptable when the shadows are very small.

However, a new technique has to be used when Hector's leg is casting on the basketball at about 8;01 and various other points where he passes the ball between his legs. The shadow needs to be drawn, rotoscoped, using the underlying original basketball shadow as your guide.

Follow these steps to get a handle on animated shadow creation for brief sequences:

1. Go to about 8;01 on the timeline and zoom into the baseball; 400 to 800% is good, depending on the size of your monitor.

2. Choose the Brush tool and make sure it's in Normal mode, not Clear. Use a 5-pixel soft tip and then double-click the Quick Mask Mode button on the Tools palette.

3. Set the color to something other than red; red is too close to the orange basketball. Try blue or green. Click OK to return; you're in Quick Mask mode now.

4. Hide the baseball layer and then paint over the basketball shadow. Then unhide the baseball and refine the edges of the Quick Mask, as shown in Figure 15.17. In Quick Mask mode, the foreground/background colors are automatically set to black and white. Press X to swap the colors and thus be able to erase any Quick Mask areas you don't want.

5. Choose Layer > Video Layers > New Blank Video Layer.

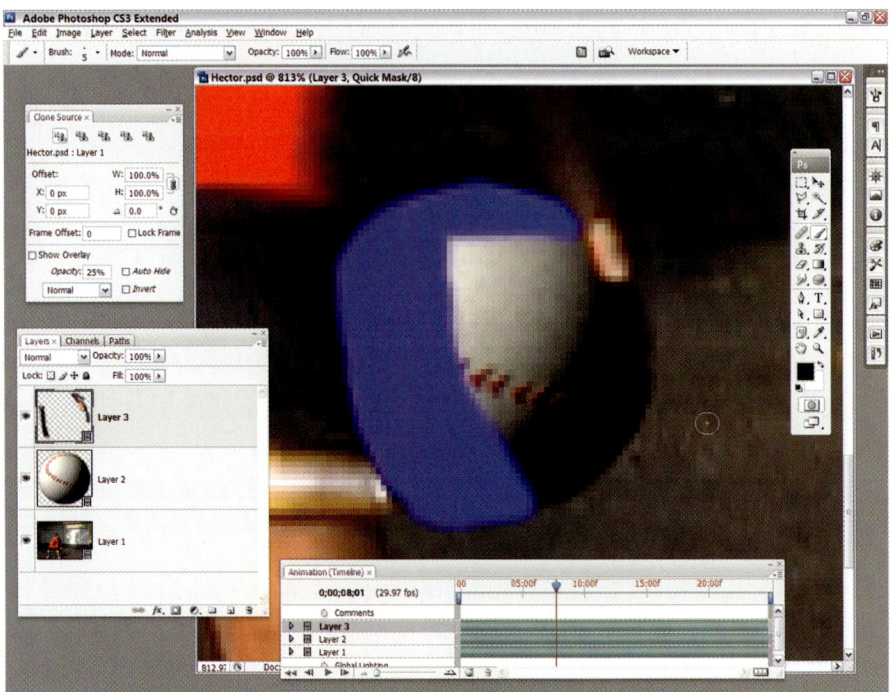

Figure 15.17
Create a Quick Mask area that defines the original shadow cast on the basketball.

6. Press Q to return to Standard Editing mode on the Tools palette, and your mask is now a marquee selection. Put the new video layer under the clone layer but above the baseball layer.

7. With the Brush tool, hold Alt/Opt to toggle to the Eyedropper tool and then click where I've marked the garage in the scene in Figure 15.18. It's an ideal shade of gray, compatible with the baseball because as you can see, both the garage door and the baseball are almost pure white (although Hector's dad told me later the garage was done in Venice Bisque, $12.99 a gallon). Choose Multiply mode for the new video layer, and then press Alt/Opt+Backspace to fill the selection with the appropriate gray shadow. Press Ctrl/Cmd+H to hide the marquee and then press Ctrl/Cmd+D to deselect when you're sure this frame looks right. Perform similar steps with all frames that need the shadow; use the shortcut Q to toggle in and out of Quick Mask mode and keep the shadow color the same, you might want to fine-tune the opacity of the Multiply mode video layer, and because you're essentially tracing over an existing shadow, your rotoscope work will be consistent and not in the forefront of the audience's minds.

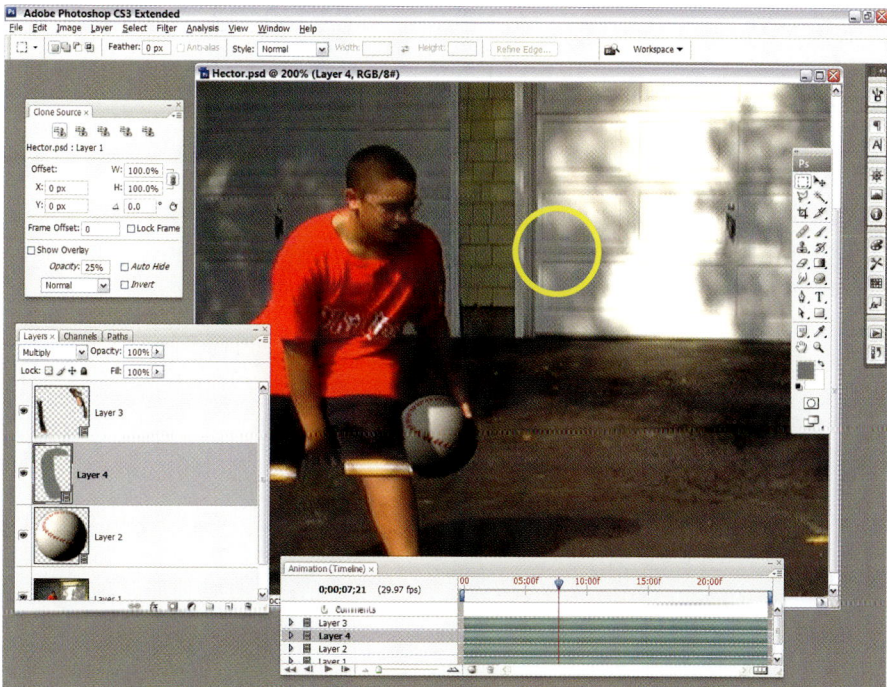

Figure 15.18
Rotoscope over areas that need a shadow.

Fading Between Sports Balls

After playing the first retouched clip of Hector dribbling a baseball, it actually seemed too subtle to me, but then again to me, mixing plaid with argyle is subtle. So I rendered a second rotating ball out of Cinema 4D, a #14 billiard ball. To extend this fantasy sequence, you do the following:

1. Duplicate Hector's poolball.mov to the Hector.psd composition.

2. Scale the ball just as you did with the baseball.

3. Key its position exactly as you did with the baseball. Let the head start at about nine seconds, allowing this layer to overlap the baseball layer in time by about a third of a second (about 10 frames). You'll create a soft cut.

4. Fade the billiard ball up from 0% opacity to 100%, beginning at the head of the clip and ending just short of the end of the baseball layer. See Figure 15.19.

5. Scrub the timeline, and you might find you're done. But if the baseball can be seen at any frame beyond where the billiard ball is at 100%, create a key on the baseball, reduce the opacity to 0% (on the Layers palette), and then right-click the key marker on the Animation palette and choose Hold Interpolation, not Linear, to slam that frame to invisibility at this frame.

6. Perform any masking you need to do to keep Hector's hands in front of the billiard ball. Save the document.

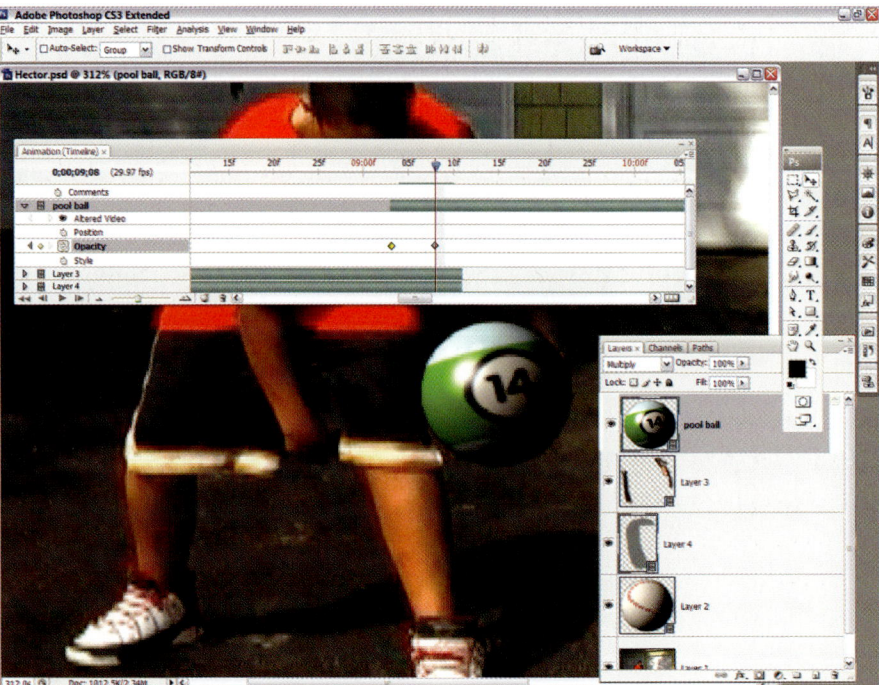

Figure 15.19
Fade the billiard ball up on its position as the top layer.

From the Ridiculous to the Sublime

I think we can take this video farther, not only stretching reality but bending it beyond recognition. I created an urchin ball that quickly sprouts its tentacles and then retracts them using Cinema 4D's Hair module, shown in Figure 15.20. The baseball and other sports balls could in fact be spun in a stationary position by green-screening them while spinning them on a spike, but you can't really shoot footage of this urchin ball; additionally, a green screen setup would take hours, while an adequate 3D simulation took me perhaps 10 minutes.

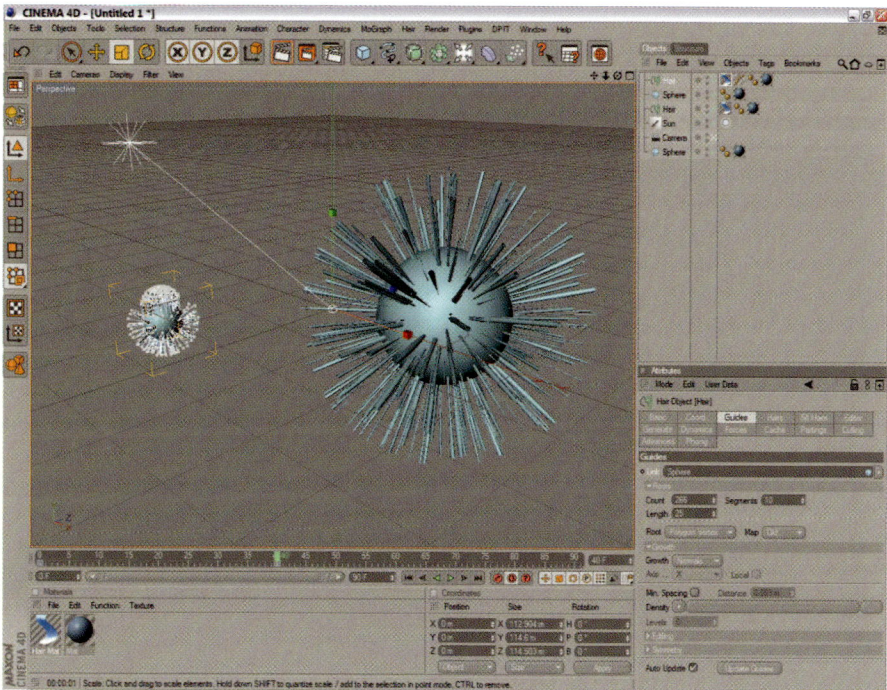

Figure 15.20
The impossible takes a little while in Photoshop. The *ridiculous* takes a modeling app.

Because of the dramatic transformation, the urchin ball clip proved ungainly and unacceptable in quality to give it to you as a QuickTime movie. Instead I picked up more than a MB in compression by writing the sequence out to still frames; I then used SuperPNG, a freeware Photoshop plug-in, to distill the frames to PNG file format with transparency. Unpack Urchin ball.zip to a new folder and then follow these steps to complete the video part of this composition:

1. Choose File > Open, point the Open box to the folder to which you unzipped the urchin ball frames, click the Image Sequence checkbox, and then click Open. Choose 29.97 when prompted for the fps value, as this is the same as the original Hector.mov file.

2. Duplicate the urchin ball layer to the Hector movie, which is now a bonafide movie layer, scale it, start it at about half a second before the tail of the billiard ball, and then key its position until about one-half to one second before the tail of the composition's Work Area.

3. Let the urchin ball layer fade up at the head, a soft cut from the billiard ball, as shown in Figure 15.21.

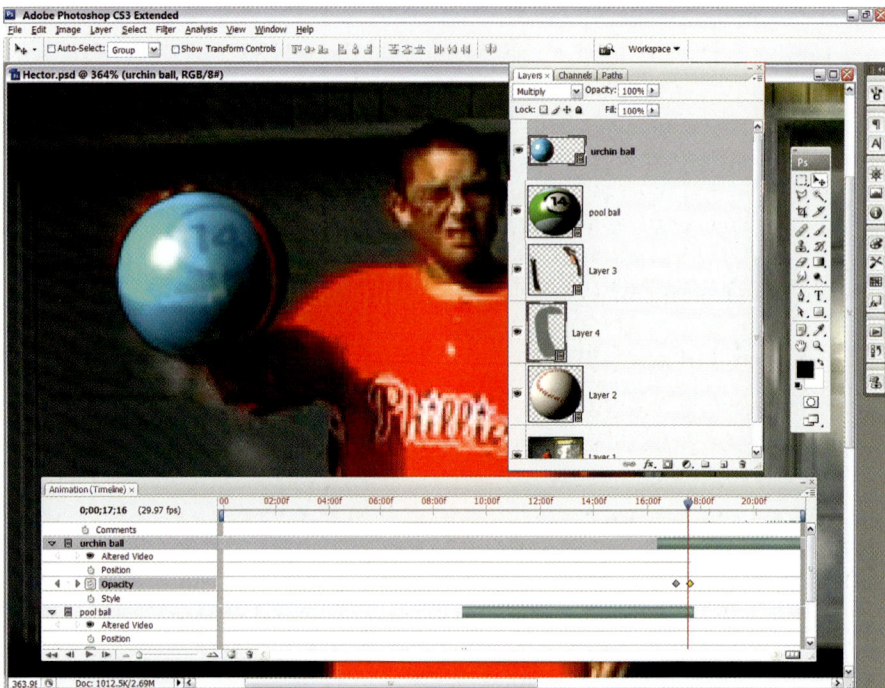

Figure 15.21
Fade the urchin ball in to replace the billiard ball exactly as you faded the billiard ball up to replace the baseball.

4. You'll notice a pleasant perk to concluding the video's silliness with the expanding urchin ball: There's no masking needed for Hector's hands. At this point, when you've played the video in Photoshop and corrected any possible misalignments, you should write the video out to QuickTime with no compression. Hold Alt/Opt when you click the Play button on the Animation palette: Notice that there's ambient sound but no basketball hits in the audio. You'll want to add the hits as I guide you in the next section. Archive or delete the composition once you're certain the QuickTime movie was rendered out of File > Export correctly, just to conserve disk space.

> **Note**
>
> The reason why there are no sounds of the basketball hitting the driveway in the original video is because I took the entire video track out and replaced it with a half minute of ambient street sounds. If you have a recording of street sounds, to do something like this, you write the video out to AVI, which is rendered without audio as per Adobe's design, then bring the video back into Photoshop, add an audio track using File > Open As, choose QuickTime as the file format, then choose an MP3 file you've recorded, duplicate the audio track to the video import, and then use File > Export > Render Video, but then use QuickTime as the render file format to keep the new audio track.
>
> Alternatively (more simply and more expensively), use a program such as Adobe Audition to perform audio editing on movies. Audition was originally Cool Edit, and prices now range from $139 to $349, depending on where you buy and which version is available. It saves to Apple QuickTime lossless file format.

Adding Sound Effects

Armed with a keyboard synth, a microphone, and a few pots and pans, I created a number of different, often humorous sound effects you'll now add to the video to hone your skills as an audio editor using Photoshop. You can't alter volume, but only specify a specific time at which an audio layer in a composition happens, so I kept the sound levels consistent in the MP3 files and also trimmed the audio clips so there is almost no lag time in the file for the sound to play. You'll want to do this in your own work because there is no audio "profile" for audio in Photoshop's workspace, no waveform graphic that tells you when a passage begins.

Open the rendered video from the previous tutorial, and here's how to add hits to Hector's strange sports equipment:

1. Windows users should choose File > Open As (Ctrl+Alt+Shift+O if your digits stretch this way) and then choose QuickTime movie as the file type, then choose one or several MP3 files from the ZIP archive's Sound fx folder. If you have color management enabled, just dismiss the attention box. Mac users need to choose QuickTime as the file type but needn't bother with Open As.

2. Let's start with the beginning two hits or so; they deserve the appropriate Basketball hit.mp3 file. Duplicate one to the video composition.

3. On the Animation palette, move the head of the audio layer to the frame where the ball hits the driveway. Actually, audio typically leads video in movies because audience response has shown over the years that sound reaches the ears a little later than visuals. Drag the Work Area head and tail to surround the basketball hit; this reduces Photoshop's need to buffer playback, and you'll get real-time playback a lot faster.

4. Hold Alt/Opt and then click the Play button (or press the Spacebar on your keyboard) to see how well the audio synchs with the video. When you're happy with this, just duplicate the audio layer by dragging its thumbnail into the Layers palette's Create a New Layer icon. Then move the clip on the Animation palette to the next instant where the basketball hits the driveway (or a squeak before).

5. As the ball grows weirder over time, choose a different sound effect. In Figure 15.22 you can see I've timed an MP3 called Blip to the moment the baseball hits the driveway. You have several hits to key, and hopefully I've provided enough different sound effects. Render the file to QuickTime, use any codec you like, amaze your friends, and then you can save the composition to rework if you care to in the future. A saved PSD of this composition contains only links, no altered video, and so it's quite small.

Figure 15.22

Blat, Squoink, and Bleep is evidently not a law firm.

Creating a 38-Second Situation Comedy

I originally got the idea for the example to follow from two sources: the late, great Henson Productions' *Dinosaurs*, a situation comedy that ate its own, lampooning how lame situation comedies are. And *Space Angel*, a 1959 Cambria Productions five-minute TV show that was done by superimposing live-action human lips over extremely limited-motion animation or even motionless animation cels. Ad agency art directors will be reminded of *animatics*, filmed storyboards to sell clients on filming the commercial.

Love on the Rocks, the mini-sitcom in this section, hopes to prove that entertainment can be derived from just about anything speaking a corny line, in this case a pair of talking lawn ornaments. What makes this tutorial different than the preceding ones is that there is a camera pan from one lawn ornament to the other; the video superimposed on the still life ornaments will need to move in perfect synch with the camera pan to pull off quite an extraordinary illusion.

What I did to gather the resources for this mini-episode was to get cheap greasepaint and mix it to generally match the color of two lawn ornaments we have in the back yard. My wife and I painted ourselves up and then ran lines with a locked-down camera. Then I used a hand-held DV camera (so the pan is not quite steady) to capture the ornaments to put behind the painted faces. And so here comes trick number 1 in this section: The hand-held quality of my holds on the ornaments outside of the pan was not steady enough to carry the illusion of a locked-down face shot superimposed on it. I did this, and you can, too, when you need a pan followed or preceded by a lock-down sequence:

1. Bring the footage into Photoshop and then duplicate it twice to layers in the same document.
2. Move the timeline to the frame just before the pan.
3. Right-click the top layer and choose Rasterize from the context menu. The layer is a still image now, perfectly locked for position.
4. Move the timeline to the conclusion of the pan, then choose the layer under the rasterized one and rasterize it.
5. The video layer that's still a live video layer is the hammock between still frames. On the Animation palette, drag the ends of the layer timeline in so the first frame of the pan butts to the beginning still layer and the end butts to the end still frame.
6. Write the composition out to video.

In Figure 15.23 you can see the unedited footage of the character "Rocky" and the footage that you'll composite Rocky into. Bear with me here; the original footage is not what you'll be using.

Chapter 5 covers a lot of color correction techniques for video that I used to make my face blend more thoroughly into the fake rock house key holder I portray.

Tip

A decorative rock, particularly with a foolish grin, would be the first place a criminal would look for your house key.

Figure 15.23
Try to match lighting and come close to matching color values when you need to composite a live actor into a mostly still scene.

In a nutshell, I masked everything around the face with a color I Eyedropper sampled by using a 5 by 5 pixel average. Beneath this layer is an Adjustment layer for Hue/Saturation. I've been known to do strange things but one of them is *not* putting theater greasepaint too close to my eyes or on my tongue. As you can see in Figure 15.24, I knocked the color out of only these areas. You might ask, "Why didn't you just do the footage with no makeup and then use Hue/Saturation?" For tone; human skin (or at least my own skin) is not close to the lawn ornament's luminosity values. Additionally, the greasepaint added texture. Finally, I distorted my face using the Spherize command, which turned the video clip into a Smart Object layer. I then rendered the video out, and as you'll hear in a moment, I went

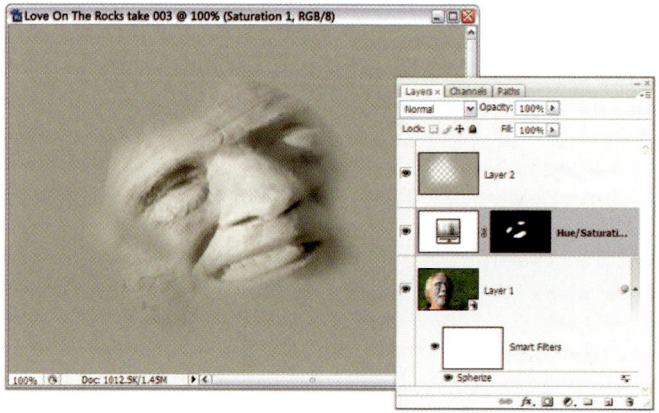

Figure 15.24
Add some stage makeup and Photoshop to your subject and suddenly you've got a talking rock.

into an audio editor and noise gated the monologue and dropped the pitch by a third to give me a gravelly voice.

I did a similar procedure to the footage of my wife as Porcha. Let's get down to some serious fun now. Notice that there's a hard edge at right above my eyebrow. I put this here deliberately; it's a reference point for changing the face's position relative to the pan in the Opening with pan.mov clip in the following steps. By writing out a 30+ second clip without an alpha channel I was able to provide you with a relatively high-quality video that you'll mask yourself to create the sitcom.

Clipping Masks and Initial Composition

Let's begin with the most difficult shot, the pan from Rocky's opening line to the reaction from Porcha. You want to introduce the first character to your composition, then add the second character, so duplicating and masking come first.

1. Open Opening with pan.mov and then Rocky.mov. Turn View > Pixel Aspect Ratio Correction off for both imported movies, and this is DV Widescreen in file format, a 720 by 480 uncorrected aspect formatted to 1.2 (approximately 853 by 480 pixels if measured using square pixels).

2. Duplicate the Rocky layer to the Opening with pan composition; the video automatically duplicates to the head of the Animation palette's Work Area.

3. Create a new (normal) layer below the Rocky layer (currently named Layer 2).

4. Press Q to switch to Quick Mask mode and then with the Brush tool and the 65-pixel soft tip (on the Options bar), paint over Rocky's face for a coarse mask you'll refine in a moment.

5. Press Q to toggle back to Standard Editing mode and then choose the new normal layer on the Layers palette.

6. Fill the selection marquee with black, then deselect.

7. Name the layers so we're on the same page in the following steps: Rename the top layer "Rocky," the clipping mask layer "clipping mask," and the bottom layer can keep its default name. Hold Alt/Opt and hover over the edge of the layer titles on the Layers palette between the Rocky layer and the layer underneath until your cursor becomes the icon I've enlarged in Figure 15.25, then click. You've created a clipping mask from the layer you painted on in Step 3. This is 90% of the integration technique.

8. Chances are the clipping layer's good but not flawless; you really need to see it in place to get an idea of the composite to then finesse the edges. Use the Brush tool in Normal mode to extend the mask—you simply paint on the clipping mask layer—or use Clear painting mode (on the Options bar) if you want to contract the mask and see less of Rocky.

Figure 15.25
Use a clipping layer (mask) to hide areas above the layer you've painted on.

9. Chances are also excellent that Rocky doesn't align to his stunt rock on the bottom video layer. You can Shift+click both the Rocky and the clipping mask layers on the Layers palette and then with the Move tool, move them both in synch to perfect this video illusion.

10. Save the composition to PSD file format; name it Love on the rocks.psd so I can refer to it in the following sections. Keep the document open.

Creating the Pan

Click on the top layer to make it active and then bring Porcha.mov into the workspace now and duplicate her video layer to the composition. Perform the same clipping layer masking on the character and then name the layers "Porcha" and "Porcha's clipping mask." Move to Frame 225 when the pan settles in for the placement of the face and the mask. Remember to Shift+click to select video *and* mask when moving them; alternatively, you can create a group from the Layers palette and put both items in a group (then move the group).

Begin at the beginning; Rocky needs to start moving out of frame at 188 and be completely out of frame at 196; fortunately, Photoshop supports Big Data and does not clip a layer's contents when you move it out of the document window.

1. On the Animation palette, move to Frame 187, the last still frame I built into the video before the pan. Click the Position stopwatch for both Rocky and his clipping mask to set a keyframe.

2. Advance to the next frame. Shift+click to choose both the Rocky video and the mask. Choose a reference point for the Rocky layer. Earlier I'd recommended keeping the hard edge above the eyebrow—this is a good reference point; you'll need to keep the relationship between Rocky's face and the rock that pans in this frame absolutely rock steady. Choose the Move tool and then use the keyboard arrow keys to nudge both layers.

3. Advance to the next frame and then repeat Step 2.

4. Continue until Rocky and his mask are completely out of frame at 196, nine critically important editing moves. See Figure 15.26 for the work in progress.

   I've included Figure 15.27 as an intermediate reference point, and you can see the complete position movement for Rocky should take about a dozen changes, accomplished through keyboard arrow nudging. Also, you might want to turn on thumbnail options via the Animation palette's Palette Options box accessed from the Palette menu, but I suggest you choose small thumbnail size. The other thing I did was alter the opacity between the last and next-to-last position change to ensure Rocky's face was completely out of frame at 196. You might not need to do this, but it's difficult, even when you extend the edges of the document window, to get a good idea of the accuracy of the position change between Frames 195 and 196.

5. Enter Porcha: once you have a key set at the frame where you aligned the face to the background sculpture, you're free to move on to the motion tracking. Begin at Frame 198; nudge both Porcha's face layer and the clipping layer almost completely out of frame, and also try keying the opacity of the

Figure 15.26
Move the video layer along with the mask to match the changing view of the panning footage on the bottom layer.

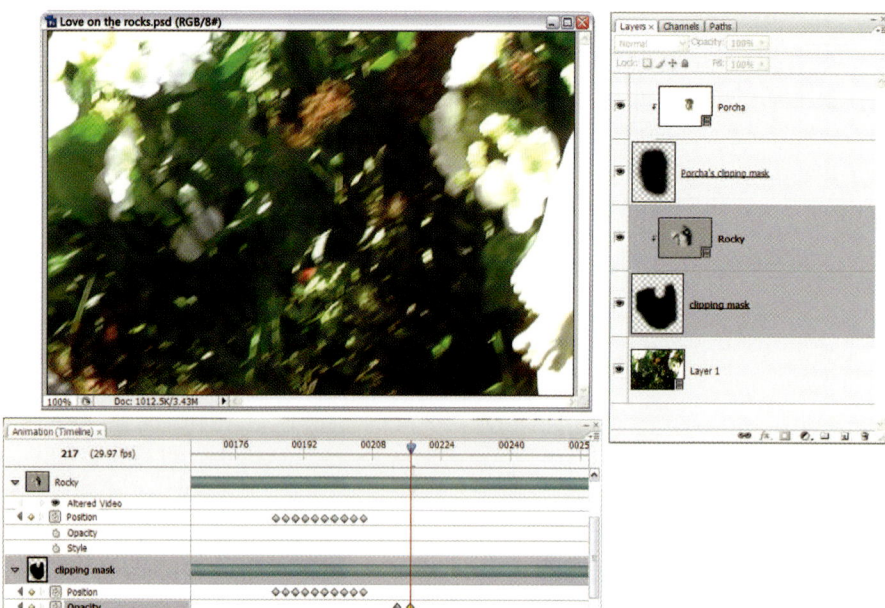

Figure 15.27
You can decrease Opacity to 0% on the last frame of a character's presence to ensure it's completely out of frame and will not accidentally pop up later.

clipping mask layer only. When you adjust clipping layer opacity, it affects the layer it clips. I suggest this because you'll note that my camera auto-adjusted exposure during the end of the pan, opening up for a few frames, slightly overexposing the background lawn ornament for Porcha, which settles back to a good exposure by Frame 209. Therefore, if you reduce the opacity of Porcha's face slightly (the lawn ornament's face is almost completely bleached out with almost no detail) at her entrance, bringing the opacity up to 100% toward the end of the pan, you'll match motion while faking the proper exposure change. See Figure 15.28.

Figures 15.29 and 15.30 are for reference to better show the position changes you need to make for the face video layers. In Figure 15.29, the pan is complete, and if you hold Alt/Opt while clicking the Play button on the Animation palette, you'll see and hear Porcha's lines against Rocky. This is an important step because shortly you'll exchange your special effects role for one of film editor, and the sections to follow show how to make good cuts from the footage I've provided. Where should you cut from Porcha's little tirade to Rocky's response?

Figure 15.30 is a map of where the motion matching travels from frame to frame, with the center of the faces as a reference point. Clearly, there is easing, acceleration, and deceleration, and clearly if you performed the preceding steps and the playback looks good, the motion matching does not travel in a straight line.

Figure 15.28
Try bringing the opacity of the face up at the beginning of Porcha's entrance to better match the exposure of the background video.

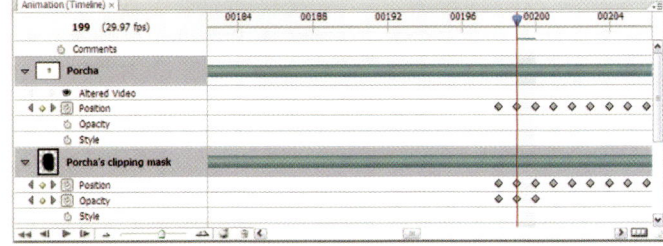

Figure 15.29
The Animation palette shows that at least 22 moves are necessary to move Porcha's face into the scene.

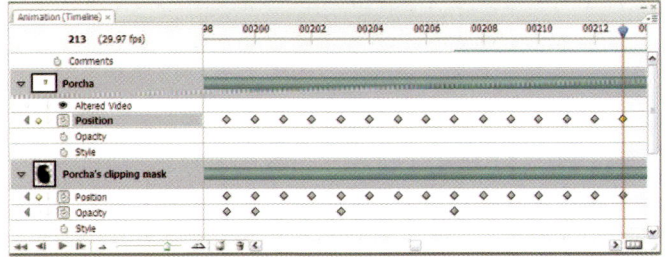

Figure 15.30
The anchors in this figure are a graphical representation of the motion of the faces relative to the panning background.

6. To keep this project lean so you can work without stressing out your system (and your computer's system), I say you should mark what you feel the end of this piece should be with a comment; you move the thumb to the area where you want to make a note and then click the Comment stopwatch on the Animation palette. My estimation from a film editor's position is that after Porcha's line, "Make sure your friends stay in the bushes…" is a good place to make a cut. Frame 400 is the place to put the comment because it provides a little wiggle room to cut to Rocky's response. Also, the film has been playing for more than 10 seconds from the head at this point and even with snappy dialog, today's audiences tend to fidget after 10 seconds without a cut.

7. Drag the Work Area end marker on the Animation palette in to 400.

8. Choose File > Export > Render Video. Use QuickTime format to preserve the audio track, don't use compression because compression should come last in the editing pipeline, and make sure Range is set to Currently Selected Frames. Now, if you don't like my recommendation for the cut, you can always go back to this PSD file and change the Work Area markers. For now, just render the file and keep the document open because you can cull additional cuts from it (it contains the sum total of the dialog for the finished sitcom).

Repurposing a Special Effects Setup

Figure 15.31 is a storyboard of the finished 38-second sitcom. I show my "director's cut" here and now because every cinematographer from Hitchcock to Spielberg found the need to pre-visualize a film to keep the budget down and to keep the editing tight. You haven't created the clips following Frame 387 yet, but if you play the current document with audio, you'll see that I'm *cutting on action. Cut on action* is a technique for keeping a scene fast-paced. Instead of waiting until an action is completed, or in this example a line of dialog is completed, you make an anticipatory cut to the following scene. Even the best actor or actress will appear a little stiff and rehearsed if you let the camera linger after a line has been delivered.

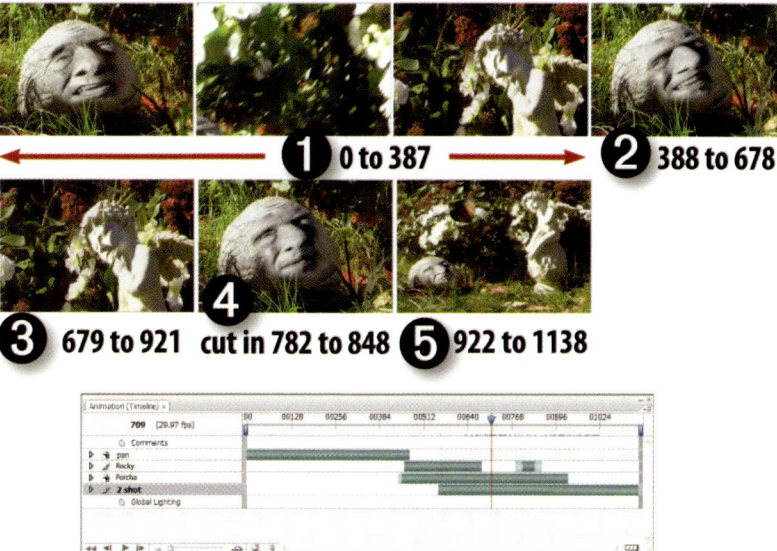

Figure 15.31
Storyboard your video at the planning stage so you know what to shoot and retouch and your editor has some insight to the flow of the scene.

First things first: Save a copy of the pan composition and then use it instead of the original to create the insert close-ups shown on the storyboard, marked with 2, 3 and 4, like so:

1. In the Love on the rocks.psd file, scroll the thumb on the Animation palette to where Rocky's face is center screen. Then click the stopwatch for position on both the face and the clipping mask tracks to remove motion. The close-ups on Rocky are static.

2. You can safely delete the background pan video layer.

3. Hide the Porcha layer on the Layers palette. It's not that her face will be visible, but her audio track will be exported unless you hide the video layer from Photoshop's QuickTime rendering engine.

4. Choose Layer > Video Layers > New Video Layer from File and then choose Rocky's background.mov from the ZIP archive. Put the layer on the bottom

of the stack, and then move the head of the video layer on the Animation palette to about Frame 380.

5. Position the mask and face properly for the new background.

6. First, choose document Settings on the Animation palette menu and extend the document to end at Frame 855. Drag the Work Area handles in to bracket Frames 380–685. This will include all of Rocky's reply to Porcha plus a few frames to spare.

7. File > Export > Render Video. Name the file something easy to remember such as scene01. Export using NSTV DV Widescreen from the File Options Size drop-down list (to match the original video), no alpha, no compression, and use QuickTime file format to preserve the audio.

8. Drag the Work Area to bracket 775–855.

9. Export the video with no compression; call it scene 02.mov. Actually, you can export to AVI or QuickTime for this clip because Rocky has no lines.

10. Scenes 3 and 5 are ahead of you now. Choose Layer > Video Layers > New Video Layer from File and then import Porcha's background.mov. Put it on top of Rocky's background layer. Off the menu for the Animation palette, extend Document Settings to 1138 frames.

11. Unhide the Porcha face layer and then hide the Rocky face layer. Drag the Porcha track on the Animation palette so its head is at Frame 675. Scroll the timeline until Porcha's face is fully onscreen (about Frame 388 or so) and then kill the position changes for both the face and the clipping mask layers by clicking their stopwatch icons on the Animation palette (just like you did with Rocky in Step 1).

12. Make sure Porcha's face is aligned with the underlying background video and that the background is present at Frames 675 to 935. Therefore, drag Porcha's track on the Animation palette so it starts at 675.

13. Move the Work Area handles to bracket these frames and then export to QuickTime, no compression.

Usually, an establishing shot would occur in a segment at the beginning, but I thought a reveal of the garden using a two-shot at the conclusion of this uproarious comedy would work better. Now that you have removed motion from the face video layers, it's easier than you'd think to create the end, Frames 922 to 1138. Follow these steps:

1. Open 2 shot background.mov and remove aspect correction from your view.

2. Put Rocky and his clipping mask into a new group on the Layers palette. Click the New Group icon, double-click the title on the list to rename it Rocky, and

then Shift+click to select both layers and drag them into the group icon, the little manila folder.

3. Do the same with Porcha and her clipping layer.
4. Drag both Group folders into the 2 shot background movie, then save and close the duplicate composition you worked on in the previous steps to save resources.
5. Save the new document as 2 shot.psd.
6. Choose the Rocky Group folder on the Layers palette. First press Ctrl/Cmd+T to Free Transform the group and then scale the face and mask to I'd say about 35 to 42%.
7. With the Move tool, reposition Rocky's face so it's on the rock.
8. Perform Steps 6 and 7 with Porcha's Group folder.
9. Because you duplicated roughly 30 seconds of characters and dialog over to a 7.2 second video layer, much of the character footage is clipped outside the Work Area, and this is actually good. But you need to shift the character tracks so Rocky is making faces at the head of the new composition, and you can simply scoot the tail of the Porcha footage to align with the end of the Work Area, as shown in Figure 15.32.
10. Export the video to QuickTime, no compression. You can close this composition after saving to PSD.

Figure 15.32
Shift the video layers on the Animation palette so that the conclusion of the bickering happens at the end of the bottom video layer.

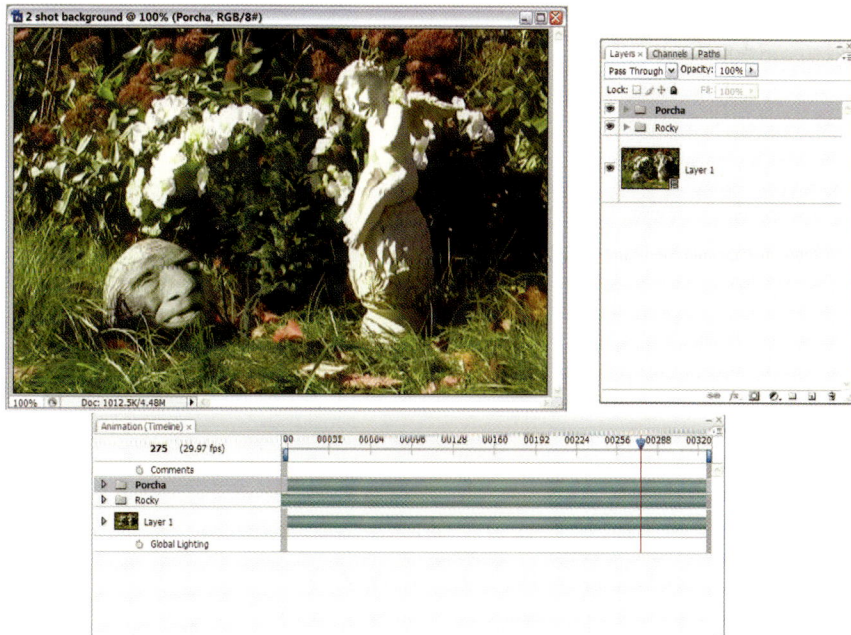

Editing the Clips Together, Adding Sound fx

By exporting the clips as segments that were storyboarded, editing the clips together is going to be a piece of cake. Wait; do you hear something? No you don't; there's no canned laughter! Yet. In the ZIP archive I've included three outbursts of laughter that, while you're editing in the following steps, you can add to appropriate places. I've also included a humorous soundtrack that has a strong introduction but then fades so it doesn't step on Rocky's opening line.

Surprisingly, the audience clips were fairly easy to create. First I found yesterday's Op/Ed section in the newspaper before our parakeet used it, to give my wife and me motivation to do some serious chortling. Seriously, the laugh tracks are only two people, overdubbed three times, with a little reverb added. You'd think six voices are too little to imitate a studio audience, but at low volume it truly works.

As for the music, it's a heartfelt tribute to Jim Henson, who wrote the theme to *The Muppets Show*. Jim had an excellent ear for humorous, squishy music that perfectly reflected his creations. After studying the music a while, I used a digital audio workspace along with some Virtual Studio Technology (VST) plug-ins that emulate real musical instrument sounds to create Love on the Rocks Theme.mp3. It's a hybrid of vaudeville and Dixieland-style jazz, with a bucket-muted trumpet, a raspy bass line, and the obligatory fruity tenor saxophone.

Here's how to put the whole deal together into the completed composition:

1. Refer back to Figure 15.31, the storyboard. At the bottom you'll see the Animation palette, whose tracks correspond to the storyboard appearances of the characters.

2. Open your rendered video clips, undo Pixel Aspect Ratio View, create a new video composition that's the same size and pixel aspect ratio as your rendered clips (I used D1/DV NSTC Widescreen, approximately 1.2 aspect ratio, 720 by 480 to film the original clips), and then duplicate them over.

3. Click the menu icon on the Animation palette, choose Document Settings, and then specify 1138 frames (38;00 seconds) or a little more for wiggle room.

4. Here is where I leave it to you to create split-second timing to suit your own creative taste. Use the storyboard as a guideline; you have the leisure to shift tracks on the timeline and to hide video layer areas by dragging inward from the green video layer edges on the Animation palette. You can see I did this to make the Gallery movie in Figure 15.31.

5. Open (Open As QuickTime for Windows users) the Love on the Rocks Theme.mp3 file, Short laughs with giggle.mp3, Short laughs.mp3, and 4 sec audience laughs.mp3.

6. Start by duplicating the theme song layer over to your composition. It should align perfectly with the composition start on the Animation palette's Work Area.

7. Add a short audience laugh (the short or the short with giggle work fine) after a frame you feel probably doesn't deserve a laugh; there are many such pieces of dialog, and that's what makes sitcom laugh tracks so irritating and your composition so authentic! See Figure 15.33's Animation palette for a suggested entrance for a laugh.

Figure 15.33
Add bursts of audience reaction after dialog lines in the composition.

8. Laugh it up; pepper the Work Area with guffaws, and finally, use the 4 second clip to conclude the composition.

9. Export the composition to QuickTime file format. Use compression; I got the file down to about 3MB with decent quality using the Sorenson 3 codec.

10. Save the composition to PSD file format, and I seriously suggest you back all the resource files, mine and yours, off to a DVD sometime soon to save on hard drive space. Your files won't add up to as much as mine, but we're talking at least 5GB.

> **Note**
>
> Earlier in this section I mentioned that the pan footage was created by placing the pan itself between two still images to better stabilize the takes where the characters have their lines. However, you might notice some motion in the background. I did a little enhancing because although the focus is supposed to be on the lawn ornament characters, I felt the audience's eyes might wander and detect a still background. I used Cinema 4D to animate an xFrog bush and to animate some blades of grass I created, similar to the hair technique I showed earlier to build the animated urchin ball. Additionally, I animated a butterfly during the two-shot sequence and rotoscoped a few falling autumn leaves into the background movies you worked with. I made certain I blurred the CG effects a little to blend more completely into the background still images. As evangelical as it might sound, 3D animation applications can indeed help enhance your video work in Photoshop; the cost can be as little as $900 for a full-featured modeling/rendering/animation application, and the learning curve is about as steep as Photoshop itself.

Add motion matching to your bag of tricks now! I find it less of a challenge than rotoscoping, and as with all digital media, the illusions you create are virtually undetectable to audiences. Like anything worthwhile, your admission ticket is a little patience and marginally more time.

Part VI

Output

16

Codecs, DVD Authoring, and Saving for the Web

You're reading this book from cover to cover, and now you have several gigabytes of your own edited, enhanced, and special effects videos. This chapter shows you how to do what every content creator wants to do: *publish* your work. Whether it's to YouTube or an e-mail attachment to a friend, an authored DVD for commercial release or a straight write to DVD for archiving, Photoshop and third-party software can make beautiful copies of your digital masterpieces to assist you is getting your work outside of your personal computer.

Different Recipients Require Different File Formats

Once your composition is complete, regardless of your audience, the route to sharing your video work is File > Export > Render Video. In previous chapters I've provided basic export settings, but these have been for instant personal gratification, so you can play your video on your system.

The recipient of your video dictates the type of export you define, and I see four distinct segments to the publishing pipeline:

- **Publishing to the Web and as e-mail attachments.** This includes YouTube, MetaCafe, and other video parlors online, video tutorials, embedded objects on Web pages, and videos you want to share with friends and family. Codecs are a must for prepping a copy of your video, and I explain codec technology in the following section.

- **Authoring a DVD.** Commercial DVD movies you rent or buy are pressed, while DVDs you generate using your computer are burned, but the only real difference is the predicted life span of the disc (home-burned DVDs are anticipated to degrade, and the layers might separate after five years or so). You can't author a DVD that the recipient can play back on a television's DVD player straight out of Photoshop, but you can indeed prepare the video for burning using third-party software I discuss later in this chapter.

- **Creating a video for collaboration work.** If you were commissioned to create a title or special effect for a client that will be composited by a third party, you have a number of options here. You can write the PSD composition and the associated video clips to DVD or other mass storage (professionals have been known to mail hard drives), you can write a video that requires compositing to uncompressed video file format with an alpha mask, and you can also use a codec that supports alpha masking if video quality is of little concern (for test footage and proof of concept, for example).

- **Archiving.** Archiving is simple and straightforward. You probably don't want or need gigabytes of video snippets on your hard drives after you've finished a video. You write the finished, edited video to uncompressed file format, gather all your resource files, organize them in a folder structure so they make sense four years from now, and then write them to DVD. As a backup, you'll want to also write the media back to DV tape. It's the reverse process of downloading DV footage from your camera, and although the jury is still out, DV tapes can possibly retain data longer than DVDs you burn.

I've organized this chapter according to specific export needs and not a laundry list of codecs and video file formats, although I do discuss the particulars of video formats as they relate to the quality of a finished copy of your Photoshop video work. There are a lot of good video file formats you can use; I'd like to show you what they're good *for*.

Examining the Structure of Digital Video

Before getting into compression, it's a good idea to understand what digital video is, how it's *structured*, because you have options in Photoshop and other video applications that have an impact on the quality and general playability of your video for presentation. By knowing how digital video is compiled, video compression through codecs will make more sense, and you can make smarter choices for exporting video compositions. Like still images, every video is unique in content, and content has a bearing on which codec and other setting you should choose.

The easiest model to intellectually grasp that represents digital video exists in three dimensional (theoretical) space. Two dimensions represent the horizontal and vertical extents of video, and although we can see that we can measure a video composition using pixels as an increment in Photoshop, the dimensions might be more accurately expressed as directions and not dimensions—video pictures *move*. The third dimension is that of time. Therefore, when rendering a video out of Photoshop, you have control over the height and width of what programmers call a data frame, and also of its duration, how long the still picture remains onscreen. All digital movies are collections of still images, although this might not always be apparent because of the method by which the still images are encoded into a video file.

When Is a Video Still Not a Still?

If you bring a video clip into Photoshop and then stop the video at any given frame, you might see the effect of *interlacing*. The still image isn't exactly a still image at all, but rather *part* of a still image.

Interlacing was originally developed as a television broadcasting technique for reducing flicker without the need to expand broadcast bandwidth, particularly important in the nascent age of television in the late 1930s. An interlacing scan takes the image data from a data frame and creates an image (historically on a cathode ray tube) for every *second* line. Interlacing is written from the top left corner to the bottom right corner of a display. This process is repeated again starting at the second row, to fill in the gaps left behind while performing the first scan on alternate rows.

A good question is why on Earth would a video camera perform interlacing when you the user have no intention of broadcasting your video over a television network? The answer is that, because digital video has its roots in traditional video, older video cameras that record analog signals to videotape (not DV tape) use a scanline tube called a vidicon tube to record data, and today videographers are migrating to progressive scan encoding (I'll explain this in a moment) because the historic problem of flicker has mostly been solved through increased broadcast bandwidth and improved refresh rates with monitors.

In Figure 16.1 at left you can see a field from a video that was originally from videotape and was digitized. A field is an image that contains half the lines needed to complete a data frame. At right is what we see as a complete image. What I did was use Photoshop's Filter > Video > De-Interlace. Photoshop does not reconstruct the data frame using two successive fields, but instead you have the option to reconstruct the image using interpolation (smart duplication of existing visual data) or duplication (dumb duplication of existing visual data). However, the resulting still image looks good, and this is what you do if you want to pull a still frame from a video that's been interlaced. Your other option in this box is odd and even fields. Most interlaced video was created by separating the lower field first so Even could be your first choice; if the resulting image looks wrong or awful, undo and then try odd fields.

Interlacing, when watched as a video, produces less flickering due to two physical phenomena: There is an afterglow to the phosphors on a TV tube that carries the first field over to the second, and the human brain has something called "persistence of vision," which helps bind the two separate video fields.

Fortunately, today's video uses progressive scanning, transmitted and displayed line by line top to bottom, no alternating of scan lines, and each data frame contains the whole picture as captured. Interlacing for broadcast TV is still used for standard definition TVs and the 1080i HDTV broadcast standard, but not for LCD or plasma displays, which take a progressive scan signal.

What this means to you as a video publisher is that you should not choose interlacing for videos you write out of Photoshop. Use progressive scanning for all content you know will be published on the Web and viewed on a computer monitor. If you're authoring a DVD, covered later in this chapter, the DVD authoring software will give you the option to interlace the media.

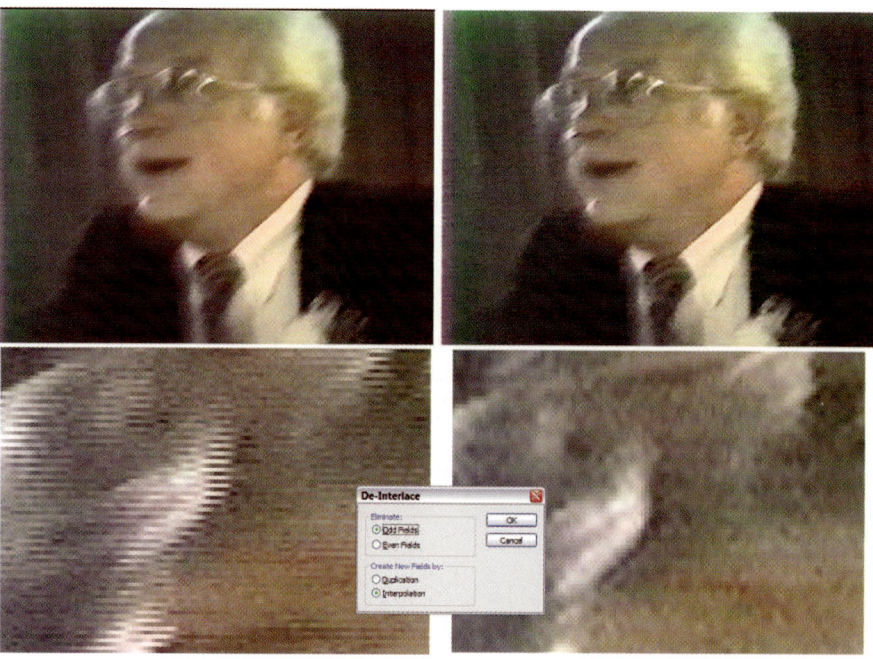

Figure 16.1

Interlacing separates a data frame into two successive fields, each containing half the total visual data.

A Primer on Codecs

If your intention is to deliver a copy of your work via the Internet, you'll definitely need the assistance of one of the codecs that ship with Photoshop Extended. The term *codec* is an abbreviation for compressor/decompressor; it would be inefficient if not downright impractical *not* to compress a video during the encoding process and to then let it decompress (and temporarily expand in file size) when the audience watches it. Video compression, just like with still image compression, comes in two flavors: lossy and lossless. Two different recipes (algorithms) are used for these compression types, but essentially it boils down to making your video more efficient for transmitting purposes.

Video compression algorithms usually begin the routine by examining a block of pixels at a given point in the video. The block of pixels is then compared from one frame to the next, and the codec writes only the differences within those blocks. Successful compression, as you would imagine, then, depends on all three dimensions of video content. For example, a video of a snail is boring as entertainment goes, but it would compress well because there's very little difference from data frame to frame. The same is true of video titles. However, when more pixels change, the codec must send more data to keep up with the number of pixels that are changing. Flames from a campfire, a distant shot of an enthusiastic crowd, and similar scenes require ever-changing pixels.

Compression Types

With any compression, there is a trade-off between saved file size and quality, and this is where lossy and lossless compression come into play. There is a third aspect to add to the equation: You can improve the playback quality of highly compressed videos by increasing the *bit rate*, an issue I cover later in this chapter.

Think of JPEG and PNG compressed images; video compression's two types are:

- *Lossy*, where some of the original visual data is discarded to afford a compression ratio you define, but typically is 5:1 and better. Lossy compression at high rates causes poor overall focus and video artifacting (flat blocks of color popping up where there was originally image detail), but I have posted videos to YouTube and MetaCafe using 10:1 compression ratio, and the flicks look pretty good. When you hear "lossy," think of JPEG-type compression.

- *Lossless*, where the video is compressed without losing any of the original data. When lossless compression is used, during the encoding process redundant and inefficient code is replaced with more efficient code. Some forms of data compression are lossless. This means that when the data is decompressed, the result is a bit-for-bit perfect match with the original. While lossless compression of video is possible, it is rarely used. This is because any lossless compression system will sometimes result in a file (or portions of) that is as large and/or has the same data rate as the uncompressed original. As a result, all hardware in a lossless system would have to be able to run fast enough to handle uncompressed video as well. This eliminates much of the benefit of compressing the data in the first place. For example, digital videotape can't vary its data rate easily, so dealing with short bursts of maximum-data-rate video would be more complicated than something that was fixed at the maximum rate all the time.

For example, an RGB still photograph saved to TIFF file format might have several sequences of identical pixel values; suppose for example there's a completely black wall behind a person—we're talking R:0, G:0, B:0. Uncompressed files write *explicit* data, and this uncompressed TIFF image would have thousands of color entries that say the same thing, "Give this pixel R:0, G:0, B:0" for row after row. A more efficient coding would be, "Start R:0, G:0, B:0, continue value for the following 15,000 pixels, end pixel value here." You can't expect the magnitude of compression with lossless as lossy, but you do ensure original video fidelity. When you think of lossless compression, think of the PNG file format, a highly efficient file structure for still images.

In a nutshell, by the nature of video, it contains redundant data relating to similarities in color within a single frame and similarities between neighboring frames. In many codecs a scheme similar to that used in JPEG lossy compression is used, and it's quite effective. The human brain is less sensitive to changes in brightness than differences in chroma (hue and saturation). By averaging the unique color areas from image area to area and from frame to frame, a codec can take massive amounts of video data and present it with varying fidelity (depending on the content of the video) at very, very small saved and transmitted file sizes.

Codec Quality Concerns

Even if you believe you have plenty of free space on your hard drives for storing uncompressed videos, don't let the purist in you keep you from compressing video files. Lossy compression actually occurs when you capture a video with your DV camera. Your original files, right off the DV tape, are compressed—it's unrealistic to think that an affordable DV camera can capture a 720 by 480 pixel RGB image (a 1MB file) at the rate of 30 per second. Some discarding and short-handing is performed to record digital video.

Understand that there is no such thing as "uncompressed DV"; when you capture DV over your USB II or Firewire connection, you're not actually digitizing the video, but rather performing a file transfer of the DV compressed files. As I get into explaining and defining codecs, take heart in this reality, archive your originals on DVDs and DV tapes, and know that compression truly is in the eye of the beholder. The purist in me used to run away in hysterics at the mention of making JPEGs out of my precious uncompressed TIFF still images. Then I read up on what JPEG lossy compression actually does, and then I mentally filed the information and took a good look at a JPEG of an original file with my eyes. Hey, for 99% of my still images, at 8:1 compression, JPEGs don't look bad! Similarly, with compressed videos, you evaluate your copy of the original by itself, experiment with different compression levels until you're happy, and you do yourself a disservice by sitting there and comparing the original with the compressed copy. It's an exercise in futility because the compressed copy is never going to look as good as your original. You get happy with the compressed copy; YouTube is never going to air your uncompressed original, so your goal is to deliver the best looking compressed copy of your video.

Publishing for the Web: QuickTime Codecs

Photoshop's video rendering engine is built in part on licensed Apple QuickTime technology. QuickTime is not simply that player Macintosh and Windows users can run to watch QuickTime and other file formats for video and audio, but a self-contained rendering system. Because Photoshop uses this technology for all high-quality video renders, Windows users need to intellectually walk away from the Microsoft AVI file format, because although Photoshop can render to AVI, audio is not supported.

QuickTime features 26 different compression schemes, as you can see when you click Settings next to File Options in the Render Video box. Out of the 26 choices, several are not what the industry considers a true video codec so much as a coding scheme for the frames that is then compressed using a codec. For example, Targa, TIFF, BMP, and JPEG options use the compression supported by these still file formats. Unless your client specifically states that he needs a certain codec (and you're certain he knows what he's talking about), you are usually best off with a handful of codecs that provide good quality at relatively small file sizes.

The following sections cover the various codecs and their strengths and weaknesses, and I've listed them in descending order of general professional popularity.

Sorenson Video

Occasionally referred to as the Sorenson Video Quantizer (SVQ), the Sorenson codec was devised by the company Sorenson Media and is the best general-purpose codec Photoshop supports. Not surprisingly, it is also used in the core of Adobe Flash (originally licensed by Macromedia as Sorenson Spark). The Sorenson codec comes in two flavors in Photoshop: Sorenson Video and Sorenson Video 3. The plain Sorenson Video is version 2, offering less quality and larger file sizes; I see no reason to choose this option unless you have a client with whom you need to be backward compatible.

Sorenson Video is the Basic edition in Photoshop; you have options for quality, frame rate, data rate, and frequency of keyframing, all of which I cover later in this chapter. Sorenson Pro can be purchased in a standalone application (Sorenson Squeeze Suite) at about $500 and offers not only QuickTime but Microsoft WMV and several other file formats, along with a range of compression options and settings.

Although the Basic codec in Photoshop is compatible with all versions of QuickTime, the Pro version is not currently compatible with Intel-based Macintosh computers.

H.264

Here's where naming conventions might get a little confusing: H.264 compression is called MPEG-4 in ISO (International Standards Organization) terminology, and the natural question that arises is, "Why then does Photoshop offer MPEG-4 as an export option in addition to MPEG-4 for QuickTime, in addition to H.264, which is MPEG-4—for QuickTime?"

MPEG, the Moving Picture Experts Group, has been working for years with the Video Coding Experts Group and other partners to devise a portable standard for digital video. As a result, there are many versions of the MPEG codec. If your client wants an MPEG file without the QuickTime "wrapper," you choose MPEG-4 in the Render Video box. I recommend that if your client needs a QuickTime with MPEG-4 compression, you can safely choose H.264 as the codec, it has more formatting options than MPEG-4, and don't sweat the naming discrepancy.

Previous versions of this codec include H.262, which is also known as MPEG-2 (currently used to encode commercial DVD movies), and H.261. Unless your client has a specific need for these compression types, stick to H.264, which offers better quality and larger frame dimensions. Apple has embraced H.264 as the codec of the future. Apple implements H.264 as MPEG-4 in QuickTime, and a high definition version of H.264 is in the works at the time of this writing.

In addition to the massive amount of work put into this codec, it is also the work of several different ventures, and not a sole one such as Sorenson. You might therefore expect more improvements more quickly and a more competitive price for the codec in future releases of professional standalone products.

Multiple Rendering Passes

When you choose H.264 as a codec for QuickTime export or if you use a post-editing standalone codec such as Sorenson Squeeze, you have the additional option of having the rendering engine perform a single or several passes in the encoding. This has to do with bit rate, which I'll get to later in this chapter; bit rate is related to compression and quality.

An innovative thing programmers have developed is *variable bit rate*, where the rendering application examines segments of the video and decides whether certain passages can use more or less visually unimportant color data averaged. For example, you might have a video of a fellow sleeping, waking up, and then going out for a run. With *constant bit rate* (CBR), the default for many codecs featured in Photoshop (nowhere in the interface does it use this term, but technically this is what it's doing), you are locked into a scheme of compression versus quality and might waste precious MB documenting the fellow at sleep, where there isn't much change from frame to frame, thus wasting compression. However, VBR, which is called Best Quality (Multi-pass) in the Compression Settings dialog box, can lower the amount of data written to accommodate video passages that have little or no changes between neighboring frames. During the subsequent passes, the data rate is increased when more scene change is detected. The overall effect is smooth, and you get both quality and the amount of compression you need.

All the parameters for writing a video using a codec are interrelated: bit rate, key frames, and frame rate.

Other, Less Preferred QuickTime Codecs

There are codecs for DVD authoring in the QuickTime codec list, and I cover these separately in later sections. There are also codecs for collaborative work; outside of these categories, there remain codecs whose quality I find unacceptable and whose compression ratios make it daunting to send the compressed video to a video café or as an e-mail attachment. But they're part of the QuickTime codec bundle, and I cover them briefly in the following sections purely as points of interest.

Graphics

This codec handles only 8-bit (256 color) video; if your video is RGB as most are, the codec brute-force dithers the colors down to a 256-maximum color video. Saved files are uncompressed in standard video terminology—the compression is achieved by dithering down the unique colors to this comparatively small palette.

If you created an animated GIF you want to save as a genuine video, the Graphics codec works fine, only because GIFs are limited to 256 colors.

Component Video

Intended for re-rendering video whose native source is broadcast television that uses the YUV color space. YUV color space is similar to LAB color; it contains one channel of luminance and two channels of chromacity (color). However, due to an inherent lack of reconciliation between digital imaging and broadcast video, don't equate YUV with LAB color; YUV was created when color broadcasting came into existence. The Y channel was broadcast for years for black and white reception, and then the color channels were cobbled onto the standard. YUV has a narrower color space than RGB, LAB, SHV, and other models used to describe what we call 24-bit color, and the luminance is higher than digital standards so analog TVs display bright colors.

Component Video encodes luminance using four passes, and the color channels get two passes, very similar to what an affordable DV camera writes. It offers poor compression, it's lossless, and I see no reason to use it for other than archiving existing broadcast video.

Motion-JPEG

The A and B varieties of Motion-JPEG are available due to the differing chip sets on relatively old video capture cards (mid-1990s). This is one of the oldest QuickTime codecs and saves data frames as progressive scans using 4:2:2 color and luminance passes to generate, as the name suggests, little JPEG images. Quality and compression are not nearly as good as H.264 or Sorenson, but for archiving, if you use 100% quality, there is no data loss (85% quality produces small video files with decent quality).

In short, it's a legacy codec.

PNG

The PNG codec is a lossless one, using the same algorithms as still image PNG technology. It is also a CBR (constant bit rate) codec, which means that all frames are rendered to the same quality, making a video primarily of unchanging content impossible to compress to send as an e-mail attachment.

It's a good archiving file format, but so is archiving your original, unretouched footage using the None option under Compression Settings.

Cinepak

Cinepak was one of the first codecs for the personal computer. Today it's legacy; poor video quality and comparatively large file sizes do not compensate for the sole virtue of being readable by Macs, Unix, and Windows users.

Intel Indeo

You don't achieve as good compression or quality with this codec as you would using QuickTime H.264 or Microsoft's WMV (an implementation of MPEG-4; Photoshop cannot read or write WMV because its rendering engine is based on QuickTime). Therefore it's not suitable for Web distribution of videos, but it does support alpha channel transparency.

Après-Codec: Setting Other Parameters for Publishing

Compression/decompression schemes are important, but not the sole determining factor for quality viewing of your work on YouTube and other video parlors on the Web. The following sections cover your other settings in the File > Export > Render Video box in Photoshop Extended, and after that I guide you through uploading your video masterpiece so the world can appreciate it.

H.264 (MPEG-4) and Your Options

I need to choose a specific codec to demonstrate the additional settings you want to consider. H.264, also known as a special flavor of MPEG-4, appears to have the most options and therefore affords the best opportunity for getting your video up on the Web with good playback quality.

Choose a video you'd like to render for Web viewing or as an e-mail attachment. Choose File > Export > Render Video, choose QuickTime Movie from the File Options QuickTime Export drop-down list, and then click the Setting, button. Click the Settings button in the Movie Settings box, and then in the Standard Video Compression Settings box, choose H:264 from the drop-down list.

Frame Rate

The frame rate of the video you want to export is expressed in fps (frames per second). You can change this to anything you like; you might actually want to do this for videos with only a little visible motion, but typically if your DV camera recorded at 29.97 fps, you set the frame rate to 29.97 fps.

Frame rate is the resolution of the motion in your video in very much the same way as ppi (pixels per inch) is the resolution you use to measure still images for printing. You don't increase the playback speed of a video or decrease it by specifying different frame rates; I discuss slow motion and other time effects in Chapter 13, and warping time has nothing to do with frame rate.

By resolution, I'm referring to how smoothly or jittery a video plays back. For example, 29.97 fps is the NTSC standard for broadcast playback, and its smoothness is as technologically advanced and aesthetically acceptable as we have to date. I explained the odd number of fps for NTSC earlier in this book, but it deserves repeating again here.

Black and white broadcast and color broadcasts are usually transmitted simultaneously to conserve bandwidth. However, the specs for B&W and color are different, and to reconcile the difference, 29.97 (not quite 30 fps) was settled upon.

This is called drop-frame frame rate, not to be confused with frame-*skipping*, where your system can't keep up with the video throughput and segments are skipped over. Drop-frame broadcasting is merely a convention; frames aren't actually dropped but rather reconciled between two different standards, and PAL standards actually use 25 fps for broadcasting.

You don't gain anything in quality or playback smoothness by increasing the fps value beyond the native film speed (in this box within Photoshop). Therefore, it's a mistake to write a DV segment that was captured at 29.97 fps to 30 fps, and the resulting file will be larger than necessary. On the other hand, you can save a little upload file size for your video by *decreasing* the fps value. I don't recommend this trick capriciously, but here's something to be aware of: Researchers discovered that the lowest resolution for video (before the audience gets annoyed or develops a headache) is somewhere between 12 and 18 fps. Part of the reason why Flash animations are so small is that one of the settings for SWF files is 15 frames per second. Can you or should you do this with full-action video footage?

It depends on your needs and the content of the video. Some gifted special effects videographers created an *American Idol* clip in 2006 featuring a duet between Celine Dion and the late Elvis Presley through advance compositing techniques and a stunt body-double. When the video was broadcast on YouTube, it was done using a Flash Shockwave file (SWF) playing at 15 fps, as many videos do. The reason it worked and looked good was because the song, *If I Can Dream*, is a slow ballad, and there is very little frenetic motion in the clip. Also, we accept Super 8 video transfers your parents or grandparents took with a silent home movie camera in the 1950s and early 1960s. However, Super 8 typically traveled through the gate at 12 frames per second (18 with the more expensive cameras). Yet our minds tell us this is okay video because it generally has tons of emotional impact to distract us from the overall jerkiness, and typical home movie content is waving at the camera and blowing out birthday cake candles—not a lot of dramatic motion.

If your video is mostly "talking head" in content, try rendering a 15 fps copy of the video and see how it plays back; judge it as the audience will, on quality, presentation, and content. Try to use whole number incremental divisions if you're degrading the fps; for example, PAL broadcast at 25fps will degrade better to 12 fps than say 18. Similarly, try a value of 10 or 15 for 30 fps NTSC videos. You will conserve saved file size, just as the videos from space were narrow-banded back in the late 1960s; the astronauts took breathtaking footage at little more than 8 frames per second to conserve on transmission bandwidth. Just remember that you can't regain what you lose when degrading the resolution or frame rate; always back up your original file.

Key Frames

Key frames when rendering a video has a different meaning than key frames in Frames mode on the Animation palette. In rendering, a key frame is a reference frame for rendering and codec calculations. For example, a cut to a different scene in a video clip requires a key frame; without one, the codec will get confused over which frame to reference when it then averages color and composition similarities in successive frames. As you might expect, key frames get the least compression; therefore, the more keys in a rendered compressed video, the larger the saved file size.

The automatic key frame option does exactly what you think it does, and perhaps it's not the best option to let a software program evaluate the aesthetics of your valued composition. Generally, with Talking Head videos, you can get away with a key frame every 10 seconds or so, while action scenes require more key frames. Use a multiple technique when manually setting key frames: a moderately paced video can use one keyframe every 5 seconds. A video that has a lot of visual changes and importance should be keyed every one to two seconds.

Frame Reordering and Streaming Media

Streaming media is one of the twenty-first century buzzwords that loosely interpreted means, "it starts downloading as soon as you click the Play button on a Web page and continues downloading in the background. No wait to watch!" A more studied look at the term reveals that *all* Web media is "streaming"; videos stream when watched on a PC, and they don't stream when you play them from DVD.

However, to better optimize your video to stream efficiently, the H.264 codec in this example has a Frame Reorder option. What this does when enabled is code your video nonsequentially when necessary to provide an optimized stream. Although your audience will see Johnny get up in the morning, shave, and then go to work (if this is your video content), this sequence is not necessarily what Frame Reordering will code to optimize your file. It's sort of black box technology, and it'll speed up the stream for sequences that contain a lot of static content, so use it when you use this codec.

Data Rate

By default in Photoshop, the data rate is set to Automatic and Optimized for Download. Most of the time this is okay, however you should understand a little about data transfer rates because it's *your* video.

Because the saved file size depends on frame color averaging (you set this using the Quality slider, it's how much lossiness is written), plus fps, plus the dimensions of your video, the data rate can be used as part of the equation to improve quality and/or to help keep large saved file sizes down.

How do you measure for the right data rate? First of all, because data rate measures size of transfer, it's somewhat dependent on the dimensions of your video, but Table 16.1 shows overall quality of a video (regardless of dimensions) using MPEG-4 as a benchmark codec for the video.

Table 16.1 Video Transfer Rate versus Video Quality

Cell phone/iPod streaming video	16 Kbps
Video conferencing	128–384 Kbps
VHS quality (common and quite acceptable)	1 Mbps
DVD quality	5 Mbps

As a rule, the higher your frame rate, the higher the data rate should be. If you don't specify this, you'll get less visual quality at a high saved file size price. Table 16.2 shows the video frame dimensions versus a data rate recommended by a friend in the trade I trust:

Table 16.2 Frame Size versus Data Rate

320 by 240 pixels (typical Internet size)	300–500 Kbps.
640 by 480 (720 by 480 by .9 aspect ratio)	1,000–2,000 Kbps
1280 by 720 pixels (high definition)	8,000 Kbps

Tip

In addition to the settings options for QuickTime codecs, in the Settings box after you click OK there are filter and size buttons. Where available (depending on the codec you choose), the Filter box enables you to tweak Saturation and Sharpness and even offers a few filters from Photoshop's Filters menu. You have a preview of the filtered video, but it's so small you won't get a good idea of the filtered video, so it's more or less trial and error. You might consider sharpening your video as a means of compensating for a lot of video codec compression and also increasing saturation as codecs tend to dull the resulting video.

Also, you can specify standard sizes for your exported video. This can also be done in the main render Video Box, overriding any settings in the Settings box.

Figure 16.2 is the Settings box in Render Video.

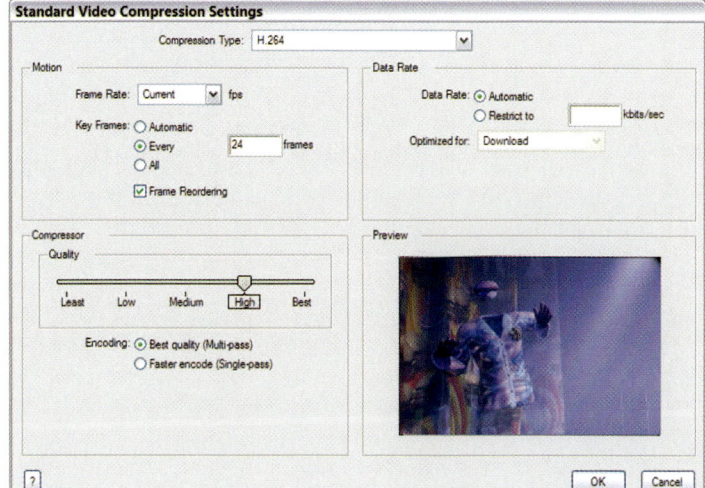

Figure 16.2
Choose your options manually for the most quality and smallest exported video.

A Benchmark and Summary of Render Video Options for the Web

Like anyone who is proud of their video work, I send e-mail attachments of little funny snippets to my friends. They look good and play fast, and here's what I use:

- Sorenson Video 3 when I'm striving for color fidelity and H.264 when I need smaller files that are guaranteed to be compatible with all operating systems.

- 29.97 fps for DV video and 30 fps for digital 3D animations. 30 fps is perfectly legitimate for the Web and e-mail because there is no drop-frame to reconcile; my animations are only in color and not to be broadcast on the airwaves.

- Variable Bit Rate (Multi-pass rendering).

- 640 by 40 pixels (or 720 by 480 by .9 pixel aspect ratio for DV). I drop this to 480 by 360 (532 by 480 at .9 pixel aspect ratio) for videos that are long and have a lot of close-ups.

- Through trial and error, I play with the quality slider until I get a file that's under 2MB as a courtesy for friends (and to keep them as friends). After a while, you'll be able to estimate as a sixth sense approximately how large an exported compressed video will be.

To summarize a lot of the preceding information, here's what your options are and what they mean:

- A codec is a compression/decompression scheme that can greatly reduce the file size of a copy of your video work. Codecs achieve compression in either lossy or lossless style.

- Frame rate determines the smoothness, the resolution of motion in your video.

- Key frames are frames in rendering video upon which a codec evaluates how other frames of similar visual content can be efficiently compressed.

- Data rate specifies how large a chunk of video streams through the audience's video subsystem and affects saved file size and image quality and is dependent on fps.

- Constant bit rate requires a single render pass for the codec and treats all data frames with equal emphasis (except key frames).

- Variable bit rate takes more than one codec pass and results in smaller file sizes with better video quality because it emphasizes dramatic changes in segments while discarding more redundant data in places where there is not a lot of action.

E-Mail Attachments and Cross-Platform Issues

When I receive a video as an e-mail attachment from a friend, it's a cause for excitement, and naturally I want to see the mini-masterpiece in its best light. Unfortunately, there are so many standards for DV, so many different file formats and codecs used, it can be a challenge, for example, for a Macintosh user to watch a Windows WMV, and the converse is true when a Windows user wishes to see a QuickTime movie.

Apple's QuickTime Movie Player is available for free to all Windows users, and there is a Pro version for $30 that enables users to download content from the Web as *.MOV files, convert audio streams in videos to pure audio files, and more. The only "gotcha" with viewing QuickTime movies using the player that I've discovered is the gamma. The Macintosh OS uses a gamma setting of 1.8, while Windows uses a higher gamma of 2.0, and QuickTime movies, although they look fine in Photoshop Extended in Windows, lack a certain crispness derived from the higher system gamma—and this is an option you can't change in the free version of QuickTime Movie Player.

A simple, fast, and very good workaround if you're concerned with the fidelity of creator content is to download the free VLC media player from www.videolan.org.

It plays various file formats including QuickTime, and it does so with higher video fidelity than QuickTime Movie Player. In Figure 16.3 you can see the same video clip displayed in QuickTime and in VLC media player.

Figure 16.3
VLC media player automatically adjusts the gamma of Macintosh MOV files to play beautifully in Windows.

As I mentioned earlier, Microsoft has co-opted some of the MPEG-4 technology to bring the Windows Media Video (WMV) file format to the forefront of Internet video distribution. WMV files are very small, typically smaller than QuickTime files using H.264 compression, with very high video and audio fidelity; I use third-party software to write WMV copies of my Photoshop rendered QuickTimes. The problem is that not all Macintosh users can access this file format. Microsoft has discontinued support for the Mac with a media browser that can play WMV files. The solution is as easy and inexpensive as the VLC player for Windows; www.flip4mac.com offers a free WMV utility that plays this video file type directly inside the Mac QuickTime player. They also offer retail versions with more features, but this free player does the trick and helps bridge this unfortunate schism between content creators who've decided on different operating systems.

Publishing for the Web

YouTube, MetaCafe, Photobucket, and other video parlors on the Web are actively helping to level the playing field with independent, new videographer talents. Legend has it that the way Steven Spielberg broke into Hollywood was by sneaking away from a Universal Studios tour into an abandoned backroom that he fixed up as an office and arrived at the gate every morning in a suit to look as though he belonged there—hanging around until someone mistakenly gave him work—and the rest is history. Fortunately, you don't have to live remotely near Hollywood today to get your stuff viewed by any of the over 800 million personal computers worldwide who have an Internet connection.

Almost ubiquitously, the video salons require a registration for content providers, some sort of assurance that you own the content you upload, and that you upload your video work in any number of file formats. You read the requirements, and I estimate that within a half an hour, you're a published director/producer.

The following sections contain just a few refinements on the settings you'll want to use to create video copies that you can publish online.

Recommended Codecs and Settings for Video Salons

Adobe's Flash video file format (FLV) is commonly used as the final display for videos you upload to YouTube and other sites. This calls for an explanation of the file format and a strategy for ensuring that the recoding of your uploaded video shows the best video quality.

The Flash Video File Format

FLV is a plain "wrapper" for video; in contrast to Shockwave files (SWF) you can produce using Adobe Flash, SwishMax, and other products, FLV was engineered using Sorenson Spark for Flash originally, a variant of H.263 codec, currently moving to On2 TrueMotion VP6 compression technology. In short, FLV media can be embedded in an SWF file, but SWF files can be interactive or contain animations and other niceties, and SWF files cannot be embedded in FLV media.

- FLV is a highly compressed file format that has good video quality.

- Photoshop can write an FLV file from your video composition, but doesn't support audio export because Photoshop uses QuickTime technology for video renders. It's puzzling because Adobe owns Flash technology; I presume there wasn't time in the CS3 Extended development cycle to implement full-featured FLV export, or it's a call to buy Adobe Flash in addition to your other software.

- The video salons don't accept FLV files. They all have automated routines that accept *.MOV, MPEG, AVI, WMV and other video formats they in turn convert to FLV file format.

- If you're a wiz at coding HTML pages, you can embed FLV files rendered from Photoshop without audio, but it's a daunting task, and SWF files are much easier to embed.

- It's not a smart idea to send FLV files to friends because neither the Mac OS nor Windows has a native player for FLVs. However, with a little surfing you'll find self-contained third-party FLV players such as Wimpy FLV Player, about a 2MB executable program.

Video Settings for the Salons

Here's your checklist to run through in Photoshop's Render Video box to make a Photobucket and YouTube (and other video site) upload:

1. YouTube prefers but doesn't require your video to be 640 by 480 pixels, 4:3 aspect ratio. Anything larger will be auto-scaled down, and anything smaller will be auto-scaled up to fit their player window. Scaling a video to be larger produces hideous results because the software needs to guess at the pixels to be added, while scaling a video down to size loses a little focus but overall is acceptable because software guesses at losing pixels much better than creating new ones.

   Now here's a potential showstopper: *Videos straight off your DV camera are not 640 by 480 pixels, square pixel aspect ratio!* They're 720 by 480 by 4:33 pixel aspect ratio, commonly called .9 in programs by Adobe Systems, for which you can thank the NTSC's failure to reconcile broadcast aspect ratio with digital over the years. What this means is that if post to YouTube without correcting the aspect ratio, your subjects will look noticeably smooshed, more so if you use a different, common setting on your DV cam, NTSC DV Widescreen, which has a pixel aspect ratio of 16:9, almost 2 to 1, and measures in square pixels as about 853 by 480.

   You have two solutions for "getting it right" for posting: cropping or letterboxing. Letterboxing can be performed manually; you add Canvas Size to the height of the video, and then use the rectangular Marquee tool set to Fixed Ratio (4:3) to crop the composition. You can then add background color, a title, even an animated title, as shown in Chapter 7. Automatically, letterboxing can be performed through the size options in the Settings box; see Figure 16.4; it's the 640 by 480 VGA option.

   In Figure 16.5 I wanted to show you visuals of the "smooshed" conversion and a cropped and then a letterbox treatment to fix the aspect ratio discrepancy. Cropping is not always an option; you probably don't want to compromise a composition you carefully set up.

2. YouTube prefers the Sorenson codec, although they'll accept variations on MPEG-4, preferring compressions *other* than H.264 for reasons unknown. They accept MOV, MPG, AVI, and WMV file formats.

3. You're safe and sound with audio tracks exported directly from Photoshop. YouTube and the other parlors expect MP3 compression on the audio tracks, and Photoshop is compliant in this regard. If you're using third-party software to compress your work for uploading, be very careful about the compression scheme for the audio. If you choose something other than MP3, which is a "layer" of MPEG technology, the best that might happen is that the video won't have an audible audio track on the Web; the worst that can

happen is the folks at YouTube will yell at you for not reading the FAQs on uploading files. YouTube prefers mono audio at 64K, which is an attribute you cannot set using Photoshop. I've uploaded stereo at a bit rate of 128K and received no complaints, and the playback is fine.

4. Use a frame rate of 30 fps or 25 fps if you're in Europe and used to using PAL standards. The video salon's conversion process will in all probability scale your fps rate back to suit their bandwidth standards, but this is nothing you can control.

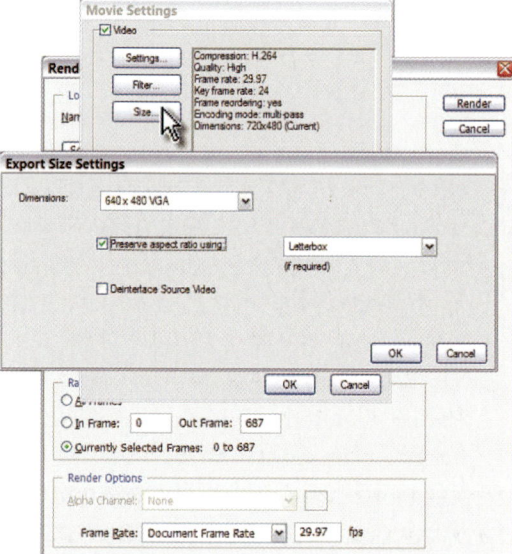

Figure 16.4
The pixel aspect ratio and file dimensions for a video you want to post must meet the host's specifications.

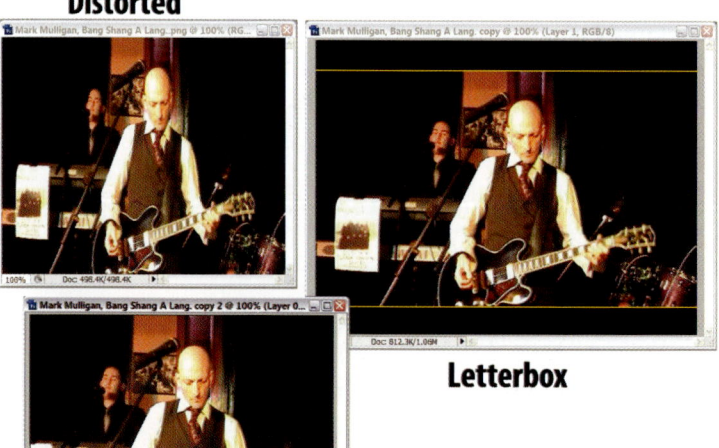

Figure 16.5
Cropping and letterboxing are two ways to standardize a video that has a pixel aspect ratio other than square.

Exporting for Collaboration

Occasionally I need to send an uncomposited special effect to an editor. More than occasionally, the special effect needs to be superimposed over a video layer; this means alpha channel transparency masking, and there are really only three visually acceptable file formats in which to render the clip:

- QuickTime 32-bit uncompressed. You choose None in the Standard Video Compression Settings box and then choose Millions of Colors+ from the Compressor > Depth drop-down. When you've made your other choices and return to the Render Video box, make sure you choose Straight-Unmatted or other alpha option from the Alpha Channel Render Options drop-down box. I'll explain the other alpha options shortly.

- QuickTime with Animation codec. Animation supports alpha channel transparency, and also you pick up a little compression, lossless compression, if your video contains several lines of identical color pixels the codec can "shorthand."

- Windows AVI. With None as the Compression Type and Millions of Colors+ as the Depth, Windows AVI file format does indeed support alpha channel transparency. However, not many software manufacturers outside of Adobe Systems today leverage the alpha capability. I recommend QuickTime unless you're using Windows, your collaborator is using Windows, and the both of you own Adobe video editing software.

Alpha interpretation is accomplished using one of two methods when you render a video you want to use as a composite later. Straight-Unmatted produces a "What You See Is What You Get" alpha mask, and you might get a little unwanted fringing at the edges of your composite video as nontransparent pixels might not quite blend into the background video. Premultiplied is a good choice when you know in advance that a composite piece will be laid on top of a specific color, such as you'd do with video titles. The edges of the composite blend well using Premultiplied, but you need to specify the matte color, and a Premultiplied alpha-enabled video clip is useless for compositing, for example, if you've chosen black as the Premultiplied color and your collaborator has chosen a pink background video.

Codecs for Authoring

Photoshop cannot write a DVD. You can preview video through File > Export > Video Preview—if you have a television monitor properly hooked up to your video card. You can choose File > Export > Render Video to hand-held devices such as palmtops and cell phones if they, too, are hooked up correctly, but you need video authoring software to burn your compositions to DVD.

That's the bad news. The good news is that Photoshop can format your videos so they'll go straight to DVD with little or no reformatting (transcoding). In the following sections I'll explain the DV codecs available to you and the third-party software you can use to author a DVD title.

Exporting to DV

In the Render Video box under File Options QuickTime Export, you'll see DV Stream as an option in the drop-down list. This is not what you want to export video with audio to author a DVD. Photoshop doesn't support audio with this option; you have to use QuickTime (again, it's Apple's QuickTime engine that renders video with audio support from Photoshop).

Click Settings, and then click Settings for compression type and then choose DV/DVCPRO from the drop-down list of Compression Type. This codec is based around MPEG-4; as a result, you can bring the rendered video back into Photoshop with no hassles in the future. However, some authoring software such as Nero (for Windows) cannot parse MPEG-4 encoding, but others such as Adobe Premiere and Premiere Elements and iDVD for the Mac handle the file with no complaints. Ultimately, video is encoded to MPEG-2 for burning to DVDs; commercial DVDs also use MPEG-2. MPEG-2 is sort of an albatross today, and new technology is bound to eventually replace it. MPEG-2 files cannot be imported to Photoshop, and the MPEG-4 files written by Photoshop for DV export need to be transcoded to MPEG-2 by authoring software to be burned to DVD.

The difference between DV and DVCPRO is that DVCPRO can produce higher quality videos. It accepts 4:2:2 color coding, which samples color channels twice as much as DV's 4:1:1 scheme, and the data rate can go up to 100Mbps and supports data frame resolution exceeding the standard 720 by 480 pixels.

Third-Party DVD Authoring Tools

For all I've covered in this chapter, DVD authoring is quite a simple and relatively inexpensive process. If you want to slum it, you can use your system's utilities to burn a DVD title. A much better solution is to buy a simple editing package that has DVD burning capabilities.

For Windows users, there's Nero (about $80) and what you get for your money is not only a DVD burning utility, but it can also stitch video clips for one seamless DVD play, it can break clips into menued segments the audience can browse at the beginning of the DVD, it can create a fancy title menu with animated buttons and music from templates or your own creations, it can create chapters so the audience can pause and fast forward through videos, and my experience is that it's fairly idiot proof.

For about ten dollars more, there's Adobe Premiere Elements, which not only burns DVDs but is a real mini editing suite for video. Heavily menued with lots of templates, Premiere Elements has a semi-hidden "pro" interface that displays video tracks and audio tracks exactly like its big brother Premiere Pro, and you can do some serious video editing and authoring with it for about $100. You have automatic cross-fades, animated special effects such as Lens Flare, rudimentary audio editing features, and alpha channel support. Not only can you composite videos that have transparency, but just like in Photoshop, you can composite and animate still images, such as you might save to PNG file format. It's a terrific little accomplice to Photoshop. You'd be getting a head start on the pro world of video editing because the UI is very similar to Premiere Pro and After Effects, but Premiere Elements lacks any of the paint and sophisticated selection tools in Photoshop. Figure 16.6 shows the interface.

On the Macintosh side of things, of comparable cost are iDVD, part of the iLife 08 bundle (about $80 with a very attractive family multiuser bundle pricing) and Apple Final Cut Express. Final Cut Express is a pared-down version of Final Cut Pro; it's a little more expensive than Premiere, and it uses the paradigm of video and audio tracks that you layer, just like the more expensive video editors. See Figure 16.7.

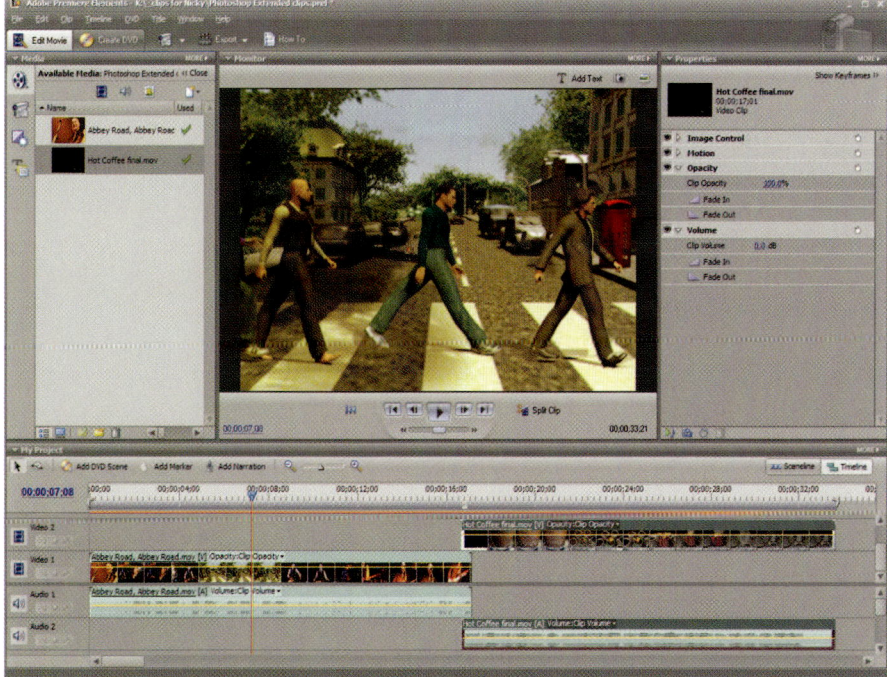

Figure 16.6
Premiere Elements delivers your Photoshop video compositions to DVD.

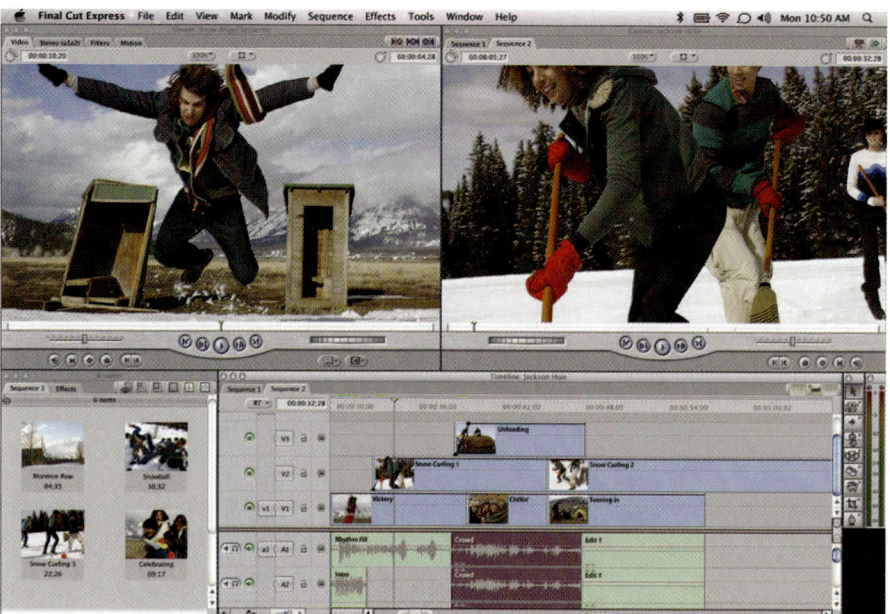

Figure 16.7
Apple Final Cut Express is a DVD burner and also a powerful introduction to video editing.

All the DVD burning programs I've mentioned in the previous sections run on "auto pilot." Burning the DVD is not an intellectual challenge once video that's been formatted properly in Photoshop has been imported (placed). For example, in Premiere Elements, the Project Settings box looks like that in Figure 16.8. It should look familiar, quite similar to Photoshop's Render Video options, except these options are for writing to disc instead of to file.

It's nice every once in a while to feel confident that a software application can make the right decisions for you.

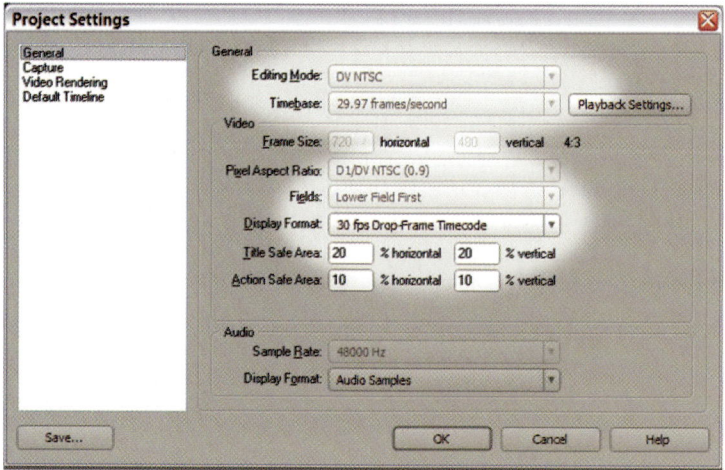

Figure 16.8
Choose from NTSC or PAL display format; choose a quality setting and Premiere Elements does the rest.

Archiving Your Video Work

I mentioned at the beginning of this chapter that archiving alternate takes and other snippets of video and Photoshop composition work you'll no longer need for weeks or years is essential for good hard disk management. Archiving requires almost no technical expertise and absolutely no artistic flair. However, archiving has an importance to your future career as Video Guru as significant as the skills you've learned by reading this book. It's Sock Drawer Psychology: Owning several pairs of socks is a sign of prestige, wealth, and often good hygiene. But it's all for nothing if you have a messy sock drawer and can't find the pair you need for that big interview in 20 minutes!

I encourage you to organize files by project and not by file type. For example, I have a composition that uses two video clips, three audio clips, and several still PNG files with transparency. I have the PSD composition file, the PNGs, the WAV audio files, and the MOV files all in one labeled folder on my hard drive.

Saving to Removable Media

After I've rendered an uncompressed video I'm pleased with, I can make compressed ones using Photoshop later or a third-party utility. Therefore, it's time to archive the folder with all the component files onto removable media, the non-spinning, failure-resistant, no moving parts type. If I need to rework the Photoshop composition in the future, I have all the resource files in one easy to locate folder and can back the data back onto my hard drive in five minutes.

However, let's talk about stability of removable media for a moment, also known as "protecting your investment with the best technology."

I recommend that you back up files to DVD *and* to tape. Why both? DVD is easier to use because it is random access, but until HDDVD burners become commonly available, they don't really hold the magnitude of data that's commonly written for digital video. Also, the life span of a home-burned DVD is *not* the 100 years some developers originally predicted. Some DVDs go bad in a year when stored improperly; humidity and exposure to directly sunlight are two common killers. Then there are the usual problems with scratching. Finally, when you look at technology, players tend to go extinct way before the media. Try buying a Beta videotape player today, or a record turntable. DVD players may not be available 15 years from now, no less 50.

Tape, the kind you taped the original material on, has a longer documented storage life (10+ years) using average care for storage, and the tape holds a lot more data than a conventional DVD. You can record back to your DV camera using a few steps that are in effect the reverse process of writing data off your camera and onto hard disk.

1. Put a fresh tape into your DV camera.

2. Hook the camera up to your computer using the DV cable appropriate for your camera. If your camera can download video to your computer using USB or Firewire (aka IEEE 1394 or iLink), you need to use the Firewire cable. You can't use the DV/Composite RCA or S-Video cables to make this kind of connection.

3. Use the software that came with your camera to write your files to tape. Alternatively, you can use Movie Maker (Windows) or iMovie (OS X).

Duplicating Your Archives

Heartbreak number 1 for content creators is misplacing a finished video; well-organized archiving of your media is the remedy. Consider what content creation today would be like for photographers without products such as Bridge and Lightroom and catalogers such as iMatch.

Heartbreak number 2 is *losing* a video; the remedy is local and offsite backing up.

It's a good idea…no, make that a "career-critical idea"…to have external drives that are dedicated to local backup/archive duty. Video files in particular are much easier to work with if they are stored on a fast hard disk; having local duplicate files of your work saves all sorts of investments, time, work, your hair *when* a hard disk dies; not *if*—*when*.

However, in your media protection scheme, local backup isn't enough. All you have to do is think of the phrases *tsunami* or *California wildfire* to make you appreciate the value of off-site backup of your work. *Out of region* backup is even better.

I recommend subscribing to a service such as Carbonite or Mozy. These services encrypt and then upload files and folders you've tagged to their servers. You'll see a virtual drive on your operating system's directory window, and these services dynamically update in the background any files, folders, or disks that you have specified as you work. Mirroring services will hold on to your file for as long as you are a customer, and you keep the file on your hard disk; it's exactly like a RAD except the striping hard disks are not at your physical place of work.

If one of your hard drives fail, or you accidentally delete a video clip, you can restore the file to your hard disk by downloading the backup copy of the file from their servers. If you delete a file from your local drive, the service holds on to the uploaded backup copy of your file for at least 30 days in case you change your mind.

Fade to Black; Roll Credits

That's the pipeline. You begin with media and a concept, you use your talents and capable software to bring your vision to a silver screen of just about any size, and then you publish. Digital video requires massive amounts of processing and storage compared to even two years ago, but the rewards are correspondingly massive.

There's nothing quite like the moving picture; it's a rollercoaster in your family room, it's comedy and tragedy spliced together to happen quicker than possible in real life, it's entertainment, it's education.

It's the logical next plateau for any individual with the time and patience and sensitivity. You reach for the application that continually reinvents itself to make it the first, and often the only, one professionals choose. Then you communicate ideas that strike the audience in an intriguing, profound, emotional way.

Index

A

A-D converters, 162
   filtering, starting, 167–169
   FireWire connection from A-D to computer, 166–167
   host application for transfers, 168–169
Ablan, Dan, 334
actions. *See also* **green-screening**
   to animate objects, writing, 215–216
   background colors, removing, 224–226
   live action as rotoscope, using, 286–297
   sparkle animation, driving, 431–433
adjustment layers, 135. *See also* **black and white TV**
   animating, 146–148
   blurring, 147–148
   cleaning up, 137–138
   Color Overlay, using, 148–150
   colors, correcting, 134–137
   for edgework, 281
   for motion pictures, 170–176
   renaming, 136
   traveling masks, setting up, 143–146
Adobe After Effects
   green-screening and, 478–479
   radial wipes, 124–125
   spill suppression utility, 478
   thumb, 14
Adobe Bridge, 576
   builds, creating, 42
   RAW files, working with, 42–44
   reversing footage, 108–109
   and warping time effect, 465–466
Adobe Flash, 557
   file format, 568
   media-based camcorders, 5
Adobe Illustrator
   for bouncing ball animation, 251
   layers for, 398
   rotating in, 243
   for sparkle effect, 430
Adobe InDesign, 15, 196
Adobe Premiere/Premiere Elements, 163, 572–574
   as host application for transfers, 168
   motion picture clips to video, rendering, 184
After Effects. *See* **Adobe After Effects**
AIFF format, 23
Alias! Wavefront OBJ file format, 314
Alien Skin Exposure 2, 158–160
aligning
   layer stacks, 44–49
   subtitles, 194
alpha channels, 449
   building movie with transparency, 200–203
   for CGI animation, 376–378
   compression and masking, 414
   Intel Indeo codec supporting, 560
   Xara 3D and, 223–228
alpha interpretation, 571
ambient sounds, adding, 100
Anamorphic aspect ratio, 124–125
animated overlay, creating, 348–352
animatics, 534–535
animating in twos, 235–239
animation. *See also* **cartoon animations; effects (fx); GIF animations; motion cycles; rotoscoping; text**
   adjustment layers, animating, 146–148
   building movie with, 200–203
   crawls, animated, 203–205
   cycle, 232
   of filters, 16
   fps (frames per second) and, 18–19
   holds to animated titles, adding, 226–228
   lightning, animating, 442–443
   logos, animating, 209–212
   neon sign in video, placing, 388–397
   offsetting time and, 422
   one way sign animation, 398–402
   photography, mixing with, 264–273
   3D animated text, 223–228

timelapse animations, 52
typewriter text, 220–223
Animation (Timeline) palette, 3, 11–12, 14. *See also* **GIF animations**
  buffering in, 17
  features of, 13–19
  trimming footage in, 19–22
  zoom in, 15
Animation under Compression settings, 414
anti-aliasing text for titles, 187
Apple. *See also* **QuickTime**
  Final Cut Express, 573–574
  Final Cut Pro, 14
AppleScripts, 103
archiving
  duplicating archives, 576
  file formats for, 552
  removable media, saving to, 575–576
aspect ratio
  Anamorphic aspect ratio, 124–125
  correcting, 11
  .9 pixel aspect ratio, 67–68
  standard aspect radio, choosing, 186
  and trimming footage, 20
  for YouTube, 570
attachments. *See* **e-mail attachments**
audio, 23–26, 100. *See also* **green-screening; rotoscoping**
  AVI files with audio, exporting, 77
  with Canopus ADVC 300, 167
  with cartoon animations, 258–259
  for CGI (computer generated images), 371
  checkerboard composition, adding to, 86–89
  to duplicated layers, 123
  editing, 87
  frames, adding, 139

Love on the Rocks tutorial, adding sound effects (fx) to, 546–548
motion matching, adding to, 533–534
PAL standard and, 67
in potter's wheel animation, 40
for push-in transitions, 129–130
retaining format on exporting, 24–26
royalty-free songs, 23
with scene props, 416
subtitles, creating, 190–195
texture exercise, adding to, 354
for time-warping movie, 471–472
trimmed video, adding music to, 24
for YouTube, 569
Aurora, Digital Elements, 55
AutoDesk products, 317
AVCHD (Advanced Video Codec High Definition) cameras, 5
averaging, 252–253
AVI format, 4, 77
  alpha channels, support for, 449
  audio and, 557
  collaboration, exporting files for, 571
Avid Studio thumb, 14

B

background colors, removing, 223–226
backgrounds. *See also* **green-screening; motion matching; rotoscoping**
  for cartoon animations, 252–255
  for motion cycles, 260
  still image animation, scrolling in, 246–249
  wire removal and, 307

backing up. *See* **archiving**
barrel distortion
  in motion picture clips, 180
  in panoramic photomerge, 60
basketball to baseball animation, 520–534
Becker font, 214
Bend Text Wrap setting, 206–207
Bible Script font, 214
Big Data, 56, 143
  in *Love on the Rocks* tutorial, 538–539
bit rate, 555
  multiple rendering passes and, 559
black and white
  fades to black, creating, 141–143
  H.264 and, 561–562
black and white TV
  blue effect, 154–155
  ghosting, adding, 157
  plug-ins for effect, 158–160
  raster pattern effect, 155–157
blackouts, 372
blending layers, 97–101
blending modes and alpha channels, 449
blossoming, 152
blue-screening objects, 357
blurring. *See also* **Motion Blur**
  adjustment layers, 147
  in Venetian blinds animation, 117–118
BMP format, 557
bouncing ball, creating, 250–252
bracketing production, 100–101
Branches Wafting movie, 413–416
Bridge. *See* **Adobe Bridge**
brightness, 150. *See also* **vignetting**
broadcast frame rates, 18
Brown, Russell, 368, 478, 481

Index

browsing the Timeline, 21
Brush tool, 279
   for cartoon animations, 256
   in fountain animation, 423
   irregular outlines, creating, 285–286
   photography and animation, mixing, 265–267
buffering
   in Animation (Timeline) palette, 17
   fps (frames per second) field, 17–18
building blocks, designing, 384–387
builds, 42
   fades, adding, 49–51
   with layer stacks, 46
   repairing frames in, 48
   tweening function with, 46–49
bunraku theater, 496
Burns, Ken, 29, 53

C

caching, 17
CAD (Computer Assisted Design), 315
camcorder shopping tips, 4
camera RAW. *See* RAW format
Camera tool, zoom for, 318
cameras, video quality and, 481
Canopus ADVC 300, 162
   filtering software, 167–169
canvas of composition, resizing, 55, 151–152
capturing. *See* importing/exporting
Carbonite, 576
cartoon animations, 231, 249–259
   audio, adding, 258–259
   backgrounds, adding, 252–255
   embellishing, 257–259
   shadows, adding, 255–257

   squash and stretch bouncing ball, creating, 250–252
   tweening for, 252–255
CGI (computer generated images), 69, 355
   alpha channels, creating, 376–378
   audio with, 371
   compositing 3D animation, 378–381
   compressing file sizes, 361–363
   duration in CGI animation, 374–375
   easing in/easing out at keyframes, 375–376
   editing, 365–366
   exporting, 365–366
   falloff, light with, 376
   final right-to-left CGI pass, creating, 367–368
   flower growing video, 358–361
   fuzziness values, 368–370
   lighting in CGI sequence, 372
   movement in CGI animation, 374–375
   position CGI animation, 376
   rendering video, 371
   second pass, setting up, 368–370
   setting up CGI composite, 363–365
   textures for animation, creating, 373–374
   3D character animation, 372–381
Character palette, 196–198
character shading, 241–243
checkerboard composition, 66
   audio, adding, 86–89
   beginning/ending work area markers, 79–80
   clip dimensions, editing, 70–73
   concept and, 70
   entrance, editing, 70–73
   finishing, 81–82

   freeze-framing, 73–75
   playing, 79–81
   rendering work, 86–89
   second element, adding, 75–76
   shifting time with clip, 79–81
   signature shot, adding, 83
   starting video, frames for, 73
   titles, adding, 84–86
choreography, 354
chroma keying. *See* green-screening
chromacity in YUV color space, 559
CINCH/AV connectors, 163
Cinema 4D, 298, 317. *See also* CGI (computer generated images)
   alpha channels, support for, 449
   flower growing video, 358–361
   fps (frames per second) and animations in, 18–19
   and Google Earth model, 333
   HAIR module, 359
   orthographic perspective, 318
Cinepak, 560
The Civil War, 29
clapboard wipes, 124–126
cleaning film, 170
Clear painting mode, 278
clipboard, killing, 478–480
clipping masks. *See also* split-screen effect
   cleaning up, 137–138
   for composite work, 133
   in *Love on the Rocks* tutorial, 537–538
   for push-in transitions, 129
   with rotoscoping, 290–291
   transitions and, 118–120
clips. *See* video
clock sweep, creating, 110–112
Clone Source tool
   editing with, 412–413

in fantasy composition
  exercise, 301–303
with rotoscoping, 272–273
for scene props, 407–410
Clone Stamp tool, 279
  in fantasy composition
    exercise, 301–303
  with Google Earth structure,
    331–333
  and motion matching, 519,
    523–524
  with panoramic photomerge,
    61
  retouching rendered videos,
    305
  with rotoscoping, 272–273
cloning. *See also* **Clone Stamp
  tool**
  at partial opacity, 412–413
  in rotoscoping, 246–247
**clothing, green-screening
  with, 496**
**Clouds filter with 3D model,
  325**
codecs, 41, 555. *See also*
  **H.264; Sorenson codec;
  Web publishing**
  Cinepak, 560
  Component Video, 559–560
  for DVD authoring, 571–574
  Graphics codec, 559
  Intel Indeo codec, 560
  Motion-JPEG codec, 560
  multiple rendering passes,
    558–559
  PNG codec, 560
  quality issues, 556–557
  structure of video and,
    552–553
  for Web publishing, 551–552
**coily cord frame element,
  adding, 137–141**
collaboration
  exporting files for, 571
  file formats for, 552
colons, reading, 18–19
Color Balance tool, 136–137
color keys, 476

Color Overlay, 148–150
colors. *See also* **black and
  white TV**
  adjustment layers for
    correcting, 134–137
  background colors, removing,
    223–226
  broadcast-legal colors,
    152–153
  composite video, correcting
    within, 131–143
  effects with color correction,
    153–160
  fades to, 101–103
  motion pictures, fixing in,
    170–171
  moving video area, colorizing,
    143–152
  NTSC standards, conforming
    to, 152–153
  for panoramic photomerge,
    55
  for still image animation, 33,
    50
  for titles, 188
  TV blue effect, 154–155
  for video layers, 269–271
comments, 14
  rotoscoping live action, using
    with, 295
  for subtitles, 192
  and trimming footage, 21
Comments stopwatch, 17
**component video data, 164,
  559–560**
composite video data, 164
compositing
  CGI 3D animation, 378–381
  green-screening, elements for,
    487–489
  sparkle effect, 433–435
compositions. *See also*
  checkerboard composition
  black, creating fade to,
    141–143
  broadcast standards and,
    67–70
  canvas, resizing, 151–152
  cleaning up, 137–138

clipping video layer for, 133
coily cord frame element,
  adding, 137–141
color correction within,
  131–143
concept and editing, 70
duration, choosing, 69
frames, adding, 138–141
in *Love on the Rocks* tutorial,
  537–538
NTSC base layer, creating,
  68–70
outline for, 66
safety zones in, 68
setting up for transitions,
  115–116
stretch room, creating, 116
transitions, editing, 115–123
traveling mask, setting up for,
  143–146
compression. *See also* **codecs**
  alpha masking and, 414
  of compositing file sizes,
    361–363
  keyframes and, 414
  for potter's wheel animation,
    41
  Settings box, 564–565
  types of, 555–556
**computer generated images
  (CGI).** *See* **CGI (computer
  generated images)**
concept, 30
connector cables, 163
Constant Bit Rate (CBR), 559
  PNG codec, 560
**Convert to Timeline
  command, 432**
copying/pasting. *See* **crawls;
  subtitles**
Core Duo, 462
CorelDraw, 209
**Correct Levels for motion
  picture clips, 172**
**costumes, green-screening
  with, 496**

crawls
    animated crawl, building, 203–205
    creating, 195–205
    in green-screening, 488–489
Create New Layer for Each New Frame, 31
cropping
    duplicated layers, 122
    layer stacks, images in, 45–46
    YouTube, video for, 569–570
cross-dissolves, 83
cross-fades, 98–101
cross-sections in 3D, 323–324
cross-star sparkle. *See* sparkle effect
cuts, 95–97
cutting keys, 475–478. *See also* green-screening
    quality of video and, 481
cutting on action, 543

D

Da Vinci, Leonardo, 318
data rate
    H.264 and, 563–565
    measurement of, 564–565
DAWs (digital audio workspaces), 23, 546
degrading video. *See* black and white TV
Digital Anarchy
    Knoll Light Factory, 436
    Primatte, 486
Digital Elements, Aurora, 55
directory structure, setting up, 6
dissolves. *See* fades
distortion. *See also* barrel distortion
    in panoramic photomerge, 62–63
DISTRESS texture, 325
dithering, 559
docking strip, 13

docking/undocking palettes, 13
Dodge tool, 242
downloading. *See also* importing/exporting
    Dr. Brown's Background Remover, 368, 479
    SuperPNG, 414
Dr. Brown's Background Remover, 368–370, 479–480
drop-frame broadcasting, 562
drop-frame timecode, 18
drop shadows
    for subtitles, 191
    to 3D text, 226–227
    video layer, adding to, 269–270
dulling spray and green-screening, 477–478
duplicate layers, 120–123
    with first transition, 127
    for motion pictures, 174–176
duplicating. *See also* CGI (computer generated images)
    frames, 279
    for wire removal, 308–309
duration
    changing, 48
    of composition, 69
    of fades, 51
    for panoramic photomerge, 57
    split-screen effect, trimming durations for, 459–460
    of subtitles, 191–192
DV-AVI format, 4–5
    digital video stream, 163
DV cable, 163
DV Pro camera, 481
DVCPRO, 572
DVD authoring
    codecs for, 571–574
    exporting to DV, 572
    file format for, 552
    software, 183
    third-party tools, 572–574

E

e-mail attachments
    file format for, 551–552
    standards for, 566–567
    summary of rendering options, 565–566
earthquake simulation, 450–455
    matte, creating, 450–451
    motion blur, adding, 453–455
    waveform, motion as, 451–452
easing in/easing out, 521
    at keyframes, 375–376
edgework, hand-rotoscoping, 280–285
Edit Timeline Comment dialog box
    with subtitles, 191
    and trimming footage, 21
editing. *See also* checkerboard composition
    audio, 87
    CGI (computer generated images), 365–366
    clip dimensions, 70–73
    with Clone Source, 412–413
    concept and, 70
    downloading capability in programs, 7
    in Frames mode, 39
    Smart Objects, 434
    3D objects, 315
    transitions, 115–123
effects (fx), 427. *See also* earthquake simulation; lightning effect; sparkle effect; split-screen effect; warping time
    with Adobe Premiere Elements, 573
    with color correction, 153–160
    eggs, reversing cracking of, 473–474
    ghosting, adding, 157
    in *Love on the Rocks* tutorial, 543–545

raster pattern effect, 155–157
reversing time, 472–474
TV blue effect, 154–155
in Venetian blinds animation, 116–118
eggs, reversing cracking of, 473–474
elliptical Marquee tool, 49
End Work Area marker, 14
evil twin effect. *See* **split-screen effect**
Export Clipboard option, 479
Exposure 2, Alien Skin, 158–160
extracting work area, 94–97
Extrude feature, 406
Eyedropper tool, 172

F

fades, 105
  black, creating fades to, 141–143
  to colors, 101–103
  cross-dissolves, 83
  cross-fades, 98–101
  in motion matching, 530
  in panoramic photomerge, 56, 58–60
  rotoscoping life action, fading in with, 294–297
  between segments, 99–100
  in still image animation, 49–51
  for subtitles, 193
  for wavy text, 208
falloff, light with, 376
fantasy composition exercise, 297–303
  Clone Source tool in, 301–303
  garbage matte, creating, 298–300
  partial opacity, blending with, 300–301
files. *See also* **importing/exporting**
  for still image animation, 30
  video from file, creating, 77–79

film warp, manually correcting, 180
filters
  animation of, 16
  Offset filter, 246–247
  with panoramic photomerge, 56
  photo filters for motion picture clips, 176–178
  post-production filtering, 60–64
  Smart Objects, application to, 378
Final Cut Express, 573–574
Final Cut Pro, 14
finding misplaced resource files, 26–28
FireWire connections, 162–163
  for A-D unit to computer, 166–167
first transition, adding, 126–128
fisheye pan, 63
Flash. *See* **Adobe Flash**
flower growing video, 358–361
FLV file format, 568
flyout menu button, 14
focus
  enhancing, 181
  fixing in, 171
folders, setting up, 6
FontLab Studio, 209
Fontographer, 209
fonts
  logos, fonts for animating, 209–210
  for 3D models, 326
  for titles, 187–188
forced perspective, 318
foreshadowing, 448
fountain animation, 416–424
  water to fountain, adding, 420–424
fps (frames per second). *See also* **warping time**
  field, 17–19
  H.264 and, 561–562

NTSC standard and, 67
PAL standard and, 67
and rotoscoping, 235
Frame Number display, 233
frame-skipping, 562
frames, 47. *See also* **fps (frames per second); keyframes; rotoscoping; still image animation**
  coily cord frame element, adding, 137–141
  compiling video from, 77–79
  composition, adding to, 137–138
  data rate, frame size *versus*, 564
  duplicate frames, working with, 279
  in potter's wheel animation, 35–36
Frames/Animation toggle, 15
Frames mode
  editing in, 39
  reversing animation in, 218
  text, building frame-based animation for, 216–218
Frames to Timeline command, 432
Free Transform feature, 72, 89
  for checkerboard composition, 71
freeze-framing, 73–75
fringing, cleaning up, 484–487
Futura fonts, 188
fx. *See* **effects (fx)**

G

Garamond fonts, 187
garbage matte, 276–279
  for fantasy composition, 298–300
Gerotype SE.otf font, 209–212
ghosting, adding, 157
GIF animations, 29–34
  blinking effects in, 34

pedestrian crossing animation, creating, 30–34
potter's wheel animation, creating, 34–38
writing to disk, 33
GIF format. *See also* **GIF animations**
Graphics codec, 559
moving from GIFs to video, 38–42
Google Earth model, 314
buildings in scene, photorealism in, 338–341
contextualizing of pre-viz, 331–333
importing data into, 334–338
photorealism in, 333–341
Photoshop, working with, 329–330
pre-visualization of structure, 327–333
resurfacing structure, 327–329
and 3D architecture, 327–342
grain, sharpening, 181
Graphics codec, 559
green-screening, 475–478
audio
distorting, 504–505
foreground, adding to, 500–503
checklist for, 476–478
clipboard, killing, 478–480
compositing elements, 487–489
costuming for, 496–498
crawls, adding, 488–489
and Dr. Brown's Background Remover, 479–480
dulling spray and, 477–478
finessing the key, 484–487
first key, cutting, 478–492
foreground, 498–509
music, animating, 500–505
variations, adding, 506–509
fringing, cleaning up, 484–487

graphic elements, adding, 487–489
guides, using, 481–484
hair, cutting key around, 486
headlines, adding, 490–491
inset video, adding, 494–496
Layer Styles, adding, 502
lighting, 475–478
and costume keying, 497–498
for live actions, 286
motion matching and, 531–533
outdoor green-screening, 476–477
polishing production, 492–494
quality of video and, 481
rainbow, adding, 491–492
running background removal script, 480–484
shadows and, 477
size of files, 484
snapshots, saving, 478–480
spill, 478
static graphics, adding, 490–492
talent, stand-ins for, 478
variations, finessing, 503–504
White Matte option, using, 499–500

H

hair
and CGI modeling, 359
and green-screening, 486
hand animation. *See* **rotoscoping**
Hand tool, 279
hardware for video transfer, 162–163
HDDVD burners, 575
HDTV, interlacing and, 554
Helium-Neon laser tubes, 164
Helvetica fonts, 187–188
Henson, Jim, 546
Henson Productions, 534

HiDef original data, 5
hierarchical nesting, 243–246
High Definition (HD) video, 4–5
High Dynamic Range (HDR) images, 338
highlights in lightning effect, 448
History, purging, 480
Hitchcock, Alfred, 424
Hold and Linear Interpolation, 58–60
Hold Interpolation for typewriter text, 220–221
holds, 73–75
animated title, adding to, 226–228
for subtitles, 193–194
HTML pages, embedding FLV files in, 568
H.264, 41, 558
data rate and, 563–565
frame rate options, 561–562
frame reordering with, 563
key frames and, 563
streaming media, 563
Hue/Saturation adjustment layer, 143–146
TV blue effect, 154–155
human skin tone, 536

I

iDVD, 572, 573–574
IEEE 1394 interface, 163
iLife 08 bundle, 573
i.LINK, 163
Illustrator. *See* **Adobe Illustrator**
Image Size command, 38–39
ImageReady, 29
iMatch, 576
iMovies, 163
downloading, 9–11
importing/exporting. *See also* **H.264**
aspect ratio, correcting, 11
audio, exporting video in format retaining, 24–26

camera software, using, 6–7
CGI (computer generated images), 365–366
collaboration, exporting files for, 571
DVD authoring, exporting to DV for, 572
layer stacks, 44–49
Mac OS, downloading videos in, 9–11
MIDI tracks to DAWs, 23
motion pictures, 181–183
paragraph text, 196–200
recipients of, 551–552
3D, objects into, 320–324
videos to hard disk, importing, 6–11
with Windows Movie Maker, 7–9
InDesign, 15, 196
Info palette, 144
inset video, adding, 494–496
Intel Indeo codec, 560
Interactive Layout feature, 60–61
interlacing, 553–554
International Organization for Standardization (ISO), 558
inverting layer masks, 135
iris wipes, 103, 112–115
with duplicate clipped layer, 121–122
irregular outlines, working with, 285–286

J

Jackie.mov. *See* green-screening
Japanese *bunraku* **theater, 496**
JavaScript, 103–105. *See also* **CGI (computer generated images)**
Dr. Brown's Background Remover, 368–370
for live actions, 287–288

JPEG format, 5. *See also* **warping time**
lossy compression, 555–556
Motion-JPEG codec, 560
for panoramic photomerge, 54
quality and, 556–557
justifying text, 197

K

Ken Burns Effect, 29
creating, 53–60
kerning text, 198
keyboard shortcuts for keyframes, 192
keyframes, 15
compression and, 414
H.264 and, 563
keyboard shortcuts for, 192
markers, 193
Knoll, John, 436, 496
***Knoll Light Factory,* Digital Anarchy, 436**

L

LAB color space, 559–560
LaserDiscs, 164
layer masks. *See also* **fantasy composition exercise**
adjustment layer masks, 135
color corrections and, 134–135
softening hard edges, 137–138
layer stacks
aligning, 44–49
importing, 44–49
Layer Style dialog box, 188
Layer Styles
with green-screening, 502
for title text, 188–189
layers. *See also* **audio; green-screening; motion matching; rotoscoping**
duplicates, 120–123
persistent layer properties, creating, 38

Layers palette, 11
Propagate Frame 1 checkbox, 38
LCD displays, 554
legacy technology, 161. *See also* **restoration**
Lens Correction
for motion picture clips, 178–179
in panoramic photomerge, 62–63
lens flare, 428
letterboxing, 569–570
Levels adjustment for motion pictures, 174–176
lifting layers, 94–97
lifting video segments, 85
lighting. *See also* **green-screening; vignetting**
in CGI sequence, 372
3D, light and appearance settings in, 317, 322–323
lightning effect
animation of, 442–443
building strike scene, 444–446
creating, 438–442
prepping original video for, 439–442
scorched earth/smoke, adding, 446–449
Lightroom, 576
line breaks, creating, 197
linear interpolation, 520–521
live action as rotoscope, using, 286–297
Load Files into Stack script, 36–37
Load Layers dialog box, 36
logos, 85
green-screening, adding in, 491
Text Wrap, animating logo with, 209–212
lossless compression, 555–556
lossy compression, 555

Index

Love on the Rocks tutorial, 535–548
  sound effects (fx), adding, 546–548
  special effects setup, repurposing, 543–545
Lucas, George, 123, 195, 476, 496
luminance/luminosity
  PAL standard and, 67
  in YUV color space, 559
Luxology modo
  exported model, building model based on, 406–407
  green-screening, creating graphic for, 492–494
  motion matching, creating clips for, 517
Lynch, Michael, 496

M

Mac OS, downloading videos in, 9–11
Macromedia Fontographer, 209
Magic Eraser tool, 55
Magnetic Lasso tool, 281–282, 284
manually animating text, 213–220
marionettes, wire removal and, 307
marquees
  in layer stacks, 45–46
  for text, 197
masks. *See also* adjustment layers; clipping masks; green-screening; layer masks
  traveling masks, 143–146
mattes. *See also* garbage matte
  in earthquake simulation, 450–451
  traveling matte, 277
  White Matte option, 499–500
Maya, alpha channels support in, 449

Merge Visible tool, 55
MetaCafe, 567
  file format for, 551–552
  lossy compression and, 555
Microsoft MovieMaker, 163
MIDI tracks, importing, 23
MiniDV format, 4–5
mirroring services, 576
misplaced resource files, finding, 26–28
modeling. *See also* Google Earth model
  CGI character animation, 372–381
  combining animation with models, 416–424
  flower growing video, 358–361
  importing data into modeling program, 334–338
  photorealistic modeling, 333–341
  texture replacements exercise, 342–355
  3D objects, 315
Motion Blur
  in earthquake simulation, 453–455
  for photorealism, 340–341
  with sparkle effect, 436–437
motion cycles, 259–264
  backgrounds, creating, 260
  Determinator video, 260–264
  seamless loop, creating, 260–264
motion in earthquake simulation, 450–455
Motion-JPEG codec, 560
motion matching, 513–516
  audio effects, adding, 533–534
  basketball to baseball animation, 520–534
  cloning away unwanted areas, 523–524
  complex processes, 520–534
  exposing elements in, 524–527

fades, creating, 530
green-screening and, 531–533
hiding elements, 524–525
shadows, working with, 527–529
for sparkle effect, 433–435
video clips, 516–520
motion pictures
  adjustment masks for, 174–176
  color correction, 170–171
  duplicate layers for, 174–176
  exporting, 181–183
  film warp, manually correcting, 180
  focus
    enhancing, 181
    fixing in, 171
  Lens Correction for, 178–179
  Levels adjustment for, 174–176
  photo filters, working with, 176–178
  polishing presentation, 181–183
  restoring video clips, 171–174
  retouching, 169–180
  Smart Objects, placing in, 170–171
  traveling masks for, 173
MOV format, 4, 11
Move tool, 188–189
MovieMaker. *See* Windows MovieMaker
moving
  colorizing video area, 143–152
  static layer contents across time, 410–412
Mozy, 576
MPEG-1, 4
MPEG-2, 4–5, 163, 558
MPEG-4, 4–5, 163
  DVD authoring and, 572
  for e-mail attachments, 567
  H.264 codec and, 558
  motion picture clips to video, rendering, 184

MP3 files, 23
MTV, compression for, 414
multiple split-screen, creating, 456–458
Mummenschanz, 496
music. *See* audio
muting audio, 87

N

naming/renaming
 adjustment layers, 136
 warping time effect, renaming files in, 465–467
neon sign animation, 388–397
 motion matching for, 513–516
 sizing up proportions, 394–397
Nero, 183, 573
.9 pixel aspect ratio, 67–68
NTSC (National Television Systems Committee), 18
 Adobe Premiere/Premiere Elements and, 574
 aspect ratio, correcting, 11
 base layer, creating, 68–70
 color adjustments, conforming, 152–153
 compositions and, 67–70
 fps (frames per second) and, 561–562, 17018
 screen safety standards, 185–186
nudging video layers, 452

O

off-site backup, 576
Official Luxology modo Guide (Ablan), 334
Offset filter, 246–247
offsetting time, 422
Ogg-Vorbis files, 23
one way sign animation, 398–402
Onion Skin, 15, 236
 for character shading, 242

opacity
 alpha channels and, 449
 in fantasy composition exercise, 300–301
 in *Love on the Rocks* tutorial, 539–541
 stopwatch icon and, 15–16
 tweening function and, 47
Open GL, 317
Optima fonts, 188
ordering layers, 97–101
orthographic perspective, 318
outdoor green-screening, 476–477
Outer Glow, rotoscoping with, 290–292
overcranking camera, 461
overlapping segments, 98–99
overscanning, 185
Oxberry animation stand, 231

P

painting 3D objects, 403
PAL standards
 Adobe Premiere/Premiere Elements and, 574
 compositions and, 67
 drop-frame broadcasting, 562
Palatino fonts, 188
palette display tips, 13
Panasonic AVCHD (Advanced Video Codec High Definition) cameras, 5
panning. *See also* motion matching
 elements to pan, adding, 511–520
 Love on the Rocks tutorial, 535–548
 tracing and styling, 512–513
panoramic photomerge. *See also* Ken Burns Effect
 arrow keyboarding, moving with, 57–58
 documents, setting up, 56–60
parsing MPEG compression, 5
Paste Keyframe(s), 391

Path Selection tool, 267
Path Styler Pro, Shineycore, 213–215
patterns, creating, 155–157
Patty Duke Effect, 397
PDF files for subtitles, 190
pedestrian crossing animation, creating, 30–34
Pen tool, 265–266
perspective
 forced perspective, 318
 orthographic perspective, 318
 in 3D, 317–319
perspective shadows, 239–240
 with live action rotoscoping, 292–293
photo filters for motion picture clips, 176–178
Photobucket, 567
photography, mixing animation with, 264–273
Photomerge Automation, 54
photorealism
 buildings in scene, 338–341
 in Google Earth model, 333–341
 tips for adding, 337–338
pincushioning, 180
Pixel Aspect Ratio Correction, 20
pixels. *See also* aspect ratio
 Info palette in, 144
plasma displays, 554
PNG format, 560
 Adobe Premiere Elements and, 573
 for archiving, 575
Poser
 alpha information, video rendered for, 377
 fps (frames per second) and animations in, 18–19
post-production filtering, 60–64
potter's wheel animation
 creating, 34–38
 video from, 39–42

pre-visualization
  of Google Earth model, 327–333
  3D object, pre-visualizing for, 402–405
Primatte, Digital Anarchy, 486
Profile Mismatch attention box, 320
profiles, 406–407
progressive scan signals, 553
projection spill, 186
projections, 324
Propagate Frame 1 checkbox, 38
props. *See* scene props
prosumer MiniDV camera, 4
PSB (Photoshop large file). *See also* 3D
  for 3D work, 314
PSD files, 26–27
  restoring, 27–28
publishing to Web. *See* Web publishing
Purcell, Henry, 129
push-in transitions, 128–130
Pyrus Software, 209

Q

quality
  codec issues, 556–557
  fps (frames per second) and, 562
  green-screening and, 481
  transfer rate *versus*, 564
quantizing video, 168
Quark, 15, 196
Quick Mask tool, 49
  for colorizing moving video area, 145
  for wire removal, 308–309
QuickTime. *See also* e-mail attachments; H.264; Web publishing
  alpha channels, support for, 449
  and audio files, 23

CGI (computer generated images), rendering, 371
collaboration, exporting files for, 571
motion picture clips to video, rendering, 183
for potter's wheel animation audio, 41
video engine based on, 11

R

RAD, 576
Radial Gradient, 175
radial wipes, 124–126
RAM frame buffering, 17
raster pattern effect, 155–157
RAW Editor, 42
RAW format, 5
  Adobe Bridge, working with, 42–44
  preparing for animation, 42–44
RCA phono connectors, 163–165
rectangular Marquee tool, 45
  for letterboxing, 569
removable media, saving to, 575–576
Render to Video dialog box, 41–42
rendering
  checkerboard composition, 86–89
  flower growing video, 360
  motion picture clips to video, 181–183
  retouching rendered videos, 303–306
  textures, scene with, 346–347
repeat cycles in rotoscoping, 239–240
resizing canvas, 151–152
resolution and H.264, 561–562
restoration, 161. *See also* A-D converters
  color-coded cables, 164–165

  connections, setting up, 164–165
  hardware for video transfer, 162–163
  motion picture clips, 169–180, 171–174
  of PSD files, 27–28
  software for video transfer, 163
retexturing 3D model, 324–327
retouching rendered videos, 303–306
reversing footage, 108–109
reversing time, 472–474
RGB images
  alpha channels and, 449
  compression of still photographs, 556
Ring Around the Rosie music, 472
Ring spin movie, 264–268
Roman fonts, 188
rotating
  3D objects, 315
  in Venetian blinds animation, 117
rotoscoping, 231–232, 357
  animating in twos, 235–239
  audio, 272
  for live action video, 296–297
  backgrounds
    creating, 239–240
    integrating subject with new background, 289–290
    static background, adding, 243–246
  character shading, 241–243
  clipping mask, working with, 290–291
  Clone Source tool with, 272–273
  cloning scenes in, 246–247
  edgework, hand-rotoscoping, 280–285
  fading in second video, 294–297

fantasy composition exercise, 297–303
first frame, building, 232–235
fps (frames per second) and, 235
garbage matte, creating, 276–279
hierarchical motion, 243–246
integrating subject with new background, 289–290
irregular outlines, working with, 285–286
live action as rotoscope, using, 286–297
off-seamless background, eliminating, 283–285
perspective shadows
  creating, 239–240
  with live actions, 292–293
repeat cycles, 239–240
retouching rendered videos, 303–306
scrolling the background, 246–249
simple, fast-paced video, 264–268
static background, adding, 243–246
styles to video layer, adding, 268–271
transparency for live action, 288–289
tweening and, 235–239
unwanted scene areas, 276–286
for walk cycle, 232–239
wire removal, 306–310
royalty-free songs, 23
Ruler tool, 144

S

S-Video cables, 163, 164
  jacks for, 166
safe-falling animation. *See* earthquake simulation
Salvation Army, props from, 35
sans serif fonts, 187–188
saturation, 150
  blossoming, 152
Save for Web and Devices, 33–34
saving. *See also* archiving
  green-screening, saving snapshot for, 478–480
scaled footage, 11
scaling video, 70–73
scene props, 383
  audio, adding, 416
  cloning source, 407–410
  combining animation with models/video, 416–424
  exported model, building model based on, 405–407
  finishing touches, adding, 412–416
  fountain animation, 416–424
  hiding moving image areas, 407–410
  neon sign animation, 388–397
  offsetting time and, 422
  one way sign animation, 398–402
  placing props into scene, 397–416
  pre-visualization for, 402–405
  shadows, suggesting, 407–408
  static layer, moving contents of, 410–412
  time, moving static layer contents across, 410–412
  Vanishing Point, working with, 383–387
scratch disk allotment, increasing, 17
screen safety, measuring, 185–189
scripting, 103–105
scrubbing, 21
serif fonts, 187
Set Current Time dialog box, 13
shading characters, 241–243
shadows. *See also* **drop shadows; perspective shadows**
  in cartoon animations, 255–257
  in fountain animation, 418–419
  and green-screening, 477
  in lightning effect, 448
  motion matching and, 527–529
  white from shadows, removing, 365–366
Sharp anti-aliasing setting, 187
Shineycore's Path Styler Pro, 213–215
Shockwave (SWF) format, 568
shortcut keys
  for Brush tool, 267
  for Path Selection tool, 267
  for rotoscoping, 279
showing/hiding
  portion of video, 76
  scene props, hiding moving image areas in, 407–410
signature shot, adding, 83
sizing/resizing canvas, 151–152
SketchUp. *See* **Google Earth model**
slipping video, 28
slow motion footage, creating, 466–471
slugs, 199
Smart Guides for checkerboard composition, 71
Smart Objects
  for checkerboard composition, 71–72
  direct editing of, 434
  filters, application of, 378
  loading time and, 421
  motion pictures in, 170–171
  video layers as, 16
Smith, Alvy, 449
Soderbergh, Steven, 481
software
  DVD authoring software, 183
  for video transfer, 163

Index   591

Sony
    AVCHD (Advanced Video
        Codec High Definition)
        cameras, 5
    HD hardware, 4
Sorenson codec, 89, 557–558
    YouTube and, 569
Sorenson Spark, 568
Sorenson Squeeze Suite, 558
sound. *See* audio
Sousa, John Phillip, 272
Spacebar, toggling with, 279
sparkle effect, 427–449
    action, driving animation
        with, 431–433
    compositing, 433–435
    creating sparkle, 428–430
    finishing, 436–438
    motion matching for,
        433–435
Spielberg, Steven, 567
spill, 478
spinning text. *See* text
Splatter brush tips, 256
split-screen effect, 455–460
    dividers, working with,
        456–458
    durations for clipping masks,
        trimming, 459–460
    gathering elements for,
        455–456
    multiple split-screen, creating,
        456–458
    second character, adding,
        458–459
splitting layers, 94–97
spotlight effect, 49–50
squash and stretch bouncing
    ball, creating, 250–252
Stack command for still
    image animation, 36
stacks. *See also* layer stacks
    Adobe Bridge creating, 42
    Bridge image stack, 43
    for panoramic photomerge,
        53–54

standard definition (SD)
    Digital Video (DV) format,
        4–5
    televisions, 185
Star Wars films, 96, 123, 195,
    357
starfield, placing movie on,
    200–203
Start of Work Area marker, 14
still image animation, 29–64.
    See also Ken Burns Effect
    backgrounds, scrolling,
        246–249
    editing 3D objects, 315
    fades, creating, 49–51
    GIFs to video, moving, 38–42
    interlacing, 553–554
    mixing animation with,
        264–273
    Offset filter, using, 246–247
    pedestrian crossing animation,
        creating, 30–34
    potter's wheel animation,
        creating, 34–38
    seamless backgrounds,
        cloning, 246–249
    10-second commercial with
        stills, creating, 347–348
    timelapse animations, 52
    tracks, moving, 40
    video footage, adding frame-
        based animation to,
        39–42
    warping time, splitting image
        layers and, 462–464
stopwatch icon, 15–16
streaming media, 563
strokes for neon sign prop,
    390
structure of digital video,
    552–557
styles
    for logos, 210–212
    video layer, adding styles to,
        268–271

subtitles
    creating, 190–195
    fades for, 193
    holds for, 193–194
Super 8. *See* Video 8
SuperPNG, 414, 531
SwishMax, 84, 568

T

talent stand-ins and green-
    screening, 478
tape, saving files to, 575–576
Targa format, 557
television. *See also* black and
    white TV
    interlacing and, 553–554
    standard definition (SD)
        televisions, 185
text, 200–203. *See also* crawls;
    titles
    actions to animate objects,
        writing, 215–216
    compositing animated text,
        219–220
    frame-based animation,
        building, 216–218
    handsome text, creating,
        213–215
    importing paragraph text,
        196–200
    line breaks, creating, 197
    manually animating text,
        213–220
    spacing between lines, 199
    spinning text, 216–218
        compositing, 219–220
    3D animated text, 223–228
    timing animated text,
        219–220
    tracking feature for, 198
    typewriter text, creating,
        220–223
    video clips for text, creating,
        215–216
    wavy text, creating, 205–207
Text Wrap
    logos, animating, 209–212
    wavy text, creating, 205–207

textures
  animated overlay, creating, 348–352
  audio, adding, 354
  in CGI animation, 373–374
  exercise for replacing textures, 342–355
  finishing exercise video, 352–355
  overwriting, 344–346
  placing textures, 346–347
  rendering scene, 346
  10-second commercial with stills, creating, 347–348
  for 3D model, 324–327
  transition scene, building, 347–348
The Thieving Magpie (Rossini), 371
3D. *See also* **Google Earth model; scene props**
  animated text, 223–228
  CGI character animation, 372–381
  cross-section options, 317, 323–324
  defined, 313
  experiment for working with, 319–324
  flower growing video, 358–361
  importing objects into, 320–324
  legend for tools, 314–316
  light and appearance settings, 317, 322–323
  Line and Face color options, 322
  navigating 3D objects, 315
  perspective in, 317–319
  potter's wheel animation, creating, 34–38
  primitive shapes in, 320
  retexturing 3D model, 324–327
  texture replacements exercise, 342–355
  tools, 314–319
  views in, 316–317

3D Camera Settings, 321
3D Studio, 314, 317
thumb, 14
  dragging and, 21
TIFF format, 557
  alpha channels and, 449
time, 13. *See also* **warping time**
  reversing time, 472–474
time echoing, 469–471
timecode values, 18
timelapse animations, 52
Timeline Current Time counter, 13
Timeline Editor, 11–19
Timeline palette. *See* **Animation (Timeline) palette**
Times fonts, 187
titles
  adding, 84–86
  fonts for, 187–188
  holds to animated title, adding, 226–228
  legal title, creating, 187–189
  subtitles, creating, 190–195
  typewriter text, creating, 220–223
Tools palette, 13
tracing the pan, 512–513
Tracking feature for text, 198
transcoding MPEG footage, 5
transferring. *See* **importing/exporting**
Transformers, 423
transitions, 103–105. *See also* **fades**
  building, 105–115
  clapboard wipes, 124–126
  and clipping masks, 118–120
  clock sweep, creating, 110–112
  duplicating layers and, 120–123
  editing, 115–123
  first transition, adding, 126–128
  iris wipes, 103, 112–115

  push-in transitions, 128–130
  reversing footage, 108–109
  venetian blind wipes, 103, 105–108
transparencies. *See also* **alpha channels; green-screening**
  animation packages, support from, 84–86
  compared to alpha channels, 449
  live actions, creating, 288–289
  2D objects in 3D space, 405
traveling masks, 143–146
  for motion picture clips, 173
traveling matte, 277
trimming footage, 19–22
TrueType fonts, creating, 209
turtle pond exercise. *See* **fantasy composition exercise**
TV blue effect, 154–155
tweening, 46–49
  for cartoon animations, 252–255
  and rotoscoping, 235–239
twittering, 188
2D objects in 3D space, 405
Type tool, 209
typewriter text, creating, 220–223

U

Unify icons, 38
Universal 3D file format, 314

V

Vanishing Point, 60–61, 318–319, 383–387
  building block, designing, 384–387
  exported model, building model based on, 406–407
  in fountain animation, 418
  perspective grids in, 385–386
  pre-visualization with, 402–405

Variable Bit Rate (VBR), 559
VCR area
 audio, playing, 23
 controls, 15
venetian blinds animation, 103, 105–108
 effects in, 116–118
VHS playback devices, 162
video. *See also* **codecs**
 combining animation with, 416–424
 editing, 296
 inset video, adding, 494–496
 interlacing, 553–554
 motion matching for clips, 516–520
 structure of digital video, 552–557
Video 8, 164, 165, 562. *See also* **motion pictures**
 professional services for writing DVDs from, 169–170
Video Coding Experts Group, 558
video layers. *See also* **green-screening**
 icon, 15
 motion blur on, 454–455
video salons, 567–570. *See also* **YouTube**
 settings for, 569–570
video service bureaus, 169–170
video tape decks, 164–165
vignetting
 motion picture clips, fixing in, 171, 178–179
 in panoramic photomerge, 63
Virtual Studio Technology (VST), 546
volume of audio, adjusting, 87
Vue 6, 377

W

walk cycle, rotoscoping, 232–239

Warp Free Transform, 180
warping time, 108, 461
 accelerated setup sequence, creating, 467–468
 assembling time-warping movie, 471–472
 audio, adding, 471–472
 compiling frames, 466–471
 fast times, 461–462
 renaming files for, 465–467
 reordering files, 465–466
 slow motion, creating, 466–471
 slow times, 461–462
 splitting still image layers, 462–464
 time echoing, 469–471
Watercolor Artistic Filter, 170
WAV format, 23
 and archiving, 575
wavy text, creating, 205–207
Web publishing, 557–560, 567–568. *See also* **video salons**
 Cinepak, 560
 Component Video, 559–560
 file format for, 551–552
 Graphics codec, 559
 H.264 codec, 558
 Intel Indeo codec, 560
 Motion-JPEG codec, 560
 multiple rendering passes, 558–559
 PNG codec, 560
 Sorenson codec, 557–558
 summary of rendering options, 565–566
wedge for clock sweeps, 110–112
white
 fades to, 101–103
 shadows, removing white from, 365–366
White Matte option, 499–500
widows, avoiding, 198
Williams, John, 129
Wimpy FLV Player, 568
Windows AVI. *See* **AVI format**

Windows Media Video (WMV), 560, 567
Windows Movie Maker
 downloading video with, 7–9
 as host application for transfers, 168–169
Windows Visual Basic Scripts, 103
windshield reflectors, 497–498
wipes, 105. *See also* **iris wipes**
wire removal, 306–310
 assessing damage, 307–308
 cleaning up, 309–310
 duplicating selected area, 308–309
WMV format, 560, 567
Wondertouch ParticleIllusion, 416
Work Area
 End Work Area marker, 14
 extracting, 94–97
 hidden area of placed video, 14
 Start of Work Area marker, 14

X

Xara 3D, 223–228
Xara Xtreme, 138
 for bouncing ball animation, 251
 for lighting effect, 438

Y

YouTube, 567
 compression for, 414
 file format for, 551–552
 lossy compression and, 555
 royalty-free songs and, 23
 video settings for, 569–570
YUV colorspace, 559–560

Z

zooming in/out
 Camera tool, zoom for, 318
 Onion Skin, 15